THE FOUNDATIONS PROJECT

Harvey Sarles

Copyright ©2014 Harvey Sarles

Published by Trébol Press

Los Angeles, California

www.trebolpress.com

All rights reserved. No part of this publication may be reproduced or transmitted in any form or by any means, electronic or mechanical, including photocopying, recording, or any other information storage and retrieval system, without permission in writing from the publisher.

info@trebolpress.com

ISBN-10: 0990360725

ISBN-13: 978-0-9903607-2-8

Printed in the United States of America.

For Janis

Preface

The *Foundations Project* is an extended work-in-progress which attempts to *lay out* an encompassing philosophical anthropology.

It is motivated by the attempt to reframe some issues of human meaning which have, in this complicated moment of great felt change, come into a virtual crisis. The narratives and stories which have previously sustained our Being no longer offer or yield to us theories which frame any idea of a future in which we can see ourselves clearly.

This is a moment within the history of thought when we need to rethink who and what we are, tempting as it is also in this moment, to reclaim other stories from earlier times or outside our human experience. The overall aim of the *Foundations Project* is thus to address the questions: what is the human nature? What is the human condition?

Its most ambitious claim is that we can retrieve and/or invert the (Western) foundational architectonic of thought about the human without falling into limiting positions or presumptions which have captivated most thinking at least since Plato.

It is not, I think, motivated by any wish to capture the foundational idea of truth as existing somewhere beyond sophistry. Rather it aims to take seriously the puzzle stated by Protagoras as (hu)man being the measure of all things, asking critically about this human which is the experience and the shaper of its measures and measuring. In the American Pragmatist tradition, Dewey expressed it to concern the mostly unasked questions of "human agency."

Although we are in a period of postmodernized forms of battle between rhetorical and metaphysical approaches to being, this project takes the view that some critical and/or new ideas of the human condition are available from comparative study: what I call the *ethological critique* of the philosophy of language.

To approach this retrieval/inversion requires various forms of long term commitment to (ongoing) observation—of others and of oneself; better, in the reverse order – of oneself and of others.

As well, it necessitates a comparative and developmental visioning of the human, trying to position and relocate one's viewing from as many critical experiential perspectives as one can muster. Else, as Nietzsche teaches us, we merely refresh ancient questions within (post-)modernist themes and variations, or seek interfaces within the geographies of polar axes of the several paradoxes which rule most of our thinking to this day.

It derives from a person trained to be a comparative field-oriented linguist-anthropologist come upon philosophy and metaphysics only upon experiencing the power of a thought revolution in which foundationalism was invoked to beat down my form of scientific/scientistic investigation.

Only much later, following the Chomskyan (Cartesian) revolution in linguistics, psychology, and philosophy, that I began to become educated to the sociology, history, and politics of ideas upon which my life and career had become impaled. This work represents *my ways out*, as it were, of the formalisms and idealisms which have so appealed to the vast majority of those concerned with issues of being, truth, knowledge, etc. (i.e., the human condition).

Two orientations from comparative thought direct and frame this work: one is to always attempt to relook at my/our experience (the *ordinary*) from the (possible/likely cognitive) perspectives of the other; animals, other languages and cultures, ways of thinking, being; machines/technologies. The second comparative revision is from the *Weltanschauung* of other traditions in which I have lived or read: from the ethnically and religiously diverse households and companions of my youth and an ecumenical marriage, to the ways of thinking of my own culture within the perspectives of other cultures, other academic disciplines, fundamentalisms, the variety of thought modes of others and of my students over many years, and the ways of thinking of disciplines which have changed or not, over a similar span (and always of J.).

Within these contexts are many stories. Some of them I have tried to describe and/or virtually enter. Especially relevant in this project, is my orientation as a (sometimes) performing musician, and an ongoing examination of the body in performance: an aspect, most closely, of the *engineering* approach to artificial intelligence (AI), expert systems.

My biology is especially a *biology of form*: the question is how to see the human from the outside, then from the inside of experiencing: how does a small body become larger? What and how does it know? What do we know honestly/precisely in distinguishing human from other animals? Rather than moving from the prevailing dualistic approaches to development which proceed within foundationalism—from biology to rationality—I concentrate particularly upon form and appearance, inspired by Darwin's late works on human nature and (emotional) expression: its readings and interpretations. ("Expression of the Emotions in Man and Animals,"1872.)

This places this work, then, in a particular form of another argument which has raged for centuries, between metaphysics and rhetoric as determining the human. Here, I find myself working out the ideas of the pragmatists from Mead and Dewey backward to Peirce and forward to this project.

But this is not born from any direct resistance or antagonisms, near as I can tell. Rather, it derives from the comparative knowledge that we humans are a social species, like other species. And this means that I/we are body in the world with other(s') bodies. Including, most importantly, the fact that we are of two kinds/genders, and the emergence of "attachment theory" (between m/other and child) addresses the obvious of our being, which has remained somehow "hidden" to biologists and psychologists (particularly) as they seem to be captive/captivated to and by rather ancient ideas of human nature.

Being is, as Mead says, 'emergent," but never, I will claim, remote or born free in any Rousseauean senses. Indeed, I explore being as the human necessity or habit to create the emergent individual-person-self within ongoing cultural-social living.

Another, more temporal comparative perspective of this project, concerns this moment of the globalization of the world: especially its peoples; most especially its ideas. It presumes and attempts to consider critically many of the narratives and ideas which have informed the human condition. As the world's theo-political traditions are now coming into mutual interaction, awareness, complementarity, contrast, and competition, it is timely to gather the different perspectives which have sustained (human) being. This project seeks some (new) syntheses which may filter the human experience through its characterizing descriptions.

It also responds to a felt sense that this is a moment of unclarity and possible crisis as (older) ideas come into this moment of vast change, driven much by technology and the recasting of the human within sharply contrasting ideas of present and a deepening sense that futurity is no longer clearly *scripted*. That is, the very *idea* of the future is at some risk.

In this extended work, the principal task has been to consider the global variety of ways of life, of world views, of depictions of purpose and directedness in order to (re)discover the ordinariness of our experience and existence. Reading and thinking across ideational traditions provides the critical expanse necessary and useful to see and probe smaller or more particular modes of thought about the human. Coming as I/we do from within Western thinking, thinking across the globe also sets the Western tradition in sufficient relief that we may recover a fuller and more complete sense of our own being.

More specifically, I have discovered that the various traditions—large and smaller—provide both meaning within life experience, and some sense of the power of futurity that we go on and on. While the larger (in terms of geography and populations) worldviews seems to provide *a sense of utopia* within or after life, a sense which can gather large groups of adherents and believers, the smaller also give meaning to being; at least within certain moments or runs of history. As we (have) come into global contact, some of these traditions gain or lose power and adherents, depending on their power to inform current understandings of, and purpose to being, thence to futurity.

The *incommonesses* have to do with their referents to fairly particular aspects of life experience, namely what I will call *life paradoxes*; the differences have to do with how the various traditions *handle* some twenty or so of these paradoxes such as life/death, man/woman, sleep/wakefulness, one/many, change/permanence, and so on. Most of the global traditions *resolve* these paradoxes on one side or the other; others *complementarize* (some of) them over time and experience.

This admission of paradox will allow us to re-see Western thinking from the perspective of its *favorite* paradoxes and their resolutions: i.e., change/*permanence*, the one/*many*, life/*death*—at least during much of its Christian history. And it will urge us to expand or make more encompassing what we mean by reality, tied as its definition has been to a narrow and particularly Western set of understandings.

More to the point of the *Foundations Project*, the ideas which are coming at us from the deeply different global traditions also provide a critical perspective from which to rethink Western ideas which have so far captivated our thinking and outlined/framed/restricted the study of the human condition.

In this sense, a major attempt of this project is to *invert* and/or *retrieve* the foundational ideas of the Western tradition resting most clearly within Plato's dialogic works, especially the *Phaedo*. The placing or positioning of the so-called philosopher is raised into critical re-questioning.

Rather than positioning the philosopher within the idea—that is, the idea of the viewing of the present from the afterward of death's visioning—here the philosopher takes the position of Teacher in Dialogue with her/his students; perhaps a more existential/experiential reading of Plato if we wish to remain within his metaphorical spinning (Sarles, 2013).

The philosopher qua teacher agrees/admits that s/he exist within life's ongoingnesses of older and younger, of (teacher's) present and (students') futures.

Rather than banishing the changeable and fractious body from our minds' thoughts, the being of our ideas and the ideas of our being flow within our being as bodies—finding ourselves in the world with other(s') bodies. Within the idea of teaching as dialogue, it attempts to expand the necessity of human relationship, of a sacred within the secular; of keeping life experience within life by increasing and expanding the importance of being.

The *retrieval* aspect of this study entails a positioning of the thinker just at that moment when Plato (*Phaedo*) banishes the body, resolving the problems of life existence within the contexts of timelessness and the presentiment of ideality: the "is" as what-would-be.

It admits the presence and gendering of human being, and opens the questions of knowledge as located within all of experience, including our bodies; rather, flowing from our bodily being.

This project thus resides within the experiences of being without the intellectual *luxury* of resolving a/the primary paradox of life and death as a beginning point for settling the course of human existence. It asks about the human condition by pondering the nature of our nature as a mode of inquiry, pushing us inevitably to relook more widely and inclusively at our being than ever we have before: who and what we are, how do we create and understand, what is the nature of our meaning, the movement and towardness of our ontogenesis; an *anthropology of the ordinary*.

This is no attempt to enter the dialectic of existence vs. essence, to solve or resolve the mind-body problem. It does not deny the human capacities for imagination, thought, or logic. Nor is it an intellectual play between materialism and mentalism, within the structuration of being one or the other or some compromise at an interface.

Rather this project admits and explores the nature of our being, urging us to observe ourselves and one another in the fullness of being terrestrial creatures moving in gravity, noting that the judgments and ideas of our being actual to ourselves and to others is a complex mesh of knowing, imaging, and imaginings.

Motivating this project is the claim that the ideas which have underlain the (Western, but now also global) examination of our being have been narrowly crafted, relying too much and too often on some notion of humans being unique as the beginning point for its exclamations (and residing often within a limited politics of a bounded city-state). Such uniqueness claims have already selected and prejudged the statements and studies of our being. We remain unable to surmount the walls of separation, nor to deconstruct them *bricolagically*.

In effect, we in all the world's traditions have discipled ourselves to particularities of approvingly or disapprovingly viewing our own viewings, less to explore being human in its fullness and ongoingness.

Study of the human within the purview of the remote philosopher has focused primarily on the ideas associated with language as a/the defining characteristic of the human. Our (actual) bodily being and experience have been largely overlooked or cast within an oppositional mechanical depiction of the human.

It is as if we only discovered the problematics of our being after we had each come to hard and certain judgments of who we are: quite *late* in the actualities of experiencing; already grappling with the puzzles and paradoxes of being anyone/someone in particular. This narrowness in orientation and perspective has limited study and understanding of our human nature and proclivities, and has more often than not taken some notion of human essence removed from experience and existence as the principal characterization of our being.

This project locates itself instead within the notion that our habits of thought flowing from the Platonic tradition can (need to) be restrained and reconsidered: a philosophical anthropology; but one which takes into account a consideration of the thinking in whose terms the problematics of this project arise.

The locus of study, that is, needs to be set within the context of comparative thought in which we observe other species and critically rediscover rather than presume the attributes which might distinguish the human.

In a similar critical vein, we can (need to) rethink the theories and stories which have informed our thinking about our human being: the history and politics of ideas and the sociology of knowledge as they have framed what has heretofore been almost at the level of the *obvious*. How to see through our own seeing? How to distinguish what we can/do know from the theories and stories which have previously informed the characterization of the philosopher who would know knowing?

As the *Foundations Project* is a retrieval in the sense that we enter Platonic thinking just before the moment in the *Phaedo* where Plato banishes the body from our being, one notes, for example, that humans *love* faces; that the eye of the mind developed its clear visioning within the socially-interactive journey each of us has taken from birth to present being; that life is no metaphor for metaphysics or for any metanarrative constructed from our ideas of death; it more simply is. We need to re-gather being without losing any aspects of ourselves or giving them up to others' *stories*.

The *Foundations Project* is an inversion. The *Project's* ideas and critique flow principally from some of my earlier work on language and the questions about human nature which are implicated in its various definitions. As this attempt is cast within an *anthropology of the ordinary*, I recognize that we only come to the questions of being—after we have made many formative judgments about our being.

This means that our experience and judgment is (already, by the time of our recognition of the ongoing problematics) mediated both by experience and by the metanarratives in whose terms we construct and interpret that experience. How narrow, how comprehensive our understanding of being, have only been addressable within theories of rationality and maturity which are tradition—and age-bound.

How, the *Foundations Project* asks, do we see ourselves within the ordinariness of our experiencing, as we (more) truly are; e.g., body within a world of other(s') bodies.

The dialectic of this project is calculated to unpack our (particularly Western) propensities to compare our human bodies with (the bodies of) other species, to locate the presumptive bases of our knowing. In order to do this, we must acknowledge what we know and can study from what we have been told about other species: their putative languaging and awareness is not available to us, so far at least; and to tell false or presumptuous tales about others redounds to our feeding precooked theories about being, not to see us *as we are*.

This is to say that the *ethological critique of language* will lead us inevitably to seek new ways of observing/understanding the human. We have come to judgment about (inquiry into) our human being from over-specific and largely incomplete and/or incorrect visioning of other species:

More directly, what I have called the *Question-Response* (Q-R) *System* in language is a way of understanding human language which clearly inverts (some of) the primary ideas of our being which have flowed from the either/or's of metaphysical mentalism. Rather than language (logic, rationality, etc.) being located within each individual, Q-R shows us that most of what we call language is learned/obtained from our mothers/others: rather than each of us inventing or having languaging propensities *built-in*, we come to know the world principally as our parents know it. Our individuality *emerges* from this sociality—not the other way round as our tradition from Plato/Aristotle to Hobbes would have it.

Q-R inverts or elaborates several other puzzles about our being which have so-far formed the foundations of our thinking about ourselves. The rethinking of these puzzles sets a principal context for this project:

1) Q-R explains, better *accounts for*, our ability to be symbolic/infinite without having to invoke a given or *a priori* mentalism within a dualistic dialectic.

Our apparent *infinity* is located within the response sets which are responses to a fairly small number of question words—we can conclude that there is no necessity to explain our transcendent directives by seeking agency outside of human being. It suggests that the universality of language we have sought is located (primarily) in the processes by which (each) language is taught/learned in the contexts of interactive ontogenesis; thence language translation.

2) Q-R shows that sociality is prior to individuality, that we (primarily) emerge from sociality, inverting the Aristotelian presumption that physics (our physical being) is prior to metaphysics (and within the ethological critique, it opens a comparative study of social species in which we can reframe questions about human nature, about meaning, transcendence, context, etc.—the various sections of the *Foundations Project*).

3) It reframes Plato's epistemological puzzles by obviating the need to raise the question of (our knowing) other minds—the problematics of being are, reasonably, redirected to a prior necessity of understanding ourselves/oneself... in relation to others as well as to ourselves. Individual knowledge emerges from knowing other(s') minds. Knowing is primarily a partaking of others' knowing, descriptions, seeings of the world.

4) It shows that language in any sense per se, is not the (sole) wellspring of meaning: the principal locus of meaning is within the larger arenas of *context*. The study of meaning must derive from issues of context (indicating the necessity of studying the development of meaning in ontogenesis, rather than from the formal or other analysis only of language— words, sentences, what have we). It helps to account for the apparently rapid development of language at certain points in development. And it leads us to new ways of investigating questions of *origin* of our being: showing that we seem to conflate individual and species history when(ever) we come face-to-face with certain puzzles (such as the *origin of meaning*, and *being and identity*).

5) It redirects most questions of historical development from any sense of primitive to civilized, or biology to rationality—thus recasting issues of morality, politics, and so on, all of which flow from any reexamination of human nature. Within the ethological critique of language, it raises the question of human morality as morality (of the individual) within sociality; not as the morality primarily/exclusively of the (rational) individual.

6) From Q-R, it is clear that logic is an aspect of our knowing and understanding, rather than determining of it. It asks us to rethink how we think about human nature.

7) The question of human *consciousness* is recast in the sense of the emergent individual as a demand of mothers/others that we be/become propositional/responsible individuals. This understanding obviates the necessity, for example, to attempt to explain ourselves as unique either by postulating mechanical metaphors (umpteen neurons organized in parallel processing) or a primitive cognitive matrix seeking syntactic/semantic organization. As well, it opens the possibility of understanding other social species (directed) in their own terms: as raising the young to be competent adults of any species, further informing Protagoras' idea.

8) As universality is not to be studied or found in language per se, Q-R redirects us to study the foundational similarities (thence differences) across cultural-intellectual traditions, thence to see Western thought comparatively and more clearly. In reading and studying broadly across the various world traditions, it has become apparent to me that the most general (and most immediate) insight into various traditions is via the recognition that the differences among the traditions have principally to do with the fact that the human condition consists (especially) of a number of commonly experienced *life-paradoxes*; that the various traditions have chosen to concentrate and/or celebrate certain of these to the neglect of others, and to effectively *resolve* these on one or the other pole of our being (paradoxical): e.g., we in the West concentrate especially on paradoxical issues of the one/many, change/permanence, life/death, sleep/wakefulness, male/female, form/content by granting the status of more certain reality to the one rather than the other - but usually not both as the Confucian tradition is more wont to do, complementarily.

9) And so on...

The sensibility of this project flows, as well, from the recognition that the world is moving, apparently rapidly, into an era which seems quite distinct from its recent pasts. We in the West, at least, are in the midst of what I am calling a *crisis in meaning*. The conditions and narratives which have supported and sustained us no longer seem to provide the impetus and energy which underwrite futurity; we are moving into an *unscripted time* in which the temptations to hold on to past theories of our being are at war with the sense that we are moving and changing at an enormous, probably unprecedented pace.

(Some of) the technologies which have sprung from the ideas of the Enlightenment are so powerful in their effects that they are reframing the ideas of our being: especially, television, but also transportation, and the rapidly developing transformative fields including information technologies and genetic engineering. The question of the human condition demands serious reappraisal and study during this fragmenting and fragile moment.

Plato and the Unreal Real: In the dialogue *Phaedo*, Plato attempts to place the philosopher in the position of having effectively accepted the fact of his (sic!) own death: he would then look back at life and his life from the perspective of a forever after. One must first accept fully the idea that death is no big deal: Socrates' death wasn't. And, in this way we can fully and cleanly get to knowledge of the real, the ideas and the forms without the problematics of body: desire, sensory information always nearing overload, sickness, sex and the other muck of having to maintain a life which tends to overwhelm and to confuse seeing clearly with seeing the shadows of misperception.

We see as well, from *Republic X*, that the life of being before accepting fully the position of knowledge from having died, is organized hierarchically: the real which is the form and ideas of continuity and universality are the highest, life and being are themselves mere copies (Pythagoras) or, even less, merely partake in the real. Thus it is necessary to go with the mind alone (from the position of having accepted one's bodily death) to knowledge. Granted all this, the path from ideal hierarchy to Realpolitik is very short in Aristotle's body politic.

In the *Foundations Project* I reject the idea and the possibility of having fully accepted my own death and coming to experience in the *as if* of refusing to confuse body and (spiritual) being. I reject this notion on various grounds, each of which seems sufficient in itself, but as a group of reasons to be simply descriptive of the human condition within the contexts of identity and being (our life, as Kafka says in his *Parables and Puzzles*, which is the only life we have).

In my study/understanding of being, any existence or experience within the concept of our own death possesses, as it were, its own domain; and this is not my/our business. It is not accessible even though it may be interesting or otherwise informative...or a palliative to increasing fears. The concept of death we deal with is *from life*. If this concept of death shapes or forms horizons of our lives, so be it; and this is important to understand, to critique, and to see that and what it consists in.

But our concept of death being from life, does not take us outside of bodily being, does not declare that there are two domains to our individual bodily being body and mind; nor does it declare that knowledge belongs to the mental, the imaginative. It is a philosophy of denial of existence and experience even as it takes aspects of them, narrows and particularizes being, knowledge, and existence, and expands such narrownesses to the infinitude of the universe. Granting agency to the products of this invented infinitude takes our being outside of our existence, to tell us how we are and ought to be.

Instead, I propose a different locus or removal or grounding from which we might be able to observe ourselves observing ourselves—of the being of our being.

I propose that we take seriously a kind of (for lack of a better terms) *as if existence* which might stem from the complete acceptance of an *intellectual nihilism*. (Perhaps, in some kind of agreement with Plato that we need to find a locus of removal from the usual/obvious grounding of our own being, that we need a form of death = a nihilism. Whether to agree with/co-opt Plato needs its own Foundations Project... a counter-foundations project...)

What I mean by an intellectual nihilism has to do with beginning our retrieve of the body and existence from as complete as possible an acceptance that there is no meaning in the world which we can take as a given; that the world is only us humans/terrestrial creatures; that the entire human condition is *as if*, stories, myths. And if the world is mythical; so what?

Coming and emanating from this acceptance we now note that most peoples operate as if the world is real, has meaning, needs and wants meaning located within/without, in their bodies, imaginations, in relationships to mothers/others, to place, to history,...to their (our) own being. (Different from Socrates, death is a tragedy, life is to be lived, celebrated!)

I think, as well, that we are describing loci of existence which take us out of the ancient Parmenidean/Platonic paradox picked up by Heidegger in *Being and Time*'s reference to Plato's Sophist, where being is placed in some dialectic with non-being. This has led to our having an affair of love with the *imaginative* abilities of being human, pushing to rid ourselves of our bodies and whatever is linguistic but not symbolic (i.e., *paralanguage*).

And this re-cognition of the imaginative should ask us to ask how we both live as body and think infinitively, rather than acting as if (Plato was truly positing an *as if*, you see!) the body grounds our essential being, and then we can act as if this body which is our life, is somehow non-essential to actual being. I am not trying to resolve some paradox of life and death, but to focus our retrieve upon the fact that our concepts of being are from life.

As a kind of strategic position which might extend the power of the acceptance of this extreme of *as if* being, it seems also important to deal with a couple of other paradoxes which have captivated Western thinking, linked as they have been with Plato's acceptance/proposed solution to the problem of death: the problematics of the one v. many; and of change v. permanence.

With respect to change, I think it important in order to remain clearly within life, to retrieve the Heraclitean position in a very strong form. This involves the acceptance of the time paradox: that life is both changing and it is/has many senses of permanence. I want to place the paradox with life experience; i.e., that the experience of the time paradox actually occurs— whether continuously in our awareness or, more likely, from *time-to-time*.

The strong form of Heraclitus is that we take change to be the governing actuality from being within life. But this does not require explanation or accounting. What needs accounting is that we find much of existence to be (now, *apparently*) stable or continuous. Since this cannot be true (from our Heraclitean pinnacle), all such stabilities need accounting. If, that is, there are no powers continuing to support or regenerate (frequently) the apparent structures, they would change. So our primary questions have to with the infrastructures—intellectual, bureaucratic, etc.—which themselves structure permanence: structures, and the senses of being within such structuring in whose terms many of us calculate being.

Within the paradox of one and many, it is crucial in providing critique of the Platonic pursuit to note that the Phaedonic split of mind and body and the subsequent banishing of the body from the realm of philosophy, epistemology, and so on for us to re-cognize and accept the importance of the locus of being as the physical body. This acceptance has been surreptitious in terms of its power to define the entire Platonic enterprise, but nonetheless powerful in its defining and attracting power: in effect, then, taking us outside our bodily being to locate our being. The fact is that with this surreptitious locational move, we have accepted the body as a kind of mistaken but certain existence—only then to deny it as we then see the mind as being located/placed within the body; but not exactly of it.

We are bodies, as Nietzsche so boldly stated in *Thus Spake Zarathustra*, and mind/soul is some story about the body. But he missed, being in the end an inescapable Platonist, the idea that we are by our nature social creatures: that we/I are body located in a universe of other bodies. He had accepted uncritically (but how could he not have in the 19th century?) the notion that our objectivity—the very basis for the possibility of epistemology—that the development of human language has enabled sociality, not the other way round.

The body—located with a universe of others' bodies is the scene, the setting and locus for the problematics of our being, of knowledge and identity and existence.

L'chaim!

A Foundational Mode of Inquiry: Although it is difficult and presumptuous to approach even one's own tradition critically and sweepingly, it is timely to attempt to re-consider the foundations of thought at this historical moment when the theo-political traditions of the entire earth come together: the great/powerful traditions as well as those which never attracted the followings of Plato-Western-Judeo-Christian-Muslim or Confucius, Buddha: indigenous Amerindian, African, animist, shamanist...

This project consists of several aphoristic works which move toward the study of what I understand to be the foundations of thought. The various projects take up the modes of inquiry, the framing questions, and the directions for search which have shaped the ways in which many/most of us think about the nature of our (human) being. They attempt to approach these critically, and to extend the foundational issues so they may possibly stand somehow, somewhere outside of any particular history, politics, or sociology of thought. Though obviously deriving from a particular place and moment in the sweeps of history, the *Foundations Project* attempts to consider thinking about the human condition from as global a set of perspectives as I can muster.

The second event-insight-critique-understanding which frames the *Foundations Project*, has to do with the (Western) understanding of what constitutes the human condition. It is now clear that other species are (also) social. I have called this insight the *ethological critique* (Sarles, *Ethology and the Philosophy of Language*)

In this context, it attempts to avoid any intellectual slippage into the earlier foundational ideas that we humans have body in common with other species. It admits, precisely, that the human (or any other species) body is how we identify ourselves and others; that the body is central to our being, intellectually... and every other way.

The ethological critique reframes in the spirit of comparative thought and inquiry much of what we think about being human. It takes us into the behavior and being of other species in the form of a fieldwork excursion, offers an immersion in the being of other forms in the world together with their conspecifics, watching what and how they do and are, how their young become adults. Then we *return* to our own human world, having placed new lenses upon our inward and reflective eyes seeing humans in newly critical ways. It is much the same as fieldwork among seemingly *exotic* human cultures: i.e., in languages and cultures which are very different from our own. It is the attempt in developing a philosophical anthropology, to do an anthropology of the *ordinary*. How to see our own habits of seeing and thinking, especially our thinking about ourselves?

Upon our return, we discover in this critical vein, that we have received and endlessly repeated stories about the human condition, many/most of which have assumed and believed that only humans are social. These stories have elaborated in a powerful but speculative way how humans could have become social, building upon presumptions of human uniqueness, especially language, symbolic behavior, and human knowledge (Aristotle, Hobbes, especially).

As these stories have been elevated to the potent status of *theory* and encapsulated in history as *natural law*, they have persuaded us that we know in some deep ways what it means to be human; as opposed to being other species or supra-human. It is precisely in this arena of presumed human uniqueness that our stories about boundaries and their maintenance have to be restudied critically.

Within the ethological critique it is clear that we are and always have been social; that we evolved to the present already as social creatures. The import of the ethological critique is to force us to rethink what we have considered to be uniquely human: language, symbolic knowledge, logic, rationality, natural law, politics, morality, being and identity, transcendence, and so on.

As well the ethological critique leads us to examine critically what has been *essentially* (a technical term critical of Platonic idealism) left out and omitted from our thinking about the human condition: namely, the fact that we are bodies living in the world with other(s') bodies. There is much about the nature of the human body whose study will prove critically interesting. And its virtual omission within the Platonic dualism of mind and body—where mind has become the principal study arena of the human condition—directs us, literally forces us, to this foundational rethinking.

As works-in-progress, I consider that readers will not only enter the *Foundations Project* as a set of limited narratives. Rather, I hope that you will enter with me into the thinking and observational self-critical positions and locations.

These projects are set within the form(s) of writing which are spare and aphoristic, leaving at least some space for readers stimulated to enter their own perorations and searches parallel to and critical of mine.

The writings are bounded and limited by their orientations within a variety of forms particularly of Western thinking to which I am heir, and whose breath I literally breathe—although with a stance which I couch and variously aggrandize as visitor, participant/observer, interviewer, and student-thinker of the writings and peoples of the earth. It is also informed by reading widely into other traditions, as well as having lived for a few years in the mixed cultures of Southern Mexico, working in the Mexican Mestizo world, but especially as an anthropological-linguist with speakers of a Mayan language. As important, is my attempt to enter cognitively the thinking of various different groups with whom I have lived and studied, including ethnic, gendered, generational, religious, linguistic, disciplinary, collegiate, and professional groups.

Context: The *Foundations Project* considers a variety of topics as writings-in-progress which wonder how we are as human beings and how place, history, language, and traditions both divide us and make it obvious that we are of a single strand of being. They seek for the *Ursprachen* of our commonesses as well as for the variety into which the vicissitudes of being human direct us. They wander upon the lines which have divided us, attempting to see and to *see-through* them.

Perhaps it is (yet) another mode of deconstruction for which the *Foundations Project* yearns; one which attempts to stand as much as possible outside of the history/culture of its tradition, so that it can reread/retrieve them as much as is possible. It surely is an apologetic of the visitor-intellectual who would live in several worlds but is not exactly at home in any or *one's own*.

The *foundational* aspects of the projects are that they try to discern the ancient discussions of the human condition at a most general yet penetrating level of analysis. Especially they consider to be foundational those ideas which have been able to capture thinking as virtually framing the idea of reality (Parmenides, Pythagoras, Plato, Aristotle in the West). As different traditions seem to have done this differently, the comparative thought which reflects one tradition onto another reveals that the notion of *reality itself* has (had) various possibilities, further pushing me to explore the human condition foundationally rather than totally relativizing our being. I presume, that is, that we are! (Sarles, *Cultural Relativism and Critical Naturalism*, 1991)

We are most certainly physical bodies living with and within the presence of other(s') bodies. Our *knowing* our bodies constitutes the groundwork of being and reality.

And we have extension. While it has been the notion of our extension *beyond* the physical that has excited most (especially Western) thinkers to characterize this especially as *the* human, I think that the physicality of our being is our being, and is much more interesting and complicated than the merely mechanical/material we have usually considered. We are—particularly our faces—mirrors of and for one another, and complicated in the dynamics of living.

An important aspect of this larger project will be to recomplementarize the mechanical/mental/spiritual aspects of being human. In various ways it will be a kind of return to a Heraclitean holism, in which experience is not at philosophical war with *materiality*. These dualistic polemics have taken us to the various edges of understanding whose unpacking has no further directedness. Instead, they have blocked us from examining various questions, directing human agency away from being.

But I realize also that time and place and various personal and collective histories direct us and our thinking to frame being in marvelously different ways. At some moments life is enjoyed and celebrated; at others it is feared and lamented, occasionally cursed. Sometimes we have invented and concocted stories to explain our feelings and to move ourselves on; at other times we have looked inside our being or totally away from being to explain our feelings, or to explain them away.

Particularly in those world traditions which have become *powerful*—those whose heirs are presently meeting in the literal classrooms of our collective lives—some moment and character of history has expressed the nature of our being in ways so powerfully convincing that the nature of our being is to a large extent lived within the framework of an historical-textual rendering of being. The world of any *actual* experience is often virtually subsumed to its textual descriptions: that is, as we are all students of existence, the text-as-world (*TAW*) has usually ruled over the world-as-text (*WAT*).

And there is the question of paradox. Apparently, for most of us, some aspects of our lives are lived—as it were, singly. Other aspects are multiple. Still others seem to us have or to develop themes which are, at once, one and another. In some traditions, for example, we try to remain fully awake and praise that as experience; in others, we find in the dreams of sleep that which we call experience. What is, for example, male is never exclusively male, nor female a way of being unto itself. Similarly with time, and with change, with life and its perorations upon death.

We humans have and continue to understand and experience the passage of time in quite different ways. Sometimes life seems viscous and slow; at other times one may effectively live two days before noon. Various traditions have attempted to stop the experience of time, or to discover ways to effectively banish time and change; others have attempted to make time cyclical, effectively containing time and change within a framework of permanence. Yet others have said (Heraclitus) that our condition is change. I add, agreeing, that we then must attempt to explain that which seems to us permanent.

And, in the traditions to which I also am heir, many of us find the fullness of being only when we no longer exist in our bodily form. And so the *Foundations Project* grapples with the paradoxical aspects of being, wondering especially why paradox has so often tried to explain itself away.

Content: This collection includes several foundational works which are variously complete (and continuing) because the meanings of our being are various and alter considerably as we move on in life. Questions about our nature, about the ways in which this nature is constructed, lived, interpreted, given and sustained in being and meaning are explored.

The problem for the thinker-about our being is to find and to occupy some critical position(s) from which to observe her/himself viewing, else get waylaid within some particularities of perspective, history, or limitations of knowing.

The common ground which they attempt to occupy with some discernable consistency has to do with the facts of our human physical presence in the presence of other physical beings in relation to the ability of mutual understanding. Our ability to understand others irrespective of language or culture or geography, history, or preferences, teaches us that understanding is possible if not always likely. The current conceptual shrinking of the entire earth which brings us together in our being, thinking, knowing instructs us of this possibility. But we must work at such understandings.

As well as certain particularities of experience and intellectual training (much of it as an autodidact), I rely on several simultaneous positioning in considering the human condition: 1) comparative thought (thinking across traditions, disciplines, species, and machines); 2) history of discourse/ideas; 3) politics of ideas/discourse; 4) sociology/marketplace of knowledge.

I am neither structuralist nor anti-structuralist, but do note that much of the human condition operates much of the time *as if* it were structural. I presume, like Heraclitus, that change is the nature and the directedness of being, but note that permanence as the antinomy of change as well as cycles of change, perforates and precludes change.

I further presume, as in the telling, that these are active principles in the human condition rather than givens. Much of the problematic of what is form and what is substance, for example, is that they often operate (as if) in some unfolding dynamic processes, rather than being in some opposition to one another.

Much of the ground of any understanding thus lies not in answers or solutions to paradox, but to the grasping of the foundational solutions of various traditions to the facts of experiential puzzling. We are creatures who experience paradox at various moments in existence. The habits of solving/resolving apparent oppositions does not tell us much about paradox, but instead directs us toward the issues and questions and their directions for solution which various traditions have effectively adopted over the centuries, and made the basis for the computation of the very idea of reality.

These studies, then, attempt to see-through the boundaries of our being to gain new appreciation of their nature. They explore the framings and architectonics of being which have informed the stories we tell ourselves as well as of the contexts of *context itself*.

These studies approach the major categories of discussion as broadly as has been possible within the time of my life and life-studies. It is informed as well by the major dialogues of my life, especially with Janis Sarles (J.) and also with Philip Regal, Gerald Timian, Glenn Radde, and Judith Martin. Others with whom I have talked include Dean Oyen, Spero Manson, Jean Cameron, Stanley Williams, Mischa Penn, Wlad Godzich, Yi-Fu Tuan, Burton Shapiro, Robin Brown, Karl Rogers, Rod Sando...

The Foundations Project is an extensive exploration of changing times. As we are exploring the idea that the world is becoming an encompassing concept—the means to understand what is happening—how to enter, to help create a global world has become a possible and urgent undertaking.

In addition to the so extensive development of new technologies, so many media, we are parts of the world driven—perhaps principally—by the vast changes in issues of gender. The other major gathering force has been since the 1969 "man on the moon" insight that all people(s) are parts of the same world. Here, *the Foundations Project* is a series of ways for exploring how we are, how we think, how we are changing just as we are coming together globally.

The ten chapters of *the Foundations Project* help us to re-enter our own thinking, hoping to deepen, expand, and grow ourselves as significant players/members of these coming times. The titles of the chapters are illustrative of the journeys upon which we are exploring: our world, and our thinking. They are a collection of ten arenas of thought—written as prose/poetry aphorisms which are "designed" for us to explore global being, even as we explore our own thinking. I suggest that these reading-thinking aphorisms will open our reading to our thinking as we move... forward toward a "Global Present."

Harvey Sarles, 2014

1.

CONTENTS OF THE MIND

1. The Adult Mind, the Individual, Me: A great deal is *memorized*; already "in" the mind (or bodymind: Dewey). Presumably, this is either "held in check," not interfering with what "enters" perception and/or knowing in each moment, or forms some kind of "filter" through which present perception is ameliorated. (J.J. Gibson 1963)–(but currently "changing with aging—I'm 80+).

I "read words," do not see merely lines and squiggles while I think about what I am writing and watch it appear in black upon the screen in front of my eyes.

Simultaneously, I am listening to some music on a disk, which is also the music on which I am working in order to rehearse tonight with a music coach. Not too difficult to do both, and live within two (three or more?) contexts at once. (For I am also drinking coffee, sitting on a Scandinavian bench, etc.)

While this is all "ordinary," it is not uninteresting, nor non-problematic. And—as processes—they are likely to occur much faster than we usually imagine.

2. Seeing Faces: I have memorized—they *reside* within my mind—the faces of, say, 1,000 persons, whom I can and do "recognize" when I see them. Some of these: those I know well, like...fear, hate...I can "run" in my thinking through fairly elaborate, if brief, events. How they (will) react, smile, frown, I can "see" as literally as I can image the screen in front of me, upon closing my eyes, now.

Every person I see, I seem to "judge" and note whether they have (are) faces I know, recognize, have memorized. Most of these I "greet," saying "Hello," or signaling somehow that we have crossed paths and entered "mutual space." Some of these I recognize I do not greet, others I avert my eyes from—a form of positive non-greeting.

Many faces I see (in this city of some size), I do not know to recognize. They are not within my mind's recognition. Nonetheless, I can/do judge something about the face: whether young, whether female, whether attractive, whether scary, whether "successful."

Judging faces, I simultaneously judge "persons."

Do I see faces with respect to my memory, to my matrices of judgment: whether I know the person, specifically; whether I know (judge) the "type" of person? Are these judgments, mere types? Or are they "stereotypes," against which I see and judge most faces? Do I have in mind, a set of faces (facial images) against which, with respect to which, I see and judge each (new) person? How many of these do I "keep in mind," how are they altered or updated? What is the relation between what I see and what I do or say; or not-say?

What, if any, is the relation between faces...and ideas? When I see or imagine another's face, does this cue much beyond the (idea of) the face, itself?

And as I have wondered elsewhere, do I see faces, or do I somehow "read" the changes which my faces undergo as I see others' faces?

And currently – approaching 80 years, retired two years ago – I've "dropped" quite a few faces "from" my memory…

3. Here and Now: Though I can "run" in thought thousands of years and micro-seconds, the infinitude of the universe and the infinitesimals of microscopy, I sit here in full realization of the gravity of my body being pulled down. I resist, sit up, my hands poised above a keyboard, fingers moving down occasionally to type this note.

If I move, I "must" set my feet, push up upon, along, my toes and leg muscles, and raise myself to full height. I can run this possibility in my thinking about doing it. Most important, I can "decide" to do it… and do it!

Here and now, I know as muscles and tissues, and gravity, the possibility and necessity of movement.

Front-facing, facing front, I see what my eye(s) see, and hear all-round. But I know more than what I see (hear), for I have in mind (memorized) where are the walls, and doors, and furniture - approximately, but surely and securely.

This knowledge, these ideas—and much more—I not only have in mind, and can run myself running through the spaces round me, but have an assured confidence that: all is approximately true, correct; that I can move through it when I want, "decide" to; that I can "locate" myself here and now.

Whether bounded, how well bounded is this here and now is set against the world being in flux, the stream of consciousness which seems to have no obvious resting places. As gravity and I are in some continuing dance, it is this choreography against which I judge Being... anywhere... any time. (See: 2 *Context*)

4. The Concept of "Being":

"Philosophical speculation began with the concept of *being*. In the very moment when this concept appeared, when man's consciousness awakened to the unity of being as opposed to the multiplicity and diversity of existing things, the specific philosophical approach to the world was born...The philosophers attempted to determine the beginning and origin, the ultimate `foundation' of all being..." (1893 Cassirer - p.73)

In my mind there runs constantly some awareness of this thing I call me; myself; I. It feels to be central to all else, at least much of the time. I can always (I tell my self) *locate* this I/me and do not seem to reinvent it each day, or even frequently. It is I; I am it.

But I am also many, and most of those which I am to others in some relation I know full well, too. Father, husband, teacher, friend, confidante, my (now dead) dog's companion, son (still, to my parents, also dead), neighbor (and still a significant ex-neighbor to many). I am in some relation to my memories of earlier selves, how coherent the 30s, the 40s, 50s, 60s, 70s, 80s, 90s 2000s, 10s all have some lively place in memory... to be conjured up when? (A recent retrospective of the songs of Irving Berlin, and I know still almost all the lyrics!) All of these memories I have and am, and can usually "find" when I will.

Being: this philosophical fundament, seems engorged and full toward bursting.

But, I agree with Cassirer, that Being (or much about being) is fundamental to philosophic thought—to much else, too. And it emerged at a certain point in history, not merely because some particular geniuses arrived or the history demanded it, but because human *scale* changed dramatically at that point. More people lived, lived longer, lived together. (Agriculture was the major culprit!)

One's personal Being, one's self and sense of self, emerges at a point in social life when there are too many others to keep track of in the fullness of their existence, and in the fullness of our relationships. It is at these points when we begin to deal (1000, 1500 persons) with more and more limited aspects and features of "others"... limited aspects of ourselves. This is true personally, and historically as well.

It is with this increase in scale, when there are too many, that Being emerges. In dealing with limited aspects of other: as a friend's mother, (only) as a teacher, a sale's clerk, a boss; when we do not know these others (also) as child to their person, as husband, father, daughter, friend, companion to their pets, then we begin to deal with others much more as objects, as persons, rather than as particular people, in the particularity of their relationships. As we deal with others in the narrowness of Being, we begin to see ourselves, as well, as being the limited features with which they deal with us. We become objectified in the sense of being congeries of features, rather than as the full person we are/were.

Once law emerged, we could frame and restrict the aspects of thought which we call "rational." Reason began to stand on its own, as we stood outside of ourselves, as it were, watching our selves watching. We came to take the limited features of our Being, which others treated us as, and reconstructed who we are; who we must be.

As the Pythagoreans elaborated the formal aspects of "things," we began to play with temporality and the indefinite as if they were, like the limited aspects of persons-not-people, delimitable. And, like persons, they are!

What we (that is, Cassirer) are calling Philosophy, began with the habit of raising a limited set of features of objects and of persons, to a reality which was granted hegemony over all else. This was called Mind, and reason, and was declaimed as *the real* in all of thought. All else became a kind of intellectual residuum, which nonetheless floats about in our minds, trying to find categories which it fits; which fit it.

Being, in this formal (universal, infinite) sense, has developed beyond belief, perhaps beyond recognition. All else, all these primitives of mind content, float freely; or not so freely in the 30s, 40s,...90s, 2000s, 10s, not so surely finding a homely set of categories, not always so willing to stay out of the way of Being.

Grant Being "agency" and the contents of the mind begin to appear explicable? Grant agency to any idea and the superorganic will rise again!

5. The Mind-Brain Problem: For some, this is a deep problem; for others, it melts toward one "side" or the other. Usually the question is how a finite, material "grey matter" can entertain thoughts about an infinite universe; or, how to imagine imagining?

The materialist, neurological "solution" tends to deny the problem, or to delay dealing with it, "until we understand" the brain (in terms of whatever the current research uses). Most materialists (I have known) have also delayed dealing with notions dealing with or deriving from the "mind." Either they are naive and simplistic (e.g., uncritically claiming that "only humans have Language = an aspect of mind), or they seem to deny that humans have "minds." Some expect, that is, a thorough materialist answer to "how we think." For them, there is, effectively, no "mind-brain problem."

The "anti-materialist" position also holds that there is no "mind-brain problem," but for quite different sorts of reasons. Most of these partake of one form or another of philosophical "idealism." For some of these, the brain occupies one (categorical) domain, the mind another, and these are (to be) kept quite separate. They are not to be considered together: the brain is in the domain of "nature;" the mind is in the domain of "culture." And one "should" not (following Durkheim 1893, as I recall) analyze different things of these sorts, together. They each "exist," and each has its own terms - different, non-comparable.

Other idealists are Platonic "formalists"; formalists in the sense of judging the reality of things not by the particularities of what occurs in any moment, but in terms of the forms or ideas which are "deeper," and non-finite. For them, the brain and its workings are aspects of superficiality and momentariness. What is real are the permanent aspects of thought and reason; for Cassirer, the symbolic forms. For them, the study becomes one of "pure" thought (Kant 1959), or of the forms... of symbols. For these, the contents of the mind are these aspects of pure thought, which "operate" essentially independently of the moment, of the dynamics of the brain. Not only independent, they are also primary to knowledge: knowledge, per se.

So, in a certain sense, the mind-brain problem (if it is a "real" problem) is a debate over the hegemony of what is knowledge, and, derivatively, what is truth and reality.

Others of us do not consider the mind-brain problem to be a good or useful way of stating what is problematic.

Minnesota Public Radio just began playing the Mozart Clarinet Quartet which I performed (as 2nd violin) some years ago. As I am typing, I hear each note often in the detail of each instrument's playing, and the entire ensemble performing as a unit. However much detail in running in my head (while I am typing this, still), I really know this piece in a fairly great amount of detail, moment-by-moment in a stream of multiple consciousnesses (I'm still typing; they're still playing.)

Even as I press down my fingers on the computer typing-thing (I don't necessarily have all the names down to the letter), and perhaps my mind and thinking is somewhat cluttered, even as I get off on the melodies and accompaniments—thinking also of the characters with whom I performed. One just died; one just retired; I know them also in some detail (their characters, the politics of two of them with whom I have disagreed to a large extent over the past few years: they now moved into the *allego finale*, even as I am playing in my mind the melody and at least the 2nd violin part and typing. Just finished, they did. I can still run almost entire piece, but it's difficult to begin it again without halting my typing.

I have the violin in mind, playing it, my history with it, with some cellists, with only one clarinetist actually, the other violin who was a musicologist; none of them very easy for me (nor I for them, probably; but maybe I wasn't much of a counter for them). The violist I didn't know well, but he introduced me to R. Zabinski who turns out to be a great maker of bows, and on to his friend who does the Ballet of the Dolls; and the question of my violin—playing it, repairing it, how much is it worth, and am I worthy of it. Why don't I take some lessons? I am hardly focusing at all on the music they are playing presently, don't know it, I don't think, and find it difficult to get my focus back to it (I actually do know it, heard a familiar passage; but not in the detail that I know and can sing and hear and gush over the Mozart, over my participation in it, the other 4 players, the setting in which we played it).

6. The Homunculus: Our theories of mind often come down to the nature of the "interpreter," the homunculus or little person "in" the brain/mind who takes in this sensory information from the world, casts it in some forms that our mind "understands," and interprets it so that it "makes sense."

What is the nature of the homunculus? Is this the only way to think about how we "understand?"

The (intellectual?) problem with the notion of the homunculus, the steerer-interpreter inside our heads, is that it (he/she?) appears to be a solution for how we understand anything, but it is (really?) just another name for something which merely appears to be a solution. By naming it, we have appeared to solve something, while just making the problem disappear, or remain hidden in the excitement of claiming a notion or level of solution to an ancient problem (or offer promises for the proximate solution, just now via brain scans).

Computer scientists have tried to solve this problem by making a program "work like the mind." If such a program were to do what we do, think like we think, then we could examine the internal dynamics of the program, and gain some insight into the way a brain might work. At present, these programs seem to be at some impasse, because the model of "language" which has been chosen to "represent" the homunculus, seems too simplistic. It by-passes the facticity of the human body, paralanguage, context, etc. It begins with the ancient (honorable?) notions of words referring to objects or ideas, which seem (to me) to form a grand tautology.

What are some aspects of the homunculus problem?
How, for example, can the movement (vibration) of air waves be interpreted as words? How are these words "constructed" (in our minds) out of the variation of sound "pressure" (amplitude of noise) and duration; i.e., how do we "entify" sound? What is acoustic; what "psycho-acoustic?" (—another "word-substitution" or naming, without much substance?)

Are "impressions" or "images" of "objects" "copied" in our minds? It is not clear whether this is one question, several, or a non-question! Even assuming that we "know" "objects" objectively, do we see direct images of them? e.g., do we have a pictorial image of a cat, when we see a cat (a direct copy); do we "see" the cat in terms of impressions—size, color, 4 legs, not-a-dog—which we then "construct" into the whole (image) of a cat?

The experiential answer is, obviously, "yes!" We see the cat; we also see its "component" impressions or qualities. What is the difference between the "real" objective cat and the cat we have in mind? (From the social-emergentist position of Question-Response grammar: we see as and how our parents see! *See below.*)

It has seemed to me that a number of these terms and questions get gathered up into some surreptitious or hidden concept. We have a need to resolve some of these experiential responses (these wonderments) into the concept of the homunculus or interpreter; often, we seem to place these in a kind of "no-person's land" between the brain and the mind. Then we back off, as it were, and make some intellectual jumps, or side steps which seem to solve/resolve these problems. There are several ways or moves which have seemed useful—at least for some thinkers.

The materialist move: to report on all the wonderful things which we are learning, recently and day-by-day, about the workings of the brain. When we know "enough" (it is said, in the form of an intellectual promissory note) about the brain, these problems will have an obvious solution. We will know! Some place, some connections, some whatever! While this is, in a sense, no doubt a truth of sorts—concepts most likely have mechanical or material correlates—the brain-solution thinkers seem to be offering a direct causal explanation, which will (someday) explain all this. But my suspicion is that their explanations will not be much better than the homunculus they (also) have in mind—a concept as well. These brain solvers of the interpretive problem seem to be reductionists whose occasional claims to be holists grants them some credibility... But I think the problem gets begged.

I propose that the solution is that Q-R *forms* the brain, rather than the reverse.

The idealist solution: This has several apparent possibilities, which look different in different settings. Basically, this solution is to attempt to by-pass the problem by attributing most or all aspects of knowing to the "mind, itself" (granting in some *a priori* way that there is an entity such as the mind). It grants (up-front or surreptitiously) that there is, indeed, an interpreter; and that it is an inherent feature of our being: we are born this way; our mind's understanding is a feature of our being.

What happens now varies considerably. Most (Western) thinkers, in considering this issue, have a more complicated conceptual matrix in which this problem is placed than might be noted at first glance. The homunculus which we Westerners seem to depict is, first of all, not like the "interpreter" of any other species. This is to say that our homunculus is bound up already with what we consider to be particularly, uniquely human; that which is (significantly) NOT like any non-humans. I think that this is terribly important to ponder when considering this issue because the apparent paradox of the finite-infinite abilities of humans (only) pervades our thinking about the interpreter/homunculus. Indeed, the idealist solution rests (always?) on removing the mind from "experience" and granting it some kind of "independence."

Well, the deity-as-explanation hovers here. What we call the interpreter, the homunculus, the solution to this deep "mystery" (Elevating this conceptual problem to the level of "mystery" already moves the problem toward a deific solution!) is some form of "God." Some thinkers of my acquaintance, call this the "Archeus" (or originating principle [Leibniz 1686]). Others derive their thinking directly (or indirectly) from Genesis: 1:26. Here the distinction is drawn between humans and others: made in the "image" of God; having "dominion" over all the "animals." What this does—in any event (in all events?)—is to re-place the problem within a new construction, namely within the concept of God, or the Archeus. As I have seen, the usual move then is to by-pass the problem by claiming to have offered a solution. Thence forward we are directed to examine the deity, or world-spirit. And the issue disappears while we probe the nature and possibilities of the selected principle. This also seems not to be any solution, in the name of offering an explanation.

Another idealist solution—usually without exclaiming a deity—is to claim this conceptual territory for the mind—as opposed to the brain. Cassirer is a modern proclaimer.

The mind has its own, proprietary stuff; since Kant it has been called pure reason. *It* has rules, structures, internal coherence, etc. Cassirer calls it "symbolic forms." These moves put (at least appear to put) some conceptual baggage upon a sphere of being which is, at the outset, dubitable in terms of any existence. In either case, these appear to be virtual synonyms for the homunculus, the interpreter of old. This move is somehow taken to be rock-bottom, ground for all of human knowledge. And it has directed thinking about thinking in the Humanities at least since Kant, mostly since Descartes.

Here the subject matter of human nature has either by-passed materiality completely (from brain to body), or promised to return to experience once the important work of thinking, knowing, etc., has been sufficient to some larger task.

Are there other (alternative) ways of dealing with the homunculus? How do we know: ourselves, the world, others? How can we simultaneously think our internal thoughts and let the world of experience and the senses enter thought? Do we "run several tracks"? Does the comparative ethological insight that we are (primarily!) social creatures, provide any framework for thinking about thinking?

7. On Sociality: Thinking socially, comparatively, looking "back" at humans, it seems clear that we have been considering "the human" as coterminous with individual (bodily) being. Many of the philosophical "dilemmas" which have arisen have found problems and paths toward their solution within this very particular portrayal of the human condition.

How can we be, simultaneously, finite and infinite; think and experience; be material and be persons? Where is the self which is continuous, whilst the stream of consciousness flows on carrying us with it?

To rethink comparatively, socially, it is useful (probably necessary) to suspend judgment about a number of things, some of which have seemed basic or obvious.

(a) The human "individual" is not survivable. In crude terms, "life is lethal." Our parents, the prior generation not only granted us life, but MUST sustain it for several years. Our "independence" is emergent; our "individuality"—its primariness and centrality—is itself a "social construct." This is not to deny that we have or possess individuality, but that it is enmeshed from the beginning of our existence in social construction and definition; basic notions such as existence, experience, and essence of being human, require re-consideration. The dualisms which have underlain Western thought such as mind-body, individual-society, finite-infinite are not "opposed," but complementary in various, often "surprising" ways.

(b) As we derive "being" within social relations and social matrices we are "students" and "interactors" with others. As we suspend judgment about the nature of "individuality," we consider that the infant does not stand outside of his interactions but "becomes" them. The infant, as student of m/other's face (especially), mimics it, moves as it moves, enters "into" it as much as "responds" to facial movement (expression). Whether the infant understands itself as a self or an aspect of the m/other's being must remain an open issue.

(c) Infants (we as social beings) are primarily—as survivors—students of our parents. We do not "know" the world directly but "as they do." As we study who they are, we are students of what and how they know and do. The "environment" in which we live, our *Umwelt* is not that which surrounds us, but precisely that which our parents define, already. We do not, that is, learn to refer to objects as our beginning language lesson or language game, but learn how our parents refer, and what they consider to be objects. Whether we (each infant) does this properly, well, or morally depends primarily on how the parents define the infant's behavior, study it, move it on, in some sense of development and progression (Q-R System).

(d) As we are students of parents' definitions of being, and of their descriptions of the world, we do this primarily through (as a "mechanism") mimicking their facial expressions. (Language, even, is facial mimicry in its primary senses.) Seeing them, seeing their faces move, our faces move as theirs. (Note: opening infants' mouths in response to parents opening theirs in feeding.) That is, the individual moves its faces (external, internal facial muscles), with respect to, in response to how they see parents moving theirs. In a deep (I think) sense, facial movement and facial "formulation" is how we "see."

We obtain knowledge of others, thence of the world, by facial "modeling" of others' faces, of their changing expressions, interactive and with respect to the external world. We learn, in a sense, to become (like) they look and appear. We move our faces as they move theirs, look outward at the world, as they (almost literally) look out. In a sense, we "suspend" our facial movement from the remainder of our being. Our faces act as if they possess a life of their own; a life, that is, which models parents (mothers)—both anatomically and in dynamic movement.

Knowledge of the external world must then be some "second order reading(s)" of the changes we experience in our faces (tongues, facial muscles, eye blinks, lip striae...). The problematic of epistemology thus shifts to questions of how this might happen (does happen). What are the (some) mechanisms? What is the nature of expressive change and dynamics; what, the base of a constancy in terms of which change might be noted (muscular, most likely)? How does this external muscle facial structuring of other faces, articulate with deeper muscles (e.g., breathing, tongue...) so that we form "images" of objects, words, etc?

The homunculus, then, begins with the facial muscles, at least for humans. We do not "see" the world directly, but through a matrix of our faces seeing other faces seeing the world. Similarly, we "hear" through our tongues' movements imitating the sounds of those others we hear (i.e., our dialects are part and parcel of articulating and moving our vocal muscles approximate like the others around us). We "let loose" of our external facial muscles and "read" them—either "as they are" or how they have "changed" is an open question, perhaps both.

Examples abound: our virtual inability to "resist" the smile of another person, by "smiling" ourselves; having to whisper when another person whispers.

What is the nature of the "second order" reading? Where do we gain (sustain) the constancy of self, from which (facial) change is read? Should we read "body" for "face," in a more general sense? Is there a mechanism for the second order reading (or several)? What is the nature of that reading? How related to the homunculus or interpreter by which we internalize the external?

(e) Body Image: In this semiotic universe, where we become, in a deep sense, the way in which we see significant others' being, we are defined—in a consistent sense—largely by those others. Who we are is ("inside") largely in flux...actually. We keep ourselves "in balance," requiring large and small muscles moving and holding, and keeping us upright or moving. Yet we have ("keep") a fairly constant image of ourselves which includes: where we are (orientation), how we move or are in balance (navigation), what we look or appear like.

Our "judgment" of ourselves is constant and consistent enough, in an imagistic sense, that we can judge change of at least many sorts. Much of this is, no doubt a sense of muscular consistency with which we are "comfortable." Comfort, in this context, means just a continuity which "feels like us."

It is imagistic, probably in several senses: coherence and integrity. "Insults" (lesions, paralyses, etc.) to the body are likely more insulting to the integrity of one's image of self, than to the body "itself." "A broken heart" is less a cardio-vascular problem than we have a deep concern ("need?") for keeping a sense of who we are; damage to one's integrity.

Appearance to self: we are "susceptible" to personal facial changes during each day, yet often find our appearance "surprising" as we look in the mirror. The relation between "inside" imagistic senses of facial appearance and how we actually reflect in a mirror are often strangely out of sync. During each day we are dancing partners with gravity, responding to external (and some internal) changes and a quick dynamic—each of which alters our faces in small ways. Each change is, in a sense, a change in a changing, a not-quite-the-same return to a previous state of "hold," of "neutral," of who I am. When I glance in the mirror, I am looking through the "filter" of some kind of memory of how I look (from the last time, in some idealized sense). What I see often is different from what I "expected" (remembered).

The social aspects of our body image are, no doubt derived from some sense of how others saw/see us. Whether our parents "liked" us (& how we appeared to them), whether we responded to them in ways which enhanced their dealings with us, played a part in gaining an imagistic sense of how we now appear.

As Kant portrayed pure reason, the image of the body—in the context of relating the image of self which we "carry" and what we "see" in the mirror each time—is an issue of "judgment." Thus the study of appearance will turn out to be the study of how we come to judgment—and how we judge those judgments.

8. Consciousness: Within traditional philosophy, the issue and nature of consciousness had to do primarily with the contrast between the operation of the mind in the immediate, contrasted with the longer terms aspects of memory and internal thinking or reason.

In the notion of the individual "mind" understood to exist within a social matrix, the mind is seen more as an existent within and among a universe shared with others, not as emanating "outward" from itself. The mind is not seen primarily as existing in any direct or singular "opposition" to the body or other material aspects of being; e.g., the brain. We do primarily see or sense the world, construct it in any purely individual sense, but see and construct the world much as others do. Much of what is "consciousness" is thus an ability or "skill" to shift into others' knowing of the world in shared terms. As stated earlier, we do not learn first the objective world, and come to study others as (like) ourselves, but we come to know the world already as others know it.

Casteneda has claimed in "The Second Ring of Power," (1991) the most difficult thing in life is to believe what is happening to us in the immediate. However much this describes the actuality of our lives, it does remind us that we come to each moment, live the stream of consciousness, within complex social notions. Not only do we experience what we do in any immediate, for example, but we are likely convinced that others experience the world in approximately the same way. Further, we remain mostly convinced that these immediate events are not only shared, but communicable from me to you, and vice-versa.

Since we know full well that the immediate is in some flux, perhaps the beginning question of the nature of consciousness is to look for the factors which form a constancy or backdrop in contrast with which we even acknowledge the momentariousness of immediacy. (Again, contrast this with the philosophical psychology, which grants primariness to immediate "perception." Somehow, in some conceptual corner, we have swept away the need to postulate and theorize how we know that the present is, having granted it surreptitiously to the body, which we then give back to "nature.")

It seems obvious, within a sociality of knowledge, that there is not one (track of) consciousness, but several: knowing ("tracking") on how/what others know; knowing where my gravity/balance is and where it is about to go (knowing where I am); knowing that I have access to language, to talk, to action or to none; knowing that I can detect change, danger; knowing where and how to locate my esthetic and judgment; knowing the event-space and the context (where I am, others are; walls, time-of-day, situation); knowing that I know...

Moreover, these so-called tracks of knowing and of consciousness may be of various sorts, or modes. In the context of sociality (The Q-R System), perhaps the primary track has to do with being able to know how others know, what, when, etc. "Consciousness" (to provoke some rethinking) is the ability to cue-in to others' understandings when it is situationally appropriate.

The notion of consciousness—traditionally having to do with knowing self-consciously what one knows in any moment—resides upon the constancy of self-knowing, which is that self-derived relation to others' visioning of oneself. It is not an inherent aspect of each individual, but a semiotic aspect of the successfully socialized person (i.e., all of us who survive, learn language, etc.). When I see an object, refer to it, intend to talk about it, I see it mediated through the knowing of others who taught me to refer.

There is, no doubt, an individual track of knowing, but it is one (are ones) to which we have less direct and/or articulated access. As we learn language, learn to refer to objects (both the particular and the universal meaning) the how of how we analyze, the what-we-see-in-particular into sense impressions simply does not arise in the interaction. As long as we identify objects properly (using the correct word), we are seldom asked how we analyze and re-construct any entity; we are only asked to do it. Each of us has developed ways of naming, which "contains" many idiosyncrasies. In this, a great deal of individual "freedom" may be located. An irony is that we have not articulated this arena of "howness" to anyone else; neither have we articulated it to ourselves. Much of what we may call the "unconscious" thus consists of the ways we have, individually hit upon aspects of naming and language use which simply never arise in interactions.

Other tracks are related to or defined by (roughly) context and situation: how we locate where we are is no "mere" matter of physical orientation, but also one of complex social/personal definition. Issues of "concentration" are also important: how do we "set bounds" upon any situation and select what we see, simultaneously *dis-attending* to "extraneous" issues? What is "attention?" How do we enter certain tracks of our thinking, pick up yesterday's ideas just where we left-off; stay "in there" and rummage around, whilst excluding whatever else? What are the relations between "feelings" and thought: certain feelings (e.g., depressed) seem often to "own" certain thought arenas in my life?

Thus, to state what is conscious, or consciousness, what the contents of the mind in any instant, what is hidden, unavailable or lurking with latent and possible horrific powers in the depths of psychic meanderings, so far at least, is to postulate a non-social mind. Traditionally, this has excluded (or brought in as epiphenomenon or afterthought) sociality; it has excluded aspects of the body (except as they have been useful to account for what has otherwise been explicable).

9. Consciousness and Culture: Part of the Romantic reaction to the Enlightenment mechanistic depiction of the mind as geometer, was to worry about the human spirit. Where did we come from? How powerful is this history of the question of origin, especially in relation to some sense of destiny, deity, or world spirit! How do we go "beyond" any mechanistic "present" into the "transcendent"?—by any definition of "beyondness" and "transcendental"!

Within this reconstruction of the mind, the issue of history—of time in many of its senses—gained importance. What remained essentially the same was the sense that we were individuals (primarily, essentially) and that the individual "I" consisted of a dualism, the two-ness of mind and body. Where the earlier concern of the Enlightenment rationalists was with the nature of how and what we know about the real/external world, and they "backed-in" to a description of the mind as a tool to explain human knowledge and judgment, the Romantics dwelt upon the mind as having dimensions of tremendous scale and scope.

Noting the world's different peoples, cultures and languages, the sense of history playing a grand role up to the present, gave writers like Herder (1791) and Humboldt 1836) the sense that some destiny was ever-recurring in the present. Like the differences among species in the natural world, the differences among peoples was writ large into some evolutionary frameworks whose explanatory power would tell us, somehow, who we are—as who we are *meant to be*.

The world of reality, directly apparent to the mind of man, had been replaced by Kant into a study of the mind; a prior study, whose elaboration and elucidation must precede any hope to apprehend the world. The change—in the possibility of its apprehension—from Aristotle's object, whose purpose had its immanence within our minds, to Hegel's phenomenon. It was to be the phenomenology, a temporal unfolding of the mind's increasing ability to know, which dominated the thought about thinking, from then to this day.

It was to be a concern with Culture, a name for this unfolding from the "naivety" of the body's direct, momentary investiture in the present, to the synthetic frameworks of thought's consciousness about itself, which would gain definitional hegemony over our conception of mind. The distinction between the world and mind, object and subject, nature and culture would take a difference, turn it into an opposition, and create a chasm between a biology and an anthropology. Each word became super-organic, gained its own substance, to be examined in "its own terms," never again (to this day, at least) to understand the human condition except through some conceptual filters which separate us from our nature. Still the mind-body dualism, but now each occupying an unbridgeable domain.

Culture, the heir to and co-communicant with Language, has become bound-up with attempts to show how humans are... all on the (critically unexamined) assumption that humans are unique in the terrestrial scape. Reason, thought, modes of moving away from our natural selves, where we seem to find ourselves, as Plato claimed—as spirit and soul placed and virtually trapped—within the body, which is nature.

Now the subject is self-consciousness, the movement of knowledge away from the naive present, into the ideational networks which take us away—in the sense of an alienation from self—from our nature. But what do they take us toward? What are the contents of consciousness? What is its oppositional category—*the unconscious*? Will history determine us? Do ideas clash in some dialectic which is progressive? What is all there in our minds? What have we forgotten? Unfolded in our own unfoldings? Is this love affair with categories useable toward our understanding of thought?

Can we do anything in the here and now, which is beyond the naivety which is our destiny to escape? Stay tuned!

10. Matter and Form: "mere" matter and the "purity of form," an embattled categorical distinction which has been hovering about Western thought since Parmenides was first uncertain about whether he could distinguish—in his imagination—between being and non-being.

Some sense that physics is primary in the order of things, and humans, especially the aspects of humans knowing, is "after" or "meta" to that physics. Mirrored in our thinking about ourselves (aspects of the contents of the mind!) the body is mere matter, the mind is what makes us heavenly. (One can imagine some Maileresque quotation about bodily odors and the attempt to deodorize the pits of existence... as if smelling good perfumes the conceptual detritus.)

Driven by angst, probably a foreboding of mourning for the existence we do not permit ourselves to live in any entirety, we have seen life as a drive to remove us from mere matter. Always it has some veil of history cast over us as if its befogging of us hides the purity of form which will reveal itself when the shroud lifts... as if life were statuary cast within a bed of sands whose aggregate will wash off, any day now. Rather than wanting to live, exactly, we are on some search for the Holy Grail whose notion of existence will free us from life itself.

This veil, as it were, of history, has—in its rootedness—a dual life, whose propagative power so ensconces the imagination that it boggles thinking. The root of angst? Life and death? Matter and the mind? I think what we call religion has taken the first question, and philosophy the latter, as its separate locus for determining being. The path of exploration has been conceptual: to free the mind from the body by whatever means have seemed "reasonable." Or, within some sociology of knowledge, whatever would "sell" in any particular era. Yet the overarching conceptual architecture, the duality driving being, remains, in creating the very definition of life's problems.

Perhaps, to probe further, the amazement of the mind-matter philosopher, that mere matter could become conceptual; the finite become infinite. How could that be?

The ordinariness of the two-year old who already knows the finite and the infinite belies the conceptual astonishment that this is at all difficult for quite usual little humans. Has this problem of mind and matter been miscast?

11. Pure Synthetic Apperception: If we assumed, like Kant, that the central problem of epistemology is in determining how we—at once—think our ongoing thoughts, and receive momentary sensory information, then we would no doubt postulate some internal mechanism. Such a mechanism 1934would likely consider that our mind possesses pure reason, a mode of thinking which is effectively independent of the senses, and an "interrupt" mode, which can suspend reason, at will, and "judge" in some relation the ongoing, new information, compared with the workings of the reason. There must be some "I" which runs the program and can interrupt it when it judges it useful or important, or is occasionally "overridden" by excitement. This "I" has, historically, been granted to the individual as an inherent aspect of being, with a sense of some constancy and integrity: an aspect of the mind (in a mind, not body, dualistic framework); a grounded aspect of self which is evident to the self.

Instead, the fact of the matter is that we begin life in some complex of relationships, in which the self is the "reasoned;" the center of one's independent being is more a semiotic fact than a fact inherent in bodily being.

The self-which-is-the-judge is—in my view (Mead 1934)—a social derivation; a process which is so ingrained as to seem instantaneous. That self which is constant, which is available to think thoughts, as well as to judge the instantaneity of a car's onrushing presence, for example, is a "place" in our being which is constant in the social sense that we are considered by others to be who I am; a name, an integrity, an ongoingness, a presence to the others who judge me to be me. The ego, the "I" which my name reminds me that I am, is derived, yet is as constant as any aspect of one's being. The bodily I, the other side of the dualistic opposition which stands aside but never gets any rest, is in various aspects of flux, but the mindful "I" seems constant.

In rethinking reason and cognition, then, we must first suspend the notion that the self, the constant judging "I" is inherent in being: it is a process which we know as well as how we chew or swallow or breathe. Probably it partakes of these processes, as well as of our balance and gravity: our abilities of orientation and navigation, knowing our gravity, the constancy of the muscles of support. Its apparent depth in our being has more to do, I suggest, with the fervor and frequency with which we peruse its constancy, that with a constancy, per se.

This ego, this story we tell ourselves about who I am, this consciousness which I trust to judge judging, is a semiotic fabrication. (Is "fabrication" too strong a word?) Our certification, our validity, our existence in the world is our existence in the social world. The ego is emergent, its constancy a desire of all parents; the honing of its raggedness is an aspect of the socialization which is towards its being who/what "they" declare it to be. And we have no choice, no particular interest in being anything other. (Freedom is fairly abundant, it turns out, but not located in the formulation of the self or judging ego. That we become ego, that we can find an "I" which is worthy of our trust, here there is no other possibility!)

The Q-R System, is part of the story, at least, of how we become cognitive "agents." The infant, endowed with the ability to "read" its parents (m/other), practices movement, studies others bodies and its own, and it able to "bootstrap" itself to "reason" like others reason. It enjoys movement, studies and loves the facial movement which it can mimic (in part) at birth; loves sucking, vocalizing, centers itself within gravity, and it moves around that center; yields aspects of its being to the movement of others' faces.

Rather than to postulate an inherent constancy within the flux of (bodily) being it is more useful to explore how we actually are, to see that we are inherently creatures who are simultaneously both constancies and in some flux. By thinking of this simultaneity of change and constancy as some forbidden intellectual paradox, Western philosophy has taken us to places which remove us from our own being. Instead, the infant, the infant which we all once were, is and lives that paradox.

We have overlooked many of the aspects of being which are aspects of the human experience because we have been busy—perhaps preoccupied—trying to respond to our questions derived from a very particular philosophical-religious history, rather than attempting to see how (successful) humans become, sustain, and find meaning in a complicated world.

12. Form and Content: The prevailing depiction or vision of how the human mind gathers information, unfolding and developing from a biological-reflex (unthinking) creature to one which is reasoning is of some unfilled vessel, which becomes filled. The problem, given this sense of being and development, is how this intrinsic and inherent individual, takes in information, processes it properly, and becomes rational.

Piaget's representation of this problem is well done (1952). Instead of, or in addition to, the interpretive self (a pre-homunculus) which takes in information, there are "stages," each of which has some sort of inherent shaping: a set of reinterpreters which are triggered at various ages. Schemes derived directly from Locke's (1690) notion of "experience," Stimulus-Response Psychology in its variety of modern workings out, try to by-pass the notion of a mind at all, but it hovers, and is susceptible to being replaced by a "mind scheme" (Chomsky 1966) which proffers a way of generalizing and universalizing knowledge.

In a deep sense, however, each of these developmental schemes postulates an inherent self or knower which somehow incorporates the world into its thinking mind. That self seems determinate, constant. In this sort of scheme, it apparently must be. The world is environment; the self selects what is interesting or important. The problematic of knowledge seems to reduce, often at least, to the efficiency of learning, rather than to a more general sense of the nature of knowing and of knowledge.

Given a vision of the human spirit as primarily social, however, the question of the development and accumulation of knowledge appears quite different. "The individual" is an emergent notion, shared as it were by parent and child. The constancy of being is similarly a social notion: the individual's gradual coming to call and know him/herself as an "I" is ensured and reinforced by others' constant definition and treatment.

Thus, there is no "self" which knows what to know, inherently; no person whose intuitions form some ground upon which to plant knowledge of the correct seed for the right varieties. As environment, the world has no compelling structure whose appeal is self-evident. Indeed, the "world" of the developing child is structured—not in any inherent material sense—in certain proclivities of the (human) child and in the conceptual and experiential structures of the adult generation.

The child is not directly a student of the world, but of its parent(s); through this study, thence of the world. Knowledge is not directly of the world, but of other persons, thence of their study of the world.

The process (no doubt there are several) is one of "bootstrapping" what is already conceptualized by the parents into the being of the developing child. The child's senses are not directed toward the environment in any simple, general way, but are particularly oriented toward the study of its mother's face and facial changes. The child is also student of "itself," its gravity, balance, orientation, and movement. How the child comes to know—especially to interpret—is mediated, however, through knowing how others know.

The principal "method," the structure which enables knowing of the world, of the structure and meaning of meaning, is what I have called elsewhere (Sarles 1985) the "Question-Response System." It is a method by which the mother gets the child to enter into the world as a set of mother's queries to which the child is to respond. Mother's queries are, indeed, about the world; especially, early on, about objects and reference and naming. As the child comes to know the questions, the sets of responses to any question, the meaning of the sets becomes available. It is in the meaning of the response sets to parental questions, that meaning is located: space, time, persons, objects, cause (and effect), action, choice, relation, and the quantifiers of number, color, size, etc., which we call in other contexts, adjectives and adverbs.

What is "inherent" in the human condition is an infant who possesses the ability *to want to* study its mother, who can (as example) transduce mother's opening of her mouth to feed, into opening its own mouth—a complex mimesis of internal muscular response to changes in mother's facial surfaces.

Now the infant (I suggest) has no particular sense that the content, the knowledge of the world, what is "worth knowing," is apparent or obvious. As "student," the child is curious, engaged, moving, excited, especially by facial surfaces. What is exciting, I will define as "form" or "style"—what is attractive to the child. The parental "problem" is to translate or transfer what is attractive to the child into a conceptual structure, which is precisely that one which the parent "possesses," concerning the world. This latter is the "content" of knowledge.

But this is no direct road, no strait-gate, from form to content. Indeed, I suggest that the development of knowledge consists in a number (kinds?) of form-content shift from what is attractive or interesting at any point of development, into a next kind of content; at which point, something else becomes attractive (a new sense of what is form), to become content, and on... and on.

For example, once the child "possesses" the ability to name objects (the content), the question of number (How many...?) begins to be interesting. Once the child can stand, the possibility of raising the arms to be picked up becomes possible and interesting; the very nature (content) of movement has altered. Once the notion of responses to (Who is...?) person is filled-in, the possibility of naming oneself as "I" first arises; the constancy of the self, each an "I," thus requires much prior bootstrapping.

The "style-content" analogy in teaching may be apt: students are, primarily, students of their teachers, trying to "please" them (at least the student's version of them). The pedagogical problem: to use the attraction of students to the teacher (style or form) to attract them to the teacher's subject matter (content).

The study of language, from this perspective, shows it to be a kind of "rigid," absolute structure in many ways; e.g., the way in which questions and response are structured; but they have a great deal of flexibility ("relativity") in others. Once the child has embodied (to possess content is, in a deep sense, to embody that content, to be it, rather than having "learnt" it as a process of memory, as an attachment to a deeper or prior sense of self), that structure, there is an openness to the response sets which is indefinite → the infinitude of language which theology has attributed to the extra-natural in the human.

This depiction of development—one which is more than a summative sense of a process of learning, which is itself a singularity—raises a great deal more questions than it answers. But it also provides a critique of previous thinking about cognition, lays certain questions to rest, sets some directions for new inquiry, and begins to account for some human propensities which have seemed mysterious, and needing non-rational explanation or seeming to remove the human (especially "intelligence") from the terrestrial bed whence we derive.

Especially, it begins to account for some of the complexities of the contents of the human mind. Many of our ostensibly internal conversations are a kind of discourse with others; meaning involves reference to situations, including entire landscapes of concepts and occurrences, as easily as it involves reference to objects; we can act as if we are non-finite or indefinite creatures even as we exist within any here and now, because the response sets to definite (finite, fixed) questions are open (infinite), able to generate maps in our imagination and to actualize any step on the path—simultaneously; we keep many other faces (bodies) alive in our thinking, with exquisite detail, seeing others apparently with reference to these facial memories; etc.

The human psyche—because it has not taken in its development any straight, summative path towards knowledge—is no mere dual or trial entity. We are creatures in process in various senses: form becomes content, even bootstrapping is probably never a finished process. Most anything can (once again) become form, an attraction, a style toward which thinking directs itself, once again to redo—always becoming. What fills the consciousness, what lurks in the whatever-*elses* are recessed in thought and reason and unreason, is never all that clear. We "keep track" of a great deal... merely being two-legged creatures perpetually seeking balance; just because we may be "unaware" of what we know as doing, does not mean that it is not deeply part of us. To explore knowledge, we should examine the most talented humans, in all dimensions; not just extrapolate from some partial theory of meaning to grand schemes of the meaning of meaning.

What is astonishing, to me, is that within the complexities of thought which race around our mind's eyes and ears, that we can mostly "find" the rational, find the world, distinguish between ourselves and others and where is here, when is now... and what this all means for being and acting. To do all this, we must, I think, be creatures in process, with abilities to restate to ourselves the grounds of our existence. Being is never a state, not any place, nor a looking-out from any fixed entity which we call our selves; being human is paradoxical in its social derivations. Yet we are and continue to be... and can contemplate "not to be" from a findable locus in our existence.

13. Feelings and Emotions: Whether from the perspective of the definitiveness of the material brain or the infinitude of the idealist mind, there is a sense that there is some independent "agency" to this aspect of being. From brain perspective, the body is the "site" for the nervous end organs; from the mind, the body is "other" and opposed, or parallel and different... of merely some "place" into which the mind is set.

Within a similarity of dualistic thinking, the emotions form a kind of "interface" category: a mechanism which connects categories, or provides some "explanation" of the one to the other; particularly it explains the body to the mind, which most mind-oriented thinkers wish to be quite independent. Or it exists simply as a kind of connective between body and mind: the emotions are said to affect the mind, to cause the reasoning mind to become irrational; for some it is also a place, an entity, where, for example, "faith" might be located.

Some of the complications in talking about this may be illustrated by the sorts of historical stories or metaphors which most of us have heard, concerning the development of language from pre-human to the "truly human. These "a-ha!" stories postulate that pre-language (=pre-mind, I guess) creatures, walking in the forest primeval, began to vocalize their feelings ("Ouch!"), and these began to turn from the (mere) expression of feelings into words: thus, us. In another version (human history and ontogenesis—the history of oneself—always seem to travel together!), we go from pure reflex biology-body (=nature) to rational, going from infant cries to toddler's speaking and naming. Vocalization "begins" with feelings and emerges into language. Body, more natural, is also more primordial in this vision of becoming human.

Because the categories of mind and body have been reified and universalized, the emotions, too, are often thought of as being universal: general to human nature. In recent times, Ekman's work (2007) in particular has taken as assumption the notion that there are 8 or so human emotions which are "expressed" on the human face. These show up on the face, directly or "masked," as one or in combination. Only recently has he taken seriously the issue of the nature of these 8 emotions. These emotions, like the body and mind which they interface, are assumed to be properties of each individual; aspects of the "package."

Sometimes these categorical arguments seem to mask the fact that emotions have to do with the body, and particularly self-readings of the body, and judgments based upon these readings. Having been enamored with the primacy of the problem of knowledge meaning knowledge of the external world, the question of reading one's internality in the context of knowledge, has been less interesting.

Reading one's body (and others') is an ongoing set of processes. From what we think of as physiological, "reflex" processes of breathing, salivating, swallowing, blinking, tensioning our muscles (especially, perhaps, the tongue) to more self-aware functions as eye-focus and head direction, muscle movement, reading and hearing in a self-conscious way. We read, update, judge, vary, readjust—at rest and in movement. To say that any ofthese is "reflex" or automatic does not in any sense lessen its importance in the dynamic processes of knowing.

As language (itself, essentially muscular) is an aspect of the sociality of being, our very physical bodies also partake of social interaction. Even materially, we are not self-contained, self-bounded creatures, but readjust our faces frequently, for example, in discourse with others. Even in thinking about others, we may smile, or imagine ourselves frowning if the interaction does not please us; or we may move those muscles which may be judged and called a "frown." And, as I have pointed out elsewhere, looking like we do, our very facial appearance, is dependent upon holding our muscles very much in relation to how significant others "tell" us we look.

This is to say that the feelings and emotions, which have generally held to be essentially individual and "private," also partake in social interaction. Like aspects of language, it is difficult to separate oneself in any totality, from others: one's self is an emergent phenomenon. Similarly, as Darwin's very title: "The Expression of the Emotions in Man and Animals," 1872) shows us, the emotions are semiotic. They are expressed; they are read... and reacted to, shaped, restructured. Whether we can restructure our bodies, whether we restructure or interpretations of our feelings, is most interesting and problematical.

In social perspective, we deal with a "person" whom we characterize at birth as "just like us" (potentially at least). We see and read and feed this face(body)-character and imagine in any momentariness that this person will "grow up" to be just about like us. How to get from here to there; there to here?

Whatever any infant really feels (like), we parents busily interpret its behavior via our interpretive frameworks. To what extent do we see directly what the infant "wants," to what extent the infant comes to be (form → content) the framework and filter through which we determine the meaning of the infant's behavior—this is as aspect of the process of the discourse of becoming. Often, it seems, this area particularly is an area of personal complication and difficulty in life, where it is never clear whether we read and respond to our "own" (private?) feelings, or are reading our bodily responses through the virtual gaze of some other(s). As illustration, I still (some 15 years after his death) think about my father, and would prefer that he (my version of his version of himself judging me) not be displeased by what I do. To what extent, do I bend present judgment and action in his direction? Why would pleasing him "please" me still? Obviously, this issue of the emotions is no way-station toward knowledge, but is an ever-present aspect of being and of knowing.

Partly this is an area of life's complications, in as much as the feelings are not like objects which we can locate materially; yet they are given names much as if they were. It is difficult to say if we (all) experience the same feelings as, say, "sadness" or "elation." No doubt we can read others' expressions as being relatively sad or happy. Probably this causes us to "empathize" by recalling within us (can we, do we "cause" our bodies to experience what we experience as that emotion?) that feeling. But we, in fact, do not know full well whether they are even very close to the same experiences.

Indeed, it is right here that the problem of personal integrity becomes interesting. How do we read others and understand them, without "becoming" them? How do we become them sufficiently to understand them, yet retain our own personas? To what extent, in what senses, do we become (like) others? Precisely where does the boundedness of our individuality find its integrity?

In a way, within the problem of knowledge, the emotions are important early in development, then they seem to disappear as problematical. Just as intellectual development is depicted as progressive movement toward rationality, it is seen as movement away from nature, from biology, from the body—via the emotions—on the way to knowledge. In fact, the body and emotions (are they different, from mind, from one another?) are always with us. They are us, and are aspects of what and how we know the internal and external worlds. Curiously, and importantly, within the epistemological problem stated as the psychology of knowledge, emotions seem to fill the "anti-category" of knowledge: the irrational, to the mind's rationality.

14. The Brain-Mind Problem in Semiotic Restatement: The human brain can, perhaps, go in an astounding number of "directions," in many "modes." The fact is, however, that the directions and modes in which it goes (may go?) are sharply delimited by its bending in the direction of the mind, defined as like the minds of successful adults.

The brain does not directly analyze all of the world to which it may be "receptive." It analyzes the world as that world is presented and represented by others. It comes to see the world approximately like those significant others see it, organize it, and label it. It is not necessarily "unreal," but is more like "selective." Its form—the world, that is—is not necessarily unlike itself, but is placed even its perceptions and lookings-out, into frameworks and systems which are akin to those which are the frameworks and systems into which, by which, others organize it. The mind, that is, is like the minds of others. The brain is limited early on and "grows" in the directions which satisfy the worldview into which it is socialized.

In being inventive and creative, once the language and cognitive structures are in place, and match those of its parents, the brain may (once again?) be allowed to roam "as it may." We don't need to think that the mind is the source of all of thinking—that mind which is social in its necessities. Perhaps the pre- or un-socialized brain retains some possibilities which are "untamed" in its development.

In attempting to rethink the brain-mind problem, to wonder how a finite mass of gray cells can imagine and think beyond itself, we may think of the major aspect of the consciousness as, in effect, belonging to the world already constructed by previous generations. Most of this, we must come to share, to partake in. But the logic and categories and possibilities which reside within the structures of language and interaction probably tell us more about the way the mind structures the world, than about the interconnections and ways of the manifold of neuronic relations.

What we have been doing, that is, is attempting to model the brain, when what we have really been doing is modeling some aspects of the semiotics of the mind. The brain must have the possibilities of representing the world—in itself, and to itself—and it may have other or additional possibilities as well. This still leaves moot, the question of reality, of what is nature or not. Clearly, to the extent we have survived and do so still, we deal with reality quite well. What more there may be, what the totality of the physics and geometry, may have to rest until we learn to query the other terrestrial species... or we learn to rethink our thinking.

2

CONTEXT

Context: a Residuum?—Leave it to context! Meaning is given by context! – In another context, it would mean something other.

Is context something, some entity, a process, a mode of being? Where is it? How do we know which context we are in, which to apply? How do we learn context? Is context anything; or merely a convenient notion to apply when nothing else will do?

Is context, situation? Is context, bedrock, underpinning?

Is context a notion which is "around"; available to fill, available to invoke—like G(g)od—when one needs or demands explanation? A quality?

Is context for ourselves? For others?

Where to begin, to consider context? Some entry point, some issue or example, better, more persuasive, more expansive, pivotal, than others? (e.g., language/thought as a pivotal arena from/in which to enter Human Nature argumentation, understanding!)

When Context Matters: 1) when the "same" event means differently because "it occurs" in different contexts: e.g., swinging a wooden bat in cricket and in baseball; addressing a group of people for the first time, for the nth time; therapeutic talk, friendly talk; hitting to punish, to correct, to vent one's anger; 2) when the "same" event means differently to different interactor/observers; e.g. a lover's quarrel inside, outside an ongoing relationship; a slap to instruct a child/to punish it; violin playing to the player or other experts, to the listener; 3) when "different" events mean the same: e.g., a period in hockey, a quarter in football; talking for the hearing person, signing for the deaf; 4) etc.

Context and Form: is the Form-Content problem a sub-issue of context? I think that form and content are not always in any opposition, but are often in some process: form→ content→ form→ content→. This is not exactly a change in the notion of what is a form or formal or formalism, but a change in one's being. Or form-content is paradoxical, not any mere antinomy. The attempt to remove one from the other seems (always?) to lead toward the transcendental winning over and replacing the actual in various ways; e.g., granting agency and causality to a deity who tells us how we are, even that we are creating vast layers of Angst even over the facticity and experience of our own existence—e.g., of death over life, of permanence over change, of the universal over the particular → the disappearance of myself. If, on the other hand, content wins in this game of apparent war, then we believe that we must believe in order to exist. Either way existence is problematized; probably cheapened and weakened. A problem in being and becoming?

Context and the Scene: Where are we? How do we locate ourselves?

"It was a cool, overcast morning..."—the reader is to inject oneself into this scene, as if she were there, observing actually or magically. Once there...

Once where? Is an aspect of context, placing ourselves in a particular event-space? Once there, do we know, within some limits, what is likely to happen in that setting: what will not happen: what is unlikely, impossible? Is this (some of) what we mean by context?

Is the world divided up into some number, some kinds of context? What parts of this translates across cultures, across languages? In what senses can we "enter" any scene—metaphorically, a bodily "transport"?

Do contexts, say sports events, possess "time" dimensions; or parts, innings, periods? If an event will end with winners and losers, is that context? If so, knowledge of outcome determines as well as interprets? Does context determine as well as interpret? Or is it such that context is a larger, wider principle, a question of procedure or outcome, and somehow both subsidiary and different?

Once we possess an axiom system, a mode of proceeding, we can do/generate a geometry. But how do we know enough to do geometry? Or to know that is what there is to do; what we are supposed to do; can do?

Malinowski and Context: "...the study of language in the context of culture...no future study of language except as an aspect of culture!"

(Appendix to Ogden and Richards: *The Meaning of Meaning. 1923*). I was trained to believe this: that to understand, one has to understand the background, the experience, the...?

The battleground Malinowski created was over the definition of culture. But this languished, and gave way to some "universal" notion of language-as-human nature, and culture, particularly as-context, was lost.

If, for example, the virtues of a particular society are stoical, then the notion of "tragedy" is very different than where the cultural outlook is frenzied. Thus, it would appear, the study of culture includes such (habits of) outlook, of vision, of "virtues" and of motivation. A word, a meaning, a concept is to be located within such frameworks. Here, the virtue of the concept of "culture" is that it provides and portrays the human condition most widely. Large (potentially) numbers of people sharing common outlook and/or experience—different from some others—are to be understood, collectively. The "psychology" of a person, how one means some word or idea, is to be considered only within that cultural vision.

The advantage of looking most widely, and *early* in the task, is that one notes the commonalities within which to both notice and interpret differences. One also discovers (perhaps) that one's own context is so second-nature that one does not consciously observe one's own habits. (Easiest to learn through doing a phonemic analysis of other languages: self-insight!) And the quest to pursue context devolves equally on finding ways to observe one's own habits of thought and being: consciousness vs. self-consciousness.

An Ursprache: at some level of being and understanding, I seem to have little problem communicating with persons of extremely varying backgrounds. With some others, often "of my own kind," the troubles of communicating, of mutual understanding, seem insurmountable. Perhaps it is a question of depth, of willingness, of some context which sets the scene in which we will "work" at the understanding... or not.

To get a baby fed—in another land—is very easy. The task is well understood—the context (perhaps) is clear, clean, well-defined.

In "body-work"; e.g. violin play (Isaac Stern, the movie—*From Mao to Mozart*), the fact of understanding is easily communicated by the students performing in a "new" way, thinking (virtually), as Stern had suggested.

Is this a case of recognizing large differences—e.g., in language—and being willing to act in terms of other kinds of analysis? A question of a mutuality of knowing, of strategy, a similarity of "politics," an acceptance of others-as-oneself?

Time and Place: What can happen at 3:00 a.m.?—In the middle of a forest, of a small town, the desert, the city?

What is the range of "possibilities," of likely events, of the family of events in which certain unlikely events, make sense, and others are remote or ridiculous? Which, of this range, is "actively" within our thinking?

Notions of time and space set off our thinking in certain, delimited lines. Once there...

Most persons I have asked about how they remember themselves at say, eight years old, think first about one or two specific people (school teacher, mother,...), or places (at home, school), then proceed to think about events. These "entry" memories are the metaphors, the "events" in terms of which we, perhaps, pack or organize our memories. They are like access codes: what we decide to remember, or what we decide *not* to forget; a way to gain entry to a story. They are like the index to a book of maps.

Once "in": how do we proceed? What do we look for? Do we have principles of organization, of how to find where we are, and what we want? (Why is the obvious so difficult to articulate?)

Once "in": there are (apparently) likely events, those which derive from those events (going to the bathroom at 3 A.M., and falling in the toilet). How do we shift—from gaining entry—to remembering where to go, how to move on?

Is form-content itself a shifting dialectic in our conceptual dynamics?

How do we remain in/on the map which we have chosen?—e.g., in teaching, having such total "concentration" that all other thoughts disappear;

that my memory of the course becomes enhanced, possibly "total" during the teaching?

Is it that we shift from form (map) to content, over and over? Is form-content itself a shifting dialectic in our conceptual dynamics?

Which Key? In music, the key signature signals the context: how particular notes will be played, in relation to which others; which will be dominant, where "home" will be. And it certainly makes a difference to the music, to its hearing, to "what it is," what the key is; like a "law."

The announcement of a theme, the timing, the length of a phrase or a stanza: everything seems to be heard in relation to these. Do we, hearing a particular (sort of) pattern, then seek to hear it again, or some limited sets of variation upon it? What's "interesting" in music, is when this pattern which our minds seek is altered or broken in certain ways?

If this be true, then any/every note, every event in music must be heard in relation to, in the context of the piece of music. (And when I practice to perform any particular piece, I have to memorize—virtually—the relation between each note, its preceding and following, in order to "play in tune").

This sets or confirms my notion that we operate, in some senses, in absolute-relative fashions: i.e., we decide quite firmly "where we are" (the "context"), then hear always in relation to some ongoing, some phenomenology, of the context. Its dynamic requires, apparently, some updating and re-invention of the "absolute"; perhaps this is what we mean by a short-term memory. In any case, the context must be kept "in mind," while the "content" is heard/experienced in some relation to the (outline of) context. (As well as in relation to other, "internal" events of contiguity, etc.)

Several orders of question arise:
1. Does the dealing with each "internal" event ever alter the context? Or do we keep the context "pure," as it were? (We must operate in at least two different sorts of time mode!)
2. Do we keep the context in memory as some sort of constant, or do we remember to recreate it; e.g., when we "need it"?
3. How do we go from one "context" to another; i.e., give one up as our absolute, or take on another one? It doesn't seem difficult to do most times

(more difficult: to shift from Western Classical to South Asian to Amerindian music!)

The Seat in the Movie: A young woman was seated in a not very full movie theatre. There were five seats in her row. A man with two young (11-12 years) girls sat down next to her; she moved over to the end seat. Why?

The context: she would not have moved if the theatre were more full; i.e., as the theatre was mostly empty (the context?), the man's sudden presence was felt as a sort of attack upon her, an assault.

She would not have moved if one of the girls had sat next to her. (As far as we could tell the girls sort of pushed the man to go in first; i.e., he recognized that this would not be a good move).
1957
So here the context had to do with the fullness of the theatre, the fact that, 1) it was a man moving, 2) next to a young woman.

Visions and Context: Are there world visions (Ashley Montagu 1957)), somehow larger, more encompassing than contexts? They are not merely visual looking-out, tendencies to see or to sense certain events rather than others, but ways of organizing what there is, what there can be. Maybe visions are ways of reducing/enhancing surprises. Visions are outlooks, orientations, ways of thinking about self, time, life and death, others; what counts, what motivates, whether there is the concept of success and failure; what is love, what is virtuous.

Is the relation between vision and context akin to that between cosmology and metaphysics?

Isn't it that context-is-context because—within a shared vision—it is fairly clear where we are, what the context can be that everyone somehow knows?

Vision is like that proverbial conceptual bedrock, underlying.

Vision and judgment are the same/similar because the possible, noted, counted, interpreted events depend; e.g., on whether one assumes he is conceived/exists in sin or is neutral: whether God is and is supportive, loving, vengeful; whether one's family is loving, punishing; why life is, and what is worthwhile.

Experience: it all comes down to what (I think) it comes down to. What is context is what I treat context as: how I (you) see and agree that a context is; where we are, when, the conditions, what happens here usually, what is likely, not likely.

So, you ask, what is experience? Is it everything we are and do? What is, then, not experience? Is experience a *reductio ad absurdum*, a nothing-else-left? Then isn't it nothing? Because we have to list everything we are, and by the time we are half way through, it is all different?
So it is salient, significant experience! The kind which is knowing-what's-going-on. It is selective, it must have its own life, its own patterns, rules. What are they; where do they derive; do we learn them; do we remember them—or do they arise, naturally, when the conditions are right, when the congruencies congeal?

When I hand something to someone, how do I extend my arm the "right" distance; how does the other know to take whatever it is *and not to drop it?* Is it an awareness, a knowledge of someone else, about what "I" will do, or how I am aware of what they will do? An agreement to...? Based upon?

I go to play the violin, now with an organist—we have a text. She recognizes me—large, hulking me, moving slower than usual into the empty church spaces of mid-week, mid-day. "Hello," she says. "Hi," say I. The organ turned-on, breathes and heaves, the blower hissing, the air changing in pressure, a mass of metal tubes, a balustrade of oak, all come to life. I take out my fiddle, apply a tiny bit of rosin to bow, and begin to tune. "A please." And the organ plays "A" as I twist my left hand around the neck of the fiddle to disengage the peg which winds the string called "A."

I listen, she listens, while I move the peg very slightly, carefully, fully controlled, and stroke the string with my bow. "Too high, just a bit low"; moving around the organ's "A," trying to match timbres: vibrating air, vibrating string, in pipes, resonating wood a century old. "O.K.," we agree. Tune the other strings to "A." What do I hear? Fifths, I hear fifths. Hm-m-m.

"Let's play the 7th Corelli Sonata."

I say, "O.K."

"Take the first section twice, the second, once!"

"O.K."

The text I have is short, a single melodic note, no double-stops for violin. Her text is three times mine, and includes mine. I see mine, only.

We begin. The sound, what a sound in that room. We are both transfixed, looking for Corelli's ears, making sounds that would sound right: pure, lovely, wonderful.

The context? The church, us, the instruments, the texts, the acoustics, our level of ability and of knowing?

We play - da, da, ta, ta, da-ta—da, da, ta, ta, da-ta. I play, but these syllables are the way I phonate. The violin plays other. I know what I sing; I know, too, what the fiddle sings. They are similar, but we are different, my fiddle and me; and we are one. The organ plays, too, in relation to the violin. It, too, is other, and the same.

We follow the texts; we play the first section twice, the second once. "Comments?" I ask. "Good speed," she says, "maybe a slight bit faster." "Terrific" I say. "Terrific," I think. Ready to perform... And we do!

The audience, come another day, hears what we do, and enjoys. But their experience, while like ours, is also different. They do not perform; they enjoy, are critical. They love the space; think of it as a church (which it is, too), or they do not. Two persons performing: they know us as other besides as players; or only as performers. They do not have the text, do not know Corelli—confuse him with Tartini or with Tarentella. But we play, we perform, and it is good.

What context? How many?

How many shared, which ones? How many differ—which?

Context and Confidence: If the audience is nervous that the actors are less than competent to do whatever the context "calls for," then the nature of what is context becomes interestingly problematic.

If the musicians are not sufficiently competent (or have a really "off" day) then the audience finds itself becoming, first critical, then embarrassed, possibly distressed. Why?

Well, everyone has heard poor performances, amateur music. What did they expect? And do expectations have much to do with context?

And the other side of the coin: what if we are (of course we are) more competent than they have any "right" to expect? We're not professional full-time players. In this case they come into the context with lesser expectations, and will be relieved to realize that we can do what we claim, and that they can "relax and enjoy." And it will be better than if they came with high expectations and were "disappointed." (I try to perform "beyond embarrassment!")

In any case expectations affect context; not in the sense of what will happen, but of how the audience will deal with the experience that, indeed, will occur in that context. Do expectations have much power in actually defining the (boundaries of the) context?

Well, that, too, depends. If my friends come to see me play, they may not expect too much (not too much enjoyment, neither much embarrassment). For them, at least knowing me in other contexts, they come to watch a "me" they do not know well, another persona—yet they will have to respond to me-as-friend in later moments, after the performance, and in other settings. So, for them, the context of musical performance includes their knowing me in other contexts, and having to deal with me and their own embarrassment if the musical performance is below some "standard." (How do they come to such a standard?)

For those in the audience who know neither player, they will judge the performance in terms of their experience, bounded fairly cleanly already within the context of the playing of the music.

All of this to say that there is some overlapping of contexts which depends on the experience(s) of the audience, potential futures, relation of audience to actors, and of the expectations with respect to the actuality.

More Complications of Context: The performance (violin and organ—I have a musical recital in mind), will take place in what is otherwise and obviously a Lutheran Church. From my perspective this is convenient (being at the corner near where I live), there is a new organ, a good and willing organist, and the acoustics of the room (the Sanctuary) are extremely good—at least for organ and violin. The baroque literature is extensive and rich. (Some years later, playing in the romantic: baroque tends to sound "all the same.")

However the fact that this room is a church will have several effects, depending on the nature of the audience. Some will find it especially edifying because it is a church; others will have to overcome some feelings of improperness; others will find it convenient being next to an urban lake promenade; others will like it because it is convenient, in the neighborhood, and I am a neighbor, known—if not very well.

For the church-positives the music will be "inspirational," the meditations will be divine, spiritual, etc. For the anti-church the music may have to be better to captivate and capture their thinking. They will have to be "enticed" to enter the situation fully, to suspend the notion of peculiarity upon finding themselves in a church.

And if money is asked?

On the other hand, the context is clear: performing baroque violin-organ music. And it would be the same; anywhere, everywhere.

One more complication: what if we gain a "reputation"?

(Not to worry!)

How Large is Meaning? Take an ordinary word: e.g., "table." It is a thing upon which I write—we eat upon the "same" table, at other moments. It is a verb: "to table a motion." It is other objects: "a table of contents, of numbers." It goes in many directions depending upon context, situation, neighborhood. Confusion?—Hardly. Why not?

Meaning is as large as usage.

A Critique upon Criticism: yesterday I was an actor in a doctoral thesis examination. The rules of this game are well-known, were played well by the two "outside" examiners (I was one). Two of the "inside" examiners were troubled (probably) by us outsiders, and they were exercised by some aspects of the thesis, particularly the uses of certain, apparently idiosyncratic terms which seemed "loaded"—biased.

I reacted or generally attempted to control the scene in the Rhetoric Dep't (and so I tried to stretch the notion of rhetoric back upon itself, several times over). (See how difficult it is to "set" this context in writing, briefly and interestingly!)

My critique was a critique of the notion of criticism, attempting to show, to ponder what criticism is, that the rhetorician-critic uses a mode of analysis to "control" the definition of the situation or subject matter (here, TV ads); that criticism thinks it exists, has a history, essentially independent of the observer-interactor-viewer; i.e. that the critic has knowledge or method by which one (thinks she) can judge what is good, what works, etc.

This was a complicated discussion because I asked the candidate to defend both his thesis and his field, when, in fact, he had taken on a role of critic and was not exactly in any position to defend anything. And, in fact, his was not a critic's view, but the view of a teacher and maker of ads. So his analysis was more of "how to do" as an ongoing process, rather than an analysis from hindsight. "His" examiners, in fact, got upset when the analytic position was "revealed," naming itself and calling attention to the rhetorical aspects of the analysis, and they, like many other "critics" like to remain "experts" without probing too deeply or broadly into the nature of their expertise; particularly into their claims of expertise.

The complications were various, but especially because the context and the grounds of the discussion kept changing. (I plead guilty to helping this process along.) But this is inherent in any rhetorical discussion, because it is presumed that thesis is an interaction; and that 1) one interactor "knows" something the other does not, and 2) that the nature of the interaction also affects the communication of that message. (A third issue is that the interactors have different "orientations" or "outlooks" as well as experience, but this does not seem to concern these rhetoricians too much).

So the interaction is assumed to be out-of-balance in some sense or other, and there is (at least) a double sense of context: a content and an instrumental or processual aspect.

It seems to be that context can easily shift between these two (at least two): that the nature of the "content" is not ever crystal clear in any sui generis sense, and this is not any mere form-content debate because the "form" is not clearly separable from the relationship between the interactors. And there is always the possibility that one interactant can "call attention to" the rhetorical aspects of the situation, shifting what is content, or shifting the very grounds of the discussion of what is content, what is form, even of what is context. And this is part of what makes life interesting and the study of context complicated.

But we didn't (at least I didn't) get lost. And that's not bad. "Home" must both be "somewhere" and "where you find it."

Context and Mind: in a general sense, every discussion of context is a wonderment about how minds work or operate.

How do we know: where we are; how a context is "set"; how do we shift into a particular scene and stay there, play within the rules, etc.? What happens to "minds" when a player shifts the context "in mid-stream," etc.? (Answer: those who are "rigid" get apopleptic!—Most technician-academicians).

Example: Much learning, conceptual change does not (cannot?) take place within a well-defined context. Most (in my experience) takes place when the context is ambiguously presented, and the students have to search for the rules which define the nature of the context (most will do this). But a nihilist will delightedly find that this teacher must be a nihilist, too, masquerading as a person of knowledge.

So—mind! Ha-ha, did I take you to another context? Are you right back here? Do you smile? Do you frown? Should you read this aphorism once again? (Where are you now?)

My Dog and Context: usually when we walk at night my dog is off his leash. When he greets other dogs, he does well if the other dog is also free. However whenever either dog is put upon the leash, the very next moment growling ensues and a "fight" begins. Is the "same" dog on a leash a different entity? Or is the perspective from the leash (and person) so different that a "friendly" encounter turns sour? Has the space altered? Yes, yes, yes!? Is a change in perspective of this sort, say a change in context?

Boundaries: when does an event begin, end? How do we know? And what difference does it make? In driving a car, will a merging driver "let me in?" How do I read their intentions?

Generally there is "sufficient" time for decisions, retractions. How do I know that one is thinking about the same thing I am? Only negatively; i.e., there are few accidents of this or of particular sorts, and any "competent" driver... So it must be that drivers are either operating within very similar contexts, or they are different, but similar enough.

And their "decisions," when there are conflictual decisions, have sufficient time for no accidents—mostly. Thus the world operates, and boundaries are just enough bigger than our thinking about what to do that it usually goes on smoothly; except when weather conditions change, and some drivers either do, or do not sufficiently.

In violin play the transition from down bow to up bow, (etc.) has many possibilities with respect to what is a beginning or ending; what is smooth/rough, silky, seamless, etc. In a string transition segment it is possible to play two melodies on the alternate strings by moving each string in its (own) distinctive way, of giving a tiny added length to each note in an internal melody. Or by getting louder toward the end of a note's duration, it appears to transit toward the next note, more than from the previous, and so on. The setting and continuity of context, of different melodic elements, has practically infinite possibilities—and most listeners can hear the differences, even though they can't specify what their cause or mechanics.

Depth of musicianship is to find, through study, and to be able to play (in performance) as much, thoughtfully and well, as one can find "written into" the composition.

Equally, playing with particular instruments and in certain spaces "makes" the experience different, and one must study how to play well with, e.g., organ—as I am doing now, in the small church on the corner where I live. Example: very little vibrato, the violin wants to be "pure" in relation to the reedy, breathy organ. Are these examples of context? Both organ and the room, and each particular composition force me to alter and to learn new techniques—especially, in this case, bowing (right-hand). The intonation problems are severe, but more like playing in other settings, and with respect to each piece—but less affected by the organ and the space.

My bowing has to be much quicker at boundary points—in order to sound "clean" with the organ. Also I have to get louder toward the end of each bow, rather than the reverse—I think because the organ amplitude is constant on each note and a relatively "slow" instrument and I have to make my "bright" (i.e. quick response) violin act as if it is slow by enhancing end-duration. So, the question of boundaries, contexts, etc., is a somewhat shifty business, and is relative—in certain terms. But that there are boundaries, that we note them and can operate within their terms (hearing music, reacting in driving), suggests that the effective or working boundaries in our lives are well within our sensory possibilities and must be in order to function in any real world. (It may well be, however, that we work at extending them by study and experience. But if no one can get to especial points of seeing or hearing or whatever, then they would not enter and remain in general domains.)

Episodes: Certain (types of) events are episodic. Within (the way we experience) time, they are short, clearly finite. In sports, I am thinking of ski-jumps, diving, and weightlifting (perhaps dashes in track), television ads, etc. These are different from performing music or teaching. (I suppose love-making can go in either mode or manner, and maturity is "anti-episodic!")

The episode-as-context, especially as discussed in sporting contexts, is interesting because of the way participant-performers claim they think about them. In ski-jumping, e.g., the thinking-out is done the previous night in the hotel room. The "ideal," perfect jump or lift or dive is constructed in the imagination, they say, by specifying some three or four event points in the episode (the most "significant," crucial, difficult, troubling—perhaps the least of these), and imagining how to do them as perfectly as possible (out of much prior experience—a distillation?). During the episodic performance the athletes do not actively "think-out" the activity, but try to get their bodies to match in actuality these 3 or 4 moments with their imagination of what they ought to be. And if they match very closely, it will be "a champion performance," they will say, both champions and ex-champion/coaches alike.

In episodic events, nothing is (intended to be) random. It is clear what the event consists of, and it is easy to judge it well or badly, because I guess, it is so clearly specifiable. (Playing music, teaching are not episodic.)

Nostalgia: whenever I hear some music which I have performed, I not only listen and enjoy the music but find myself reliving the performance out of my past; its preparation and so on. In this sense the music is not mere music, like much other music, but a study and a "getting off on" my earlier experience with it. Thus the "same" event—by objective standards—resonates very differently in my experience than in others'. So the relation between context and experience may be full of, and informed by, particular history.

Similarly the performance of music which is well known by the public, is very different from mere music. This week we are performing Pachelbel's *Canon*. It was recently the theme music for a popular movie and has received radio exposure as well. In this context, the public "has" the music memorized, and wants its memory, apparently, titillated. The difficulty, for the performers, is that the audience in such cases turns from hearers into critical listeners.

Such musical moments have become "clichés." Like other moments and notions excerpted from ongoing experience, they become counters and filters through which and in whose terms other experience is now interpreted, detailed, counted, and understood. Heard prior to such clichés, or after they have matured or altered or been forgotten, the experiences are other.

The Contexts of "We": what you and I know and have experienced together; that which we regard as both of us knowing; that which I can as well ask you to refresh my memory, as to query my own memory. How much can I, how much do I, must I, rely upon you? You upon me? How much do we work at remembering together, tracking upon the context of "we"?

Here there are two senses of Culture: that which we share in common because we have shared the earth at the same period, and that which we have decided to share together, to entrust the knowledge to the other as to ourselves. They end up being similar; the first more passive, the second a common acquiescence: "a contract."

The "Contexts of "We""—what a wonderfully peculiar usage of "we"!

Context and Culture: what remains, for me, in any theory of Culture has to do with the shared contexts of persons of shared (cultural) backgrounds; seeing boundaries, knowing what is happening, where they are, likely and unlikely outcomes; what makes sense, what does not: what is hope, guilt, justice, the future; why is life, death; what is sadness, a tragedy; what we deserve, what luck is; what is competition and why, or why not; what is a friend, are there enemies; what is human, what not; health, pain—what is there to do? Why should I do anything? Ask this sort of question? To whom are my loyalties, under what conditions?

Why culture fades, for me, is that many of these questions are indeed shared by members of different cultures—at certain times in their lives—and some vary widely within what were previously thought to be monolithic cultures.

Differences, on the other hand, can fade or be downplayed in dire circumstances, or where a Messianic or other rallying cry is heard. (For example, in modern fundamentalism all differences can be relegated to false or satanic interference).

"Culture" can be used as "Race" to oppose, to explain undesired behavior; to place persons on some ladder of progress or evaluation behind wherever we want "our side" to be found. Culture as concept calls attention away from a changing world, away from existence, experience.

If the question is: why are people(s) different, the response is that there are many sorts of differences. What question do you ask; and why? We differ—all of us—day by day. Is that what you meant? What do we worship? At the feet of? Because our parents do/did! These questions/answers no longer seem very difficult. The difficulties are in knowing generations (i.e., having lived long enough to watch the amazing differences within those whom one knows well-enough) in believing one's own observations; in continuing to query the world and seek to question what is going on.

Urbanity and bureaucracy are, after all, very similar the world around; and democratizers of experience in interesting ways. Life is always and everywhere an ongoing translation. The question of Culture comes down to the nature of translation construed in the broadest sense. (See Question-Response System, "Human Grammar," in my *Language & Human Nature*, 1985)

Who Owns the Context? In some cases, in some places, not only do persons share an outlook of common vision and insight but they believe they have a proprietary right to that idea. Anyone who differs from them, they think, actively disagrees with them. Any disagreement becomes an argument, not only between the discussants, but about what is right and what is wrong.

Currently there is such a battle already waning into disinterest and unimportance, between the disciplines which presently call themselves Anthropology and Biology. Anthropology believes it owns the concept of Culture; Biology, the concept of Nature. The human condition they have divided roughly and unevenly into two: Culture and Nature. Both assume that each humanoid is some combination of the two. The argument that seems to be taking place is over how much Nature vs. how much Culture; or how changeable, how fixed is the human condition, as if Culture means learned, plastic, changing, and Nature is predetermining in "its" effect.

Since, I think, this way of thinking about human nature is prejudging and silly, and has its roots in ancient thinking and metaphysics, this "debate" forces me to wonder who I am as an anthropologist: to seek out (good, thoughtful) biologists and to ferret out the underlying arguments and unpack the discussion, both to see why it takes this form, and how to alter the way we think in order to probe human nature without taking all this intellectual baggage into the fray.

This has turned out to be difficult, particularly because of the proprietary nature of the discussion. If one criticizes, he is placed—as an antagonist—into the "opposite camp." That is, since both sides are dualists and have made up, to a large extent, their opposition, whatever they perceive as opposition (including criticism of every stripe), they take the argument to belong to the opposition *as they have defined it*. Neither the biologists' Theory of Culture, nor the anthropologists' Theory of Nature has a great deal to do with how thoughtful practitioners of either discipline experience their respective worlds. (Except there is a tendency for some younger persons to become the opposition as defined from outside, rather than from inside the discipline.)

What, then, is the context for the discussion of human nature, behavior from the perspective of the anthropologist, the biologist, or the critical thinker? Now that culture has been co-opted by business and literature how does it play; what does it mean?

The critical thinker ends up being a pariah to both proprietary camps and must either leave the fray or seek to write for different audiences and/or in different times!

What Generalizes: Consider an infant, relatively isolated, reared in a home with three or four other persons; brushing briefly, occasionally upon others of diverse interests. About three years of this experience, limited and bounded, and this child can speak to a hundred million persons; to everyone who speaks that language. That's amazing!

Does anyone know how to grasp the nature of being, of language, which enables this to occur?

Consider: here I sit in my kitchen artificially warmed by flowing electrons, listening within a mode of non-hearing to morning classical music (today mostly Christmas), writing to you, and to you, and back to myself; imaging all things, all of us. Writing, a way to enter your mind; a way to enable you to enter mine. And you can do this without electrons, without music, not even in your kitchen (perhaps without even knowing writer, kitchen, or what classicism is!).

How is it that I write to you such that you can see it, take it into your thoughts, and make my thoughts yours? Is it what it is? Or what we know about what (it) is?—Or?

Experience: The organist with whom I perform violin sonatas is conducting a group of about ten strings in playing Pachelbel's *Canon*. This canon doesn't have a melodic "center," exactly, so each pair (of three pairs) of violins, either have to watch the conductor, to listen to the previous melody two bars earlier, (the canon repeats every two bars) and perform the same music in about the same way; or listen to the cello which provides the "coherence" to this music.

Experienced players can do all three. But the less experienced (and less adept) players, tending to play fast passages even faster that they are supposed to be, are "stuck" in the technique and can neither watch the conductor nor continue what they have been hearing in its own terms. But, we discovered, they can "correct" themselves by listening to the cello. The problem is in getting them to remember: 1) to listen to the cello; 2) and then to correct themselves.

The less experienced players seem to get "stuck" in technique, in hitting the notes in tune and on time, and have little excess energy, or conceptual being, left over to watch the conductor, etc. Performing enhances this tendency to "concentrate" upon technique. (Music without technique is, perhaps, "worse" than technique minus music—but players tend toward technique rather than toward music.)

There are various ways to get past such problems, to "gather" experience. Most obvious, of course, is to have sufficient technique, so that—in any moment—one can rely upon the ability to perform within smaller and smaller limits of "correctness." (The notion of "sufficient" technique itself changes in many and various ways with practice, improvement, etc.—and is its own long story!) With this technical sufficiency and a trust and confidence in it, one can release oneself from a technical reading of the musical text, and can "learn" to watch, listen to others, to predict (a lot of experience involves various sorts of predictions), etc. So in much of musical performance and playing in groups, "experience" consists in extending oneself from the literal text to attending to many simultaneous occurrences.

Concentration: A Sunday morning in the neighborhood Lutheran Church, I was to perform Corelli (7th Sonata) and Handel (F major, 1st movement) at 10:30. At 7:30 I arose and proceeded to warm up, doing mostly bowing exercises and concluding that I should have been doing intonation exercises to make me more secure in performance.

Our 18 year old son had gone—in our car—to ski in Colorado and hadn't yet called. Between preparing to perform and considering at some level of my being what could have happened between here and Vail, I kept calm as well as I knew how.

At about 8:00, he called and said all was well except for one spin-out into a soft snowdrift going up the mountain from Denver. He had forgotten to call the previous afternoon and had gone to sleep after driving all night.

My relief carried over into my violin preparation; my muscles relaxed, apparently; my thoughts dulled, and I had a good deal of trouble staying consciously in my practicing. I ran through the exercises, but they were not done particularly well or thoughtfully.

I went to the church at 9:30 to rehearse till 10, then relaxed. Perhaps I was too relaxed.

At 10:22, we began the Corelli. I remembered to tighten the bow for the "Marcato" first movement. "Ba, ba, ba,ba, ba, ba, ba,...!" and I was pretty much in control. Repeat; go on. People now streaming in to the Sunday after Christmas. The sound of the organ wonderful in this church. The violin, resonant; just wonderful to hear, and to play.

"Me?" Stray thoughts creeping in. "Me? What am I doing here?" The organ in a funny, off-balance counterpoint with violin.

The 2nd movement, a run (*corrente*). My right hand, not so secure. A trembling. "Steady down, little finger! Relax wrist! More shoulder!" "O.K." "Da, da-a-a." The next note, the note after. All of a sudden, the next page, the trouble-spots overlaying each note. "Will I do O.K., there?" Yes! No! The present, each next note, still playing, still being played. Still, creeping in; "What will happen?" Now, thinking the last movement, "the string changes, E to A to E, so fast."

Each note, now overlain with the fingers on my right bow hand tightening when they should relax, preparing for the disaster of futuristic images. And I want each next note to sound just "out, out! Here I am. I am right here. I wanted to be here. I wanted to perform. I was trained to do this. Love each note! Stay here; right here, right now!"

"Listen to the organ." Mary, calm, steady, beating out that fantastic wind reverberating. "Take it in, my little mind. Love this note. Give it everything it deserves. There is no better sound. Keep here. Keep here. Sh-sh-sh. Build now to crescendo. Breathe. Repeat. So lovely. Later. Later, all the stray thoughts, all the random worries. But, now, listen, play; make each moment, every note as beautiful as I know how. Take the energy of the audience into the sound, play the violin into the edges and depths of their minds."

And so, I drew into each moment the curtain round my thoughts, concentrated, played. The piece became of-a-piece. The faltering, never out-of-control, steadied into a performance. Compacted, concentrated.

Congruence: My Teachers (anthropological linguists Henry Lee Smith and George Trager) used to talk about "congruence" as if it were a major concept, perhaps the principal conceptual area to be considered in understanding.

Congruence means, I think, that what is going on in any interaction (especially), has to be understood with respect to whether it "fits," is congruent with whatever else is happening.

It signals, I think, the notion that context is a multi-layered, many-leveled sort of thing, and that within some larger context(s), events can be seen as fitting, being congruent with or not. It suggests that some events with some larger context(s) fit one notion, some fit another notion of what is going on.

If, for example, two persons do not go "outside" some rules or boundaries (the idea of the "breaking of context"), and maintain a conversational pose, they might or might not be dealing in communicative behavior. They might, for example, be deep into their own minds, blocking any communication; they might be talking at several levels within the interaction, each connected with any future possibilities (e.g. if "you" understand me, really, you'll be able to separate what I "really" mean from what I am saying). The question of analysis (and description) comes down to whether and with respect to what, the events are congruent.

In any event there is thought to be a level of context which "contains" all ensuing events (like a sporting event-which has its own rules for continuity), for what constitutes it - and within that, much can and does occur at many levels, of various sorts. The clue to analysis, to understanding, splitting up the complex into its event-forms, was said by my teachers to be congruence.

My trouble with this is that congruence demanded some (I think a lot of) surreptitious theories of meaning, even of context, in order to say what event was what, belonged with or to which others, etc. That is, in order to "know" congruence, one would, already, have to know what is context, presumably what we were trying to discover... eventually.

So within the concept of congruence we find ourselves caught in another circle, much wider, perhaps, than the ones others are caught in, and holding-out much long-term promise (and, no doubt, a truth of a sort!)

Context and Linguistics: On comparing words within a sentence as a part of my studies in linguistics some years ago, I realized that there was variation in the sounds depending on the *location* within the sentence. Whether a word was initial, medial, or final (say) in a sentence, made a difference in the sound of any/every word.

Whether this has to do with the "form" of a sentence or with other factors (as well), it suggests that we have in mind a much more complicated notion of languaging than had been noted previously. It means that location (within certain structures?) and context are intertwined in interesting ways.

It means, also, that any observed "word" not only is that word (i.e., contains within its duration information specifying that it is that word and not any others), but that within its duration there is also information about where it is in the sentence. Thus, every linguistic "event" (e.g., a "word") is both event and context for itself and what surrounds it, or it is somehow "about" the structure within which it is embedded.

What this could mean, to generalize, is that many/most events we note or observe are not only or merely those events (i.e., what we think, for whatever reasons, is that event), but they also carry information about structures and context.

Why I think this is complicated: in contexts that we already operate within, the fact that, e.g., words vary (phonetically) according to location in a sentence, was not before noted. So we are (we must be!) the kinds of observers who accommodate at least some sorts of contexts already in our observations. That is, we do not self-consciously note the dynamics but somehow act as if they are not there while simultaneously taking them into account in our own familiar worlds. In others' worlds we do not take them into account, but act as if we can observe clearly; i.e. outside of context. (Our tendency is to apologize for this by assuming whomever or whatever we observe is simpler than we are.) So the problem is in "knowing" what we see, "learning" how to see/observe as if we are within the proper context and structure, etc.

Consider the problem of seeing so-called retarded or autistic people as they really are. What we "see" in their behavior we label to ourselves as "retarded." While such persons are "different from ordinary" in certain physical ways (which we're studying now), the notion of "retarded" is our designation, and may not fit them very well, if at all. It has much to do with differences in muscle structure and in dealing with gravity. Here, we can both study them, and learn about our observational habits and tendencies.

Problem: How to examine (re-examine) our observational categories, habits and tendencies, especially as we are "bound" to certain contextual habits, or see with respect to our own categories.

The World Works: The work of the world yet goes on: "it" knows what it is doing. Most people, however, seem deeply suspicious (pessimistic?) of this and think that the world is much too complicated to work. Or they think it (our institutions, etc.) has no flux, and will break before it changes. Or they are narrow thinkers, or historical thinkers.

In many senses the fact of the world ongoing seems very simple. Children get born, raised, etc.; marriages, society. There are some theories— we may assume—by which this happens; or there are no such theories necessary. If, we assume, the world works, there are theories underlying, and our job is to understand them, see when they get into trouble, see ahead, etc. (Machiavelli, Martin Krieger).

Where are these theories and how do we locate them become the principal questions. And "context" is at least the residual answer: context is (about) the sorts of knowledge by which all of us know where we are, and how events are to be considered and understood, within. It is or contains frameworks, perspectives, theories of architectonic and directions for moving in these.

Assuming all of this to be generally correct, the lack of explicit work on context is likely due to several factors: 1) we are context-congruent observer-interactors; i.e., we are creatures of context and become aspects of it rather than (remaining) observers who update ourselves at all points within some process. Our possibilities of consciousness, objectivity, etc., are suspended with respect to whatever is contextual; 2) our attentions are positively directed to other sorts of issues and problems (e.g. toward individuals rather than to relationships between persons), and we never "get back" to contextual issues; or we fall for content rather than form or the reverse; 3) whatever is context changes in such ways that it is, e.g., "form" in one "instant" and "content" in another (e.g. language, music); 4) context is many modes simultaneously and we don't know how to direct questions at its "essence"; 5) context is a residual notion invoked to account for whatever seems to be left over (and we hope this is small); 6) etc.

Process and Memory: in, for example, teaching, the teacher goes through the process of teaching ("change," "learning," etc.) with the students to at least some extent. After the course, as/when it resonates still in memory, the course changes somewhat, and becomes an event, a product, a kind of unity (I think).

As teacher, I have in mind both the process (multiple, manifold, ongoing, altering) and the outcome (say six months, five years later). I "teach toward" a desirable outcome and bend the process in that direction. The students, having no real sense for that outcome, experience the course very differently from the teacher; while it yet appears to all that the course events are identical for everyone, including the teacher.

The process, the teaching, how I'm going to "get to" those particular students, that particular class, within the range of my desired outcome, depends on the weather, the students, the times, the mix of many, many factors. All of these I try to take into account and keep my eye on the afterward of the memory of the course: an example of how form turns into content; and of other things as well.

(Why do I think this is somewhat accurate?—Returning students, sitting in on the "same" course the next year, have a very different notion of the course, and are surprised [annoyed, upset, challenged] by the experience of the process; i.e. they had "redone" the course in memory.)

Deep vs. Surface: a diversion away from contextual issues. Since context "is" residual, the data, the observables (it is assumed) cannot possibly be anything but "form" (like the telegraph wire, carrying the message/context).

Therefore we must look deeper to see what rules "generate" the observable (e.g., like algorithms for numbers, forgetting that behavior is not exactly as formal as numbers; grammar for words, forgetting that words are noise are representations are discourses with other persons).

These rules become, then, the data, the reality which governs, and the subject-matter of our lives. And we forget the context, the nature of the observer (by which the surface is described, and the forgetter of the context). And we spend the next eras seeking to define and refine what is either not there to begin with, or what we believe will yield some truth if only we define the right "units," analyze them "correctly"—never getting back to why we thought about anything "that way" to begin with.

Becoming a House-husband: J. with whom I share my life, went to work in 1981-2 and I remained mostly at home, arranging, cleaning, cooking, etc., etc., etc.

Since I had cooked and cleaned previously, this was not all new. I knew the various rooms, what is in the house, where most of it "belongs," what to get rid of. What is new, from a contextual perspective, is that I am seeing so much more than I had previously, that it is difficult to believe and to fathom.

Before, I could do my chores, perhaps like it was an assignment; a task carved out by J., out of the range of whatever good-housekeeping is. Now I am the one who assigns to myself, the manager I have become.

And I see so much more: what is out of place, what is a half-done job; what clean and neat is. I have developed, by now, a fairly complete, fairly "enclosed" aesthetic. Having vacuumed the floors for many years, the most astonishing newness is to be actually able to see dust as I vacuum, and note what is then clean - or not.

Thus what was, what I was as observer of the familiar, has altered radically. My house—a home of 15 years—now new, now enclosing a similar store of events, now all expanded, turned somewhat.

Has this filtered into the other concepts of my life, my observations? How was it that I saw so little then, so much more now; that I then (also) accounted myself a careful observer? What else do I not see, enclosed in a vision of implicit knowledge, boundaries in so far from the edges? (Jerry Timian: "Becoming a wife-boy!")

Form become Content become Form: it is clearer to me that context is at once real and a will-o-the-wisp.

Like bed-rock it is always presumed to reside "at bottom." But when we attempt to pull away the coverlets of our lives, we always get closer in some senses, but never seem to arrive. Either there is no bottom, no bed-rock, no basis for the assumptions in terms of which we (science, experience) proceed, or we don't know how to look; or somehow the bed-rock is itself in some senses "in flux."

Example: hairstyles—what is "in style" now, comes "in" and will be what is normal in several months. That is, what was form, through the adoption by sufficiently many persons, becomes content: what is and what is real. After a while (days, months, centuries, millennia), via various processes, what was real, content-full, becomes form once again, as the underlying acquaintance with the content is lost, forgotten, abandoned, and once more in the categorical world of what is attractive (alive) or not (merely lost).

Example: language learning (development): based on some (intrinsic) interactional propensities of the infant, the infant begins to exercise its vocal chords (form), and this is responded to by parents as if it has content (meaning); the infant somehow learns that this is to be used as meaningful, expands the repertoire as sound and muscle use, given meaning by parents, accepted as meaningful, and so on and so on. Form become content...etc. The infant-which-survives principally is that "one" into which the parents have read personage which is interpreted by them as the actual person (...on the complications of being oneself).

Example: rhetoric, the style of speech, of teaching, is for some reason or in some senses "attractive.' The student-listener attends, the message-content is packaged, but remains ill-understood. The stylistics of the teacher change to assume, to act as if the content was/were understood; the nature of the teacher-student relationship changes; the student comes to believe that she understands, now has to take on a proprietary relationship to the content of the course, and so on. Form become content.

Example: Greek Dance Poses: Diane Watts, teacher of Isadora Duncan. Instead of worshipping Greek statuary, as many 19th century idealists did, she recreated the poses as a dancer.

But this is true of any writing or of any speaking in which the ideas, the content, are not yet known or understood. And, perhaps, this is why context is both bed-rock and non-existent, depending on perspective, time and place, what is already understood.

(In this sense, in this context, does context "progress"? Is context a paradox? A parable? A paragon?)

Example: Plato's Dialogues. Plato runs a double-game (at the least). The "form" of the dialogue—what dialectic "does" to our minds in engaging in it—versus the "content" of the dialogues (Western thought is essentially Plato's "content.") In some places these seem parallel or complementary; in others they seem opposed, and seem to have little to do with one another. A student of dialectic who studied pedagogy with me, took the notion of the dialogue to be the whole of pedagogical dialectic, and taught teaching in terms only of the quality of dialectic (to engage people-listeners-students). I, who operate in terms of the content principally, always directing and redirecting in terms of the underlying ideas I was trying to teach, found myself at great odds with him, who seemed to me to be always manipulating form—to enhance the attention and enjoyment, irrespective of subject matter, ideas or content. In the end (I believe), his students would end up "empty" and tending toward nihilism, for which it is unclear why anyone does anything; except as theater. (Formalism → nihilism → boom!)

Searching the Unknown: it may well be that our methods, our ideas about the unknown will not illuminate much more broadly, especially more deeply what is not yet understood. Whatever our methods, some of them hide or obscure as much as they may direct. Or there may be arenas of thought and experience which we do not know because of our linguistic habits, social experience.

It has seemed to me that there are several processes for pursuing the unknown, which I gather under the concept of *locating* problems or issues. First I speak with, interview, practitioners of various disciplines and orientations to find out what they do, what they know, and if possible, to move to the "edges" of each discipline to find out where their methods and knowledge direct them. After a while, with much experience, one can sense where they tend to move, what they might or ought to inquire about, but in fact do not.

Example: neurology has a "circular" view of mental retardation, which supposedly "explains" that "retardation and/or autism" is due to neurological, unchangeable disorders. This belief directs them and their followers away from observing, once the diagnosis has been made. Thus what is actually different or peculiar about such "funny-looking" people is never well-described because neurologists do not believe it will tell them/us anything. (Wrong!—in my view.) Especially, it is useful to compare different disciplines who claim to study the same subject matter (e.g., human behavior) but from different orientations or disciplines.

After a while, also, one is driven to reading the writings of those who formulated the questions and answers, the visions and modes of inquiry. One begins to discover what was bothering them, what their intellectual-temporal histories taught them. Perhaps it is correct to say that one studies what the contexts of anyone's lives consisted in: what they loved, hated, feared, for what they worked, for whom they could succeed, fail; what gods they had, what illness, and so on. And one can begin to see what was invented, when a concept gained strength, fell, was objected to, was replaced, forgotten, and, to some extent, why.

Then, with luck, one can rediscover "today"; where we are now, how we got here, where we might go, and of what the "proximate" unknown might consist. One studies the forces for change, equally those for stability, and notes where the weaknesses are; which aspects of life are and will be fought for, defended seriously, and not so seriously.

Perhaps one can then begin to see what is not yet seen, imagine the unimagined. (Mysticism as another response to wanting to know what there-is-not-yet).

Life in the Interstices: like Dostoyevsky, I used to think I lived in the underground, waiting there till it was dark enough not to be seen. Then mole-like I would poke up my head and look around. Since my vision was not too good, especially in the zones of twilight, I was assured that nothing much was going on; not too much, that is, that was interesting or important. I retracted, pulled myself back into my hole of protective self-satisfaction, and continued on with my tasks some of which were, no doubt, calculated to plug up that hole, once and for all. Even when I had encounters with the lighted world I remained hidden, having learned to pass in the world as if I were one of "them."

Then there was some trouble, and an invitation. I emerged, got a lawyer, found a new friend, and began to look at where I had gotten. No longer underground, a fantasy no longer sustainable, I awoke to find myself inside yet not exactly any place which I could specify. And not any place where there was company. It was, I discovered, within the structures and organization of some entity, some thingness called a university. But I was somehow in-between, in the interstices.

Now the view from the interstices may not be clear; objectivity may be more vain than vision and observation from some place, or from some usual location; but it is not uninteresting. For one thing I now wander abroad in the world, and others with "place" think I am somewhere, as well; and treat me as if I am just like them. But I know that I am not and do not belong anywhere. And so I have, in many senses, rejoined, but live still in the interstices. Attempting to locate them, I walk in their ways, and parallel ways as well, living in the interstices.

Metaphor: metaphor has something to do with something which it isn't exactly. Like a dictionary this is somehow a large, perhaps unabridged circle; stay on the journey long enough, everything will be revealed in terms of other things, and the ride will be sufficiently heady that we require nothing more: "The Glass-Bead Game." (Hesse, 1943)

Instead some of us prefer to stay at home, looking for the *somethings* which metaphors are metaphorical to. Often, it seems, context is invoked when is becomes finally obvious that everything/something is something else's metaphor. Or at such points we deny that there are any *somethings*. And we get worried about whether we are anything either. (If you don't "believe in" reality you may pick up your pay check; but you may not cash it!)

It seems that context will never be able to tell us that we are, but its study may enable us to locate ourselves. Its solution will be located in the kinds of thinking which will show us how we both are and are our own metaphors, simultaneously. We must be continuous enough, sufficiently "absolute," that we are—identifiably—in (almost) all contexts. (There may be contexts in which we "give away" ourselves but know how to get identity back.) That is, memory (its bases) must be sufficient that we always find ourselves; know who we are/who I am.

The strange power of metaphors is that they often work to convince us that someone knows something which—if it were said "straight"—would be totally unconvincing. (Any metaphor in a storm!)

The use of metaphors historically, within the discussions of what it means to be human, is quite amazing. We are dual; we are speechless statues; we are culture, language; phalluses when we have lost our tongues; assholes when we supersede being pricks; heads when we are stoned; tool-makers when nothing else convinces; brains when we look at ourselves and forget we are looking out as well.

Context and Meaning: But this is Malinowski's problem. If "we know where we are" (already; to begin?) then we can analyze the meaning pretty easily. If we don't know the context then the analysis is not grounded anywhere, at least not anywhere where we can be secure in knowledge. The same "word," the identical concept, "mean" differently in different contexts. The problem is what is it to locate ourselves (or anyone or anything) and how do we go about this? (The fact is that most living creatures, even humans, do this quite well, most of the time.) A problem in the nature of orientation and navigation (Donald Griffin, 1976)?

Ambiguity: Life is not so sparkling clear as the beer ads would claim for their water, but neither is it so murky, in any sense constantly or consistently.

It is tempting to build a theory of meaning by matching, arranging, resolving what appear to be ambiguities (Chomsky 1966). But the mere fact that they are (apparently) resolvable, at least arrangeable, should tell us that we operate within some, probably logical frameworks of even recognizing an ambiguity. It seems, to be, to require a great deal of various sorts of knowledge, to recognize ambiguity.

Perhaps the study of context should begin with developing the idea of the necessary frameworks to recognize (and to resolve?) ambiguity. (My major teacher, George Trager used to deny that there were any actually occurring ambiguities in living; I think he thought they were all "structural.")

Context and Logic: raising the issues of context seem generally to be part of an attack on logic in the sense of the possibility of abstracting (from contexts) statements being capable of being, say, clearly false or true or at least resolvable.

The intellectual difficulty and trap is that the concept of human rationality (so far) is tied intimately to this limited notion of logic. And as questions of meaning have arisen (especially, perhaps, within the notion of language translation), it has become fairly clear that there is more both to logic and to meaning, than any mere truth and falsity.

Also clear, from geometry, that certain sorts of pivotal assumptions—shifts in these—provide logical algebraic systems. Within each geometry, algebra, truth means differently. A question about context, here, is how we know/are told which geometry we are (to be) within?

Being Human: one of the residual senses in which context remains secreted, is Human Nature. Apparently we hold out some promise, some wish, that the facts somehow implicit in being human "explain" a great deal of life and of life's experiences.

"That is innate; this is inherent; a universal"—meaning that it is shared by all humans somehow as an attribute of whatever being human means. The practical result is that a number of problems remain hidden, obscure, unrecognized: but in an insidious intellectual sense: fixed, predetermined, life experience continually blurred.

That is, that since they are (assumed to be) inherent, they need not be raised to actual, rational, conscious or conscientious discussion; moreover, we apparently assume they form a bedrock, an assumptive foundation which will/can/must explain whatever is truly deep and profound. Somehow all of this seems to make present experience pretty banal. Or we look for causality, for being and experience in externalities: God, death, ESP, all of which we seem to use to provide us categories and gathering principles within which to place experiences—again, as if these notions will explain life's experience beyond which they (the categories) are and (life) is.

And all of this obscures, in a variety of apparent ways, the senses in which we are inter-personal; in which we experience the world in ways others claim it is to be, and force us to organize how we(I) contemplate experience.

This notion of Human Nature also seems to have persuaded us to seek for Self-Knowledge from within the categories, the experiences, and thinking-about that we already somehow possess: because we are human. As if this will tell us a great deal we don't already know: a search for exactly the correct method, a seduction of the philosopher into believing that knowledge is (already) within oneself (Rorty's (1967) review of Derrida's *Of Grammatology*, 1967)

Ongoingness and Context: The notion of context implies some starts and stops, some divisions of time/space, of eventness, into discreta both similar and different; and in ways that we can find, and in places where we can find our way, where we are and what we are doing.

But like the chicken and egg, the whole business is ongoing. There is no obvious beginning, and the endings are not so clear either.

We construct life—or life is—such that there are different times, and we construct rituals—or life is—to state these times, to celebrate them, to announce them, and to convince ourselves that they are and are real.

Context and Confusion: most of the time in most circumstances we are located within, we invent ourselves within several contexts. The difficulties, complications, ambiguities, have much to do with who I am and who we are, and what we are doing, because the situation is multiple—in form, in logic, in relationship.

Every human relationship has, within it, so many possibilities that it seems impossible to proceed with almost anything at all: everyone can be friends, lovers, enemies; instruments to use, to love, to hurt; students, teachers, doers, the done-to; the in-this-moment, the past, all tomorrows

So which ones are we in? What is this moment, this time? In ordinary English, for example, the common past tense is multiply ambiguous: "She was here" could be yesterday or 2000 years ago. And we need more to know which is meant; or even if she is properly female—or even what female means.

Who then decides what context this is, who delimits, who confuses?

Mistakes, Confusions: There we were at a high school hockey game, an intersectional game with the crowds of people from a town to which we are now "tied" by marriage. All was fine, a good game, a happy crowd.

But sitting next to me and in my line of vision to the ice and hockey action was a youngish man whose saliva was being created in the most gigantic proportions known to humankind. Chewing tobacco, we thought. And how did we know this? Because he had an every-two-minute's bolus which he emptied on to the floor beneath his facial orifice. Yecch. A virtual lake of sputum.

I thought of what to do, what to say, appalled as I was. And did exactly nothing. I thought to say, "Sir, your sputum stinks!" But since his friends said and did nothing, neither did I. A problem in context? His behavior so awful, so improbable? (My esthetic? My problem?)

Instantaneous Stimuli: psychologists (always) trying to bound the stimuli to its smallest possible dimensions, zero rise-time, then immediate fall—to set boundaries to the immediate, to know when precisely is now. The problem is to know what is a stimulus, then we have a chance of knowing what is a response, and what it is a response to (...trying to "locate" or pinpoint causality).

Here context, history are problems. Stimuli are supposed to be context-free, to stimulate their (particular) responses, to cause clearly and cleanly whatever they cause; and the organism is presumed to be always in the same state, a zero-state, or a state whose activity does not interfere with receiving the stimulus.

Remarkably eyes and ears act as if they are clear, at least much of the time. Pain, too, except that acupuncture seems to confuse this tendency of ours to be able to cleanse our "pain states." Perhaps it is that we are very good at cleansing ourselves of context (blinking, swallowing!?), preparing ourselves to see and hear, thus to be cast within each next moment and to be creatures in-time and simultaneously open to stimuli (i.e. outside of time).

In this sense, context is the ways in which we are: 1) not free to be open in each next moment; 2) the senses in which, from which we must "cleanse" ourselves, to be open to instantaneity. (How, then, are we continuous—lacks of instantaneity?) Is such cleansing the same as forgetting?

Space and Context: Certain events happen in certain sorts of space: often, usually. Certain events do not, definitely do not happen in particular sorts of space. The space "itself" tells us a lot about context, perhaps spaces "set" context.

Is this all because of experience and expectations? Is it because of how we use space, how we react and interact in particular settings? Is it how space manages, permits, forces us to be or do, in certain ways? (P. Wilson "The Domestication of the Human Species" 1989—in which it is claimed that we became "geometrized" in our thinking when we humans became domestic, living in fixed settlements with insides and outsides, and privacy). Is space then, real, related to our being and moving within "it"? Or is it (another?) form of *agency* in which we have come to exteriorize our being by placing causality outside, then finding ourselves inside of?

A Musical Program: how to organize the recital we are going to give next month!

Two sonatas are "good introductory pieces," thus they will begin the concert (Telemann) and begin the post-intermission (Handel). The Bach is "too hard" on people's ears and minds and they will need the rest (and us too); so just before intermission. The Corelli is easy to hear and a "crowd-pleaser"—good to finish and leave them with a lot of energy, looking still for more. So we have been operating in terms of some notions of how audiences' minds are, and will experience listening to music of particular sorts.

Bach is "difficult to listen to" because there are no "anchors" exactly, where the beat is obvious in any continual manner.

The organist will introduce the concert with pieces "in keys which will transition the music from one mood to another." And everyone will love the experience.

So, people (friends mostly) will come to a concert knowing that music will be performed, probably in a good mood to enjoy, ready to sit for a couple of hours. And we hope to entertain them, and to have them wanting more? Thinking it was wonderful?

The audience who knows me, mostly don't know me as a violinist (already some shift of context).

Velocity and Intensity: Performing for a (student's) wedding with a neophyte but eager organist I had to play a Corelli Sonata, (Opus 5, #7, final allegro) at about half usual speed.

At "ordinary" speed the music has a wonderful intensity, particularly good and well-suited for recessionals and other sorts of *finishings*. But at half speed it lacked intensity and continuity (though still being lovely). I tried to compensate by being very "deliberate" with my bow, attempting to increase the amplitude from softest to much louder within each stroke of the bow. Apparently this worked to (re)create the notion of a lilting song, and as effective finale. What is the "ordinary velocity" of the world and experience? How does this affect our lives: perceptions, experiencing, etc? What do velocity and boredom have to do with one another?

Illusions: do we experience them? Do we seek them? If there are illusions, is there a reality opposite to, or in dialogue with the illusion?

Are we used to seeing at a particular "velocity"? If there is a slight change of speed, do we "notice" it, a "just exactly" rapid enough change? Is there a human "time," in other words; a time and a timing in which we do not note what is normal or usual but only the deviations?

Is illusion a perception; i.e., a raw perception devoid of context (like a reflex); or is illusion dependent on context in some senses? Do we, accepting (some definitions of) context predict next events such that illusion as a change is in opposition to those predictions?

How is it that some "people" on a stage turn into "actors"? Is the cinema or TV different from actuality?

Lighting (illumination), timing, depth of space...?

Is illusion a boundary on what is reality (much as death may inform life)?

Observation: what sorts of contextual observers are we? Do our (raw?) perceptions change through, say, the duration of what we consider to be a single event? In the duration of a spoken sentence do we hear amplitude of pitch in some constant way, or somehow in relation to what has happened and what is about to happen?

Does this "truth" (that we are contextually-bound) claim that we are "relative" rather than "absolute" observers? And that we are relative within contexts, but observe "extra-contextually" in pretty constant manners? How can we "break context" to discover the nature of our own contextually-bound observations?

Escape from Context: in a sense, context is both relative and simultaneously the notion which everything else is relative with regard to, and we are caught within smaller or larger circles of thought and of being: the reductionist and the holist seem like vortices of equivalence but opposite in direction.

But there are constancies, moments, senses in which we are placed in surety, in some senses of absolute: some sense like the tuning of my violin A. That is all I need; and everything else is played in relation to it; in harmony with it. But that A, that is my life-line. That A, I can take anywhere and everywhere and it is sufficiently the same to act as if it were The Place; the escape from context. And it works. Is the world like playing the violin? (Would pianists agree?)

Searching for Bed-rock: where, what does it all come down to? Where is bottom, the foundation; what is fundamental, where do we begin, when did it begin? I keep sensing these are the wrong questions, looking for some surety, some purity: then it will be clear and we will know.

But isn't "it" already clear in various senses? Are we looking for the world to hold, for a time to stop (again!?) so we can see how it starts or was started?

Humans (others?) construct the world fairly sufficiently. Living within some senses of our senses we know beginnings and endings, are as amused as enraged by ambiguity, have our worlds mapped within a complex of cognitive frameworks. The bed-rock is ourselves, and that usually works, except as friend Martin Krieger says, when we are in trouble and need "advice."

Flow of Conversation: conversations and discourse seem to have a certain direction of flow. Once a context is "set," the participants knowing and agreeing, then there is/are progressions or movement.

But there are various pitfalls, where a conversation enters a morass; an area of quicksand where ideas do not "follow." That is, there is a (several!) kind of logic of process and flow: where the focus, the context has been forgotten or lost; where an unrelated idea comes in from "nowhere"; where there is a "disruption"; where one gets into a "side idea," and no longer can get back, not "realizing" where one is, or not willing to admit one is lost, or not knowing how to get out of such quicksand, one gets deeper into arenas of confusion.

This illustrates that ordinary/usual discourse has "rules" of *ongoingness*—of flow. Usually this works sufficiently well. Only sometimes there is trouble.

Editing: When there is too much, where something has been left out, where ideas do not follow well, where there could be better flow; where there is some elapsed time between writing and re-reading, then one enters into an editing mode: the same reading, yet different in perspective, in purpose. To write is to create something "from nothing"; to edit is to possess that something, that writing, and to "improve" it.

Problems in editing: often, I read what I have written to confirm my ideas or myself—not editing, but some form of self-love, of having memorized my previous being, of flattery. A different "frame-of-mind" is necessary, to see it as a critical reader; not merely the audience which is the writer's mirror-image. "Distance" of time, of attitude, of context.

Multiple Sclerosis: a loss of context. An inability to place one-self in context? Some years ago a woman who had developed symptoms of multiple sclerosis studied a course on Kinesics with me. Like many other persons with symptoms, she wanted to rid herself of them (to become well, whole) and possibly to become famous for developing a "cure"—all at the same time.

The usual neurological "explanation" is that the nerves become demyelinated, thus incapable of transmitting nervous impulses as they did earlier. Various forms of paralysis develop, often beginning with visual problems (holes in the vision) and moving to either or both sides, developing muscular weaknesses (due to lack of nervous innervation), etc. The disease may be rampantly "progressive" or very gradual.

Working together in an interview/dialogue mode we did note several things, and raised various questions which may have to do with context. Indeed, we wondered if the disease is not somehow a contextual pathology. First, it was clear her "memory" was spotty. She had little "access" to the memories of where and with whom she was at age four, seven, ten. As we interviewed others to see how they "construct" their personal histories, most of them seemed to "begin" this process by locating themselves somewhere: home or school, and/or with particular others, family, friends, or teachers. Once they begin this process—reported this way—then they could go on to elaborate various events which unfolded more or less like other narratives.

Since these are processes occurring in the ongoing present, we (all) seem to have ways of (re)constructing such stories to ourselves which we believe to be fairly accurate history (or we construct these histories in the form of narratives which we then check with family, friends and conclude they are accurate. One of the problems of moving and aging is that the others are not available to check one's stories and theories of personal history, etc.). Whatever is considered to be MS, the student had no history available to her, and this seemed somewhat disorienting for her in her ongoing present. She could not, that is, be secure in her having an accounting for how she "got" here, and this seemed to carry over to knowing what was happening right now; perhaps increasing or enhancing her sense of pathology.

We did not get very "far" in our understanding except to wonder about some contextual issues: do the so-called symptoms occur frequently in all of us, but the person who develops progressive MS will become "literal" or infatuated with these symptoms, or can no longer "turn them off"? That is, are the processes of the ongoing context merely continuous and obvious in the human condition, or do they require a frequent re-generation of "orienting stories" to oneself? Do most of us have occasional symptoms, but somehow "work" past them? How do we become, maintain, sustain issues of identity, orientation, location, navigation, which seem to be necessary for knowing who and where we are at any moment—how active are these processes?

Titles: beginnings, announcements, locators, statements about what is about to happen, how to interpret them; what is "in" and what is "out"; endings of whatever else, calls to dis-attend to whatever runs downs one's stream of consciousness. Perhaps titles are calls to halt, much as calls to begin. They focus, concentrate, announce that for the next "interval" the events will hold together, will follow, will belong; there will be an introduction, middle, (a climax, perhaps), an ending, a termination. And we should be "on the alert"...

Titles carve niches into the banks along the various streams of consciousness—indicating that the ongoing being and thought of anyone is not any single dynamic process, but some mess and mélange. Some of them seem to wander in quite obvious, at least known and tracked cycles (sleep/wakefulness, menstruation, micturation, hunger, thirst). Others seem aspects of the (re)generation of identity. Some may concern "themselves" with internal dialogues or with internal dialogues to others of one's imaginings and realities.

Some titles are announced: ladies and gentlemen; dear mother (now quite dead for many years, but still she demands some place in my thinking, at least occasionally, and how "I" do this remains somehow important); to myself; to Plato and Confucius whom I seek to understand and often refute; to Descartes whom I laugh at and with; to J. with whom dialogue is...; dear students, children, neighbors; dear those who do not understand me; dear president, pope, saint to whom I aspire to be; dear jerk, dear sick and dying; dear deity in whose name...

Some titles are "given" or "learned" or "happen": duke, or Nobel or poet laureate, parent, wise person, buffoon. Some of these remain active in one's life and in others' thinking about them, and acquire power or they do not.

Some of them are 'circular" like this one which both begins and ends with the bold-faced...**Titles**.

Titles (stories, poems, aphorisms): I choose the name of a topic to pursue thinking/writing that day, any day, every day. It begins the topic, the title does, portraying a domain of thought, signaling a discussion to come. In the old days—before computers—it would be as if there were a blank page to be filled partially...or mostly. Now, I merely type in the word "Titles,"

67

place it in bold face, and go on as long as the blank page of my former meanderings will take me.

The first sentence/paragraph depicts the problem, lays out the domain of the pursuit of an idea, a thought, something which needs at once to be expressed and thought out. It (the reference of the title) needs to be of a size and scope which can possess a beginning, middle and end—like some logical narrative, but with condensation, a certain parsimony; the attempt to get to the bottom, the centrality of whatever the title represents in the world, in my thinking and analysis, "should" (if I understand any potential audience now or in some futurity or in some past from which I live my present) resonate in your reader's mind as well. It should carve out some issue which is clearly problematic—or one which I can convince you might be problematical.

The first sentence/paragraph states approximately what the issue is and why it might be problematic. In an aphoristic work (such as the present one on "Context"), the title might draw its problematicity from the previous ones, hinting strongly that this one is a further unpacking of some underlying issue. It might repeat a previous one (Titles) by showing/claiming that the titled problem has a variety of possible resonances, allowing me the author to go somewhat further afield, perhaps deeper into a question whose understanding has perhaps a simple or more superficial arena, but one which also goes in various other directions, gathering ideas as it circles back upon itself or becomes its own self-reference, sometimes causing/enticing the reader to go back to see how the piece got here, and even getting the reader to look for deeper questions than had been seen previously when the beginning and the title led in one direction whilst the piece was moving (also) in others.

In the first paragraph of this aphorism, for example, I tried to conflate a writing with a day, suggesting that my life (thence the reader's?) has duration akin to the duration of the study of "context." This might give the reader/thinker (another attempt at conflation and the development of linkages—and, I think, more properly in the domain of pedagogy than many other aphorisms which are more exploratory and internal rather than this piece which is self-reflective) the idea that the reading of an aphoristic essay is an aspect of one's lived life, occurring over some time sufficient for the ideas to enter and penetrate and be reflected upon, gathering whatever it is that ideas gather. Indeed, I think I am trying to get and give some sense for the duration of thought occurring over the decade this has been in the thinking and writing. (Is the writing up to the portrayal of the ideation? Which is knowledge, which skill; is there any difference?)

The title has, I hope and expect by now an increasing set of dimensions from subject to object to self-analysis to a wondering why I am pursuing the issue of "Titles" even when I merely use the title to discuss how to think out such an aphorism. Actually, the issue of the term is the sense in which it sets a context in terms of which what follows is to be interpreted and understood. And here I am trying to stretch the possibilities of what can be "included" within the topic of Titles, to attempt to entice the reader to read the damn thing yet again, to see how we got here, reflexively giving it its own life while complicating the thinking of the reader perhaps to the point of breaking, or of utter boredom.

Counter-Intuition: Though it remains murky to me that there is some obvious sense to the term "intuition," it has often been clear in my pedagogical practice that there are some powerful moments in the teaching art which I understand to be "counter-intuitive."

What I-the-teacher seem to discern is some "direction" or directedness to the thinking of many of the students in some particular course. Having seen this displayed in several students, I seem to track on its course, and am predicting how and/or where they will go, next. Once engaging in this observation and surmising, I then guess what will be counter to their mode and direction of thinking, and spring this on them. See my *Teaching as Dialogue* 2013.

Facial Expression: A proportion of whatever is context concerns the nature of our presence—bodily, occupying space, "able" to demand the attention of others, and so on. This complex area of our being has been backgrounded within the import of literature, narrative, and the excitement which symbolic extension has created in our theories of human nature. In the idealist tradition in which abstraction has meant so much, it is also worth recalling that Plato "got rid of" the body in the dialogue *Phaedo*, at least as having much importance in the exploration of our being, which he pointed toward knowledge of the formal, and always external to our bodies. (This has much to do with the intellectual "wish" to banish change from what is knowing, and the body is certainly changing and changeable—but Plato did not see the Heraclitean notion of knowing truth, that the changing body like the proverbial "river" also has duration and stability of sorts.) Nonetheless the cliché that "a picture is worth a thousand words" embeds itself in the hard facts of presence and the power it has in the providing of context.

This area of our being is extremely complex (at least intellectually; practically much of who we are resides here), having apparently multifold senses of meaning including quite basic issues of how we see others (and ourselves), but also including a variety of judgments actual and metaphorical.

It is not so clear to me how to provide written contexts to explore and underline the import of presence as a central focus of our existence. Surely one can proceed by examining the variety of literary approaches to "setting scenes," i.e. "locating" the action (time, place, occurrence, variety, absence) much of which is "unnecessary" when one is present and "in person." Much of what we mean by "following" a scene seems to be "derived" from experience in being with others; especially faces, but also presence more generally.

An analogy, perhaps, to illustrate from "later" experience how much of the knowing of our presence is already backgrounded by the time we learn to read: at first letters are quite abstract to the learner—little squiggles which have no obvious meaning. Gradually they are "learned," become parts of words; words are attached to meanings the child already possesses, become aspects of sentences. All of whatever letters symbolize become facts to be used in reading (or writing—think of the strangeness of the typing keyboard), and their complexity becomes quite unapparent. Their actual complications may be "recalled" in the attempt to learn to read in another orthography. In any case, the complexity of the body in its presence (with others) is much more complex than the quite complicated learning of reading, but is so much background that we have quite literally read it out of what we know about knowing.

So, the face and facial expression: to begin, the presence of someone's face seems to "demand" that we actively look at "it," look at her or him, or have to take quite a lot of energy to deliberately 'not look'. Unusual faces also capture energy—"pathologies," the "mask" of death; we invest being in persons essentially "as their faces." Perhaps it is not too strong to claim that context "begins" here and returns here. As I (the narrator, the reader, the observer) "face the world," read the book. I locate myself and others and the seat of actions, "decide" what is real or surreal.

And I decide not how the world is, but primarily how others (and I, thus I) will decide "how it is," where I am, you are...

The "I" of my presence is much more the "body in the mind" as I look out, interpreting the world with my bodily presence being there. (See: my *Body Journals*), ms. 2014. With respect to facial expression, context is quite paradoxical, perhaps multiply paradoxical, "using" a "fixed" gaze (a person who has enduring duration) to signal and determine the locus of being in the present, but also seeing and looking at what others look at, and interpret, and give meaning to, and change, and change the rules for seeing what there is and what is happening.

Prediction and Prophecy: Entire eras are given over to theories and practices which portend and portray our notions of futurity. The two which are most clear (others?) are prediction and prophecy. These seem to embed, as sort of meta- or master contexts, the ways in which we cast our being "forward" and interpret how the future will be, and, reflexively, how to understand the present.

Both of these (importantly?) have to do with modes of knowing: do we judge the past and present and cast these judgments into our sense of futurity → prediction, or do we call upon some agency (deity, chance, personal destiny or vision, a shared spirit or nagual with another dead or alive person or demi-person or animal) to interpret what will happen at least in terms of who/what keeps the world afloat.

These modes of future interpretation are akin to the geological theories of catastrophism and uniformitarianism, where these have been granted historical dimensionality in interpreting why the earth came to have its present form: e.g., from *Genesis* or from the study of "nature," as well as why and how life is (humans and our presumed relation to other species: we "have dominion," are related to them, should live in harmony, etc.).

In the context of the study of context the important aspect is the sort of outlook we take to the interpretation of our experiencing: the questions we raise about our very existence ("do we exist?" is quite recurrent in eschatological Platonic traditions—abortion issues); how do I relate to myself, others, to the world; why is the world the way it is, and how does this reflect on and determine what I do; how do I ground knowledge and myself; etc.?

Beginning and end-of-life debates are illustrative: is the fetus a "person" or an "individual"? In predictive eras, this is not ever very clear, but it seems that most persons gather meaning to others the longer they endure beyond a few years of age; in prophetic eras, the judgment is made based on an interpretation of external (deific) agency; e.g., returning the soul to heaven. Similarly with euthanasia.

But the powerful potential of prophetic thinking is quite apparent in the context of millennial moments. At this moment, the prophetic thinkers find no end of sport in interpreting changes (especially plagues and other disasters, but not necessarily) in the context of expectation of the return of the deity, our "release" from this existence, and so on. Since (the thinking goes) what is happening is forewarned, there is nothing much to do to stop or redirect wars, pestilence, or epidemics: they are "supposed" to happen within the prophecy (mostly from the *Book of Revelation* in this case). See: my *The Crisis in Meaning*.

Similarly the effect on our thinking and activity can be framed in very different ways depending on the context of prophecy or prediction. Some of them easily come over into self-judgment: what was I "meant" to be, what is success for me, etc.?

Tai Chi: The study (and practice) of the Eastern martial arts is interesting and illuminating both for what it consists in, and what it offers as critique and lessons upon being and upon society. The Confucian setting (only?–what of Buddhist? Jewish? Islamic? Taoist?) is the major tradition which is at once utopic and within life: that no matter how much we know, there is more to learn; however much we can, there is more. Life is a directedness toward a perfection which is always in the doing, becoming, and being. Moreover, there is always a mentor, a teacher, a person of some more advanced age who knows more than I, and can do more; can "do me in." It is a tradition in which futurity in located within the practice and persona of a teacher.

Like the other healing traditions which involve bodily movement, it consists particularly in stretching and relaxing (rather, relax then stretch) movements which help us deal with the inexorable pulling and compression of living longer in gravity. Tai Chi particularly is the "yielding" art, while others (e.g., karate, judo) are more externally directed, linear. Yielding involves a study of one's standing body, especially the support of legs in the various directedness of 360° of movement. It involves the exertion of the muscles and limbs, as well as the release from tensions, directed as it were by the breath. In its yielding, it is the preparation and preparedness for any attack or onslaught while standing well anchored and flexible, and at the ready to effectively absorb any movement directed at our bodies. One deflects and absorbs the momentum and turns it into one's own defensive deflection. The "form"—it usually is done in a sequence of movements which are calculated to exercise the entire body in all possible dimensions—is a set of movements which are often "named" to enable the person to concentrate on the doing, rather than upon the details of memory and analysis. Like the other martial arts, it attempts to downplay any rational analysis and to direct all energy to the moment and the performing.

It appears to be very slow, but the slowness is experienced very differently from the observer and the person who is doing the form. One attempts to both move and to release tension in the moving, and this requires a way of moving which uses minimal energy to accomplish any moving, and this appears slow to the observer, but correct and necessary to the doer.

It is a recipe for a long life with a sense of directedness toward a/the best possible mode of living. It is a doing relying on a well-trained and confident body sitting upon a most firm foundation, always at the ready, but never needing to strike out unless provoked. When provoked, it this is unavoidable, one accepts the attack, turns it about into one's own energy while apparently yielding.

Tai Chi is a useful example/metaphor for the study of the grounding of one's being within the mores and morass of contextual being.

Grudges: Castaneda's 1968 observation that "the hardest thing to do in life is to see what is happening right now" is well illustrated by considering all the grudges we develop in life and in its living; grudges against others, against ourselves and our histories, with respect to what might have been, and the variety of vengeances which seem to offer to us ways of reducing or ameliorating the sense of anger or whatever we call grudges.

Something happened once upon a time, and entered our memories with a vengeance like concretions dropping upon our heads from the tops of mountains. They got our attention so fully at that moment, and that moment persists in our thinking in each right now, crowding our thinking, and pushing the possibility of concentrated action toward the peripheries of our being. That hateful person, and what one did to me, against me. Grudges toy with concepts of justice, asking and bending in some dance with whether what happened was deserved.

In the context of context, grudges frame and shape the experiencing of each moment by offering to us interpretive accountings of what is held and balanced against what we see in the judgment of our memories. I see not a person free of my venom, but of someone I yet owe, of someone who virtually owns my interpretation of present representations of her being. I want to hit back at him; he who hurt me or didn't appreciate my being or good works or hurt someone I love or whom I depend on.

Grudges provide a shaping of the present in which the variety of the contexts of my being are (subtly?) not free to be fresh or very new, but always contain the press of the history of my thinking which didn't go in the direction I might have wished at some earlier moment, but was controlled somehow by someone against whom I yet hold a grudge. And I wonder, in each next moment, what new grudges are accumulating in what I am destined and burdened to hold in memory, while I tell myself I walk anew each day.

I wonder, too, if vengeance will end the sense of any grudge, or merely deepen its effects in my being, will lead toward some sense of vindication and protect the grudge, or help it to be satisfied and thence to disappear.

The '80's, '70's, '60's,...: Time and history are the fuller, the longer we exist and walk upon this earth. Each moment of my being is full now of some sense of the '90's, but also of the '80's, back even to the '30's. And this is just in the experiencing of my being, and of being in the world: songs, ideas, images, experiences, wars, and fantasies, all and whatever. In talking with the young, the sense of each moment differs so radically, talking with those whose each minute stretches so long, while my time races, and my times race.

All of this does not yet begin to touch the sense of vast scales of history which float in my mind's being and seeing the rock in front of my foot and wondering whence it had come to this place and how, and how humans began and endured and what does this have to do with me. Thinking of precisely where I am, and where anyone is, the question of the analytics of histology and multi-micro seconds, and how quickly eventness occurs tends to overwhelm the scale of my being, and to look to see how quickly/slowly is the human.

The pace is blinding... or boring.

How tempting to balance some sense of the eternal and the infinite with the rush of present being. Looking to my history, looking to history while trying to walk in the myriad contexts of each day and each person whom I know, while trying to sort what is significant from what is meaningless, I can appreciate how the turn of the millennium is at all moments so close and so far, and just who is counting... what? (See my *Next Places*.)

Facial Expression: Gray's anatomy discusses facial expression as being the muscles of the emotions: happy, we smile; sad, we frown, grimace—as if our being resides in some more-or-less permanent state which is punctuated occasionally by our emotions acting up or out.

The fact is that the question of expressions on our faces underlines some complications and peculiarities to the general consideration of context. Where to begin? This is difficult because there is no beginning, no clear boundaries. Our faces do not move from some neutral or zero state in which there is "no" facial expression to smiling states of happiness which are somehow observable and measurable to any external watcher. The face is already always in some muscular tensioned state(s): at "rest" the tongue is not flaccid, the lips are in some particularities of lateral or raising/lowering. Facial expression is not movement from nothing, but from some already/constantly held muscles (principally around the mouth and eyes).

The issue of expression is further complicated by the fact that what "we look like" is some congeries of the external facial "showing" of these muscular tensions, with respect to or in the background (context?) of facial hair, eye placement and directedness, etc. We remain looking "like we look" as a sense of identity to others, even when we express ourselves in some sense "emotionally." Like age, gender, (social and cultural background, etc.), interpreters of our facial expressions "read" our expressions within a fairly vast number of characteristics which are at play upon the facial mask.

Faces are (this is difficult to state with precision) expressions which are seen by others. Thus it is not clear where the facial expression is located exactly—upon the face or within the interpretation of the observer and/or both. If one's face is understood (to oneself) as being seen and interpreted by others and at least partially defined by how they see our faces, then it seems not so clear where is the seat of the emotions: within the expressing person, within the interaction, within the imagination of the interpretation of the feelings which then show up on one's face. How continuingly important is it in one's life (for example) is it that one's significant other interprets one's expressions "positively" or not?

Some thinkers have attempted to take the dualism of mind and body and find a third or "interface" arena in the emotions and in their expression. This has been accompanied by a quasi-historical story that humans got to be human (uniquely, to have reason, etc.) as they learned to speak as articulations of the emotions. The "status" we assign to facial expression thus plays intellectually into the question of the harder (less changing) reality of the body. We find ourselves, in this argument, not very able to discern the contextual issues which are framed or at least illustrated by facial expression, because the questions are seen as either-or's rather than as issues of relation, of context, and of the (dis-)confirmation of one's being as being important, worthy, credible. (See my *The Body Journals*)

Identity: Caught in myriad swirls of context defining context and being defined leaves one flying, hopping, and never thinking that ground is anywhere exactly, or that there is any ground upon which I stand, upon which I find and locate myself. Yet I am who I am.

The "me" I call myself, the identity, picture, social security number, address might remind me and reassure me that I am who I say I am. But that all seems fragile, especially now that I try to state it as some fact. Some fact of philosophical and religious history, the notion of the individual is so taken-for-granted that I can get lost without ever being exactly sure that I am not lost.

At play with words, the issue of context would have no discernment unless I am findable; surely sure that I am who I am. The clue is not located within myself - as the individual that is the body which contains the soul which Plato told me I am, and Augustine told God to tell me that I am. Rather my/me is at once caught within the swirls of contexts, and interestingly extricated by the others who tell me that I am who I am, over and over again as the I who I am changes drastically and grows from seven pounds to one hundred seventy, from 15 inches to five feet fifteen. Who I am is who I am... treated as being.

Identity is the basis, the ground, the place to begin to unravel context, the where that circles swoop come to rest to start again: the focus and locus for change and continuity, for boundaries and the peelings off of paradox. It is less a specific place, not so specified, but a sense that there is such a center to one's being, and that there are modes of finding "it" every day, often, from time to time. It is the focus of an internal dialogue where many voices are mediated and demand a singular one: I am who I am. And it/I take this notion into a complex world and move on, changing rapidly and radically while being like Heraclitus' river contained within the banks of my being.

It is this sense of confirmed identity which can analyze, interpret and act in terms of the varying contextual issues and meanings which so complexly intertwine being with being who I am. (See: 10 *Identity*.)

Clericy: The fact that identity is granted and confirmed by others—how strong equals how significant the others are—is shown by the development of conscience, perhaps also of consciousness. We live as beings independent only to some degree—and sustainable as such only within specific and bounded contexts. I am who I am is an "I" which is fragile at many moments of being.

The boundedness of myself contains within it only so much power of self-definition, only so much strength and willingness of self-declared and sustained. For many of us this is not sufficient, at least at some times in living, at some moments in history, when we feel afflicted and sense our energies' waning. At different moments, in different settings and cultures—all contexts of sorts—we long to believe that our insufficiency is proper to our being, and this can be garnered less from within, more from without.

The power of self-definition is diminished as we yield the "who I am" to some notion of externality. The concept of conscience, of doing what our parents told us to do, of not-doing what they told us not to do, is translated by many of us into longings and belongings. In most settings, we are at various moments in life not-so-complete within ourselves as we are led to want to be: thus love and marriage and intimacy and family. But in the context of clericy, we long to believe in believing (See my *Next Places, 2006*)

It seems less important—viewed globally—what we might believe in. Rather the wanting to exteriorize, to locate reality or authority outside of me or us, to become a supplicant to our own imaginations as our cultural-significant others also seem to define this, leads us to deities and ideologies: power less shared with others, but deriving from them as if we are small and weak and "they" can tell us how to be and what to do.

In the context of context, the power of clericy is to reduce possibilities and to confirm and strengthen the lines in terms of which we see and interpret: particularly issues of being.

The positive aspects of clericy with respect to being and deepened understanding and human possibilities are that we use the power we have granted in our believing to treat others humanely or well, to deal with ourselves with patience and humility (in Judeo-Christian contexts).

But the dangers of clericy are all too powerful, leading us to abandon possibility and responsibility to deity, bureaucracy, cult: to kill in the name of (holocaustic murder reduced to policy necessity), to commit suicide (Jonestown), greed; to shift radically from political left to reactionary right without ever giving much notice because all is clericy, and I have no position from which to judge seeing what is and who I am.

The boundaries of communality of individuality are never very clear, nor is the firmness of our identity always so assured that we are not susceptible to finding ourselves so attracted or so repelled that we join with others in exteriorizing all our beings, thus reducing being and the variety of contexts to a very few problematics: e.g., Do I exist? Will I die?–Rather than giving care to how I am living today.

Surreal and the Avant-garde: I tend to liken these concepts or notions to issues of "counter-intuition" and "learning," which I use in my pedagogy to get students to call their critical attention to what they already accept and believe. If the opposite, or the inversion is seen to be at fairly direct odds with what they (must already) think and believe, then they begin to see how they have thought, and the way is open to move on. This does not necessarily mean that they are wrong in any overarching sense; merely that they have gone in particular directions or made certain assumptions. And I want them to open up, think more broadly and critically, in order to move on. Pedagogically this is a complex problem: the teacher has to set-up the reality of the presumptions, then get the students to question it; to question themselves without undermining the authority of the teacher. The teacher has to be pretty sure of their intuitive modes of thinking at some point, then think oppositionally and state a counter-intuitional point in such a way that it will be "heard"—realized.

Similarly, the surreal seems to call attention to one's own and prior thinking about what is the real; to make one realize in fits and starts that one has seen the world in one way, when it can be seen other ways; otherwise. On seeing one thing, the surreal causes or forces one to see that one is seeing the other as well. The surreal is thus peculiarly contrastive: like, perhaps, seeing a gorilla "causes" us simultaneously to see the gorilla and to see both its likeness and difference from humans, and to wonder how we see humans. Whether all humans see gorillas in this way is dubitable. Thus when I/you see a gorilla and experience the contrastive moment, it seems to have much to do with the intuition we have (as Western thinkers?) about the juxtapositional relation between humans and non-humans.

Contextually, the surreal seems to cause/allow us to see ourselves seeing, to multiply our modes of seeing and to further complicate the world. Similarly with counter-intuitions, the recognition of the intuitive in one's thinking explodes possibilities, and methodologically seems to open one up to be able to further explore how one already sees and thinks. What was obvious now becomes problematized; what is problem may lead toward new knowledge.

The complication—perhaps this is an appropriate term—is that the surreal and the counter-intuition seem to lead many to question the very nature of reality rather than to enjoy its further explorations. Perhaps this occurs to those who approach the world through fear rather than wonder. In the teaching context, the fact that the teacher has some sense of how to utilize the insight into one's intuitions to further conceptual change, seems to ensure development, rather than to arrest it, and to cause many to enter severe doubt about the grounds of their being and knowing.

Here context seems to bend to and within the outlook of the observer-interactor: whether the surreal destroys the real or opens it radically, whether the counter-intuition moves on and becomes the future direction for thought and development and is judged good and interesting and progressive!?

On Seeing Faces: (on seeing what there is...) The question had arisen in my life as I pondered my daughter's appearance at the age of 19, and caused me to say that she hadn't much changed in looks since I had seen her first at the age of 15 minutes new. J. remarked that she had changed vastly, radically, but that my image and imagination of her hadn't much altered during that period of growth and change. It was as if my vision was—in part at least—quite fixed and placed in some mental compartment which was not very easy to open; which I didn't want to bring out into today's light.

On this same daughter's adopting of a Korean infant, we went to hear an author speak about adoption. She confirmed that one is not very good at "seeing" much about one's family members. How they might appear to others, whether they are "attractive" in some larger sense, or even that they appear culturally or "racially" different, if they do. One sees one's significant others not in social terms of categories, but as the person to whom one relates closely: a spouse, child, parent, or friend. This identifying someone as some one seems to leave no space for categories, even though one might be very sensitive to social categories shared with others when seeing others with whom one has no "special" relationship.

Therefore seeing others is itself a contextual issue. I wonder how far and wide this applies to other aspects of being and of the world, and how to go about seeing through my seeing!?

Paradoxes and Parables: and aphorisms, psalms, lamentations, meditations and whatever may be which gets us to think, rethink, think again, and move into futurity differently than we would have before their contemplation.

The paradox of paradox is, I suppose, that we begin to make a method and critique of being by thinking that any and all oppositions need to be resolved. This is restrictive and falls within the logic and method of logic, itself. Instead, the pleasure of paradox is that "it" (whatever we experience as paradox) extends however we were thinking, showing us that what we thought formerly was one, is not one plus, or one and its inversion, or opens us to futurity which is more textured and complex, hopefully without being overburdening.

The point of paradox is to show us that we had fallen into the limiting trap of believing that what we had accepted as a truth had taken on the clothing of who we are: we wear it rather than think it. Paradox mirrors our thought in appearance so we can see our seeing. "One cannot step twice into the same river" extended to the human face has not been nearly as obvious. My face changes as it remains the center of my identity. So it is that paradox, even when it is clear and clean, is contextually laden: face it!

Parable is a story (a story which works!) which illustrates to us that we have other similar stories at work in our thinking and being, and teaches us; lessons about what we are about; how to see our seeing without the oppositional and resolutional power of paradox; gently and without the guilt of logical error as its lessons may lead us to reconstruct memory as we alter the experience of being, and the experience of experience. Even here, context sits about parable hanging onto some dirigible of sun's setting reflections or hovering above directly like a personal black cloud just about to spit upon our heads. As death is parable, we cannot hear it when it is overwhelmed by feelings we call fear. For as Kafka says (*Parables and Paradoxes*): "in this life (which is the only life we have) many of us Western thinkers do not even see the parable." (1961) As structures (political, religious, educational, etc.) are parables, we concretize them like they are aspects of the built world, and seem wont to find ourselves actually in the mirror, so we know what self to be.

3.

RETRIEVAL OF BEING

In the beginning was the deed. –Redner

The Frozen Moment: the just-in-time as Plato banishes the body in the dialogue *Phaedo*. Contemplating personal death outweighs the desire and necessity to move on in one's Being and Becoming; the means to overcome (any) fear of death transcribe, place structures and strictures on present experience. Outweighing all else, the fixation upon the eternality of death, the always growing sense of temporality snuffing out time itself, the time in and within which I know that I am turns a corner, abruptly.

I look back, now, me the philosopher-Teacher from the ever-is of the hereafter (Sarles 2013). The hereafter is called wonderful, heavenly, at one with the Being of being my soul, my mind, my spirit which has - at last longing - found its sense of truth, unmixed and unmired with any feelings; no more feelings, particularly those of out-of-control, desires, longings, fears, wishing to be or not to be, of sickness or health, of debts and owing to the being of our Being all banished. The sense and senses of body borne and born, gone. Not to worry Being, but being freed of Being, ideality. Being is diminished radically into a partial partaking of the realm of ideality, of what would be... if...

The question of life circumscribed by a definition of death by Aristotle in *de Anima*, as the moment when the soul or spirit, the animating life force leaves the body: the body presumed, taken for granted as the locus of our Being: a place, a container or package. But/And the body is somehow prior: physics prior, a priori, previous to life (itself) As *de anima* is *me ta physics*, talk about the body, about the world is also *me ta physics*.

The ground of reality (and nature) thus *is* physics). We muse endlessly about our place *within* it. Within *it*. In various ways we question existence as a quest for the reality and solidity of physics via its descriptor languages and logics; and we are somehow left-overs, residual in our very being, trying to

83

figure how and what we might know, deriving the facticity of our existence from the idea that we are aspects, but principally descriptors, of some-thing which is essentially independent of our Being. (See: 10. *Identity*)

Beyond Finiteness: Caught within some Parmenidean necessity to resolve and to solve the interiorities of our experienced paradoxical being: logic vs. rhetoric. How can this finite being body, know, have imagination, scope beyond the bounds of my bodily Being? Bodily Being?

Instead, (I observe that) we are bodies, we are time, we are feelings, in gravity, well and sick, always on the edges and verges of control and out of control, is and will and would be, and we are of two kinds: not merely, not only mind, soul, spirit. We are male and female. Do we not notice?

We must retrieve Being, becoming, and knowing just at that regnant moment when Plato *solves* the problem of death by banishing life, by banishing the body, leading us to not note gender and what else do we not notice?

The body is the truth, it is knowledge; it, I endure as I am. It is imagination, infinite, and transcendent; it is the terrestrial, the solid, the place, the beauty and the changing I; the believing and the disbelieving, the ugly, the rotting, the control at war with, in accord with desires, sickening, curing... dying, birthing; new-old, old-new. It is not eternal; it is eternal. It is the paradoxes of our Being which we must seek to understand, in order to know that and who we are; that and who we are... we are.

The Invention of the Mind: the problem is/was of the nature of human transcendence—how is it that we possess imagination, the ability to get beyond ourselves (Parmenides). The body appears incapable of moving beyond itself—a materialistic assumption that what is, is what is (defining the nature of "is-ness"). Physical bodies –a foundation based upon physics as the primariness of the universe—are what they are. But life is different; especially human life.

In order to account for the animism in humanity, the mind was posited as the word repository for the concept of the transcendent; that which gets us beyond the finite. First the notion of the mind, filled by whatever turns out to be definitional of "language" in any era. Then rationality, then life beyond life—it turned out to be a solution to (fear of) death—mostly by turning its back on life and living, and making life itself a puzzle which was (best?) answered by Augustine's "Confessions" - of the "fall" to earth. What a deal! Make sure you purchase a return ticket!

That fact: that the body is what there is, and "must" (therefore) be transcendent of itself (in the world with others' bodies). How can we "imagine" that possibility?—is the question of Western metaphysics, without the meta-? (We know other animals and ourselves as bodies. We infer our Being.)

Permanence and Universals: The issues which arise in our thinking are inevitably shaped by the early Greeks, whose ideas (still) permeate our own. Attempting to recreate their thought, we enter with Thales into the idea that there is some "truth"—some particularly enduring or overarching architecture or unity to the universe. Muse on the name of the concept: universe. Another paradox uncovered and resolved in the same moment as our Being beyond the finite.

One infers that the early Ionian and Milesian philosophers who came upon the notion of philosophy, of having happened upon a "ground" or position through which to see-through their own commonsensical observations were the first "comparatists." Having traveled far and wide, having noted that various peoples think differently, having figured out many of the rules of navigation, they return to their own "native" thinking with lenses newly colored by their sojourns in different places, in some immersion in different systems of thought; looking for *incommonesses*.

The principal or primary insight, perhaps, is that there is some ground to see-through one's own native or naïve observations. Secondly, a set of questions (now) arise in thought which cause one to wonder both about the world and about oneself:

1) Issues of change and permanence—if the world (actually) is totally in flux in some Heraclitean sense, then issues of identity and continuity arise. What is the same; what keeps things the same; maintaining, sustaining; structures, processes? If the world is inherently static or stable, then why is there (does there "appear" to be) change? Something about us; something about the world (its "unity")? What is form, what substance; style or content? What is either/or and what is-not? Paradoxically, if the world is (we are) inherently

85

changeable, why does much of Being seem continuous, stable? Have we invented structures which we raise then to the level of what is?

2) Questions of the real—if the world; if us—in which order? Which is primary: physics or that which is beyond physics (*me ta physics*)? If the material is primary, then what factors are at work in *not* allowing us to see it; what are causal factors, what is their locus → "infinity" arose quite early as an explanatory notion (and called "the deity").

The idea that our Being is an issue of causality which is somehow beyond the world (God: an Aristotelian *self-caused first cause*), or lies within the world at an encompassing conceptual level (a world mind—a heavenly mind). Once this move occurs, then concentration is upon the nature of the transcendent, seeking out its nature (always presuming that the body is not itself, cannot be transcendent).

3) If the transcendent exists in some sense, then the issue of how we (can) know it assumes great importance. There must be, within us (bodily) an aspect of our Being which is, variously, like the transcendent, open to it, an aspect of it, etc. The Platonic solution is to deny the "truth" of our senses, and to look for those aspects of our being which are permanent—to foreswear whatever is changing within us to look for the permanence which organizes the universe, and which is external to being—in which we partake, but do not constitute. Banish the body and everything is solved.

4) The grand issue—within the permanence/change paradox—came to be the question of knowledge, but in the following way: we "know" in two senses—the immediate knowledge arriving at our eyes and ears, versus the knowledge by which we "conjure up" images of knowing. Which is the true image, the imagined and remembered from some other time and place—or that which is immediate? Within the search for the transcendent, the image which is already in the mind, has clearly been the winner. (Again, the "fact" that we do/are *both* more-or-less simultaneously—that we *are* paradoxical creatures—does not seriously arise within this mode of thinking, as it is cast within the either/or of permanence versus change—the world seen as oppositional.

5) Within the notion of material physics being in deep ways unchanging, the human body... Only rarely noting that we (our bodies) *develop* into the adult which we judge to be the human.

The Architecture of *Legitimate* Issues: The history of thinking about the human condition is focused particularly upon a small set of questions concerning what and who we are, how we are like and different from other species, and how we think and know. Especially is this true of what has come to be called metaphysics, in which the human condition is contrasted with, or more literally, with what *remains* "after" physics: i.e., the aspects of human life which are *beyond* the physical or material. Thinking about human nature has concentrated on the mental—the "left over" or the "more than" the physical—and is delimited by the obviousness of the individual; it is, as Whitehead (1925) says, "the philosophy of the organism."

In these contexts it is the "relationship" between the mental and the physical body, and the ways in which individuals come together in social arrangements which have delimited the exploration of the limits of the human condition. The curing arts have taken over study of the physical in almost an *exact* opposition to metaphysics. The philosopher and the physician meet only rarely in discussion, having divided up the organism into two categories, each of which remains in its own domain. Following the ancients Plato and Aristotle, they all presume that our very nature is located within and about each individual: a mind and a body. Somehow, there seems to be a veiled presumption that the two categories will someday meet and add up to a total being, always at war with the idea that the mind *or* the body will explain human nature. The relationship *between* individuals—questions of interaction and discourse—have risen relatively recently as definitional of the individual.[1]

In Western thinking, where we are heirs and students of the Platonic-Aristotelian tradition, concentration upon metaphysics has been delimited and carved out of the larger senses and contexts of being human, to reside in the domain of the mind or soul or spirit. Here we have taken Being to be the non-material, in which it is considered that we are different from other species in terms of human "reason"—and the issue of our particular human identity has resonated within the sphere of reason's domains: e.g., language, symbolic thought, knowledge. Whereas the physician can practice surgery upon other similar species, the metaphysician has held that humans are essentially unique, non-comparable with other species, however similar in

---

[1] Reference to the ancient and now recurring battles between philosophy as metaphysics and rhetoric. G. H. Mead.

other respects. (Until very recently, the anatomy of the cadaver has been idiomatic of the description of our bodies... interestingly. Now sports medicine, alternative medicine begins to admit, even acknowledge, that body moves upright and within gravity, contributing much to its adult form.)

Within these metaphysical domains, the mind and body are ensconced within the individual organism. Where the individual is the beginning and the end, there has, historically, been little sense of reflection upon the organism as anything interestingly problematic within some more extensive or prior contexts.

Within some cycles which occur over several centuries, questions occasionally arise which seem to engulf the notion of metaphysics and reduce its possibilities of *solving* the "what" and "who" of "being human."

Such times—we find ourselves within such, right now—are moments in the broad sweep of history when the edges of being seem to come to the center; when any meaning in and of life loses its power to inform and sustain; when the possibilities of annihilation overtake life itself, and make problematic the nature of our existence (Buber 1937)). At times like these, the broad history of great traditions is, paradoxically, both spurned and held up as paragon, in some epic battle in which the present moment finds itself at war with its history. Here, and now, is rediscovered cosmology and the questioning of existence itself. Here and now, is problematized the metaphysical questions of the very nature of Being, and of being human.

Retrieving the Framing Questions: In the midst of this "era of problematization," a number of inquiries are set in motion. Some of them are paradoxically historical *and* anti-historical: attempting to "retrieve" a prior time, a "classical" age when we were alternatively innocent or wise beyond present imaginings; e.g., a return to the *Great Books* of Western civilization (Bloom 1987), or a return to the Biblical texts in the hope of a messianic return in an approaching millennial moment. The retrieve/return is paradoxical because it "uses" historical sources to (re)define or revise the present, thus destroying, perhaps, the very concept of history. As a *return* to a putative past, it seems to be destroying or radically diminishing the concept of the ongoing present. As a retrieve it may open up the present to its possible impossible. The skepticisms which usually inform reason and rationality—not accepting whole-cloth the superstitious and unexamined and beyond nature (irrational, paranormal)—turn guarded and secretive. The skeptical tradition since Hume has argued that reason itself resides upon a foundation of feelings, passions, and intuitions.

"Reason is and ought only to be the slave of the passions and can never pretend to any other office than to serve and obey them." (Hume, *Treatise of Human Nature* Bk. 2, Sec.3)

Do we, can we know about the *external* world? If not... our bodies?

If not, can we believe in, can we prove, our own existence? Descartes' *cogito* no longer serves, no longer satisfies.

The skeptical tradition wrestles with a thoughtful and critical wonderment about fact and proof at war with an increasing puzzling about the possibility of knowledge: not only Plato's truth vs. opinion, but ways of doubting doubt itself in the postmodern co-optation of science into the history of narration; just another story; all of Being is stories... All of knowledge is politics; esthetics; reality is virtual.

The skepticism grows: there is actual doubt about externality—and, I infer, also about our own existence, in spite of Descartes. The failure of Husserl's phenomenology to positively construct the real continues to haunt us (and instruct us that all forms of idealism and formalism, including logic, are derived rather than central to or explanatory of Being).

The thinker yearning after truth, enters into a self-telling which begins to find success in showing that the very possibility of truth is itself problematic. In this era, Hume's 18th century skepticism cannot find this self I may call myself, nor can it find any solid basis on which knowing may ground itself. The skeptic turns cynical—first wonders that anything may be known in surety; then in a mood of self-protection of the self-denied, dwells upon the death of the very concept of existence. If rationality is uncertain, if God is seen as dead, the very concept of meaning recedes, and as Nietzsche tells us, there will rise a form of (European) nihilism. An unrequited positivism, a visitor to its own life, finds its solace in an intellectual nihilism!? Fun?!

Physical being is no longer proof of itself! Life and being, socially constructed: deconstruct meaning and find meaning? (The question of the socially constructed body arising recently within the re-discovery of gendered being, is an intellectually constructed body which forms an oppositional category *within* the mental, leaving the original mind-body dichotomy fairly intact; as usual.)

As the self-telling skeptic engages in an internal dialogue over what she/he knows, as well as the very notion of knowing, the business of our engagement is both psychological and metaphysical. As we follow Hume, this relies on some notion of the human individual, the organism as a composite which focuses upon how each of us gets knowledge perceptually, and molds it into knowing: as metaphor, it is a story of how we *look out* from the primary position of observer of the world and what we do with this knowledge in our minds' concatenations.

Its central Parmenidean puzzle has to do with how a finite creature of flesh and blood (you/I) can exist "outside" of the present here and now (our inherited notion of *this time*) transcendental with respect both to space and to time, able to approach the gifts we reserve for our deities: eternality and omniscience. Indeed the very ability to conceive of this deity has been used, often, as proof that God exists, and that we are conceived in His(!) image. (Anselm, 1033-1109)

But this story is narrow and limited in spite of its acceptance as commonsensical. Many of the "facts of life" have been omitted or circumnavigated in our enthusiasms and fears. The rhetorical aspects of our Being have been seen as derivative, reaching-out from each individual, rather than seeing us, primarily, as children of our parents.

How to see us as we are: first, we need to retrieve Being.

Our conceptualization of Being has been guided, frequently, within the context of a vague theory about nature: usually so-called *natural law*, in which the issues of psychology and metaphysics are extended directly into politics.[2] But the politics have begun from the notion of the adult (male) being totally "free" in nature, and "chained" within the contract of our becoming social (Rousseau 1762))

Instead we are most likely creatures who have "emerged" from sociality into individuality, and are dialogic in our very beingness, rather than Hobbesian "solitaries." (Mead 1934)

---

[2] The line most directly from Aristotle's *Politics* to Hobbes' *Leviathan*.

Within this context of retrieval, many of the problematics of earlier philosophies will see themselves altered, dissolved, or recast. Whether skepticism about knowledge, about the reality of the external world, can be made to vanish, at the least we will see that knowledge does not *begin* from individual being (Sarles, 1985, chap.1). We are not primarily individual students of the external world, but primarily of others and of their views of reality; more emergent than given.

Enlarging Being to its Proper Dimensions: There is an undercurrent, at times an undertow as swift and powerful as the ocean currents off Monterrey which robbed, too early, the life of a friend. This undercurrent lurks below the surface, nibbling at the concept of (one's) Being, and circumscribes the very size of Being.

As a lying-under, I can address it only by circumlocution and by example or metaphor. With the victory of a mechanical notion of the human body standing outside, as it were, of its own observations in the 18th century, a victory, that is, of the heliocentric theory of being, the size of being was significantly reduced. From a deity who had created the world, this earth, specifically for us, for me, now we humans all seem infinitesimal and Lilliputian.

It is no longer enough to be concerned with death as a major shaper of life, now we have to fight for some self-respect, and seek to become celebrated within our earthly existence. And in the modernist sense of the postmodern critique, the implosion of *belief* in science and rationality further raises the pathological and the narrative to central determinative status, taking us away from any sense of (willful) self-determination.

The possibility of knowledge in the sense of wisdom further fades as we operate from a nagging yearning, more than from the strengths inherent in Being. We tend to be impressed by devices more than by Being; by the proclamation of others upon our Being, rather than from any voice within. We have undermined the nature of Being by attacking reason or faith, faith and reason, and are threatened with the loss of meaning, even as we find selfhood reduced. (That is, in the Meadian sense, emergence does not mean merely that we are derived.)

(But there is a lesson in this: if Being can be diminished, or in any way altered, it can no doubt be increased!)

Sunderings, Thunderings: In a form of parallelism, there is also a wondering if our understandings and perceptions of where we are is bound-up restrictively by any particularity of our thinking; particularities which are capable of being seen, being studied critically, of gotten around, beyond, or simply passed-by. Here the concept of the postmodern offshoots of Heidegger's wonderings about Being, claim that the history of (Western) thought has strait-jacketed thinking.

To think critically, its seems necessary from this perspective, to enter into some mode which will be revolutionary, explosive, and de(con)structive; to declare the present to be a "new" time: post-modern, *after* metaphysics.[3]

If, as Buber (1934) claims, we are not now "at home" upon this earth, how did we come to this so sorry state? How, where were we misdirected, misled? Studying this history of ideas, can we now locate ourselves in any ways freshened, cleansed, newly naive and open? Or is the critical approach itself so jaundiced that it poisons clear vision? Can we retrieve our history to make the present? Indeed, just how would we like the present to be? (Or are we too comfortably bedded-down within the architectonic of historic edifices to inquire?)

Alternatively—associatively—we can attempt to grasp the present by studying its workings, by noting what has been emphasized, and seeing if—and what—has been left-out, omitted from our purview. We note that the history of ideas about Being, about being human, has been selective and restrictive. It has been more wishful, exuberant, and excessive in certain narrownesses, hoping that some reductive notion—brain, behavior, rationality, mind; language, society, culture, a deity; history, purity, ideality, normality would sufficiently characterize what is human, that it could/would tell us who and what we are.

We note now that there is a *marketplace* for ideas, in which skepticism suspends itself, that success in that market overwhelms knowing and the

---

[3]*After Metaphysics*: the original title of my book republished under the title, *Language and Human Nature* (Sarles, 1985).

possibility of human wisdom. Success and integrity? Diogenes's tears snuff-out the candle of truth just as it is being lit.

There is a *politics* of ideas: what power do particular ideas yield to its promoters or detractors? We note that the application of these ideas, themselves, is used for self-promotion or control.

Most recently, we note that there are parallel ways of thinking about the human condition, many of which have survived and inform the thinking and being of countless humans: a *comparative study of thought*: a search into the likelihood and actuality of humans understanding in a mutuality of their Being.

Rhetoric vs. Grammar: history and her/his-story. Much of the last three or so centuries of thought about the human condition, has been about human knowledge, and especially about the place or position in which we find ourselves: alternatively viewing the world from a place suspended, seeing objects, objective; and entering actively into the unfolding, with no obviously privileged locus of removal or safety.

While the story called science and technology has been very successful in considering the observer to be remote, suspended, removed and outside, always the same in his(!) objectivity, the humanities since Rousseau have entered the human psyche by as many routes as imagination has been able to conjure. Life is variable, changeable, intuitive; knowledge itself a form of desire.

What (I think) is a paradox which enters into each of our lives more or less strongly at different moments, has been raised to the level of the metaphysics of Being. What constant; what changing—and the "so what" of either position. Heraclitus haunts Being. The body changes, but the mind does not? Or does the mind not notice? Do we construct narratives whose self-telling completes itself? I am where? Where am I to go?

If we are communicational, rhetorical creatures by our very nature, can be (also) be individual: priorities, reconnections, dialogue and discourse within an ongoing present? What notion of grammar could account for what and how we know?

Parallel Living: To enter (literally) into the science-humanities dialectic is to find the position of objectivity, of removal, of constancy, having had the size and importance of human being, ignominiously reduced. As a sideshow and accompaniment to the mechanical model of remote observation, there has been a sense that this observer stands outside of history, of culture, of language; indeed, outside of his(!) own life.

We have learned, since Plato (*Meno*) to live "outside" of our own lives, parallel as it were to experiencing. The issue of our Being has been retranslated into active "living" of our lives, where we were trained somehow to live "outside" of ourselves. (Humans are unique, mentally, logically; study logic, discover myself? Me? Myself? I?)

How did we purchase the list of oppositional categories in which human "objectivity" seemed to raise us "above"—above nature, perhaps, even while seeking nature? In a quest for determinate truth, his(!) objective, rational truth has led him ironically to be hand-maiden to the devices which have resulted from the endeavor. Occasionally—and then only briefly—has the human perspective arisen to the position of its own examination. Will we all get swept away in the 3rd wave of technology? Won't we...? (Toffler 1980)

What seemed a freeing from textual truths, from the oppressions of organized churches and never-so-benevolent despots, turned instead toward a self-imposed diminishment in which the replaceability of everyone by everyone has created a smallness of being which does not note its own bondages (excepting when it "feels" frightened, and moves rapidly from objectivity to a full removal from the self: toward mysticism, the deity, the bureaucratization of the mind, Being as a cog on the assembly line...).

In the Humanities: The complications, and powers, the involutions, and possibilities of the human condition have focused upon the mental—textually tracing knowledge to its human focus and concentration in the transcendental sphere of being which Plato first created in the dialogue *Phaedo*, in which the realm of mental being is somehow beyond or transcendent to actual construed as physical being.

But where/how do we seek our "the truth" about Being? As Heidegger said:

"After all, it is the subject who knows, and it is in the subject that the criteria of truth are to be found." (Heidegger, 1929)

Or is truth located somewhere/somehow outside of Being? The dialectic between the sciences and the humanities arises quite differently within each perspective, and the question of Being, of the human condition and of human nature finds itself stated quite differently—neither parallel nor complementary—beginning from the different notion of the locus of truth: in nature, or within individual (knowledge). (Ongoing struggles to understand Protagoras' paradox: man is the measure of all things.)

The battle for the truth of truth resonates increasingly within the breastplates of truth's detractors, being caught in a paradox which turns into a dialectic from which removal seems the only option: there is no truth, there is only politics, narratives, history...

But the loss of the possibility of any universal, rational truth, various forms of intellectual and/or critical nihilism, has different paths within the humanities, leading only sometimes to similar endings, but via different routes: not from the diminution of Being, but because Being has become located in various texts; or because each super-organic notion in turn (Society, Language, Culture...) has been used as definitional of the entire nature of our being.

While we rejected the supernatural as explaining human nature, we replaced it with various super-organic transcendentals; each, in turn, has promised to explain fully ourselves to ourselves. And the question of textual interpretation has become problematized, problematic, impossible; because the temptation to return to classical texts as defining of existence, of the diminution of the spirit overwhelmed by Plato's systematics, seems to leave less and less room for now or for newness—another form of the impossibility of change, newness, or originality (ironically at war with the vast developments in new technologies).

Grounds of/for Being? In this mélange of controversy with no possibility of meeting except most briefly in the whitewater downstreams of nihilism already accepted, it is useful and necessary to reexamine the very grounds of our Being: to see, for example, that we are physical, that we do change; but that we live as well, as persistent if not constant, exactly. (There is much to be studied in our ability to see *ourselves* into our childhood photos!)

We know a great deal, so that knowledge is not only possible but interesting. Hume's skepticism, for example, does not follow the human condition, but particular ways of philosophizing about it.

The skepticisms about knowledge, of the impossibility of knowing or of being oneself, are not aspects of Being, but of having-been. By entering into history, critically, we do not necessarily have to become victims of that history, mere footnotes to Plato or Aristotle, but thinkers who can walk-with them in these complicated times; an attempt not to purge, rather to domesticate and walk hand-in-hand in the ongoing present with these original thinkers.

Now is, perhaps, the time to examine critically those defining aspects of Being which have "hidden" from us the rhetorical and discursive aspects of our Being: the surreptitious elements of being human which have included powerful theories of nature, of our Being-not the other creatures in our world (two-year olds know this; why have we forgotten or downgraded such forms of knowing?).

It is a time to note that we are, in the very terms of our Being, in discourse with our m/others from the beginning of Being: the individuality we have merely presumed to characterize Being, is emergent, not given. The logic of our "object" or "idea-formal-sentence" grammar which we have thought to characterize what is human—by the hiddenness of our presumptive characterization of what is not-human—will be seen to be an aspect of a grammar of rhetoric: the basis and "how-ness" of how we come to possess knowledge (e.g., Q-R). Any so-called *universality* of language is due primarily to m/others in every society teaching their children language/understanding via very similar Q-R processes.

In the actual world, much as the organism as individual seems to occur "self-defined," primary, irreducible, the facts of our Being are that we survive (literally) within the contexts of m/others (parents) giving us life; then "granting" us life.

We, I, you, are not survivable creatures alone, as individuals: not the feral children in some pre-human time, not the "speechless statue" of Condillac, to which we add attributes and needs on the way to defining what is human. Rather, we are creatures who are defined, seen, treated through the (complicated and growing/changing) screens of our parents' conceptualizations—not merely their conceiving of us.

Whatever the features of the (physically bounded, individual) organism in some senses per se, they are structured in great force by others. Our individuality has as a major source, their defining and treatment of each child; not arising from the individual in any primary sense. If, as has been said, logic is the defining characteristic of what is human, it is at most a subset of a more encompassing grammar of rhetoric: the grammar of Q-R (Sarles, 1985, chapter 9).

As the debate to which we are heir, of Descartes, Locke, Hume, Leibniz, Kant et al, has told us, it is the question of how we know and possess knowledge of the external world, which has virtually defined Being. This debate must be now recast by considering that the individual is (always) in some relation with others. Indeed, I will suggest that the "individual" (now italicized as a concept) does not directly study the world, but that she/he is an eager student of m/others'—parents'—conceptualizations of that world. The grammatical and conceptual structuring of the world as we experience it, are derived/shared with others.

The categories of "pure reason," the ontic and transcendental categories of Kant do not come ready-to-wear in the infantile package as some given of the human intuition, but are aspects of rhetorical-developmental processes. Even questions and knowing of the nature of space and time, of causality itself, are garnered from parental definitions of the world.

What is innate, primary, or primitive in the human situation characterized often as a form of Euclidean geometry, will remain moot: but, in any case, it is pushed, pulled, shaped, refined and defined in the direction of knowledge which is characterized more-or-less well by the notion of language in the rhetorical sense of Q-R. Children study parents, thence their knowledge of the world, thence... knowing. (Most of what we call individuality comes later in development, the propositional person, much *demanded* by mothers/others!)

If there are in-born or *given* some thousand features of the individual organism, it is those (fewer) which parents select, frame and shape, in whose contexts and terms we survive actually and literally. The Aristotelian notion of human "potential" was, at the least, over-stated, presuming as it did, that we were primarily and exhaustively composed of mind located in body. Purpose, futurity, we understand within their (mothers/others) framing of our Being.

As knowledge—rather the accounting for knowledge—is not located within the individual, a number of problems inherent in the earlier organismic metaphysics will be seen either as non-problems in the context of a rhetorical grammar, or will be re-directed: e.g., the *problem* of "other minds," questions of the finite and the universal, whether words and signs are "natural" or "representational," whether we are changing or unchanging, etc.

In addition, I will attempt to show how and why metaphysics has taken certain turns, directions, and paths toward the nature of human understanding, and why these are incomplete, following the notion of language (thus Being) as primarily logical rather than primarily rhetorical. (In the context of the grammar of Question and Response, logic is an aspect of the structuration of Q-R responses.)

The attempt will be to suggest a coherent human study which matches more closely the experiencing of the human, rather than one which concentrates upon one side or the other of the several (metaphysical) paradoxes which have plagued thinkers since time immemorial; and which have been used as the architectonic framing and explanatory of what is human.

In the cases of some of these paradoxes, of the various logical antinomies, the development of our thinking occurs within, perhaps in spite of them. To claim that we are not paradoxical, or that paradoxes need to be resolved, is not to mirror, account for, or explain the human condition, but to attempt to resolve paradoxes in favor of one or another path in solving or handling any human dilemma. This is precisely what has happened historically in our coming to the study of Being (seen most clearly be comparing different theo-political world traditions with the Western).

Rather, paradox will be treated as natural to Being, requiring study toward its understanding, towards its existential working-out: but not toward its denial or any solution which favors one mode of existence over some other, and some particular architectonic and understanding of human nature.

Students of the World? Or, Students of our Parents' (visions of the World)? Since Kant (in terms of Heidegger's retrieval of Kant, at the least), the question of the ontic, of the necessaries of human knowledge, has been stated in such terms, as "laying the foundation of human knowledge."

What is the "intuitive" (Leibniz), what the features of Kant's notion of "pure reason" which grant us the "possibility" of human knowledge? Why these questions as *the* questions of epistemology?

I will claim that there is very little "built-in" to the human (infants') condition beyond the ability to relate to (love, attend highly to) m/others highly contrastive faces, be fascinated with the sound of the sounds of questions to be answered by responses, be fascinated with their mouths and tongues and sucking...

Infants are in some very intimate relationship (from the "beginning"), with their m/others (parents, previous generation). They are eager students, entranced and delighted with others' faces as a very central feature of their (own) lives.

Indeed they become individuals in some emergent senses only from and within the dialogic. They gather/gain a sense for Kant's categories from discourse with their parents: even learning what is time? What is space? What is the question and answer to "Why?"? (The roots of causality located here?) Here, belief in Being and in the world take root (Hume, 1748)).

If any infants are, indeed, skeptics about knowledge, they do not survive in any sense, usually/normally. (Survival, that is, is problematic in the human condition, and we must study how it occurs and when it does not.)

The gaining of language and of knowledge are neither direct nor linear, but exist within a number of processes by which our infants-children "bootstrap" knowledge: undergoing vast, even radical changes in perception and outlook, as they *advance* through a series of "form-content" alterations. (See: 2 *Context*)

To study the development of knowing, we need to observe the dialogues between mothers/others and *their* infants/toddlers. We need to critique the sort of thinking about development which already constructs the outline of the nature of the ontogenetic processes as toward the mental-rational-symbolic from the bodily bound-in-time.

To begin to rethink (invert) our thinking and learn to see what is happening in the infant-parent dialogue, we must query the observational construction of mothers: how and what they see/sense; how they respond; how they not only see *their child* in that present moment, but also projected into the future as a person essentially like themselves. The parental side of the dialogue, the construction and interpretation of their child, is way beyond the organismic. The infant responds in kind, and becomes much like s/he is constructed. (The child's *contribution*...)

To enter critically into rethinking the nature of Being and becoming, it is important to rethink how each of us constructs an infant: what it/he/she is and will be; lift it, feel, smell, imagined into the future of walking, thinking, all impressed in one instant upon the babe of our viewings. Interesting, treasured, already with a future history projected rearward into this moment, and each next moment, and...

Admittedly, it is difficult to unpack and become critically aware of what we observers already bring to our acts of seeing. It is useful to observe the young and their m/others in some other species; and to enter into the projected imagination of those mothers as they cajole, correct, caress their young not out of some inner necessity, but out of the *desire* to see them as future adults of that species; correct, decent, theirs (the ground for any truly comparative study).

To see humans as already distinct from other species in our beginning observations is to have accepted the metaphysical explanatory scheme of our Being, to collect data within a schema of thought, but not to *see*, necessarily.

It is also helpful/necessary to rethink the nature of various (apparent) paradoxes; importantly the *form-content* paradox. With respect to a growing/changing infant, our ideas of form and content need to be rethought as a kind of (set of) process: what is (attractively!) form at one moment, becomes content in a next. What is then form is perceived from a "new" notion of content (of one's being).

No direct analysis of the adult content of language will be able to characterize this actual ontology of knowledge, indirect appearing as it is. Nor is it obvious how to characterize the experience of various developmental "stages," because the perception of "form" from each, differs when one is "within" from when one is "past" that life-moment. (It is similar and comparable to the "plateaus" of, say, musical performance skill, where one does not improve, does not improve, then—"of a sudden"— there is a "break-through," and one moves rapidly beyond these halting places, reconceptualizing, regathering, being different, thence regathering the next set of form-problematics.)

It is not knowledge of the world which (individual) children gain during development, but knowledge of their parents' view of the world. Whether this insight leads us beyond Hume's skepticism, or not, each infant finds language (in its widest senses) to be sufficient, inviting, and engaging. They are (including each of us in our own ontogenies)—if they survive—not skeptics in the Humean sense.

(As we will see there are a number of moments (later) in each individual's psychological development, where there comes a "realization" of a number of life's "paradoxes" which often inspire review, updating, and, often, some "resolution.")

Without a dialogic, rhetorical sense of knowledge, there is (and has been, historically) the urge to raise some of these life-paradoxes to philosophical heights, and to construct great systems of thought (theo-political-philosophical) based upon one or another resolving of a "felt" paradox; e.g., the paradox of the finite/*universal* or of the changing/*unchanging* character of being which have been favorites of the West.

Although the wish to de(con)struct idealism and metaphysics may lead to a Meadian notion of the emergent individual from the rhetorical and communicational aspects of social existence, this is not sufficient to move us beyond various architectonics of human existence: directions, purposes, presumed uniquenesses.

Much of the impetus for my dialogic-rhetorical view derives from the investigation into the actually observed lives of other species, where we come to see that they are highly social (following Darling, *The Red Deer*), 1937). That is to say: in the context of the history of thinking about human uniqueness due to the acquisition of language, it was not language which made us social as Hobbes and natural law claim. That is, the human uniqueness of language remains undetermined; part, so far, of our Western story of difference between humans and others (Griffin 1976) .

This recent insight into other species should lead us to rethink our thinking about Being, not only within the individual vs. rhetorical models of being, but also comparatively when we are able to rethink our own thinking by accepting (if only as thought experiment) the idea that other species (also) raise their young to be much like they are (purpose/progress). (See: 8 *Morality*).

The conceptualization of what it means to be a person, adult of whatever type or species...

As Western thought developed its particular form having assumed that only humans are (intrinsically) social, this sense of the sociality of others and of humans should considerably alter our thinking about what is human: I call this sense that other species' sociality casts doubt upon previous analyses of human knowledge via language, the *ethological critique*. Others—notably Bahktin (1982) and Buber (1937)—came upon this notion from other inspirations, so while there is much parallelism in the direction for new understandings of the human condition, there will be also inevitable differences in focus, and in the nature of our accountings.

I THE ENIGMA OF BEING

Enigmatic Being: Having pursued the notion and question of Being to its sources in Plato (*Sophist*) and Aristotle (*Metaphysics*), and to its presence in each moment, Heidegger's devoted tenacity leaves us still with the *enigma* of being: we exist, we understand at some level that we are in each moment, and deal with existence and the world through such an (implicit) understanding. Yet the ground, the being of our Being remains somehow vague, elusive... an enigma. Yet it is *the fundamental question* (Heidegger, 1927: 23-24).

The skeptic hangs heavy about the necessities which underlie the very possibility of knowledge: what is to be "'taken for granted in all our reasoning' - amounts to two things: acceptance of the existence of body and of the general reliability of inductive belief formation [which are]...ineradicably implanted in our minds by Nature."

Wittgenstein "speaks of our learning from childhood up, an activity, a practice, a social practice... [which] reflect the general character of the practice itself, form a frame within which the judgments we actually make hang together in a more or less coherent way." But, the skeptic remains unsatisfiable!

Can we not prove that we are? Yes? How? How, then, are we? What is our nature? What is the (ontic) foundation of our knowledge? What is the relation between Being and knowing?

We must enter warily and critically into the history of thoughts which have led us to this state in which we cannot exactly ferret out the nature of our Being, and enter into an intellectual "de-struct" mode to peel off, as it were, the layers of concepts which ensconce this most basic of problems, this most hidden and enigmatic form of intellectual grail.

Our concept of Being is so layered with the paints and elaborations of history that we can no longer discern the original or originary structure. Is there such a structure? (In a deific context, we might ask if Adam would recognize himself in our Being.)

The journey is heady. Its map leads beyond metaphysics, towards escaping the mined fields of conceptual war which have led us to this necessity for destruction of our antecedents: they who have contaminated our being able to think in clean and perspicuous ways. It is largely a critique of thinking about the nature of language. What is it that simultaneously enables thinking and directs it into tortured paths? How, as example, can we know the truth of any false statements?

When we name things, call things, do we name the thing in terms of its "limits," or in terms of what it is, here and now?

If the namer—that thing I call myself—is in this moment, then how is it that I know more than what is, in this moment?

How do I know the limits, *the aboutness* of the thing, beyond the thing itself?

Which is real, more actual; and where am I? What is (in) my *immediate* consciousness?

How do I know and think, gather my memory and make judgment upon the world of "right now," simultaneously see and hear what is externally immediate and available to my senses?

How do I "incorporate" this "new" knowledge into Being, whilst swimming (ahead?) in the stream of consciousness?

Memory? Forgetting? Being?

The search for the understanding of Being entails an examination of our virtual presence, looking out at the visible aspects of the material and personified world, attempting in each moment to fill our Being with a fullness which realizes in the consciousness of our own thinking, that we are here...and now. Realizing its own realizings...

On the journey it re-discovers the body, an unveiling; as if we were once again and still Eve and Adam. How had we lost sight of our bodies; of the concept of our being bodies?

Yet, to remain in some Jungian universe of what once was, may cripple the phenomenological and existential which is us as well, and lead us away from today, bureaucratizing the mind, and destroying the nerve to see our seeing.

Uphill, over dale, we note that there is some possibility, some opposition, some antinomy between what is visible, and how it has emerged from the shadow of non-being. The visible world has, at all moments, various possibilities, only one of which is that which is. In its turn, it calls our attention to our own presence, as the namer, the see-er, the observer, who is subject to each named object.

Our attention is directed to the billboards and footnotes as if a moving trajectory propels us, and directs us to the engagement with the knowing of each moment: the present linked to our presence. We are puzzled about the precise locus of our Being and wonder whether we move or we are moved; whether we are conscious and reflective as we look out;

whether we are bombarded by sense impressions and "raw" percepts which overwhelm our reflectivity; how we can be both sensitive and reflective... puzzles all. How do we know that the youthful appearing subject of our own childhood photographs is continuous with who I am, here and now? Subject; object? Yes, a paradox...

Moving thence, our awareness of our presence disengages our presence—by our "difference" and "separation"—from the materiality of the substances of which (by which) we name and call. Knowledge, knowing, just how do I know where I am as I move along? Am I no more than the stream of *impressions* which Hume says I am; leaving no I, no self, whom I recognize as me, as I? Is there only a single pathway, or do we live within and as several simultaneities? (Lewis Carroll). Do we *have* them safely in the hard disks of memory; or are they generated old/anew each day, frequently, set in the contexts of context in which meaning and Being find themselves? Body loci of memory: tongue, eyes..?!

If, to push the intellectual skepticism to its ultimate de-lights, there is no self, is there ought but relationships between things—say, cause and effect, contiguity? Is (to extend this to its n-th) there any external world which we can know directly, which we can know exactly? Not only (Hume's) skepticism about knowledge, but a severe skepticism about the possible objects of any knowledge, remains a cloying puzzle. Though Becker says the world can be calculated just fine, whether or not it actually exists (Becker 1932), it leads to a nihilism which gnaws at being.

So what: if being and objects are all *arbitrary*, all re-presentations whose solipsistic leanings know no ground? (Saussure 1916). Im-pure reason? Categories categorized?

So what if it is all *semiotic*? What if the world presents itself to us as some systems of signs? By now, that statement or claim is no surprise. It does not lessen the skepticism; perhaps delays it, suspends it by asking: what sort of creatures are we that we respond to signs?

It doesn't melt away the skepticism, but holds it in abeyance while we search anew for the sense of meaning which we had thought, and hoped, was located in knowledge, in language. Now, we wonder about our own presence. Are we satisfied by Derrida's notion of "differance"? Being: a kind of subtraction? (Living, breathing, joyous...?)

Just now we begin to sense that presence of our Being notes the presence of the being of others (Habermas, 1976, *et al*). We are in some dialogue with them; our Being is discursive, somehow. My journey, mine alone? My journey, defined, directed by others? Is my very Being emergent (Mead)? Is it only/merely derived? What concepts fill the notions of conscience, love, mourning? Not, as Heidegger, claimed (1927): "Being is always the Being of an entity."

For this moment: Stop! We have uncovered and recovered "rhetoric" which is "not a matter of pure form but has to do with the relation of language to the world (to life) through the relation of linguistic expressions to the specific circumstances in which their use makes sense."(I/we are body in the world with other(s') bodies. I am! But who? How? What are the "contexts" of our Being?

In many senses, it is language which is the culprit who has hidden our being from ourselves and has left it enigmatic. The metaphor of moving upon a map, upon a singular trajectory was deceptive; moving is not only singular, but in concert.

Heidegger attempted to link Being with time, to base a theory of being upon the notion of time. As we will see, the very notion of time has been linked, surreptitiously, with the notion of the human body. Surreptitiously, we hide the body from our mind's eyes.

Thought's Culprit: The locus of the enigma is in the Western depiction of substance, (Aristotle's *Metaphysics* especially) which discusses the notions of primariness and irreducibility of those *things* we name as objects. Our Being is thus derived, in peculiar ways, and is "after" physics (*me ta physika*), because we (as heirs of Aristotle) have presumed that the materiality of the world is somehow prior; primary, "before" Being (and "lesser"?).

Our Being—the bodily aspect of Being—is cut of the same cloth, but our spirit, the locus of the ways of our knowing about the world, stands *outside*. But, again the enigma, asks "Where?" and "When?" (And non-being lurks in our thinking about being, as well. Has the enigma overtaken true, actual, experiencing being? Why do we love the enigma more than we love bodily Being?)

The originary depiction of Being found in Plato and Aristotle's metaphysical works is compounded in Aristotle's *Politics*, in which the notion of individual is *presumed*. Once presumed—so clear at the level of the obvious—it is divided into body and mind, thence taken directly into the realm of politics: it is stated that the master rules over the slave, the king over the subject (man over woman, etc.), in direct analogy with the mind "ruling" over the body (*Body Politic*) as director, leader, chooser, the source of the will.

Physics, materiality thus accounts for being, but then *submits* to the rule of "mind over matter." So presumptive and obvious is this to us that the current version of skepticism asks whether we can know that we are body: is the mind *embodied*? (The inverse thinker asks, in some sense of spite: is the body "*enminded*"?)

In the 17th century, these ideas are modernized in the conceptual basis of *natural law*. Hobbes presumed a world of nature in which Being human consists of adult male "solitaries," who upon developing "reason" (differentiating them from non-human males), enter into society: giving up their complete freedom to love and to leave in competition with all other males, in return for safety from the death, which reason now tells them may ensue from this ungentle competition to win.

Much of the subsequent discussion of human nature follows from these metaphors of nature, freedom, society, and reason. Though it now appears very unlikely that this depiction of nature is at all accurate, since we have been social creatures since pre-human times; this grounding of the ideas of nature and of what is human reappears in our thinking, willy-nilly. The enigma of Being has been traveling the conceptual road for some time.

This conceptual journey has led us to see all individuals as primary: no gender, no age. What paths have each of us traveled upon, not to see much of what there is to see and to be, not well fixed to see history or the present?

An example: in a postmodernist battle for equality of the genders and the right of the present to own knowledge, Hobbes' depiction of natural law is never distant from modern thinking. The present times become *worrisome* times when the rise of crime and terrorism seems rapid. Lack of responsibility and obligation by the criminal and/or those opposed to the currents of power, make Hobbesian thinking newly attractive: competition is the law of life; the political is economic is rational; power is in the hands of those who deserve it; are it.

Enigma? In considering the nature of Being, it can arise as enigma only in response to some prior notion of Being, not from a sense of Being "in and of itself," or as each infant lives/experiences it. What prior ideas of Being wander within? Are they (world) historical or lying somewhere in the memorized experiences, in the nether regions of each of our Being?

More: The rationalist impulse has awoken us (in us?) only as adults to discover that Being is in some senses problematic. That life has paradoxes, or that life is often paradoxical, requires awakening and discovery, a sense that one's prior and earlier Being was wrong, naive, incomplete, a step on the way to... "Ah hah!" and "My God, I'm going to die," and "I am girl, or boy," floats above being just as we had come to think that life is interesting and good, and being 7 or 4 or 60 years *old*.

Just as we have (but recently) discovered that the promise of progress from technology has been broken by its own success producing too much garbage, we awake puzzled that life's journey is not all linearly forward. It is a life-strangeness that all is not progressive, a building toward. We grow up—mature. But in whose terms? Being as epidemiology? (See: 5 *The Ideal*)

There are shadows, places which lurk around next corners, which turn us around and cast us upon wavy waters. The present, our presence, looks out from under wispy clouds. The signposts do not stand out so boldly as we had (once) thought, and our desires to see clearly are often molded into translucent yearnings, repulsions, delights, or fears. Yet we often come upon scenic outlooks where we gain oversight of our Being from whence the enigma melted, fades. Vision, clarity, surety?

Certain people in (un)certain times seem desperately to yearn for the days of *innocence* before we were conscious of our destiny. How often do such yearnings govern thinking about the nature of Being?

How so? Where are those places whose brilliance of light and transparence of the air between here and there frees us from Plato's burden of obscuring shadows? When we find them, will we recognize where we are; that we are... there? Where do I stand? Is my ground firm? Does the light enlighten or merely play with the shadows obscuring Being?

What has perplexed the mighty thinkers, those who began from the irreducibility of things, is how a thing is at once particular, yet partakes in universality. What perplexes us, their intellectual heirs, is much the same. Why this paradox? How do we resolve it so we can solve the enigma? (Is resolution of paradox and de(con)struction of texts, approximately the same? Does the dualism inherent in Western thought prevent us from grappling directly with the paradoxes of life? No two-year old I have seen, by the way, has any difficulty with the paradox of one and many! The great paradox, an adulthood reflection on one's ability to know that of which one was once clear and sure? Maturity?)

It has been the Western impulse to side with the universal, the species of things over against the particularity of Being in time, which has done the most to tell ourselves that Being is an enigma. From granting the primariness of being substance, we have told ourselves that it is human destiny to see beyond the moment. Only humans. If our Being is able to be beyond its time, then where am I, right now? The paradox resolved not so happily by postulating that Being is two, or three, or... The enigma of Being, a problem in intellectual-bureaucratic management of its constituent *parts*? (And if the greatest historical contribution to knowledge by Plato is his *solving* the problem of death by banishing the body, isn't is obvious that Being remains an enigma in this line of thinking?)

Whether students of Aristotle's more practical approach to knowing, or of Plato's concentration upon the universal forms of the things which populate the world, both traditions are of one mind in wishing to resolve the paradox of Being one and many at once.

May it be that this paradox is not so puzzling? Is it any more difficult to live with, than these other "facts of life?" such as gender, death, sleep...? Is this really a paradox: being finite, being infinite? The finiteness of our being has seemed sad?

Has it seemed so obvious that to examine it in greater depth is only to prove that life is, at best, banal! Whence does the paradox arise, that it is at once so subtle, and so (apparently) convincing?

Models of Pure Being: Within the notion of Being as substance, as the irreducible individual, there has been a great temptation to deal with the concept of (individual) person as pure and isolated. In Hobbes' depiction of nature, it is the male solitary wandering in the forest primeval, totally pure and free, doing what he(!) wants, lacking language and thought. (Born free? I muse with my students that many men often seem to *forget* that their mothers were present at the moment of their own births. What a forgetting! What else is *forgotten*?)

Obtaining language and thought—by becoming human—he(!) now glances at the notion of the future and, foreseeing his death, desires the safety of society: the social contract. (Obtaining language? Mothers?)

Another persuasive metaphor of Being is that the (hu)man of our imaginings in the context of the enigma of Being, is always already adult: Adam of Genesis, created fully adult; or in imagining the origin of (hu)man, the metaphor of Condillac's "speechless statue," an alabaster figure fully grown—the problematic of Being is what does the statue need to become fully human?—like the story of Pinocchio or the lion in the Wizard of Oz. No wonder Being is an enigma. (We have *solved* the problem of Being but remain without personal history!)

(Go home, philosopher, open your eyes! Look at your own child! Look at yourself as if you were as a child! Look at your spouse; yourself; your child, your own child within. Enigma?)

It has been, and remains for many, the contrast between some such notion of pure Being—isolated or unsocial—and what we see as (minimal?) for human being and human interaction that has guided much of our thinking about Being. Language, whatever has raised us above what we granted to our stories/observations of other species; whatever has been the grand narrative of becoming human; whatever has *sold* in any era (What will sell *in this bull market* for the definition of human?)

Especially it has directed thinking about the relation between language and Being; language used as a kind of mechanism to account for the difference between the individual's mere existence qua individual, as a *pure* Being, and the possibility of communicating, of knowing, of understanding. (Descartes' *problem of other minds*. Being *is* enigma!)

The nature of what is human is thus linked with several other concepts: language, especially its origin; politics and the notion of what is freedom and the social contract, differentiating us from other species; time as definitional of human and of Being; a sense of purity which includes the *clean* boundedness and uniqueness of humans, and of unchangingness since we became human —thus, a sense that deep within us is the *pure* human; the idea that the locus of Being is the individual-organism.

What is missing, in an obvious sense whose inobviousness continues to amaze, is the presence of woman—the concept of development and the phenomenal-existential in each person's life; the fact of relationship, that we are born of mothers/others, thrive and live within their terms, somehow. What is missing, inobvious, is also a major aspect of this *Foundations Project*—this exploration.

How has this been elaborated? In one of its forms there has been added another powerful metaphor in terms of which many of us think about Being, especially when placed in some sort of (pseudo) historical dimension. It is related to Hobbes' metaphor of nature, but also picks up a theological dimension, related to Leibniz' argument with Locke (1703) over the "naturalness" or the "representation" of words and ideas.

What is the originary or creation of Being? And meaning?

Consider in *the New Testament* Paul's 1st Epistle to the Corinthians 13:11-12: "When I was a child, I spake as a child, I understood as a child, I thought as a child: but when I became a man, I put away childish things... For now we see through a glass, darkly; but then face to face: now I know in part; but then shall I know even as also I am known."

We have inherited the story of Adam (thus "Adamic language"), who was created in Genesis and was told to "name" all the animals: this, the story goes, was the originary language, in which the names he knew and chose were totally *natural*, before any "corruption" had occurred.

In this metaphor of pure Being, we have *fallen* from the use of natural sounds and words (God-given), to varieties of "artificiality" (art = man-made); thus the 19th century (and continuing, in some circles) attempt to find in *savagery*, the originary or purely natural and/or deific language. To solve the enigma, we need to *return* to...

In the Christian *re-reading* of Genesis, this notion supports the idea of the human *fall* to earth, with the apparent promise of a return to purity, naturalness, Heaven, and God, if we but determine what really is language, mind, and so on. Purity seems to represent a solution to the enigma of Being: when we reach the pure state, we shall know: 1) who we are really; and 2) what we should do.

The way in which the question of Being is posed in these notion of human purity, the nature of language and knowledge is of something added on to our originary nature: enabling or corrupting, depending on whether one is (I suppose) pessimistic or progressivist concerning the human condition.

In either case, the metaphors have been very important in guiding our thinking, not directly about human nature, but in pointing out problematics and directions for their solution. What is human nature, what is Being, having been cast within these metaphors have in fact directed us considerably away from observing our actual nature.

The Circle which is Telling: What is most "obvious" is that we are. Body *in* time; body *is* time.

We have privileged our participation in discussing Being, as we seek to stand outside of Being here and now. The so earthly presumption of our substantive Being always being in the present, has convinced us to explore our *essential* nature as those aspects of us which stand outside of our materiality. Thinking about Being always flirts with the notion of time and location. Thus the discussion of Being begins with a grounding which seems preternaturally actual: some "primordial" (Heidegger, 1927), a firm *grounding* to Being.

As anatomy, physiology, as neurology, we are here; and here we are, precisely in the present moment. Materiality is all; the question about Being, any quest for reality and authenticity, we impute to neurology which will inevitably unlock any remaining mysteries. (Dretsky, 1999; Demasio, 2010) With patience we will come to know what's what! Questions of Being will dissolve. The self-convinced materialist understands this problem to be either/or. What enigma?

The enigma is banished; put out of mind! (What mind?) The individual body planted so firmly within the notion of nature which states that time stands outside of Being, urges us to return to some simpler mechanistic vision of cosmology: once the heavens were set into motion, clocks work, and Being remains an enigma. But we no longer notice. The computer has taken over the enigma of Being: an expert system is me; I am.

This is to (re)state that the concept of being human as a body has been cast within a categorical argument about the nature of Being at once mind and body, and individual.

As we Western thinkers have equated body with nature and with other species, we have directed consideration of our corporeal being in the direction (within our metaphors) of our thinking about other species: bestiality, animality, etc. (Haraway, 2008))

Importantly, we consider the human species as unique—not with much reference to our bodies (which is how we *actually* differentiate amongst species, no small knowing), but with respect to our idea that humans alone, uniquely, possess mind and language. This has placed our conceptualization of time, itself, into some sort of primary categorical or definitional counter: the body, that is, *is* time, but a time-outside-of-time; namely, the body literally defines our notion of the present here and now.

In considering Being and time, we have (inadvertantly? thoughtfully?) decided that our Being is constituted within an already given framework of time: the Body = here and now, as if Being is a frozen snapshot taken at the speed of 1n-th of a second.

The intellectual mapping of this move has had to do with the presumption that the (human) body is essentially like the body of any other species: other species lack a sense of time because they are body alone, living in/as time but not being aware of it; humans know time because we alone possess language. The difference between humans and other bodies-species is in our knowing.

What is a somewhat complicated circle of definition of what is human—within a dualism of mind and body—has been raised to the status of defining the body as co-extential with (a very limited) concept of present time. Much of the sense of Being as enigma resides within this conceptual move. This has misled thinking, including Heidegger's, about the actual human condition.

Aristotle's substantive irreducible potential embryonic being, bursting forth into life, so casts our focus upon the materiality of each individual that we have seen the living context as afterthought, as happenstance; residual or inconsequential for the materialist. The fact is that as irreducible individual bodies, we are dead in the conceptual water, soon upon arrival! For and from a species which is social, this clean materialism seems not to notice that it is mothers/others who nurture us and desire our Being; living, ongoing. (Example: from the study of identical twins whose authors have not yet noticed that identicality—primarily facial—is expressive and rhetorical.)

The view from the penthouse of substantive Being, is: "feed me, clean me, touch me, talk to me, love me, and I will..."

The conceptual either/or of mind versus body is not precisely *incorrect*, but its elevation to the status of an entire solution to the problem of Being obscures much/more than it illuminates. As a position it is self-justifying as the opposition to what is, is (in part) no doubt *incorrect* (not the human condition); partial solutions to particular questions—acting as if they are the entire answer. (Some Western habit of invoking omniscience when the going gets tough?)

Much of the human condition and experience remains outside of the metaphysical discussion: unnoted, hidden, downgraded as unnecessary to accountings or explanation of what is human. Like the history of neurological thinking, where the brain and nervous system are reified and rarified, as if that is what we are and all we are, the shape and size and expression of our heads which encase that brain, remains unnoted: we infer Being from pathology. Or the idea of genetic predetermination which claims that all of our Being which is significant to the human condition is already decided at conception or some other moment prior to the ongoing present; i.e., Being is not an enigma, it is a predisposition. (And it solves any issues of experience by reducing life to chimera! Mind? Does/is anyone?)

In the linear depiction of the history of human development, the brain expanded; the head followed suit. But we know now that bone, too, has its *own* story which is ongoing. Its narrative forces a rewriting of bone as a fundament, and convinces us even that bone's hardness is processual, viscous... *Bone and Being*? (If this seem far-fetched in this context, remember that the idea of skeleton as fundamental was used by Konrad Lorenz (1966) in his grounding analogy of why he claims that behavior is genetically predetermined in his attempt to proclaim that human reason has crippled us! Are we battling over what constitutes an architecture of Being?)

Just as there is no brain which does not live (hidden) behind a human face, there is no completely independent human individual. We are not, like named objects, irreducible or primary. The question of our Being is, like the brain, ensconced in bone's story, and masked by our faces' expressions.

Offspring of living mothers, are we ever exactly or totally independent of others? Do they nurture us merely with food and material sustenance? So an embryo grows, frees itself physically; is there not some conceptual discontinuity between (mere) existence and Being? Are our bodies just like tables, or chairs, or circles?

Whose here? Whose now? How tempting it is to conceptualize us within the Platonic-Pythagorean sense of pure forms, whereby the very notion of reality is defined as the immutable intelligible-mathematical over the changingness of the sensible. Not body, not in the here and now, unchanging, eternal, the path lengthens.

Having developed (grown?) conceptually to that point in our lives where the paradoxes register upon Being, we seem able to abstract our bodies from the presence of our Being. Grown now, adult, we act as if our Being is like the brain: independent, somehow, of all the contexts which encase, in which it lives. (This is not to say that we are not, paradoxically, *independent* in many senses in our ongoing experience.) How did we reach that place in life, where we could imagine knowing knowledge?

We have found places of rest and observation from which to observe Being: our Being. And we have found, from that perch, a place *outside* of Being. If the view of being ourselves is derived only from ourselves, this is astonishing, a major accomplishment. Again, where is the viewpoint from which our Being is derived?

What have we unwittingly attributed to that substance we call the body: time, place, the concept called "now?" What superstructure have we built upon that frame, which has enabled us to leave materiality an unexamined terrain? We do not exist for long without others? How is it that they nurture this thing I call my body? How is my bodily being organized as it includes others in its Being?

The circle of thought in which our Being comes wrapped already presumes the body to be a ground of sorts. The enigma of Being, so called, begins after physics; after, that is, the locus of our Being is defined implicitly. But we do not survive (merely) as body; nor do we survive alone. To oppose the metaphysical definition of Being as the mental, must we grasp literally Nietzsche's dictum that "body is all we are, and mind is some story about it?" Thus Spake Zarathustra, Pt.1 (1883).

Savage Substance—Being as Polemic: As Plato equates the knowing of *aborigines* (Sophist 247) only with the lowest aspects of Being, materiality is set against the higher (soul); as theories of pure Being are contrasted with human experience, materiality is akin more to (other) animals and to an exteriorized sense of nature, than to what is human. Immediately the body is cast into a kind of comparative and historical (in these days) mode, where most of the senses in which we know, especially knowing about Being (*Dasein*: Heidegger), is attributed to the higher; a sense of consciousness over against some (implicitly lower) residual category. (The being of Being was much easier to dispense with when homunculi were assigned this role!)

Indeed, Plato's attribution of *lower* knowing to the aborigines is analogous to the history of the origin and development of language and mind. On the road to becoming human, we (in this story) are likened to the human infant becoming knowledgeable—toward rationality. The presumption is deep in our thinking: that infant is like aborigine (like chimps and other primates); that the path toward adulthood is analogous to animal becoming aborigine becoming fully human; infant, aborigine is fully body— the path toward rationality is contra the body, or is an "overcoming" of the body (*Phaedo*), or a denial of its continuing place in our being. (Importantly, this conflates in our thinking the development of the human species with each of our individual histories! Perhaps this drives the agonizing sense of the enigma. See: 6 *Origin of Meaning*)

Within this mode of thinking and it complicated labyrinths of thought development, it becomes almost impossible to stand outside of the Platonic formulation: almost any opposition of the essentialist position thus is likely to *oppose* body to mind (as, e.g., Lorenz does 1966), and to retrace the same labyrinth to its sources, without getting off on some sidetrack, losing labyrinth itself.

As example, consider how Freud approaches the aboriginal mind: "Above all the problem of death must have become the starting point of the formation of the theory [animism]. To primitive man the continuation of life—immortality— would be *self-evident*. The conception of death is something accepted later, and only with mentation, for even to us it is still devoid of content and unrealizable." (Freud, 1918) Self-evidently?

In my own understandings of animistic thinking, from reading and from two years' experience in Southern Mexico working with indigenous Mayan persons, their primary (intellectual) problem was not about death, but about the nature of reality. Being: when we are awake, or when we are asleep?

Indeed, a close reading of Heraclitus—a most important figure in the development of Western thinking –shows that he, too, was very involved in this wonderment: commonsense, in its Heraclitean usage, meant when we are awake, and in *conscious* in-common contact with others; asleep, we are truly individual.

In my understanding, animism *resolves* the sleep-awake paradox on the side of actual reality being when we are asleep: i.e., when we are *open* and our spirits and others' can enter and leave; e.g., animal spirits (*Naguals* in Mexico). (Western thought has resolved the paradox on the side of reality when we are awake. But the notion that sleep and wakefulness are paradoxical and important in defining Being only became clear to me in comparing different intellectual traditions.)

Death, for the animistic mind, seems less a principal direction for or occupation with thought than for us, whose concern since Parmenides and Pythagoras, have considered most seriously the possibility that transcendence is within our possibility.(See: 5 *The Ideal*)

I think, contrary to Freud, contrary to the Platonic theme of the hierarchy of rational thought from animal to aboriginal to us, that death and immortality are relatively recent human concerns—just pre-Platonic. The sorts of skepticism about knowledge to which Plato reacted (as do we, still), seem to arise post-animism, thence the retrieval of Being. (*Fear* of death an historical phenomenon?)

Similarly, the very concept of immortality depends on a strong notion of the individual, salvation, timelessness, and so on. That is, we seem to have made our predilections for a supernaturalism which our rationalism has sought to overcome, into an attribute of human nature.

However the Platonic depiction of the aborigine still informs our thinking, as it did Freud's, whereby we confute and conflate our story of human development with the (folk-) history of our youthful memories. This story is powerful in the very directing of our thinking, often blinding us from seeing much of what is obvious: that we are bodies, that we are always "in-relation" to others (no matter how free or independent we might have become, paradoxically).

Indeed this is the center of Plato's argument that some (at least) aspects of Being, can exist as essence, outside of substance, as immateriality: viz., the soul. In *Meno*, Plato's story of the slave boy, who is given some *new* notions from geometry and led to a proof from *reasoning alone*, has been persuasive is assuring us that the human senses (the body?) is not the source of external knowledge, but the *intelligibility* (rational knowledge by which we know the circularity of the circle) is the source of knowledge of reality. Body, slave, lower, you, me? We are caught in our own webs.

It was this insight, this noted antinomy between the particular and the universal that has led and directed thinking toward the rational as the center of the quest for human nature. But, again, the hubris of insight into its own foundational importance, has so focused thought as to eliminate what is otherwise apparent in the human condition.

Any argument which in this fashion considers the nature of human knowledge as definitional thus bypasses considering the body (and experience) as having any more attributes than its (purely?) physical being. Especially it/body does not, cannot possess knowledge. (Keleman, 1987)

(I suspect that to even attempt to raise the issue of the knowing body is to enter into the labyrinth on some path which is often/usually political rather than cleanly metaphysical. As Aristotle (*Politics*) tells us, the individual is mind and body, but the mind has hegemony over body *just as* master over slave, man over woman, society over individual.)

To enter into an epistemological dualism is to take the general framework of oppositionism; more likely, to enter into the discussion from political motives without being very knowledgeable that these are analogical arguments within the general framework; commonsensical and separated as metaphysics and politics may seem.

Thus, for example, the concept of the *knowing body* may be seen to be an attack upon reason or of any of its associated conceptual domains: language, masculinity, humanism, Western thought, civilization, the deity, and so on.

(Recent attacks on this issue which raise to our consciousness the facticity of gender, thence of body, also seem to be of the form of retrieve of Plato: retrieve the body, rediscover gender (Helen Longino: former colleague and friend: Philosopher at U.C. Berkeley). How odd of us to act as if our human bodies are of a single kind. Reviewing our implicit acceptance of the arguments which have hidden gender from our view in the name of philosophy should instruct our thinking, critically! Some ancient puzzle about the paradoxical duality of our being male and female resolved into the less paradoxical mind and body dualism?)

The development of the concept of the soul's knowing time, seems to have most to do with the notion of the soul being immortal, thus *existing* outside of time, being able to stand outside of Being, watching. The soul possesses memory (past). The body, solid and stolid, exists within time, or as time. The transcendent soul, some notion of the being of Being, *Dasein*—in which life somehow "participates,"—has been a guidepost to the formulation of many of the ideal-essentialist notions of being as rational, from Plato to the present.

Thus to oppose the mind is, in the context of the development of the transcendence of the human soul or spirit, often seen as necessarily being anti-reason, anti-rational, necessarily mystical, political, etc.

And—it must be admitted—most of the extra-normal, or super-natural ideas which have entered Western thinking have been precisely these: embedded within the general Platonic framework, now at the level of commonsense. They have not been refutations of Platonism, but opposing responses to, or transliterations of, the hegemony of mentalism.

Descartes—the Essential Existential: Since Descartes, there has been some shift, a change—more or less large—but also *within* the essentialism of Plato. As the sense of the universe made for humans by a deity acting precisely for us, altered to a universe in which this earth seemed small in comparison with a sun-centered system, Descartes expressed an urgency born of diminishment. All that is, all that is knowable is within *me*. No longer what is the nature of externality, but what is the mind, what is in the mind, has directed mentalism towards it own reflection. The ultimate temptation: to think that (subjective) mind is all; that there is nothing but...

In refuting Plato, as responses to his dualism, the choices have been few. Like Epicurus, we could be materialists, who claim it is all somehow organic, natural. The soul dies with the body, and is no more than some aspect or feature of the (usually) brain. Here, neurology rather than philosophy, holds "the key" to understanding human understanding (Damasio). (The only fear is the fear of fear, itself!?)–and Descartes' "I think therefore I am."–Humans: body, bodies-in-interaction – m/others??? See: Sarles, 1985: Chap. 12)

But, as heirs to Plato, placing knowing within the body seems *dumb*, anti-rational, and in the schemes of ontic history by which we know we are here, it seems immature or baldly political. If knowing presumes thinking, knowing the body (or the knowing body) seems thoughtless. (We are urged to revert to some pre-determinist, social-Darwinist scheme of the best genes for: money, power, virtue, intelligence...)

These materialist solutions to Plato's independent, immortal soul, trying to place them within the body (the Aristotelian tradition), making them an aspect of the body, have tended to diminish the human condition. Even/especially the modern metaphor of the brain as a (most) complicated digital computer, reduce Being to something both tactilely and intellectually palpable.

We are obviously very complicated conceptually and to argue one side or the other of a philosophical dualism does not uncomplicate us, actually. But, in our complications, we seem willing (eager and earnest, perhaps, in difficult times) to buy a solution which satisfies our queries, rather than that which is more actual: which explains ourselves to ourselves.

How can a material object, the body, appear (be) so complicated?

Heidegger, doggedly, insistently, demandingly attempted to ferret out the senses in which we are: from how Being thinks about itself, to its own awareness of the problematics of Being. He placed us (back) within ourselves, not merely naming objects, but being fully present in each situation where we are. Why, he asked over and over, do we not know this? To this Derrida added: how are we different from that which we see? In this "differance" we emerge more fully.

Still, however, we do not see our reflections in the mirrors of our thinking about Being, expressed as thinking about Being.

Therefore...I am. What: therefore? Why this question riding on the skepticisms about existence and Being?

Being *As* Time: Even if body defines the present here and now in some complicated fashions, it is/does more. It is (to some extent?) memory: it is and has absorbed others—myriad faces it has memorized at the very least; witness the literal pain of mourning, having somehow absorbed the Being of another into oneself. (Who am I?)

The body is/has developed a vocabulary (Keleman, 1987)—think about how one might, for example, enclose a fluttering butterfly in one's hands without damaging it; or think about what our body does as we are reading, or how one (as body) focuses one upon one then the other of a paradoxical image where one shifts one's seeing from foregrounding one image then the other. We have so backgrounded the body as merely *there* that we forget that we all have ways of Being, doing, and organizing each idea, every metaphor, can redo and rework our bodies in becoming joyous or frightened, seeing our bodies seeing a good friend; the rat, spider, or snake which gives us the *willies* or shakes.

This is to reiterate that to claim even on a simple level that the body defines here and now is but a partial truth. The problematic between subjective and objective, between perceptions and knowing (and learning) has been poorly/incompletely cast, and much has/is been overlooked concerning the nature of Being: questions of context, of the transcendental temptation, of the theories and stories in whose terms we experience Being, all of these remain too simple. Heidegger's realizations of Being as enigma as cast within the available theories of Being need to be understood as reasonable. Some necessary correctives are available within the outlines of the *Foundations Project*.

To begin to resolve the sense that Being is enigma, it is useful and necessary to review our own knowledge. We have, for example, vastly underestimated the complexity of being human or any other species. Looking at ourselves from the position of adult, for example, we fail to acknowledge that our experiencing the passage of time is very much *quicker* than for young children, and continues to hurry up as we grow older: i.e., much happens that we discount, from the perspective of streams of time flowing and passing quickly. We undervalue the discovery of one's own body, interpreting necessities of controlling one's bodily functions, for example, by incorporating them into some easy psychosocial accounting which apparently satisfies most of us that we understand them. Or sleep (or wakefulness), issues of the context of context, literally moving the body, keeping it in balance, knowing the subtleties of gravity when walking downstairs, or upon any uneven surface, our intimate balletic knowing of the insides of our mouth so subtly articulating, eating, breathing. We background such knowledge as implicit or innate to the organism even as we tend to deny aspects of our very existence.

Whether such linkage between our theories of Being as enigma and our more actual Being is to be located in some facticity about the present—our being in the world at this moment—or in a sense of personal (phenomenal, existential) being—where am I, and how did I get here—is beyond the merely problematic. The linkage between Being and time seems more a framework of thought and approach to understanding, than any direct path for (re)solving the nature of Being, or even of elucidating the problematic within this conceptual arena.

There are quite distinct differences in historical outlook and predilection, which frame the nature of (present) Being. Some of these differences seem large, almost but not quite obvious; others are subtle, nagging rather than gnawing at Being.

The subtlety of one's historical position (or, of the historical thinking of entire disciplines in some cases) is due to the pervasive orientation of thought which characterizes the very aspects of what one may observe, the frameworks in which one describes and interprets, even the locus of what one considers to be knowledge or data; the appreciation-depreciation of what is even problematic, the nature (acceptability, reasonableness) of a proper question or solution.

And we live as bodies in the world of other(s') bodies. We (must) accept the present of present Being which we share with others in order to enter into dialogue and discourse with them. Simply knowing when we are, what may/will likely happen or not, is not simply knowing. In this sense, Being is time and delimits the domains of meaning located in the breadth of conceptual stuff we call context.

Historical Thinking: How to rethink our thinking about Being? Most of the informing narratives about Being are enclosed within the problematics drawn by the foundational thinkers.

We have, presumably, disciplined our thinking to theirs. But this insight or declaration gives us little to do in rethinking foundations, beyond rejecting some of their thinking as it resonates within ours. More useful, perhaps, is to find some contemporary thinkers who are clearly historical, to attempt to study historical thinking: to enter their thinking in a comparative vein such that we will be able to return to our own thinking, critically and renewed; wearing new lenses.

The historical thinkers who are *large* in our experience and thinking seem to be of a few major sorts. The distinctions I have seen to be drawn has to do principally with the scope and pervasiveness of historical dimension as well as to certain habits of thought.[4]

---

[4] I have spent a good deal of my investigatory life in wandering across the disciplines (at the University of Minnesota and elsewhere) seeking to understand how various modes of thinking and investigation approach their putative subject matters, especially but not limited to concerns with human. I have approached them within the context of depth interview, much as if I were engaged in fieldwork in different human cultures. I teach about interviewing across the curriculum regularly and have written about this work in *Communicating Across the Disciplines* (ms).

In addition to historians per se, among historical thinkers I include most evolutionary biologists (but not genetic engineers-microbiologists), geologists, and astronomers; and many, probably most, literary scholars.

The mode of thought to which I refer, is the orientation—e.g., of biologists—to be concerned overwhelmingly and amazedly with the fact of all the prior generations of all species who had to have survived in order that the present generation could exist. They call themselves *ultimate* biologists, and differentiate themselves from *proximate* biologists, who (if such even exist) would deal with the ongoing present. Importantly, they depreciate the present and are chary, even, of being able to characterize it; not much interested in it having lessons to teach concerning the human condition.

In other words, this orientation or self-depiction diminishes in importance any context of the processual or dynamic. Rather than focusing on present Being: "How did we get here?" is asked; not, "What are we doing, here?"

Important is the fact that the very issue of Being—as well as its attendant enquiries—seem not to make sense or are reduced in their potential salience for the historical thinker, because the issue is constantly reflected or redirected toward the necessity of *getting to this moment*. More provocatively, the historical thinker is anxiously awaiting this moment to pass, until it *can* be studied judiciously and meaningfully. The present is not, simply stated, a reasonable or possible subject matter. (And, existentially, it is never clear when or where such historical thinkers locate themselves: what is the nature of their position, being, observing, judging? Being?)[5]

Many, probably most other scholars are historical in a somewhat different sense, than those who truly remain unconcerned about the present. Most scholars find themselves within a tradition of thought, bringing it into the present era, updating it, criticizing it, but remaining within the Western tradition.

Possibly the difference between historical thinkers' intellectual orientation and others can be understood as in the contrast between *reading as phenomenon* and *reading phenomenally*: most thinkers attend to the authority of

---

[5] E.O. Wilson, who *has* dealt with this issue in *The Naturalist*, blithely claims he can and does suspend his own Being as he engages easily and objectively in observing other species.

the writing they take seriously as phenomenon and content. To enter into the rethinking of the *Foundations Project* it is important to place oneself into the position of the various authors, and to read them phenomenally.[6]

In the issue of Being, the tendency to concentrate on aspects of the present is paramount; historical study aids and aims toward an understanding of today. The evolutionary questioner tends, on the other hand, to regard present existence as *fuzzy*. She/he is impressed to the point of being overwhelmed by the obvious fact of all our antecedents having had to survive, in order that we might exist. Self-authority—in present experience—diminishes itself in its very thinking.

These two kinds of thinker are both often immersed in history, but their problematics often pass each other by, directed as they are toward stating then solving different sorts of favorite or *obvious* questions.

In the context of whatever is Being, for example, the evolutionary thinker is directed toward causality as determining how we are. A primary solution to what is our Being is to be found by examining the genetic make-up of our micro-structure, and to concentrate upon what is stable, continuous in being.

As the power of determination grows conceptually, the size of our Being in the experiential sense, diminishes almost directly in proportion. For such historical thinkers, their virtual presence in the classroom teaching about being is fuzzy. To be sure, the biology of form or structure has received attention occasionally in the field of biology, but the very anatomy of humans, the body, has until very recently been the literal dissection of the cadaver, rather than of the living body being and moving. The facticity of our body being and moving with other humans in actual discourse, remains mostly neglected; its literature fairly empty (D'Arcy Thompson, 1917)

The *"who we are"* thinker in literature, basing Being on prior texts seems to approach Being similarly. She/he often feels that Being in the present is so determined by the history of thought, language, ideas, that it is contaminated. For such thinkers, history and the world-as-text has, yes, determined who we are.

---

[6] Personal Communication: Martin Krieger in trying to explain me to myself.

In the context of the politics of ideas, the issue of determination and cause is quite similar for both these historical thinkers. What is contrastive is how each approaches present possibilities. For the historical determinist, the present is some continuing (mere?) aspect of the past, and there is not much to do, actively: acceptance, passivity will emerge from understanding our place in the sun. For the historically determined, who is determined to unravel that history, freedom from history is finally possible via retrieval, inversion, and comparative study.

Perhaps the issue is about limitations vs. possibilities. (Or, for Kierkegaard, approaching Being through fear or through wonder.)

Perhaps there are other sorts of historical thinkers: those who are *classical* in the sense of thinking that the present era is a pale imitation of the past (many religious Fundamentalists, Rousseau); those who are thinking about the present as our principal problematic, but informed by history; those who seek prediction... prophecy, teaching of the young. (...comments drawn from the observation that the Present Age is drowning in some current *Crisis in Meaning*, including the rise of history in reaction to the death of the idea of progress.)

Cant Since Kant: Knowing and the possibility of objective knowledge: the question of whether we (can) have objective knowledge seems quite interwoven with the question of whether we possess a philosophy which can account for this capability.

Many "believers" in philosophy seem to think that not possessing such a philosophy is equivalent to our not having objective knowledge. Hume's skepticism about knowledge attracts more thinkers than the human condition *itself*. Yet one more kind of historical thinker...

A philosophy, a philosophical "system" which would account for what does not seem at all difficult in the doing; this seems to be an enigma which runs somehow parallel to the enigma of Being.

Just look around, not just at us hyper- and post-moderns, but at the people and peoples of the world who have only recently come upon high-tech. *They* grow food, hunt. *They* are easily capable of "standing outside of themselves" to examine the habits (thought structures) of other creatures, and to defeat them in their own terms. *They* know about crops and seeds and "improving the species," if they do not know always how to articulate their knowledge. Most peoples can construct houses and artifacts, have in mind mappings and blue prints. *They* are, in many respects in their lives, just that: capable!

Full, perhaps, of superstitions about certain things, having "theories" of disease, of life and death which are not so 18th century European-scientific, they nonetheless survive. They read and know the universe in which they find themselves. They have survived; they live still. Do we do more? Are they not, in many senses, objective?

Is objectivity a problematic notion? Is there more to it than knowing one's surround, adapting to it, using it to live on and on? Or is there some sense of objectivity which is, say, mathematical, which demands that we transcend the ordinariness of our being, to see clearly and consistently what is there, unbesmirched by memory, or the vicissitudes of desire?

Are we, then, still engaged in a search similar to a proof of the being of the deity, which can verify our own existence, that we find it compelling often to be skeptical about the possibility of knowledge? The path from what, who, and how we are—to why are we, thence often to "are" we?—Well, "you can't get there from here!"

Once the question and problematic of our existence enters thinking, however surreptitious the path, the potential solution will already deny its own possibility in the very questioning. If we are, that is, searching for personal salvation, then "acceptable proof" is merged with whatever allays the sorts of fear which drove us to ponder the issue, in the first place. Objectivity?

Or is it that scholars spend much (too much?) of their lives reading the words and thoughts of others, to seek their own being? Does the classicist, looking backwards to the great words of great thinkers, downgrade the present? How many of us read past thinkers to ponder how they would walk with us on this day into the future? How many of us, that is, have cast the present only as some extrapolation from the past?

Is the question at issue something like: how can we both partake of our own subjectivity yet see what is happening in each next present as if we could stand outside of ourselves?

Can we learn, change, move on? From Schopenhauer, Nietzsche, Emerson, Kierkegaard, more recently Camus, reacting vigorously to the dispensation of Being by the dialectics of Hegel's process, the lingering wonder is of what keeps us going at all? Is it will, power, self-determination, a rejection of suicide? Between Hume's skepticism about the very possibility of knowledge, and Schopenhauer's pessimism about Being sustaining itself, aren't we caught teetering between the demand to understand knowing, and its application to our very being? If not knowing, is there no Being?

Always, I am driven back to that well-worn meditation upon the finite and the universal, that paradox whose (falsely motivated) resolution so feeds upon itself that it can overtake Being.

In medieval days, we were only trying to prove the existence of the deity. Now we seem to be flirting with the necessity of proving Being. Was Nietzsche correct in reporting that the death of our belief in a deity would lead tortuously to a nihilism which would overwhelm us?

Isn't Being sufficient proof of itself, that we are busily trying to offer other kinds of proof? Isn't Philosophy saying: "No!" rather than affirming Being?

Language: Mortgage or Lend-lease? A corollary to, an aspect of, an addendum, a definition of whatever is human "nature," language is virtually a metaphor for itself. Toward an inversion...

How do we engage in Heidegger's de-struct mode when we consider language?

Surely we must be suspicious that language is held out to "exemplify" precisely the sense in which finite and universal demonstrate themselves. Language is "creative" (St. Thomas 1274) thus allowing us "to know" God the infinite; language is infinite because there are an infinite-indefinite number of sentences whose grammar is coterminous with being human (Chomsky, 1966); language enables us to think, which Descartes (1644) claims to prove or justify existence. All the languages of the world possess a grammar, all are somehow translatable one to each other, thus proving that we are all humans.

Or: Language has so taken humans from our natural instincts that we have moved to an extremely dangerous time, from which we can extricate ourselves only if we pay attention to our pre-language, animal-instinctual selves. Lorenz (1966) sees language less as leading toward deity and salvation, more as the fall from Edenic bliss.

Or: Language is natural to humans; at least to those who are "normal"; proving in the same moment what is human, what is human nature, how we come to be fully human, and who possesses language in the proper degree (Simpson, 1966). Language is (fundamental to) logic, thus to knowledge and the possibility of objectivity. Language enables us to be objective, thence to stand outsides of ourselves and to know ourselves as others would, enabling us to know ourselves subjectively.

Language is linked further to the historical development of humans from our (non-human!?) antecedents, as we came to be bipedal, upright, and got ourselves a big(ger) brain.

Language enables us to know objects: language is; language does; says. Most of what is called philosophy is the analysis or philosophy of language in one form or another. A promise: that if we analyze language correctly, we will understand the human mind.

For the humane scholars, language is so bound to texts that we probably cannot "get to" language, until we deconstruct the texts into which they are so bound → Derrida's (1966) "railings" against language.

If, as some hold, language structures thought (Sapir-Whorf), then we are virtually not (yet?) human until we possess language. Piaget (1952) holds that ontogenetic development is from a purely biological-reflex creature toward rationality, via language and thought.

Like the circularity by which the human body is granted substance and time in some irreducible sense, the soul and language of humans is simply presumed. We have, by some—again surreptitious—presumption based on what we have (already) decided to see, granted humans some unique properties, while taking the human form and equating it with the body of (every?) other species. Instead of studying humans in some direct sense of appreciation and wonder, we have "juxtaposed" humans with others within this circularity of body and time.

Other species (all?) now appear much more intelligent than we had earlier expected (Linden, 1974). If they know, are they alive (is survival in uncertain universe a reasonable measure of objective knowledge?)? They cannot speak just as humans do. But their bodies are different, and their ways and abilities to speak are, no doubt different. What difference, these differences? (Adler 1993). In thinking about other species, have we included them in our circularity about ourselves, then extrapolated from our views of other species back to humans?

I posed the question: *Could a non-H?* Could a non-human of our imaginings (an average Martian, for example) possibly "discover" whether or not humans possess language, if they brought to the study of humans the presumptions we take to the study of other terrestrial species. This is underscored by the work of Sagan *et al.* (CETI) who fully expect to communicate with Martians (sic!) via mathematics which they assume to be a mindful universal (in the BIG sense) language. Our minds remain Platonic souls placed, *haphazardly* I feel confident, in the body which happens to encase it. The answer to *Could a Non-H?* is *No!*

But this era, footnotes and highlights to Plato, is just now at a moment of discontinuity. Some analysis or other of language is going to replace human thought; some "artificial" intelligence which will by some future date teach itself to learn.

Language which once powerfully elevated humans into sub-deities, now will enable us to diminish ourselves to hand-maidens of "friendly" machines. What a massive irony, this seduction!

But like the circular placement of body into the surreptitious present, and the mind allowed to freely float in its own hithers and yons, our analyses of language are bound intimately with mothers/others' constructions of our Being: those who bore us, nurture us, how have they and their definition of our Being affected Being?

Is language a way of knowing the world; a way of knowing others; ways of knowing how others claim the world to be? Do we possess language; use it; borrow it? Is language a thing, a process, a structure? Yes? How? Does Language exist anymore as an object of Being than our own human individuality?

And: If not Being? What if we cannot, somehow, "prove" that Being *is*? It has seemed to me that this question drives the (re-)discovery of cosmology, rescuing it from the oblivion into which metaphysics has driven it. For I think that there is some overarching sense in which the enigma of Being is no mere enigma. That is, there is a sense in which there seem to be three (at least) modalities of thinking about Being, only one of which is being possibly an enigma. Much of the apparent confusion is, I think, due to mixing of these modalities, rather than to the nature of the question.

In metaphysics, as Aristotle shows us, the notion of Being presumes that the individual is the central (be-all, end-all) figuration of Being, the irreducible originary thingness which forms some groundwork of our Being body and mind. History has thus proclaimed that the mind is different from the body in some essential form, as the Pythagorean concentration on "universals" is different (and elevated) from the body which is a particularity.

Metaphysics is a modality of thought which concentrates (so to speak) on the quest for generalities: a world-spirit, an eternality. Being is, "itself," not problematic, but the body is displaced from the issue of our Being, or it may be merely presumed and left philosophically "empty"—a residuum.

The body fits (as Aristotle tells us) into the realm of physics, which is at once prior to Being, in various senses "necessary" to Being, but it is not itself, Being. Here, the realm of Being easily may include pre-life, post-life. Space and time may expand or contract in various schemata, and there is often (usually? always?) a sense that we stand outside of Being, observers to Being. Metaphysics may include a mode of "perfection," though it is not (in most traditions) available within life. (The nature of history, as well, depends on how the various relations between Being, space and time are organized in any scheme—that the problematics of history and historicism depend on how Being is "defined" or construed.)

The kind of nihilism which may arise within a metaphysical modality, is (like the Christian) a notion that incarnation, the body, is chimerical, and that the soul, this most general aspect of Being is the real and enduring. Our essential Being is the question of life and living becomes problematic: a kind of oppositional Satanism. It "dwells" upon life "outside" of life, and places its "politics" in those who construe life as subordinate to "salvation."

Cosmology is concerned with the very nature and possibility of existence, not beginning with Aristotle's irreducible "things," and human body to be understood as (one of) thingness, but whether (or NOT) existence is; how it may be, etc. Though it is wider in its notion of physics ("What is the universe?"), the nagging question with respect to Being, is: Do I, we exist?

Cosmology is not, at least in the "animistic" theo-philosophies, very concerned with matters of life and death because change is ever-present; space and time not very clear as categories. It tends to begin with the question of reality and Being, but focuses on a world which is very full of Being.

Amerindian: is reality when (I) am awake or asleep? One's Being is "permeable," not just irreducible to a oneness of bodily substance, but shared with the Beingness of other creatures on this earth; not the "holy" spirit of a deity, but the actual spirit and aspects of, say, eagle, or bear, wolf or coyote. They enter (my) Being, and I enter theirs, when "I" am asleep. The dead are transformations of the alive and vice-versa; they "hover" all about, at least in their places (why land, place is usually construed as sacred or sacrosanct, and cannot receive monetary valuation).

When metaphysicians (re)discover cosmology, they seem to fall easily into a nihilism, in which the question of existence is often answered, No! And they spend much (most?) of their remaining time, trying to find people, stories which will (re)assure them that they are. As the body is not irreducible in cosmology, their potential groundedness in metaphysics is no longer available, and they have a tendency to "float" conceptually or to wander into non-Western traditions for some solace. It does not appear (to me) that there is any notion of perfection within cosmology, which is out of the ordinary, which—in cosmology—is so inclusive of the universe that it is beyond the ordinary in any other modality.

Ontology, in Western tradition, is a kind of discovery of Being (actually a rediscovery of one's Being, which one "possessed" prior to one's discovery of consciousness about one's Being!). It (merely) accepts Beingness and goes on from there. Body and mind am I, and it is in some pathness (some Way: Confucius) toward becoming who I would be. Life is, what there is; usually all there is. Its form of nihilism is in losing the sense that there is a (progressive?) path: a towardness in this life (which is the "only life we have"—Kafka *Puzzles and Parables*).

In the Confucian form, it is a utopic, progressive, a path toward a kind of perfection, but in this life. As I have written (*Next Places*), this notion is more akin to the rhetorical, semiotic sense in which we gain meaning in life from our parents and communities; a less self-conscious way of Being. Here, the enigma of Being seems to melt.

Since these "modalities" of construing Being are so over-arching, so basic to the very imagining of ourselves, one can only "discover" that there are differing modalities when they come into contrast or clash, as they do in this global moment. The present age is a time of such clashes as world traditions are beginning to rub against one another in quite constant, and in quite common, often serious circumstances. When the Jihad of Islam is, for example, invoked against some perceived enemy, it may take the person directly to his destiny, which is metaphysically construed death: which is, paradoxically from ontology, (true!?) life.

When a metaphysician discovers cosmology, the oft-occurring result is to seek for the greatest sense of permanence available: usually, a return to the texts of religion or other "classics," which seem remote enough from the present, to have a kind of validity over and above experience. When the accountants of Western medical practice discover ontology, they discover that "wellness" is literally cheaper than symptomatic treatment; and are busily altering Western metaphysics in the name of economics (Health Maintenance Organizations as the locus of ontology?!).

The issue of *authority*, which I have suggested (from the perspective of ontology) now requires a thoughtful teaching tradition, disappears through the cracks, as it were, in a time of modality clash, where the sense of a scripted future is vague at best and ever-reducing as the notion of the present moment stands in some paralysis of the enigma of Being. This is so because the modalities "possess" the power "to enlarge or to reduce" the "size" of the human, thus granting more or fewer possibilities of entering into our own human destiny.

It also becomes clear (if not obvious) that the question of modalities is a study in (philosophical) psychology and/or anthropology. It is comparative thought through which one can explore the ordinary or usualness that one lives within or has constructed: in the sense that one cannot "discover" one's air or water, so enveloping in a modality as a way of self-construal.

If (when) the politics of each modality differ (even, in odd moments, when they appear to be the same), they swell up from different notions of Being (human), and how this translates into communal arrangements...

II Conceptual Chicken Coops

The Egg and I: Heat an egg properly, incubate it just so. It will hatch and, well fed, become a chicken. It lays eggs... is Being a chicken and egg story?

A cycle, merely? The "all is vanity" of Ecclesiastes, whose life is a dully cyclical version of Camus' "Sisyphus," simply submerges the question of Being to a standing outside of ourselves. Like the deity, we watch ourselves coming in and out of Being, in some harmony, perhaps, with the remainder of life's processes. But, without much hope, and with the deepest irony, we usurp the heavenly position from which the deity views us viewing, and swallowing stoically, we proclaim life—all of life—to be Narcissus, looking out wanting to believe that the reflection is all. Being is image, re-presentation.

Like our too easy acceptance of the notion that the brain exists in most senses independently of its surroundings and contexts, we find it easy to believe that the egg-become-chick is (already) a Being, a thing. It is, is it not? In fact, we have (surreptitiously) broken into the cycle, metaphorically calling Being a thing. In accepting, uncritically, Aristotle's idea of body and Being as an irreducible thing, we have chosen to represent the very basis of Being at once falsely and in a way which leaves us as enigma.

In Kant and Heidegger's parlance, the question prior to the consideration of Being is placed or relegated to the transcendent or ontic: what are the conditions necessary to Being and knowledge? What is the nature of the "intuitive," or of the "pure reason" which permits the knowing which is particularly human, they ask.

They proceed by an exploration of Being and decide upon its necessary antecedents. From Kant to Heidegger, this has become more complete, more flushed out and filled in. Yet, there remains the sense of enigma, of a coming forth into the world, of an unease of Being which is at once more than, yet less than. Completeness, integrity of Being seems somehow unfulfillable. Does it need more analysis, a new mode of de(con)struction to see what is Being? Or have we been overly loyal to our presuppositions and need to rethink them? Are we on the verge of a post-Copernican revolution in thinking about Being, whose malaise is overly apparent? Yes, of course.

It is necessary to begin this rethinking of an enigma, to enter into some mode of Cartesian doubt about things; doubt that we are so assured that Aristotle was correct in thinking that material objects—here, including the human body—are so irreducible, so primary. In the context of a rhetorical approach to existence, it is apparent that others not only conceive us, but conceive "of" us. Materially they look at faces, but "see" a person.

Perhaps there are "magical moments" in life; perhaps the instant of seeing one's newborn child is one of them. In that moment, the infant is seen by its mother (parents) as *someone*. But, perhaps, this is extending, but not critically opposing Aristotle. Let us see.

Already and always, in discerning other people, we transduce the facial surfaces of others into a Being, a character, a person beyond the materiality of the reflection of light off chin, cheek, nose, and see within their eyes a *who*. This *who* we see is displaced and expanded in time and space. It is not a thing, irreducible, primary. It is a person-in-relation whose history of relationship with us frames our seeing; a person whose futurity in the world joins with ours. There is no simple materiality in seeing persons. We do not exist "after" physics, as Aristotle claimed; mind, to our materiality.

In the context of our Being aspects of life—preceding and, to follow—we partake in (of) an existence which is heavily defined and delimited by discourse; within the rhetoric of others. It is simply not clear whether the person is an individual in a preliminary "ontic" sense, or the notion of individuality which we ensconce ourselves in, is largely derived and emergent. Did Heidegger simply expand Aristotle's notion of the individual and move to "reconcile" Being as enigma? Or did he?

Here, it is useful to (re)consider the first (physical?) emergence of Being. Often we are lulled into the obviousness of our adultocentric notions of Being, and cast them about loosely as if existence began conceptually when our bodies were fully grown. Rousseau's "Emile" reminds us that development is long, and quite full, and "necessary" to (present) Being. It is not philosophically prior, ontically prior, but *a sine qua non* and perhaps heavily constraining upon how we imagine Being. Perhaps we have been overly impressed with our first becoming fully conscious of our Being, at some near-adult point in life, and have not wished to remember what Being needed to prepare for its own awareness.

When first we emerge in the world, expelled more or less graciously from the womb of our formulation, we are "seen" by our mother who sees from within her experience. Her seeing is not spanking "new," not "clean," not in any *mere here and now* of the newborn substance. She lives as memory, of myriad moments of any present, and toward the varieties of futurity an infant—*her* infant—represents: her life, its life. She lives in relationship to her own mother, updated to now, yet variously in memory; and to all the others who defined and delimited, excited and extended.

Does she act in terms of such conceptions? What does her seeing her new babe, conceptualizing it as him/her, treating it as a person essentially as she is, have to do with Being? How powerful in terms of our ("individual") Being is her conceptualization? Do we not, very basically, "survive" in the terms which she grants to our "Being"?

Is an aspect of the "enigma" of Being that Being does not inhere precisely within the individual, but also rhetorically within the mother's (societal) conceptualization, treatment, and constant defining of "our" Being?

If we are "seen" not as the material faces from which the light reflects and outlines our visages, is it not true that our very Being is, from the beginning of life, semiotic? No mere object am I, but some complex of attributed signs? Being is no mere thing, beyond physics, but of others' representations of Being.

Where, then, am "I"?

Historical Yearnings: An aspect of my Being, is that I got here: and here I am!

But each of us, an "I," seems not to be so clear about which (sense of?) history to invoke, to state that "I am here". Which history: my "own" personal history? the "species"? Whence did I come, now that I am here? What paths did the journey take? Which is "my" journey? In what "archetype" do I partake? Could it have gone another way? (Borges 1985). Whose today is my today? Paradoxes to be solved or resolved? Paradoxes to be studied; lived? Tomorrow?

If causality, if effect, regressed back to my beginnings: what is the origin of Being? Child of my parents, they of theirs, ultimately we proclaim a "self-caused" first cause and name it the deity. The deity a mere logical necessity for the need to explain causal linearity? "Because" is a mere response to asking, "Why?" The thinking of Aristotle carried to its (logical?) boundaries... Because.

But what of Being? What of my Being? If I do not know so clearly how I got here, how can my Being now be but an enigma?

We had hoped to account for being human by asking the question of the origin of the mind. We had hoped that being human means having language, because mind and reason and language seems to be what makes us different from other species. We want to know, to know what is human, what is man-alone, says Aristotle; what is "nature"? the in-common with other species (*Politics*)? Then the origin of language would tell us whence we came, thence where we are. Imagine the "first" humans. Compare our language with the "non-language" of other species, of our long ago antecedents. Have we thought well about this? Need we deny any languaging to other species to justify ourselves to ourselves?

One story which resonates powerfully still, is Rousseau's, whose notion of nature has us in touch and in tune with the primeval. And we were, naturally, happy. Born free! Born free? Only society, the urges and demands of others upon personal freedom and destiny, has enslaved us.

We forget (Rousseau did not know) that humans have evolved already as social species. We never were alone, solitary; we never are, alone, solitary. Our independence, and personal freedom develops (as it does!) within sociality; within the discourse whose rhetoric and sense of futurity demands that we become individual.

But Being is (always) also rhetorical within the contexts and definitions of who we are, by others. There is always some "tension" between definitions of Being which is a story I tell myself, and stories told to me by others (including many in memory).

Within small societies, where we are always known in great detail and extent, the modern notions of individuality remain muted, the tension directed to Being's sociality. Within large scale society, where we are often more anonymous, individuality as Being strengthens, the impersonality of formal law emerges, and the "freedom" of the individual becomes problematized as it never was in earlier, small society, times. The paradox of large-scale society: the more individual "I" become, the more problematic is its very definition.

Being as Body: Perhaps (as heirs to Aristotle) we forget to remind ourselves that the enigma of Being human, also has much to do with the human body, the human form! Because we had been awestruck with the paradox of Being here and everywhere, we came upon an Aristotelian path and found it inviting, enticing even. If body is (in) the here and now, prior to our Being; if the body of other species is also and only in the present, then our bodies are "like" the bodies of other species. But, man-alone possesses...!?

Part of the circularity of thought which grants substance prior to Being, makes the human form "just like" the form of other species—irrespective of snouts, paws, trunks, fins, feathers, beaks and claws, tentacles and suckers, different from human faces; unawares of the relation of bodily form, movement, and gravity. The enigma of Being we have located in the "difference" between humans and others.

We imputed our notion of body being in the present to other species when we granted ourselves symbolism and reason; to others only the signs of each present moment. From the circularity of time and body we granted humans in order to account for Being; we then imputed here and now-ness to other species, and somewhat ungraciously decided that the significance of being human was located in the differences between us and others; a difference we had already presumed in the priority of substance. The circle is complete (and unending... no place to begin...)

Thinking historically, we invest Being with the emergence of the universal and non-finite, from the very same body in whose terms which we implicitly "touch" ground.

Do we, at some level of Being, tell ourselves an historical story, a "how I got here," often? Is it updated frequently? Is it revised to suit the present time? Is our reading of the present revised to satisfy our historical yearnings? Or have we buried it deeply, so deeply that its surreptitious applications no longer seem problematic? Under what conditions do we admit that (our theory of) Being is an enigma?

Being... on Time: A caution, a reminder, perhaps a self-scolding: the temptation of the primariness of material being is to conceptually make that Being real, but in a primary or mathematically "primitive" sense; a "given," a locus or place to "begin." An entity, a person; a person, an entity. It sure *seems* reasonable (is this the enigma?).

(Is our conceptualization of Being the same as, does it jibe with whatever is our actual experience? Or does the conceptualization arise from particular problematics which occur in life, only after one begins self-consciously to reflect upon life? Are we not, once conscious of Being, surprised by the paradoxes we light upon? What is the particular; the universal, which is the real, is change or non-change, the permanent, the eternal? Am I bound (forever?) to try to cool a burning foot in Heraclitus' river? Can Being live with paradox, with a doubling, a re-doubling of itself, and retrieve transcendence within life?)

From this (tentative?) ground, we grant Being the possibility of a platform and a podium, and wish it to discourse upon all sorts of topics. We even seem to grant it advanced scholarly degrees and a sense of professorial authority: Being is → Being does → Being says! Hush! And Listen! Take notes! Truth speaks Truth! It must! (Applause!)

Its tentativeness fades from practical memory in our zeal to believe our beliefs until Being becomes "the" subject matter upon which all else rests. Much of the enigma resides here.

A disquisition upon memory, upon the future, upon the very nature of time; we sit back passively, waiting for our intelligence to quote itself and tell us something we do not know already. There is a temptation to equate, since Parmenides (Frag. VIII), knowledge with the human imagination. What we can imagine, since the human mind is the man-alone repository of knowledge, is what there is: Anselm's ontological proof that the deity exists because we can imagine Him(!). Examine our imagination and discover Being? Lo and behold, the truth is a chimera. Language is, the mind is, Being is infinite?

Heidegger, a refreshing breeze, unsatisfied, restless, gnawing at the knots of Being—on Being itself. Heidegger, an unraveling of Being's discourse upon itself, looking away, looking back with wayward glances attempting to steal away the podium from which Being proclaims its own truths verified.

The recognition that Being is an enigma, the attempt to problematize whatever is ensconced, however surreptitiously, in the concept of Being that we have "received," this unraveling and de-construction, it is necessary for us to see ourselves.

(Kierkegaard's "solution" was somewhat more certain. In the light of not-knowing whence we came and are bound, he urges a rejoining with the life of a Christ. Live as he lived! Walk hand-in-hand with him; enter his life, rather than letting him enter yours as a believer, a worshiper. A trust in... a distrust in...? (Akin to an "expert system's approach" to Artificial Intelligence: mimic our definition of the nature of an infinite intelligence, rather than craft it).

So... Being on time? If the (bodily) ground of Being is not already defining of the present, then it is not so clear what, when, where is time. Having presumed (at least we can possibly re-discover when we have assumed) that the individual body is time, in time, or somehow "with" time, the issue of time is not merely enigmatic, problematic, but does not seem very capable of understanding, much less of "solution." But this simply underscores the sense of enigma, in which we are intellectually increasingly unsure of where we are, while it seems quite obvious experientially.

Might we be like Kierkegaard, who understood this dilemma, and sought to resolve it by standing outside, as it were, of time; for Kierkegaard time dissolves, melts. We can enter the dimensions of all of time by taking the ethical path of standing outside of life, projecting it elsewhere; e.g., into the life of a Christ... living as Christ lived. Time itself is time-less. As the deity is eternal, so we partake of it, catch-as-catch-can. By Being a Christ, can we re-enter our own Being? Doubtful?

But this cannot be, we say with Heidegger, glancing at our analogue watches which march about their faces dutifully, in time with... time? We know where we are, when we are. But now that Being is an enigma, does time seem to move ever faster?

Knowing...as Being: We begin life a "purely biological" reflex creature (Piaget, 1952). We do not "do." Rather, "doing" does us. Doing "becomes" knowledge. Thence knowing enters Being.

There is a story. Bodily gestures translate into oral phrases somehow, we begin to name things and to say them to describe the world (St. Augustine. Being is in this sense some reflection upon the things of the world, and the names we apply to them. Knowing them reflects upon our Being, and defines it: knowing... as Being (Aristotle: "Metaphysics"). "Words and Things." (R. Brown. 1970))

Experience with objects, hearing their names, we "associate" thing with name, gradually constructing language... rationality. Language becomes a model, as it were, for thought and knowledge. Skinner, 1938). How do we "associate" word with word?

Knowledge, thence Being (knowing thus Being?), is an (one) analysis of language. Nouns are (stand for?) the irreducible things; verbs, what can be done with and to the things; adjectives, adverbs, the particularities of things and their predicative possibilities. When we sought for the deity through language (do we often "give-up" on Being via increasingly complex circumlocutions?), we imagined that the first "man" spoke the language of true nature: Adam, Adamic language would lead us right back to nature (to the deity)—Boehme in Aarsleff).

Come lately, Wittgenstein (1953) proclaims that knowledge does not completely define Being, but also that Being "uses" names. Being, earlier derived from knowing, now wanders in the world, knowingly. Is this an extension of logic? Or a "bashing" of logic?

Peirce (1878), buried in the nineteenth century—disinterred in the twentieth—wondered if things and their names weren't reflections of ourselves seeing them. We see, he thought, not things "themselves," but our designations of them. If Being isn't knowing, reflected upon itself, if Being only sees "signs" of things, then Being is only (merely?) "semiosis." Last century's (bleak?) translation with the introduction of television: "The medium IS the message." (McLuhan, 1967). Here, Being is no enigma, merely a derivation. I/we are video's viewers. Lazy enigmas, at that.

Bleak! Where once the individual was primary, now we are derived, merely. Being reduced to poop. Better off, we were say some, with God. At least He gave us the earth and the heavens. Now, where are we sitting, couched as potatoes, in front of the world as video? The truth is what motivates us to buy? A capital idea.

Our theories of knowledge cast within these various circularities only heighten the sense of Being as enigma. Should we, like Kierkegaard, throw up our intellectual hands in cynical dismay? Why do we take so seriously our theories about Being, rather than letting Being speak to us; observe Being more closely, in its own terms? If only the Delphic admonition to "know thyself," could escape the history of its theories of Being.

How do we (permit ourselves to) listen, freshened or with an innocence similar to that which once was our lot? Must we "burn" the texts of all of time which have determined some oughtness to our thinking? May we expand the sense of text to knowing: the world-as-text?

De-struct this text? How?

Looking-out (Phenomenology of Normative Thinking): Looking-out "from" those senses which extend the bodily geography I call myself, I am able to see what is and hear what is being said... or so it seems.

This greatest puzzle which whirls over Being like some crazy-quilt of jargon, wonders how we are "inside," and how we get "new" information from the world; how are we, really, and what is the nature of that externality. How does this brained blob reach "outside" itself and know what is going on? And how does our internal mind converse with itself? At the least since Descartes, we have been concerned with that existence-guaranteeing process called "thinking": the famous "cogito ergo sum."

From a discursive, rhetorical perspective (which is the human, social perspective), this is a narrow visioning of Being. It raises the study of thinking to an epitome, and implies that the reasoning, knowing aspects of Being are paramount in the study of Being. They not only constitute its *sine qua non*, but call our attention "away from" many other aspects of Being. They infer a process of thinking held to be universal to (hu)mankind, and entail the notion of a Platonic formal truth which is "ideal" in its core. It derives, perhaps, from Plato and Aristotle who want to consider the "ideal" human being, in considering the nature of politics, ethics, etc. (And, in oppositional Western thinking, it sets up an anti-reason, anti-knowledge, category: usually, some form of "values," "passion," "morality," etc.) Not wishing to derogate the study of thinking, of knowing, I prefer instead to suspend these issues, and to point to some other, perhaps very important but

I paraphrase an essay I wrote some years ago, which showed that there is a "phenomenology" to "normative thinking," a type of thinking which we "construct." It is a kind of walking-through our paths of thinking, much like a dancer may walk-through a new routine before doing it up to pace. However, it is not our only path of thinking; it may change; and it leads—in its workings out—to quite particular ways of judgment. It is, in many senses, a habit of thinking, not a model of clear thought, and often varies "with context." And it contextualizes Kant's "Critiques," especially of "Pure Reason."

The view of language which was pervasive in academic circles for many years (Chomsky and Halle, 1968) was characteristic of "ideal" thinking. It postulated some notion of an "ideal-normal" language grammar which each normal human learned intuitively. Language, it claimed, has a formal grammar, made up of rules which generate the sentences of any natural language. It reacted to a reductive model of language (Skinner 1938) which stated that all knowledge is experiential (the mechanism for knowing is some form of stimulus-response learning loop). Instead, this "ideal" grammar allowed us to be "creative," to speak and to understand sentences we had "never heard before." It implied, among other things, that Being has an "inbuilt-intuitive" character, an innate human disposition to language grammar, much like Kant's notion of "pure reason."

(In fairness, it argued for a much more complicated notion of being human, than that of Skinner, which seemed to rob us of our minds and/or wills. The difficulty of criticizing it, in the context of oppositional thinking, is that is seems to argue "the" idealist position against "the" empiricist position, as if one or the other encapsulates either the concepts or the total human condition, both standing *outside* of experience—as if this is a human possibility.)

What this model of language entails is a habit of thinking by which we look-out and judge things, issues, people with respect to some ideal notion. Certainly there are good reasons to do this. In considering the ideal air foil, for example, we may disregard actual conditions of friction. In judging anyone's state of health, a physician judges with respect to some normal-ideal of health, versus, say, some observed pathology. However, this ideal-language notion also lends itself equally well to judging presumed normalcy of any speaker judged against, or with respect to, this ideal.

It is right here that some of the sometimes insidious entailments of this mode of thinking take on a reality. Those who differ from the ideal, who speak a different "way" (a geographical, social class dialect), may be judged by the ideal-thinker to be non-normal; non-normal in the sense of deviant, deficient, "pathological."

(Historically, the application of physical/mathematical notions to society have been frequently problematic, assuming as they do, that society "obeys" natural law(s) just as an airplane does. While there are many reasons to think that society is natural, "it" is not so clear that a society is just like an airplane, and that the direct application of geometrical thinking (as, for example, in Hobbes or Spinoza) to theories of society is correct or legitimate. Here, it has been more a case of applying some "partial truth" as if it had very general applicability, than of imputing falsely or falsity, to society or culture. The base or root- metaphor for this thinking is found in Aristotle's "Politics," where he presumes the body-mind dichotomy, then attempts to show how politics "works" just like the relation of mind over body—men over women, master over slave, etc.)

The problematic of thinking "ideally" is located in the selection of what is (categorically) held to be "ideal," and in the phenomenology of judgment of what is observed "against" that model of ideal. While a good thinker and writer may strive in her/his own life, to work at clarity of expression with respect to, say, a well-educated audience, taking this notion of ideal into the social world is often to discriminate against those who differ, in some way, from the putative ideal.

It is a way or mode of thought. It is one way of thinking; there are others not merely opposed. One could, for example, simultaneously think and judge with respect to some ideal structure, while also considering that dialects differ according merely to geography. In fact, most educated persons do entertain more than a single mode of thinking, although those who tell themselves they ought to be committed to an absolute/ideal, seem to deny to themselves that thinking is a bit more complicated.

Thinking is (often) contextual. What is ideal with respect to the purity of some aerodynamic forces, is not ideal with respect to the nature of health. What is anti-ideal is pathological with respect to health, but has no relation to pathology with respect to dialects. Any notion of an ideal-pure language is bound considerably to time and place, as well as to the context of thought. Why, for example, when we think of persons who differ from the majority (normal-ideal?—G.G. Simpson (1961) do we infer from a handicap (deafness) or unusualness of facial appearance ("retarded" persons) to their capability of intellection or mentation—before we have undergone thorough examination to see how their physical difference affects their ability to, say, speak or communicate?

In this context, it is obvious that we have taken our thinking habits about the normal-ideal or pure types, to attempt to explain how others are different. We have not (until quite recently) been "willing" to step outside of our models of thought to actually explore and describe the nature of "sign language," or what the appearance of so-called "retarded" persons has to do with some inability to articulate sounds. In both these examples, we have been quite mistaken in our judgments based on normal-ideal theories of language. It is time to re-examine our models as well as the persons to whom we have applied them, incorrectly.

But for the thinker who is "pure" in her/his holding out for a singular notion of purity in all her/his lookings out, judgment takes on a sense of values and a sense that the thinker is a "moral center" in all she/he does. The ideal thinker is engaged, looking out, in some version of a Kierkegaardian "either/or."

Much of what goes on in life, in the world, is literally "missed" by the ideal-thinker who wants, like a Chomsky, to consider ideal-language as a thing-in and of itself; per se. The fact of one's body being in the world with others, that language is an aspect of this human discourse; all of this is missed, thence dismissed as "irrelevant" to the bounded, pre-packaged ideal structure which is seen, looking-out, to exist—even when it never does. At a limit, an idealist point-of-view can make all of life and existence, seem like an illusion!

There are (at least) two senses in which it is dismissed: 1) the ideal-absolutist thinker refers to the non-absolutist as a "relativist"; but relativism in the thinking of an absolutist seems to be "twisted" into "there is no truth!" The absolutist, that is, constructs her/his version of relativity as opposed, an anti-absolute, but (necessarily) a different kind of absolute: like the religious view of evil, or of Satan, or of the anti-Christ—no possibility of an "agnostic" position; 2) the idealist-absolute thinker has already selected a notion of truth in terms of quite rigid categories, and the battle is only over these categories (in various ways).

That the categories, themselves, may be ensconced in a particular tradition (say, Western thought as different from Confucian thinking), simply is not a possible counter in any such argument, because the conditions of any discussion are already fixed, at the level of (usually surreptitious) presumptions; not open to discussion, but only to opposition and/or argumentation.

Here it is useful to (re)read Aristotle's "Politics," in which the nature of politics is to be referred to some ideal, always and eventually reducing to the hegemony of mind over body. Poor Being!

Doubt about Existence: Buber (1937) thought that this is one of those times in which we are not "at home" in our lives upon this earth. Indeed, such times have come upon us before. They occur when the possibility of the destruction (literally) of the known earthly universe, finds itself as an idea meandering in our minds. Now that the earth has shrunk conceptually so we can imagine it in its entirety, now that "the bomb" is a reality, the issue of its destruction lurks... once again.

Such times occur as well, particularly in the West, when the pace of felt change accelerates to the edges of our tolerance. Why the West, particularly? Because we are, since Plato, essentialist idealists, residing principally in a static world, in which change is to be re-incorporated into unchange, into eternality. (Nietzsche's claim that we needed to pursue the truth.) In the experiential, "felt" paradox of change and unchange, in which we retain a constancy of identity and integrity with some occasional difficulty and disbelief, Being seems sometimes diffuse, fragile. We teeter on a precipitous and poorly balanced axis of permanence and change. When change is perceived as "too large," we do not merely rush back to a sense of permanence (texts, the deity, a messiah, some human Archeus), but feel that some surreptitious axis lay unrevealed behind our notions of change: chaos, an abyss into which we may fall, in each next instant. Some say (Bloom 1987) that this is true, particularly, of Americans whose banality is so deep that it can hardly recognize an abyss until it hangs precipitously over the edge.

The self-discovery of our lemming-likeness occurs only after we have fallen, and are lurching full-fall to grasp for any edge of safety.

In times as these, the question of existence—the very question pops into our thoughts—and begins a wrestling contest for control over the coolness of reasoned consideration. The question of existence, whose appearance arises in each person's life as a youth, as a to- be-uncovered-paradox, now engages all our other thoughts. It enters not as the scientific question of "how," or the existential question of "why," but as the cosmic question: "Do we exist?" Not "where am I," or "how do I know I am here," but: "Am I?"

The West, the Christian tradition from Augustine, the wedding of the Greeks with the Christ, thought they had "solved" this question by saying that we "fell" to earth. We are the incarnate soul, "placed" here out of some sin of our parent's (parents'), and the "reality" of life is in heaven. We "exist" only as souls, in a diaspora from paradise, embattled with life and evil, so we may be "saved" and "return" whence we came. Life is a chimera; an illusion. "Do we exist?"—gets an always wavering response. Always there is a nagging, niggling sense that the very next time the question pops into thought, which tends to be always closer in time, the answer will be: NO! WOE! WHOA! Stop, time!

The perennial freshman question: "Well, can you PROVE that we're here!?" fills our aging lives and any sense of true maturity fades from possibility.

The question increases its resonance and frequency with the fears of change/chaos, the possible destruction of humankind, of today, of history, of any tomorrow, of me and you of meaning.

The question of existence, the "do I" of a sharply abrupt cognizance, begins to pervade thought, and cries out for answers, for some way of allaying fear. And we are in some wavering state of oscillations, where knowledge, observation, human reason and human authority, are as often on a downward slope, as the yearning for the salving of fear is rising.

There is trouble, right here, in River City.

In such times, Being is no enigma, merely. It is a desperation!

In the context of the cosmological question of existence, it is so clear that the history of ideas is crucial in understanding present times. Other traditions simply do not get into this fear-driven notion that life is chimerical: many "animistic" cultures are cosmological always, and distinguish less than we, between humans and other species, between life and the dead; in the Confucian tradition, the facticity of each person's existence is where thinking and philosophy begin. On the other hand, we share much with Buddhistic thought, where "present" existence is one of many "earlier" incarnations—literally "placings" in the body. Rather than denying bodily Being, however, the "Zen" way is to enter into (bodily) Being as totally as possible, in each moment. But, ideas are these all. Once we recognize them as ideas, which have been invented, we can "deconstruct" the contexts in which they arose/arise, and with hope, can "construct" others which will serve us in these "hard" times.

The form in which the cosmological question arises in Western thought underscores the Aristotelian concentration upon the thing and the individual as the primary, the irreducible, the analytic "unit" into which all issues are to be broken. In Christian thought, the question is not, "do WE," but "do I," exist? Literally, the universe begins and ends in the thinking of each of us about our personal destinies. Salvation is mine alone. Community (charity), any "covenant" between persons, any relation to the history of persons in whose terms I have been "created" and survive, these all diminish to the vanishing point. In Western thought, we live literally in two universes: of ideas (as pure individuals), and of actuality (of and with others). Cosmological fear seems to "drive" most of us eventually ever more deeply into our individual selves as personal death concerns win out over the comforting others may provide us.

In the over-arching divisions between the curriculum of life being logical vs. rhetorical, does this comment prove that cosmology is an aspect of logic? Or are there other cosmologies: discursive...?

Existence vs. Being (a digression): Being is some large encompassing idea which includes all of my existence and experience/experiencings. From the light in my parents' eyes contemplating the babe and person to be, to the fetus and embryo begun on a path to here and now, to everyone's seeing and imagining me to be the one which/who I think I am, willing to be what I am willing to be as struggle toward resuscitating the concept of wisdom which has virtually been lost in these times thinking out the present and its becomings, I include all this in Being: all that I accept, and (knowingly, often unknowingly reject).

Existence and experience have some overlaps: existence is created as a concept from and within the antinomies of Western dualism opposing any foundational essentialism, formalism, or idealism. Experience is ongoing in the present and my presence within it; what and who I am-not in any positive sense, all the paradoxes of Being which I reside upon, the ideas which make no sense, and the very idea of sense made or not. I try to live carefully and with some integrity; but am always questioning their inclusiveness and exclusiveness; living with another with whom I share thoughts, my boundaries also blur and blend, the discourse of Being inner and outer also in dialogue with the critical mind reflecting joint history, futurity, and family, and all of Being.

Visitor to the world, renting rather than owning, the study of my life engaging in life is my vocation. Happiness is doing, writing, teaching, living who I would be at least occasionally.

Being includes all of this and these and more.

Four Models of *Rationality*: The notion of "rationality" has been quite powerful in its relation to Being and existence. It appears in various guises when any notion of what is nature or natural, what is human, is being discussed: in Kant's notion of "pure reason," Locke's concepts of "human understanding," Descartes's "...therefore I am." It underlay thinkers like

Nietzsche and Kierkegaard, whose work reacted against a felt narrowness in the definition of human and rationality. Today, it inspires a pessimism among some behavioral psychologists and comparative biologists who claim that rationality has led us into deep trouble and should be "abandoned," virtually before it is too late. Modern religious fundamentalism of most stripes is also a reaction against various notions of rationality gone too far. If God gave us "free" will, the range of its application has overbounded "faith," whose domain has been shrinking.

There is, however, a deep set of complications in understanding and deconstructing what is rational, and disentangling what is human, what Being, because there are by now (at least) four quite different concepts of rationality with which every educated person is familiar. Indeed, they are aspects of each of our thinking, and we easily dredge out one or the other, whenever the congruent situation seems at hand.

The "oldest" Western model of rationality, derived once again from Aristotle directly (*Politics*) and from Plato less directly (*Sophist*), begins from two linked presumptions: 1) that the human is composed of (can be "analyzed into") two parts, the mind and body; 2) the comparative presumption that humans "alone" possess the intellectual capacity to think out things for ourselves (other species, slaves, barbarians, women, and children in different "degrees" do not).

In its Aristotelian form, which seems to lurk at various levels of (un-)consciousness still in our current thinking, this presumption is developed and argued philosophically in the domain of politics: politics ranging from the analysis of the state and its component parts (including the household and the relation between "master" and the others in the household) analogized to the notion that the mind (or soul) "directs" the body. In its elaborations it is an argument and justification for male "dominance," for slavery, for aristocracy and kingship (as opposed to democracy). In arguing the opposite way, from the "weaker" to the stronger, it attempts to show how the body, thence "different" (from "ideal," "pure," male, aristocratic, masterful) is "inferior." It sets up some notion of the "ideal" and contrasts every (thing, -one) difference as partaking of some related degree of inferiority.

Thus, in one of its critical modern forms, Bloom (1987) may discuss the "closing" of the American mind (cynically: "mind"), and following

Aristotle, "blames" divorce, Blacks, an insidious weakening of the "master" class (young males), a disenchantment of differences between the sexes (due, for example, to the constancy of rock music = simple sex). This is not to say that intellection in modern America is at some acme (here it's difficult to disagree with Bloom), but to see how Bloom argues his case in the Aristotelian mode still. And, as in Aristotle, intellection and politics are interwoven, with great intimacy.

As in the Greek mode, the development of what is a good life, the greatest happiness, and so on, relates directly to contemplation: being able to have and take the time to think hard, to study, to argue with the "great" minds. As abstract thinking is linked with a suspension of "doing," there is an oppositional relationship with those who work and do—the "pragmatic"—being anti, being incapable of contemplative thinking. To become truly intelligent, we need "time out" from ordinary life. Lastly, it equates being rational with a thoughtful life: being "reasonable." Rationality → reason.

This complex of ideas remains central to our thinking about the nature of rationality, what and who is rational. It remains in our being at some level waiting, as it were, for the invocation of any of its grand themes. These, in turn, seem to bring out many of the remainder, depending often on the times: whether this is a time of "revolution" against a monarchy (18th century "Enlightenment"); or a time when we worry lest the sense of some former political-intellectual hegemony is at risk (America during the last years of the 20th century); whether we are brave, frightened, bemused, looking to think-out our futures, or waiting for deliverance (the "Messiah" will return!)

Ensconced within, as well, is the issue of what, in any era, is "virtue"; what, whether we "aim" our lives in any particular direction, and what is that direction. And there is hidden here a sense of what is "nature," what is human nature, and whether this should affect our thinking about ourselves and how to be.

As I said earlier, this is one of four, by now rather ordinary notions of rationality. It is the one most often regarded as logical, philosophical. It is the one we invoke when thinking about the nature of intelligence, of what (good) thinking is, that one which has gained some great measure of authority=truth value, as the foundational mode of scientific thinking. In the 18th century, this mode of being rational seemed obvious and rather complete, and quintessentially human—as well as related to a variety of notions of "progress": social, political, technogical. By the 19th century, its "optimism" began to be tempered...

But the tempering, the "attacks" on this mode of rationality, do not at all begin to account for the other "modes" of rationality. They seem to exist in most of our minds' eyes, not as any opposition or attacks upon rationality, but simply different. They are all apparent at the level of what is, by now, commonsense. They do not seem, usually, to interfere with one another. But we seem to invoke one or another in the proper situation or context. They seem to pass-by one another, much as airplanes at night flying different patterns to different places, at different altitudes. I have occasionally noted, however, that arguing in one of these modes may of a sudden bring out one of the others. Thus it is difficult to know where one is "standing" in this ground which seems murky.

The other three "ordinary" modes of discussion about rationality are: 2) the "clinical" notion of insanity or craziness, the irrationality which is not merely against the rational-logical, but which is not at all in the same realm— hallucinatory (not even objective about the shared objectivity, etc.), out of control of the thinker; 3) the "economic" mode of rationality, in which the individual who is most rational (!) attempts to maximize profit. It is more (than the others) about motivation; not how a mind "is," but what a rational person will do, to benefit (him)self. Modes (2) and (3) share the feature that if someone does not act rationally, in either sense, there is something "wrong" with them, similarly to the logical idea of being rational: they are thinking "poorly" or "wrongly."

Mode (4) is different, but just as commonsensical about being rational. It is the sense of rationality involved in legal thinking: what would a "rational" or "reasonable" person do, or think, or act, or react?

While it has many strong aspects, and has undoubtedly led to a legal code which acts in terms of fairness for many citizens; it requires in its formulation a consideration of what is a "reasonable person." And this often is restricted to those (kinds; sorts of) persons whom lawyers and judges are familiar with, and respect (or dis-respect).

Thus, there are these four "modes" of thinking about the rational, which almost all of us have gathered into our thinking. They reside in each of our thinking, occupying most independent conceptual arenas, and rarely interfere.

However, sometimes they overlap. When one is (apparently) in one arena, someone begins to argue in another, as if the elaboration of one is a direct or genuine response to another. If some persons (peoples) in the world, do not seem to act to maximize agricultural profits, American economists do not always find it difficult to label them as irrational: if they were rational, they would think differently about farming (and their mode of existence); something is "wrong" with other cultures who do not act as we do, as we would. They "should" change, we should change them... the slope is slippery.

In defending against the accusation of some modern (apparently) neo-conservatives that the American mind is "closed," that intellection is not at an all-time high, some (lawyers) are tempted to argue the legal notion, not to respond to the accusation. That is, intellection is not all that important, what is important is being a reasonable person, to engage in interpersonal "equality," in some sense of mutual understanding toward greater community, toward more reasonable behavior. Here, what John Gardner called an American balancing act of cycling between "excellence" and "equality," tips toward "equality," and leaves the question of intellectual excellence hanging in the wind.

In "confusion" between modes (1) and (2), American political administrations seem to find it easy to accuse those who think quite differently from them, as being crazy, and uncivilized: either insane, or like animals, perhaps both: witness attacks upon Libya.

In an ultra-competitive era, we seem to find it easy to justify increasing poverty, by labeling "the unfortunates" as being less "capable" than those of us who succeed, invoking the economic sense of rationality to justify what "we" do, while labeling others in terms of mode (1), being less rational or intelligent "by nature."

Without complicating this aspect of the discussion of being beyond its possible disentanglement, it does seem important to go often through the exercise of approaching the contents of one's thinking and experience with respect to the issue of what is the rational. It has had a long history, even in each life, in each of our educations, as we have been drilled to make judgments about what is better or more advanced thinking, what is simpler; what is clear, what murky; what is the sense of self each of us carries at some levels of Being, by which we judge ourselves as reasonable. Which of these notions of the rational do we invoke, under what circumstances? How do they reside, often separately, but sometimes overlapping, in our conceptual Being?

Are there other modes of rationality?

Bloom (1987) claims that Freud (one of Nietzsche's heirs) brought to us the notion of the rational as "rationalization." Rather than being concerned with being rational=thinking logically and well, we invoke various sorts of rationales to account for or to justify what we "want" to do anyway. Thus, contends Bloom, the 19th century notion of Enlightenment rationality, of the best uses of reason, have turned about some 180 degrees, into the use of "reason=rationalism" to justify our passions, desires, mistakes.

Relativism versus Context: There is some confusion, some sense of overlap between the notions of meaning of how the world "means," or how we understand, as different from how we find meaning—how we lead meaningful lives. What is real, what is unreal; or not so real? What is genuine, authentic? Sometimes these notions are the same, and collapse into one another. In other senses, in other contexts, they seem miles apart. Rather than attack this puzzle directly, I wish to "back into" it by considering the (apparent) opposition between absolutism and relativism, to show how slippery is this arena. After this, I will introduce the notion of meaning change with respect to context, to begin to show how complicated is ordinary life, which, I think, we have tended to narrow and to underestimate in our concentration on certain favorite categories and "party lines."

Some of the complications and circularities of thinking about Being are wound up in issues which are often given names like "relativism" and "absolutism." With little further ado, these names slip and slide into strong opposition as if they are necessarily at war with one another. To "be" one or the other of these is strongly to take upon thinking an entire framework and approach to meaning. One cannot be a relativist about one situation, an absolutist about another: at least from the point of view of absolutists who, of course, are true to their appellations.

And the relativists are tempted to be equally absolutist in their judgment about judgment: the world "should" be open, pluralistic; there is no single perspective which is the right one. Logically, there is abundant irony in the absolutism which convinced relativists fall into. There is (can be?) no clear relativism which opposes absolutism directly and consistently. Either we might search for some middle ground to resolve this apparent opposition, or begin to rethink the issues which seem to be involved and entailed here.

Some discussion of these arenas is in order. The usual argument in the public domain, is between religious "believers" and the others. The religious who are absolutists hold that God is real; further, that He is the truth. Anything or anyone who opposes Him (rather, some relativist in me is urged to poke his nose in, to say that God is their construction of some transcendent idea), is against God. Further, the opposers (the a-theists) "must" also oppose what God "represents": e.g., truth, morality, values, light, good, eternality, salvation, the soul, *and meaning*.

It is thus difficult (virtually impossible, but there are some ways "around" this), because this oppositional absolutism already embraces in its thinking and in the Being of its followers, the categories of its opponents: evil, Satanic, anti-Christ, anti-truth (lies), immorality, lack of values, darkness, sin, the body, the present (Being in the moment)... nihilism.

Not only does the relativist fall into the absolutists' notion of what s/he is "really" like, but it is easy (too easy) to convince the convinced absolutist that anyone who exhibits any of the anti- or oppositional characteristics, is at once an a-theist, and partakes in all the other oppositions as well. Any expression bordering upon nihilism, a non-judgmental stand about the morals of other peoples (e.g., the anthropologist who describes "other" marriage types, but does not judge them as being "wrong"), and a person is cast into a Satanic, anti-Christ barrel.

Will a thoughtful agnosticism please stand up, and identify itself? This, as I recall, was one of Nietzsche's plaintive wails; that there is no thick and pungent form of suspending thought about the deity of Western thought, which can yet yield meaning to life. For whatever reason, the sense that God is alive and well and doing His incantations and omniscience grants us meaning in our lives. That worry, the loss of meaning, the "Rise of European Nihilism" (*Intro: Will to Power*) was what led to Nietzsche's announcement of the "death of God." Can we not create or observe other transcendental elements in our Being? Can we not find meaning, some sense of "ultimacy," of towards which in whose terms we can direct our lives and find meaning? Perhaps the central question about Being in such a time as this is how do we come to "have" meaning in life; perhaps, more usefully, how do we "lose" meaning?

What or who grants us meaning? Who or what sustains it?

Somewhere there exists a kind of wrap around the question. Call it "context"; "leave it" to context; "it changes" with the context. What changes; what is "it"?

The "same" word, the "same" gesture means "differently" in various situations. Some "different" ideas "come together" in certain contexts. Enter a house filled with family at a holiday; enter the same house just upon the death of an elderly mother or a child; enter the same house devoid of furniture. Each entering may be identical, the steps taken, the greeting. But each entering is quite a different sort of event, they "mean" differently. Is the meaning in the context, in what we "know" about the context, in our "interpretation" or "perspective"?

What theory of meaning tells us about context? Where, in our Being, is this knowledge derived? kept? Is context a kind of relativism? Is context partaken in by those who are (otherwise) absolutists? If so, of course, the relativist/absolutist debate is not how it appears!

Human Rights: Since the beginning of the United Nations and its Declaration of Human Rights, the question of these Human Rights seems to have been directed principally by Western Democracies against other governments who have been dealing with some (groups) of persons in ways we consider inhuman, especially inhumane.

This Declaration culminated practically a century of a distinctively "American" approach to anthropology developed by Franz Boas and his students. It incorporated an approach to the study of all human beings, everywhere in the world, which was three-fold: Language, the Physical ("Race"), and Culture.

It argued, and argued quite successfully in the long run of the 20th century, that all of the peoples who speak language, have human forms, partake in the "family" of humans: *homo sapiens*. By virtue of their being born to human parents, and entering into human society, all humans have certain rights. They all have sufficient similarity of form. More importantly they all possess and speak languages which possess grammars of equal complexity with Western languages, possess logic, etc. They possess, that is, identity of mental operations, capacities, abilities, and so on. Whatever differences there may be in physical form or appearance, seem small or unimportant in the identity of all as partaking of human nature.

These ideas developed during the centuries when an empirical approach to nature sought to determine what is the nature of being human, over and above the theo-political "arrangements" in which people found themselves? As well, it argued against the concepts of "race," of human ability and capability being granted only, or principally along familial, national, ethnic, geographic lines. It argued against some of the foundations of Western thought, against, for example, Aristotle's claim that: "...those who are sprung from better ancestors are likely to be better men, for nobility is excellence of race."(*Politics: 1283a, 35-7*)

It argued, that is, against certain forms of Greek idealism deriving from Plato and Aristotle. To resuscitate those Greeks, without very careful criticism, to proclaim their thinking as some ultimate flowering of abstraction, to often to carry with it a parallel renewal and revival of Greek philosophical politics: a state which presumes slavery, one in which women do not partake in its deliberations or administration.

While much is interesting and admirable in the works of Plato and Aristotle, their political thinking presumed that the "state" was the category which contained, as it were, all its citizens. Moreover, it presumed a class of slaves and other lesser types such as women and children. The Greek notion of Being thus rests upon presumptions which are inimical to rights belonging to all humans, but argues that they pertain only to a favored few.

Much depends, since the Greeks, on what is the nature of Nature, what is the nature of humans (within nature) and just how do we ascertain these? From Aristotle, we derive the most popular method based on the oppositions between a sense of the "best" (ideal) humans in the ideal state, metaphorized to the assumed division between mind and body (*Politics*). In a complex of logic alluded to earlier, the nature of humans is taken to be unique from other species due to our mind (reason) and elaborated into human sociality or culture. As critical as I am of this entire line of thinking, my main objection is to the presumption that the human body is not of major importance in this determination of what is human. Somehow the bodily form of humans, and its ordinary juxtaposition with other species' forms is hidden within its ordinariness. For the query of what is human, we have relied on the elaboration of a story which is a partial truth at most.

Out of this depiction of individuals wandering in the forest primeval, primordial man came upon language (mind) and gradually became social. Sociality, politics, the state are derived from the evolution of humans from pre-human to human. In this story, there is the dual story of ontogenesis, each individual's growing-up, wherein each of us has become "chained" (Rousseau) after being "born free." Freedom and human rights demand that we remain "free." And in the light of the theo-politics and monarchies of 18th century Europe, this was indeed an informing, revolution-making idea. As a critique of modern Republics of Western Europe and America, however, the invocation of Rousseauian ideas flies in the face of what we have come to know about other species, thence about humans. What was, two centuries ago a politics of nature, now seems contrary to nature; opposed to nature, particularly as we have come to know other species in some detail.

Other species (any exceptions?) are already social. They were never, and are not now "solitary brutes" wandering in the primeval forest. We did not evolve as solitaries either. The notion of social contract is present already in other related species. The problematic issue in human existence has to do with the "emergence" of individuality, not of society. Whether we are only derived from others as some Marxists hold, whether our individuality is "demanded" within the social structure, as seems clear to me, the issue of what is particularly human, what individual and what social, requires much rethinking in the light of modern knowledge of the sociality of other species and of "primitive" peoples.

What is happening in the sphere of the politics and sociology of ideas is, however, a kind of "revisionism" of political theory, in which the sense of universal justice present in democratic states is presently being challenged. Equality for all is, in Bloom's (1987) terms, causing us to "close our minds." Some deep sense of "inequality" which is imputed to "nature" is being held out as the "true" salvation of the state from: nihilism, stupidity, anarchy, etc. The theory of "social contract" has come full-circle and is being utilized in the present to re-establish the senses of aristocracy and monarchy which it originally opposed. Enigma become irony!

Truly, I love this notion of freedom of each and all individuals. But I think freedom occurs in approximately the opposite direction: that we are born in-relation, and gradually become the individual who is independent, capable. We do not even survive as individuals. The possible physiological survival of a "wolf-child" is, though probably mythological, impossible toward a languaging, interacting, thoughtful Being in a human sense. Many of us have a habit of mythologizing nature to fit the model of human politics which we desire.

I respond to the human rights claims about human nature, as well, because they are being undermined as they are being proclaimed. They rest (from Locke) on a notion that there is no carry-over from one generation to the next which is determinative of anything essential to our freedom of thinking. The "tabula rasa" was calculated to defeat the concept of hereditary kingship (again, all of this is laid out in Aristotle's *Politics*) and it was used by Jefferson, effectively, declared to the heavens in the Declaration of Independence. But it now is being undermined.

In the modern form, called the nature-nurture debate, the rise of genetics has rekindled the determinist theorists, to claim that freedom is "freedom." Our behavior, our thinking, our intelligence is related to our parents', they say. This thinking will, in "hard times," be used to justify idealist Western thinking (the mind) over and against others" thinking (3rd World, non-Western), who, if we look at them straight, look differently. It is their bodies which are different (physiognomy) from those who proclaim Western hegemony intellectually (Bloom, 1987). It is this which will undermine eventually the claim that we are all human, all have equal rights, and so on.

It is a complex road from proclaiming the excellence of abstract thinking by studying Plato and Aristotle (the "great men") to noting that this argument is deeply enmeshed in politics. From Aristotle, we learn that this is because it is the best men (sic!) who will rule best; the closest to the ideal judged by Aristotle's methods, which presume a slave state, a place for women which is "different from that of barbarians," but indeterminately lesser. In this thought line, we get what we "deserve"—we are not "self-determining"; human rights revert, once again to those rights which flow in family lines; the aristocracy of birth is restored.

The Individual—Aristotle vs. Marx: The Aristotelian version of Being is being an individual male. The notion of I Being who I am, in a deep sense independently of all others, seeking my living and my dying (salvation), relates knowledge directly to this (concept of) being an individual. I exist, primarily. The world comes to me; or I wander, variously, "through" it (perhaps I am a planar figure, entering constantly into next planes). Other persons are like the remainder of the world, like objects, like world-fill. I become the actor, the hero, the goat, the savior of myself. Others... well, they are problematic, fading in and out, like planar ghosts extending across, or running parallel to my trajectory. I am my life trajectory; or, my life trajectory is me.

In Marxist thinking, there is a transposition, an inversion of Being. The individual is derived, a construct which "I" match, seeking out Being within the congeries of social roles which exist in the social construction of others. This view is not necessarily a "weakened" view of the individual, but one in which the very notion of the individual has little meaning. Being, here, is less an enigma, more a wondering.

In the ordinary social=parental construction of the world, it has seemed to me that the notion of the individual Being is one which parents at once desire and work-at. But they also work-at its counterpoise: varieties of "conscience." Individual Being, directly associated with bodily Being, is less the parental-social notion of the individuality of their child: it is much more the "person" whom they see in the faces (& body) of "their" infant. This parental idea of Being has extent, in every moment into the reaches of an entire lifetime (maybe, beyond). It has, as well, extent into the congeries of relationships into which they themselves are placed (place themselves?) In a (deep?) sense, the individual is treated as a particular person and a social (=universal?). In actual life, Being is not an either/or. Being is more a both/and.

Skepticism, Cynicism, Nihilism, and Slippery-Slopes. Beware men (and women) quoting Nietzsche! (Dare I trust myself?!)

Frederick Nietzsche, author of some 20 books, announced and noted the "death of God." He did not "proclaim" it, but noted incisively that many Europeans had "lost" their belief in a form of the deity which had previously "given" meaning to their lives.

In his final book (save one, written from the confines of the asylum), edited by his sister, Mrs. Foerster, who married an anti-Semite with Nazi leanings, he considered at some length the "Rise of European Nihilism."

In these days, these days precisely, when the remainder of the world seems poised to "displace" the hegemony of European thinking (so it seems to some), the sense of nihilism can be found in many places. What Nietzsche announced, was the realization finally after almost two millennia of Christian piety that "meaning" is a life problem. Formerly the question of meaning and the quest for meaning had had a kind of specificity and directedness toward the nature of God. Man—in Western thought—was composed of two (always two) aspects of faith and of reason. In centuries previous to the 19th of Nietzsche and of Kierkegaard (and Schopenhauer), the quest for reason had become the stronger; the nature of reason was thought to be grounded and to be "located" in nature.

Now that God was dead as a concept which lends meaning to life, Nietzsche wondered that those most basic of concepts which lend direction and "values" to life—good and evil—were indeed no more than human values. They were not linked to knowledge or truth in the sense that God was eternal, truthful, and omniscient, but to be examined within the psyche and psychology of what is human. The darkening, brooding of what it is that maintains and sustains humans had been raised in its glory and gory details since Schopenhauer had worried about the "will to live." What is it which "keeps us going"?

This question of and quest for the will had since Plato and Aristotle seemed "backwards." The soul, the animating force which is the oppositional force between what is life and what is death, this life-fragile concept had earlier motivated the question of knowledge. Now, some two thousand years later, it had suddenly become obvious that life must sustain itself; death is always ready, around the next corner. Life without the concept of God has only itself to fall back upon.

Knowledge without God? Always knowledge, reason, the will of humans had been problematic since the story of Eden; linked with the will of (wo)man to disobey good and to embrace evil: the tree of knowledge. Man had gotten haughty, seeking the power to compete with the God who had given (him) life, and whose languages were mystified and made incomprehensible, as he (man) tried to erect the Tower at Babel. Now, without God, are we, as Nietzsche asks, "Beyond Good and Evil?"

Skepticism, abounding since the Greeks, addressed in such brilliant verbiage within the dialogues of Plato, and the mundane but no less powerful notes of Aristotle, was pushed back. The quest for the human was to be found somehow, somewhere within the concept of the soul. Skepticism about what could be known, translated into the eternal concepts of "truth" guaranteed by a hovering God, elides so gradually in thinking into a cynicism in which doubt could be celebrated as dissent against the "knowers of it-all." Of a sudden, fear rises to its occasions.

Then there was the question of texts and truth. What is there to do when skepticism elides into a fear-driven cynicism, which doubts various possibilities, and turns into the face of the abyss: life as an infinitesimal within the two-folded eternities surrounding it? What to do, to seek knowing the truth, and Being. Go back! Return! To what? To when?

Ensconced as we were within an optimism bred of a youthful and progressive time, we have little self-protection against the sort of pessimism bred in bureaucratic life, where we do the same every day; some days more, some less, but every day forever more. The drama of life is turned upon itself and is bored to tears; just then, fear enters! Perhaps it is the fear of fear, a fear that will not go away, that presses upon Being like a twelve-ton press pressing upon my soul; my soul arises to protest, to protect. What roads will I travel now, so little space left in life, a wandering amongst the crackled walks, full of hidden falls lurking just beyond? Go back! Return! The past beckons.

The texts of all of time: the Bible, the New Testament, calculated to "solve" the fear of death, elaborates fear so it may relieve it, relives fear so that fear, itself, may die lingering. Go back to Socrates, the classical knower who was wise for all of time, for all of us within time. Texts become the real. We enter them, the black upon white; the world become fuzzy, background to the drama of the textual characters who lived that we may now live. Here, meaning resides truly; the truth of life's experiences fades into the background, unfocused, disappearing; going, going, gone.

Do we gather present strength in this way? Or do we weaken ourselves in the present, while laying praise at the feet of the masters who reside within some theory of the long-past, remaining alive in ways which we find to resurrect them? Coming from a skepticism, have we so "reduced" ourselves, our strength and resolve to live in each next present, that we began to doubt knowledge itself, a cynicism bred from fear... and, of a sudden, fear-driven into a nihilism in which doubt breeds only more doubt until we cannot stand it, and cannot withstand the fuzzing of time and today and ourselves?

What was once an intellectual disposition, a skepticism about what we did not know, how did it take those peculiar turns, begin to slide and to elide skepticism about our knowing, to skepticism about knowledge, to a nihilism which hollowed as it hollered for...Help!

A Picture worth a Thousand Words: My major mentor (Kinesicist Ray Birdwhistell – my teacher at U. Buffalo, colleague in working...) once quoted his friend Margaret Mead as saying that we never use our primary sense to test reality. Those of us, that is, who are "primarily" visual, tend to play with auditory or perhaps tactile stimuli; similarly, those of us who primarily "hear" the world, may tell ourselves that we are visual people. But, at a level deep to our individual Being, we ground ourselves in some particular sense, which we keep steady, "safe" from play, from puns and the vicissitudes of everyday life.

Whether or not there is some basic sort of truth to this statement, it is at once critically stimulating for self-review, and important in calling attention to how we are in the world. It is also, perhaps, metaphorical for the complex aspects of Being which remain at a level out-of-awareness. For the linguist-in-me, it may be likened to the kind of knowledge we possess in terms of which we articulate speech, a balletic virtuosity of the tongue, lips, teeth which only come to our attention when there is something wrong (a caught food particle, a broken cusp).

While I find it easy, persuasive even, to be drawn into a wonderment about how I am "really," setting me upon a path of self-observation and no small amount of personal history, I find it also fascinating to be drawn into the formal world of Plato's caves, wherein the senses do not reveal, but can only mislead. This contrast, which has virtually defined the history of Western thought in many ways, has had many entailments in its workings out. They can be expressed, again metaphorically, by referring to that great puzzler who thought all was change, Heraclitus, who said: "I trust the senses best."

Plato, the idealist, the formalist, seeing in shadowy particularities only a sense of chaos, sought to find the universals, the spiritual aboveness and overall. But in this adventure, he "lost" himself, banished the body, and praised that sense of philosopher which stood outside of Being. For him, the introductory phrase "a picture is worth a thousand words" could have no meaning.

Yet, it is a truth of a sort. But, what sort?

If it is the case that we take in through the senses, external information which is passed through some nerves into the brain, then interpreted somehow, somewhere in the brain, we could guess that there must be more nerves taking in visual information than auditory. Or, we could guess that visual information is less complex than auditory, needing less interpretation, thus being more potent in its effect upon us. And there could be other explanations of this sort. But, again, of what sort?

These explanations are all of a single piece, presuming that the individual (organism—not person!) is an open, passive thing, taking in information via external nerves into some central interpreter.

Instead, as J.J. Gibson (1963) instructs us, the senses are to be considered as perceptual "systems," already in some ways interpretive and cognitive beyond mere open perception. There are no "raw" percepts, coming at us "cleanly," exactly as they "are."

Moreover, these theories presume that the individual is the center of her/his own universe, open perceptually to the world "as it is." However, from the rhetorical, discursive perspective in which life is lived "truly," the question of "how" we see takes on greater power.

The rhetorical fact of humans seeing "persons in faces"—if it is metaphorical—is the human metaphor. It is the basis for the semiosis of our

Being in which the human face is transformed in our seeing: "it" into "whom." It is in terms of this human metaphor in terms of which we live, indeed survive at all.

Does this mean we see the world not as objects in the Aristotelian sense, but primarily as pictures? Others, thence ourselves? Do we see the world as pictures; through pictures? Does the brain then interpret our pictures?

The face: a mask; an expression? A picture worth a thousand words?

To the extent that we live as formalists, as universalists, are we to this extent so vulnerable to the attractiveness of pictures floating past upon the video tubes in our private places, that we cannot use our critical judgment to remain resistant to such attractions? Has, as my colleague Jochen Schulte-Sasse claimed, the capital which was money, now turned into images which are now the only capital of worth left in life?

Death... on Being: Talk about paradox! Talk about enigma! Wow! Death!

There is some sense upon studying the sorts of glyphic references which the ancients attributed to Heraclitus, that the earlier yearnings of civilization were infested still with questions about Being that derived from a kind of "animistic" outlook.

There was a sense that a world-spirit existed which invaded, pervaded, determined and sustained life; indeed, sustained the entire world. (Collingwood 1938) reminds us that Aristotle too lived in a universe which was "full" of purposeful spirit(s). This ended with the Newtonian "mechanical-mechanist" view of the 17th and 18th century. It left our bodies outside of our Being, still, but in a new way: a kind of geometric extension.)

Rather than "naming" objects, it was more the human way to "look-out" of one's eyes and note the "world-fill." Each of those irreducible substances possessed spirit—much as we. For some, each substance-possessing spirit also has had a "purpose" in some grand scheme of things.

The thinkers we now call philosophers were just awakening to discover themselves. They did not merely do, but they began to watch themselves doing. Watching, in a sense, replaced doing, as the technologies of agriculture and civil engineering enabled the contemplative life to feed upon itself, and proclaim its virtue above all others.

The issue in Heraclitus' time (as it is still among many animistic thinking peoples) has to do with this world-fill full of spirits. At that time, the dead "remained" amongst the living, also as spirits. (If grandma is still "floating around" the house in our thinking, full-time, or she is "reborn" as my little sister, then "death" is not an "end" or a return, but perhaps another state of Being.)

The concepts of "eternal" and "nothingness" remained to be invented. "Everything was something," in a universe which was likely much more "full" than the one which our eyes look out upon these days. Instead of life versus death, engaged in some infernal war, death and life were (perhaps) aspects of one another. Grandma's and Uncle Joe's (positive and not-so-pleasant) spirits kind of "hung around," their "energy" joining with those of their descendants in ways to be "divined." Humans shared, as well, spirits with other species, whose life (and death) were interwoven intimately with theirs. If, as a young person I am told that I possess (also) the spirit of some powerful animal, whose identity I will someday discover upon a "vision quest," then this is probably "as real" as anything else.

The major question (was it, to them, a paradox?) was whether reality was an aspect of the sleeping world, or the world of wakefulness? Sleeping is a solitary activity, wakefulness is about the in-common sense of our Being. Although the world was in (constant?) flux and all was change, there was a sense of permanence (*logos*), usually characterized by some version of Heraclitus' most famous maxim: "You cannot walk twice into the same river." It is this sameness, this sense of constancy in a world in flux, which so attracted Heraclitus' intellectual descendants. (Me? You?)

The problematic of sleep versus wakefulness was replaced by the question of death versus life, as the reality. The Pythagoreans thence Plato chose death as the primary metaphor for life; the formal or limiting aspects of things over the particularity of material objects. Life became a preparation for death. The infinite and universal, the logic (logos) of grammar, became the path upon which the resolution of reality was to be discovered. Time was exteriorized from experience, and change was illusory. Zeno's arrows which never got to where they were "going," is an apt metaphor for the life of contemplation.

The queen of the disciplines, philosophy, held that the proper perspective for viewing life, was to already accept the fact of our own personal deaths, and to view the present from that moment looking backwards to the present (this present).

Change reveals itself as an axis opposed by permanence. The experience of living, the existential by any definition, had to banish the body, and reveal that notion of soul which is the sameness of the river. Change is not merely rejected, but (re-)interpreted as some sense of chaos; chaos, that is, which destroys any possibility of Being.

Only in death is there life...

Death... on Being.

Identity and Masks: I have always been in some peculiar relation with my face, at least since I have (since age 7) "worn" an artificial eye, a prosthesis, a glass (now, plastic) eye. My face I have always known looked, appeared different to others looking at me than to myself looking out. But, for me, this was always somehow cosmetic, a way of not displeasing others' looking, a way of not calling attention to an anomaly, an unusualness, of seeing a freak, an incompletion. It was never/always a mask, a deceit. But I have *passed*! Do we (don't we?) all pass? And I am who I am? How do we appear to ourselves; to others? What is a face that humans seem so much to love; to study; to find personage and Being within them?

Others (Ekman 2007), come at the face differently, so it seems. They see always a mask, a deceit, a covering which is different from some sense of a substance, a substantial...truth. The face, they seem to think, is some congeries of facial "expressions," painted upon... upon what? The face is not what it is, in any clear sense of identity or of its nature, but a locus for deceit, for masking.

I think they come to this position from some sense of disappointment, or from a sense of human nature that states that only humans can lie, cannot tell the truth. I think they bewail the notion that we have become alienated or inauthentic in our Being, and study the face to prove what they do not find provable. I think they think that other species' identities are "what they are," somehow irreducible, as if old Aristotle were still painting them into Being.

But, I think, it is not very useful to search for Being by beginning from Being as a deceit, a masking, whose peeling would reveal something/nothing? As for me, I am fairly secure in knowing that my depiction of my facial appearance is different from others' seeing it, but the deceit, if it is that, may have to do with something about the psycho-social me, but not about my true, deeper Being or identity.

As I have written before (Sarles, 1985), the face is many-faceted, a locus for light reflection, a statement of age and gender, a presentation of health, of linguistic habit, and on, and on. A face is not, merely. It is not a cover up. The face is a human study. We seem to love faces, from the moment of birth. They fascinate us, and we memorize them, and see newness through some mental arrangements of them. We respond to them, see in them love and hate, besides masking and deceit. They are routes and directions for interaction with others; they are rhetorical devices; they are ornaments; they are scary, they are images. We record persons as faces, and store their photographs to identify "them." And they often transcend life, in the conjuring of the yet living. Being, identity, surely they are all of these and more.

It is, perhaps, not too strong to say that we have love affairs with our own images of our faces, and a facial accident, a partial paralysis of facial muscles is often an "insult" to our entire Being. For we "construct" self-images, derived from the mirrors of glass, and the mirrors of myriad others' faces facing our own. Narcissus is at work within, but she/he is no mere muse. We (learn to) look like we do, remain (for others/ourselves?) consistent, as our Being is continuous and consistent.

It is likely that the sense of identity, integrity, continuity, wholeness, coherence that we do possess is at once quite real, yet quite fragile. It derives, as J. has said, not directly from the Aristotelian irreducibility which is the individual (we call ourselves) proclaiming its own integrity. It is not, as Marx would have it, derived totally from a congeries of social realities and roles from which it emerges as a consciousness. Rather it is rhetorical. It emerges from the sense of personhood granted us by our parents, who also grant us individuality, and place upon us the necessity/burden to be individuals. Its continuity is certified by the constancy which others tell us that we are who we are. But it is internal and internalized by each "I" in an ongoing interaction with our significant others. It is the search for some evanescent notion of authenticity, of an inalienable self, an archetypical human Being, which detracts us from developing a strong-er sense of Being, which is always humanly possible, but no integral given.

This is to state that the face is, like Heraclitus' puzzle of the river in which we cannot twice step, at once constant and changing. It is both seat and situation; a paradox whose ancient Western wish to resolve takes us away from entering into our lives, and worries that life is (no longer) genuine.

Yet here we are, I and you. We both are our faces, and, no doubt "wear" them as well. We know them deeply etched in our mind's eye, yet never see them except that we are mirrored or photographed or otherwise removed. The fact is that they change commonly, and often, responding not only to the gravity's of standing or lying in repose, but to the seeing of others seeing us, our faces. They live out situationally, contextually in the various lights/darks which reflect and illuminate them. They are neither genuine; nor are they ingenuine. Only in some essentialist ideality, can we discuss masks and deceits and disguises as if they reside in truth, somewhere else in another time.

Disguises "work," deceits deceive only within the perspectives of others' imaginings and calculations. We who love magic, who pay homage to the illusions of the stage and movies and video; we, the bearers and the wearers of the masks, looking out, still think we look like we look. It is others looking at the appearance and expression which they call our face, who see lies and deceits; or who cannot discern some truth for which they search vainly.

Like the sage sayings of Ecclesiastes, it is a vanity which causes us to seek what is not there. Instead, we might search for Being within its paradoxical aspects. Like the simultaneous particulars and universals within we are always taught thinking and seeing, we are simultaneously who we are and who others see in us. In Nietzsche's sense of the *bermensch*, to move on in life as an overcoming, rather than a resolution of the paradox(es) of Being, better we should contemplate our Next Places, rather than bewail some Lost kingdom of the genuine.

Is it some sense of "imperfection" which drives some to wail that the expression is mask to the person; some wish to destroy the present and the future, to assert that Being was, but is not now? What sense of the enigma of Being emerge within this wish?

Immediate Consciousness: Recently I saw a picture of a "kitchen-nook" built-into the bungalows of some houses in America in the 1920's. Memories poured back of five or so years of youth (6-11 years of age), when I passed many hour and many meals, thoughts, books, radio serials, family gathered or alone. I hadn't seen such a room, very much like mine, in many years, correct in most of its details: the benches, the windows, the table, and me.

What it brings to mind, in the present context, is that I remember distinctly a thought that even now pops to mind: that I never did or thought a single thing, but three at least, which were distinct in thought and in activity. I read voraciously, listened to the radio, and often ate all at the same time, and learned, attuned my ears to the nuances of sound which later made me a linguist, and became quite hefty. All these concentrations, and their attendant difficulties have stood by me during the ensuing years. And I am still wary that there is a singularity which might be called the contents of "immediate consciousness."

I come at this problem primarily, perhaps, as a descriptive linguist whose notion of language is from some other culture, where an unknown tongue is spoken, looking-back at the English of America. I approach it, as well, as a would-be violinist whose bank of techniques is, though lacking a certain polish, quite formidable. In either of these contexts, I am aware (at once, I think) that a great deal of what I do and know in order to speak or to play the violin, is quite immediate, but more is "out-of-awareness."

My English-speaking tongue and articulators are all poised, with a kind of knowing which is in sharp contrast to the tongue of any other language: it knows not only what to do in this moment, but in all moments; it (my tongue) is so well-knowing, so habitual in its journeys, that to speak another tongue requires very considerable "retraining," a suspension, as it were of immediate consciousness, and a re-placement with another. My violin playing thinking sees black notes upon staffs, and creates through my arms and fingers stopping strings, drawing bow, music that Bach would say he dreamt of and wrote down.

What, in all this, is immediate; what is not? It is not so much, in any instant, that I do not know what is knowing, but that so much knowledge, so many perspectives come to bear upon each instant that to bracket out "right now" seems paradoxically obvious and complex beyond imagination.

By now, in violin play, I bring to each next note, various perspectives, an interplay of considerations which go together to make this next note "musical" and "correct." In each (next) moment there are years of practice, various heard and studied performances, much experience, which come to focus upon this instant. What, then, is immediate? What conscious?

I think there is some story which comes into this notion of the stream of consciousness, some sense that our non-conscious is not so readily "available" to consciousness that we call it the "unconsciousness," and analogize it to the world of vision: the visible versus the invisible. But here again, the world is quite "full." The visualized setting is no monolithic picture, but one with details that we can manage and manipulate, and turn-about this way and that, create characters that we engage, and create a "oneself" who enters in. What is immediate?

It seems that the immediate is much more complicated than we had thought. Having presumed that the body is "in" the immediate, that the groundedness of time always had (has) some immediate reference to bodily being, the problem of consciousness has appeared to (re)solvable by positing a sense of continuance (Kant's "pure reason," Chomsky's "innate grammar") which was a feature of human Being, and various ways in which this "opened" to each moment, or brought "judgment" to bear on the moment. It seemed, like our depiction of the content of language, a kind of single linearity: one message at a time, which we could abstract from the remainder of Being and focus upon independently. As Plato had told us (*Republic*: 9), "nature" has created the ideas prior to our Being. Being is somehow to "fit" ourselves to these pre-arranged ideas. Immediacy is some way that perception can enter into this arrangement, and be up-dated, resisted, or even denied.

Instead, it seems clear to me, that we have other "positions": other ways of "standing outside" of the present; places, groundings, from which we can view viewing; perspectives which are comparative, historical, mutual, rhetorical. If, as it seems to me, the notion of Being an individual is indeed emergent within the infant-parent relationship, that individuality is largely "defined" by others, that we Become an individual always in interaction with some notions of ourselves as others (would) have us, then we are always and simultaneously one and many. What is "immediate" consciousness partakes of the semiotic rhetoric of Being. The very notion of the present, of immediacy is thus, and remains, problematic.

It is not at all obvious, since our "bodies" do not necessarily partake of/in time the same way that we all come at the immediate in, even, similar ways. How we are able to (ever) find the same present as others, engage in any mutuality of understanding, becomes extremely intriguing.

Where does consciousness reside?—not what is "in" it—seems a more productive question.

How do we find the present of others?—seems to be a locus of what is even meant by the term "consciousness." That we can come into mutual contact with others, in contexts where this is "called-for," seems—like the nature of sleep—so ordinary and obvious and second nature, that we find them easy to do, and think that we have some way of "understanding" them.

Even Heidegger, accepting the enigma of Being, tried to fill-in all those aspects of Being which would account for Being and Time. The answer, the resolving of the enigma, resides in my view, in the rhetorical-semiotic nature of Being, not in the Aristotelian acceptance of Being as primarily an individual. Here, in rhetoric, in the notion of the sociality and contextual aspects of Being, the philosophical problematic and enigma of Being dissolve, and bring us forcibly into the existential problematics of, as it were, Being-proper.

The Problem of Evil: Niebuhr (1941) praises/damns the rise of science as substituting for the presumption of evil as a feature of our human nature, the presumption of good, at least, of our being, by nature, neutral.

It is as if, he worries, that by praising our rational aspects, we too easily presume that knowledge begets virtue somehow. Indeed, he claims, it simply removes the problem of evil from our direct sight, and hides it to arise again, ever more viciously. Similarly, Rousseau in his First Discourse, claims that knowledge (of the Arts and Sciences) really is "based" on or underlain by the virtues. Thus they are fundamental to and prior to knowledge, and we must attend to them: the passions, the virtues, the dangerous aspects, the edges of our Being.

Instead of being concerned that evil resides somehow within us—in our nature—the rhetorical approach to Being notes that we are, from the beginning, political-interactive creatures. The question of individuality, of what are its features, is emergent. Individuality, rather than being inherent within (each of) us, develops with the notion of conscience an aspect of that individuality.

By conscience, I mean that the individual is (always?) in relation to others, having to get some sense of boundaries and of extension: where one is, where one cannot go, how one is to behave are all notions which emerge along with the person's individuality. As the (developing) child is treated as if individual, the nature and extent of this aspect of oneself is not so clear: how "far" it goes, how to gather things and other Beings to oneself; how to get attention, how not to stretch demands beyond the respondents' willingness. The "discovery" and elaboration of one's concept of oneself is complicated, alternatively clear and fuzzy, and it changes with increasing size and age: a two-year old can do some things (e.g., "impinge" on others' space) which most four-year olds cannot.

Much of ontogenesis is in the play of discovering boundednesses.

Conscience (approximately "superego") is not an attribute only of the individual, but emerges along with individuality, from one's discursive in-relatedness. The "definitions" of the boundaries of one's Being—what is too much, not enough (and of what...)—are located within the discursive "field." Parents "grant" one's individuality, but simultaneously limit it.

It is delimited—in their terms—but gradually (much of what we call time and progress is located in these processes and/or reconceptualizations.) Much of what we call "evil" develops within the "negotiations" for this rhetorical notion of the individual: just how "conscience" is doled out, demanded, integrated into relationships: if a child "oversteps" some (parental, socially defined) notion of its Being, how is this conveyed, enforced, reinforced.

If, for example, a child in encouraged to do something, how far is this encouraged; is it discouraged, in the same breath; is it "allowed" to go way beyond the parental sense of proportion?

Here is the seat of evil: in the discovery of one's individuality; in the politics of one's Being; in the parental letting-go and pulling-back-in; toward a child's sense of individuality which the parents find not too uncomfortable, but "interesting" in the sense of that child becoming a person. Tantrums develop right here: given more "rope" than one can "handle," then being reeled back in like a caught fish, just as one is exploring its new dimensions. Behaving "badly," while the parental eye glints with mock anger and a hint of pride is another mixed message like Bateson's "double-bind." 1969) All in all, this involves politics; the search for the possibilities of one's extent and extensions into the world...but, defined discursively.

One cannot "know" evil, as a child. Nor can she/he know goodness. I observe that each child is bound within the logics and politics of that family, and is forever working out one's Being within the traces of that early context. In any case, evil, goodness, the virtues, the passions, and how these are handled as aspects of one's Being, are not built-ins, not aspects of one's Being in any sense *a priori*, but aspects of the negotiations for one's sense of her/his own individuality and Being: questions of "will," of the sense and largesse of one's "responsibility" and "conscience" are worked-out and worked-on as narratives of "who I am" in the oft times paradoxical context of questioning "who am I?"

Only in the rhetorical accounting of emergent individuality, is it at all clear why there is often the "twinning" of two such opposed notions as evil and love. Both are "explorations" of the edges of one's Being, of the boundaries of oneself. (In a sense, both evil and love can be seen as aspects of the "size" of one's Being, and of one's being able to find contentment or restlessness, a sense of being at-home or in exile from others; from oneself...) Here, Being truly finds itself to be an enigma: especially from the "inside" where one find her/his Being to be much in flux, one's boundednesses unclear and debated even within consciousness; while, externally, in others' view, one appears as continuous and as constant as the irreducible "thing" which Aristotle went on about...

Perhaps (I have thought) the "size" and boundedness of one's Being is most truly observed at the moment of the death of one's "significant" others. To the extent that we mourn, to that extent we mourn the "loss" of another within our Being. The moments of the day when we might expect a call to be received with a joy, a fear, gladness or sadness, these moments must be themselves "deadened." No more... no more! What is it to mourn well or poorly? To "bury" the dead, truly; or to keep them alive in Being, to transform them in ourselves? Here there is no enigma of Being: but there are endless puzzles whose power within us often takes on a life of its own, and evolves in the memories of narrative. The fact of Being, which reveals itself within mourning, is that we are (have become) others; that we are, at once, ourselves and others, and that the enigma is in the construction of self and individuality that we are "told" that we are, to be...

The Size of Being: An aspect (linked to the problem of evil!) is of the "size" of Being. Where—if anywhere—are one's "limits"? Can we (must we not) compete even with God (as in the Tower of Babel)? Can we (must) compete with, or merely become as big as our parents, our friends, our children, our teachers, the King (Queen), Captain Marvel? SHAZAM! How big am I today? Will I grow or diminish? Is this a question of stature? Or of power? Or of its felt lack?

In a God-given sense of Being, where God has given us (me/you) this earth for my domicile, I am at least as "big" as I am. The earth is my home, it has been constructed for me.

In a scientific, Enlightenment, mechanistic world, I am much diminished, my existence not even present within the cosmology which informs the very conditions of Being, but leaves me without.

In a "fixed" society, or in a "high-context" society where everyone is "known" to everyone, and is always in "contact," I am who I am. This has been determined and known since I was little: if it fits, I am who I am; if not, then I can (at least possibly) change my size by changing society; killing the King, I can revolt.

Where we are all equal, the temptations are more complicated, the passions more far-reaching: "I can become all there is," is at war with, "there is no more becoming." The awesomeness of democracy, the possibilities at war with: risks, responsibilities, the dependence on oneself to judge one's own Being makes the notion of one's size continually problematic. Whether one can even achieve the authority over one's own domains, fades into the temptation to bureaucratize Being, and fix one's boundedness yet again, as if the King (Queen) had her/his royal guns sticking in our ribs poking at Being. If only, Kafka (1961)—if only Kafka were here to tell us in some parable that "waiting at the door of Being" does not banish the problematic, but merely makes it wait... until Being is no longer.

This dilemma is a general case of Freire's (2007) "problem," where the oppressed upon gaining power, in turn oppress all the others in order that their demands for size and for its concomitant authority be served well and properly. The path toward solution is in the direct study of authority with teachers worthy of that name; not merely in the substantive tradition of Socrates, but opening up the possibility of (self-) empowerment within, and emerging from the Socratic dialogue.

The problematic of the size of one's Being can be likened to the two-headed beast who is (often; usually) busy devouring the other end of her/his self.

Love ya... Language: Western thought has been largely a temptation to by-pass our engagement with any actuality, rather to analyze the language by which we know that actuality. Only in the later Wittgenstein, beginning with a quote from Augustine's "Confessions," do we begin to grapple at all seriously with the "use" of language. Even here, the dance of Being with what is called "language" seems exterior to our Being.

Has substituting language for Being contributed to the enigma? Has it merely extended the enigma with a (constantly renewable) promise that the proper analysis and understanding of language would lead to an understanding of...?

Whereas Heidegger is concerned with the fundamentals conditions of a theory which would create an ontology, the use of language as metaphor for Being seems to by-pass the grounding necessary to that ontology. Or does it?

If we remain within the metaphysical tradition of Aristotle, at once problematizing Being, then seeming to offer a path towards its understanding via language, probably any solution to the enigma is no firmer than the quality and nature of its presumptions. They are briefly: language is the set of all sentences—or the rules of the underlying grammar which generate all those (indefinitely large set) sentences. The units are names of objects and their predications. Human development is via naming objects toward understanding of the world. It (language) is "located" in the individual; in each individual. That this statement of what is language seems so self-evident may be taken as an indication of what we believe already, and what must be questioned to its core, in order that we may (re-)solve the enigma of Being. The path of Being human involves some simultaneity of finite and infinite, and that the study of language stresses the universal, infinite, and ideality of our Being.

Instead, I want to consider what I have called elsewhere "the Human Grammar." It is calculated to resolve all the problems mentioned above, but it is rhetorical in its essence, just as the human condition. It is, at once, individual and interactional, finite and universal, and is analytic into nouns, verbs, and so on. It (like its materialistic "orientation") is more powerful than "sentence" grammars in its analysis of semantics, showing that different aspects of language operate in different modes, and that language syntax is primarily interactional, only secondarily individual. It hints, at least, at how intelligibility works so well, so quickly. Rather than an end, in and of itself, which will somehow apply to and account for understanding and Being, its analysis seems to be self-limiting, pointing out other paths for further study: toward the study of context, toward the non-verbal, gestural, and tone-of-voice aspects of discourse... hopefully, towards its own self-criticism; towards some fuller understanding of "primary" categories which we have tended to attribute at some intuitive level to the conditions of being human, rather than to the processes of living. Finally, it shows how Being is semiotic in its core. Does it solve, resolve, make the enigma of Being disappear as a problem? We shall see.

4.

ON HUMAN NATURE

I Entering the Human Nature Issue

The Apology: In Plato's dialogue *Apology*, Socrates refers to what is the nature of humans: why they act and think like they do; how they would respond to his defense of his being and teaching; why they condemned him. In defense of his life he praised his dedication to the truth, rather than pandering to the opinions and praises of others. Socrates, in his "apologia," eloquently spells out what is the best life, toward integrity, virtue and wisdom. He says, also, that he is a good citizen—praising the gods and the city-state of Athens—that he worked not for riches, but for the good of humankind.

In the *Apology*, Socrates was accused of mis-education, corrupting the thoughts and knowing of the youths of Athens, and being godless, against the best interests of Athens. He was convicted and sentenced to death. In his last speech to the tribunal of "justice" he explained why he would not avoid death: death being either nothing (like a good night's dreamless sleep), or an adventure of deepest and most interesting dimensions.

Socrates, the teacher, a person who thought himself and was acknowledged by others as a person of wisdom, thought he could improve the state of being human by good laws, a good education, and laws well-constructed in a reasoned manner by those philosophers who were dedicated to justice and to truth. Wisdom was less a matter of knowledge, and more of critical thought. Human nature was complex, but able to be altered and directed well—by the highest and clearest reasoning and good laws. Plato's *Republic* is a model for a series of utopias in which the "best" sort of society is depicted.

Some modern "constructors" of human nature are opposed to the Platonic. Reasoning, in the minds of some, is exactly what we do *not* need. Reasoning, rational thought, is just what has gotten us in a huge mess, and should be disregarded or overcome. Inferring, we are told, from other species who do not (it is claimed) even possess reasoning, is where our only future lies. We are on a path toward self-destruction because that is our nature, and we have become self-destructive and must be controlled. This notion of reason, which has led to a "false" construction of "freedom" is no longer tenable. In the words of a behavioral biologist (Lorenz, 1966) we need a group of philosopher-biologists to see our "true" nature by inferring from other species; in the words of a behavioral psychologist (Skinner, 1938), we need a group of philosopher-behaviorists who will lead us to control ourselves.

Things have not worked out vs. things can work out: the juxtaposition is not exactly opposed. But what these depictions of the future—one wonderful, the other bleak—have in common is the concept of a privileged few: the philosopher-kings who will lead us via their wisdom, on proper paths. For truth and knowledge are, on both sides, hidden to ordinary view; privileged and open only to the seekers of "truth." Obviously there is some disagreement as to the truth nature of truth, knowledge, thence to the nature of being human...

"Step by step we have become habituated to the idea that the wretched state in which we are living is the natural condition..." (Kierkegaard, 1845: 302)

"In the old days they believed that whatever one hears concerns the individual himself (de te fabula), that everything concerns himself: now everybody believes that he can tell a fable which concerns all mankind but not himself." (Kierkegaard, 1845: 394)

The Dilemma: The difficulty is one that constantly dogs the thinker of any sort, the artist included. Any effort to evolve categories or forms adequate to the job of making sense of one's experience eventually threatens to backlash, affecting the quality of experience itself. Reflection and the things it brings to us as important does, in time, tend to occupy center-stage in our view of the world. We begin to see what we are looking for, and look for it because we have come to think it is the thing worthy of primary notice. Not even in our earliest years is experience a totally undifferentiated field, unstructured by such foci of importance: language, the cues of elders and companions, the myriad features of environment in the widest understanding of that term, all serve to direct our attentions, influence our valuations. As life proceeds, it becomes increasingly difficult to avoid, in T.S. Eliot's phrase, the fate of having "had the experience and missed the meaning." For the meanings we have progressively imposed upon experience place certain landmarks in the limelight, leaving others cloaked in shadow. A truncated theory of friendship, marriage, or art can in time blunt our perceptions, blind us to the shifting tones that for another man, or for another age, become the very focus of contemplation and evaluation.

"This problem of experience and meaning only complicates when the thinker involved is at the same time trying to see his world in the light of a religious revelation. How does human experience relate to the experience of the world that revelation suggests should be the experience of the Christian?...How is human life to be understood, when some at least can claim, and believers themselves be sometimes tempted to think, that the understanding proposed in revelation is a different one from that which man, left to his own resources, could arrive at?" (St. Augustine, *Early Theory of Man*, 386-9 A.D.)

"The Fall" into the human body implies a rejection of sense data and truth.

"The fact is that we have no first premise." (Becker, 1932: 16)

"There really is no occasion for despair: our world can be computed even if it doesn't exist." (Becker, 1932: 27)
"...when the mind is satisfied with the pattern of the things it sees, it has what it calls an 'explanation' of the things—it has found the 'cause' of them." (Becker, 1932: 29)

Some Issues which Move this Author: 1.) The current attack on reason! (See my *Nietzsche's Prophecy: the Crisis in Meaning"*) 2.) How one comes to "possess" enlightened self-interest (or any other interest)! 3.) A "bodily" view of morality. (See: 8 *Morality*) 4.) Notions of culture, "race," and other categories.

"I am not so irrational as to despise Public Opinion; I have no thought of making light of a tribunal established in the conditions and necessities of human nature. It has its place in the very constitution of society; it ever has been, it ever will be, whether in the commonwealth of nations, or in the humble and secluded village. But wholesome as it is as a principle, it has, in common with all things human, great imperfections and makes many mistakes. Too often it is nothing else than what the whole world opines, and no one in particular. Your neighbor assures you that everyone is of one way of thinking; that there is but one opinion on the subject; and while he claims not to be answerable for it, he does not hesitate to propound and spread it. In such cases, everyone is appealing to everyone else; and the constituent members of a community one by one think it their duty to defer and succumb to the voice of that same community as a whole." (Newman 1902)

"Now it is impossible for existence to be caused only by the essential principles of a being, since no being whose existence is caused is sufficient of itself to cause its own existence. It follows that a being whose existence is other than its own essence has that existence as caused by another. Now this cannot be said of God since we say that God is the first efficient cause. It is impossible, therefore, that in God existence is other than His essence." (Thomas Aquinas, *Primacy of Existence*; Banez (1966))

Essence is form; existence is actuality—primary.

Human Nature: as the history of (the definition of the) virtues and the emotions? What necessarily constitutes a theory of Human Nature?

On Universals: in Human Nature...the Species

Miriam: There are three primary sorts of people: men, women, and children. Of these, two are constant throughout, and will always be: male and female.

Janis: Yes, but...

Miriam (breaking-in): What we want in any accounting is what is everywhere, in all times. Do you know? I was in Jamaica living in the hills with poor people and they, even they, are talking about the survival of the species. Everyone agrees that we are in dangerous times. And we must survive!

Harvey [an observer]: (to himself): Oh? Why?—*must* we?

Miriam: The trouble is, the fact is that the question of survival arises because the "construction" of the world, the actuality, the ideas, power, the will to hurt and destroy, are in the hands of men. The only chance we have is to attempt to take the power which men got... and give more, take more for women. Not only change their power, but in the change, alter the nature of men-women relationships.

Janis: How will we do that? Will it help? Why do you think there are only two kinds of humans?

Miriam: That's only too obvious! Male and female. That is the basic, the fundamental and foundational.

Janis: But, they never exist, except with respect to one another.

Virtues and their Motivations: Much of the history of the idea of human nature is filled with notions of what is proper or good or excellent vs. bad types of persons or personal Virtues might be. Schemes of the good life, the "ends" of society and nations are constructed to enhance or control whatever virtues were "in" (popular) in those times (are "in" in these times). One approach to the study of human nature is by considering: (1) the virtues and (2) how they arose, were maintained and changed—with respect to particular societies and times, their provenience and descendance; how this affected their ethics/politics, esthetics, education toward these virtues, schemes of "having" or obtaining them. They are underlain, usually (but perhaps not always) by motivational or "impulse" theories of various sorts; active vs. passive (theories of "will" vs. predetermination and certain environmental theories).

Will (Schopenhauer): The psychological-social question? Do individuals/gods "possess" wills? If no, then why do we do what we do?—life is an illusion! If yes, then of what sort(s), how "caused," how broad, where reside, how plastic, how motivated. Theories of life mean theories of positive will (theories of life-as-death may contain theories of will; but may not!)

The (Social) Reality: Those who stay alive demonstrate what parents (sponsors) consider to be active wills. This is not an exhaustive truth (i.e., we are more than mere wills), but it is a way of the world, of this and probably other social species. The rest do not survive.

"In fact contempt for the political process is a very widespread method of masking subordination to those who direct it." (Jaworsky, 1980)

Will: Parents teach, look for, observe, and believe that their children possess a will—an active, dynamic sense of self which talks, thinks, does, has power over itself (and them). The children accede to/accept this picture of will, and come to act as if they are actually in possession of will, mostly in the same senses as their parents' observations and reactions. A great human fiction? Perhaps. But one which *is*... which *works*.

Life and Death: Two "great" theoretical traditions about the nature of being, of life. The tradition of and from death creates (from time-to-time) the notion that life "is" deeply an aspect of death; a preparation, a very small moment in some eternity - life, an illusion, the body, a testing; unreal in any experiential sense (certain exceptions á la Kierkegaard).

Life theories which are mirror images to the death theories (not all are) try to make death an aspect of life in the sense that it is life which goes on forever—or at least till it seems to be beyond interest. The body is all (non-dualism), each moment is forever or all there is. But neither of these has a strong theory of experience "in" the world.

Conjunctions of Existence: To be alive while particular others are alive is in many senses less important than the particular histories through which each of them has gotten here. Those histories are so powerful that they can enable us neither to see nor to appreciate those conjunctions which some spiritual (e.g. Native American) traditions find overwhelmingly obvious.

Spirituality: In a world full of different, often opposing and contradictory religions, one can still appreciate that others believe in their own traditions, that they each try in some sense to transcend their experience (some altogether, some in each moment). To be spiritual is to appreciate this without being captured by any specific tradition, but to dwell on the wonders of being and becoming; and to not be so frightened that one has to accede to pictures of being which are not honest to oneself and best friends/spouse.

Human Nature and History: ...many questions. Are humans the same in all eras? Does different life experience—individual, age grades, etc.—make one different? How? Strength? Gullibility? Openness or resistance to certain ideas? Different histories, languages, traditions—in what senses are we children of our parents? Are these senses always the same? Or can they bring us up to not be like them? Do we have equal access to the stories we are being told, as, for example, the tellers of those stories? (e.g., Confucius). In what senses do we learn from history? Can we imagine, usefully, what great figures would have done in this era, in one's own setting and experience? How does the nature of how we see ourselves affect our theories of human nature? Are these so inexplicably intertwined that they cannot be disconnected? (e.g., is what it takes for a "humble" persona to discuss world-class theories the same as what it takes for God's "chosen" to do the same?)

Why the Human Nature Discussion? Because questions/observations of other species are quite different from the stories we have told ourselves about them: they (many) are social, communicative, possess something like knowledge; learn, change, survive in an experiential world. Because these stories we have told ourselves about other species become important/are important in delimiting what we claim to be human and uniquely human. So the discussion arises because the delimitation of what is human appears to be *incorrect* in some possibly deep senses.

How, a rational person asks, could one's theory of human nature be said to be "incorrect"? How could one claim to know what is correct since we live out our lives with respect to being theorists of our own nature? The question thence comes down to: what sorts of human nature theorists are we and why? That is, there must be some slippage between what we believe and what we believe we believe!

Human Nature and Gravity: More than 3 centuries it took to discover that Newton's apple applies to the human condition—except that we grow on the ground, not above it, and falling is a relational factor, not a free-fall. Always in some gravitational dance, we spend our first two decades defying it, the next acceding to its power in counts of years and eras. The apparent paradox is that we are, at once, gravity and users of gravity. Aging is gravity!

Social Reality: The nature of experience is determined, it is said, by what others claim reality to be. But that claim cannot be anti-real, anti-physical in any critical sense. And where do "they"—who determine us—find out? Isn't it a question of infinite regression?

Who, on the other hand, can deny that we are aspects of a history and language which is deeply social: agreed-upon if only to talk, about? There remain questions of will, of determining what one can determine about oneself, how one comes to conceptualize possibilities of becoming (also social?), how one pursues them...

If I say to myself that I *will* do something, is it only or merely because others have willed me to will this or that? What difference does it make, if I can and do act out of this will to action, the exact senses in which it can be said to have been *determined*? (And, e.g., what do teachers do in the world?) Doesn't death, e.g., become a determiner for the Christian?

Illuminating the Human Nature Discussion: I presume that our neglect of the argument indicates that it has been considered "well-understood" until now; that we have assumed that we knew the nature of Human Nature in essential outline, and were merely filling-in detail. Good times push large problems into obscurity and bad times unleash those aspects which had been presumed banished, or merely personal and personality quirks. To me this merely indicates that we have infinite ways to hide; to develop theories of our being which manage to take those aspects of the human condition we dislike in any era, and create a theory which declares them abnormal, thus not me, not us.

The problem is how to illuminate an issue which we hide so well, or even deny is an issue (except in bad times)?

Natural Selection:...is invoked to demonstrate, against the view that species are continuous and fixed forever; that the "mere" workings of nature are sufficient to "cause" or otherwise account for evolution; that the natural world is sufficiently harsh that many individuals of whatever types do not survive; that those who survive are either fit or capable of adaptation to a harsh (and/or "new") environment; that those who are fit are individually or collectively at least slightly different in certain ways (minimally in ways which permit survival) from their brethren and cousins who do not survive; that these differences "move" in such directions as to "produce" offspring who are different from their collective antecedents sufficiently that they are a "new" species.

This is not to say that *Nature caused selection*, but that the vicissitudes of life (due to weather, volcanoes, disease, or chance) caught some creatures unprepared, unaware, or that it could have. Whether evolution actually happened *because* of natural selection is moot, and remains debatable, and to be demonstrated—if possible (e.g., changes in response to modern antibiotics).

As an argument against the fixity of species, it is plausible and generally persuasive. It is not an argument against theology in general, but opposes certain particular notions of the deity as ultimate, once-and-for-all creator. It is not necessarily anti-theistic, nor atheistic in principle; it opposes certain forms of theism, most particularly (so far) those concerned primarily with the "origins" of humankind, of life...

The entire argument depends, of course, on definitions and conceptions of "nature," most of which (all of which?) seem debatable at the present time.

The biologists' "present" is a period of at least 10,000 years!

Existence: Why are we here?—Often couples itself with questions of: Are we here? Do we exist? Isn't "this" (worldly apparition I call myself) an aspect of "death," of non-existence?

The question implies (already in its asking, because its posing already entails a world-view; i.e., why would anyone ask about his/her own existence unless s/he expected a form of negative answer?)—A reason, a cause to our being which is more/other than the so-called "biological facts."

What is the form of an "answer" (more than, perhaps, a mere response) to such a question? God created us; Eve sinned and we "fell" into our bodies? Always "more than" mere biology—and it raises questions of what is a biology, and how do we claim that we know? It entails theories of "time" (e.g., when is the "present"? and what is an *observed*; what is observable?)

The biologists' answer: to survive! We are here in order to survive. A trivial fact, from many points of view, becomes fascinating when one begins to realize the travails through which we must have gone, in order (merely) *to be here* (and why the theologian-anti-biologists want to shorten the history of being; i.e., to again trivialize evolutionary survival difficulties).

But: why pose this question?—Why we are here? Why is this not sufficient being? Will wishing change the actuality, or (merely) change our perceptions of it? (And/or will the perceptions lead to actual changes in its reality?)

Virtues and Emotions: Either/or, in various combinations structure the visions of our worlds. That which is prized, those to be avoided, to be sought, to be frightened of this comprises the bases of our world-views. Fear, courage—here, axes of being reside: to overcome fear—a powerful principle; the awesome power of the fear of fear.

One more piece: what to do with/about pain?

Biology—A Critique: To use the term "biology" or "biological" in reference to the human condition is at once to inform, to demarcate, and to obfuscate. Like the use of the term "anthropology" to talk only about "others" (exotic and/or dead), the history of the term is taken as the study not of life, but of other species. In both "biology" and "anthropology" we become residual beings, defined and existing only in contrast with the focus, the subject matter, the others. More ways to lose meaning?—To be the leftovers in our own perorations?

The fact is, in Western thinking, that there is no biology without anthropology, no anthropology without biology because humans are juxtaposed with other creatures in this tradition (body=animal/nature). Any change in our knowledge, even in our conceptions of others or of what is human, affects our thinking about the others. To state the primacy of one, to even believe they are independent subject areas, is a high order of fakery. To study one *is* to study the other. To not know this, to hide or deny it, is delusory or a lie.

"Biology"—used in isolation, rather *as if* it is isolable, is already to have assumed much about the life of other species (thus, about humans), that probably ought not to be assumed.

Life's Surprises: 1.) There is continuity. 2.) There is change. 3.) There is death. 4.) There is life.

Entire visions, whole eras are constructed herein: which questions are considered; which ones seriously; in what order?

Epochal Battles in the Shrunken World: 1.) *Justice*—by those who feel downtrodden. How do people(s) come to perceive themselves as "downtrodden"? What will get them even, ahead, justified, treated fairly? Do some want control, or a little more, of what they think they deserve, or what they see others have, or riches, or to be left alone, or...? "Terrorism," civil disobedience, mutiny, martyrdom—attempts to "win," to call attention to... to make the world more "serious"? 2.) *Existence/Reality*—in a world of different, perhaps competing "-isms," the wonder of what is... right... real, of what is life, and what is it worth. To be some -one, some nation, some caste: to *not* be...

To live right vs. to die right!

Truth vs. Opinion: Absolute vs. Relative: Are these, indeed, the same arguments? Or do their overlapping semantic fields blind us to their arenas of difference?

Example: of the string player whose intonation is very good: I tune my A string to 440 Hz (give or take a few Hz). I tune my D and E to the A; listening for the best 5th, I turn the pegs aft and yon, surrounding and dampening the relationships until they are very good (and depend, obviously, on my aesthetic—but good intonation is not so difficult to discern). And the G is tuned a 5th down from the D and in-relation. Then, I try to play "in tune," a notion which is "fairly" absolute, even if based, in the first instance, on a set of relationships. It leaves a great deal of room for illusion and trickery, but the limits of in-tuneness are very narrow. And, it is in this sense, that we are both absolutists and relativists, simultaneously.

It is an empirical question—and an important one—which is which, however.

The Superorganic (Agency and the Agent): ...or how the underpinnings of social science have become bureaucratized! It was "Grimm's law" 1822 (or Law) which did us in. It stated that language changes. Language has an evolution; language evolves. This was the essence of the study called philology. And it was interesting and important news.

It meant, among other things, that questions of meaning, translation, and history are intertwined; that a literal understanding of ancient texts is impossible, but can be possibly elucidated by careful scholarship into the study of language and cultural change; that life is ongoing, processual and not fixed or essential—at least with respect to whatever we base upon some arche-language (e.g. Adamic) notion of human derivation whose supposed elucidation would be through etymology.

It meant also that to whatever ever extent the human psyche is dependent upon or intertwined with language and linguistic processes, it is probably also changing and evolving, almost in spite of itself. Some aspects of the zeitgeist are due to linguistic change. And that's interesting.

What Grimm's Law also did was to persuade many thinkers that language has/had an independent existence: that it can be characterized, grasped, and studied by itself, *per se*; that it is a "force" which exists independently of "its" speakers, and lately, that the study of language is the place to go to study the human psyche. Language *is* the mind, is like the mind, establishes the mind, or controls it. (A corollary is that as language becomes Language, the existence of "the mind" is also reaffirmed.)

Carried along on these enthusiastic wings were other superorganic concepts such as: Society and Culture, each of which was given *its* laws, *its* evolution. But...

But there are no people; only Language. No people → no existence; it has led to a new and modern form of nihilism.

The fact that people(s) are dynamic, and change in what/how they hear and speak, and that turns out—on a large scale—to be what we observe or realize as Language changes; that fact of live humans disappears from our remembering... as with Society, Culture...

The invention of normality, statistics, etc., also derives from this notion of superorganic, and appears to give it substance by providing an underpinning characterization of it, which further appears to be mathematical, thus really lawful.

It used to be that we gave "agency" only to the deity; now we give agency to any gathering category → the Transcendental Pretense! (Solomon 1979)

Libertarianism: The only problem with libertarianism (Ayn Rand) is that there are other people in the world (individualism gone wild!)

Enlightenment and Society:

"But this [neglect of society] left the Enlightenment with perhaps an impossible task, which we are still trying to carry on today: to develop a theory of society without first taking the concept of society seriously." (Solomon, 1979:31)

Human Nature Theories: What do human nature theories include (explicitly or implicitly): a theory of the world, a theory of time and space (not always interlinked), a theory of society—a theory of the individual; a theory of causation; of history.

Do these theories differ on where one's assumptions begin, how they are put together? -- e.g., in Western thought, physics is primary, being is meta- or after- physics.

Empty Categories (& their Importance): What is not there, that is "left out," that we do not notice (because of our predilections or our perspectives, etc.)? How important are these omissions; how would they change our ideas and theories? Are certain things "left out" on purpose; or do they not get noticed because they seem trivial or something other; disconnected? Similarly there are "residual" categories like "bit buckets" in computer jargon and "wellness" in the context of pathology-as-medicine.

The Meta-Curriculum and the Interstices: I work in the places between, the subjects between—what there is and what there appears to be. Where (they say) there are boundaries, edges of subject matters, of inquiry that is where I dance. Asking the proprietors of subject areas: Why don't you ask? What about?—within the logics of their subjects, and they don't and they won't, often because an outsider asks; the queries which count have already been decided upon and the matter is closed. Those I ask have no nerve and are producing for the ghosts of their youths. They own what they have, and any new query threatens ownership—and because they all have an imperium—to take the rightness of what they own—and attempt to own all inquiry thereby increasing their holdings, but particularly justifying what they do and who (they think) they are.

Human Nature and Nature: In meta-physics, where human is some sort of residuum, human nature is related to, derived from our notions of nature and all that entails: what is life (for)? What is the nature of existence? (How) do we relate to nature?—causally, likeness of bodies, susceptible to the same or different "Laws." So in this important sense the issue of human nature is the issue of what is nature, how do we know and study, and what is our (human) place within/outside of nature.

But there are several competing ways of thinking about nature (and some others we haven't considered yet, I'm certain), and each of these directly affects how we think about human nature. And, vice-versa: how we think about nature depends on our orientation; habits, what strikes us as important questions or observations, from sickness/health, life/death, from a normative model; also how we solve these questions.

Does, e.g., nature possess—or is nature governed by laws (*logos*)? Where does *logos* reside? How do we locate "it"? Is it a constancy for which we seek—and find? Is it caused—or does it somehow merely inhere?—in nature, in our observations?

Does this entire orientation or vision depend on a zeitgeist (e.g., does the question of "existence" now arise?)—when? why? when not? why not?

Heraclitus vs. Plato:

Heraclitus: "Whatever comes from sight, hearing, learning from experience: this I prefer." (XIV; Kahn, 1981))

Plato: "...have sight and hearing any truth in them? Are they not, as the poets are always telling us, inaccurate witnesses?" (*Phaedo* 65)

The Problem: have we fallen in love with our imaginations?

Logos vs. Chaos: The (mistaken) interpretation of Heraclitus which froze his experiential oppositions into some natural dialectic: where opposites exist, merely are, rather than as being derived from experience (e.g., the notion of "wellness" derives from the experience of being sick within allopathic medicine).

The taking of the opposition between continuity and change as somehow being between continuity and chaos: that is, if the notion of change, of history is considered, it would lead to chaos, to a kind of falling-off the world, into an abyss, out of control. The rejection of (the experience of) change, the creation of metaphysics in which change and experience is to be considered illusory, death is banished, as in chaos. Thus any and all experience of change. Thus the creationist battle against evolution is against chaos, not against the experiential, observational idea of evolution as mere change. The danger of admitting any change is that we are in constant danger of loss of control: of chaos.

Culture: About 1962, I *lost* the anthropological concept of Culture. At the least the report that a group of macaques in Japan seemed to be handing on "new" habits or customs from one generation to the next, raised the question of whether humans possess Culture in any sense uniquely. Not that I didn't (and don't) believe humans are unique (I actively identify humans and non-human; I must possess such categories in my deeper being), but that the notion of Culture (and, for me, also Language) no longer seemed sufficient to account for such species differences.

By now the concept of Culture has been claimed for other social animals (E.O. Wilson 1998), and the notion of Culture has moved from anthropology to literature (as have I). In the present context, the sense of Culture is that it is an omnibus notion accounting for human-group-category differences, but seems to gather very little with it.

On Embodying the Human: What a strange notion, embodiment. Somehow some of us have discovered the philosophical problem of life and of living. Somehow this directs us to realize that we have/are bodies. The strangeness, having accepted this view always (at least many years ago) is to note that the "philosophers' vision" is that we *are* and we are continuous, and now we have bodies; at least our concepts of being are *embodied*.

How—I have been wondering—did the facticity of our bodies ever get sidestepped; how did they not appear in our theories about human being? It was, as far as I can tell, because the question of our abilities to imagine, to live outside of the here and now, struck thinkers (especially Parmenides) as wonderfully remarkable. Thence, the rest of our being was, somehow, kept in the realm of the ordinary or mundane. Even now, we are still kept busy trying to explain how the "mind" works without noting clearly that it, as Nietzsche says, is some story about the body (TSZ, I, 1883)).

To embody: what a wonderful and strange notion.

Next, we will rediscover experience.

Observation: We are neither passive nor constant observers. If violin practice is exemplary, I have to "warm-up" each day. This entails the stretching, use, extending of myriad muscle groupings, some very subtle, some still new and surprising. But it also involves hearing and seeing. Both have to be re-exercised, recalibrated, re-established each day. Visually, for example, I work on my "eye muscles" to see faster (literally, to see more notes in any unit of time). There is nothing direct or obvious in this. I am not merely faster because I was able to see at a certain rate yesterday (though this is a skill at which I have become much more proficient in recent years). Whether I actually see faster, have confidence I can both see and play faster, or know how to re-study velocity better, or... I do not know.)

In hearing, I have to rethink sound relationships each day: I usually begin practice by tuning my strings to my A (often leaving the A as it is, unless it sounds awful to me). I alter the D string, first sharp, then flat with respect to its 5th with A, studying to hear the best harmony I can find; first by what is decidedly off, then gradually discovering what sounds "best."

So I think observation is not so passive, and not so constant and we have to restudy, relearn, and practice each day. We apparently change somewhat just by our mere being (due to gravity and other bodily changes, forgetfulness.) While this may be unobvious in ordinary tasks, it is certainly true in violin play at my level, and I think it is true generally that the bodily arts require "warming up" before one can regain the "form" sufficient to perform at any previous level; certainly it is necessary in order to "improve."

Are Other Species Rational?: If other (any other) species were rational, I am convinced that we would not be able to realize that fact. Taking this as a given: why not? What is it about us (and/or them) which would obscure their rationality?—A major problem in our thinking about what it means to be human!

Loving Porpoises: Jean Houston told me that it was true that the women (on LSD) who worked with porpoises under John Lilly, fell in love with them: (Personal Communication). She offered two reasons: 1) their skin feels unbelievably good to the touch; 2) their shape is exactly how a human can imagine being, having remained in water and changed to a perfect shape: human → porpoise.

Power of the History of Ideas: If I re-organize the fragments of Heraclitus, to "show" that he was basically an existential/experiential thinker, who was misinterpreted throughout Western thought to be the master perpetrator of logic, rather of the axis of logic vs. chaos, then it seems to be easy to show how particular ideas can so dominate thought as to have become the obvious, our *commonsense*.

Searle's Biologism: Having abandoned the computer as a metaphor for knowledge/intelligence on the grounds that the test for Artificial Intelligence (AI) is a "syntax without semantics," Searle ("The Mind's I" - NYRB 4/29/82) wants to replace this with some notion of the brain as "causing" mental events. This invoking of the brain, a nod to biologism but not to experience or to existence, is another form of essentialism.

Offhand, I prefer AI because the rules are able to be discovered; that is, I can inspect the wiring, the programs, and see if it mimics whatever we imagine human intelligence to be. (Make the AI test more experiential!) For 25 years the field of linguistics which was praised uncritically, attempted to generate a kind of semantics cleanly from the rules by which we put phrases together into ideas and sentences, as if we already knew what grammaticality is, free of surreptitious theories of meaning.

Searle, instead of wanting to make AI more like humans, wishes to abandon the enterprise, and to invoke the brain. I think he wants to bury the problem once more, hoping to cast a new essentialism upon us: ironically, now, in the name of "biology."

II Human Nature Arguments

The Quest for Universality: What is the same or in-common among some of us, stretched to "all" of human-kind, in all the world, now, in the indefinite past, toward an indefinite future?

Expressions of Human Nature Claims: All humans are, do, will, think, believe...e.g., all humans "have" religion, "have" language, souls... The same claims often work in the obverse: if they have religion, have language, *then* they are (must be) human.

Exclusions: Those humans (i.e., born of humans) looking like other humans, who do not speak, are anti-religious, etc., are not admitted into human being, or are kept in some sub-category (e.g., "retarded" persons, children, slaves) which is almost human (or almost non-human). What is an "interface" category? a.) *Appearance*: bodily, especially facial .in Western thought, made in the "image" of God (*Genesis*: 1.26); usually means in the image of the "visage" of God: looking like "God looks" (face, eyes, expression) → fear of the study of expression? → entering into God's domain?—not to be tampered with? b.) *Different Aspects or Attributes*: different language (un-understandable, thus unintelligent?); different visage (color, facial features, looking "stupid," looking like...?); different beliefs: different God(s); different habits/histories.

What Motivates the Quest?: (a.) *Religious/Personal*: if God(s) and humans in some (causal?) relationship, then if I am human, I partake in all of what Human means: God, Language (e.g., eternity, blessedness, etc.—depending on the "attributes" of my God(s)). (b.) *Metaphysical/Political*: if I am human, then I (individually) partake in the *essence* of what is human. I can do, be, look inside my own being, and be secure that I "know" who I am and what I do: justifying thought and action. (c.) *Psychological/Individual*: fear, guilt... A "set" of bodily feelings which some/all of us find annoying-to-disturbing, and which may seek relief or justification. These feelings accompany or are accompanied by thoughts/internal images which interact with the feelings: driving or driven by them. New or substitute thoughts can be used, often, to manage or alter feelings, or vice-versa: e.g., fear of "death" can often be managed or shifted by images of "salvation." Sometimes these become quite derivative: e.g., the fear, of the fear, of death, may itself be very powerful and we may be *moved* to control or to flee any sense or feeling of fear (perhaps no longer knowing what it is a fear of).

Purpose of Universality Claims of Human-Nature Arguments: Once the claim of Human Nature is made and secured, the circularity of its logic is obscured: e.g., if God, then Humans. Now, if Human Nature essence is shared by many, then a search for causes; thus the necessity for the cause of the (human) design; thus God.

A lack of the necessity of responsibility for one's own character development: aids in extinguishing blame for one's failures, weaknesses; leaves self-understanding shallow, tends to objectify self, to stand outside oneself watching, removed from action and from time.

Justifies any (political/moral) treatment of those who are excluded: "partial" Humans, non-Humans.

Comparative World-Visions: *The Pursuit of Life*: Not the cosmological question—of the nature of existence, because it is ours already—but "What is life in its living?" How "far" can anyone go in the direction of a good life toward perfection, or toward perfectibility? Can perfection be achieved or gained within what we call Life—or can perfection be achieved only upon/after death? Is life—being born—"neutral," or already laden with some aspects of an existence cast more widely: other lives, some notion of a pre-formation?

What is the good life? How does anyone pursue it? Is it available to all and to everyone? What is the path? Who will help us, teach us, criticize us, return us to the correct or righteous way? Is the way the same Way for everyone?

Perfectibility: 1) If available within (what we call) life, how to pursue it? A doing, a mode of being, of "seeing" (sensing), of knowing? Is there a model (e.g., Confucian) who has achieved a state of human perfectibility—or who has moved "as close as possible," who continues to pursue perfectibility? Is this a "human" model? i.e., does the "perfect one" exist essentially as we, human as we, born of the ordinary, partaking of the same life as we? How has this one (these ones) moved toward perfectibility? Can I/we merely "copy" (mimic?) that one; at the point of perfectibility (i.e., with the same attitudes, outlooks, thoughts, practices); or must we pursue a similar path or path-processes? Can we (ever) find our own paths (our "characters")? Do these change; in any obvious or particular directions? Do we use/need teachers?

If existence "includes" death (or any states of being or non-being as we know it, or preformation), then is perfectibility achievable? If NO, we are, possibly, forever "damned," and there is nothing to do—then this leads to slavery or to anti-social and/or to a self-destructive sense of being.

If "existence" includes death, is perfectibility available within "existence," within life (not usual in such a scheme), only within or upon death? By approaching a "perfect" deity? That is, what is the model of perfectibility, what path (if any), what to do: study, pray, etc.—or is there "nothing" to do?

Time and Existence: if existence includes pre/post life, then the time of life and living tends toward the infinitesimal; each moment very tiny;

diminishing perhaps. If our "souls" exist "forever" then today is very short, indeed, as is a life-time. We tend, in these schemes, to move toward metaphysics, to stand outside of our own being, to live life as if it were symbolic, to objectify ourselves; to separate being and existence, and to separate these into (usually) mind and body.

If existence remains within life (in some sense of being available within the "longest" lifetime), then we tend toward ontology: being in/as process, with life as a particular kind of development/progression (or regression).

Within these schemes the question of what is a good life, what is progressive (transcendental?) differs, often radically. While life may (appear to) be lived similarly, the valuation of self, of others, of acts and of being, the judgment of self/others, may be quite different. That is, hope and the future, may dwell within a person, or be kept outside—the concept of futurity dependent upon our fears and faiths, rather than within our Being.

Sleep unto Death: From Heraclitus to Plato, the dualism once-established, persisted. Two categories, only two, to cover all of being and experience. What evolution that the sense of two-ness, of the one and its "opposite," reigns, while the apparent substance, the concentration of our thoughts, finds its focus changed?

Life and Death: the questions of the Socratic sickness unto death; the aged, threatened Socrates who proclaimed himself the master arbiter of all of knowledge, these he left us with. But in any earlier age, and "still" among many peoples, particularly those native to the Americas, the question of being and experience (which may indeed be the ultimate-ultimate), was whether our human reality really occurred while we slept or while we were awake.

Among the Mayans I have known, it is during what we call "sleep," the sleeping state that we are "open" to the fundamentals. Sleep is when our true knowledge is 'awake," that the spirit of life (which in Mayan lore we *share* with some other species—or they share with us) may enter and/or leave us. Awakeness, when our bodies are abroad in the world of what we Westerners call experience, effectively stops movement in the true-spirit world. Knowledge, true knowledge, occurs then only while we are asleep.

Heraclitus pondered this state of affairs at length and concluded, it now appears, that he "liked the senses best." I surmise that by the senses, he meant the senses when awake (but this would mean the opposite among the Mayans because the true senses are "open" only while we are asleep). But Heraclitus was taken with the difference between the aloneness of sleep--its individual-ness—and distinguished this being and knowing from the waking state when our knowledge is "in-common" with others. Through some ironic *trick* of historical fate (i.e., the rise of the metaphysicians), the in-common sense of knowledge shared by persons became the "common sense" by which every individual now believes s/he knows what is basic truth. The "common sense" grounded itself within the "*logos*," the "logic" which became the property of each individual, and the waking state became *Phenomenon*, while sleeping became epiphenomenal: commentary upon being and experience. But sleep and dreams were/are not touchstones of being, nor related to actuality in any clear or direct sense. The individual-ness of our aloneness in the sleeping state became the central aspect of our being...

Having lost or given up the meaningful comparison between sleep and wakefulness, finding ourselves (as it were) awake, and still not able to account for much of being and experience, the problematic was to account somehow for our being—for the deeper sense of some underlying dualism about knowledge persisted. And the quest for knowledge now concentrated itself in the formerly (sleeping) individual.

The problematic became cosmological rather than ontological-in-common-sense, and we began to question individual existence. Parmenides (*Fragment VIII*) invented the deity which corresponded to that question and which would then provide "solutions" for several millennia, and whose notion of the human spirit of our sleeping state, metamorphosed into a notion of the continuity of this spirit within the concept of time which "logos" promoted, and a sense of a deity which "caused" existence turned to a depiction of time-as-eternal.

Within this construct of time-as-eternal, and the question of existence as the cosmological "why," the focus of the solutions to the why-ness of life turned toward the notion of reality as enduring as the concept of the deity whose existence was postulated to explain ours. The real became (Pythagoras, Plato) the forms behind any actual object or event. The world of actuality, of waking-sleeping dissolved, as it were, into a world whose reality was no longer how it appeared to us; i.e., to our senses of seeing, hearing, touching, etc. Knowledge was removed from any immediate sensing, and skepticism about any present, about time and about our being became attractive as a solution to the cosmological, "why."

The enduring deity, of which we were part and product, gave us life as one aspect or part of our existence. The greater part, the life of the spirit soul which endured, was to be accounted for as prior to life, or as after life. As death reigned, life became the incarnate aspect of life everlasting; i.e., death, grotesque or paradisiacal.

The quest for knowledge, heretofore concerned with sleep and wakefulness, now turned upon life and death. The body, the senses, the actual of here and now, of change, being and becoming, became distrusted: actualizations of the underlying, enduring forms and little, in and of itself. The question of what is the aloneness of sleep, what is the in-common of common sense and logic, disappeared, replaced by the question of why we exist, whose final solution was to claim that life is an aspect of death: an illusion; a time to prepare for the truths of final judgment. But life, in-and-of-itself, weakened.

The dualism, the sense that what is, is duple, somehow paradoxical, that experience is not what it seems, but has a second, hidden part... persisted. The foci, the quest for what is knowledge as a metaphor for what is life, also persisted.

What changed, however, were the salient, sapient, significant questions. From an acceptance of life within which is the problematic of sleep and whatever else is its "opposite," the concern evolved to the problematic of death—and whatever else is its opposite. (The notion of duality, of opposites, as encompassing the entire universe of possibilities, continued... continues!)

Changing Conceptions of the Entire Earth: From time immemorial, the quest for what is Human Nature has extended to the entire earth: as far as it was known, and—for the rest—from hearsay. As the world is now shrinking in our concepts, as we can move easily and swiftly from place to place through the air, as we can conceive of missiles moving across vast continents or satellites circling the globe in 90 minutes, the sense that all is known or, certainly, knowable, impresses upon us.

As the earth has become effectively smaller, as there is actual movement from place to place, the experience with exotic peoples who derive from other, distant homelands, has become usual, perhaps ordinary. With the people has come ideas and knowledge whose interchange with our peoples' ideas and knowledge is affecting the world in various ways. From South and East Asia, different concepts of the body, of medicine, of experience and outlook, have inspired us of Judaeo-Christian derivation, to lives of exercise, of a new sense of awareness of self, of responsibility for our own health and well-being.

It has caused a tension, as well, between our concepts of being, of purpose and meaning in life, in some, as yet ill-defined conflict with other ways of being. While we join some concepts, others seem to cause some vague dis-ease to which we react by seeking firmer ground within our own traditions. A sense of differences on the earth, among its peoples, translates often into a sense of moral relativism where foundational issues of being, of reason, of law, of any "oughtness" in our lives, seem to be without basis, except that we claim them to be.

As technology has shrunk the earth in our ability to travel, to know at least in possibility, who and what it consists of (including television reportage instantly from everywhere on this earth), an ecological sense of the relationships of place and person and the rest of life's processes and the inorganic, these have shown us that there are some parameters surrounding being, some limitations upon the earth, to support and nurture us. The technical-mechanical knowledge of life processes and how to alter them, has grown, apparently far in excess of our knowledge and/or ability to understand the relationships between humans and other life forms.

Similarly these technical advances, deriving from a view of human nature which, in many philosophical-religious-political traditions, is opposed literally to such mechanical views, has fought the impingement of the technological outlook, while surreptitiously accepting some/much of the technology. This seems often to result in social theories which derive historically from pre-technical eras, while our actual lives are conducted in the brief interstices among micro-chips.

In this sense the shrinking earth has caused many of us to live our lives from at least two vastly different and often opposed outlooks which we keep in separate and distinct modes in our lives. While this cultural schizophrenia does not often conflict directly or overtly, the disparities are felt by some people(s), especially as the sense of accelerating change and increasing complexity of our lives pushes us in many directions, often at the same time.

Also in this era, the ancient questions of social and political arrangements are given radically new bases. The notion of the State, the pledges of allegiance which we accept (or reject) to some idea of a flag which represents place and history and shared outlook, is in some relation to the fact that the earth is geographically and economically ordered in different (and new) ways; i.e., the theories of the State—which still govern our thinking—derived from other times. Minerals, goods, knowledge, etc., flow like osmotic qualities in the cells of our bodies. Cells, like States, are differentially permeable. They exist with respect to some configurations, but have no being with respect to others. This fact, also, is conflictual, but not always and not in any direct or obvious sense.

The temptation of State-National Governments to attempt to seal boundaries in some actual or conceptual sense is at odds with the ease and necessity of flow. We find that governments increasingly try to proclaim simultaneously the firmness and the openness of their national boundaries: war, of course, "enemies," etc., being metaphors for the closeness and existence of clean boundaries, to be invoked in times when the diffuseness of the State seems to be problematic.

As knowledge of a variety of ways of living and thinking enters the mentality of many peoples, the questions of justice arise in new ways. Who has, who has-not, who deserves what, why; all these questions gain a new backdrop against which to compare any particular situation. The interaction between perceived and actual repression, their moves to action and counter-action, tends to form many splintering factions; paradoxically, as the world gains a sense of oneness.

Historical-religious-political-linguistic claims to political dominance are argued against other cases. Local and international harmony and peace are motivated and reacted to with more strength and violence, as all claims have global cases to support or to defeat their own claims. Virtually every claim can find a precedent claim somewhere.

The shrinking earth notion, actual and conceptual, the flow of ideas and peoples, also possesses its paradoxes. While we believe we know in some depth of our experience how others live and think—we can get instantaneous video virtually from anywhere on earth—the presentation of the people and ideas is easily shaped and limited by governments, the nature of reportage and what is news, and by our critical sense, knowledge, and ability to conceptualize differences among peoples. Since these are presently extremely limited, it is comparatively easy for even "free" presses to shape news, reduce it imagistically, so that understanding in some critical depth eludes any public.

It is in this context that the question of how to educate, to understand, to conceptualize the entire earth, gains new meaning.

The difficult questions: will understanding lead towards mutual respect, or to more subtle attempts at manipulation or control? When/how can we pursue some vision(s) of future which can listen to the voices of all the people, and accommodate to them; advance them in some sense of life and justice which sustains and grows?

Shadows and the Sources of Light: We find ourselves, awakened, ensconced in Plato's Cave of Shadows. What we see and hear, when we sense and know may be only shadows; merely shadows. Not knowing whence the light derives, we do not know whether we see what there is, or some complex effect of the light, things, and events, and ourselves. We must therefore seek the sources of light to begin to know what is, what is actual, what is shadow, where and who we are, having arrived in this Cave before we could know about knowing.

The shadows, sometimes larger, sometimes smaller than what they reflect, may be more attractive and enticing than any actuality. How they move, dancing; a kind of superordinary quickness, flickering, too thin, too thick, looking like mostly whatever our imaginations conjure. Now they dance, now they embrace, now they threaten, contact, disappear only to reappear with an eerie suddenness, always the same within their differences; always different within their singularities.

What's shadow; what's actual? Where is the source of light and what see I, watching? The path: from shadows to the obscurity of what is shadowed; to the source which illuminates, casting shadows. Perhaps it is the space about the shadows which reflect, outline, highlight, but only figures as some whatever-is-not; to us watching. What trust in what we see?

Shadows are not nothing: not illusions, nor chimeras, nor tricks, nor deceits.

Let us, as Plato pleaded, seek the light, bright—too bright, that it might be—remembering that it is we who know light and darkness, actual and shadow. Let us seek after the sources of light and we may determine who we are, and how we happened into this Cave.

On Good and Evil: The ideas and definitions associated with the words and concepts of good and evil are very powerful in the world and in the minds of people. It is, however, clear that even such basic concepts change! What is included within the notion of the good, whatever is its opposite—evil—what is their relationship, varies in time, in place, and in each of our lives. This fact of change, even in such basic ideas, does not diminish the importance of the words and their meanings, but asks us to consider them in the broadest contexts possible.

Very generally it is clear that good and evil partake in some common domain of meaning; i.e., they are similar, but opposite. Like the notions of other similar oppositions such as big and little, light and dark, it is the contrast, the opposition which impresses itself upon our thinking. Nonetheless, the similarity is also clear, and we should seek out its nature. Indeed, where we attempt to understand meaning, where similarities and differences are already important in our thinking, we should make every attempt to note similarities, because the contrasts always seem very large and important, and will impress us even if we concentrate first upon similarities; whereas the opposite is seldom true, as we noted above. In this general sense, then, the question of good and evil is concerned with the nature of concepts and words which partake in similar domains of meaning, yet seem to be definitely opposite and contradictory to one another. Where do such domains of meaning reside and arise?

Grammatically, good and evil are adjectives or adverbs which describe or delimit something about a person/object or some event: to live a good life—to do evil—I am good. The pair is generally interchangeable, and this is a part of their similarity. Whatever can be described/delimited as good can also be evil (and vice-versa). Part of the similarity, then, partakes in those objects, events, persons which can be/are described as good/evil.

Part of the differences between them reside in the objects/events which are *not* described this way. Many things or objects are "neutral" with respect to good/evil; others do not partake of good/evil, or good/evil do not exist within them. Usually, for example, paper, or, say, a cup, are neither one nor the other; except that they may, and such conditions help extend the notion of the domain of good/evil.

Paper, which is ordinarily neutral, may be good if utilized or conceptualized a particular way, depending, that is, on its "agency." Who uses it? What it is used for/against? Paper used for a holy text may be good; if used for bad ends, may be evil. (There is, of course, a separate domain of "good for" some purpose, or good in relation to something which is not very good for that purpose; here evil is not an opposite.)

The similarities, then, reside partly in the notion of the object/person/event which may partake of good/evil, and in those which do not. Also, the similarities reside in our minds, knowing that as descriptive terms, they are usually a *pair*, i.e., interchangeable one for the other. Much of the rest of the similarity resides in the senses or circumstances in which these terms are invoked. It is in these latter, the situations or circumstances which call to mind judgments of good/evil, where most of the (cultural) change occurs, and why the notion of such a basic pair, may actually change.

As an example, consider that the oppositional pair is invoked in a time and place where humans being on earth is considered to be positive or neutral, compared to one being considered to partake, already, of some evil (e.g., the pre- and post-Christian interpretation of the book of Genesis).

If one is (...I am, you are) generally neutral, then any act or thought may be judged, in some sense, in its own terms. If one is already evil, by dint of mere being, then most acts/thoughts partake in evil, and judgment is quite another business. It may, for example, be impossible to be or do "good" in a world where our corporeal being is a "fall" (evil) to earth. Or it may require herculean efforts to be good, when, it is assumed, so much evil must be overcome.

Indeed, historically, Humanism has attempted to override the "already-evil" notions of our being, and to substitute for it a neutral idea. None of this discussion, of course, either confirms or denies the notion of good/evil, but is concerned with "locating" it, in order to see what it is, in an overarching sense, irrespective of temporal or cultural particularities. Why a two-opposed category system, a dualism which posits either one and elaborates its theology through the other? Why attach a dualistic meaning scheme to our very existence?—e.g., to ward-off (fears of) death?

Beyond the taxonomic-category assignations of terms to our being and/or reasons for being, arises the question of the nature of morality. Are good/evil ensconced within some encompassing contextual idea of morality which has to do with how one ought/should be? Or is morality derivative somehow from a primary existence marker for which the categories of good/evil provide a framework of understanding or interpretation? Do either/both of these considerations of morality inhere in our very existence; do they partake in judgment, interpretation, and valuation of our being; do they provide guides for determining or judging the activity in/of our lives? The nature of morality differs considerably according to which notion of morality (e.g., as context for good/evil vs. aspects of a good/evil primary framework for interpreting all acts and being) informs thought and judgment; as well as the sense we have/develop for the oughtnesses of our lives.

If we situate morality external to living, we are likely to attribute the qualities of good/evil to some force exterior to our own existence (God, Satan, "the Force," etc.), setting up a moral theology which we invoke to explain or judge life and activity. If we situate morality in each life and in the relationships we have with others, then the locus of the study of morality is in the development and maintenance of moral judgment between others and oneself; e.g., morality overlaps with justice. The reason to explore this latter notion, locating moral study within (human) existence, is not to deny any notion of a transcendent deity, but to attempt to understand how different outlooks, markedly different ideas of deity and of morality, have in fact sustained life/sustain life, and to explore those aspects of the secular which involve the *shoulds and oughts* of life, and how we maintain justice in our lives.

In this context, of an agnostic, "secular" morality, the clearest point of embarkation in the moral sphere concerns "the next generation." Why do we choose (when we do) to support and nurture infants and children to the point of self-maintenance? Why do we sacrifice self-interest to nurture those who would perish without the concern, interest, and quite constant nurturance of (our) children? This we seem to have in-common with other (social) species, and may mark, as well, a comparative biological notion of morality.

We raise the next generation because we will/want to. It is from this notion of willing, and how this will is maintained/supported in real-social life, that morality gains its force and power. That is, we are not only committed, as Schopenhauer put it, to will our ideas and lives, to will our futures in the Nietzschean sense of overcoming our present, but also to relate to particular others—our children, who would not survive without us—to will their lives as well. This is the kernel of morality; not merely good/evil, no mere invocation of any deity to pray tell us what should we do, but the constancy of willingness to relate to the not-yet-self-maintaining, and to maintain them.

True morality is located in these relationships, in the aspect of ourselves which we transform into the necessity to parent/maintain. The prevailing morality in any time/place has to do with how the morality of generation is maintained, supported, its costs and satisfactions. Herein are good and evil located, as aspects of the human condition.

Who We Grow Up Among: Many of those "kinds" of people now missing in my life, so I seek the faces and characters of my youth's experiences. I think I liked the Irish best: the Nelligans who lived across the street; O'Leary down the block; McDonough, Fitzpatrick and Boyle, a couple of blocks away. Today, even, I seek out those characters who are much like those of yesteryear: Martin, McCarthy, Gearity...

Others, too, are missed more. All the Mediterranean peoples who found a home together, all those faces and laughs, the black, black hair of the beauty of my teen-age imaginations never settled in my present home. Whenever I travel, I seek them out, merely to look at them, see them, and wish I was among them more, with their intensity and spirit, which I miss in this land of blonds and coolness of disposition, the self-contained appearing taciturn in comparison with my retrospective visions.

I remember that many kinds and sorts lived together; that I loved seeing and smelling and being amongst them, wondering who they were, what languages they had by now forgotten, how they lived and thought and loved, trying to find meaning in a land whose life they shared through some historical quirks.

What difference, what effects, who we grow up among? Why, what I saw, who I knew, who laughed and played and let me into their lives still resonates in my looking-out. A kind of love of all people, different, but each a sense of beauty and dignity which I could find if I saw correctly through the drab and dung of surface smiles.

Who I am now reflects itself against the mirrors of the others who saw me as they saw me, emerged to study and judge, to look for the beauty that is there; and that, that may yet be.

On Reading Texts (...the Bible): "Vanity, vanity. All is vanity," says the Book of Ecclesiastes. I love the mellifluous flow of words in the English version: "A time to sow, to reap, to live and die." The words sing, a kind of poetry whose penetration into the soul of my being is as beautiful and as deep as the deepest sky of blackness's starlight. They carry, as well, a sense of content, of meaning. "What is vanity?" my heart murmurs. Is my reading, my hearing and loving the sounds, is that also vanity? I look in vain at the reflection of my image's visage: that, too is vanity? "Here, I think," is a good beginning. How I am, what I am, is not so very deep. It is vanity, surface. Where is the "I" which watches myself watching, knowing what vanity is, and searching for more?

Texts which are mellifluous, which carry meaning, also remove us from ourselves, watching, hearing the form of words, flowing, laughing, crying, they enter our thoughts, moving at first between them. Then, joining sounds which dance already inside, enter thinking, repeating for the joy of the sake of repetition: vanity, in the beginning, all the world, he came upon a midnight clear, woe is me... a time to sew, to think, to know. They ring, and ring... and gradually they ring true.

What vanity, what beginning, what paradise? The experiences of life, the dawning of the "I" who I am, ponders. I learn to look at myself, looking; to see the world in its reflections placing myself outside looking in; to sense what was and will be; where I am, and am not. Sense, where does sense reside? What do I see that I do not know? Hurt, sickness, death, I often mourn being...

The texts, the Bibles, they sing the songs which are the sounds in my head. Vanity, in the beginning... God created. Which phrases ring more loudly? I? In the image of a god?

The text resounds in the largeness of the heavens, echoing, echoing, as in my inner thoughts. Yes, in the beginning... no, what is a beginning? Whose visage is the image, where is my vanity... beginning, was the Word?

Which lines, which words are the ones, precisely, that are God's? This line, is mine: vanity, vanity... the vanity of my talk, of writing, of claiming to know, this is my text, my primary, my beginning. And yours? Where do you begin? What do you tell yourself, that you tell... yourself?

What then? What interpretation, what exegesis?—in the image of God? What god?—of the Day of Judgment, as in the Koran? What God—of today and yesterday? What death; what life?

Words...become more than words. Life, become more than life. In God's image? Vanity?

What is Human Nature? This question has several sorts of answers or responses, because each word "Human" and "Nature" and their juxtaposition have both simple and complicated histories and present realities. In addition there is a somewhat peculiar history and framework from which the question is even posed or asked; e.g., as rhetorical; as problematic.

The importance of the question and of the concepts may be drawn first. It appears clear that every social philosophy—politics, ethics, law, theory of individual and of society, etc., contains, rests upon, presumes, implies... a theory of Human Nature.

Whether humans are "by nature" indolent (Augustine) or desirous of hard work, whether we are "by nature" evil or good or neutral, whether perfectibility can be achieved within life, whether we are like other species or are particularly not like them—each of these notions (and many others) is used to construct a vision or practicum of the social order. Thus the posing of this question seems to run through our thinking, consideration, and judgment of who and how we are in the world, who we are not, and why. Indeed, we can understand to some great extent, how and why societies/nations are the way they are, by understanding how this question and its solutions (directions, paths...) are conceived.

To return to the framework of the question, itself, the notion of "What is Human Nature?" usually presumes that there is some notion of Nature which is *not* human. Thus, most systems of accounting for our being (usually, metaphysics), juxtapose what is Human with respect to Nature, with what is not-Human.

Here (as in many of the H-N theoretic frameworks), responses to what is not-H may include a notion of other live creatures, or aspects of them (e.g., their bodily forms, their "spirits"). Responses may also include machines (e.g., computers/Descartes), notions of the deity or other "Human-like" entities which have extra-ordinary presence or powers.

What these have in common is some aspect of what we see as human, or consider to be "particularly" or "uniquely" Human... and transpose to some other "entity": a god, a machine, a non-H animal. Thus, "What is Human Nature?" generally carries in its posing, some (often unstated) premise that there is some significant non-H-N, with which any solution is to be *compared*: implicitly or explicitly: like us, but not us.

Confucianism, which is a humanism, does not seem to embed itself in an H-N comparison: other species are simply not human, not comparable. Most other traditions have humans and other species with some aspect(s) in-common (e.g., the Body in Western Thought, the "spirit" in Native American), but what is then Human is what is considered to be different—a "large" difference, or not so large.

What is considered to be N, then, concerns what is not-H, that which occurs without the intervention of humans (e.g., machines are not *in* Nature or natural). In this context, N includes other animal species, elements, flora, and objects. Probably most important in the H-N discussion, however, are those aspects of being H which we juxtapose with what is significantly non-H.

In Western thought, we are dual or duple: the body is considered to be natural—we have it in common with other species. But the rest, the mind or spirit or soul, is what is considered to be especially H. And since this dualism runs throughout Western Thought, the mind is what is considered to be outside of N and uniquely H. That is, what we *attribute* to N is taken to be totally distinct from what is then considered to be uniquely H; what is now called "Culture."

Culture is then, in a dualistic framework, *opposed* to N by contrasting aspects (elements) of what is uniquely H (i.e., "mind"), to what we consider to be "natural"—e.g., aspects of the body. In Christian theology, this metaphor of mind (=Human) and body (=Nature) is carried on to a kind of war (Plato)—the body impinging on "pure thought" where the body is considered, "like Nature," to be bestial, to be anti-Human... thus sinful. The theology we have inherited is thus an H-N theory, in this case a dualism, in which we are "pitted against ourselves" in a most complicated fashion.

In other, non-Western traditions, the question of "What is Human Nature?" arises somewhat differently. Some (Amerindians) contrast *sleeping-waking*, as others contrast life-death (Christian, Muslim), and do not distinguish between humans and (other) animals in the sleeping state. In Amerindian traditions, humans *share* spirits with other species. These spirits move freely whilst we sleep, but are distinct when we are awake. Thus Humans are "closer" to Nature in these traditions, being—at least part of our lives—aspects of Nature rather than in any sense distinct from Nature.

In South Asian, Buddhist traditions, humans have a kind of hierarchical progressive journey through several lifetimes, from "lowly" animal up toward a kind of humanly transcendent perfection or Nirvana. Thus we are not different in any deep sense from Nature, but attempt to move beyond it. To eat of animals is thus to eat of some sense of spirit which is human... or potentially or once-was human.

What is Human? What Nature?—varies considerably in different theo-philosophical traditions. Some traditions, especially Confucian, do not seem to even raise this as a question or issue. For the rest, we construct theories of what is human, based on what we decide is not-H or Na. Depending on how we juxtapose H and not-H, entire theories of being (metaphysics) follow from what we consider to be human: how we are, how we should conduct ourselves, are there slaves?, extending even to questions about the nature of time, of experience; what is life? Death? The nature of deity? And so on. Thus the question of "What is Human Nature?" remains a puzzle, in actuality, but has received grand elaborations within most theo-philosophical traditions.

Recent (1930's to the present) studies and reconsiderations of non-H species have cast new light on the *question* of Human Nature, at least for Western thinkers (revealed, in part, by which thinkers join in conversations concerning the so-called "origin" of Language—Americans and British, for the most part.)

While it was formerly presumed that the in-commonness of H and non-H was their "body," field observation and description of non-H's and the consequent observation of H's from this perspective (ethological) has altered the sense of boundary and uniqueness of what is Human (=Culture?).

It has even forced us to re-look at the history of the H-N argument, to see why H-N has been cast as it has, and to ask quite fundamental questions about the "large" world theo-philosophical traditions (e.g., Western, Eastern, Amerindian, African, etc.), and what is the relation between the truth as we observe it, and how it has come to us, historically.

Thus, for example, the recent wonderment about dualisms, about so-called human uniqueness due to "mind" or "culture"—i.e., the other side of the dualism of what was presumed to be "animal" (=N). It now appears that we are similar to, have in-common with other species, more than or different from what was earlier presumed. The question of what is H-N has shifted, at the least because our view and knowledge of other species has changed, much through observation, new instrumentation, etc.

Some examples: other species seem to be social, in deep and complicated senses. This is important in the H-N discussion because of the history of what has considered to be uniquely H, particularly "language," as well as the entailments of what the notion of Language has meant.

Language has been "used" as a metaphor for the human "mind"; it has been claimed that human knowledge and objectivity are especial to humans, and due to a uniquely human *sociality* (i.e., Language "made" us social, or enabled us to be social: knowing objects, we could come to "know" ourselves from the outside—objectively—and thus became social). If other species are social, then they must communicate, teach, change, possess "Culture," by most definitions.

The clear inference is that humans possess much more in common with other species than had been thought; thus Human Nature and Nature are, at the least, in different conceptual places than had been thought, with attendant implications for other aspects of life: politics, theology, morality, etc. To act "bestially," for example, was considered previously to be totally impulsive, tied to the present, to be body (=sex); and sinful = against God. Now, this is all not so very clear, as other species seem to treat their own con-specifics with "care and love," teaching toward adulthood = the future!?

Moreover, since in Western thought we find ourselves in-common, juxtaposed with other non-H creatures, changes in how we think about them will affect how we think about H's. Such changes have occurred already, particularly in the past decade or so. Since, as Western dualists, we have contrasted H's and non-H's as being "cultural" or "natural," the population of "abnormal" humans has been calculated to be "less-than-human," toward (how we conceptualized) other species.

This thinking was applied to so-called "retarded" persons, to deaf (and dumb) persons, to handicapped persons in general, to women, and to children... and to the elderly, sometimes. As we have been thinking differently about other species (i.e., more like H's), the group of "peculiar" humans has been de-animalized, reconsidered, and gathered into the human "family." On the other side of the coin, the "Animal Rights" movement has burgeoned.

We are now conceptualizing H's and non-H's differently from previously, with at least two schools of thought pushing their theories, but both agreeing that H and non-H are more similar than earlier thought: (1) the "biological determinists," who still consider non-H's as fixed in outlook and composition, who want to consider H's as also pre-determined... a kind of bio-politics of global control; and 2) the "culturologists" and "ecologists" who wonder how to re-construe the world of H and non-H with responsibility, compassion and understanding, given that we have underestimated non-H's, and (probably), by juxtaposition, also underestimated the complexities of the human condition.

In either case (and more positions may develop), since H-N theories underlie theology and politics, we now witness and may expect a good deal of activity and change in these arenas, as people react to these changing conceptualizations of who and what we are, in actuality and potentiality.

Morality: Absolute, Relative...Other Species: As we (currently) re-estimate other species, a number of issues about who and how humans are, arise to new questions. The question of how we "should" be—"what is morality?"—reoccurs in all its complications. Since, it was believed, only humans were moral—capable of thought, of decision, of considering issues of good and evil, right and wrong—the issue of morality was taken as a given or ensconced within whatever notion of theology was prevalent in a given era and locale.

Since the idea of deity usually included a moral imperative, and the deity in Western monotheism was considered to be a timeless ideal, the notion of morality was given a sense of absoluteness: right is always right, always the same; evil is evil in all senses, places, and conditions: opposed to the good (which is the deity).

Any code or notion of morality which differed from a prevailing one was/is considered immoral, or less than moral. This has entailed a judgment about other peoples and cultures: if they have different customs from us, we (the "moral") have tended to judge them as lesser or wrong, and have, indeed, "missionized" other peoples within the concept of the correctness of *our* moral-theological ideas.

The concept of a "relative" morality—of other cultures' customs being merely different, but equally legitimate or moral as our own—has been reacted to with a virtual sense of horror. And all ideas which have supported a "relative morality" have been seen to be Satanic (evil, somehow: the opposite of good), and against God in a very direct sense. Thus, any shift in the concept of morality from a particular ideal/absolute has been considered to be motivated by anti-God, anti-human motives.

Until very recently, the notion of morality was considered to be "safely" within the realm of H-N. Morality, like, language, rationality, and sociality, was seen as uniquely human. With the rise of social-behavioral observations of other species, it has become clear that other species are social, and that this sociality includes the politics and ethics of how any one animal of a particular species relates to other con-specifics (same species members).

Since prior depictions of other species had animals being "bestial" in the senses of each animal being alone and "out-for-itself," unthoughtful, tied to the narrow here-and-now, the wonderment of considering other species' survival has shifted.

"Individuals" of other species "take care" of one another, do not seem to hurt or kill, seem to partake of "love," raise their young when it "costs" great amounts of energy, even in dangerous situations. By most definitions of what is moral behavior, many other species seem to be moral, at least to act morally! (They are "altruistic"—in current parlance.)

These observations and questions raise several issues and ask us to ponder, as well, how our own moral judgments are situated. For the absolutist moralist the notion of other species being possibly within any moral order, seems on the one hand ludicrous, and on the other to be an attack on (the concept of) God-as-absolute.

Since most Western theology grounds itself on the text of Genesis, especially Genesis I: 26—humans in the "image of God"—any shift in the "image" of human may be taken as an attack on the "image" of God (often, on the very notion of God). However vague or abstract the Judeo-Christian idea of the image and visage of God may be, it has generally been within our concept of a human body/face. For those who are absolutists, the importance of this idea of human uniqueness being in the image of God is very powerful, and any shift in it may presage an attack on the concept of God, of associated notions such as salvation, and all those ideas which apparently give deepest meaning to their (continuing) being, and to their lives.

To image the visage of God as being non-H (or even imagine God as not male) may be sacrilegious in the deepest senses. (Associated here, as well, is the other phrase of Genesis I: 26: man having "dominion" over the other species. To conceive of other species as merely morally different, not necessarily lesser than human, places severe strictures on the definitions, rights, responsibilities, etc. of what is human!)

Within the context of other aspects of H-N, namely that the mind/soul is "pure," it is the body which is impure or sinful, anti-God, anti-Christ. Also, it is the body that has "linked" H's and non-H's. Thus to suggest that other animals are moral in any (strong?) sense, is to weaken the foundations of morality and the concepts of sin and evil, because it is to suggest that the human body is, in some sense, either moral, or at least not immoral (i.e., "bestial").

For the absolutist, this represents another relativism of the worst sort, since it must be interpreted as anti-God; an attack on the possible purity of our souls—a severe diminution of (the concept of) human being. Literally, it is an attack on the Genesis notion of Creation, especially on the Christian "re-reading" of the story of the Garden of Eden: the cosmological answer to why we humans find ourselves (corporeally) upon the earth, the foundation of sin (sex), the very notions of morality...etc.

In a global context, it is by now obvious that most of the "great" world religions are absolutist in outlook, but differ from one another in various ways; some contradictory. These areas of contradictory differences, based upon absolute notions of correctness, may lead to very deep and powerful clashes. If none is willing to yield, or to leave other religions to occupy (de-)limited areas, then the politics of the religious outlooks may well lead to (religious) wars.

The only alternative seen thus far is to embrace some "relativism" which permits others to follow their own outlooks. In a time of religious ascendance and messianism, however, this relativism of leaving "well-enough-alone" is construed as an attack on the absolutist foundations of the fundamentalist religions, and may not be tolerated.

To avoid the Scylla of contradictory absolutisms and the Charybdis of the moral relativisms in which there seem to be no moral bases for living (properly), the notion of H-N seems to provide a context for a query into the very nature of morality which may permit us to understand the arguments, positions, differences among the religious (and other) outlooks.

It is clear that virtually all humans have some sense of morality with respect to the treatment of others, and of themselves. Morality has to do with life-sustaining, with fairness and justice, with the ability and necessity to judge ideas, outlooks, and actions.

Morality is also a social notion: a taking from oneself a sense of sacrifice, even, to give to some other(s), especially the dependent, especially the next generation: our children. In this last sense, it is now clear that morality is not confined or unique to human nature, but to all social species. In its essence, perhaps, morality is the answer, "Why," to the moral question: "Should...?"

In the widest sense of biology—the sense of how life goes on and survives—morality is a key concept, devolving upon life and generation. The question of raising each next generation within some shared vision of one's own life and of the next generation, suggests that the nature of moral judgment beyond the absoluteness of the nurturance of the dependent, is often circumstantial, depending on the times (climate, seasons, available energy), upon outlook within the experience of each present adult generation (each present measured against the past, but confined to current actualities), and upon some sense of sociality (place, role, strength, experience, expectations), and within some sense of what is proper and virtuous.

Within this sense and context of morality and judgment, the sense of a clear, absolute commitment to generation, a comparative study of morality may help further to illuminate what is the "human" in Human Nature. Why do humans get themselves (ourselves) into wars? Why, that is, can we behave morally towards some people (ours, like us), yet kill "others," with little moral revulsion? What are the moral "habits" of other species? When do they act war-like? How do they distinguish between "their own" and others...?

Absolute and Relative: Clearly there are differences in the ways various humans approach life, the world, self and others. There are also limits to life: whatever is a poison will end life; mechanical problems similarly, too much or too little heat; and so on. From life's limitations, from a rejection of alternatives, we humans have derived some senses of the "oughtnesses" of life, a tending toward an absolute code of living and of conduct. Other ways than our own tend to be rejected, much as if they were venomous and life-threatening. Often we call them "backwards" or "primitive," and talk of the need of others "to develop"—to become more like us = modern.

The "psychology" of the absolute is deep and complicated, and reflects some sense of an arrogance which seems self-serving, either to justify itself or to assure oneself that he/she possesses a certainty of being or of proceeding in living. The purveyor of the absolute—at least within some dialectic between some one way (an absolute) and the knowledge that there are others—tends to equate simple differences with some notion of opposition to the absolute. If, e.g., my belief is "good" then whatever is different is opposed, thus "evil." The absolutist seems to move within a dialectically dualistic sphere of: "with me, or, against me!" Done in the name of oneself or of a deity, the effect is the same, and the outlook seems little different.

On the other hand, those who point out that there are differences, the so-called "relativists," are also likely to forget that life/living have "limits," and to downplay various aspects of our being which demonstrate a great deal of variation in particular planes of existence. While the students and observers of the differences among humans know fully that life exists within particular boundaries, they may also be eager/or be forced within various dialectics, to promote the notion that a variety of religious dispositions will (and have) "work" to promote and sustain life; that the range of the customs of life arrangements is extremely wide. The outcome of these dialectics has often been the sense that relativism translates into "anything goes"—that there are no limits or boundaries on our life-ways.

The absolutist further translates this into an attack upon the surety (even, on the possibility) of knowledge, especially on the texts which inform the absolutism leading to worries about "false" gods, and seem to the absolutist to either be an aspect of "evil" opposing, or of a necessary decline into a nihilism; a nihilism in which no meaning in life or in destiny can be grasped and held.

Partly, this positioning into an oppositional dialectic between absolutism and relativism is due to a kind of technical posturing, especially of the relativistic scholars who want to demonstrate differences and complexity. In their understandable zeal to show, for example, that different world-visions have sustained life in major human populations, they are likely to downplay what is similar, what are the bases for comparison among different humans and their groupings, and to stress the differences.

The naïve, in their turn, not understanding the human commonalities, see differences as extremely large, and as necessarily opposed to their own schemata, particularly if they judge people primarily within a moral outlook, where "different" often translates as morally lesser. This is to say that most ordinary persons tend to judge other major outlooks within the same moral scheme as they judge other persons whom they know (...or themselves).

So, the problematic of the absolutism-relativism arguments must avoid an oppositional dialectic if we are to shed any light on what human outlooks and possibilities are and may be, particularly as the global village inevitably pits peoples of quite different habits and outlooks against one another in public forums; including wars.

With respect to absolutism, the notion of human, the very idea that we (can) group some several billions of persons under this rubric reasonably and concretely, means that there is a common basis, an in-commonness among all these persons. It usually implies (but not always) a set of differences between humans and "others" by which humans are distinctly or uniquely human: different from animals, transcendent deities, machines/computers, etc.

What is considered to be in-common, particularly human, has been called "essentialism": some set of unique aspects which are essentially Human (and not-non-Human). And, of course, most (major) traditions have interpreted this within their own systems of thought, and usually from the chauvinism of their own particular outlooks, assuming and believing that their inspirational visions were the universal truth, for everyone.

Thus, what we have had is a number of absolutisms judging one another from the position of judging themselves and their perspectives well, and others as lesser (or totally other); each possessing an essentialism which consists of their particular version of human uniqueness. The question, a continuing problematic, of what is really, truly essentially human, remains, and the problematic is continually enmeshed with respect to racism of a most general sort; i.e., the consideration of some (other) humans as being "not-quite" human, not (as in Western thought) in the "image of God."

Some events of the recent past, especially in America, demonstrate, I believe, that our views of absolutism which may seem totally firm in any given moment, in fact are alterable and changing, as regards Human Nature. Especially I refer to physically handicapped and so-called "retarded" persons, but this covers, as well, the "women's movement/feminism."

As we have become more familiar with the habits and life-ways of other species, it has become clear that some/many of the aspects of essentialism which have traditionally been considered unique to humans, are shared or are in-common with at least some other species: aspects of sociality, interaction, communication, etc.

This has "forced" kinds of re-evaluation not only of other species, but also of (some) humans. The outcome of this has been to note the inclusive humanness of some "different" humans who had previously been considered lesser or inferior, in the direction of how we considered other species!

The deaf, for example, who were considered as "deaf *and dumb*," are now conceived to be fully human, merely, non-oral. Sign language is widely taught in schools for the deaf, whereas formerly it was suppressed. (Sign language is an aspect of the body, thus in the opposition between mind and body, thought of as an animal-less-than-human skill). Many formerly "retarded" persons, who looked "peculiar" and "spoke poorly" or were "mute" are now living in the community, whereas previously they would have been in protected institutions, and considered less than competent to do or learn much.

Thus, while our concepts of Human Nature "seem" (in any era) to be stable and well-bounded, a number of formerly "marginal" persons have been included in our definitions of an absolute essentialism. And it is not clear how else our notions of H-N are altering, except to say that there appear to be attempts both to enrich our concepts of what is H, and to tighten them; depending, it appears, on the theo-political and other entailments of the meaning of what is H, absolutism in our being and our well-being.

All of this is to state that a kind of absolutism which recognizes what is H, what is humanly possible and potential what are the boundaries of life, is one aspect of thinking about human being. Beyond this, however, there appear to be many ways of being and becoming which sustain and give meaning to a productive and satisfying life.

The problem in global terms is that some perspectives which sustain may contradict or clash with others because each may be based on an absolutism which grants its own philosophy some necessary hegemony. Unless there is to be a global conflict of grand dimension, either one of the absolutisms will "win" over the others, or a new way(s) of constructing meaning-full life-ways must emerge...

Racism and H-N Arguments: Racism directed toward various kinds or types of human beings has been implicit in the sorts of H-N arguments which have pervaded many of the large theo-philosophical traditions on earth. If the question even arises concerning what is Human Nature then there is an (implicit) notion that someone or something is to be distinguished, is different from human, but is, at the same time, somehow the same or similar or there are some features "in-common" in some respects. (Confucianism: an exception?)

In Western tradition, the major distinction is between the sorts of mental and /or animating attributes of humans which supposedly differentiate us from (other?) animals. The in-commonness is that we all possess or are "bodies."

The particular and pervasive form of racism which emerges from this depiction of Human Nature has to do with a hierarchy of superiority that we attribute to the differences between mind (=human) and body (=in-common) where we already assume humans are "above" and other species are "below"; thus, what we think of as mind/human is better, more advanced, progressive, closer to perfection (= God?), etc.; that the body/shared or even, in some traditions, a mere "location" for the mind.

The tendency toward racism thus has had to do with peoples/persons/types who seem to those who attempt to "control" the definition of what is human, so some humans can be less perfect, less mental; thus, within this dualism to be the opposite—more body/bodily and more "animal." Or in other dualisms which seem to spread from this, more natural as opposed to more cultural with elaborations of what Nature-Culture means or implies.

The racist "strategy" generally is to elaborate the Human side of the dualism and to decide that other people(s) are more "like" or closer to Nature. Again—in Western tradition closer to Nature has meant being more like bodies, like other species who are presumed to be less mental, thus more stupid than humans, etc.

Thus, for example, the depiction of deaf persons - who have a bodily "imperfection"—not merely as different and handicapped, but as "deaf and dumb": i.e., like other species are presumed to be mute, dumb, without the intelligence and oral language that are presumably aspects of the (human) mind. (The story of William Stokoe–a personal friend–and how he, principally, managed to get Sign Language to be taught and used in schools, is quite fascinating! 1960) Although resisted for many years, American Sign Language has become routine, ordinary, and taught at most universities where deaf students can usually "find" an interpreter to accompany them in their coursework.

In these forms of racist thought (& practice), there is a sense, like Aristotle's "Great Chain of Being," of perfection, of some ideal against which we judge. We judge ourselves (usually, in racism, the judgment is with reference to "ourselves," as some paragon), to be clones to, or approaching an ideal or perfect type or form, or judge others to be "lesser" than perfect, thus lesser than we.

Since, in Western Thought at least, there is a hierarchical dualism which lends itself well to higher-lower, we have generally judged things or aspects of being as higher which are more like those aspects of mind or soul which we consider uniquely human; those to be lesser which are like body or animal. A biblical Old Testament text is often used to justify this type of judgment, both in the sense of the identity of humans and the politics of being able to do as we like with lesser creatures. Genesis 1:26: "Man has dominion over all other species; man is created in the image of God."

In exegeting this statement, there are always problems, traditions and habits of understanding how "God's image" is reflected specifically in human being (e.g., pertaining to both men and women, being a God of a particular color or visage, a God-in-process or God-everlasting, etc.), and what "dominion" means exactly (e.g. the "right" to eat other creatures, to sacrifice, how to deal with them with respect to treatment, funding, space, responsibility for them). And the perennially tricky problem of the borders between human and whatever else: e.g. must they "talk" to be human, assuming other species do not/cannot; must they have bodies just like "us"—color, size, facial appearance, hair type and distribution, two opposable thumbs, upright posture, a similar or shared history (for "religious" or materialistic reasons). Not to downplay the issues which still shout between men and women's equality.

Given Genesis 1:26, that "we" have dominion over all other creatures, it is clear that by defining any person or types of person as non-human, we grant ourselves the right to treat them as without rights; i.e., any way we wish to, up to and including annihilation.

Given the history of Western racism, granting "ourselves" the patina of identity, being like God, it is clear that we have defined as lesser in the sense of as inferior "race," those whom we regard as more like other species, compared to the "ideal" us who are more like, and in the image of (our) God. And why it is important to think about how God and Gods have gotten endowed with their particular attributes in various religious traditions—see my *Religious Point of View.* ms)

As much, perhaps more, it is important to consider what our views of other creatures are and have been, and to remember that intensive studies have shown that other creatures are more "like human" in most respects than we had believed earlier. As dualists, Western thinkers have extended the mind-body dualism to a culture-nature and to a good-evil dualism where we have considered other creatures (non-"ideal," non-"perfect") as being like animals (i.e., as we have believed other animals to be).

This racist outlook, this judgment of others who are deemed to be inferior, has been applied (is being applied) to many persons who differ from "us" (i.e., the ideal) in various respects. Most important, perhaps, is that the judgments have almost always, been judgments in the direction of how these "different" or "important" persons are more like "animals" than those of us doing the judging. Imperfect has thus meant: like bodily attributes; e.g., more "natural," less intelligent or rational (e.g. "retarded"), more like we have considered other animals—e.g., less civilized, more tied to the present here-and-now (e.g., impulsive, athletic); less like God (e.g., ugly/anomalous faces or other physical handicaps). So the way in which we have made racist judgments is essentially the same as the judgments we have made about other species.

Several quite recent punctures in this racist outlook: (1) *Other animals* are not like we have depicted them. This has shown us that racism has constructed a depiction of those it deems "inferior," not on the basis of descriptive fact, but with respect to an historical depiction or a dualistic category construction of other species. By understanding other species more accurately in their own terms, (as social, relatively peaceful, communicating, etc.), racist thought can be shown to be inaccurate, not as being about persons or other species, but about an historical tradition in whose terms we still think. (2) Many people formerly considered inferior in an intellectual sense (like we considered animals to be), have been shown to be capable of intelligent thought once we considered their handicaps; e.g., the deaf, many so-called "retarded" persons who can communicate their often complicated thinking by the use of sign-language. That is, we have learned that different or peculiar or anomalous human bodies or facial appearances do not (necessarily) imply any mental inferiority (like we had attributed to other species), but morphological differences which can be transcended once they are studied, described and understood. (3) The "animal rights" movement has caused us to consider that Gen. 1:26, which may give us "rights," power and control over other species, also makes us responsible to these creatures. (4) A new sort of appreciation of the human body (deriving, probably, from ideas of South and East Asia), where many persons' conception of the body has altered into some sort of holism, an anti-dualism, and a sense of a healthy life. The "Special Olympics" aspects and feminism counter this dualism. (5) An increasing realization that the racist judgments we have made, as inference from, say, facially "peculiar" looking-people to lack of mental ability is an outcome of dualistic thinking of the observer, not an accurate depiction of the situation. The mind-body dualism had led to a conceptual habit of judging mental attributes by facial (bodily) appearance, and this is now changing for many persons, aware now that this inference is incorrect in many if not most cases.

It is important to return to the exploration of Native American cultures and languages–led by the "papa" of American anthropology: Franz Boas–who urged his students to explore all native groups as having/being fully cultural/linguistic abilities and practices.

It is clear that racism is part and parcel of H-N arguments; the politics of personal relationships have been and can be heavily affected by theories about human beings which may be incorrect or misleading. We see and judge within notions of observation and evaluation, especially when we judge ourselves as (close to) an ideal, and others to be *lesser.*

Individual *or* Society: To some large degree, the H-N discussion is placed, caught perhaps, on the horns of a dilemma concerning the essence or primariness of humans as individuals, as opposed to humans as social creatures. Within the dualisms which abound in world philosophies, the opposition between such outlooks tends to favor one or the other, and usually obscures the fact that these are not mutually exclusive categories of being. However it is important to note that concentration on one or the other of these categories as *the* locus of our essential being heavily influences the ways in which we approach life in all personal and social terms.

Factually or descriptively, it is clear that humans are interactive. We are generational, born of others who not only give us life, but enable us to sustain it. Even though it is the individual bounded by or contained within its skin which is born and dies—and why most theories of essential individuality dwell upon or derive from death—we are seen, conceptualized, trusted, cared for, responded to within the contexts which are at once individual and social.

Moreover, they are both present and future-directed—infants and children being treated within the futurity of their becoming adults essentially like the present adults. And these time-minded dimensionalities of being individual/social already complicate fitting humans into any neat, clear, or closed categories of being. Whatever we may be—potentially—when we are born, much of our upbringing is restrictive, constrictive and shaped within limited notions of what any society regards as *normal-reasonable* human behavior.

It is not overly strong to report that parents, upon seeing the visage of their newborn for the very first time already *read/project* (future) character into their (social) judgment of the infant's face. Parents see an individual in only some senses, but also what/who that "person" will be like into the vague future. Thus, whatever an individual might essentially be, however clearly that individual may be a singular entity, all or most of its relations with others, including sustaining relations of feeding, loving, talk, are construed within more-or-less complicated social-temporal matrices.

Language, even, deeply reflects social agreements. The division of the world into particular objects, events, types is a social division which might be construed differently by different linguistic systems. A child is constructed, shaped, limited in many senses, by having to speak like those around him/her, in order to talk "sense." That is, the very notion of sensibility, of being a reasonable, rational person is constructed upon a set of social agreements which we tend to call linguistic categories or parts of speech.

But all of this may seem, so far, to say that there is only sociality; there is no individual except that defined or attributed by social interactions and definition. This may be incorrectly construed to state that the individual is only, and no more than the social "roles" attributed to her/him by society—via particular other "social individuals" (also defined by society).

Instead there are strong senses in which individuation and individualization exist. For one thing, an individual is treated with a strong sense of "constancy." Even if all of individuality does not emanate from the individual, others treat oneself as a particular "I," a named person who was, is, and will be. Even in small societies where everyone is "in relation" to others s/he knows personally, all one's life, still s/he has to come to a sense of self, an "I am," who can think, reason, propose, answer, respond and be. The "I," the individual is her/himself... plus.

The older empirical arguments for perception and cognition seem less true today in the sense that cognitive systems are to some extent socially mediated: to see, for example, what others see; to articulate language approximately as others do. The arguments from death and sickness are more persuasive, in the sense that they strengthen the notion of the individual person, and turn each of us "into" ourselves to see "our being."

However the important notion here is that no one is an either/or in actual life. We live in some ongoing/changing complex of individual and society, where neither definition nor delimitation can be taken as a given, and the other a gloss upon it. Who I am (or anyone is) is always in some interactive processual mode, between factors such as how I appear to others, how I have defined myself, history and future and what is happening in any present moment. So it is difficult if not impossible, to discuss being (only) within the context of this sort of dualism.

What is the case with respect to *theories* of our being, however, is that life events and social conditions can drive or push us into a dualistic framework of interpreting self-hood: within a dualism, toward one pole or the other of (in this context) individual or society. Sickness and old age tend to push one to dwell on his/her individual self, or occasionally to seek social "solutions" to these problems of living. It is interesting that theories of individual/society often interact with theological outlooks: my God/our God, and that this intermeshing is equally interactive and complex as our (strictly?) experiential theories of being. (Sarles: *The Body Journals*).

A major difficulty with theories of individual vs. society is that they also "inform" politics or political theories, and policy. If the world is assumed to be composed purely of "free" individuals with society imposing on this "natural" freedom (Rousseau, 1762—*Social Contract*), then each individual should be able to follow his/her (unique) potential to some ultimate point.

The social difficulty here, of course, is that this defines other persons as some diminishing or controlling force upon the individual, creating a fragile sense of family and society. In the reverse theory, of the individual as no more than what society defines him/her to be, and any personal sense of freedom or justice can be legitimately diminished in the name of some social "good." Bureaucracy fits this well, with the individual being defined as a job description, with the often consequent diminution of self.

The existential problem, the problem in living, is also a set of problems in individual and society, but one which is not only more complex than any single dualism would suggest, but one which changes at least occasionally throughout life. One is always, say, a son or daughter (a social notion), but is also a particular person of a particular age or size or expertise. Parents die, one marries, expanding, changing social relations: one's children grow up.

Existentially, humans seem to (attempt to) create coherent senses of self, to remember/forget aspects of this, and to carry at any and all points of life a sense of "who I am," and who I am that others are not; who are others that I am not. It is this coherence of self which is, to the greatest extent, the individual self: who lives, loves, moves on in life, creates a sufficient sense of love of self to continue to will living to move on to his/her "next places" (Sarles, 2006)

But this is always also interactive: constructed within a sense of continuity and coherence which others attribute to anyone by naming, by consistency of treatment, by entering into varieties of contractual arrangements (marriage, etc.). A set of existential, interactive questions remain active in our lives: who am I (not) that my parents, friends intended me to be? Who am I (not) that my work is for (self, children, others); what will I attack/defend, in what "cause"?

All of this to state that, existentially, the reality of life's experiences is perennially enmeshed in problems of self and society, often further complicated by living within theoretical outlooks which may stress one pole or the other exclusively.

To pose a notion, for example, of a deity which is exclusively personal (much of fundamentalist New Testament interpretation) is to not be able to explain or understand the existence of others (family, community), irrespective of the existential *facts*. So the facts, existentially, can be downgraded (via Plato's *Phaedo*), and a kind of extra, invisible existence posited which reinforces the individual interpretation, but leaves the "facts" of actual life in a place of suspicious limbo.

Similarly in a social-role interpretation of the individual as entity, a creature of external definition; the facts of existence, of any sense of "I-ness," are publicly denied, driving the individual "into" himself or herself, limiting the possibilities of actual experience, or severely shaping them (e.g., celibacy).

Finally, it is necessary to point out that almost any theory of existence such as exclusive individual or social, can sustain life if it does not totally "interfere" with the kind of interactive actualities by which living and generation and sustaining of persons continues to persevere.

The Cosmological Question: The Cosmological Question is the human posing, seriously, of the question: "whither existence?" Do I exist?

Proposed solutions to this question, which seems to arise in epochs of deep uncertainty (Buber, 1937), are often very powerful. Witness Descartes' "I think, therefore I am."—a solution which has set off several centuries of investigation into the nature of the human "mind," trying to account for whatever is thinking (underwriting and guaranteeing *being*, as it were).

The general search for causality of the "whither" of existence arises from the (apparently) associated existential questions of why do I exist? Do others exist" What is the nature of this existence?

The "why" of existence in Western Thought, where the existential-cosmological question has been most persuasive, has apparently grown out of the Western sense of an order of the world—from things (physics) to humans ("after" physics).

The things, the physics is the simpler: we humans are the end result, the after-ness, composed of things, plus some animating force which leaves us upon death (Aristotle: *de Anima*).

The ways in which the cosmological question arises also has to do with the finiteness of things and the "infinitude" of the human imagination. To be both "here and now" and "in" the entire universe at any time in our thinking has impressed thinkers at least since Parmenides (*Frag. VIII*) first wondered if we could distinguish between being and non-being.

The dichotomy, the dualism between "now" and "forever" is an associated theme since Pythagoras posited that the "now-ness" of our being and existence, is underlain by a permanence of the form of ideas (e.g. number, geometry, objects, musical harmonies) in which humans partake.

It was to account for this "permanence" of forms that the essential idealism of the human "spirit," "soul," or "mind," from which the idea of a deity which was enduring and "forever" arose. It was this deity-as-solution to our question of the dualism of now-infinity, which underlies much of Western thought, and led to a depiction of human metaphysics which was dual; the dualism being in-time (the body), and out-of-time, enduring (the "mind").

As well, the question of *human* existence was separated from the problems of living, as we excluded other species from the enduring, calling them "bodies" and comparable to our bodies, which are aspects of us which are "in-time" and led to the construction of philosophy which is mostly about human "language,"—language and logic being, it has been said, uniquely human because they are/allow us to be both immediate and infinite.

The Comparative Vision and Human Universals: What are the bases for comparing humans, and to what extent can these be extended to all people(s): everywhere; in all times?

Solomon Asch (1990) criticizes this tendency to say we humans are all the same in some essence, as the "transcendental pretense" emanating from Kant. He implies that different "cultures" have to be seen in specific or individual terms as do people, and that the universalization of the human condition is an intellectualization. The notion of "pure" reason" is not sufficient.

Though I am critical of the notion of some human essence related to "reason," I think the idea of human nature in a universalizing sense is indeed, rich and, even "correct."

The criticism of "reason-as-essence" is related to the idea pervading Western thought which claims that humans are unique in soul/reason, but like animals in bodily attribution: the "juxtaposition" argument.

Partly this is shown to be incorrect by ethological studies of some other species, showing that they interact, communicate, and understand one another, possess "culture" in at least some ways which have been claimed to be uniquely human: apparently, some other species are more similar to us than this sort of uniqueness claim would justify.

Secondly, it is clear if we spend some time and effort studying the bodies and behavior of other species, that the bodies of humans are a/the locus for what we regard as human. Whether our minds are unique in some transcendental sense, or unique due to our bodies, or not very unique at all, remains not very well known and moot. Even including severely "retarded" persons, they are still "retarded" humans, not to be judged as more "animal-like" because of their peculiar faces or physical anomalies. (Indeed, they have been misunderstood exactly because of this false thinking, inferring from imperfect body to "defective" mind.)

So there is good reason to believe that all humans are much the same (i.e. universal) because of their sameness of body. The differences among human bodies shrink to nothing, especially in the comparative framework, seen in comparing any/all humans to any other species.

But to return to the arguments deriving from dualism, even if we agree within the context of the "essentialist" line, there is good evidence to suggest that humans all "raise" their children to become human in approximately the same senses as all others. Whatever the potentialities and propinquities of human infants (and I presume they are extremely large), the learning of the world is shaped by adults to a remarkable extent.

Development is not to go from "biological to rational" (as Piaget (1952) would have it), but to become like their parents, the adults of every today. This means that they learn or otherwise come to understand the world in turn sufficiently the same as their parents; so that they will understand one another in great breadth and depth.

That is, knowledge-epistemology is not about each individual knowing the world in any direct or objective sense, but in knowing the world through others, and as others know it. It is the world of in-common-sense (as Heraclitus used that concept.)

The reasons this turns out to be universal are of two sorts: (1) humans come to the world in sufficiently similar terms that they are mutually translatable, and (2) each individual must come to think of him/herself as an "I." I will call this "the essential act of human discovery," because it can nowhere be taught.

The usage of "I" and "you" is everywhere reciprocal, and each person must, in essence, "discover" that the pronoun "I" belongs to each person, self, especially him/herself. This notion of the individual, of each "I" is demanded by the parental generation, including the making of statements, of propositions, of intending, of explaining, of working at an understanding of who is that self, that individual who I state to be "I," that I who I am.

Each and every "normal" human being comes, through language and the pronoun "I," to conceptualize s/himself in a sense sufficiently similar to all others that it is possible to state that humans are essentially the same: conceptually universal.

But, this is a dynamic, processual sense of "I," of self. The sense of constancy of any self, a continuity throughout life is not merely built-in, but has to be worked-at in living. Much of the sense of self-constancy is provided by each person seeing s/himself as "I," but also because the significant others in one's life regard one as the same; the same person, the same name, the same relationship. It is not anywhere fixed, one's individuality attached to one's morphology, one's body, but because others treat each person, each "I," as that person (grant personage).

This (not alone, obviously) seems to allow each human being to be like all others; sufficiently for us to talk about some *essential* notion of Human

Nature, and to state that there are indeed, some human universals. But these are not fixed in a "creationist" sense, or predetermined in any "biological" sense, but aspects of the dynamics of "generation" (i.e. being children of functioning social adults), having particularly developed outlooks upon the world, a sense for theories and problematics of being.

How do Humans Differ?: Granted that there are dynamic senses in which all humans share some (*essential*) features, still humans differ from each other. How do we differ? Are these differences fixed? Are they insurmountable; transcendental? To what degree can we change, in any time frame, to move towards or away from others?

Consider language and linguistic "habits": surely any human infant can come to speak any (or several) human languages. This is a matter of experience, exposure, and a kind of muscular flexibility which being an infant is; or enables. Speaking a given language is not only a set of rules, but particular muscular habits (of use and disuse) which become relatively well "set" at any early age (6 to 10, or so). These habits "result" in some large degree in what we "look like" (the way we use, e.g., our lips and hold them in some particular degree of roundedness, say, or tension), and also in some well grooved dynamics of tongue and mouth articulation which is so artistically precise as to deserve to be called "balletic."

Why these are difficult to change after age 10 or so is that these habits have to be altered, to be suspended (so to speak), and this turns out to be difficult, at least for most people, for several reasons: (1) to attempt to speak another language may require great change from a set of already well-accustomed habits, which may be difficult to overcome; (2) in some cases, there are new muscle movements which require (literally) new strengths whose ability is not obvious; (3) in other cases, to learn new/other sounds, one must suspend well-grooved habits, and one essentially "loses" some function—most people resist these sorts of changes (in my experience gained from violin study).

With "good coaching," however, these habits can usually be overcome or altered. Attributes of good coaching include: knowledge of the first and "target" language; analysis of both, including the ways in which any particular person (language: i.e. habits) may change efficiently or effectively; confidence in coaching and in getting the "student" to be confident of one's ability to change; an analysis of each student. Whether this sort of change can be effective for all persons through all of life's seasons remains moot. But if people are "motivated" to change, to attempt new/other ways of speaking, then most speaking habits can be altered or overcome. In many other cases, an interpreter can help.

This also seems true of many other aspects of our lives: including habits of thought, outlook, dealing with others, with oneself, and with the world. Some of these are questions of (cultural) identity, of religion, of philosophy; others, of how we relate to others whom we see as like us, or not like us. None, as far as I know or understand are impenetrable or non-understandable to the "outsider." So there exist "brokers," "translators" or "interpreters" who can (to whatever extent) know more than one way of thinking and being. The differences among us, that is, are not unbridgeable, but questions of interpretation, translation, etc.

This is not, however, to say that the differences are not deep, real, or unimportant. Experience also cautions us that change and/or transcendence of human differences is not necessarily attractive in every particular context.

Also, the notion of human difference has probably altered in some radical sense, only recently, within the context of the global village, as all people (virtually) are now aware that others exist who are very different from themselves, and in different ways. That is, peoples now differ from one another in a more "self-conscious" sense than previously: to some extent, we are not only who we are, but we are specifically not-like particular others: not Japanese, not Catholic, not...

How do Humans differ (from one another)? To state who we are (who I am) is to select some others—usually family or derived from a notion of generation—and to be "like them." That is, we become different not because of any intent to differ in the first instance, but because we (yearn) to be alike and to be liked. As we attach ourselves, generationally, to our families and significant others (e.g. teachers, heroes), we become more like them: in terms of bearing, outlook, questions, paths toward solutions, what we do. The differences emerge after some time, and are, in a sense, "surprising" because we had set out to become alike, not to be different. We are, in the first instance, Jews or Confucians; not non-Christians. It (merely) turns out that way, and perhaps this is a source of surprise and difficulty, and is, somehow, a betrayal of some sense of self: the first paradox of being.

Humans love touch of others, of self, of things. The world, early on, accessible. Later on much is removed, withdrawn, not available. Others' bodies, at first, given freely; gradually diminished, redefined, confined to hands or to mouths. One's own body, at first, remote, outside, surprising; gradually gains some sense of coherence and integrity, grows, weighs, analyses itself. Parts appear, some insist, others insistently urge touch to touch, touch to be touched. Much happens commonly, others are told how, when, not to touch, develop different urgencies, genders, to push or be pushed upon, two sorts: a surprise of sorts—the second paradox of being.

The Religious Outlook: The Religious Outlook: to confirm. To say "Yes" to all of being, of experience, of imagination; to "see" coherence and connection, some Grand Design, irrespective of observation or logic.

An inability (or unwillingness?) to say, "No," as if any nay-saying, any denial might topple the enterprise of being and the world. The irony: the fear and nagging worry that some (deep) sense of negation lurks within any destiny, positive when things are going well, but nihilistic in the (vague) threat that all can lose meaning. The paradox: that in the affirmation and confirmation, which it is impossible not to do (or think), there lies a hidden, denied fear that the entire enterprise can topple. Any theory of meaning which relies on the invisible-to-evidence or observation thus contains the seeds of (its own) destruction. If all apparent differences and/or discontinuities demand a coherence, then it is the theory of coherence which rules life; experience will fade when the necessity to find confirmation arises.

But life and life-with-others goes on irrespective of confirmation. Life is generally its own sufficiency and this is what's interesting and surprising. The religious outlook, on the other hand, does not want surprises, and is (always) on the verge of going out-of control.

Being and Understanding: Attempting to refute Kant's claims of human universals and the necessity for causal explanation in the world, it is evident that epistemology and experience are located (for Kant) within each individual. The individual, bounded by or ensconced— bones within skin—is the sole knowing entity, self-growing, self-defined. It is the individual who is *a priori* continuous, self-determining toward the future, getting to know about the world. In this context and concept of individuals' knowing, the notion that there is any common understanding must rely on some essentialist picture that humans are intrinsically *the same by nature*, in some universal sense.

Surreptitiously, assumptively this also carries the notion that entity-ness and being are continuous; also intrinsically.

Instead, it appears that humans are involved, in some deeply Heraclitean sense, both in change and are simultaneously continuous. Previously, continuity has been stressed and attributed, as I say, to the individual in some morphological sense of concrete being: concrete, I suppose, being hard, thus ongoing. Here I want to claim (to proclaim if I were Nietzsche) that the *individual* (now and forever more italicized) is in some complex of interaction with a few others who present and filter the world, how to know, and what is there to be known. Continuity is not (merely) within the individual but is provided by others knowing that individual as a character, as a person, as a significant someone with history and futurity.

In this context, knowing, being, and understanding are within the dominion not of the world, but of how others know and frame knowing about the world—a rhetorical (semiotic), not a descriptive knowing. This sense of knowing is not solipsistic, nor a mere imposition upon the world, but is a long-term working out of being and surviving. It is a knowing about the world, at once directly and indirectly: directly because it is sensory; indirect, because it is a human cognition within which the senses are shaped and directed by how others see, valuate and interpret.

We are universal, not because of any purely intrinsic knowledge-filter, but because adults of all societies engage in a similar process of educating their young to become propositioning, continuous individuals who learn language as they know and think it. Thus human universality is a kind of truth, a foundation from which, within which we may translate from one to another. But universality is, primarily, some sense of process toward becoming (an ontology), rather than any metaphysical sense of being. And it means that humans are intrinsically tied to one another in a variety of senses.

Within this ontology, however, a strong aspect of Being is that we are individuated and individuate ourselves: thus Being. But this is derived, not meta-physics, but meta-ontology is some sense following our sense of being as interactant. Thus, as logic is individual, logic is not any *synthetic a priori* (in Kant's terms), but requires a different notion or location within Being.

The development of the *a priori*: Though time and space (say) are usually (Kant) treated as a priori given to the human condition, they are most likely developmental. As human beings learn the world not directly (in the first instance), but as others treat the objects and categories of being, even the categories of space and time are derived from interaction with others. The error has been to consider that grammar and logic are in each individual; thus it followed that primary categories of space and time were postulated as necessary beginnings: beginning, that is, to learn to learn that/the what-nesses and how-nesses and whys of the world: how we are (and have to be) in order to know objects *a priori*.

Instead, the Q→R (Sarles, 1985, Chap. 12) system shows how a simple relationship between question and response may be developed between mother and child, into a system which is (effectively) infinite and located in each developing individual. There is thus no necessity to posit any sense of "pure reason" in the human condition; but only to posit some sense of an infant responding (acoustically) to its mother's questions. Here, "space" consists of an unlimited set of responses to "where" questions, and "time" a set of responses to "when." What humans are, then, is creatures who are in some (say) touch, acoustic, visual, etc, relationship to others, and can become, processually, total persons with sensibility, reason, etc. (Total = as their parents.) None of this has to be a priori, or pre-wired in any "hard" sense.

In Q→R, in effect, the categories are stacked by the mother; the child's response furthers the relationship as well as establishing the category: finite becomes non-finite without any claim to the uniqueness or "God-givens" of the human condition; no individual minds having to be creative to develop the imaginary and *a priori* categories by which knowledge is made possible.

This is not to say that humans are not reasoning, clever beings; only that we principally *become* human and are not merely created in full measure.

Consider the following from Kant.

"But though all our knowledge begins with experience, it does not follow that it arises out of experience. For it may well be that even our empirical knowledge is made up of what we receive through impressions and of what our own faculty of knowledge (sensible impressions serving merely as the occasion) supplies from itself. If our faculty of knowledge makes any such addition, it may be that we are not in a position to distinguish it from the raw material, until with long practice of attention we have become skilled in separating it. This then is a question which at least calls for closer examination, and does not allow of any offhand answer: - whether there is any knowledge that is thus independent of experience and even of all impressions of the senses. Such knowledge is entitled *a priori*, and distinguished from the *empirical*, which has its sources *a posteriori*, that is, in experience."

Above, I have suggested that there is no *a priori* knowledge necessary to any theory of being. The questions remain: what is the nature of *experience*? What are its *loci*? Again, even experience is not merely located in the individual, but with and with respect to social interactions. If there is an *a priori*, its locus is in the relationships between persons, not within whatever is called knowledge. This insight, along with Q→R reconciles rationalism and empiricism. Thought has its basis, its method, its impetus in Q→R, while experience informs which aspects of Q and R are propositionally appropriate and/or evident.

Why? Does the problem of existence reduce, come down, to the nature of the question: Why?

Why this? Why that? Why and why-not? All demand some sense of satisfaction. An incompletion, we suspect, wanting answers which satisfy.

"Because," that's why. Because and why occupying some special space which states and justifies that we are. Why existence? To answer the question, why, with a because that rings true.

Because the world is, we are; because we are, the world is: a story and its inversion in either order generates a world-view which compels and informs life and living. Why?

Why ask? Why not merely live? Why not live, merely?

A child asks: "why?" The parent answers: "Because." Because that is how *I* say it is. Why?—A way of relating one generation to another.

Why? In the Q-R system, not any simple question yielding a single set of responses; not a simple set of answers to a single question. Why? Derived from prior questions such as when, where, who, what, how many... just beyond, which!? Why? No simple question of existence, but a kind of conclusion which ought to confirm the "propositional person," but leads as easily to questioning the question: why-not?

Why cannot (really!) question existence because it emanates already from existence. The question "Why existence?" does not lead to: "do I exist?"! But historically it has, and the problematics of existence, of why and because, wonders us that it has caused this wonderment.

Whose fault; why? What worries, what nags at existence? Does death inform the why-not, thence the why? *To be* always in skeptical opposition with *not-to-be* from Plato to Shakespeare to Heidegger. What fear, what is fear that it poses its own why?

Where do the emotions and questions interact? Or is it that texts de-texture life, abstract and remove us from existence just so far that we wonder if we are? What is the relationship between: "why" and "if"? Do they slide upon some slippery slide from "because" to "then"? Why -because::if-then. Is the slippage of existential surety located in these four dots [::]?, which form some logical foundation? Is mathematics "iffy"?

Doesn't all of this depend on some materialist notion that physics precedes being? This is, perhaps, why "why" is problematized, and metaphysicians are always trying to catch-up, running upon some philosophical treadmill, always running in place and seeming to get somewhere.

Truth and Survival: Any species (any individual) which has survived to experience the present must have a deep sense for truth of being and of the world. Whatever is true, whatever is rational, the survivors-who-know partake of it. Each "species" owns or controls a sense of reality which is sufficient to survive (at least). Thus rationality, a sense of knowledge and truth concerning the world is not restricted to human beings alone.

This is not to say that survival is the same exact nature for all species, because the *Umwelt*, the ecology (etc.) of the world may be and is quite different for various species; only that survival, thus present or proximate existence partakes of the truth, almost by virtue of its being. To whatever extent truth equals science, then each surviving species is scientific, querying, testing, and responding to the world.

More, however, in the context of species-as-social, is that it is the adults who know, who are rational in their own terms, who pass this on, via development to their young. Becoming is not merely growing up physically, but is a particularity of being, shaped to be like that of the surviving adults.

In this contest, skepticism disappears or reduces to an experiential non-counter.

Natural:

"Natural! Natural! Yes, no doubt, natural. But what do they mean by this word? Are the sounds of a flute natural, if by this word we understand a thing that only nature makes?" (Joubert, 1803)

"Finally, when you can't find the word you were looking for, you put down the word that was there, which might lead you to it without your knowing how. This is in fact natural, for nature carries you to it." (Joubert, 1803)

Nature: Where is Nature? Where are we? Today I go to visit Dr. Mead who will do some reflection and refraction, checking the lenses of plastic which alter my own eye's lens to see what and if I see well. Would I even survive if I were truly "nature's" creature? But aren't lenses natural? Isn't plastic natural? Where does nature begin and end? Where do humans?

Nature's time: The creatures now upon this earth (or most of them) got here through some process of being, becoming, surviving, changing in ways associated with nature: natural causes, natural selections working upon struggles to continue, interests in remaining. What was natural remains in some senses and extents, but what was is not now. Pre-Cambrian, before life, is not now. Nature thus has its time, is *in* time, process, and we are aspects of it.

Nature fixed/changing:—some deep confusion between two views of Nature, depending on one's view of where humans are with respect to Nature, and how changeable are humans. Two views of biology as Nature:

one with respect to Judeo-Christian understanding of Creation, and the other with respect to biology. Here, Nature is changing, evolving for biology, yet according to Christianity, Nature was fixed once and for all by an unchanging God. But, Nature as biology is fixed with respect to an essentialist view of humans being outside of Nature, from the perspective of a dualism of mind/body.

Nature/natural: Some sense of the mechanical-material body existing upon its own "plane" within Nature: feed it right, exercise it well, it will grow properly, become strong, remain healthy. Here, Nature and Human are in some harmony of synergy. The up-side of homeostasis, a short-term view of bodily vigor.

Nature→an excuse to do what I (want; must) do. Since (it says) I am nature/nature's creature, what I do *must* be "natural." Shades of de Sade, of all those who want to live out their passions, not wondering who I am that I am at once self-contained and boundless, redounding my life on and with others. Somewhere in this mélange, the arenas of confluence of self and morality and social theories; some sense that each individual exists independently in the most "important" senses of being.

Nature→an order of physical-material objects in nature/found naturally, to the earliest = lowliest life-forms, to humans; in some Aristotelian *Scala Naturae,* a sense of history, of development, of progression which develops, infers its own causal nexus: a god; a reason; toward god; toward reason.

Nature's Laws: an always, an ever, the Laws of Physics always operate → Life: a mix of Nature/some other idea ("Culture"). The body in Nature → the mind outside; leads to the sense of permanence/change which is the dualism of Western Thought. The more real, the Natural is the permanent, the always-operates → life, less real, leads to the development of life-as-illusion.

Nature and skepticism: to whatever extent we imagine ourselves removed, remote from what is Nature, we often feel skeptical about our human ability to know anything. All this in spite, somehow, of knowing what and how we know, all this "ordinary" knowledge recedes into some crack while we sit, oracle-like, removed from Nature berating knowledge and congratulating human dignity that we are not (any longer?) bestial. Nasty beasts do not know, they are (we say) in Nature, totally in the contexts of their own being, and here we are above, beyond, outside of Nature, half self-congratulating half-wishing we could return to some Jungian before-hand where simplicity and contentment must have resided. Or we wish ourselves back to Adam's (Adamic) language, in which he was given the true (natural) names of all the things, all the species. Here we are, half-smug, half-self-doubting that we are capable of anything except doubt, even about that knowledge by which we have come to this position of arrogant stupidity doubting existence.

Nature: its invocation a bad intellectual habit? It is mostly technology, after all, which has gotten us to this place which seems outside of Nature. From writing, to levers, to replaceable teeth, eye glasses, modern medicines, most of them are technique. The claims of Culture and Civilization depend on techniques of farming, of transportation to set up the scales of living together in droves which have led to the concept of city and state which have then re-filtered our thinking about who we are and why we are not who we claim we are not.

Nature—a fear of Self: the Western (esp. Christian) worry that we (each I) is at once in Nature, but also outside. The body, like beasts of earth to return, the mind soaring cast upon the infinite viewing its own corporeal placement, yet pulled upon by the passions which are the body, the earth, Nature. "What fear?" you ask. The fear of the loss of control, the taint of evil, of the sin which the fall from Heaven forced into the loins of our parents whose minds could not control the demands of earth, and Nature upon their loins conceiving the "I" which worries about itself worrying and fears its own experiencing of fear. And where to locate those fears and worries; how to identify which are to be trusted, which not? Does evil, the satanic forces which bedevil the mind, is this the same as Nature? (The real psychological problems: that my Nature will take me over, causing me to think thoughts, or worse, to do things I—the "I" of who I really hope and wish to be, the Heavenly, spiritual I—do not want to do beyond my control... Worse, that having thought them, that having done them, I cannot relieve the guilt, cannot relieve the remorse which will ensnare me deeper, captivating me in the part of me which is Nature, which is at war with the self I tell myself I truly want to be and to love. Each day (every moment) always coveting something I am not, cannot, will not be. And who else is involved, what temptations, what weaknesses...will Nature out? If I give-in, do I die? ...if I do not?

Human Reflections: We see ourselves reflected in the surfaces of various "objects"—mirrors, robots, faces—to name some...

How real are these reflections in the insides of our mentalities? Is the face I see as me, the character who I am? Created in the image of a god whose portrayal glances back out at me when I look into the silvered glass? Do I memorize the face in the mirror, carrying that image with me, in me, as me, when I walk around unreflecting. Is the notion to reflect, a mental thought-deepening, a considering apt?

Others' faces! When they look upon me, whom do they see? How much me; how much they? Which cast of character, the sour, somber, sarcastic me; the weak, asking to be taken-care-of; the wise, strong, wondrously penetrating me—which one does anyone see? Me, I, looking at them, seeing, judging, which faces, which countenances affect me, looking back, looking inward? What power, what confusions, masks? Who is someone that s/he is not? What she, what he, what effect gender upon my seeing myself in their faces, telling me who they are they... that I am?

Dolls looking human-like, like children mostly with big heads with big eyes pasted upon them looking at us looking at them, seem almost human, yet are not. They are dolls, they do not move; yet we endow them what we want and what we will, our names, our talk, our imagination, talk, touch, little demand, less corrective. Are they more human, and we less? Do dolls diminish us? Do they provide time-out, safe harbors, where they speak out and speak back only within our own terms? What terms, dolls? Human faces, young; human-like bodies, now more and more real-like, with clothes and paper cut-outs, now able to pee and talk and do the things that humans do; still passive except in the fantasy of Nutcracker Suites' momentary movements to enlivenment, or the morality of Pinocchio's wanting the passions that most of us only test and fear and cannot recover from, often, in our having actualized them.

Now all combined in computers and robots: mirrors, pets, dolls, endowed with a sort-of thinking, a being looking back at us, who yet (as yet) makes no moral judgments. More than a doll, more than a pet—do they teach us how to touch them? As they, the ITs that were, become more like humans, do we become less, like human? Fun? Games? Serious?

Lights: Illumination, the Festival of Lights, enlightenment, a candlelight ceremony on Christmas Eve, all speak to the sense that we live greatly in darkness. From Plato's Cave where we will distinguish what is from what is shadow, there is some push upon some of us to seek the light too, in the path to the place of knowledge leading to the truth. Strange, then, the inversion: any idea which claims its own truth gathers light to proclaim itself—as if the metaphor of light is sufficient to convince us of its inherent correctness; and it often works. Is it this proprietary utilization of the metaphor certifying what is truth, which is the major mark of civilization?

Light and Life: In certain ways life is a coming to our senses. Seeing is, for many, the major sense and light is its mode and vehicle. Before life, after life, there is no sense, no light, no being. The mode of life as soul and mind takes the light of our lives and extends it into other realms of our being: into dreams, onto the before and after-life so that light is everywhere, being is all illuminated. And the world of sense, of experience is not different in its essence from any other sense of being or of knowing. How sad, somehow, that the gift of life which is ours seems to want to diminish itself.

Unnatural Light: Is not the light of day sufficient? No more do we live our lives bound by sun and moon. In the morning in the winter we arise before the sun, lift a bit of plastic, create kitchen light and the heat which keeps bones from splintering of frost's expansions. Light, heat, yet nature, occurring within my control seems somehow unnatural. Life's rhythms, now self-determinable out of sun's phases, away from the lives of the plants which feed us. Yet we seem not so tied, not so dependent, not near yet not so far from a sense of Nature empty of Human intervention. Not as before, now we seek light and find it fired by channeled elections within the houses which keep out cold. Where have we come then; by what paths; what directions hence? Unnatural light: does it cast no shadows to be brushed aside revealing Truth?

Characterizing Humans → Person(age): The symbolic self, the dual who I am that is not from my "inside," the character that others see in me, which others see me as, is endowed "upon" me in the first few moments of life's infancy. Because we are creatures of the face, because we *see into* newborns' faces destiny and destiny in the new face of each day's awakenings, because... thus, we are already in the "minds" of others, their own projections of our characters; who we are seen as; whom we are seen to be constructed out of the life experience of the viewers' viewing our newborn faces: mouths, noses, eyes constructed upon some ground of cheeky flesh—a face, a who, a person, personage is that we adults say s/he is. Genders extrapolated to a facial future, a "who" who will be like me one day looking upon a self-same sense endowing character to a fledgling flesh-ling. Thus the beginning, the origin of character, of a self which other(s) imbue us with.

Human Nature and the Notion of the State: Have our theories of what is Human and what is Nature been determined principally, primarily within the context of city/state?

What alterations, what pressures on the concepts of Human Nature within the sense of the Global Village, of the entire earth and all its populations?

It is now possible, indeed (I suspect) the information is available on who/what all the world's peoples are "like:" how they are and how they are different from "us" and from one another. The U.S. in a peculiar position because "everyone's here" in some sense or other, and we have trouble transcending local views with respect to such issues as "class," "intelligence," "habits," etc. For some of us distance from home is easier, transcendent— others, far away, are placed upon pedestals; we concentrate on their theories, and our sense of what is best, most romantic, "highest" about them. For others of us, we judge morally with us at some epicenter, and others all diminished, possibly dismissed. Many of us cannot get past the prejudices and observations from our own houses or communities.

From far away: different societies, different religious and philosophical traditions. What is a person, what is human nature, or experience, within other traditions? What alters when traditions inter-mix (as in the U.S.) with other traditions (e.g., Western medicine and Far Eastern, S. Asian views of medicine and the body)?

When they actually intermix, which notions of each are called to attention/pushed away? Do they find common grounds and focus on these; or do they, seeking to maintain integrity push these away? What do (our) Jews do in America (for example), focusing on a mutual life covenant in a Christian world which is obsessed with death? Didn't Confucianism, upon defending itself against Buddhism, alter itself drastically, focusing on metaphysics, weakening its powerful notions of a perfectible ontology?

Have our concepts of morality, the Brother-Sisterhood of humankind been extrapolated from knowing a few others (and ourselves), thence extended to all the world? What problem the differences in history which bind us (blind us?) and others to particular understandings and interpretations of human beings? What if "they" do and act differently than we thought: do we revise us; them?

What concept of "authority" is there in the world? Wise men, wise women? Do concepts of knowledge alter (besides technology which has claims to be "universal")?

Does knowledge (as Nietzsche claims 1882) simply "satisfy" the ordinary person, making the unknown appear known or controllable? In what context (state/nation) does this notion of knowledge gain power? Does each individual diminish in "size" when the sense of the state spreads to the world?—or does it enlarge as the near powers themselves become diminished? → more or less "access" to the effective world!

Proper Judgment: Why does each place and age have to think that its moral judgment is the proper judgment—for all places, all times? (Each subject, religion, discipline, each...?) What theories of being and of nature are general to all of judgment: which are particular, and how do we tell which is?

If I hated myself, my ability to judge myself, my hatred would itself always be insufficient. Not even to despise my own despising, or to love my own despising... it is a puzzle.

To write, to compose, or to formulate even two words in a row requires judgment. I do not (I think) perform *amanuensis*; no demons or gods speak to me in any language that I hear to write down, so I make it all up. My head does not buzz on its own. I think I make it talk, like this talk—talk judged.

For me, I am as large, as important as the entire universe. I say what is what each day, all the day.

But where do I garner the means to judge, to judge judging? A matter of taste? But much of what is taste seems learned?—food, music, ideas... How much, which parts are confidence and strength? How willing or able am

I to pay the prices for being wrong; for having been wrong? When do I/we cover, protect: when, bold? When should/must I change?

How much, what part, does moral judgment play in formulating, justifying theories of Human Nature? Are we talking of truth, of justification, of just keeping calm?

No More Primitives: All the world's peoples are becoming "urbanized," parts of a world culture, or living to some extent with respect to a knowledge that the world is vast and the peoples are many. While all people "live off the land" in some ultimate sense, the primitives—hunters, gatherers, those with little technology, less of the "artificial," close to the natural, those whose lives co-exist with and within the rhythm of the solar, lunar, seasonal cycles of the "world-as-it comes," such people hardly exist any longer. Perhaps they have progressed, becoming technologized, becoming... civilized; perhaps not: Aside: Or driven out, enslaved, or murdered.

The difficulty (for this is what it is) is that we no longer know how to locate Nature within the Human condition... and part of why I claim that whoever controls the definition of Human/Nature controls destiny.

When there were Primitives ("Savages") we could point to them to see, quite closely, a good approximation, we thought, what is natural to humans. We were (are?) quite concerned with notions of difference—placing them within some sense of (usually, linear) history. They, these primitives, were "long ago"; we (always we and they) were modern, today, civilized, progressed beyond and after; we-culture/they-nature. By these means, we could "measure" (and much of the theory about Human Nature concerns itself with the nature of such measures; e.g. the dualism of mind/body) and claim to be more than "they." But now with no more primitives we seem to have lost our measures. At the least we are threatened with the loss of measure and of locating ourselves—possibly why we find the reinvention of racism persuasive and important.

But the loss is not simply a problem of comparison and of difference: it involves a scheme of historical *development*. Thus history becomes problematic in some ways. It involves questions of how to live properly or well, of morality and the obligations of life, because many of these derive from notions of "how far" we are from a Nature which (we have presumed) does not give a hoot for morality. It involves the question of what is Human—anew!

Religion as Theatre: Living in a place and time where the major religion has been in pursuit of the "holy" dollar, where a liberal-secular outlook has ensconced the real work of societal maintenance in a bureaucratic outlook whose principal existential problem is boredom, it is amazing to come to realize how much of the theatre of life there can be. Here and now we seek to be entertained as passive observers watching images, listening to electro-mechanical recordings of people's talented spoorings and embroidered detritus. Yet, for the inspired to be inspired, there is much more.

Perhaps it is all imaginary; tales about the god of fear, of strength, of vengeance, of all of creation; of the god who spoke to us when we humans were very "young"; of birth and life and death and a raft of stories to instruct us in how to think and do and judge. And many people thus construct this world as theatre where each of us is in constant, that is every minute, relation to the forces and the stories and we are all partakers in the drama.

"Tell me, tell me again and again, and again," seems to the rest of us, those who sit outside of a theatre which we do not see as drama, as a boredom, a kind of weakness to be "believers," to be bowers-down-to. Yet, to those inside, it is constantly exciting, constantly dangerous, a necessity to engage, to read and think and know, a real seriousness: the space, the words, the songs and music all speak of transcendent worlds, of a beyond which casts experience right smack upon the stage; the rest of us standing outside in the marketplaces, looking, vending, selling; not seeing, not hearing the applauses of the believers whose theatre is replayed each day or week, and the believing actors are participants in their own lives. Luckily, for the *ongoingness* and presentation of self and of life, we are much more complex creatures than we tell ourselves we are.

Luckily: *For the ongoingness and preservation of self and of life, we are much more complex creature than we tell ourselves we are!*

The Second Attention (Castaneda 1): Being trained to be a philologist, concentrating on seeing what is known, but out-of-awareness, the orderliness and systematics of how we speak and hear, why we are linguistic comparators as we hear dialect differences, the senses in which we maintain life and our *ongoingness* while telling ourselves stories about being (and our own being) which are often illusory or do not pertain; how we get from here to there and back and map in the complexities of the dynamics of moving.

I write (formerly, when this was drafted) with pen, cursive squiggles in small muscle movements; squiggles that I "tell" my hand to write, and it does, and it amounts to words which mean what I mean them to mean. So knowledge—none of which I can talk about much, except in the doing and their being... and, so what?

What can it mean that my physiology has a "life of its own"? The heart is independent? What does my heart "know" about its own functioning; about "my" functioning? Does it need to know? Is there knowledge without self-consciousness about knowledge (or is this merely a question about, e.g., perspective)?

What, then; where then is our nature? Which is the strongest; which, independent and in what senses? Does knowing more (and more) about ourselves help?

According to Nature:

"You want to *live* 'according to nature'? O you noble Stoics, what fraudulent words! Think of a being such as nature is, prodigal beyond measure, indifferent beyond measure, without aim or intentions, without mercy or justice, at once fruitful and barren and uncertain; think of indifference? To live—is that not precisely wanting to be other than this nature? Is living not valuating, preferring, being unjust, being limited, wanting to be different? And even if your imperative 'live according to nature' meant at bottom the same thing as 'live according to life'—how could you *not* do that? Why make a principle of what you yourselves are and must be?—The truth of it is, however, quite different: while you rapturously pose as deriving the canon of your law from nature, you want something quite the reverse of that, you strange actors and self-deceivers! Your pride wants to describe your morality, your ideal, to nature, yes to nature itself, and incorporates them in it; you demand that nature should be nature 'according to the Stoa' and would like to make all existence exist only after your own image—as a tremendous eternal glorification and universalization of Stoicism! All your love of truth notwithstanding, you have compelled yourselves for so long and with such persistence and hypnotic rigidity to view nature *falsely*, namely Stoically, you are no longer capable of viewing it in any other way—and some abysmal arrogance infects you at last with the Bedlamite hope that, *because* you know how to tyrannize over yourselves Stoicism is self-tyranny—nature too can be tyrannized over: for is the Stoic not a *piece* of Nature? But this is an old and never-ending story: what formerly happened with the Stoics still happens today as soon as a philosophy begins to believe in itself. It always creates the world in its own image, it cannot do otherwise; philosophy is this tyrannical drive itself, the most spiritual will to power, to 'creation' of the world, to *causa prima*." *(Nietzsche 1886)*.

A Priori **Categories:** Pure reason? Space and time are givens, inbuilt, prewired, innate? No! I don't agree. Each era seems to need its own *a priori*'s; plans to begin to assist in their accounting for the human condition or what is human. Give me, say, space and time (Kant) or my right hand (Wittgenstein, 1953)... But, is this the case?

I (need only to observe that the newborn is an organism, but hardly so independent; barely an independent entity, but an aspect of its mother and others who may feed "it." What is 'innate' has much to do with the *relationship* of infant to mother. What is learning, what is knowing is not knowing the world with or from some *a priori* categories, but a learning of the world as an (in)direct consequence of knowing the mother and oneself; the mother-as-oneself...

The categories of space and time are aspects of this relationship between newborn and mother. The mother effectively poses the world as questions, and the infant "knows enough" to respond: to the breast, to mouth-openings, to a touch on the cheek. A little later, to words which elicit responses; i.e., to questions such as who? when? where? what?: persons, time, spaces, objects.

The need to postulate space and time as categories arose because the wonderment persists concerning how finite creatures (might) partake in the infinite. The solution since Kant, at least, has been to postulate an infinite (*a priori*) human mind. However, the system of Question and Response shows that a response set of infinite membership is sufficient to explain the human ability to imagine without insisting that we are created that way (e.g., in God's image).

This is neither to argue directly against any concept of an infinite deity, nor to argue that other species are or are not infinite. It is to argue that language is no less finite than any other aspect of our beingness!

Technology and Human-Nature Arguments: Why does it appear so difficult to discuss the relationship, impact, importance of technology (especially biotechnology) to human nature?

Is it the kind of dualism, the corporeality and material basis of technology which can replace or interchange "organs" and "tissues" (physics vs. meta-physics)? Is it that the human can "lose" everything except the head and its enclosures (the brain and its casing) without losing its essence: the "person"? That this physics of our being is prior in the sense of "being of the earth," thus external to our being (at least after some age and life experience: say, 5-6 years)? Is it that anyone's life can be materially altered and replaced to such an extent that the science-fiction story of the person's life preserved in the "brain and the eye" is no longer science *fiction*—at least in our thinking?

Are machines one sort of thing with respect to our being (e.g. mechanical hearts/pumps), and part replacements from other persons, other creatures (baboons, pigs?), another? When does the "essential" individual disappear?—Legs, genitalia, liver, lungs, hearts, eyes, teeth...?

When does the individual, the person "appear"—at conception, at birth, at the age of propositional languaging?—Is this the other side of the same question; an aspect of it, or something other? Should we include the question of "What is an individual?" in this context?

Is the lack of discussion due, then, to the (apparent) fact that each replacement while spectacular at first, seems not to interrupt any person's, any individual's sense of integrity and of being? (Although wearing an ocular prosthesis since age 7 has certainly affected my life, if not exactly shaping it!) Is there, do we/are we/have we some "Will to Life" (á la Schopenhauer) which permits this "mediation" of our personages without upsetting our "integrity"? Does this sense of continuity of personal integrity "fend off" any critical discussion?

Or: are most H-N arguments conducted around the issues of what is particularly human that is distinct and unique, not from physics and materiality but from other forms of life. Probably not?--Because the replacement of human hearts by baboons' is no more/no less difficult than the other, material arguments. Is the problematic of lack of discussion due thus to some issues around a species (human and not-H) argument?

Or: are these somehow moral/ethical issues which reside in some religious sphere that has been kept outside; within a medical-materialist mode which is particularly secular *and* opposed to the sacred-religious? Does the discussion fall between, through these places of Caesar and God?

Rationality and Relativism: Because human infants and parents engage in doing, learning human grammar in the Q-R system, I believe that the dynamic human foundations of language and thought are everywhere (all languages, cultures) about the same. However, it is clear that (adult) cultural thought systems are often very different from one another. If these are not somehow "due" to language, and it is (I suggest) the case that everyone goes about thinking in approximately in the same way(s), how is it that such differences exist and come about?

This is to say that languaging is everywhere rational (perhaps, equally rational is better because "rationality" is not yet circumscribed), but various people(s) frame their outlooks and (some) aspects of their thinking within different, often a-rational or anti-rational frameworks.

One "solution" to accounting for this is the relativistic one: to say that different outlooks are different in some mere or inherent sense. But (I claim) the dynamics of language and thought are the same everywhere, so what are the bases of the differences?

Much of it seems to be in how the parents conceive of, and get the developing child to conceive of her/himself, and how to go about judging that "self." How good or bad or natural: how powerful, how dangerous, how important?

Time is taught through the question 'when?' → response set, but judgment about the sense of a long or short time is quite a different matter: does eternity frame each day, making it very long/short? How does the individual learn to stand outside of self: e.g. male, female? Is a child permitted to report "evil" thoughts or not; are thoughts or actions "labeled" by parents. How often does one judge or "count"?

Within the *same* language (e.g., American English) how does a child come to be a Catholic or a Jewish or Native American thinker?

Size: It has seemed to me that a "return" to religious literalism on the part of many so moved, is motivated by a sense of personal diminution, a reduction in size or in scale.

Within a materialistic theory of human being, for example, explanations for human moral and philosophical questions often do not arise or appear, as the human condition becomes an (perhaps interesting) aspect of particle physics or biological molecules, possibly of neurons. In this material context one's sense of being, of size, of importance and power, seems to recede, not to reside anywhere exactly. To say that I am here on earth, that my very existence is some "chance" event or some congeries of carbon rings, is not uninteresting necessarily, but doesn't help much when the days are not sunny or bright. Thus it is tempting to many to enlarge their (effective, existential?) size to fill some necessity of their being which any simple pain in the back or in a tooth can easily overwhelm.

To invent or discover or preach a Godhead which says "I am that I am," the most gigantic force in all the universes of all of being, has the direct effect of making anyone larger. To think that such a being cares about me, created me, loves me, is thinking even about doing vengeance if I happen to stray somehow is enlarging. I (diminished) find whatever is a necessary sense of person or of power in this story I tell myself, that I and my self are as large as I want or need to be.

Life's Diminutions: There are several ways (at least) in which humans may become "diminished." The diminution of oneself is not an uncomplicated notion or experience, and may include a lessening of personal experience (e.g., via news media), a bending of character toward some externally imposed definition (e.g., in the military, a bureaucracy, any situation where power is acceded to some external person or agency, and one has to "go along" with it); via technology where there is a "trade-off" between, e.g., speed (auto, plane) or strength (levers), so that a better job is done, but through some external agent or tool. All of these may diminish a person.

"Scale" also may diminish. When there are so many persons that one becomes (another) member of a class, then one is not a person, but some bit of attributes or features in common with all others who are seen to fit that category. In modern (1984) America, one is not a "who," but is a what-one-does; "I am a professor" or "I am a mother"—any one of these will do as well as any other.

When agency is exteriorized from people (e.g. the university as faculty, as a Community of Scholars— Newman, 1902), to curriculum (a set of courses taught by any interchangeable persons), then a person is diminished. Students study a "subject" rather than studying with a particular person.

When the world is politicized into an "us vs. them" (workers vs. management; professors vs. administration etc.) then we abstract ourselves into a position in an argument, and we, personally, diminish ourselves. Similarly, in a world which is considered (á la Aristotle) to be material *vs.* spiritual, the materialistic urge places causality outside of ourselves as humans, and we become something extra, often, *meta-* to physics.

In this latter sense of religion-as-spirituality, humans are diminished when taking the side of materialism. Peculiarly, within an outlook which is "authentically" or totally (big "R") Religious then humans are small with respect to God: e.g., why humanism enlarges us at first, only to be diminished when inspiration which is derived from humans occasionally languishes.

...The "size" of our being.

Integrity and Human Nature: Lessons from pathology and "insults" to any sense of the wholeness of one's being. From quadriplegics and paraplegics: the notion that a person can sustain life and thought with very little of the body intact and/or in any direct realization of its parts and aspects. From pathology: the notion that insult to integrity is most powerful; more powerful, even, than the physical destruction of much/most of the body. The insult is in a sense symbolic, a story one tells oneself about s/his wholeness, and it is this story which turns out wrong, false, or loses its sense of truthfulness, thus affecting the *concept* of the will to live. The body, one instant whole, the next not intact, adjusts to itself apparently quickly not in any mechanical instant, but almost. The concept of integrity, insulted, the body's image of itself broods long: as long in alteration, perhaps, as the long of its development—the metaphor of the root of the plant being about as large as its airy aspects, perhaps being apt.

The inference, then, that the wholeness and integrity of anyone's being is that aspect (at least) of the will to live, the will to power, the will to will...

The Fullness of Life: For some people, some of the time, life is sufficient. Who they are, what ambitions, desires, how life happens, the "who" of all relationships, is what they want; it is enough. The will to power is satisfied; full enough.

Why don't some persons seek any beyond what they are and what they have? Because many people seeking to become the character which is desirable, what is sought and what they see, is who they are. What more is necessary; what more is there? Any will to live, any will to power, is full up to the brim of existence.

Why don't they don't ask? It is not that life doesn't have sadness and down days and laments, but that the fullness accommodates much else of what there may be.

What creates the sufficiency? Is it merely, only that the world-scape of desirable possibilities and possible desires is satisfied? Is it that power has come into the life of any person as it ought to have, was supposed to? Is it that fullness itself expands at all opportunities to enlarge the life it enhances, amoeboid to the edges of all of life's living? (But the Stoic, Epictetus, tells us we can live with anything, no matter how bad!)

Life vs. Living: The existential shift, to live life, to be in the process of living, not to find a position from which to judge life as if I am removed from my own life, observing.

The Christian temptation: to accept the idea of the worst, and to live in that space at any and all movements, watching myself watching myself watching. This life turns into a query: This is life?

Sufficient Space: For many, life is not at all moments full; not sufficient, not enough; yearning for itself. What paradoxes reveal themselves trapped in the imaginings of what I had supposed, been taught to imagine, to turn life's "maybes" into the "is-ness" of life itself, left not so filled?

Nature-Culture: The universe of being split into two (equal/equivalent; coherent/integral?), where what is Human removes and is removed from Nature. Humans outside of the natural world, posing the question of some mechanism of how Humans are or come to be removed from a Nature where, in some sense or other of history, we all derive. Culture did it!—got us outside of nature.

The problems remain there: what is Culture?—this problematizing a new sort of wonder concerning the nature of Nature. Before, we merely queried or tested the question; now, we speculate upon the very nature of Nature, but within the context of what is Culture, that (it) is not Nature... in this new, dichotomized sense. Some circularity of reasoning here which re-problematizes an enquiry in some dimensionality outside of itself.

This is, of course, an Aristotelian type of category argument where it is wise to examine the structure of any dualism to try to pick-apart what is the problematic, if any, and what is the nature of any dualism such as that of Nature-Culture.

The first structural rule is one of "identity"—the notion that the dichotomy exists, plus the idea that the named categories are actual entities, *and* that these are in some sense well-bounded and equivalent.

Having entered this domain—innocently, gladly, or out of some intellectual hurriedness—the usual "task" is to identify the characteristics of one or the other category. Since it is in some sense dichotomous, the observations or other notions of one category, by virtue of their being, already imply the other category as they are "opposites" or otherwise partake in the notion of "otherness" which dichotomous thinking entails.

It is important to realize that either category, once identified (i.e., named) and located within a dichotomous space, becomes a kind of transcendent notion within or as structure, because the space of the dichotomous categories seems to enlarge itself to all of thought, wiping out much else of what is actual, and acting almost magnetically to sweep any extremities within its boundedness or to make them vanish. Thus the dual categories are transcendent like a deity and seem to us to make our minds "larger" or "higher," potentially all-encompassing.

The dichotomous category "game" enlarges so persuasively, in fact, that even after the initial listings, principles, and qualities are exhausted temporarily (because the quality of transcendence is such that the dichotomy will re-invent itself in some periodic cycles) the attempt is *to wander within* their "interface."

The "interface game" is to grant, to take-as-given the two categories as axes shaping the ends of the universe, and to attempt to show how the categories fit together, inter-relate, or "affect" one another. In the "mind-body antinomy," for example, various "moves" have been made, various games have been played there; some processual, dynamic; others postulating some group of entities operating in any particular time; others, even, which seem to connect the categories of body (more "ancient," "pre-human," "biological") with the mind ("recent," "human," "cultural").

Some have been "omnibus" statements, used and useful for different things in different times and contexts; e.g. the mind is the "real" us, placed within the body, as if by accident—here the interface concerns how they march in some parallel, non-mutually destructive ways, at least for a while. Or the interface was seen in a sense of linear history when it was posited to "contain" or to consist of the "emotions." "Facial expression," (Paul Ekman 2007) in this context, is seen to consist of the emotions "playing-out" upon the facial surface, the face becoming, then, a kind of place where the mind "operates upon" the body, at least where the mind "comes to the surface." The body, historically, was earlier (pre-human, pre-language, pre-"complex" communication), the emotions were somehow the pathway, the *via media* by which body got emotional noise (ouch!) turned into language; thence the mind; the soul, sociality, objectivity, rationality, etc. ("Natural Law" theory)

In another era the interface fades as problematic and the categorical boundaries re-arise as issues: what is the mind? what is in the mind? Here, Descartes, for example, used the *cogito ergo sum* to justify or to solve the cosmological question of existence by talking about *thinking*, refocusing on the mind (as by oppositional extension, inevitably upon the body) in terms of what they "are," how they "work," etc.

But, the point is, most of this argumentation is *structural*, already implicit in the very notion of a two-category oppositional scheme. Whereas possibly the most interesting question is: "what drives the system?" from category-bounding discussion to interface discussion, cycling once again to category arguments? And this is some sort of argument about the nature of form, but, most importantly, it is located very little in any sphere of context, but is ensconced in the history and, especially, in the sociology and politics of ideas.

Finally, in the present age, we begin truly to appreciate that these arguments are structural-formal, that the categories and oppositions may be transcended or superseded by denying any necessity for the dualism as in-opposition, and begin again to observe humans in the fullness of our being in the world; cloven together as we are (or we can acknowledge that much/most of life is paradoxical, and the perceived antinomies-oppositions are "unnecessary" to explain ourselves to ourselves).

It is the same with the categorical duality of Nature-Culture. The problem is to understand the range of actualities and possibilities, of difficulties and complexities in the having, being, becoming, sustaining of life in complicated times. To split the human universe into two in some a priori or "early" fashion is to pre-limit, perhaps, the nature of what we will study and consider to be the human condition; to defend or to ensconce ideas strongly in historical settings rather than to (enable us to) see us as we are—an approach which gets nervous and retreats into cynicism and varieties of nihilisms when the going gets tough.

On the opposite side, as it were, any (structural) dualism reacts to criticism in particular ways and directions *irrespective of particular content*. This has to do with the oppositional nature of dualisms; i.e., that any criticism seen to fit within the duality (and most criticisms must be seen there, in any transcendent phase of a dualism where the categories have expanded to the edges of the universe of knowledge) is seen to oppose my view, and that criticism is always referenced to the other side of the dualism.

If, for example, "Culture" is attacked, then the attack "must" be from the "Nature" side. The insidious difficulty is that the attack is referenced not to whatever the Naturist position is in any substantive sense, but to whatever the Culturists hold to be in the oppositionist category in that particular era; having little necessity to query those who hold the Naturist (say) position, but most to do with how the Culturists are defining or delimiting Culture, and with what notion of opposition that raises in their minds. Thus, if the Culturists feel criticized, they respond to any attack by attacking in return *their* notion of Nature, which may or may not have much to do with the category of Nature which the Naturists hold to be their truth. So, often, both sides end up attacking/defending their own construction of the opposite category, a "straw-man," rather than examining the actual content of the (apparent) opposition.

Antidotes include a stepping-back from the dualistic construction of any (apparent) problem, an examination (such as this) concerning the formal structure of any categorical form of argument, a comparative study of all dualisms to note commonalities, derivation, etc. (For example, mind-body, Culture-Nature *et al.*, are usually aspects or slight variations of the identical dualism into another realm of being.) This attempt to step-back may involve finding some other "ground" from which to observe, various forms of suspension of judgment, etc. It requires, as well, an excursion into the history of ideas as well as their sociology to see whence they derive, why they "made sense" and to whom; who were they directed against, if anyone; what other ideas did they argue against or supersede; what questions were agitating the thinkers of any era?

Above all, we must begin again to observe and to attempt to describe what there is, what happens and to whom. A *comparative mode* (for Human Nature, with other species), is necessary to being to understand issues of "locus" of any problem and questions of context → comparative thought.

From Other Species (from Nature?): The Lorenzian trick is to claim a wider universality to Nature, particularly what other species presumably are like, thence to infer to humans whatever aspects of being one notes (claims to note) in other species. (Lorenz: On Aggression, Chap. 13, "Ecce Homo.") Presumably as well, we humans possess these features of existence, but we cannot observe them clearly because we are too close to them, unaware, or blind to them for other/various reasons (the "arrogance" of language, for example).

The general error is in the claim that we can see clearly what other species are like; usually, on the grounds that they are simpler than humans, or possess some archetype which is ancient, showing up in various manners in different species. Most of these arguments, so far, are basically "political" in the widest sense of politics. They refer to relationships between intra-species individuals (e.g., "pair bonding," "dominance," "caste") which, since other species (on grounds of their "simplicity" = often, non-languaging) possess them, or "do" things some way, humans (they infer) "really do," or "ought to do." We human observers of ourselves are thus misdirected or misled. We should take the categories as observations from other species, and "apply" them to our seeing of humans—buying the authority of the "naturalist" to be accurate in telling us what Nature is.

The danger, of course, is that we see in other species, categories of behavior derived from some (theory of) human politics—then apply what we think we see in other species to humans in the name of (some concept of) Nature. This is circular at best, misguiding both our observations of other species and of humans. It is political in the sense of making some *simplistic* claim about other species and (inevitably) simplifying what is human; setting up the rather easy possibility of controlling a "simple" species.

It permits a kind of thinking about humans by which we are or ought to be *controllable*. Thus it is politics.

Humankind—the Goal of Nature: (Nietzsche: *Daybreak* V, 1881) Wow! How long ago did life begin? Thousands, millions, billions of years? And here we are. All of it, life that is, leading up to this moment. Laugh for joy? Cry for the sadness of the apocalypse which is the promise of this time?

The Design of Nature—all for us? Arrogance; vanity? We create the notion of Deity which serves us. Does it serve the notion of Deity?

Nature working, burrowing in the trenches all those eons without benefit of incandescent light or the microscopes by which close becomes very close. And all leading to us. To me!

Does every single being, breathing the essences of life's impulses, believe it all led to this very existence? Is our arrogance based on the sense that we know *about* our existence? And others do not? And if they do?

Better to find a better task than to attempt to forget our Human arrogance by praising it.

Isolation of Information from Experience: Reading about the development and rise of newspapers in America late last century: the author (Trachtenberg, 1942) remarked about how this (mostly industrial) revolution, the scale of life in the city, and other factors, isolated people's information from their experience.

Whereas earlier, people, each person had to experience or to witness, or to know someone who personally experienced any event, with the advent of "NEWS" experience was reduced; perhaps greatly. Much of knowing became "knowing about," the black and white of print, then of radio, now of color video, is reportage, journalism, testimony about experience, about something which happened.

Worrying less about how truthful is that testimony (which is worry enough), what has this isolation of information from experience done to our being and thinking and evaluation and to knowing?

Are our memories lessened; have our senses gone to sleep; do we pay less attention? Surely if we read, watch, listen with some care, we know a good deal. Perhaps our scope is wider... at least for some of us. For others it is probably much reduced. Do we rely less upon ourselves—the end point in all cases—and more upon testimony? Knowing more is knowing less? Where are the boundaries between hearing testimony and hearsay?

How distrustful of technology and of the actual world have the humanities become?!

Do texts isolate information from experience also?—or do they provide some alternative sensations of experience which closely substitute for experience, lobbying even for their "superior" reality?

Arrogation of Terms: In the present age the term "theory" seems to have high value and is opposed to something lower: the "applied" or the "practical." It is difficult often to discern why something or some idea or notion is called theory, when it is hardly more general or more abstract; barely more an idea than anything else. Utopias and dystopias are, I suppose, *theories* of society, but even they possess utility—measures against which to judge what is happening now or where we are.

Aren't theories supposed to have some utility, some "for-ness"? To grab the notion of theory seems, to me, often to aggrandize the idea, and especially the aggrandizers. So it is often difficult to distinguish such characteristics of theories and theorizers from whatever the theory is for or about, how powerful or general or parsimonious or elegant or symmetrical.

To have a theory of nature or of society seems at once powerful and to mislead one either away from observing, or to observe within a constrained framework, or to be useful as a critique of something which might motivate its overturning.

On the down-side, if an idea or a theory has no particular utility but to serve to aggrandize its practitioners then it is (but) a chimera. (...but a chimera which will sustain life even while it denies it?—Nietzsche's critique of Christianity.)

Strong Will—Weak Will: Are humans, is human nature composed of individuals who possess a strong, or a weak will? Who are "possessed by" a strong, a weak will?

The loci of this question seem to be various in the extreme. 1) Insanity—do we go, become crazy or are we, do we become "sick," attacked by some pathological bug whose life overtakes ours? 2) why do we go on living?—the will to live. Will we do anything in its name, in its all-consumingness? Fraud, bribery, heroism, murder (suicide)? Here will seems so strong. A weak will, in this sense, leads to hypochondria, sickness of all sorts, psychosomatica 3) self-determination, a strong will to say who (I) am and what (I) will do. A kind of bio-politics which says this strong will is a perversity, a chimera which misleads and misdirects the biology, the brain—which has an archetypical life of its own placed in a body, perhaps, but the sense of us which "ought" to be heeded in its more truly us-ness 4) a humanism whose strength is not (merely) to deny any sense of Deity, but to trust ourselves; to query oneself, to be able to think rationally. Opposed, perhaps, to a sense of Deity (or government or bureaucracy or social structure of any sort) to which (my) will is subject, and any sense of a strong will is pretense, perversion, or worse 5) a mix, oft-times a confusion, between the verbal auxiliary, and verbal "will" (will...go, try...), the sense of futurity and some depiction of an intention slightly stronger than purely passive, a sense perhaps of hope vs. a real sense of a person "intending"... I will... certainly... a contract is drawn between me and others, me and tomorrow's myself... The distinction between a therapeutic and teaching approach to ontology, to becoming; questions of freedom and responsibility; of empowerment and the will to transcend one's willing.

Appearances: How can it be that Human Nature appears different in different times, settings, to various persons (within each of their lives!)?

Most people infer from particular and limited experiences, from talk and *grandmothers' tales*, from the fear of the odd-looking, and the fear of our own becoming lame... or worse. We invest our lives and theories with the stories and experience of who we may become, enriched (or spooked) by the memory of the now dead who were, and we knew, alive. We are told how to be, to live well with examples as well as stories; what is virtue, what is shame, how to have conscience and to be conscientious. We know who to treat well, those who may frighten us, those whom we may attempt to frighten. We live as feelings, we eat of the world, and kill and prepare what is our food which sustains us that we go on.

We know talk of other sorts of beings, from afar or abroad who differ; who may hate us; love us. And we create them out of stories of war and pestilence and the sense that we fall somewhat short of virtue... or that we may.

We see variation and imagine variety in all these directions. We know beauty and ugliness; and we judge...

Transcendence: Moving beyond oneself; as Nietzsche put it, striving to go over, to always be becoming an *Ubermensch*, going, and traveling past wherever one is today, towards tomorrow; to be engaged actively in this process. Obvious?

Why is this an issue? For different reasons in different traditions at various points in life: in dual traditions, we possess already a sense of two-ness, one which is constant (perhaps continuous, steady, outside of process), the other which is changing, buffeted by the vicissitudes of life's perturbations. Here the "I" which I am observes the changing self, remaining aloof. The problematic remaining is Heraclitus' paradox of being at once the same and not the same.

In Amerindian traditions, perhaps others in prehistoric times, a spirit shared with other species: Naguales. The problematic being which reality, which *is* reality: waking, sleeping? Asleep, my spirit wanders, its other faces join me; I become free, transcending the body which may indeed sleep, seeing more. More-ness is transcendence, transferred back to the waking body; dreaming joins the body; dreaming is the real.

Others join the dead, the deities and sundry spirits who are themselves in process, changing yet remaining: remaining yet changing, the problematic shifted beyond the edges of notice and of valuation. Others still locked in some steps, sometimes counsel with those they call relatives. Snow White's beauty eclipsing her mother's, turning mother into witch, and turning once again the cycles of Ecclesiastes whose turning knows no endings.

Transcendence otherwise knows either that today is neither yesterday nor tomorrow, or that I awake each day in a different place.

All Against All: Some sense of a global force, a super-organic invisible hand, Hobbes' Leviathan which tells each of us that each other is to be viewed with a hesitation bordering on suspicion.

Embedded, embossed in a theory of being, futurity, especially of survival, we are told that each next, each other is in some deep competition with every one for the life-space, the gladness and the goodies of life's promised lands. Each individual person cast upon life's teeter-totter: as I go up, you go down. Worse: as you go up, my life's fulcrum may hit hard upon the earth rising to meet my ass-cendent destiny; destination earth crumbled unto dust.

A sense here that communion, compassion, generation are some necessity of fate's personal creation, but not us, not me. If others do for me or I for them, it is out of some intrinsic struggle wired deep within my crudely impassioned nether-brain to keep going; to use whatever means are possible to insure that I continue. No choice have I. (E.O. Wilson 1975))

Set within a Rousseauean depiction of Nature which is bestial in this sense of world drama to hang on by the clawing which pre-figures any human existence, a kind of competition which hardens sinews into steel and casts feelings into oblivion, the only non-accidental event in the universe is oneself. But Nature is not like this within any species, within groups of smallness of scale sociality is present and highly dynamic...

Sex/Gender: Until this era, human survival has depended on sexual reproduction. Now? Differences in experience: being male; being female; being *in* a male or female body? This is what they gave me! Differences in thinking, in relation to change, to Nature (natural processes) more present, more constant, more remembered. Location of the feelings, an inner self-description of the genitalia. Others' view of oneself, their interpretations cast upon their faces which are there to be seen, absorbed, reacted to...

Objectification, a male probable? Absorptions of the other, female? Where does an individual (male/female) locate oneself? Where does any person reside that s/he is characterized as?

Generation: in relation to one's past, cast upon one's children, human nature theories of individuals surviving, a male mythos? My story... only a male story? Possible to generalize? To all males, to all people. What import, the lack of a female God?

A Capacity (for Language) vs. Innate Ideas: Some focus on the ability of humans to think, to be abstract, etc., directed toward a concept of language—now fading... To say humans have a "capacity" for whatever the metaphor is to account for human uniqueness is not to say more than that we are in some senses identifiably unique or uniquely identifiable, and is probably trivial. (The fact that humans are identifiably unique is not, however, trivial as an aspect of the human experience!)

This, as opposed to the notion of humans who possess some ideas innately, inherently. This latter has been used to justify a dualism of (human) mind and body, particularly to explain a "mind" which concentrated the ideas of Human uniqueness into a smallest packet. This shift argues a new depiction of Human Nature with two obvious directions (more like other species but stupider; or more like, but both they and we are smarter), and probably some unforeseen directions as well. The "interesting" shifts, however, will be in the realms of theo-politics and not in metaphysics, at least in the public domain.

Life is its Own Confirmation: Much of (Western) thinking about human nature has been an attempt, veiled or apparent, to *prove* that God exists: thence that we Humans exist.

This form of theorizing inevitably runs into trouble because the argument is peculiarly circular. The fact is (if there are, indeed, any facts in here) that it is our own (human) existence which allows us to pose this question—whether *or not* we are confirmed by any deity. To attempt to by-pass this fact is a (perhaps) cunning subterfuge, but a subterfuge nonetheless. It is usually to permit (the fear of) death to define or to confirm life. *But life is its own confirmation and (any) God must already agree to this as fact.*

To say this is not to deny God necessarily, but to state simply that thinking emanates from existence, not the reverse (as Descartes would have it).

This cosmological complication, the primariness of a fear of death, of attempting to prove a God who will, in turn, confirm us, derives from an outlook which is deeply, even essentially individual; where other persons (even mothers and children) are problematic, even aspects of the environment much like any other objects. Within this outlook of the universe ending and beginning at our corporeal boundaries, it is here that the questioning of existence can even arise as problematic.

But, life *is* its own confirmation! (And any actual, serious notion of a deity must proceed from this as fact.)

Criminals...by Our Nature:

"This is because human behavior ultimately derives from human volition—tastes, attitudes, values, and so on—and these aspects of volition in turn are either found entirely by choice or are the product of biological or social processes that we cannot or will not change." (Wilson, 1975)

Not being in any way certain or clear about what this all means, it certainly is a statement about the notion that crime is a question of "will." The interesting thing is that such thinking resides in some notion that human *behavior* is not merely what it appears to be on its face, but has some locus or loci of cause; here, of "derivation," which is caused, at least approximately.

If the behavior (deriving from volition) is the product of "biological processes," the assumption is that it *cannot* be changed, because "biological" = natural in this context means unchangeable, by definition.

If the behavior is produced by "social processes," then these processes are somehow beyond our own "will" to alter them. Perhaps we find them to be beyond our understanding.

Perhaps this thinking is the attempt to push our understanding of human behavior into some deeper, causal realms that we usually avoid; e.g. tastes, attitudes, values, and so on. What I think, is that there is a variety of ways to explain human nature, human behavior being a focus (particularly if it's noxious), but where to look for explanation (= causality) remains unclear.

Time: The only thing I am certain about time is that we/I-as-body exist within the gravity of the earth pulling down while I pull up and against and dance within. Time entails this as process. Existentially it goes "forward" in the sense of experiencing and telling oneself that one is here in the context of telling oneself how s/he got here. "Aging" is about acceding to gravity (or gravity "winning" over us) while development is about winning over gravity. We are terrestrial creatures and would (I feel certain) appear much different in different gravities.

Theory and Praxis: The pragmatics of being have (always) been confused with some sense of the mundane and ordinary, while theory has been held to the invention and possession of the philosopher. I think this has been a mistake. The theory of our being is how humans conceptualize and raise each next generation. Theory is thus owned by ordinary humans, not by philosophers. The problem is how to problematize and to see the ordinary without either underestimating it in its ordinariness and obviousness—or overestimating oneself as theorist.

This has gotten unbelievably complicated over the centuries by acting in terms of the history of the theories by which we have told ourselves how we are.

Transcendence (the temptation): The modern rationalist singing the Blues over the "return" of the Eastern Bloc formerly-atheistic thinkers to some notion of God: remarkably like the ones which they had presumably abandoned 70 years earlier (and almost all of them weren't even born yet; yet). No progress here from the a-rational and irrational and not very rational to logicality and experiment and hypothesis and proof. The deity has wormed His(!) way back into being: into our being.

The modern rationalist singing the hymn of humanism says, "Woe is us!" Somewhere there lurks in us, he wonders, the old Yiddish song line: "Who stole the kishka?" Our guts writhe, telling us to yearn and fill them with food for the soul → the transcendent temptation!

I sit trembling to hear him react so violently, overthrowing his own bid to rationalize the universe, by invoking human nature to account for what (for him) went wrong. "It's us, it's in us! Woe is us!"

"Whoa!" I say. "Slow down. Examine your own thinking that you trusted until the former-atheistic claimers unclaimed their own trust in thinking their being is sufficient. Examine your intellectual taste before falling once more for a full gut. There is some reason for/in the transcendental temptation.

In this life we do, after all, start little and get big; start with little knowledge and experience and increase it by leaps and bounds, heaven only knows. So when we reach "adulthood" (you should pardon the expression), when we quit growing upward and winning over gravity, it doesn't necessarily mean that we quit wanting to grow in other ways. And grow means to overcome, to overreach, to move beyond. Much/most of child development is transcendental in quite powerful ways: like puberty, like the slowly dawning notion of death, like the hundreds of conceptual realizations which may now seem mundane and ordinary, but seemed at the time of their understanding, to be revelatory. No wonder we are tempted to go beyond; why not?

To go beyond, to engage in the transcendental temptation does not seem immature, any mere carryover from a childhood filled with fantasy and the proportion of mythic reality. It was/is much of our actual experience: to wake up, to become enlightened, reflective, responsible is quite amazing. And to the extent that we were/are amazed, why not continue to seek amazement? Why do we drink, seek out drug experiences, seek to heighten, to alter?

Are not food, sex, reading, movies, stories told all "mind altering experiences"? Doesn't each day at least somewhat renew itself?

Perhaps, as there has been an anthropology primarily of the "exotic" peoples (always somewhere else, quite different), we have forgotten the admonition of the prophetess at Delphi who counseled: "know thyself." We have neglected any *anthropology of the ordinary* and did not wonder at each next day. Having placed experience into custom and habit, we forgot/forget to love each moment and to squeeze destiny into it. We have been infatuated with the reality of the externalities of life, of materiality, and have little explored the fact that life is itself transcendent.

We do not read, or do not understand Nietzsche, who proclaimed that "God is dead" would mean the loss of meaning and the rise of European nihilism. So it rose like the efflorescence of the still-warming genitalia and is now subsiding after the experience of finishing with it, but not having marveled at its experiencing.

Looking for love, but afraid of the fear, we do not see ourselves seeing. Lacking love, lacking trust, we forgot that being is becoming, and that the transcendental temptation is sufficient to life and an aspect of existence. The need to invoke an external agency—be it deity or text or magic or mystic or history or my memory of my mother comforting me or the wet nose of my dog snuggling—is to want to abandon the experiencing in favor of... of what?

It is not so inexplicable, the temptation to be beyond this moment, to have to impute it to some new mysterious space in our being. The problem is how to study it, manage it, use it, understand that others come with the same stuff. How to gain in meaning, toward one's "next places"...aahh! (Sarles 2006)

Paradoxes of Life: In attempting "to see" Human Nature in the wide, it is informative to see how all the world's (major?) theo-political systems construct themselves. Beginning from Western thought, I lived for two years in Southern Mexico among Mayan Amerindians, and discovered some things about them, and reflexively about myself (ourselves). One thing led to another. And I began to note both differences and similarities across "mega-cultural" boundaries (e.g., Western, Buddhist, Confucian, Amerindian, Africanist…).

It has seemed to me that different mega-cultural traditions are effectively world-visions which can be gathered less in terms which have seemed to characterize them when considered one or two at a time. They can be understood better, perhaps as some grand global collectivity, by noting that each of them handles or "reduces" to the set of "life paradoxes" which might be said to be aspects of our ("psychological") life experiences. This is to say that the grand meta-traditions have "handled" such experiential paradoxes in only a very few ways. The noted large differences really are due to dealing with a smaller or larger number of paradoxes, and which ones in particular seem to be "central" to any tradition. (In some cases, the most "basic" seem so obvious *within* any tradition that they are not noted as peculiar or particular; e.g., dreaming vs. wakefulness as our "real" existence. It is only when we step into Amerindian life or go back to Heraclitus and beyond that we see that this is a life paradox in the general sense.)

The central gathering issue has to do with whether any tradition tends *to resolve* or to *complementarize* paradoxes. (A life-paradox, by the way, is the experience that life consists of two apparently opposite states, at least some times.) Western thought, Amerindian, seem to want to resolve paradoxes on one side or the other—but not on both: sleep vs. wakeful, change vs. permanence. But Confucian thought seems to complementarize change and permanence: one, then the other in some yin/yang arrangement. In many African traditions, there is no particular distinction between life and death, each "new" life taking on the spirit of someone recently deceased. This move to resolve or to complementarize seems to possess the conceptual power of veritably defining the nature of reality—certainly in the traditions in which paradoxes are resolved. They are capable of "defining" or depicting the nature of deity, of existence, and perhaps of providing the effective loci of the "virtues" in any tradition.

The major differences between traditions seem to reside in which paradoxes are given primacy (in some processual or hierarchical senses): life-death, change-permanence, sleep-wakefulness; one-universal, male-female, and so on. Once this is understood, much of the rest of what are mega-cultural differences seem much more to involve the details and particularities of geography and history.

Domestication of the Species (Geometrization): Peter Wilson's (1989) wildly speculative notion that the human species began (only) to geometrize when we settled down into fixed settlements, alters radically how we might consider the human condition. For the first time with domestication, we began to have restrictions upon our experiential vision: walls, insides and outsides; inside people, outsiders; we and them. The world began to be described as geographic places: not from nature, but from domesticity. The Garden of Eden, the emergences of palaces and kingdoms, notions of hierarchy.

Not from "our human nature" but from our experience living in domesticity. Not Freud, not Marx; just process and experience. Available to all (other) species, can we move beyond/away from geometrizing the world. Or have we so altered our being, as well as the world in our geometrizing imaginations, that there is no return?

(And what theories of deity will this new speculative insight into our nature bring upon its tails?)

(Toward) a True Psychology: Nietzsche regarded himself, above all, as a psychologist; perhaps the "first" psychologist. What does he mean? What is missing as we construe the very possibility of a psychology that we don't already understand, at least know?

5.

THE IDEAL

The question of the *Ideal* is that of transcendence. What is it about human beings or the human condition that we seem to be able, want, or need to *go past* ourselves?

Responses to this question, which has entered human thought at least since the times of *domestication* of the species (Wilson, 1989), has been various. Most enduring, perhaps, is that we are the creatures who have been created by a transcendent force or deity. Our transcendence is determined by our ability and necessity to know God. In fact, much of religious thought justifies itself against various forms of Humanism with this sort of argument. The purely mechanical, objectivist Enlightenment response is that we are not really transcendent, merely some collectivity of neurons or other parts which genes, say, use in order that we survive as a species.

Other forms of argument have existentialized the human condition, moving away from fixed, essentialist sorts of explanation and have pondered how best to seek out our destiny: to stay *on the way* as in Confucianism; to seek to be an Overman á la Nietzsche, to use teachers as models for seeking the always higher and more difficult *wisdom*. Much of the current argument devolves upon the Schoperian-Nietzschean propositions that we *will* to live and the transcendent/ideal is an aspect of the human will; that the will is to seek power and to re-evaluate all values.

Some of the most powerful and enduring sorts of argument posit not experience but a direction toward the ideal: forms of utopias which, if we reach them, we will be in heaven, nirvana, or however we conceive the best of all possible worlds to be.

The Ideal: The nature of society or reality is determined by how each people, each era constructs its notion of what: 1.) should be; 2.) can be; 3) might be; 4) was; 5) is; 6) is said/claimed to be; 7) will be; 8) cannot be; 9) success(es).

Construction of the Ideal: The image and imagination of perfection. Must it imply something wrong, lacking, imperfect in what there is? Should it be an existential metaphor that times change, and we must move on? An attempt to draw out where there is to go?

The description of each people, every civilization—by how it goes about constructing the ideal: as, (for example), "real" persons, fictitious, old/young, angels, *gods* (or *rich*—as in these times).

What are the habits and possibilities by which ideals are drawn? Must they not derive from experience? Must they not, in some sense, deny that experience (at the very least, as insufficient)? Must they not include (theories of) judgment? Criticism? How do these work?

Is God the Ideal?

Does the ideal (or the idea of the ideal) exist independently from me; or is (it) our observation, our construction? Is beauty what moves us to look at it, to listen to it? Or does it exist in some other realm?

What do we note? What do we order and rank? Does this have its own history?

The Ideal, a Measure: Some notion of the ideal implies that the ideal is a standard against which to judge (actual) instances (of the ideal). A common metaphor is the ideal physical object moving in a vacuum, i.e., without all the forces of friction, gravity, etc., acting upon it. What then would it be like? Setting up this sort of ideal as a model, does it help us to infer and analyze the sorts of forces, aspects, modes of its being which cause it to be or to behave in the ways that we actually observe? And yes, it does help if we guess or infer well.

What's wrong, then, when this idea or metaphor is applied to the living condition?

Life "includes" time, is an aspect of time; the "thing," the object doesn't exist in the same senses, to be able to identify someone, some form, is already to have an ideal picture in mind![7]

Is it any necessity that the concept of the ideal rests outside of time?

The ideal—the attempt to destroy or to fix time: The absolute, eternity, what is, is what (always) was. Experience become illusion. The world is perfect—and if it is not then it is not the real world!

The ideal thus often becomes the substitute for what is experienced as imperfect. What then is experience, judgment? How do we determine what is good enough, for what and whom? When are we likely to seek permanence—fright, sickness?

The circle, perfect, enduring—all points, equidistant from the center. All harmonies (musical) in mathematical relationships (Pythagoras)—but to what *in us* that is human?

The Limited vs. the Unlimited (Pythagoras): The limited, we know, is not perfect; the world is composed of certain details—e.g., oppositions and triangularities—whereas the unlimited is perfect.

What is ideal is perfect is unlimited. It only now depends on defining the meaning of unlimited. The mathematical notion of infinity will serve: What there is beyond knowledge, to the limits of imagination and beyond?—the principle behind. What goes on forever (and when you decide to give up on any further sorts of explanation or accounting beyond that which has "satisfied" you or to which you have become "accustomed"?

On Defining the Ideal: By what it is not; by what is like it or informs it—and then the rules for arriving at that; by what is tempting and impossible; by what was and can be no longer; by what some others claim is perfect; as a circle of being of which we are some lesser part; by what is tempting and possible.

---

[7] As in the Aristotelian notion of "the self-caused first cause," there is the problem of infinite regression here: the ideal creates its own ideal—there is no end to ideality. Notions of progress and *telos* are ways of forestalling the awareness of this possibility, or to cap it temporarily or practically.

Much of what is ideal is that which cannot be—but in particular ways. Much of what is ideal is referred to something other, which we then scurry to fill-in; hoping, assuming then we will know it and have it.

Is truth that sort of ideal?—knowledge? Do we get stuck in certain (historical) notions of ideal? (cf. my view of Heraclitus as an existentialist?) Must we then fall into some form or other of nihilism when the trust in truth fails?

How can ideal theories of being take over being and inform our "actual" (experiential) theories? Is there no actual actuality?—Not to the extent that our being is defined in terms of others, and their beliefs about being.

Ideal-Normal: There is a temptation which abounds when seeing the actual world through the lenses which we call "ideal." Since what we see, if we look at all clearly and even for a few moments, bespeaks of a world which lacks perfection by some considerable amount, we have to work at observing through the ideal(izing) lenses. This "work," a remaking and reconstruction both of what we see and how we look, often takes the form of imagining what "would" be ideal, thinking of that as a kind of normal or normative against which to measure all that we observe and experience. Thus we not only see "what there is," (though the appropriate ideal lenses can obstruct our very visualization in one or more dimensions), but do an instantaneous measure of what there is, located on the scales of what there should be, if (only) it were ideal.

What is different from the ideal as seen through the lenses, is already lesser, and needs to be corrected, or to be cured, or condemned, depending on the consequences of the metaphysics within which that notion of ideality has been construed.[8]

---

[8] This notion, which I first rubbed-up against in terms of American English dialects, was where I first entered the problems of ideal-normal and noted the entailments of this as a "vision," a position through which to observe the actuality. I imagine that, deep in our thought constructions, especially those that concern the self which observes, is a self-monitor which tends toward remaking all our "negative," non-ideal experiences into whatever we would like to think of ourselves.

The Ideal-Form: The abstraction, the concept, the "picture" is such that we recognize or somehow know all actual instances, each and every position—and we do!

In this sense, "ideal" is the set of schemes we have and keep, by which we judge and classify the objects that we fill up the world with.

In this sense, too, "ideal" is the set of schemes by which we derive ourselves-as-objects (or vice-versa); a set of complex events-become-I; a scheme by which I am; a picture of self.

It is difficult (for me) to say whether these ideal-form schemes endure through time, as time, or whether we devolve a notion of time in which these schemes somehow reside. (When? → response set!) In either case the notion of ideal-form tends to exist/endure through time, and by convincing us of its generality and universality, eventually to destroy our concept of time in certain senses (e.g., essentializing being is done via a theory of time which leads us to dis-attend to experiential time as lesser, or to make it no longer appear, or for us to no longer appear).

The Image of God: *Humans are created in the image of God*, it is claimed in the book of *Genesis*. Everything else first, humans last, in the image of God. So like God, to be. (Or made by our language!)

We are, more than anything else, like God; like the image of God. Whatever the etymology of two constructions such as "image" and "God," the notion nonetheless shows how the notion of the ideal can remain powerful irrespective of the precise meaning of any of the words. That is, the notion of us being like some ideal, holds out the promise that we are not (merely) what we are: we are more, we are other; part of us is invisible, hidden, promised; more.

The story of human, of God, in different eras and constructions, is mainly concerned with the details and particulars of what image, what God(s), what hidden. The important concept is that what we seem to be, what we actually experience, is less than what there is, "really." We are some ideal, some form, somehow what we are not; not here, not now, not sufficient.

A Pure Tone: In the church on the corner where I live there is a new organ. I play the violin with that organ in the church, and occasionally (says J.), there is something like a purity-of-tone which emerges. There is something about violin, organ, and the acoustics which strikes our ears in special ways.

No doubt we are estheticians, looking, seeking for certain sorts of experience, which are beautiful; pure-in-tone.

The Music of Heaven: Modern metaphors of heaven include a sense for what would be its beautiful music; heavenly, beautiful music. The music of repose set in the *amens* of all of time creates a sense of scenic splendor, carrying our pictures of perfection forward into the rewards for a perfect life.

But the music has its own history, much of it secular; much of it composed with the notion of earthly technology in the harmonic vibrations of our inner ears. Does this depict heaven, truly? Or has a sense-which-sells grown up over the centuries, that we imagine heaven in this way?

Is this alright? Is it blasphemous? Did the God of all of time give us the harp, the organ, the strings? Or did we, seeking earthly esthetics, create them in our terms, to satisfy some human seeking and yearnings—later to find the ideal in them and to call this "God"?

What about us is there that such music works to create in us pictures of heavenly perfection? Inspired by God, or a music which titillates and vibrates our nerves in such ways that we feel the presence of God? New ways to pull our flesh, to create the eerie back-of-the-neck feelings which invade the neck's tissues in such ways that we feel that we must feel the presence of some Other. (The development of the church structure to enhance the music also to retain and maintain those self-same feelings of the presence of the more-than-we-are?)

Is the ideal a metaphor? How do such metaphors inform: life, our thinking, activity, that which will become nostalgia?

Why?—Because! The ideal is a response to the question, "why?" The notion that we are—because; that *whatever is* is caused; that if there is any futurity, we must direct it (it must be directed); that the notion of direction—of purpose—is causally provided (somehow, somewhere); that this purpose, this cause, this mirror of causality, this toward which, is the ideal.

Is this notion of ideal a circle which we invent to "motivate" ourselves? Whenever we ask "why?" we look for ideality, and come up with whatever satisfies, whatever mollifies, whatever answers that question, whatever satisfies us that it is an appropriate response. The issues, in this sense, reduce to a question-response system (Sarles, 1985).

Harmony: Pythagoras' construction of the universe is based on the integral relationships of string pitches; octaves, fifths, etc.—they turn out to be "ratios" of whole numbers—thus, *rational.* The imputation of these harmonies is that the universe is in harmony, thus mathematical, in integral relationships—rational. Because human (in this thinking) are/is aspects derived from the intrinsic universe, we are also in-harmony in an overarching sense. Thus the essential human is to be found and seen in whatever senses we are harmonic and mathematical—rational. So the experiential—*whatever is experienced*—is taken, in this ideal-harmonic notion, to be derived or to be residual. The soul or mind or psyche is taken to be a deeper reality, the real human science, and the definition of mind (in all its variations) is taken to "fit" this notion of the ideal. Here, in the world of pure, ideal form, experience is irrelevant or misleading, and we are to see-through the illusions of experience to the ideal beneath the shadows: harmonies, integral relationships, enduring without time. (Plato's *Dialogues* →Augustine's *The City of God*)

The Essential=the Ideal:

"To idealize is to essentialize—to eliminate non-characteristic elements." (Inge, 1918: 75)

But we must have "decided" at some time, somehow, obviously or surreptitiously, what is or is not "a characteristic element." Behind this decision is the scheme, method, or process within which the ideal is located. It is a refinement of definitions, often concerning words or notions which are abstract (e.g. beauty, evil). It relies upon the idea of the ideal, the notion of there being a basic, fundamental picture of reality.

The experiential problem; how we talk about this or that "table" unless there is a meaning of "tableness" which is "pure table." We *do* have such essentialist concepts in our cognitive-mappings, which we draw upon, or abstract from, in any instantiation. This is neither to affirm nor to deny this underlying ideality of forms, but to state that humans (at least through many linguistic systems—e.g., naming of any object both as particular and universal from age 2 on) operate in this fashion, and it works pretty well, especially where there is a confirmable, tangible experiential base (e.g. tables); this works less well with "abstract" notions.

It seems to me that the ideal is characteristic of "larger" (e.g., Western) traditions; either to deny the paradoxical character of life or to want to "resolve" such life-paradoxes on one side or the other (in this case, toward the universal—and unchanging).

Ideal as Progress: The "towards" which... our heading... the *telos*, perfection. Each step on the way to Buddha, Confucius, Christ, Mohammed... to a Hitler? (—worked for most Germans in the early '30s).

But if there is no ideal, no "towards" which, why do we go on? For what purpose?—we ask.

Living—life: is it not intrinsically interesting that its changes, its existence are sufficient to promote its own continuity?

If there is no notion of ideal and of perfection, where can we derive any notion of what is better-than, what is good, what is moral and obligatory? Without these, how do we distinguish, to take it to its ultimate—between life and death? (Is this particularly Western, or more universal?)

The Great Irony (in Western Thought): With religion or without religion (i.e., perfection), we can occasionally not distinguish between the *Two Kingdoms*.

The Ideal and the Will: The Will to Power, Fame, Heroism, Vanity... to Endure. The fact that we do endure, that we remain alive and kicking may, in fact, be self-sustaining, and the question of why, arises only when there is trouble. The trouble is that weakness, faltering of the will (to go on) may give rise to thoughts of the ideal, of progress.

Then, we suspend the Will, the self of maintenance and sustaining, and begin to attribute the continuity to some force (ideal) which—we tell ourselves—sustains.

It is the hint of chaos which has driven the development of ideality, at least in Western Thought.

(A confusion between personal history and social history?)

A Circle: a geometric solution, everything equidistant, a concept of perfection; everything begins, everything ends, all has a place; nothing begins, nothing ends, everything returns. Life lived upon the circumference!

Or the *yin/yang* within the circle; all is bounded, but there is the other which is something and its opposite, all in the same moment. This lends itself more to the existential because it calls attention to the present in a way which shouts: "Watch out!" "Beware!" "Careful!"

A modern tendency is to call this a *woman's metaphor*, an attack upon the linearity of thinking and of being.

Linearity upon the circumference of a circle vs. out in the world of... of what—pure time?

The problem of ideality and time: it is easier, more persuasive, to pursue ideality and to lose, destroy, not have any concept of time. Or to have time, á la Ecclesiastes, in eternal cycles—where there is a short (a moment, a second, a life-time, a...?) temporality, but "all is vanity"; i.e., the actuality is really mundane, a mere arrangement, a kind of pre-determination, a path upon which we are set (by God?), and upon which we go, like Sisyphus, perhaps, but less burdensome/no freedom; fate, Kismet.

The Ideal is a Measure: ...against which to consider all of life. It is easy thus to consider life as ugly, dirty, sinful, temporary, unreal. It is never—with respect to some notion of ideal—what it might be, what it should be. It may be a yielding to the temptation to make everything lesser; an apology (the search for the "perfect picnic" measured against which pales any actual picnic).

Or it may be a carrot, a notion in mind, to try harder, to make each moment better; to say yea, rather than nay.

If it includes the balance of the anti-ideal (utopias as well as dystopias) then the ideal may help us to determine where we are: what the present moment is...

The Existential Ideal: The notion that the ideal (anyone's concept of the ideal) differs depending on who and where anyone is. If I am, say, a curer, then my ordinary—Western--purview is (from) pathology. The ideal is less what can be, than what is not now. When what is now is no longer the case then the pathologist is done. Or, why pathology and prevention never come together, and are probably antithetical in some senses (cf. the importance of the concept of "wellness" entering medicine from S. & E. Asia).

Or say I am a pragmatist, an engineer for example; then the ideal is an arc around what works—the other side of what fails, what cannot hold up its own weight. The world in which the pragmatist lives is the attempt to widen the what-works-world in opposition to the "ideal" as what-could-be-but-won't-be. Its other side is what fails. The engineer accepts the idea of limitations and makes things work, neither falling for failure, nor lamenting in each moment what does not work (yet!—"invention" resides here.).

Ideals Which Inform: The Confucionist notion that life is at all moments perfectible, just live it right (remain on "the Way"). Here the ideal is attainable and one must study life, and live it. The self is minimally dual: who I am, who I can be. It is future-directable towards attaining the ideal when one is old, venerable—a pedagogy of dialogue! (Sarles, 2013)

The "political" difficulty in the sense of politics as present-process is that the ideal—there being a single ideal for everyone, willy-nilly—is socially very conservative=oligarchical. The goal of all of personhood, of all persons in all times, is the same; thus society remains in stasis. It allows for a highly stratified, structured society by denying any social theory (or at least dis-attending to it).

Ideals Which Undermine: If ideality, perfectibility is not possible (in this life; ever) then I must "talk" myself into (be talked into) living, especially when the going gets rough. What would convince me that one way of being is better than another? What—other than retaliation—would convince me to aid others, not to destroy them whenever I have power? (And power, in its own terms, becomes the ideality with little difficulty—Freire's (2007) problem of the oppressed-become-oppressors whenever they gain power.

If the ideal professes perfectibility, but offers no way to it, then it remains subversive because any way of being can be better, surer than any other. This notion of ideal leads to a nihilism in which one is always at war with oneself not only over whether to be somehow constructive vs. destructive, but rather whether one can tell which is which (St. Thomas 1274). Previous solutions to this "difficulty" have used other species as the examples of what is anti-perfect. But this now seems to be incorrect and no longer viable. So we must seek to re-study, re-understand, what the notion of ideality can mean, without the invention of any extrinsically-based dialectic (e.g., other species, deities, etc.)

History: Collapses into today's fantasy, in an idealist's world and each moment passes into "the next" during the time it takes to write, read this sentence. And so it is all the same, you see (says Borges 1985). Life's ambition is to make life as good (or as bad) as one desires. Since life is constructed so as to conform to what one wants, it remains totally unobvious that anyone actually possesses desires or motivations, and the psychology of being either gets buried or handled as so much disturbance and "noise," in an otherwise explicable universe. The only important question, in an ideal world, is what one fills up one's thoughts with!

Optimum: how well can anything do? What is the best there is, the best to be hoped for? A question which arose in a biology seminar. A long life, the most viable offspring, self-satisfaction, the bringing of joy or the optimum life, or to others?

The question, which is the question of ideality in actual life, is at once obvious and as obtuse as we can imagine. It is the theme of life's hope, of planning for a future which does not run continually downhill.

The difficulty is that life is not its own answer. It is a surprise. It is not isolable: its history, encapsulated as our body, does not disappear if we close our eyes, into the ideality that we can imagine… if we were not exactly as we are. ("*Next Places*"–Sarles, 2006)

And we are—with others. We imagine ourselves within the logic and constructs of life's possibilities that the others see as us, and as possible.

A Religious Point-of-View: This is much more than the belief in the divine and salvation, creation and omnipotence. It is a framework of being and interpretation whose corpus is filled from a sense of experience which has already been informed by a set of texts. It is a way, an interpretive matrix which is predisposed to see what it is seeking, and to not see "all the rest." It is interpretive already, in each experience; its framework is disposed to see ritual in movement, to take what is and transform it in its very occurrence to some other text-informed world view.

This willingness of the religious point-of-view to rely solely on textual interpretation seems un-open to discussion, discourse, much less disproof. But this is less because of what a particular interpretation is, than that all raw data is constantly ensconced in some *scheme* which is itself held at the level of what is commonsensically obvious. To attempt to argue about data, its form or nature, is not useful because "it" has, in any moment, already been joined to something else. The argument about the matrix or framework is thus the arena in which discourse may occur; but the stakes have already been raised by this time, because the matrix represents something other. Any possible argument is about the nature of why it is so difficult to see what there is.

It is constantly being renegotiated in the sense of the present updating of textual interpretation, its exegesis, etc. The religion is an impermanent state of being (if not in process), whose reinterpretation is seen through some (present) experiencing; e.g. "Orthodox" Jewish women deciding to work, then seeking texts which justify their decisions. At some point, a splintering, an orthodoxy which interprets some other interpretation as "heresy" (as "other"), and so on.

So the religion, from a religious point-of-view, becomes a stable notion which is "kept" in one's mind, one's being, to serve as some sort of existential anchor in a tide of changing winds. Or it is a mirage of eternity; a wanting to have some permanence, but also a wanting to possess a belief, and a wanting to be possessed by that belief: a form of love affair with aspects of oneself (those which one calls "unchanging"?) In a few cases, it involves a "covenant" (Jewish) with other persons—but in Western Platonism it has usually been life-denying in any number of ways.

Ritual: A renegotiation of self; saying that who one is, is the same as who one was *the last time and every time before that*. It is a way of taking oneself out of time into the universe of constancy, non-change, eternality, always was and will be. Ritual is an anchor, a mode of turning life, which is change, into the geometry of forms, the reality into the infinitude of numerology.

Ritual is also in life. It is a way of keeping some things steady, renewing relationships—motherhood, daughterhood—are forever and may allow for growth and change in other places moves into new ports from older towns of debarkation. It is not merely what it is, but a set of reminders, movements of experience from safety to be updated, perhaps to be redone.

Irony: I had thought that irony had disappeared from the world-like virtues which appear locked into "virtuous eras." But I was mistaken—I had become a non-player; rather, I had not been a "player" who had sufficient holdings in the game to be counted on, to remain vying for the pot of fool's gold. Surprise! How ironic, to note that the presence of irony is itself cyclical, depending apparently on where we are within some "moral cycles."

History vs...?:—where to penetrate the web of custom, the concept of being to which one is (I am) heir? Speak, English! Because my grandparents decided/were forced to come to America? What is the range of *becauses*? Which ones count? For what? How does one pose a "question"—*the* question? To not pose such questions is to assume (believe) that we operate externally to our own being. We do what we do, are what we are, precisely because that is "our nature." But this is no explanation (though it does seem to provide an "accounting").

The difficulty is that history, the past is no longer, and the temptation is to apply causality to everything which is antecedent. But we are not discontinuous in any clear sense. Nor are we continuous in any clear sense; nor are we either the same or different in every place and time. So theories of history falter, as they try to find a story (a theory, an explanation) which is *the* story of history; but there isn't *one*. This doesn't mean there aren't any, just not one. The usual reaction to the "disappointment" of not finding one is to deny that there are any; and entails that life is an illusion through the reactive line of thinking which flows from the disappointment; and existence—from which all questions flow—itself becomes problematic → a form of nihilism.

The Power of History: Because we think of much of our present, i.e. today, right now, in terms of how we think we used to be (e.g., in thinking of our children - right now - we think also of how we were at the age of whatever our children are, right now). These judgments seem to be somewhat "open" to rethinking and revision, depending on how we think of ourselves in the present; i.e., we tend to "update" our (memories of) our personal history (good/better ways to update?).

There is a linkage, and this linkage serves/may serve a variety of psychological purposes. The importance of history resides in the fact that any (new) interpretation of history is linked to how we think of ourselves in the present and can easily "cause" us to rethink, revalue, recast any present; even, I think, to be able to recast our ideas of truth, reality and illusion—our responsibilities, our debts, etc.

Antidotes reside in attempting to find a locus-of-permanence within the history of ideas, sociology of knowledge, and a study of one's personal historiography via a "bodily" skill (e.g. why I study the violin); or, why most people who try to keep themselves "centered" are persuaded that the only way to do so is to take oneself out-of-time by altering one's concept of time (e.g., eternal, momentary).

Living-through Revolutions: I like many aspects of life to change, but living-through the period of change is often like being totally external to one's own life. "After" the revolution is secured then we can talk! But until then I have no place, no being; I am a stereotype of the revolution, captive of my propagandistic description of someone like myself—forms of loneliness (but I am not that person!).

Toward a Social Ontology: Questions about being and becoming; the assumption of change; a description of its dynamics; the position of its static aspects, its "places" being temporary. Questions of permanence vs. change shift to continuity as aspects of change.

The anthropology of ontology has to do with the location and perspectives of the persona: the problematic aspects of life are transfigured into perspectives in living. The persona is both continuous and in-process, depending on one's "position" within some schemata of continuity and process, both about others and about the persona (more of the tensions of living-one's persona). Problematic aspects of life also include personal questions of becoming, each from the other perspectives of who one has been, is, and soon will be: how to get past, go beyond who one has been; how to find a way of becoming within others' perspectives of who one can be.

Issues of individual and society; not an easy either-or. From the perspectives of the individual, from the perspective of the individual seeing oneself as others see him, present the possibilities of seeing oneself, those possibilities, etc. → Culture and Character: Exercises in Social Ontology (see my *Next Places*, 2006).

Dualism and Polemics: I "accused" a colleague of doing politics rather than biology. He reacted by accusing me of being a "fink" and turn-coat, a traitor! He had thought we agreed.

The dualist cannot see disagreement as anything but adversarial. If I agreed in part, I must agree in whole—or else be opposed in whole. I did/do agree in part, but am not myself a dualist, and so am free to disagree-in-part; or redefine and re-embed the discussion, and can "see" politics for what it is, rather than as a mere extension of my (any) particular point-of-view.

The Platonist problematic of oppositional dualism can turn any intellectual argument into politics by taking the originating mind-body scheme and granting hegemony to the mind-like aspects of one side of the argument. Since Aristotle (*Politics*) the temptation is to take any opposition and place it into social theory.

Death: ...per se? Who knows? Our "knowledge"—what we seem to call knowing—is tied intimately, deeply to existence and/or experience. What would a "picture from death" look like, feel like? Would it have sensate properties? The pictures—living pictures—we carry with us, are derived from life, imagining, an airy image, phantoms, spirits: but these are constructed from existential theories about death; not from death. (I wanted to say "from death, itself.") But isn't this exactly the dilemma, that death is not a state which is somehow opposite to life, but different in ways not capable of being constructed in the imagination? (At least, so far!) Another reason to consider life to be paradoxical rather than dualistic! (Does the experience of "almost-dying" apply?)

Death informs life! However we construct our notions of death does, on the other hand, deeply affect how we imagine and experience life. The possibilities and variations are legion: life as preparation for death; life as bounded; as infinite in each moment; as originating in some "moment" of creation, as always was and will be; as illusion; as all there is and what there is; good/bad life, techniques of evaluation, accountings... judgment.

Death creates time! Would it be knowable which way is the future if it were not for theories of life informed by theories of death? Is this why it seems impossible to know death except as a theory from life?

Death stops time. No longer, never, ever, not even once do I have to confront (nor have the joy of seeing), e.g., my father, in any but terms which I seem to possess, to own. I may and do update him, but it is all "mine." To be redone, I will have to redo him. He lurks in no corners, across no streets; only in my imagination. I would question his ever existing, but I seem to calculate my own existence in ways which do not permit me to destroy my memories: if I forget "him," what else will I have forgotten? It seems important, right now at any rate, that there are others who remember him as well as I do, and that their pictures are remarkably/sufficiently like my own.

Form-Content: I believe that I am a "content theorist"—my good friends agree; but what does this mean?

I am opposed in certain senses to "structuralism," but am fairly certain that I entertain fine distinctions between situations which are indeed (in certain senses) "structural." Knowing, say, the structure of a particular socio-political organization, or even of the structure of a certain framework of thought, I can "predict" what will happen to particulars: ideas or persons; what is generalizable, what is specific and particular.

I understand that some structures such as languages, universities, etc., have, or at least take on "lives" of their own. I presume, however, that they are, in certain senses, perceived to exist; thus, *they are*. Is this to say that most people are form(-al) theorists; concerned principally with stylistics?—to say that they distinguish rarely or poorly between form and content?

Knowing that we (all?) treat structures as if they really exist confers and confirms their reality, but doesn't mean that they cannot change quite rapidly and radically given the proper conditions; or, from the structuralist's perspective, when the proper conditions no longer prevail.

Metaphors: "Language" doesn't change—people's hearing/judgment changes (often "collectively!").

Wonderment and Doubt: Kierkegaard's *Journals* ("Philosophy") says that Western thought has had (only) two guiding metaphors: wonderment and doubt. I am certain that I am primarily concerned, motivated by wonderment. A major problem is in inventing ways to use wonderment to deal with pain. Haven't people like F.M. Alexander (1923) and M. Feldenkreis (Ernst & Canter, 2005) been working at this, exactly? (John Dewey studied with Alexander and survived in "good shape" until age 93!) I love "doubt" as well, but it tends to feed itself, rather than to illuminate anything else: doubt begins peripherally and gradually places itself as the centerpiece in a hall of mirrors. (Western-Platonic thought as a skepticism about knowledge leading to the current malaise of nihilism!)

Puzzles and Solutions: Phil Regal–biologist and very close friend—says that he has "solved" certain puzzles—as far as he can tell—once and for all (Regal, 1990) (He referred to a paper on "why feathers evolved".) But many other biologists don't recognize that this is a "real" solution, not because it is incorrect in any obvious sense, but that they have no sharpened sense of puzzle, of wonder, of any pictures of a universe of existence which calls us to explore and explain: a major problem of scholarship if a "discipline" is sufficiently old to possess a history which has become the central subject matter! And I had thought biologists were better at spotting issues than are anthropologists. The "sciences" of behavior as an afterthought: metascience (=metaphysics?)

Form: isn't it form by which we determine who is what and for what? And whom we sleep with? Whom we eat? Human and non-human? Isn't it form which attracts us, allures us, and tells us what beauty is? Form may not be content, but it is not nothing; nor is it everything, which also leads to a form of nihilism.

My work: an *anthropology of the ordinary*. (Most "anthropology" is of the exotic). To give voice to all the people(s); all the living creatures upon earth. To problematize that to which we are accustomed.

History of Ideas: History of one's life: confusion, complications. Some issues (e.g., language-human uniqueness); I feel like I have lived so long with this issue, have solved it sufficiently that it ought to go away. In my life and history, it is already very old and from-my-youth. Older and more global issues (e.g., morality) are much newer for me, requiring perhaps the kind of maturity which may enter into one merely from having been around a fairly long time and two generations. So, in some senses, my own history of ideas is an inversion of history and I must construct them inside-out in order to keep straight where I am and how I got here (similarly: on re-considering psychoanalysis as part of humanities-literature).

Strong Will- ←→ Weak Will-Theories: The behavioral sciences divide, often, along this axis. If we explain "being" by extrinsic means (e.g. environment, stimulus-response in psychology vs. society defining persons in terms of social roles in sociology) then there is little of the self or will which seems to need explaining → weak will-theories. Strong will-theories (as in Boasian anthropology: Franz Boas: the "father of American Anthropology)) begin from the individual having some intrinsic being (biology) which the environment alters (Rousseauean social contract). That there can also be weak will-theories is attested to by sociobiology, which invokes society, once again.

Why is there such a pendulum of thinking about being? Why not a "truer" (my observation, experience) interactionist theory? Because, I think, each side tends to overlook the other side, and uses residual explanations to account for its own position (while surreptitiously accepting the same framework as its ostensive opposition). Dualists, that is, create the opposition in its own image, and rarely can step outside of its own form of argument: so that even content theorists become formalists in an oppositional dialectic.

Reactive vs. Reflective/Social Science: Responds to questionnaires all reactive—a "poll of opinion." Reflection is to ask people to become analytic about their lives. Is reflection "closer to truth" than reaction? Doesn't the market of opinion create its own truth? Or is just another form of herd behavior which we now justify on the grounds of wanting to join the market economy rather than act as its critics.

On being Re-connected: Going to my first behavioral biology discussion/lecture in 10 (ten) years; being invited to talk to linguists for first time in 13 or 14 years: strange *deja-vu*. I had suppressed thinking about such possibilities over the years, and now they re-appear. To be doused again? Probably. Feelings range from "how nice!" to "why should I care?" Like finding long-lost relatives with whom one had an (increasingly obscure) argument eons ago. But they went on different paths for what appeared to be good reasons: strange and outside of time, experientially.

Skepticism and Knowledge: Kant's response to philosophical skepticism which postulates some *a priori* form of knowledge as pure reason has unleashed its own deeper skepticism, as we find ourselves embattled over the nature of who controls reality ("if I don't like yours, I'll kill you"→ victory=proof). Survival=knowledge is as much a proof of the nature of knowledge as a proof of health through toxins. But the *a priori* is persuasive as it eliminates doubt and the skeptic; and any theory which removes doubt saves personal energy, focuses one's visions of futurity and of a derived present (derived; e.g., from other's texts) "works" for some people.

Kant's type of response also "contains" the argument of any future metaphysics since the reasonable mind is focused totally on the explanation of a particular definition or delineation of what "reason" is considered to be; itself, some variety of a derived linguistics which considers its own "primariness" in terms of nouns=objects and verbs=actions, and is itself derived from a picture of the human as reasonable in the sense of being non-animal and non-body.

But our "here-ness" is as bodily as the chair which I require to support me. (Would the skeptic reply: "What chair?"?)

The argument shifted to the nature of the "senses," but in such a way that the senses "themselves" became a derived aspect of our being. The human-as-sensate is much more complicated than the skeptic would like them to be, because the underlying problem has been to cope not with the nature of being but with its surcease. (A conflict between the fears of the almost dead and the wisdom of maturity in a world where we are not careful about the development of character!)

Causality as Personal: Why did I get into this state of being?

Derived from observations of the severely disabled (para- and quadriplegics) and from heart attack "victims." "Why, dear God, oh why me?" "Why now?" "Where did I/it go wrong?" "Whose fault?" "Quads" seem merely to die if they do not come to (evolve) a theory of causation of self-infliction in which they are primarily, personally responsible for their crippling accident. That is to say that very many of them do not survive unless they come to believe and to accept that they are personally "responsible" for causing their own injury. (This is probably because the energy necessary for survival as "a quad" is similar to, or derived from, the same sort of thinking by which they assign responsibility to self.)

In the case of heart-attack victims, it seems that they spend a good deal of time assigning cause. One suspects that their progress in recovering has something to do with how their causal thinking evolves; where one assigns blame: self, other, external events, etc.

The question which arises from these cases has to do with how, in general, we constitute our lives: assigning blame, causality, explaining to ourselves where we are and how we got here. How are we with respect to how we imagine that we could be now, or someday in the future? Some of these stories-to-oneself apparently help sustain life itself, yield energy or create the contexts in which we rebuild, recreate selfness; stories by which to find sleep and repose, by which to meditate, cure, absorb, and channel pain, vengeance, bitterness, hatred-of self and of others (Schopenhauer's "Will to Live" given metaphorical substantiation!).

How we go about doing the "willing," how we explain ourselves to ourselves, has much to so with our continuity and survival.

The shaping of personal causal explanation, the "within which" we cast our lot, our evaluation of ourselves, is not simple in any sense, and indeed has increasingly its own history in the sense that, say, success is cast within some organization, community, discipline, notion, for most persons. The evaluation of self is to some (large) extent cast within that sense of self.

Waiting for the Holocaust: More than half depending on it, I realized the other day. For good reason? Perhaps. A good friend has just died, early, of cancer, calling attention to the doom and gloom, and giving backing to the down and paranoid aspects of my outlook. In taking-over the role of housekeeper, I have become the one to dread the telephone call about the accidents my children may have incurred (and J. had abandoned the same dread in exchange!)

But reading the world, studying the transition on a day-to-day basis of the country's attitude toward anti-liberalism, noting how the forces of the political "right" are being unleashed, I am more than half-convinced we are in for dangerous times. The aspects I actually see and the daily attitude changes of academic bureaucrats reacting to changing perceptions; not probing those perceptions, why they change, whose direction are they heading.

Like the rest of us, "they" have a particular reference outside, limited and bounded, also reacting to the same world, and extending "that" world to the real world. We are in a delicate skirmish for the definition of reality and whose reality will prevail. The bureaucrats' will and knowledge to survive undermines their outlook, their representation of what the institution does and should do, who it should serve, and how.

Watching them—as I do—I am worried that "they" will make decisions out of concern for their own safety, risking ours as they preserve who and what they believe will preserve them. With heightened urgency, they will react to events more and more as if they are forced to, again heightening the sense of urgency.

Physics, Meta-Physics, and Bodies: on hearing D. Garber, a philosopher at Princeton, talk at U. Minnesota on the theory of a body in Descartes and Leibniz, a sense of the derivation of our being from some theory of existence which seems to make it obvious that bodily being is derivation from objects, and from the mathematization of object and activity useful to depict the physical world. So strange; so backwards, inverted. Could (a) physics have developed without this strange journey of disembodiment of the human condition? How? It is almost as if we have had to deny our human experience in order to reinvent it.

Continuity and Change: As the creation-evolution argument is more about the life experience—than of death—the notion of whether change is aberrant beyond some normalization points seems to be so frightening and unusual as to frame the notions of ordinary and normal. In the book *Snapping* by Conway and Siegelman (1978) the depiction is of a state in which the normal "continuous experience and awareness" is dramatically altered and one suddenly "believes" in something new and other.

That this is the way non-believers and non-converts tell the story is important; but, more important, is that the way this is argued is to posit an ordinary experience which is continuous in some static, every day, and presumably common (and commonsense way), and then a snapping occurs: a new belief, a psychotic break (but not an interesting insight, not a conceptual break-through). It is portrayed as false knowledge (="cult"), a giving-away of mental capability to a false set of truths manipulated by some self-anointed messiah who has seemed to preach against whatever the "normal continuity" is assumed to consist of.

It is also—by implication—a normative vs. relative argument because the notion of an ordinary continuity of awareness and of our inner mental life is presumed to be the relativity; the only one in which is found ordinary (non-cult?) truth. In this sense "snapping" is an argument against rhetoric, against any notion of social reality (e.g. that others manipulate our mentalities and cause us to snap!)

Positively the notion calls attention to the intellectual questions and problems of how we think: what is our inner life; how continuous, how not?

Residual Categories: In many theories of the world and of things within it, many features or aspects are paid attention to. Theories, explanations call attention to such features in ways such that descriptions are generated which account for or explain ideas and/or observations. Because theories seem to be systematic, they also urge us to believe they are true, and completely true; exhaustively true.

But most such theories, even though they may be true (in part, in some sense or other) are not exhaustively true. There are "left-overs," extrusions, things and aspects of the universe which are not included: some on purpose, others because the theory works to direct our attention in some positive sense toward something else, and we do not notice what is residual; or draw lines about our thinking for positive methodological reasons. What is left-over can become, can be what is important—even within the universe of the theory—and we will never note it, never find it worthy of notice.

An example: language is clearly an aspect of the human body. Within theories of language, however, the body is said to be "biological," mechanical, something "other." Presumably it is within the purview of other observers. But, in any case, it is not "our" business. Language "needs" an independent theory. But if the body is, indeed important, linguists will never find this out—except, perhaps in their final moments.

Theories of the Present: How long is right now? When is tomorrow? How did we get here? Where are we?

The biologists' present is 10,000 years. How can we do today whatever needs to be done? Can't, Can't, Can't? What's happening is inevitable; will have to run its course, its cycle. The best we can do is what we know to do well; carve out a niche of intellectual freedom.

Harvey. "But aren't we rational? Can't we think it out, outthink the present unto the future?—redo theories of the past, change how it informs the present? You're so pessimistic!"

Phil Regal. "I, a pessimist? I feel like I'm an optimist. I'm here to survive, and I will. The others?—what can I do about them? Today there's lots of time for me. But *what is* was foreshadowed, caused by history, for them."

Do biologists have two theories of the present; simultaneously?

How many do I have?—for me, for you, for us (for us, for me...)?

Teleology: Does the future really determine the present? Or is it purely that our beliefs about the future inform our beliefs about causality in what we call the present? (And when an era of prophecy overtakes this era of prediction? → the millennium? Then will history disappear and the present lose meaning?)

My Hands: Today, just now, I picked up my violin for the first time in a month. I've enjoyed the lay-off; my body has enjoyed the rest; and time to be. And it worked; I remembered—especially, my hands. They know. They're stunning, beautiful. They work. They're so strong, go to the right places. Gentle, quick. How can one not love such hands? (Wittgenstein on skepticism: If you so know that here is one hand, we'll grant you all the rest.)

Mysteries: This is a time for mysteries, for the occult and the mysterious; for mystical masters and magicians; for fakes, quacks and quarks; mystics, mouse-tics (and house-husbands).

I used to think that mysteries were wonderful, because they formed problems, puzzles to be solved. But now, we want mysteries to stay, to be renewed—a mental polysorbate. If, it seems, there are mysteries; well, isn't that wonderful!

More! Not only are mysteries wonderful, but if there really are mysteries, we humans must be more wonderful than we think we are...

Ah! If there are mysteries, then it must be true that we are more than we are, more than we seem to be. We don't have to dislike or hate ourselves, because those selves we hate are not our real selves. We can think ourselves into new, better, more likeable ourselves. How wonderful! How mysterious!

If wishing could make it so... Well, wishing can.

Drugs?!

(A remaining problem: How to have our mysteries and be sure that they don't turn into mysteriouser wonders which will cause us to hate ourselves even more. Heaven help us, if Heaven will!)

Consciousness: (a beginning) metaphysics (so-called) often begins with an invocation about some "facts" of consciousness, of "self-consciousness" (Hegel, Eccles, etc.), which may differ from person-to-person (or they may not → "universalism.")

It is an invocation because each of us tells ourselves some story about what we regard to be such "facts." And if we believe in universalism, some essence of humankind, then we will presumably "know" these "facts" of consciousness, because (being human) each of us partakes in the human "essence." What is 'in' consciousness, at any moment—through some stream of consciousness; the 'contents' of consciousness? What am I thinking about right now? Do I "know"? (Do I tell myself a narrative which is the one I would tell another; while in internal dialogue?)

What I think we mean or refer to is some set of stories about our thinking processes in terms of which we (seem to) speak, think about whatever, etc. It—the "facts"—may consist of the rudiments or elements or grammatical rules of speech, some notion about knowledge, and knowing that we know. Often this arena moves toward or reduces to some examination of what knowledge is, especially self-knowledge.

Why it takes certain forms, gathers-in particular facts, operates through certain metaphors and not others, is a long story about nature, especially (in Western thought) about what is human, uniquely.

Whether consciousness "belongs" to each individual, whether it is socially "assigned" or attributed to us remains a question which we don't think about very well: whether consciousness involves various forms of repression and of hiddenness; whether wakefulness is the real, or is sleeping-dreaming when we are truly "alone" (Heraclitus)?

("I" begin already within a story of others telling me I am. Consciousness must be "derived"! See: *The Body Journals*)

Active or Passive: is the human condition intrinsically active or is it passive? On any minimal observation of infants and children the human condition is obviously active—with time to nap and to sleep, to recover the high level of expected energy. If, however, one begins to think of what is human already in dualistic terms, human being is obviously passive because what moves (our bodies) is the animal, non-human aspect of our Being. Activity has to so with the wedding of the human and animal through "desire." But the human, that which is consciousness, self-consciousness, etc., is passive. So much for Western thought and the solution to the problem of Being!

Simple: As opposed to complex?—not simple in its associations of meaning. Because "simple" is so often a beginning, a lesser-than, it is not obvious that it can also be a complication. With respect to any holism, any integral something, what is simple is a part of that whole. But the something-ness, the integral whatever also can be itself, or in some relation. If whole-ness is what is at issue, it may be that integrity is a whole, irrespective of its own internal complexity; that, for example, an amoeba is equally as complex as a mammal. It *is*; it remains alive; it reproduces; it does what it does as well as any other being. The simple-complex notion should be stood on its head in order to see what there is to see. (This not to oppose analysis, but to avoid synthesizing by directly piling up its atoms and proclaiming that whole = *the* whole.)

With respect to the notion of the ideal, simple seems principally to be the hope that there is some short-cut to the nature of our nature, to experience without simply reproducing that experience. That there are structures, rules, generalities and generalizations is beyond doubt (e.g., the very notion of language, grammar, etc.), but the move toward the simple seems to want to by-pass observation, to see-through or see-into, more than to see.

Form and Substance: what if the human infant is (simply, purely) form; the substance "provided" by the "outside" definition and treatment? The form is dynamic, in flux, creating the world with respect to it-self... as its shape, its form, its "envelope." It does not "know" its shape; the world is "bent" (how: 3-D inside out?—'n'-D?) with respect to its shape, aspects of it-self. (This is to state that life(forms) is much more "complicated" than we think/have thought.)

The outside "sees" (interprets) no (mere) form but a person (somebody) already with "facial expression"; a character; a continuity; a history of having been and will have been.

The "tension" derives from the interaction of the world experienced as infant-form and the extrinsic definition, which is one of self-ness and personhood. Development occurs with respect to (a function of?) this tension, including the aspects of self we think of as emotions.

The infant (one) does not "learn" language, but becomes *languaging* → content (language). Form → content (=form → content...)

Beyond Good and Evil (Nietzsche): The question of untruth, falsity, especially (for me) of myth. The stories we tell ourselves about how it is, how we are, how we got here and where we are going, inform our thinking about "life-furthering, life-preserving, species-preserving, perhaps species-rearing." These are probably always "opinions which work," more-or-less well. Thus, morality is less a question of "truth," more of the imagination and its translations into practice (and in, the Global Village, what "works; for whom).

Against "System": Mischa Penn (friend and exemplary Teacher) urges me to systematize—to study "my" (anthropology's) formal history, and to state what (I think) I know as a series of laws, of propositions, of rules for exegesis and interpretation. Why? To become known, powerful, famous; to gain credits... but from whom?

If, as I prefer, the "world" is in flux (i.e., we are in flux and the world either goes with us or it doesn't) then, in effect, reality and truth change, at least evolve. The quest for truth, for meaning, has to be renewed, re-taken in each era. Truth—as it were—finds a "new" history, a "longer" development in a time flow whose direction is progressive; in a changing time, moving toward futurity. Truth differs in a historicist world where today is today merely, and no more than an outcome.

No—no system!

A pedagogy: a training, an establishment of teacher personae who live the past into the present, surviving and "guaranteeing" their own present, and (thence) the students' futures—that is all. That is not bad, if never exactly enough. What I can do is help the students learn to engage in their own life studies, in their own times, which are informed by me and mine; but they are theirs, and not mine. (Sarles 2013)

No system!

No…

The Invention of the Past: = the death of time?

A means for killing oneself gradually, so as to be ready for Death, whenever…?

Does each re-doing of history necessarily entail a re-doing of one's present—one's self? Likely, because an aspect of present being is the story of how we came to be here, did become as we are. (Shouldn't thinkers engage in re-thinking their own history from time-to-time, so one has a sense of how one is formed historiographically?—more sense, more sales-resistance to the power of feelings in each present moment.)

My suspicion that scholasticism, the celebration of the textual past leads to the diminution of the present, as well as the disappearance of Being, dissolves the very concept of history. Witness the millennium!

Proclaiming the past as the classical moment when the great authority appeared on earth—sacredly, intellectually, morally… tends to diminish and to disciple the present experience to the *ago* of some golden time. In contrast, the present is brass or tin, or a mere copy of the genuineness of Being. The strength with which the past appears to dominate the present (read Plato, Mohammed), leads us to believe that the past dominates this and every moment, and history effectively does not appear. If, in the millennial moment, the Christ is supposed to appear once again, it will be as if there was no time between zero and two thousand: no time for being in respect of the ideal. A matching of who I am with the ideal, and always finding my own senses senseless.

Witness to Our Own Lives: have we become voyeurs, even of our own existence?

Do we watch ourselves watch ourselves, regressed to the shadows of our being?

A cheap conversion, a cheap "lay." Is the struggle-not-to-struggle paramount?

Do we no longer believe in our own reality? Do we believe, then, in the reality of others? Are we, if anything, merely derived? Do we believe in our derived selves? Whence, this belief?

Are we afraid? Of what? Of death; of life—as Nietzsche suggests, afraid of pessimism itself? Do we analyze our own characters into some modes, aspects, parts? What do we do with these parts? Do we love some, hate some? How do we know?

Seekers after Truth? In the Creation/Science debate, it seems that there are indeed a number of "scientists" who are seekers after truth in such ways that they become seekers of certitude. Or they followed scientific endeavors because they sought certainty (a clerisy?).

These "scientists" become easy prey to the creationists who admit the search is for everlasting truth, and then flip-flop ("snap") when the winds of time turn upon them and carry the stench of (their!) flesh to their hungry nostrils.

Now they engage themselves in trying to prove the unprovable; at last convincing themselves that everything is unprovable. A rediscovery of a cosmology in which the notion of skepticism is raised from an issue of any possible knowing, to the issue of any possible existence—particularly their own.

Conversion/Snapping: To change a person's thinking, to alter one completely to see the world differently, anew; to cleanse the brain, to wash it out and take the constructs of its life-ways, and to move them into "new" horizons.[9]

Is everyone susceptible? Are there safeguards?

To whatever extent "others" can affect us, to that extent we are open to conversion.

To whatever extent we love and want love, and have once yielded the soul of self, to that extent we can see the world in new ways.

But how, suddenly; what modes of instant change?

The problem in converting—for those who wish to convert (why do they?)—is to discover the "grounds" upon which one "puts" oneself together, the "how-ness" of who I am, to attempt to grab those groundings by treating them as if they are not there; as if the "person" who thinks has *no* grounds:

Look here, I am talking to you, Reader! You think you are reading my words, but that is not true. You are reading your own mind. My words, these markings upon paper, are no more mine than the paper in your own hands. Look here, not here on paper, but inside your own mind!

What do you see? Where are the words which tell just now, you thought were mine? They are yours.

Yours? Mine.

You are my words. You own my thinking. You own my mind.

---

[9] Read Nietzsche's diagnosis, his "history of the next two centuries" in *Will to Power*, Intro. *Rise of European Nihilism*.

You are my words. You are my mind. You are mine.

The trick of snapping is in the third line. Where "I" convince you that you are no longer you, but an aspect of "me." If "you" *go* for this argument, if you can be brought to wonder if you are an independent person then you are "had," and I can re-fill your mind with whatever "I" find interesting. The procedural problem of the converter is to soften up your resistance to your being mine, my being yours.

Scientizing Morality: To set upon a scale a measure of the quality of being, which claims to be "objective," aside from its own in-built judgments; to claim that "values" can be judged "value-free" is to open the wounds of being (Kohlberg "Six Stages of Moral Development")).

To observe what is, to claim that is what has to be, to equate quality with maturity and endurance, is to claim oneself as the measure of moral perfection, and to judge others as lesser.

To take what a particular segment of a particular society has thought to be valuable, and to proclaim that is what value *is*, is to usurp ideality into pragmatics. It is to claim for some men (sic!), what others can only hope is represented by the deity.

It has no striving, no hope, no progress which is not preformed. It makes the ordinary seem out-of-the ordinary, and diminishes each person who resists or fears to be God. It proclaims morality without claiming to be moral or even that there is any such notion.

Jonestown[10]: to control the reality and destiny of others, to take them to the edges of their minds and being, to ask them to suicide—is not beyond experience—and not so difficult.

S/he who grants reality can also remove it.

---

[10] In 1979, in Guyana on the northern coast of South America, the Reverend Jones took some 1,000 of his devotees with him to await their destiny. When they were found-out, discovered by American congressman Leo Ryan, they became dismayed, and—under the influence of Rev. Jones—about 900 of them drank some sweetened juice laced with strychnine...and died.

Jones's Recipe: fear of...by subjects. A royal bearing who claims power and knowledge. The discussion/debate reigns over the ground(s) of power and knowledge. The grounds may shift—slowly, or rapidly if it is done cleverly. And gradually those grounds are taken away, or disappear. There is no perceivable continuity, and any force for life is made to seem vacuous. And so we all die; and that is life!

Heavenly. This is what they sought, from pain and out of pain. Father has delivered them. And who can say he was wrong?

The (re-)discovery of cosmology is all about skepticism and increasing doubt about one's own existence: death overtakes life as life's domain diminishes and the question is handled existentially by praying for the deity to prey upon life. The joy of life diminishes as its pain is explored and turned into a sense of joy outside of being.

Beginnings: how did it all begin? The big-bang á la Freud—something out of nothing? (Parmenides) What is nothing?—God, the creator.

The creator—God? A cheap deity—nothing more than the automatic response to a human question: something from nothing?—how? God!

Then God went into repose. Having created time, space, and being. Being?—who, why? Vanity?

Why are we here? Where are we?

Why should one stay alive? Ask Reverend Jones.

The Destruction of Time: this is what is desired. The world forever, everlasting. Today as a mirage—yesterday, tomorrow—all a preparation for heaven, for enduring being. The view of life from its demise (*Phaedo*). There being no time, there is no cause for fear, no death, no-thing...

Purity...beauty...forever.

But; today? Who I am? What to do? Pray?

But since we don't know-from-death, all of our thinking is about death is from theories from life and experience. How do such theories define death so that they can be brought to life, and truly inform experience? Is this a good idea?

Destroying Time: the existential challenge.

Here I am. The world is my invention and my punishment. Not my fault? Bah! The curse (love?) of my parents is me, is upon me. Not their fault? Bah!

It is my/their fault. All of us are to blame. Why Lord?

Death, no more. Tell me, Lord, what should I do? How shall I be? To be with you in your heaven. Not to die. How?

What do you say?

In the beginning was Heaven (yes, oh yes)—and the Earth? Oh.

Help me, Lord. Not to die, but to be with you.

No Death? No... Death! Help me, Lord.

How, no Death? Can it be? Can I learn to see? NO DEATH? Yes? Yes. Yes. Yes? Yes!

At war, am I? With... myself. Myself is a punishment? Myself is not myself? How? Riddles...

Not my fault. My parents'—Adam, deceived. Curse me, but not me! My body—not me. Kill my body—not me. Die, my body—not me.

Ah! I am not my body—not me.

A trick; a deceit. My body - not me.

Burns, yearns—my body—not me. My body, against me. At war with my body—not me.

Yes—at war. Against, opposed—not my body, *my* body—not me.

Yes—at war. Kill bodies—not me. I am not my body—not me. No, death! No death. My body—not me.

No body, no time, no me, no death. Life—that is the illusion; that is the penance. Not my fault, Lord. My body—not me.

(No time=No Evolution. A theoretical requirement!)

Questions/Non-Questions: Which of these are questions, and for whom? Are we here? (Existence) Why are we here? (Survival; "the Fall" into the human body, redemption, etc.) When is now? (Strong/weak theories of the "present") When is forever? (How long is a long time? is time an illusion? creation/evolution) Does "something" imply/entail "nothing"? (Creation-origins) What is "human"? What is not-human? How do we know? What informs us? (Texts; the world?—in which order?) What is sex for? ("The Fall"; survival) What is life? Death? Is life "informed" by death?—a *Ding an sich*? Are we deceived? (Possibility of sense-data, empiricism) By whom? (Self; others; Satan; God?) What is truth? How do we know? Is comparison possible/legitimate?

The Loss of Meaning: if meaning was lost when God died... can we get it back by resurrecting the deity? Do we require another Messiah? Do we create that one, invent it? Can we merely declare it? Use one from another "time" or borrow it from another tradition (i.e. Buddha)?

If Creation defeats Evolution, will God be where "He's" supposed to be? Is that sufficient? Yes? God is said to have said that we are, that we should be! Do we agree; do we believe that we are and should be, that He said what he meant; meant what he said?

Can we mean, as others meant 2,000 years ago? How? Are we the same? Haven't we, too, evolved—or has virtually no "time" gone by? (Authority?—Biblical?)

Can we not create our own meaning? Can we not live in our own present? Wouldn't God have wanted us to?

Can we remake, re-invent meaning? Are we to believe that we are merely who we were told to be; made to be? Outcomes of our antecedents? Futurity? All or none!?

Or is there nothing? The nihilism predicted by Nietzsche (*Will to Power*) takes the loss of meaning, and actively mourns. It would take two centuries to come about, he guessed. What he didn't guess was the Bomb and other "total" means of destruction; the shrinking of global space; the active conflict of ideas and ideologies between those who are lost, those who are losing meaning—and those who have not. How desperate are those who have lost meaning? Can we hope to regain meaning by destroying those who still believe they have it? Is there just so much meaning available in the universe? Is any remaining?

Alienation: Work, "he" said. Work will do it; give us meaning. The trouble is, we have lost our personal means of production; we don't own the goods, nor the goodies. Meaning is in making, doing, working where one owns the work. It is good and necessary to work.

Studs Terkel (1974) finds that work is "out." We (all?) try to shut off our minds while we work, regardless of whose work, which task, who owns "it." We have exteriorized meaning, even through work. No body wants to work, we believe; not for work's sake. Management (hah?) believes we don't want to work, and has to offer "incentives" to get us to work, incentives which are also non-work.

But, in the world of non-work, even those of us who "have" work find ourselves alienated. Work is nice, but it doesn't suffice.

Is it bureaucracy which provides meaning these days? We get defined by a faceless grouping, in limited ways, and get caught between that definition and our "own." The pursuit of meaning robbed of movement, robbed of momentum. Push, pull, elastic, the bureaucracy like a womb, constraining but apparently malleable. The universe expanding as we push. But the constraints: so unobvious that we quit pushing in one direction, and are pulled elsewhere. Bounded in such ways that they feel unbounded. Defined elastically on the rubber of our tethers.

Where are we? Here we are? Watching ourselves watching ourselves... being?

Moving Past One Another: We argue, fight, retreat, contradict, return to what? To whom? Do we find one another? Do we argue against you, them, or only some aspects of ourselves?

In the religion vs. science battle, do they argue against one another, or only against each side's imagined adversary? Straw arguments entail straw people?

How can we mediate, how can each of us explain and broker an apparent but deeply felt argument? Can we understand one another, in each other's terms, or only in our imagination of their terms?—only by becoming them?—losing the argument already by attempting to understand it; them?

"No," you say. The only winning is in changing, during a real conversion, that other, still alien point-of-view. To change is to sell-out, to see the new light, to become not-other, but to become *the* other.

I say, "Yes." That is my task, my job; my quest and realization of me; my vocation, to create understanding. "But, stop!"—you say, a war will result, irrevocably; perhaps with less anger, malice. "Understand, hah."

"Yes," I say. Maybe there are two, maybe 12 or 20 ways of thinking about it, about being. Maybe they contradict, but maybe we construct them, and never hear what they say. Maybe there are versions and visions. How different is different? If different is beyond vision, beyond imagination then I argue against my vision of you. Yours is truly different? But perhaps we will remain opposed, continue to hate, to vie for whatever there might be.

"So?" says J. Try harder! Capture your sadness, and hatred, and vengeance, and use it to construct; not to maintain. Destroy, if you will! But know what you will. So?

Silence-full::Silence-empty: In a room, people silent, witnessing. Taking on big issues, important problems, important persons. The crowd is silent; but how silent, what silences?

In one case, the front, the podium controlled by the power of his office. I challenged, he "stonewalled"; acted as if I had no right to question, to argue. "But," I argued, "you don't know much about this topic. I know as much, and I know I don't know much. Let's just talk. No lecture. No hortation!"

The silence. Silence so deep, so profound. The people, my neighbors, my children's teachers went deep into their mentalities. So quiet, so deep. Into places where they sought refuge from my questions. Embarrassed, morally forced, they removed their being from me, the challenger. Was I right, correct? Would they even know? So silent, they hear pins dropping in the rapidly emptying depths of their mentalities. "Click, click, click." So deep; they'll never forget the scene. So deep, they'll never know the issue, but only the nature of the protective depths into which they retreat from the challenge to "their" speaker. "Click, click, click."

Another day! Another speaker, other powers. Some challenge, same challenger, later; no wiser. Defends, but doesn't stonewall. A new era? Listening to me? Co-opting me? A critic, I am, not opposed. Let's do it better, tougher... together? A different silence, now. Warm, pregnant, no clicks, no defense. I become we. A challenge, a criticism? O.K. Another time? Other perceptions? Silence—full steam ahead!?

Inversions: ...in our thinking. To turn an idea upside-down or right-side-up. To state a counter-intuition, knowing deeply both what is that intuition, and that it is mistaken. It is to state, e.g., a question whose "answer" already proves that the respondent does not understand the issue.

An inversion is to take the "primary" of any system of thought and show that it is derived or assumptive in such a way that alternative systems are generated which illuminate the others; e.g., to show that the "individual" is within and derived from other's casting of that individual. It is to show that the sun is central, that language is an aspect of body. Inversions are powerful, not necessarily in their correctness, but in their power to illuminate what we had previously believed to have been intuition and/or obvious.

Biological Morality: If, as ethologists claim, other species than humans are social, then they must also be moral. That is, if others live together, raise their young, they must have ways of treating and of understanding one another, which is what we mean by moral. Moral is about ways of being, of being with others, of treating them and of oneself.

We thought that it was a deity, a human deity, a god for humans which informed morality. There "was" a religious base, a foundation which had to say that thou shalt or shall not. Otherwise we would be like beasts, and act like beasts, assuming "beasts" to be brutal, selfish, dealing with others by impulse and whim.

But other species are not like that! They are not the beasts of our construction; they are not humans gone rotten. They are, apparently, themselves. And they are moral as we.

Are they also "religious"? Is there a god for each species, one over all?

Do we need to create a god to tell us and command us, to threaten us, to curse, and wreak vengeance upon us? Or, can we dig within our own beingness, and come up as moral creatures?

The ultimate cynicism: that we are less than other creatures!

The Invention of Creation: Was "creation" invented? Was it always obvious in the human condition that causes went back to a first cause—that something did not come from nothing?

Was there an "origin"? Or was it a concept which was invented, had a creator, much as the universe was posited to do? (A consuming worry that a truth-telling tradition does not understand causality: Hume (1738))

In the beginning... was the chicken and the egg? (Two chickens, two...?)

The Philosophic Vision: (*Phaedo*) the acceptance of one's personal death, looking "back" at the present through that acceptance. This vision, which can hardly be denied, or said to be incorrect or untrue on any grounds derived from life's experiences, informs "the present" in very peculiar, yet powerful ways. It would not be too strong to state that Plato figured out how to frame the very notion of reality in whose terms we calculate being; our being.

Instead of merely doing, one is pushed to wonder whether he/she *is*. If I have accepted death, if I am virtually or essentially dead, then I do not exist exactly. The idea of life, of living, turns from experiencing to an idea, a theory—that one is: in each present; in each moment.

Since many ideas do not exist exactly, since ideas are in the imagination, since the present is an idea, then it may seem imaginary. If the present is, or seems to be imaginary, it is an easy step to believe that life is (merely) an aspect or outcome of the imagination. Then one's theory of life easily becomes a theory of what is real (including oneself).

If one "lives" in one's imagination, the acceptance of death, the "reality" of that death, ongoing into the indefinite, into the lasting, into the infinite, the ever-lasting, then the "real" seems, obviously, to be that which is for ever. "It" is the forms, the ideas which become and have become "alive"—for a brief moment. Life, in this vision, is not necessary. Life, for the philosopher, has become a necessity—to be endured, to be "explained away" (but hardly to be explained!).

The subject matter, the "real," is that which lasts, that which is behind, that which is deep; that which makes the timeless into time; the invisible, visible; that which gives life to the enduring forms, the pure forms; that which makes the pure, impure; that which places the timeless "mind" into these impure bodies.

Thus, a theory which "solved" the problem of death by offering us eternality, turned back upon itself to offer a vision of life, which does not observe life "in its own terms," but which concentrates upon stability, upon timelessness, upon ideality, on what would be—and, very little, upon what is. (Parmenides, Pythagoras, Plato → us – e.g. "Next Places" 2006.)

Reinventing the Present: In the vision of the world everlasting, each present is the same as every other. Our experience tells us that this is not the case, that time has direction; that to be here, in this present, is to have gotten here by routes which are/were specific; i.e., each present is not the same.

The problem: to reconcile these contradictory visions of time and of being.

A solution: to recreate the past as if it were the present; to deny time, to re-cast experience by denial or by reinterpretation of experience. It can be done by positing a "once when" which is "always" and "forever"—but how to know consistently that "once when," that messianic age when...? One can use texts, Bibles, stories, Great Authorities—but to do that, we must be constant (forever?), assume that we can gain identical and direct access to the text—especially to the mind and thinking of the writer or inspirer of the text—and, since this is not like our experience, we must deny at least some aspects of experience. But: how to do this without becoming "crazy," out of touch with the present realities? By positing other selves?—how not to dissociate?

The solution?—to reinvent the present, making it appear "sufficiently," not to change. To attribute what appears to change (evolution?) to a Satanic force, something anti-, destructive.

Its own problem: how not to destroy experience to the extent that one destroys oneself!

Origins: does the concept of heaven, of immortality, rest on the notion of causality which leads back to the postulation of the origin, creation, and a creator?

Within this, is it problematic to account for our earthly "existence"? Why?—except for sin/Satan? Is it a surprise to creationists, to discover each day, that they are alive? (If not, why not?)

Aren't there lurking deep in our mentalities a series of surreptitious issues in seeking for origins, for the "originary." In wondering about the origin of meaning, the issues seems quickly to collapse into the question of human origins, and the beginnings of my own personal memory. When, that is, I seek for who I am, the lack of memory of my early pre-articulated stories to myself of myself collapse somehow with the pre-articulated stories of the "originary" humans. To me, this conflation seems odd, but to most of us it seems, well, ordinary.

The existential issue of today is thereby swallowed up in speculation, wanting to rewrite today by recreating history. It is useful to update, to think about where to "go" next, but to want to recreate and rewrite history is to search for destiny within: another mode of essentialism versus experiencing—against life!?

The Writer: Just who is the ghost in my machine? Many writers, coming to the blank page, suspend their judgment, their critical acumen, and "give away" their hands to some other, some greater power who "takes over" and does the writing—an *amanuensis.*

Well, here I am! Sitting, drinking coffee; the blare of mostly baroque setting boundaries to my sensate tentacles; and writing. Do I guide my pen? My right hand, my "bowing" hand, guiding?—or being guided? Do I know? Should I care?

Would it help if I told myself that my story, the message, is divine; rather: Divine? But, I tell myself, it is no more divine (Divine?) than myself, and I am ordinary. It is alright (I tell myself) to be ordinary. But, irrefutably, if the divine in me tells my-self to tell me that I am ordinary, who is to say whether I am, or am not?

Who is the writer? The Writer? A puzzle or an enigma? Sacrament or sacrilege?

On Being Spiritual: In the current conversation between religious fundamentalists ("scientific" creationists) and "atheistic" evolutionists, I who used to be agnostic, now think of myself as "spiritual."

I, who used to be agnostic, and used that notion to perhaps delay grappling with life-death and other paradoxical issues till age would be self-persuasive, have found myself still occupying some ground-in-the-middle. But it is not any longer precisely agnostic. Rather it resides more on firm ground; on some positive assertion about life, and upon considerations of life informed by a wide range of specters and visions of life - from death. And, from wonder. Perhaps it is because my name is "Life" (*Chaim*).

I who used to be agnostic, and am now spiritual, try to gloss over any feelings of dread with wonderment about being, about being human; about being in the world, with others and alone. And I know, increasingly, that what I know is largely related to what others know and how they regard me. My vision of aloneness, even, is tempered and shaped, by my spouse (how much does her spirit—my thinking about her spirit—guide my pen?) who is also wondrous, also spiritual? I know, increasingly, that visions of life and of death are formed by human ideas. And I want to know what is human, because our ideas and talk about what human is and is not, what is divine and is not, is constructed within a network of webs of thought: historical, familial, sociological, economic, psychological, medical. These webs must be deconstructed to see what is in them, why they are persuasive, why they endure, why they do not; when they provoke opposition, and in what forms. Knowing if that is possible—what is human, then I can, perhaps, begin to know what is spiritual.

I, who used to be agnostic, wonder now what it is which maintains, what is it that sustains? And what it is, is stories about how we are and how we will be, about life, and frequently about death. And I wonder which stories "work" to maintain, to sustain. And their forms and varieties I find wondrous; and wonder what they are, and why they work, and when they do not. And, for now, this is what I mean when I tell myself that I am... being spiritual.

Later: much the same, but regarding spiritual as being somehow responsive/responsible for everyone's spirituality as well as my own → "the teacher."

Lessons from...: how is it possible to use the writings and thoughts of the great thinkers, and translate them into this time? Can I ask Augustine what he would do, how he would think - were he me; were I he? Or must I think like him, like I think he thought, through my study of his thoughts, and to be like him; to seek his solutions?—in his time?

But the time is different; no less frightening, perhaps, but different. And, yet; some sameness: the urge toward fundamentalism, the destruction of an established and fraying order, a dwelling upon death as the solution to life.

Augustine's solutions used the same text(s) as his opponents—complicated beyond their erudition, establishing his views as those which are necessary for understanding, even penetration of the Biblical text. ("On Christian Doctrine" A.D.426)

What text(s) do we have?—we have Nature. And the argument is about the same: who is to interpret her, and upon what grounds? (Do we usually set Culture above Nature, because Nature "is" a woman?)

Ten Years from Barbarism: In the context of human import and of human interpretation, memory, re-interpretation, a generation is about 10 years. If children are not taught, do not have access to certain aspects of the parental world, they—our children—come to adulthood not knowing, not having experienced, say, their parents' native language, or their history or culture...

Within "the whatever" is all of history, all of technology, all of Culture; all of whatever has brought us to this point of history. Lost—it could be, and in only 10 years... A report from the history of... a lament?

A Vast Unseen World: There is another world which is 'out there', invisible, yet nonetheless powerful; where decisions are made, and things happen; where chance events are determined, where the spirits reside and float close-in and far-out; where mysteries are clarities, and the faith-in-faith reigns. It is a "truer" world, where human will has no sway. (James, 1902))

(Religions: are determination of what such a putative world is like, how it intersects with the visible world, and how it decides we are!)

And *this* world...?

The Falling World: Moving downward and outward from the age of perfection. Perfection, when we were in the Gardens of Eden. And now, now we are rapidly being rendered asunder. Entropic processes, disintegration, the curse of knowledge, the curse of life.

But life is not that. Life renews; life recreates and organizes from the dusts of forever.

Why should we believe the current prophets, if they too have fallen as far as they claim we all have? Are they not also vestiges, disparate cells and tentacles grasping for a sense of wholeness which they curse us for having—for thinking we have? Must we abandon hope in order to get through each day, one at a time? I hope not!

Why Missionaries Win: Actually, I don't know with any certitude. The only idea which has occurred to me, which makes so far any sense at all, is that the encompassing visions within which most peoples of the world have constituted the meaning of life, have found Western religion to be—as "detail"—within larger frameworks of thought.

Questions of the order of "Why are we here?," informed by a cosmology, seem to regard metaphysics—being—as a way, a method of interpretation and exegesis; details of the larger questions whose minor aspects (from the perspective of, say, cosmology), are always up for grabs. Like the details of my calendars, the specifics of today - what to do this morning; where, with whom to lunch; a discussion at 3:00 this afternoon; how to get home; the bus fare up a dime today - metaphysics appears as a way through the day, and through the week, and the years. And, I guess it is very important in this case that the method and detail are very clear, concise, organized, and orderly.

What I suspect is never clear to "broader" thinkers is that process and procedure which seem minor and like detail, *have a politics*. This is true, especially, of the world religions which have already survived attack and onslaught. These politics, working themselves out from daily and weekly processes, become—in only a few years (I would guess)—what there is.

This happens with metaphysics because it freezes time and causes one to focus differently on which questions appear reasonable, within its vision. This does not necessarily mean that the earlier cosmologies disappear; they seem to endure with great and deep strengths. But many people seem to become embattled within their own visions - and, particularly within Christianity, this is an aspect of its theology - this war of the self within and against itself. The missionaries win, and the people...?

Freedom-in-Belief: The dialectic between the freedom (and the burden) to choose at-all-moments who one is and what one is to do vs. the yielding of large aspects of self to a Law, a Truth, an Otherness which lays out a great deal of what one must do to ensure one's continuity within that construct.

Yet the question of freedom is not so easy because a partial yielding, a giving-away of one's soul relieves it of so much planning, so much guilt about what one might have, should have been or done. It is so tempting to give oneself to and to be free of having to construct so much of one's life.

Freedom—it is so tempting to say, to claim and to believe that I am truly free. And the best part is that I can be and do whatever I "want." But then, whatever doesn't work out is my own fault?, my own credit? What script to follow, to be what?—successful, a good person? For whom?—for myself, for others? If I judge myself in others' terms, am I merely substituting one type of judgment for another, one set of judges who are not present in the sense of being ever/never present for another who are human, and whom I worship? Where has my sense of freedom, of worth, gone to?

Isn't bureaucracy a yielding of oneself in similar ways as yielding to any transcendent, but with the appearance and self-delusion that it is I who am deciding who I am?

An Existential Interpreting: That which endures, which is constant, forever and everlasting is the notion of myself as an independent, a persona, a vision of self which I can trust, which I can always find; and, which I believe, can always be found. It is a story to myself about my existence. It can be the idea of God-within me, or of me which is or seems very independent, or...!? It is this sense of endurance and continuity against which one constructs and argues the flux in life; against which experience rubs— sometimes soothing, at others abrasive and corroding. Occasionally both find contact and a mutuality and a loving of self from both points of view.

It is the necessity (imposed, I believe, from the "outside" in the first instance and continuing) for this constancy of persona which leads us often, perhaps usually, to 'lose' our bodies, to move away from the everyday-ness of flux, time, and gravity, and movement. It is within this construct of self that we lose time.

How we go about the loss of experiencing depends, it seems, on how we construct our constant/continuant personae. Perhaps paradoxically, whether we lose or gain a sense of well-being depends on how we "use" the notion of permanence within the (actual) experiencing. It matters less, apparently, whether the sense of continuity is attributed to self or to an external God-ness. One finds it assaulted occasionally, and must re-think? re-do? re-construct?

Much of what are called the "religious texts" can be understood precisely as this problem of the internal (and ongoing) dialectic between being-now and being-always; and its ensuing pain. (Are life's paradoxes unacceptable within our forms of thought/thinking?)

God's Truth: 1.) Is (was...) God deceitful?—If so, was humankind favored to find the Truth; or further to obscure it? Does God care? **2.)** Does our concept of God's Truth match God's concept? How can we know? 3.) If God is alive, how would we tell? By what method? 4.) Are bravery, arrogance, nobility forms of hubris? Is Faust recreating the Tower of Babel? Am I (are you) Faust?

On "Scientific" Creationism: it can't be science or scientific if there's no possible way of being wrong. The issue of the "end," the *telos,* is precisely that these statements are circular: we have already (surreptitiously) assumed what we want to prove; and have confused means and ends in order to satisfy ourselves that we know the truth. We have confused human prophecy with (natural) prediction; knowing with belief. It is as if we want to tickle our human fancies, rather than grapple critically with our notions of the transcendent.

If there were a deity would circularity be a destiny?

The Shift to Cosmology: Are cosmologists born that way, or are they metaphysicians who, looking for a conversion experience, discovered an available one in cosmology and converted to it? It means, I guess, starting from other questions, wider problems and visions of the human condition (e.g., questioning our very existence rather than accepting it).

Do questions of living become "detail" and trivial and tend to disappear? How is life and living valued within the visions of cosmology? Isn't the cosmologist precisely concerned with the nature of our existence— or of the existence of the firmament, and of humanness within that?—or of one's own individual existence? Isn't the temptation to believe that if I don't exist, the question of whether I will get (return) to heaven becomes moot? (If I exist, then of course I will return to heaven; if I don't then my soul obviously remains in heaven and this existence is apparent, chimerical. What is not?—a summational question!).

The Second Coming: We have a friend, an older woman, a 2nd generation Eastern European person of Jewish extraction. It turns out that she was born on Dec. 25; on Christmas. Is it any wonder that the thought sometimes passes through her mind that another Jew, this time a woman, should be the reincarnation of God on earth. How will she know? (How will we know?)

She is wise, at battle with society, living as best she can a Christ-like life in opposition, demonstrating, writing, hortating that the world is unjust, unfair, dishonest. She seeks a certain sort of martyrdom and often finds it. If the times are right, will she not become the next Messiah? (How will we know?) (Does she know?)

Aren't messiahs born posthumously?—proclaimed as messiah when they are no longer with us?—no longer having to be dealt with in any but our mentalities? She "loves" humanity but alienates all persons.

A Maiden/Virgin: it is claimed that a young maiden (in ancient Hebrew/Aramaic) was translated into Greek as ("a young virgin") in talking about the conception of Christ. Christianity, to some extent, the outcome of a mistranslation... Christianity, a form of Judaism which was formalized and "Greek-ized," making life into a "partaking" of an ideality, rather than life transcending its own experience? (Plato: *Republic* - Book 10)

In The Name of God?: In current debates with "Scientific Creationists," scientific colleagues claim that the Creationists are careless with facts and truths, preferring to win rather than to be precisely honest. One supposes (if this is "true"), that the cause of getting us all to accept God (their interpretation of God) overrides any particular means by which they get to their end.

But what sort of God (she...he?) would want or need to win by such means?

Death over Life=Unreal over Real? Why is life not sufficient?: If we are rational, if we can know God, why do we often prefer the Unreal; to the extent that our concept of death pervades, even determines how we experience life? Why are we weaker than our own concepts? Have our parents not provided us with sufficient spirit? Have our teachers abandoned their own teachings?

How can we believe we are rational if we abandon life, if we worship the unreal, if we do not live as fully as we can?

Is it not our duty to live? Locating the ideal...?

Individual and Society/Community: if salvation is individual, then why do/should we get along with, love one another?

What is a family?—if salvation is individual (i.e., each soul)?

If we are born in sin, then whom do we have to blame?—ourselves?

Who is anyone else?—who am I?

Who am I?—who is anyone else?

What is a priest; a pastor? Why should we listen to anyone else? How can we understand; why should we believe?

What if the priest disagrees with us? Who is s/he? What is the priest's claim? Is it pure? In our interests?

Getting Further Behind: If sex is sinful, then to engage in it, to produce offspring is further proof that we are damned; even that our damnation is increasing because we should, by now (ah, history), know better. But we can't help ourselves; our desires overtake being.

We try to justify sin by saying that the family is what (our) God wanted, and that sex within marriage, for procreation, is all right (just make sure it's not enjoyable!). But how can this not help but put us further behind? Each new life is an increase in the debt to eternity. Each new act is an act of expiration, trying to make up for lost time, which cannot help but increase. (As if God were not compromising!)

No wonder the world is running down - from this perspective!

Rape and Abortion: From a letter to the Minneapolis Tribune by a state representative.—the "baby" should not be killed, nor aborted because it might become another Mother Teresa, a Washington or Voltaire...or

But this presumes that each conceived baby (= each soul?) is self-contained, self-directed, and its genius "will out" irrespective of what experiences it undergoes. It contains or implies no theory of society, does not ask how many geniuses are ruined by all of us. But then what difference does a genius make in a world where there is no society? Why do these "contradictions" not bother the theorist of life-at-conception?

And what about the mother? Will the memory of the rape, the trauma, cause her to have difficulties with herself, with the baby, with the world? What do we owe her, the victim? Or has she now been transformed to an evil, sinful creature, for whom there is no longer any redemption in any case? What has happened to living redemption; no penance or atonement here?

But isn't this the major historical trouble with "fundamentalism," at least Christian fundamentalism—that any theory of others, of society, fades into the background, and off the map, at each and every moment—in comparison with the importance of the individual soul? Raw politics takes over while we're not noticing: how does this thinking become transformed into methodology, and to generalize to other aspects of our thinking?

Being Spiritual: I live in wonderment at the possibility and nature of life. So mundane, yet...

Is there more than this?—I don't ask very often. If others ask this, I note and appreciate their asking, and wonder what is sufficient and what is enough for them to love life; so that life is itself sustaining? (If I have respect for life, then I must respect others' thinking, even when they are wrong.)

I know and appreciate that many have been raised to wonder not about life - life is mundane - but about eternity. And I wonder if this affects how they think about many things themselves, and about people like me. I wonder how to tell them that I wonder, that I try to understand.

What If?: a religious-point-of-view is a certain, limited framework of the "what if"? What if God exists, what would God be like? What are we really like if God exists, if God created us, if God was concerned with sin, and wrong?

What if the world is as it is? What if it is not?

What if some "what-ifs" lead somewhere, and other "what-ifs" do not? What if?

Things We Shouldn't Know: From a mystical Judaism, there are certain aspects of life which one shouldn't probe, things one shouldn't study or know. Certain aspects of life were meant to be hidden, secret; life, knowledge, perhaps, included (sex, sin, fun...).

But, I said, life to me is all mysterious, all a wondering. I try to judge; it is for you to judge yourself, and to do what you must and what you can. What you do and who you are, and where you are going, I find interesting: especially perhaps because you're the only one I know who is living that sort of life. Don't be angry; don't forgive.

Someone should know; someone should think, observe, keep track. Life is what there is, and knowing is its vehicle and sustenance. (The sadness in metaphysical method is that we have proclaimed that being human is to be able to know—uniquely. Thence we have abandoned many of the questions about knowing.)

Other Realms—Labyrinths (Borges and other mystics): Concentration on the what could have been, might have been, would, should...The world filled, as well, with all the other souls, also in their entire panoply of possibilities: others' souls; the dead, angels, gods, not quite humans, other species on their way to becoming human, becoming others, becoming gods.

They, we—are all watching; one another, ourselves; watching ourselves watching. "Causality, where have you gone? You are right here? Ah! What do you look like? Ah! Green?"

Enter here. Proceed. Turn left, right, roll over. Where am I? Just ahead of where I was. How do I get out of here? The world, life, in search of a single moment, of any resolution, of a resting place. Either there is none, or there is none other.

(Myself, I prefer Sisyphus. At least one stays in shape pushing boulders up that mountain which I can always find! And the run down is often glorious.)

The Spirit: Why have humans been susceptible to/interested in believing that there is more; that what there is, is not sufficient; that we are parts, those parts or aspects having other than visible, experiential aspects?

With large (beyond the scale of being able to know each individual in great depth) populations, certainly, it is obvious that we are other, that we are somehow like certain others, members—perhaps—of groups. We are this, and we are like this and like that. Thus there is obviously more and other. Why not God, gods, spirits…?

Then there are surprises. We do not fully know ourselves, even those of us who interpret each new present from the fixed vision of self-as-past. Why are there such surprises?

Also our visages change: to others and to ourselves. Our faces, the seats of our being differ from time-to-time, even from one moment to the next. And this increases, often, with age. Who is to say that each expression is not another within? I may say that they are all myself; but then who am I to claim such a thing?

And, to whatever extent we are living within others' imaginations of us, then we are them: with them, reactive to them in response, denying their impress upon us. It is no big jump to explain all this by seeking spirits; causes who do not appear.

To blame, to assuage whatever is other, may also make the life of being-with-others more calm, more interesting, more…

Today, can I Atone?

What troubles have I caused? How have I transgressed? Against myself, my loves, my ideas, against the laws of all of us and of whoever else there might be?

Guilt, impurity—surely I have done no worse than I have done. Can I atone?

Where, how, do I invent sin?

Do I want merely to alter my feelings, to feel cleansed, purified; merely relieved? Better perhaps to asceticize being; to exteriorize, to actualize the hurt I feel, to feel hurt.

I did not want to act badly, even to think thoughts which were nasty, damaging, vengeful. But I did, and I did, to some extent because I am alive. And I decide to remain living, and these things happen.

Can I atone? Can I let go of those thoughts, self and other-damaging, which creep into my being because I decide to stay alive? Do I beseech? Whom?

Can I atone? In each end I must forgive my-self. It is the paths upon which I tread in order to invent the next how of self-forgiveness; that is where I find atonement! It is very good to seek, but is it neither where it was, last time, nor where it will be ever again. I have decided to remain, and it is necessary to atone.

The Underground Clergy: In our town the traditional preachers still sound and appear traditional, reading the old, the usual texts. They seem to be the same as always; soothing, exhorting, preaching to the haughty, the vain, the sick and the fearful. But many of these ordinary preachers live underground, the eternal deity of biblical-appearing times transformed into the processual, with-us God (and gods) of each-day living. Do they lie? Do they do their job? Are they truly religious and moral, choosing to do their jobs underground? Do they believe they do their job as they will and as they must? (Kierkegaard and Whitehead have entered the churches mostly unaware! And if they are aware?)

Exegesis: So there are texts, there are reports, there is testimony, there are stories, parables, paradoxes. Do they stand alone? Can they be simply and purely what they are; not more nor less? If we were at the beginning, perhaps; if I had Skinner's utopian "Walden Two" where everyone is, but is without experience. Ahhh! I could remake all the stories, all the texts, into something coherent, correct, whatever works!? But this assumes that every time, any time, is all of time; that the eternal God is the eternal nature of humans; and that is just one more story, good enough for the ascetic monastic, but not always good for being in life or for living.

So there are texts, and even if the right god, the True God inspired their telling, they come to us—through us. They pass by "the hot wires" of the imagination incarnate, and float upon the air of our surfaces and odors and wishes and fears. And they become interpreted and ordered into a story which works... to grant us coherence, relief, history, futurity; the gifts of wholeness in one world vision, of nothingness in another, of every-ness in yet another.

What works?—for whom?—in what era?

What is the method of interpreting, of interpretation? Are these the same: doing, interpreting, in time, active vs. interpretation—static?

How does one take certain texts, and say what they mean, where they fit, in what (sort of) scheme? Is there a "logic," a "common sense"—or are there several logics, several common senses, "common" to different times, places, contexts, particular persons, to disciplines, ideologies, to life or to death or to the imagination?

Does what comes first have to be unpacked, interpreted by what follows, thus altered? (An argument for the most "recent" text(s) over those preceding: e.g. the Koran, over the New Testament, over the Old Testament—Islam over Christianity over Judaism.) An argument also, against the equality of women: use of Genesis 2 over Genesis 1 because it is later.

What is primary, what is secondary? How is this decided?—in terms of some particular school of practice, some authority?

"Proof" of God's Existence: Is the creationism which arises now—"Scientific Creationism"—an attempt by Christian fundamentalists to prove that God exists? Here is the "strongest" claim to knowledge—science—captured by believers to bolster and/or substantiate their beliefs.

How are they better off by "proving" God? i.e., if it is true that they want to prove God by defeating or by co-existing with (evolution) science? Most likely by co-existing, because if they take over and control the notion of science it will lose its power, its belief and conviction. Thus "scientific creationism" needs a worthy, perhaps equal, certainly equivalent opposition in order to gain and hold its own convictions; an opposition which claims to have and hold and own knowledge.

Will any proof of the existence of a deity rest forever in the claim to the claim to the authority of claiming that I know what I know?

Myth-as-Truth and What Sustains Life: Whatever is true and whatever truth is, the (social) reality is the (as-if) reality in terms of which we live our lives. Individually, personally, interactionally it is the fact that we have (a) truth(s) in terms of which we operate, which work (usually) to maintain us, which keep(s) fear down and hope up or those two and others in some balance. This is how we live.

Whatever is the "external," "objective" truth of existence is and remains a particular (perhaps an "unparticular") set of truths—but a rock-bottom truth is not necessary to our continuity. We already possess it or them in sufficiency. (Ironically interesting how our worries supersede the knowledge which resides in our existence—especially of the knowledge which is the body!)

Difficulties arise because some of them do not work, are insufficient in a variety of ways, at particular times, for particular persons or peoples; occasionally they (appear to) compete, and their shape takes on political forms and entailments and there is a good deal of trouble.

The important and sustaining element is that we believe that we possess meaning, and that there are ways in which life-living can make sense. (What do we do when our theories of meaning are in crisis, when nihilism negates making-sense?)

Thieves of Existence: (1) There is a set of relativist thinkers (mostly literary scholars) who have some confidence in the idea that all is relative, there is no touch-down, no hints of being or of agreement (how could we agree if there were no common points of being?). However they sustain themselves (the ones I know, live within academic traditions and find "placeness" there), they seem to want to rob the rest of us of our own experiences, meanings, and legitimacy in the world.

For them, most of what is seems to devolve upon having an "us" and a "them"—and every relationship and all of being becomes a choosing of in or out (with us vs. against us).

If we do not choose them, to be an "in," or if we do not seem to be proper or appropriate "ins," or we oppose their allies, then their technique of dealing with us is to attempt to rob us of reality, to deny that what we know and/or experience is legitimate in whatever terms, and to treat us as non-persons. A certain sort of relativist-nihilism in which their hold is so fragile and narrow that they must confirm it constantly, in every relationship.

(Not necessarily true of relativists-in-general: e.g., string players: give us an "A" (440hz), and that is, within tradition and a good violin/bow, sufficient to make beautiful music—alone and/or with others. The music can then become its own sort of reality!)

(2) There is a set of absolutist (primarily "fundamentalist") thinkers; who think each and every time is all of time. Absolute means forever. Since each time would, I imagine, detract from the idea of absolute, or would call attention to existence, to experience in its "own terms," and never exactly add-up to forever, but only to life and to a life-time, then "each time" is diminished in its experiential power. It can have power only with respect to what it is not: what it is against (and why a theology in which the deity exists forever, gains power)—thus gaining its existence residually; what it is for (a preparation for death and what costs can and must be paid tend simultaneously to increase because death is more nigh and the costs decrease relative to the finality of non-existence).

It is easier to appeal to the anti-change theologians because being-in-opposition yields a real, if residual, being. If one is strong—as strong as they, as strong as they can imagine, as strong as Christ—then one can talk and connect. But connection and communication is different with opposing-power persons because they remake an opposing person into someone whom they construct (some new form of Satan), rather than who one thinks she or he is.

Since no one "is," there arises a problem in figuring who one is thought to represent. It is as if everyone represents a political party, except that the opposition makes up the party platform and there is no way of protesting that they have constructed you incorrectly, because you have no existence, anyway, (other than what they imagine you to have.)

The difficulty, the greatest danger, is that the absolutist gains power of the sort which will turn an Armageddon policy into actuality, in order to prove one is correct: that is, that there is no human existence. A return to Eden: on one's own terms.

The Effect of Our Concept of God on Human Nature: It has become clear to me that the way in which we think about God/gods affects the nature of how we are. How we think others are (humans and non humans, including machines), and how we construct life, death, and whatever else we can imagine. None of this is either to confirm or to deny the human spirit—life is its own confirmation!—but to state that our concepts of being are informed powerfully by how we construct God, or deny God.

The God of Creation, "in the beginning," set up the idealist notion of unreality: the idea of meta-physics, that objects precede human beings and human observation; that we are individual and dual (mind/body), that life must be explained as non-death (by heat or whatever); that how we construct God defines the rules of human epistemology; that we are observers of time, rather than creators of time; that God is whatever we/he said he was at some point in some past; that our existence, our history tends to collapse back to that time when God was: that we are damned merely for our being, and on and on. This concept of God forces us/leads us to see life as a preparation for death, principally; and leads to the notion of life-as-illusion. Within this illusion, how is one to know what she is doing; what responsibility (I exist?—do others?—what for?)

An active concept of God (Whiteheadian, Kierkegaardian) requires attention to each moment, an active growth and transcendence beyond yesterday—for today has new turns (for me). It requires more individual responsibility and strength and attention: no mere cleansings through ritual or sacrament, but constant re-evaluation and re-creation.

An anti-theism, in a theistic world, needs to create a notion of being, of responsibility, of society, of growth, of life, in others' terms. It claims a different basis for knowledge (logic, rationality?) and is currently in trouble because the attack of ethology (correctly in part) is contra-rationalism (e.g., Lorenz, 1966; Eibl-Eibesfeldt, 1989; Wilson, 1975).

An "anthropology" which examines these concepts of God, of anti-God, could (I think) address questions of existence (to confirm it) and spirituality without robbing life of life. (If there is "purpose" to life, isn't it in living?)

Religion as the Existential Outcome of Different Age-grades: It seems that the religions which have emerged in history, which compete in each age for our attention, tend to be created out of the experience of persons of different age and experience. Most emerge from "bad times."

Mosaic Law, for example, seems to be a story of older people who yet sustain life and society. It is positive to living life. The Old Testament, gradually, is a story of fright of the sick, of the young who have lived little, and fear the most, to a proposal for a life which solves death—and so begins the New Testament, a story about the beginning of youth. If death, the fear of death, results from a failure of the aged to sustain themselves, to teach the fear rather than wonder and the law of the many, then it is the first of the older people who move into an era of sickness, weakness, and pass this along to youth—both a telling through fear, and a protection against their imminent death; a concentration on what is wrong, or could be wrong: as if correction from fear will change whatever there is to fear, and what drives fear.

And so the New Testament, begun from the very old telling youth, teaching them to fear, became the story of the young, the weak; an exhortation to go on against whatever odds. And oddly, it turns out to be an excuse rather than an excursion. There are no generations; what happens is prefigured early in life...and so on.

Confucianism is a "religion" (non-divine) of the very old, who yet sustain.

Buddhism is a religion for all times, of all ages, as time is reduced incessantly into all moments being each moment. So, in a certain sense, there is no age; there are no ages.

But most religions seem to come from the experience of the middle-aged: who know life, and death, and love, and substance—who both promote and maintain.

Who Am I? The question of God, of me, of others, of myself as younger, as sane or not—how many "I"s am I? Does God/Satan enter my consciousness, or are there parts of my being and thinking which I call God? Does this, if true, make me less Godly or Godlike? Does it make God any less real, if I think a deity is an aspect of my self? And other persons? Who are they in my consciousness? If I like or hate them, is this an aspect of my self (do they bring out in me) which I don't like? How many am I?

If it is that I am many, why do I not dissociate? How do these many that I am, cohere? (If and When they do.) In what ways?

It is true, in my life, that when sad, depressed, my thinking travels into areas, on paths which I do not otherwise think and do not ordinarily explore. In good times (right now more-or-less), it is not interesting or compelling to go into sad places. I know where to find them in my being, but I do not stay there, plumbing them to the depths of their being and mine. Is the idea of God a place in my being which I know how/where to find, and which I "choose" to explore, or not? What compels me to go in one place or another, to explore, to shut off?

Is the sense in which I am many a "physical" reality, only conceptual; merely physical, "merely conceptual"? (And vice-versa: i.e., is the sense in which I am one...?)

Is it a picture of "I" which coheres, which keeps all this together? Where is it, whence did it come?—from myself?—from others' notion of me as being continuous? Why do I not lose that sense? What if I do?—is this what goes wrong after neurological damage?

Why do some aspects of self (say, God, a loved one, a "lovely" thought or memory) make me feel good, comforted? Why could/does it appear to come from the outside which we ourselves have made up...? (See my *Next Places* (2006) and *Teaching as Dialogue* (2013))

On Eternal Cycles (#272 on Pythagoras):

"If one were to believe Pythagoras, with the result that the same individual things will recur, then I shall be talking to you again sitting as you are now, with this pointer in my hand, and everything else will be just as it is now, and it is reasonable to suppose that the time then is the same as now." (Kirk & Raven, 1983)

Taken into the Bible this is the informing notion of Ecclesiastes, and reduces the primary motivating force of humans into vanity, self-love. All else is pre-ordained, and the illusion of all of time is turned into the illusion that there is, indeed, change; but the nature of change and its effects, is what is preordained. (In modern management and planning it teaches us that who controls the "plan" or "policy" effectively controls the future.)

But the notion of cycles effectively destroys time and history by admitting that humans note change, but that the change is trivial and due to human conceit. This idea robs the existential and experiential by admitting it in a partial and limited way, then claiming that it is an aspect of false consciousness, of human weakness and the passions of self-worship.

The Problem with Death: when death becomes a primary concern of life and of living and "it" pervades our (living) thinking, then life seems to diminish in importance, (its) sustenance to be toward death, and life gets lost as all is re-interpreted as preparing successfully or not for the death of eternity. Instead of living life to whatever can be its fullest, life becomes various kinds or sorts of enemies. Like a pain to be avoided and adjusted to by moving around it, life fades.

The goodness of life, whatever is positively moral or loving, tends to be overridden by some interpretation derived from whatever is personally fearsome; whatever it is that life interprets as the panic, the fear of not-living. So from a feeling interpreted as fear, the fear grows and knaws, and can be kept in tow only by a story which works to make life experience more and more illusory: life is not in any sense itself, but is some sort of punishment in return for the sin of one's parents.

A children's story—of life eternal—translated into one which sustains life by dampening fear sufficiently to keep life's "practitioners" young in mind. (If only puberty could be banished!) Life becomes a thing which can be lost, not anything in itself.

The Concept of Death in Life: The concept of death taken seriously, informs life's perspectives. Death asks us to ask where we are now; where tomorrow. What does this life do?—what are its debts, its possibilities? How does it ask us to study ourselves? What can knowing mean; what does (can) meaning mean? Meaning continually empties itself.

Death asks us to ask: why? Since this can be answered only by death, it asks us to seek provisional answers. It offers, instead to struggle with these partialities; to sustain ourselves and to help sustain those others who will help to sustain us. Death asks us to create time, history, the kinds of why-ness which will constitute life's experience.

Death asks us not to accede to it. To give-up, to give-in to death, is not to view death seriously. It is to view life in such ways that the living fear of death can be handled, ameliorated, dealt with. But not considered seriously.

Death—that is to say the concept of death, of self, of others—provides meaning to life. Not the only meaning, nor all of meaning, but the notion of life's finiteness is deeply interesting (Somehow we occasionally lose this notion). What is?—what is fearful about death?—how is it that we both are and beyond being? Are we conceptually that we are? To what depths can we reach? What is possible?—what is profound?—are these the same?

We lost meaning with the death, not of God, but of the concept of God. Be serious.

Death and Life—A Unity? Heraclitus thought they are of a piece. Plato took up the reality of life as if it were an aspect of death, a preparation, a way not to be afraid. Amerindians and African traditions understand no particular discontinuity. Philosophy, its primary basis to be a definition of death (of life-as-death) of the soul free from the body and the senses (*Phaedo*). Once we "know" what the soul is—as pure knowledge—we can understand life in its pure, knowable sense. The difficulty, apparently, is in knowing the soul, all such definitions seeming to come from life and experience.

What we decide to count as death, as information and knowledge of and from death is what *we* "decide" the nature of such a decision to be. (Better to live life!) If there were a deity we would somehow figure how to obscure the possibility within our decisions.

If God were on Earth—today: If God were ever here, s/he is here today. What solace a theory of history in which today is less than some other time, a way out from responsibility? Whether God, whether not, it is us. I and you who re-create him, her in our lives—today.

In "the Beginning" was there a beginning, a concept of the onset from nothing to something?

Or is the concept of the beginning an invention, an aspect of some theory of history?—Parmenides?—Pythagoras?—Aristotle's self-caused first cause? But, it is a concept which now convinces because the question which it seems and claims to answer has become meaningful!? A question which addresses an historical-political situation turns into a metaphysics, and the shift isn't noticed. Like trying to solve the chicken and egg story before we discovered that life is frequently *still* paradoxical.

The Solution to Solitude: Buber (1937) says that the question of philosophical anthropology, of what is human, is what gnaws at us and is solved or placated by positing some solution which suggests, claims that our place in the universe is bounded somehow. The question is provoked by feelings of solitude.

The modern problem arises via Pascal (1669) as he noted that there is no boundedness; infinity in all possible directions. Hegel's 1807 solution is to use time (history) to pre-determine all that there is. Looking for certitude, any sort of certitude will do? (If only we had not come upon "language!"—if only our concept of language hadn't misdirected our observations of self-as-body!)

If there is a solution, any certitude, it will reside in the question which the lack of certitude seems to provoke: what is human? The modern solution is very different from previously conceived solutions where we admit that we do not already know the answer to what is not-human (animals and/or machines). Thus what is human directs itself to the nature of comparison and what sorts of comparator-observers humans are.

This is very different from the so-called (reductionist) biologists who look to pre-determination in the genes, the stuffness of futurity from the past, wiping out time in yet another way. Bewailing language as having removed us from Eden (Lorenz, 1966).

My sort of solution (Sarles, 2006) is to see that we are here with others (á la Feuerbach), that they (i.e. others) grant us continuity in which an essential changing-continuing "I" is in complicated, ongoing interaction.

But, further, the notion of infinity which is already present in how we have tended to imagine we are different from (other) animals, is no longer the same notion as it was before social studies of feral species (Darling, 1937). Either other species are also infinite, or we are finite creatures who have ways of capturing some sense of infinity; e.g. via what we call language. But, in a discourse grammar (Q-R), the so-called infinity is demonstrably not that directly. We remain finite creatures whose complicatedness, e.g., as mechanical creatures, has remained underestimated by far. If only we begin study of humans by seeing how we distinguish humans from others. (And/or Amerindian ideas that we "share" our being/spirits with other animals—especially true when we are asleep...and Woman is/are the future!)

On Being Haunted: Who am I?—what enters my being? The sociality of life, of being confirmed by others, also opens up the possibility of other forces entering. What I cannot explain beyond my love and fear of self and others, I still try to explain. Seeking an accounting of what I am and what I find my self doing, there remain discrepancies. The fear of the dark banished from my childhood lingers still, but with no focus. Should I name that fear: evil, Satan—the darkness of the no-longer young? (Does Manichaeism lurk, invited or not?)

Do I own up to their creation, that evil, that Satan is me as much as any other part? Or do I forgive my self, wishing away the parts I tell my self I do not like? Do I weaken, or do I strengthen my ability to do what I want, and be what I want by thinking that Satan is not-me, but a force trying to enter me? Can I wish-away the evil in me and not lose my self, and life? (And if I define the wrong evil, or the evil incorrectly?)

Knowing What's Going On: In the shrunken world of instant communication it is not any longer very clear what precisely is going on. We get reports and see pictures broadcast as if they are instantaneous, and think ourselves across the entire earth in this very moment; just as if there are no time zones or lines of latitude which shape experience so that it is always just beyond understanding. But would we know if there were a revolution occurring 20 blocks from where we are? Whose revolution?—and who are we within it?

Riding in cars, buses, trains, planes: time shrunken with respect to the speed of movement. Instant stop, instant shock to the fabric and fibers of our lives. A lifetime to recover? A lifetime to prepare for what is increasingly instantaneous, more fragmented than ever. Do I know; will I be ready?

Smart...phones!?

Every Science (also) a Theology: I believe that one can "invent" a theology for every way of thinking about the human condition. This is not to say whether any theology is correct, or right, or... but that any and all stories and all claims we can find or observe or create about humans can equally claim a divine origin, or a theistic counterpart which is causal or anti- or cooperative in whatever we think we are like.

This fact does not lessen the reality or power of theology. It does demonstrate that it is futile to claim for, or even to seek for truth and proof from a theology. (If there really were a deity...)

The Dialogic: (Buber and Hasidism, 1937)—I and Thou, Thou with me, and in this interaction. To whatever extent it touches both, is located God; the God of being alive, in the world, with one another.

The individual, yet another myth, I must contact the soul of another in order truly to be. The soul, not clearly an entity, the "me" I experience, some aspects of my self, of my contacting others, of others defining me, and treating me as if am; I, they; I, Thou.

Well. Why not? (Ask J.)

Otherwise, in Western tradition, it is difficult to account for any one (any thing) other than my self; it is difficult to account for marriage, for family, why they are, what they might be, except to embalm it in Eve's sin; life evolved from disobedience, a mistake, an affront to God. The idea of the ideal and its perfection ends and begins in me.

Otherwise, it is difficult to account for mourning; a mystery that there is grief. Must we worship mystery?

Future-Non-Future: If we have no future, our future is assured. (If there is no future...)

Each of Us, Alone-in-Death: This notion of alone-ness, of solitude, has dominated Western thought. The body, which is the "I," the individual "me"... me is no more. What becomes of me?—I? Where will I go? Will I not-be? How frightening!

And how powerful!

What guide is this (for how) to live our lives? What room does it leave for a vision of otherness? For our own becoming-ness which is outside of, in spite of, contra the captivation of not-being. Impossible to penetrate our thoughts?

Death enters life, haunting each moment, turning our thoughts inward, and the notion of life weakens, except to get others to enjoin our own misery.

But we don't even get to live fully. Life-a-gift forgotten, suspect, as we live in the debt of the sin by which we are begotten. Dour, vengeful God, which encourages us to destroy self (and to say O.K. to others destroying themselves...what matter?)

Sadness, overwhelming.

Easier, more satisfying to bask in the vanity of fear?

Some Ways to Deal with Fear: 1.) Turn fear into wonder. 2.) Invent a deity who will tell me everything is all right—if it works, fine; if not invent a deity who will deny life, making it all (including fear) an illusion; make the illusion one which allays fear. 3.) Find a life-task worthy of my life. 4.) Banish time: each moment all of time: each moment infinitesimal within eternity. 5.) Seek fear: the Zen of fear (an aspect of self; not an enemy, not separate?) 6.) Practice yoga.

The Fear of Death: If I thought that the fear of death would help me to live better...

Creationism—A Course: The "short course" in creationism being a consideration of about a dozen vocabulary items, their histories, ranges of meaning, relationships with other words and concepts, limitations, ramifications, and so on.

Consider some of these words: 1. Continuity 2. Change 3. Origin 4. Cause 5. Experience 6. Life 7. Death 8. Fear 9. Human 10. Spiritual 11. Moral 12. Deity 13. Permanence 14. Ideal 15. Perfection

Demographics and Life: As the population bulge in this country gets older (mid-late 30's at this writing), what new effects? The fears, accomplishments of middle age, sickness, seriousness?

A sense of competition, less available success, a closed-box economic model?

Now, older (mid-40's) people search for community; preparation for retirement; personal/political senescence; yielding of power; spirituality...

A Jeremiad: We have gone against God's truth—return to God's Law, and all will be good again!

The movement from Moses to Christ: the grasping of life, hope for humankind, for a notion of persons under the spirit of God. But there are troubles, and they increase with time and with generations. The authority and leader, long dead now, venerated in memory. But the actuality seems, in each moment, to shrink.

Fear, despair enter. And the leaders try to mitigate or exacerbate, not knowing, wanting to enhance vanity, power, the gods which inform what they think - in the name of who was and what happened in the increasingly distant past. The attempt to return, like the worship of one's own childhood memories, places hope outside of life. Enter death; stalking, stomping. Pestilence, plague the natural condition. Dwell upon the worst until it pervades. Life-become-illusion to be lived through, seeking better times, a punishment. Return to the truth, and you will be saved!

The History of the Idea of Reality (Parmenides: *Frag. VIII*- D. Gallop 1991): Because we cannot imagine non-being there can be none; no such concept, no such actuality. Our imaginations (minds) being somehow in tune with the great spirit of nature, if "they" cannot imagine non-being, there can be no such thing or concept. (Death, at least as concept is banished; and concept takes over, as it were, from any experience.)

Since there is no non-being (from this theory about what "non-imaginable" means), there is no (longer) any distinction between living and non-being (non-living), and it becomes impossible to tell whether life or death is the really real. Life "cannot" inform death, but we can imagine that life is an illusion from death—thus confirming this theory. Also confirming it is the idea that death is an illusion from life. All such distinctions fade; their possibility backgrounded from actuality. The subject matter of life/death becomes the nature of the imagination (→ mind, language, rationality = the human)

And there is a necessity for setting-up to distinguish, practically, what is indistinguishable in some deeper sense of actuality.

Probably the most important note is that Parmenides-Pythagoras-Plato figured out how to "control" and define our (even 2500 years later) very concepts of reality. A story about the workings of the mind; a rhetoric which (magically?) calls attention away from itself while convincing ourselves to interpret experience in particular ways—especially to disregard "formal" dynamics in the structuration of form?

Interpretation: Here are the texts! Read them, savor them, study them, understand them, live them! The Bible, the Koran...

They describe what we are (what I am), how we came to be, whence we go; how to live, to die and what these are.

Yet, they are strangely out-of-time; they are historical. The writing, the stories about whatever events, the chronicles, are no more. The texts are their own testimonies, and we have no way to witness directly what they say happened.

So we engage in interpretation. But interpretation is a complicated journey—which can be made to appear simple—and involves beliefs, theories, observations, ideas, translations, thinking about the notion of history, of the present and future, and especially an examination of self; of subject, of the interpreter.

Do I "believe-in" the texts? Yes/No? If yes, then interpretation is elaboration; trying to make each story make sense within the larger sense of the textual scheme (especially, in Western thought from Augustine, to "resolve" contradictions). If no, then, why not? Mohammed!?

But where do I, we—in *this* time—derive schemes of interpretation? What do we know about other times, places; without radio, TV, planes, motors? What do we know about life without modern medicine and dentate fillers? What do we know about light and dark, we incandescent dwellers? We hear, read a story and place us, our experience, in the Beth – i.e. - lehems, the Jerusalems, Meccas, of other times, as we imagine other times from these times? So, who are we? And how do we know of "these times" from very limited experiences?

The Loss of Hope: Hope has been lost! The idea of a better futures—for others, for self—has dissipated within the easy relativism of a dozen "-isms," all of which claim equally well that theirs is the only truth. How do we reestablish hope?—by proclaiming the one -ism? But at what costs? Whose will be the one which emerges? –which wins? Why?

No! The secret of futurity, of hope, already lies within us and within life as its willingness and interest to have and raise a next generation. It lies within us, our will to do this, to teach what we know, to carry on—not merely because we are afraid to die or are not yet ready—but because we find it interesting, or desirable, or necessary. Continuity, survival, in its existential sense requires no particular justification, no particular reason nor any reasoning. (Is it not located already within our own willingness to have survived till now, till this moment?)

The loss of hope is not a true loss, not a permanence. It is the loss of a certain set of stories about aging, about what is for, about an ideal which informs life. But life doesn't require these sorts of stories to maintain, to reinvent progress or hope. Humankind is sufficient—within all of life—to do this yet again, and again… and always. It requires will and intelligence and some notion of rational-reflective humankind which examines itself and figures out how to move forward, and what that means and implies and entails… until the next time hope gets lost.

(Is the loss of hope, of futurity, particularly a problem of and for males? i.e., no babies…))

Dante's *Inferno*: All who enter here, abandon hope! The problem: the reinvention and re-invocation of the varieties of Inferno.

The Jupiter Effect: The morning after.

"Are we still here?" I ask, "Or are we in heaven, imagining being here?"

"If we can ask that question then what difference does it make? This is all there is. Is that not sufficient?" [J.]

The New Creationism—Anti-Progressive: A hundred years of history, of evolutionism vs. creationism, had always been the retreat of creationism toward a more "reasonable," "rational" view; i.e. one which seemed, progressively, to be compatible with an evolutionist's vision of the human condition. But not now. The historian asks, but does not pursue. (See my *Nietzsche's Prophecy: The Crisis in Meaning*, 2001)

The Existential—its Dangers: The notion of *Becoming* runs into its own difficulties, as the concern carries with it not only a lust for whatever it considers life to be, but also the seeds of its own destruction: a lust for death?

The existential, a Christology for the Christian, an ode to existing in order to control the idea of death, to keep the fear as an impetus to life, an energizing force. How?—by opposing whatever is seen to be the immoral in oneself; in society.

Politics, theo-politics, is an outgrowth of the wish of self-control, the use of a sledgehammer to hit one's self over the head in the name of *Becoming*? (Nietzsche, *Twilight of Idols*, 1889, last page)

The God Which Works: On overhearing a seminar (*4-F in God's Army* 2013), the question of having, believing in a concept of God which works to inspire us to believe. Circular, of course. But what a circle! So many questions, so many possibilities...

Does (my concept of) God change if I change? Do I change because God has changed? (Is this why pantheisms work?)

Will (my concept of) God be the same tomorrow? How will/might I be certain?

Am I (my concept of) God? Is God (my concept of) myself?

If faith falters, what (concept) have I lost faith in?

"Can't we choose life instead of death? My 14-year-old son would like to know." (From a letter to *Minneapolis Star Tribune* 3/25/82). Read the Old Testament through to the New Testament!

Here is an odyssey which begins from the choosing of life, the troubles which develop: personal, social, political, religious. Human challenges God by building a tower to heaven→ hubris. Gradually, there is a weakening, a yielding, a wish that this life would be, could be something other; a wish for a Messiah, a saving from life's troubles. Gradually sickness turns into death, and death overtakes life. The New Testament offers a solution to death, to the problem of death. Life goes its own way, or is some illusion. The boundary between life and death is blurred, and it is difficult to know which is which, or whether they are different. Life is no longer its own justification. Hasn't death been chosen?

On Being Spiritual: Perhaps it's the only way that works to get me through this life; perhaps it is that I am so curious, so full of wonderment that I strive to know what is known and what is knowable and why.

I strive to know what "invention" is, what "natural" is—and what these notions might mean. I know that the ordinary pictures of God, of death are our creations, derived from how—in various times—we have imagined them, or derived the possibility of the human imagination to be one thing or another (Parmenides); what caused fear?—what questions arose?—what appeared to be solutions?—local?—global?—and what did not?

Yet I/we go on. Managing the fears beyond toleration, yielding to the temptations which edge toward trouble in order to keep the passions of living alive and necessary, willing and experiencing in doing, teaching, knowing, studying, I think it is all somehow improbable, and want to contribute to its likelihood of actuality. I find joy in new skills, in making the mundane experientially fulfilling, in arguing against the resignations of life's maturity and carrying it off with some success.

I want to explore life in all its dimensions; to see what is, to wonder why, to know what is known and knowable, and to know why the impossible is said to be; to change how we think about that. Guardians of life? Not a mission, but in the living.

The Confucian Tradition: Its "power" in living is to hold out the idea that each of us can become as "Great" as is possible—but within life.

We can become God-like or like a god to the extent that we keep in mind and in our lives, the path (*the Way*) toward that fulfilled personage, the venerable one. The path toward the utopic and ideal can become us, we can become it—within life; within my life, your life. Not having to live "right" to get rewards after death, life is, in a deep sense, its own possible reward. Whatever is available within human being and destiny is obtainable within life. In this tradition, one needs living Teachers—exemplars, those who demonstrate and hold us to *the Way*, defining and refining the proper path as we move on, and on: but the path remains before us no matter how long we may live, and its direction is progressive somehow or other.

(It depends, also, on feeling that we are not already condemned by being alive, as the Christian tradition of "The Fall").

The question: is perfectibility available within (this) life? Confucius' solution: yes! (Tu-Wei-Ming, 1985)

In contrast to Nietzsche's criticism of Christianity, concerning humility and the weak, this demands that we always become, and become more, stronger, transcendent - in Western terms. To be Christian, to raise to the highest virtue, the weakest aspects of our being, to grant to pity of others a great deal of piety and respect, is to be anti-Human. Confucianism offers an almost oppositional path, at least to those who can remain on the path, and those who are permitted to be on the path. The utopic within life seems to require teachers who themselves are motivated to explore and to pass on knowing about becoming (Sarles, 2013).

Toward a Philosophical Anthropology: Anthropology is too important to remain only in the academy. Part of what I imagine is that (*Human Organization*—Society for Applied Anthropology) become a vehicle for the development of an anthropology of the world, the nation... the individual... the *ordinary*.

Anthropology must raise and address problems of global scope; raising problems, suggesting arenas of thought about them, and solutions or loci of solution which are anthropological. To say what is anthropological it must be "positively critical": to say both what is and not anthropology, and why. I expect it, occasionally, to be polemical; e.g., to question different disciplines as they take assumptive motivational theories to the world (e.g. "greed" in economics).

It is my hope that *Human Organization* promotes an *anthropology of the ordinary*—to examine ourselves first to promote other peoples to do similar anthropologies and not only or merely an anthropology of "the exotic" (— the *First World* looking out and judging others imperialistically).

Anthropology must be dedicated to giving voice to all the people on earth; a place not merely to describe how we see them, but for all the people to say what is the nature of their experience, their reality, and how they see one another.

But my attempts to deal with (other) anthropologists have been *terrible*. My colleagues (written during an era when I was a Professor of Anthropology at the U. of Minnesota – I "left" the Anthropology Dep't and joined Cultural Studies and Comparative Literature) are, to say the least, uninterested in what I do, or in what anyone who doesn't do what they do, or think what they think. The field has become *involuted*; internal to its own interests: fieldwork has been replaced by turf-protection, all in the name of science. (Possibly/hopefully it is "changing" during this era of completing this study – 2014).

Anthropology has, in my experience, become a discipline in which a singular point-of-view has risen to the "top," an aristocracy of sorts. And the others who derive from some earlier Boasian fantasy are *lesser*. Physical anthropology has become some methodological extension of human biology—leaving anthropology behind—perpetuated in schools of medicine or dentistry. Linguistic anthropology is just beginning to recover from the structuralist assault of Chomsky—and social anthropology has bought a good deal of that *a priori* view that an understanding of social structures provides some direct insight into those rules of linguistic structure. The fieldwork, empirical tradition is lost—the social anthropologists look at the exotic world, the more "different" the better—through fixed filters. They seem not to be open to many surprises, not to any criticism, or even to discussion, except on their own terms.

How can anthropology deal with problems of global understanding? Is miscommunication the result when it will not, or cannot deal with its own internal differences and dissensions? The aristocratic, at least, closed views of the social anthropologists appears to stop discussion, and be very like the racism one finds in the wider society.

Being the "linguist" in an anthropology department was very much like being the "nigger": the marginal other, doing the labor, preparing the ground, teaching students the skills or tools required for "real" anthropologists. Nobody I worked with wanted to talk about anthropology, about human nature. They do what they do, within issues that were cast in other contexts, in other times.

Anthropologists, furthermore, are "loners"—intellectual isolates. They do not want to work with others, or even to discuss their work. And they do not want to promote coalitions or interest groups. If we do not get along—well, that's how it is—and there is apparently nothing to be done about it.

(After 10 years, I left the bureaucratized field of anthropology to attempt to do a more genuine anthropology of the ordinary, accompanied by a increasing critique of anthropology as a form of formalistic writing.) (Written after several years of retirement I feel a connection developing!)

Übermensch: Within life, one is always changing, moving on to one's "Next Places" even as one remains consistent and oneself. The problems of moving on in life, of transcendence and beyondness at any moment are various. Nietzsche wants us to overcome ourselves (to literalize the concept of the "overman"), and to move beyond the self of any day: life as a set of problems in becoming; life as ontology.

The existential and experiential difficulties are various: developing a map of what and who one is, and where there is (for me) to go, and how to do this without damaging or destroying me as I am and have been (and the others who are in some important relationships with the character I am and have been). In a "scripted" time, this may be clear; or if one lives in a tradition which has teachers and the concept of wisdom which may offer conceptual critique and the pointed possibilities of direction and pathways: how to become "more" without becoming "less"?

If there is an ideal which is trustable and potentially obtainable, then one can attempt to define this, to grasp and grab it.

The problem of "the Present Age" (Kierkegaard, 1846) is that thinking has become cast within structured/bureaucratic outlooks which tend to look narrowly at history for possibility, and find little to do, less which portends futurity. Then one might seek "models"—for Kierkegaard, to live as a Christ lived. Otherwise one frequently constructs some sense of utopia beyond life (e.g., Christianity, Islam), and lives life only toward a "return" to utopia, compared with which this life is always a diminution. How to live life fully and in preparation each day as if I may life the longest life: life as vocation rather than technique; life in the living rather than life as a preparation?

Wisdom: Is it the *concept* of wisdom which disappeared from our ken some time ago? Maybe it was the notion of information which downgraded the possibility of wisdom. Perhaps it was that history and the texts and the authority of the past so overtook our being that we no longer pretend to some greatness, some arrogance, some ambition beyond ourselves. Maybe we have diminished possibility and futurity.

Now very rapidly approaching the age where I would be wise if the concept were available, do I now study, think, emulate? Who? What? If I live the longest life, will my vocation yet serve living? Will I find work... and work?

Does it help to review where I am, and how I got here, and think that I didn't cave in, didn't sell out, am not so much in debt to anyone or any institution or foundation or -ism; that I strive still for coherence and clarity and don't look much beyond experience to inform my being? Yes! Love today sufficiently, forgive one's incompleteneses, and seek the next day's dawning. Not utopia, not yet, not caring whether or not; but moving on each day...

The Transcendental Temptation: Even after five centuries of a humanism which attempted to raise the importance of the human and diminish the effective "size" of the deity in our comprehension of self and of being, even after five centuries the temptation to invoke religion strikes still the heart. Woe are we who thought so suredly, so delightedly, so self-congratulatedly that we would eventually become less needy of the deity, more "rational." Science and atheism would overwean religiosity. The idea of a god would surely die, as Nietzsche promised had already happened.

But it isn't merely a deity for whom we search. It is our own being and a becoming which moves past wherever we find ourselves in each and any moment. It is the transcendental temptation. It is a response to the sort of truth-telling metaphysics which is our Western heritage which has revealed its own circularities and threatens nihilism. We cannot not mean and retain any equilibrium.

It is not the loss of any sense of progress which has, by now, even infected the technologies spawned by the scientific rationalism which had emptied the universe of the necessity of the deity. It is in the aftermath of growing up, each of us, toward the pleasures and mysteries of adulthood which have, instead, concentrated often upon the attendant responsibilities which do not move on. It is a sense of movement, of towardness, of directedness toward becoming which urges and tempts us to the transcendental. It is not outside the human condition, but often invokes a response within us which we may call fear, or god, or God, or wishing-would-make-it-so. It is easier, more historically available to name some utopic moment than to live it day-by-day with the realization that the transcendental moves with us... within us.

6.

THE ORIGIN OF MEANING
(An Inversion of...)

"The Mind Speaks to itself in Parables." (Joubert, 1838)

"Our ordinary inaccurate observation takes a group of phenomena as one and calls them a fact. Between this fact and another we imagine a vacuum, we isolate each fact. In reality, however, the sum of our actions and cognition is no series of facts and intervening vacua, but a continuous stream. Now the belief in free will is incompatible with the idea of a continuous, uniform, undivided, indivisible flow. The belief presupposes that every single action is isolated and indivisible; it is an atomic theory as regards volition and cognition. –We misunderstand facts as we misunderstand characters, speaking of similar characters and similar facts, whereas both are non-existent. Further, we bestow praise and blame only on this false hypothesis, that there are similar facts, that facts exist, corresponding to a graduated order of values. Thus we isolate not only the simple fact, but the groups of apparently equal facts (good, evil, compassion, envious actions, and so forth). In both cases we are wrong.—The word and the concept are the most obvious reason for our belief in this isolation of groups of actions. We do not merely thereby designate the things; the thought at the back of our minds is that by the word and the concept we can group the essence of the action. We are still constantly led astray by words and actions, and are induced to think of things as simpler than they are, as separate, indivisible, existing in the absolute. Language contains a hidden philosophical mythology, which however careful we may be, breaks out afresh at every moment. The belief in free will—that is to say, in similar facts and isolated facts—finds in language its continual apostle and advocate." (Nietzsche, "Wanderer and His Shadow" 1880)

Origin of Human(s): If meaning is regarded as uniquely human, then any discussion about some putative *origin* of meaning is related directly to a discussion about the origin of human(s).

Troubles and difficulties abound because the grounds for deciding what is humanly unique and what is universal are debatable/contested. Our directions toward solution depend greatly on our views about what is non-human (animals, intelligent machines, etc.) and why!

A. Meaning: Humans only → A discussion of Human Nature
    1. What is human?
    2. What is not (non-) human?
        i) Terrestrial: other species (animal/vegetable)
        ii) Extraterrestrial: the *intelligent* non-human
        iii) Artificial: robots and AI
        iv) Spiritual: angels, ghosts, and gods.

B. Meaning: Not uniquely human
    1. How would we deal with this?
    2. Is comparison possible?

History of Meaning (and the Meaning of History): The question of who we humans are includes the questions of how we got here, from whence derived (or *created*). Did we evolve/change from something *other* (e.g., a smart ape)? When did meaning, how we think, understand the world and ourselves arise? Only with humans, as thinkers since Aristotle held and still hold? Or do we share a meaningful universe with (some?) other creatures, as comparatist (open) thinkers wonder: the *ethological critique of language philosophy*?

The observation spurring much of this rethinking is that other similar creatures to humans in some aspects of their anatomy/body or physiology, are also social: an aspect of humans held to be unique until the development of field observations of feral/wild animals in their natural habitats.

If, as some (fundamentalist) religious thinkers hold, we were created *de novo*, and given meaning by the creator/deity, what architectonic or theories did the creator have (in mind) for us?—a reopening or restoration of religious thought/theology?

If, as many others (rationalists, humanists, scientists) hold, we evolved from something other, some creature not yet human, how did this occur: some sequence of development (with/without purpose or *telos*); some relationship to our bodily forms (our unique faces, opposable thumbs, erect posture, brain anatomy, physiology.)? If we evolved, does any of this sequence of development toward being/becoming human have continuing resonance within our own human/personal development (from *Nature to*

Culture, as many still hold)? Is there a beast within, some primitive, savage, mythical creature hovering and beating within our (self-) conscious, rational selves: a species memory?

These issues raise, in some complicated sequences of self-analysis and discovery, the questions of identity and being: whence I/we derive? Where are we going? How do we know?

Change and Permanence of Self: Apparently we need the change-permanence dialectic for considering the origin of meaning.

The *inversion*: continuity from the outside: derived/emergent from others. Change, flux: internal. The individual, a combination of who others say one is (I am), plus an intrinsic (independent?) self.

The *important, continuous self*: an image of who other(s) see one to be; the intrinsic self in flux (an inversion?).

Meaning: sensibility. The notion (only) gains sense in a social, interactional world.

Knowing the world takes place through knowing others. Especially (for infants), knowing is through a study of mothers/others; faces (talk —as an aspect of the face, facial interaction). The mechanical-material-physical *individual* does not know the world *directly*, but as others (significant adults/parents) already consider the world to be.

The *individual*: at first, a construction, a *"who,"* a person whom others consider one to be: one's being, face, destiny as seen and interpreted by parents, family; a person who is *demanded* by others to be a proposer, a talker—an "I."

As I view the *origin of meaning*, we are not merely, only, or ever principally individuals; not merely seeking to articulate our private meanings. We are, in some (large) part, actual embodiments of others' views of us. Questions of knowing, of others, of self, of the world alter in this theory, as we are not (purely, merely) sensors or perceivers. We are creatures who deal in the world via a construct of ourselves mediated by others, which we embody to a large degree (literally!).

Our continuity, our senses of time and of memory, are a construct of "self" derived from others' construction of what and who we are. In this context the (so-called) individual relates to, is an aspect of others.

Description of the world: What is the world? What is *in* the world? How do I know? How do I tell others? How do they tell me? How is it that we understand one another and the world? (Which is the appropriate order of analysis toward understanding: society? Society → world? World → society?)

In the world conceptualized as peopled by *individuals*, each a unique, separate entity, this is a difficult problem to solve (deriving from the Aristotelian primary/originary notion of physics having precedence over *me ta* physics).

Often it seems impossible because those aspects of self which are unique and separate loom large (especially in eras of diminished meaning and crises in identity: i.e., the Present Age). Questions and theories of interaction and meaning reside often in a notion of predetermined universality, where each (*normal*) individual is claimed to be like all others, in some senses *a priori*.

Debate occurs around what is deemed to be *universal*; to be (as it were) *necessary* to account for what we seem to know, and how. The *ultimate* explanations, in this context, have pushed us towards neurology to seek what is (in) the brain, what it is which is the *same*, what is human, *rational-able*, *symbolic*, etc.

Our universality appears as a derivative of small-scale interactions; i.e., we are who we are, as others who are already like others, see and imagine us. People see others within the limits or contexts in which they have developed. It is in this sense that meaning is shared, in which mutual understanding is both possible and, to some extent, assured.

Description, then, must appeal to this notion of universality.

(This still leaves a great deal of room for an emergent individual.)

Universals: The idea (myth) that all (normal) human beings are alike in some deeply essential manner (the *transcendental pretense*: R. Solomon 1979)

My story: we are all sufficiently alike to be able to experience and to think similarly enough for most purposes; description must be experiential, entailing self-study and toward an anthropology of the ordinary.

Rejecting the use of mathematics/logic or of pseudo-math as a universal language representing some deeply essential, universal for humans (a partial truth).

Suggesting, requiring for description: the discovery, the laying-out of contexts, some common grounds, some maps or ways-through the grounds such that we (all) work at constructing them.

Life and the Origin of Meaning: Can we say that life *is* meaning in any non-trivial sense? Life is a building, a constructing from non-life, within a *plan*, or with respect to processes which work out such that they form objects which seem to have had some sense of plan, some moment within or through time and change (development, embryology... originary, architectonic).

Debate about whether change and life is somehow *within* time, or whether life creates time somehow. Any meaning to history without life? The world as independent in any important or interesting senses? The reality which is human, the only one we know; the world as depicted, experienced, understood by humans: that's all we have, so far. (Human is the measure of all things!)

We only possess an anthropology, even of Nature. Any biology is from human perspective. What does it mean to begin? This question rests upon our depiction and representation of Nature. Accurate? Truthful? Doesn't Nature change? Don't our descriptions of the world change? Doesn't experience change? Isn't Human also Nature?

The Social Birth of Reason: Originates from the demand (presumption, forward projection) by parents that the child begins to act as if it has a will; can construct ideas from the words for objects and motion which the child has gleaned from its personal world of interaction.

The concept of reason depends, too, on the notion that the child stands outside of him-herself, can construct the "I" appropriately, and begins to *state* its own existence (to others, to oneself), to speak *willfully*. This is the effective and actual-social birth of reason.

The necessity for the child to become propositional (in the terms of philosophers, logicians, will-seekers) is that one becomes trustable to take care of "self" and to become (eventually) a *proper* adult (a lens through which m/others see their children).

(The blurred boundaries between metaphysics and politics is located precisely here: where propositional meets independence and freedom in the power of exploring one's being and identity.)

Meaning and the Social World: Meaning exists already in the social world into which we are born; eggs to the universe of chickens (Mead, 1934). No origin of meaning! Does life itself equate with meaning? (Who, then, am I?)

Questions of the relation between inside (some notion of oneness, of individual, coherence, boundaries) and outside: others, the world.

Do we know the world directly/indirectly via (each) individual's sensorium? Or do we know the world via knowing how others already designate the world? The latter via the Question-Response Grammar.

(Consider the experience of so-called retarded persons who do not/cannot read others because they're so bodily different.)

Embryology: The *organization* of cells (proteins, fats, etc.) into some things—new organizations—blastopheres, etc. Memory of development? Each *new* organization, structure, a new sense of being, of emergent meaning. By being; by being located in new contexts, brings multiple meanings. (Some hierarchical notion of the self-analytic?)

If meaning is located, say, primarily or originally in each individual, how can it bootstrap itself? It is questionable whether this is likely or even possible.

Development is gradual, emergent. When/how do cells become an "I"?

In order to further explore the nature of meaning, we must study development. We need to realize how the question of the origin of meaning in the species (life?) and the question of the origin of meaning in our ontogenesis conflate, divide. That is, the question of how I got here has two (at least) radically different senses. (Is this a kind of paradox?—Like form and content?)

The Universe of Meaning: Into which we develop is only one among many (or several among thousands). In order to mean, to be and have sensibility, one must share the same/almost the same outlook, the same meaning sphere with others; or one which is translatable by someone who has the will, the talent, the patience, to act as interlocutor. Without possessing, coming to possess the same universe of meaning as others, we do not exist as meaningful creatures. In this sense the origin of meaning has to do with the willingness and ability of others to translate what we do into the (*reasonable*) process of becoming sufficiently *like them*—Interaction and sensible communication.

We are born-into a futurity which others (parents) have projected, imagined us to fit. The *universe of meaning* occurs as individuals fit into the mappings of this projected futurity. Persons are largely determined by how (significant) m/others read/project personage and character *into* us: see us, interpret our being, understand, love... grant us futurity; the idea of the future and our being within it.

Language as an Organizing Mode: Operationally, much of what we call language is a model of the world. It organizes itself (via languaging) into aspects, descriptions both of itself and of some externality. It is intrinsically finite and internally infinite. (Thus is also the world in our thinking.)

The notion of language as finite only appears clear if we begin from some rhetorical assumption: that language is for communicating, understanding, connecting between persons. (A grammar which begins from the notion of individual, seems to push a notion of language in which infinite and creative aspects appear primary: the idea that it is the imagination, our symbolic propensities, which most defines the human—Parmenides!)

The problem of knowledge: how the finite (body) can operate as if it were (at once) infinite or indefinite? How is it that we imagine the future here and now beyond the present here and now? Answer: Q-R!

Hegel and *Immediate Consciousness*:

"In my Phenomenology of Spirit, which on that account was at its publication described as the first part of the `System of Philosophy', the method adopted was to begin with the first and simplest phase of mind, immediate consciousness, and to show how that stage gradually of necessity worked onward to the philosophical point of view, the necessity of that view being proved by the process. But in these circumstances it was impossible to restrict the quest to the mere form of consciousness. For the stage of philosophical knowledge is the richest in material and organization, and therefore, as it came before us in the shape of a result, it presupposed the existence of the concrete formations of consciousness, such as individuals and social morality, art and religion." (Hegel, 1807: 58)

Hegel began with a likely error: assuming "the first and simplest phase of mind, immediate consciousness" was the beginning.

What is "immediate consciousness"? Should I empty the contents of my mind? Immediately? (An intellectual bulemia?)

When is the immediate? Doesn't *the immediate* vary with mood, with context? (What do I do/know that I don't count as *immediate*? Perorations of a violinist trying to deal with seemingly 20+ ways of considering any particular note.)

Isn't this another attempt to build a simplex-complex notion of (human) thought, needing to define the contents or to describe what is simple, thence the process by which simple becomes complex? But where do we derive the notion of what is simple?—Does simple equal few, early, primitive? Does simplex-complex entail a theory of history? (What is *in my mind* when I fiddle? How does it come to be there? What is suppressed, absent, gone? Of what am I aware, but not aware that I am aware?—rules of linguistic articulation, to begin.)

In this context, the quest for knowledge points to an examination or elaboration of what we mean by/is meant by *consciousness*. An antidote to this is *phonemic theory* which shows that some aspects of the *unconscious* are rule and pattern related or generated; that these unconscious or *out-of-awareness* patterns are powerful in our being, at least with respect to language. For example, we take a particular *phonemic-cognitive map* into a new language and thus speak it with a particular, discernable accent; we hear it, speak it through the phonemic filter of our native languages. What else, what other of our being and knowing is out-of-awareness?—that of which is knowledge which is not consciousness/not in consciousness? The process of language articulation/speaking is highly balletic, yet we do not usually include its knowing/doing in immediate consciousness. How much of our being is out-of-awareness? (Stanley Keleman, 1987)

Each Era = a New Meaning: Isn't the experience of life such that meaning, i.e. the grounds on which we construct meaning, differs, varies in place, in time, in different societies, different histories, different concepts of history? Isn't this what the history of ideas tells us?

The ongoing dialectic, the way in which ideas or meanings progress, is not the mere correct or logical resolution of conflicts, a discourse on what follows what; but what sells in any era, in the marketplace of ideas. And what sells has its own, often independent rules and criteria; e.g., driven by economic woes, positive and progressive outlooks, its understanding of its history...: the *Zeitgeist*.

Thus the origin of meaning—as an idea—itself must alter in time and context, even if it may appear to remain the same! (But why would it appear to remain the same? And why in asking this question about the origin of meaning, we seem to impute to history some power over our understanding of the ongoing present?) (Berlin, 1990)

Development is Progressive: The idea of development, of growing up from infancy (conception?) to adulthood, is a *progressive* notion (its study invented by Aristotle. Development is not merely preparation for a static (and senescent) adulthood, but a kind of guide or map toward futurity. It is a theory of time and history, which presumably informs. (And why we are enmeshed in the transcendental temptation...always.)

Parents (and society) assume progress toward adulthood (defined as being in many essential senses *pretty much like them*). So progress is no mere philosophical outlook; it is an aspect of life; toward the past, perhaps, as adults consider their own growing up (*generation backward*). But it is an aspect of our own being which is within our experience and may intrude upon us in all sorts of ways.

(Is the metaphysical attempt to *halt* time also an existential attempt to keep one's youth from intruding upon the present; trying to keep forgotten what has been? Plato at play in our lives? What do we do when experienced/felt change exceeds some limit?)

Meaninglessness: If being is meaning, meaningful, then the notion of meaninglessness is, like the notion of zero, a dislocation from what there is to the concept of being-not, or not-being (Parmenides *Frag. VIII*).

Or it is a concept *from* death? Unless there is a G/god, some supernatural aspect to being, there is no meaning, and we are enmeshed in some sort of nihilism (Nietzsche: Introduction, *Will to Power*). There is, it can be claimed, no meaning which is inherent: the problem of life, of society is to create meaning. But is it enough, is it genuine, authentic, or real? The existential difficulty with this is that if life is not sufficiently self-sustaining, one tends toward desperation, toward fear, and despair, and will grasp at a (any) solution which convinces, which keeps the fear *managed*. For the person-in-process, this is likely to be day-by-day; who knows how tomorrow will be, and will feel?—Tomorrow? Future? ...fades.

A Tabula Rasa: An argument concocted by Locke to beat down hereditary monarchy (*Two Treatises of Government*, 1690). If true, the origin of meaning problem is solved by positing some mechanism(s) - e.g., S->R associationism to account for how to fill-in an empty vessel. For reasons I don't yet understand, a most parsimonious approach is often considered best/convincing; and the same mechanism is taken to explain all of learning and development. (Psychology emulating mathematics emulating proof?) It seems clear that operation modes change significantly at various points in development, and that events which were one thing earlier, are of different kinds/arrangements later on. The process is directional, if not exactly progressive!

The opposing argument (Chomsky: *Review of Skinner*, 1967) notes that children of four or five years can understand and construct (*create*) sentences they have never heard before. That is, the tabula rasa theory presumes that living (social?) experience is everything; that unless the organism experiences new stimuli, associates objects with meaning with words, it does not/cannot develop knowledge (= meaning?).

The creative theory, in its zeal, seems to want to oppose the notion of experience within S-R theory, and posits some innate or in-built ability to each individual, by which it develops language: i.e., the origin of meaning took place only once, exactly/precisely at the moment of origin of the first human. (A corollary argument has to do with the *status* of humans vis-a-vis other species: all other species learn by S-R, only humans are creative.)

In creative theory only one sort of ability is posited to account for the entire human condition. Both of these theories seem to imply a rather simple notion of language. (Language = the set of all sentences (Creative) of the entire lexicon (S-R): i.e., these two theories argue past one another, and are not directly opposed and as contradictory as they often seem to be!)

The interactionist-emergence position claims that new infants are already (innately?) interactional: they exist in relation to m/others. They are students of the faces of the m/others who read/project personage *into* them: the m/other of all constructivists? S/he: the ultimate philosopher?!

The notion of meaning, I suppose—to whatever extent it is to come into the meaning construction by other (rational) humans—is to take the interactional relations, and to alter, extend, fill-in, using the abilities and propensities already in the interaction. (A corollary argument has to do with what is reality, and whether it is intrinsically individual or intrinsically social, or intrinsically some interactional mix. If, e.g., reality is intrinsic to each normal individual, then development is a story about a maturing individual, essentially irrespective of others' input, or others' construction of reality. Both the S-R and creative language theories seem to strongly believe in a logical reality which is intrinsically and universally human, whose locus is (in) each individual *subject*.

In this sense, there is no precise *origin* of meaning; our existence is already meaningful is several ways different for the infant and the m/other (who represents a socio-cultural view). The very notion of origin implies the picture of rational reality which also implies or presumes that only humans have language, rationality, reality (i.e., there is no *origin of language problem*, either!)

Thus, the origin of meaning is transformed, for me, into the development of meaning—*as the adult world considers meaning to be*. Successful adults (of whatever species?) agree and define reality. And it is this adult-centric definition of being which is the one which is meaningful, and which each infant must accept if it is to endure/survive as an also successful person. (There may be two, or ten, or thousands of other meaningful human realities, but this is essentially irrelevant in human—or other species'—development! It is the parental view which wins.)

Meaning and Existence: I exist! Whenever the notion of existence arises as seriously dubitable; whenever we are pulled into debate as to whether we exist, whether there is existence, whether you or I are here, or have ever been, then there is trouble! Serious trouble (Buber 1937)! (Witness Wittgenstein's 1953 lament or plea: grant me the right hand and then... If he can't...

The question of the *origin* of meaning can be related to problems of existence, rather to the problematics of existence, because it is meaning—in various senses—which is often offered as some kind of proof of existence. *I think... therefore I am.* What is thinking? What about? Why is it convincing? Proof?—for whom; when?

Or—*God says that I am?* Who am I to say that my notion of God says that I am? Was not God deceitful? Perhaps testing us? Perhaps I am not, perhaps this life/existence is no more than an illusion, some story I tell myself that I am! "If," the thinking goes, "God says that I am, then I am!" But, doesn't the notion of God require my prior existence and knowledge of the notion of God?... A paradox; a logical circle?

What if I say or think that I am, but really I am not? —But, then, who is doing this writing? Or this reading? Whom do I write for?—me, you, me-as-you or vice-versa? Don't I need you, as least my notion of you to confirm that I am? You—the real you, just like the real me, exists.

But why does doubt ever arise that I am; that I am and that there is meaning? Fright, guilt, fear of life, fear of death. But what is fear?—a bodily state, a loss of meaning, a sickness unto death? What sustains life?—meaning, a control of fear, a balance between life and death? Some harmony of being? (Purpose, progress...?)

Is life/existence *what it is*? Is it a set of paradoxes? Isn't it (precisely) these paradoxes which yield meaning, at least increase the power of the notion of meaning, because they raise questions: I am, vs. I am not; I am good, I am afraid that I am not good.

Doesn't Western thought raise (what I think are) paradoxes as opposites *to be resolved* (since Heraclitus) one way or the other? Legal, adversarial ways of thinking about life? Life as conflictions of opposites. Why did we go for oppositional thought? Because Heraclitus stated the problem of permanence vs. change, as one of stability vs. chaos. And, in lieu of chaos, he chose *logos*; the logic of our being as the true us, and the problem of meaning came down to specifying what is logic: truth vs. falsity—as if these hold for all of us in all times and places. Laws of Nature constructed as if Nature is primary, and we are some sort of after (meta-) thought. I am not anti-logic, or anti-rational, but I am for broadening the concept of logic to include the sorts of truths, of meaning, which sustain life, both physically and physically-conceptually.

Nihilism: The destruction of meaning! Nietzsche says, in the first part of "Will to Power" (*Rise of European Nihilism*) that the next historical periods will suffer heavily from nihilism—his interpretation of his declaration/diagnosis that Europeans believe that *God is Dead*.

Not having God is for such nihilists the loss of meaning; at its outermost, the loss of reason-for-being. To whomever each day is an engagement, a search for meaning, then each day is a kind of failure. And failure—in whatever terms—constitutes its own set of meanings; and needs to be dealt with lest it become a self-blaming and in turn generates a scapegoating, of whomever and whatever appears culpable and/or responsible—beyond what the self-blamed can handle; i.e., the number and degrees of failure.

The turn we see to fundamentalism—Christianity, Islam, Judaism—is based on the need to have a most tangible God who provides meaning; a God who tells us that we are, why we are, where we are, how we got here, where we are going, etc. This (concept of) God provides sustaining and persuasive meaning, interprets pain, and holds out *extraordinary* incentives.

Its new form, Scientific Creationism, is most interesting. Not only does it co-opt today's major metaphor for real-true knowledge, but it believes that it has (I think) proven, scientifically, really-truly, that God exists. At least, it does (it says) no worse than Scientific Evolutionism, and its truth is similar, and of the same order of magnitude. "If they are right, I am right." the thinking goes. (And if science underlies rationality, it underlies meaning.)

And if they are wrong?

These two visions of life clash in the present: Life-as-having-survived (evolutionarily) vs. Life-as-preparation-for-the-Hereafter (or the Ever-after).

Note: Life-as-having-survived means that (for evolutionary biologists) it is how we got here; the fact that we are here shows that we (our antecedents) survived—an important fact. The "experiential present" is not an obvious counter or fact within this theory. That is, evolutionary biologists are sorts of "historical" thinkers, and have a "weak" theory of the present (so called "ultimate" vs. "proximate" biology).

Language and Infinity: The question which has seemed of greatest import since Pythagoras, has been: how can a finite creature (a human) have imagination?—act as if it is limitless?

It has been the notion of the limitless which has then dominated the discussion of meaning, the nature of Human Nature, and so on. We are infinite "because" we have minds. The aspect of us which was declared the opposite of what is finite (the mind vs. the body) contained the (ability to be) limitless. If time is limited, then the "absolute" is limitless. Thence metaphysics and religions derived from this question and from the sorts of responses which seemed sensible ("solid") in any era.

Language, in this sense, became a force for what is infinite about humans, and it is the attributes of language which seemed without limit (e.g., the grammar: the set of all possible sentences) and without number—likened to the set of all possible integers. (The fact that it seemed to offer a solution to the problem of death, or appeared to, was not unattractive, especially in declining times or other times of fear.)

This orientation explains why and how the finite aspects of our lives have been pursued: why the experiential first "let in" the experimental: objectivity, from the limitless world of objects, to the existential agreements among humans, about what we can observe/sense, how to pose questions of Nature, as if "it" is separable from us, from being; as if Nature is continuous always.

On Losing the Concept of Language: Though trained principally as an anthropological linguist, at some early point in my career I lost the concept of language per se, language-as-such in any well-bounded sense.

Language became, for me, a metaphor about what we consider to be Human Nature. It was a new illumination (for me) to discover that most of Western thought had developed as an analysis of language, considered per se. I began to understand that language was a formal definition of some aspects of verbal behavior which could be reduced to, or reproduced in writing; that the notion of an idea, of something actualizable, which could stand some test of truthfulness of a corresponding logic which grew implicitly upon the oblique and obverse side of language, could come to represent as well, what we used to explain ourselves, as well as what it was that we attempted to explain.

The origin of meaning and the origin of language have been postulated as the same origin; as if language were sufficiently characteristic of human beingness, behavior and nature that its examination would tell us both who we are and what nature is.

The Concept of Meaning: It seems to me that the notion of meaning, in any sense separable from experience, may well have had an origin. While I doubt that language or meaning had origins in any historical sense, the concept of meaning, of abstraction, may have arisen with increasing population, with agriculture-leisure, and with writing.

The concept of meaning may well have developed with the *problems of scale*, when people began to deal with one another as "types"—i.e., when there were too many so that one could not deal, in depth, with each person, and began to think of others in terms of categories. At this point, when persons become like (other) objects, meaning is discovered as a concept. Perhaps it is this sense of origin which should be studied and discussed, rather than the origin of language in the sense of "progressive" evolution in a direct, linear- historical sense.

(This seems also to apply to ontogenesis!)

The notion of—concept, an idea, separable from all else certainly becomes obvious with writing and history (themselves closely linked.) It is probably related to numbers of persons: when one cannot "know" all others, there develops a "they," a gathering notion which implies also a "we"—a basis for the notion of a concept, in which the "abstract" takes on some aspects of entity, of nouns, of reality. Once the notion of concept is "real," it soon appears obvious that the concept, not being continually tangible or demonstrable, can alter or be altered to fit (new) experience, reshaped by having a purpose, by getting new purposes, etc.) Peter Wilson, in his *Domestication of the Human Species* (1989), suggests that this begins to occur with living in fixed settlements when we begin to think "geometrically," and have "in" and "out" places, thence persons.

Also, in Western thinking, the move to make mathematics general and physics (objects) primary creates the notion that humans are objects, and are themselves (ourselves) composed of things, to be treated as objects, objectified, counted, and no more (nor less) "real" than other objects: ultimately composed of numbers, enumerable.

Meaning and Solitude: Buber (1937) claims that the notion of solitude, of the deep realization that we are alone in the universe, is what produces or drives an interest in the question of what is human, e.g. in a philosophical anthropology.

The realization that meaning/existence is a deeply-felt issue thus seeks an answer which solves or resolves that question. The posing of such a notion as the "origin of meaning" implies ever more deeply, that the question is, itself, meaningful. Somehow the quest is to put some bounds on the issue by seeking for some sense of creation, of origin, either of a causality, or of a sense even of the locus of the question. Where, indeed, does meaning, the inquiry into meaning, reside? In whatever we deem human in Nature, in our minds, souls, etc.

If the quest is to solve our worries about solitude, then having a locus, a potential answer to the question about the "origin of meaning," would presumably "handle" solitude, and permit us to refocus elsewhere.

Buber's solution is that we (two: I and Thou), together certify God—who, in turn, certifies us. This, I guess, "works" for some who feel this question deeply—the issue being who I am, who Thou art, and how do we connect (our souls, our beings, our characters) in some genuine fashion?(—and what is authentic or genuine?).

The Concept of Consciousness: Our stories and metaphors about what consciousness is, and how it developed throughout history, strongly inform how we go about thinking about meaning: the meaning of meaning and, for the real philosopher, the meaning of life.

It is as if being aware of being aware is a really big deal; having happened only once in the nature of the universe. It smacks of arrogance and hubris much as of any attempt to understand, because we do not know about other creatures, dead or alive, with us today upon this earth. It is as if we are so enamored of our importance that we have to proclaim our self-love over and over, rather than wondering how it may be, or what we have not yet thought about or have hidden to ourselves in our attempts to prove it.

Surreptitious Theories of Meaning: Most theories of meaning seem to rest on assumptions, presumptions, beliefs, which are themselves akin to actually hidden theories of meaning. Metaphysics presumes that the objective world precedes our being and has a particular form. When we analyze meaning, we "translate"; we do not create anything new. When we talk about ideas or grammaticality or "truth," we talk about the recognition of some process or entity which we have, or seek a method of classifying or of defining (e.g., resolve ambiguities). Rarely do we bother to look under to see our own habits of abstraction. Rather we are happy if we agree that something is or isn't notable, or even imaginable. (Parmenides ruling out non-Being as being "unimaginable," thus non-existing, leading to the invention of the idea of creation and eventually of some Creator! This notion of the "unimaginable" is already a theory of meaning.)

Instead, I think that theories of meaning come back to the human condition: what we are (physically-conceptually), how we persist and sustain. Most of our theories of meaning rely on some beliefs and partial observations about what we are not and what we are (and what theories of meaning are). These seem, somehow, to reflect or lay claim to what is residual, or what we have, surreptitiously, already decided on hidden grounds, to *be* meaning.

Aphasia: Informing from how we think about persons whose languaging abilities are abnormal, imperfect, missing, etc. (Jacobson, 1930), I conclude that we associate linguistic-speaking abilities with whatever is meaningful. Usually this is depicted as being fully human, rational, and normal. Within this thinking, there is something deceptive or wrong with the less-than-normal. And what they are like (I infer) is toward the universe of other species who (we assume) do not possess language; i.e., we assume, do not possess meaning. Thus aphasic (and whatever else we deem, in our wisdom, to be less than normal; i.e. children) is like the inabilities of other species, and whatever we attribute to them, rather than being different or unusual humans, which is what they are.

We assume (though this trend is diminishing) that lack of speech is equivalent to lack of meaning and understanding. This battle has been forged well (Stokoe, 1960) for deaf persons, and has been shown for some of those who are aphasic and deemed "retarded" to be a lack of musculature or of coordination; i.e., if they are taught sign language, they can indeed demonstrate ideation, mentation, and communication. Thus, they do not lack meaning but the means of expressing it in some ways *we* can understand and believe. Thus the trouble is somehow in their different physicality or their physical means of expression, and how we observe and classify; e.g., our habits of inferring from peculiar faces and behavior—to abnormal thus *inferior* minds.

Basic (root) meaning: A myth which claims that there is some meaning which is somehow a bed-rock that each word reduces to, when we spot multiple meanings from what is "basically" the same. Like Platonic theories of forms, this is the essence of the human condition for which we futilely search. Having found it (in a future beyond time) then we will know what is truly human, who we are, I am...

Similar is the search for "Adamic" language, the original language given by God to Adam: the real names of all the animals and things, which has by now been lost to change (from Babel to babble). If we recover the root words, then we will truly know who we are, and perhaps, salvation, or whatever we look for while we pay little attention to living.

But all words have multiple meanings. Some basic or central meaning is a myth of favorite usage. What does "mother" mean? What did it used to mean; what will it mean, in various futures? To be a mother varies as experience does—spoken as a father whose children are more-or-less adult, my daughter about to be married: a mother-to-be?

Meaning derives from and is read-into relationship, experience, interaction; not the other way around. We live in a chicken-egg universe, not one which is causally caused or self-caused.

The history of ideas, of thought, is so tortuous because words which have no tangible, object-directed meanings (which are themselves multiple), so-called abstract words, are argued over and over. The difficulties (at least some of them) reside in the fact that the experiences to which they refer, directly or usually indirectly, vary from person to person, place to place, time to time. Many of them "gain" meaning only within some gathering notions of context.

And we argue about these as if they can be purified and settled upon once and for all (e.g. good, evil, justice, etc.). American Law has, in fact, settled upon what "reasonable" people think or believe, thus dodging the question in an interesting, but useable way. From Holmes (I think), it has become obvious that law (i.e. definitions and meanings of abstract words) evolves.

Translation and meaning: Translation, especially translation machines, founded on the fact that all words have multiple meanings (and multiples of multiples because of their occurrences embedded in cross-cutting logics, experiences, contexts, etc.). So, to translate literally, word-for-word "works" for a very little distance, but soon falls apart, because neither our minds, nor language, functions in this manner actually. (See my *Body Journals* for a direction for solution to this.)

But the problems of basic meaning, of translation, symbolic solutions, religions, and so on, depend (in Western thought) on where we believe language, thought, consciousness "reside." The Western solution is to claim that these all reside, are reducible to some facts, about the individual.

The social (Marxist, etc.) attack upon this, is (so far) to obscure the individual.

The activity of human life is much more like a dialogue (Buber, 1937; Feuerbach, 1841), an interaction. This alters radically, I believe, what we mean by an individual, where meaning, translation, etc., reside and derive. Human living is much more complicated than has been assumed and believed (because, I think, we have been assumed to be humanly unique as a residual non-animal creature).

Arbitrariness: Since Saussure at least, language, words and especially meaning, have been claimed to be arbitrary. One could call a table (*mesa*) or 1,000 different words. There is no direct attachment or relationship between a bounded stream of sound we call "a word," and what it refers to. On the other side of the coin, the "same" word can, in different times and settings, refer to quite different things or experiences.

Whether this sense of arbitrariness is used as an argument for relativism ("any word is as `good' as any others"), or for freedom (the ability to choose, to have choice, the fact remains that although there is freedom in human expression, but it is pretty tightly delimited in its structurations, and in many senses it is constricted and very non-arbitrary.

So while the notion of arbitrary is correct in the context of what is human and different from language to language and in varying settings, the fact is that there is little which is arbitrary in our actual, personal lives, or outlooks. This is not in any psychological or personal sense free of "parole" as opposed to a rule-governed "langue," but how we talk to others, and, in my experience, quite probably in how we think. In my English, a table is a table, and in talking or thinking, I use the word "table" to describe or refer to it. There is not much "choice" in using this word to refer to a specific table. The so-called "arbitrariness" is not within actual (English) usage, but applies across languages. (This is not to say that there is little freedom in the human condition, but that language is not its locus: See: *Next Places*).

How, for example, am I going to complete this sentence, idea? Maybe there are five or ten words, several phrases, but they are neither infinite nor arbitrary. There are a limited—*bounded*—number or sorts of ways to say something to somebody. Context often determines or delimits—*bounds*—precisely which word is to be used, but context doesn't directly equate with arbitrary.

I may use a word in another language to convey a different sort of meaning, or a shade of meaning, but this is not arbitrary in any unlimited sense: the Yiddish word for the human "behind," *tuchus* is more "affectionate" than the word in English. So I use it, because I enjoy the human anatomy, including its rear view. But the company in which I use it knows what I mean.

Knowledge would not be possible if language were arbitrary in the widest sense of that term. (The skeptic may claim that this is true, but how would he know what I was talking about, unless he "knew"...?) We might say, then that language is - at once - fixed *and* arbitrary, and begin to study the conditions and/or contexts in which this may be true. (That is, the locus for the study of arbitrariness has been so far miscast).

The Primitive: If humans developed, as our scientific myths usually claim, from simple to complex, from stimulus-bound to rational, from thoughtless to rational, which schemes for the "origin" of language and meaning, might help to account for how we developed historically?

The Jungian notion of "archetype" is exactly this sort of scheme, and is a direct descendant of the Cartesian scheme. What is civilized? Language, conceptualization is all a gloss on our true, ancient selves which we still retain deep within us. Maclean's (2012) notion of the tri-partite brain also supports his view of bodily functions as "primitive," with increasing complexity having to do with rational thought, or whatever we believe happens in the "unique" cerebral cortex. Here we observe animals with "lesser" brains, see what they are like, and attribute the differences in brain to what we're like. (The description usually seem to confirm what has been already been decided on other grounds.)

The linguistic attempts, historically, have tended to show that it is language, with currently complex grammars, *all the way back*; i.e. language gets no more primitive, there was no such simplex-complex development, at least with these methods. And from extant literature, there have been extensive changes in language over the past several millennia. But these tend, if anything, more toward certain simplifications, rather than toward complexity.

Morris Swadesh postulating some sort of "root" or "basic" vocabulary, tried to show that through change at some sort of constant rate (of change)—if we get the right data—we can infer some human beginnings: "glottochronology." As I recall now, it was fairly obviously circular.

Berlin and Kay's (1969) schema of the development of color words (words for color) presumes that there has been a simple-complex sensory development, which had an accompanying development of words for newly perceived colors. Thus we might find, perhaps now on earth, examples of primitive and complex languages, and figure out somehow what primitive means.

The general argument against this is that even moderns perceive or experience a great deal for which we have no words (or certain "languages" have gone-in-for certain areas of experience, and have developed vocabulary extensively, and others have not, for whatever reasons, e.g. Eskimo snow). Their scheme assumes that vocabulary follows experience in some pretty direct sense. Apparently these vocabulary schemes derive from Aristotle (rather than from Plato—where the notion of development devolves upon ideas rather than words), and is the one word in the New Testament (John I: "In the beginning was the word..."), and the Old Testament in Genesis, where all the species were named.

But, basically, any scheme which propounds some process of development (Prague school oppositions), or of a simpler *Urspache* (say, 1 to 3 basic vowels; a stop consonant) will generate a developmental scheme which will "account" for what we have today. Which is right?—whether such was indeed the history of human development, remains moot within the larger contexts of present thinking.

It remains to be shown either that human development went some other routes (e.g., not simplex-to-complex) by some way of "really" understanding other species; or that the history was one way or another; there were a variety of routes, etc. Or we must revise our thinking, especially about "progressive" evolution in general, and about the nature of language, in particular.

The Simple: Most arguments about origins include or follow from some notion of what is simple, primitive. This assumes in all things involving life processes, that there is a simple; that by analyzing, dividing, reducing, we can decide what that is.

But whatever is life may, in fact, all be complex; in some senses equivalent. We may be dealing with varieties of complexity.

Perhaps it helps to point some questions which have led to notions of simplicity, in attempting to show that similar questions will lead as well to life-as-complexity: The driving questions are those of objects and description, the: what is it? Once we have decided (but on what grounds?) what anything is, then we can say what all such things are, and of what they are composed.

The study of human anatomy has, for example, been like this until very recently. It has been essentially the anatomy of the cadaver; the anatomy of process, movement, upright posture, development, all being issues which were by-passed, and literally left unnoticed (unnoted). Further, the fact (for me) that other humans enter deeply into the formulations of our substantive being, has remained unnoticed, because we decided that the thing, the object and subject of human behavior, is the individual. This has been erroneous in explaining even the material appearance of the human. So the simplex-complex notion which has guided thinking and observation has trapped us in at least two senses: the development of embryo to adult; and the notion that *the* object is the individual.

Language Minus Sound: Confused, bewildered, amused I am. I just read a book on language, cognition, meaning, etc. Nowhere could I find in some 300 pages of well-written text and analysis any mention that language or meaning has anything whatsoever to do with sound. Not one reference, no passing commentary; not even a mere dismissal. Language is syntax, a set of "forms" which exist, I guess, abstracted and independent from the facts of their existing within whatever is language, as sound in process, in complex relationships with silence, to and from persons. The notion of sound as a telegraph device which transmits or carries language, but which has no effects, no importance.

This book on post-modern linguistics criticizes Chomsky's approach as not taking into account anything in the non-linguistic environment, the notion being that semantics is not studiable; meaning not understandable within the context of independent language; language per se. And it, like other such approaches, depends on a (series of?) surreptitious theories of meaning to explain meaning. Somehow this field moves in slow-motion back to broader questions of human interaction and existence (...and its takes itself so seriously!)

Meaning, Words and Experience: Some belief that words "possess" meaning—either primitive "root-words," or more general, or within various idea nets or "spaces," but that meaning inheres in the words, somehow. This is a good example of what I mean by "locating" a problem, or issue, incorrectly. Meaning is not located in words: words are located within some "larger" gathering/organizing principle; e.g. sets of responses to question words. (Q→R System)

Or, since (it is believed) meaning inheres in words (shades of Pythagoras) and words have no ultimates then meaning is located in agreements, usage, pragmatics of language. Again, these are all half-truths, but their thorough analysis will not (I believe) tell us much about the nature of meaning or "how it works" because these all by-pass the processual, phenomenological, social, existential in life.

Beginnings, rethinkings, would include inquiry into why meaning could possibly be problematic in the human condition (and it's not because of possible ambiguities, the rare, which is supposed to outline the ordinary—a view from pathology?)!

Ambiguity and pathology: There is a view rampant in the world that the study of ambiguity has much to teach us. This is, to me, much like other fields which presume (unexamined) an "ideal-normal" notion of what is, the reality which can be illuminated or specified by "curing" the abnormal. There may well be no particular insight into the ordinary here. If medicine, modern allopathy, provides lessons, we are learning that is possesses no theory of wellness, of health. Modern medicine operates "from pathology" toward the relief of symptoms. Without pathology, medicine is in trouble. It presumes to specify what is normal, healthy, and how to remain so; but it is becoming obvious, that its models of health and wellness are weak, at best. The view of language, of meaning from ambiguity strikes me as essentially a view from pathology.

In others terms, it is a view from the exotic, the extraordinary; a view which specifies some sort of truths; but what sort, how large, how extensive remains moot, unknown. (But most of us like to extend these partial truths and methods into the widest, engrossing imperium.)

The Attack upon Rationality: The question of the origin of meaning arises presently during an era of attack upon the notion of human rationality. This attack, which may or may not be a singular sort of social movement, comes from several directions and takes such diverse forms that they may not be seen for what they are; or, at least, that they have in-common this anti-rationalism.

Probably the current phase is driven by a sense of pessimism, the threat of nuclear holocaust, global famine, the loss of progress, of hope, the worry of some "lesser" peoples taking over either by war or by reproductive fecundity, the approach of the second millennium: the fear of a necessity for a global totalitarianism in lieu of all these other possible eventualities (See: Sarles, 2001).

The attack comes from religion—the rebirth and revival of fundamentalism; from some biologists—the inability of humans to "think" themselves out of this dilemma; the same from behaviorist psychology and the sociologists and economists who have stripped the notion of "will" from the human condition; from some "therapeutic humanists" who want to manage our moods and improve our feelings about ourselves; from the occult which is more entranced with the thrills of the "invisible" than with what there seems to actually be; from the intellectual humanists who think literature is more real, at least more valid, than life and living; from the neurologists, mechanistic reductionists who believe in rationality, but believe it is a simpler overarching motivation: namely, "greed"; from philosophers-logicians who have made logic and rationality into a technique over which they have proprietorship; from anthropological and other "structuralists" who do not distinguish substance from form, but "believe" in form; from curriculists who have removed the necessity for teachers and have taken the necessity for living, away from life. Probably there are some others: marketers.

Other Species and Meaning: The myth: wandering alone, individually, in the primeval jungle, no concept of time because they are stimulus-bound, past/present/future—only "here and now," externally motivated by what stimulates their nervous systems. No mind, no sense of will, of what tomorrow may bring, or of tomorrow. Incomplete, small brain, not upright, no prehensile hands.

Hominids, big brained, upright, hands and thumbs, one day discovered they were "smart." Worrying about the future, dwelling in the past. Bad vibrations and they ask: Why? Now we are human.

But this myth of other species leaves out some possible facts: 1) they are social, thus presumably communicate; meet each other's minds, if only "by example." But they change, apparently learn to be like the adults; or like the adults "think" they should be: 2) they are, in some senses, moral. They can "read" one another, are not reactive in any simple stimulus-bound sense. These two notions of the other species being social and moral seem to raise issues in a new way about human sociality and morality. These, in turn, heavily affect what we mean by meaning.

Questions of how and what other species know, what they perceive, how they transform perceptions into cognition into knowledge; how they "understand" their own species and others.

The Metaphysics of Sociality: If it is in any deep sense true that the continuity of being is provided by others believing that you are, proclaiming that you are, then the field (arena) of metaphysics alters drastically, and all that that might entail: theories of being, personal psychology, theo-politics, possibly even economics.

The Question-Response Grammar: The issue of how we humans come to have meaning, to be sensible, is addressable if we consider that language is part of a system of interpersonal interaction. Words, statements, concepts have no "meaning" in any deep sense abstractly; i.e., outside of what other social-adults consider to be meaningful.

The ontogenetic problem—conceived from the perspective of the developing child—is to come into the universe of meaning and discourse, in which s/he finds herself; into the world as-if, as constructed by those around her. (Eventually, to emerge, be(come) oneself: conscious, knowing, moral...)

The Q-R grammar assumes no particular test of logic abstracted from the human condition (e.g., of numbers or of forms), no test of truth/falsity except that of how sensible, meaningful adults construe the world. It is that universe of sensibility and meaning in which the origin of meaning takes place—has taken place—for each of us in our actual lives.

While this suggestion does not deny truth-tests (because adults live in a world of truth in logical and other senses), it does suggest that children come to their broader categories of meaning, and to the very notion of meaning, principally by what are usually called "substitution sets." Such sets are gatherings of words and phrases, and the gatherings imply some (cultural/meaning) commonalities in which the developing child infers some meanings. The infant does not have (to have) any concept of space or of time or of number, but can "discover" that a particular set—which s/he knows *is* a set—has actual reference.

The principle by which these items gather into a set, I believe are acoustical, in the first instance. They are "responses" (and I believe we are inherently responding- interacting creatures) to a set of "noise-dynamics-words" which are "questions" and which, in any interaction, stimulate fairly particular responses; possibly they are imitative, like "smile" responses, or opening a mouth when the parent/feeder opens his or hers.

The words in a set are acoustically similar to each other (I think) and particularly as responses to particular "question words." For example, a question "Where?" stimulates a set of responses—initially, irrespective of meaning and reference. The child, now knowing a set membership, with some experience, can infer the notion of space-place, moving between the response set, the question word, and experience. Gradually the child develops a notion of concept of the meaning of place (as the adults mean place). The same, I think, is true of other adjectives, then of nouns, etc.

Thus I think the origin of meaning is, early on, inferential: having sets of responses to question words, the members of these sets begin to gain some reference; the ideas of representations are spread to the sets (and to other members of the set), the sets become "meaningful," the child possesses meaning. Each response set is indefinitely large, thus solving the ancient problem of how a finite creature can simultaneously be non-finite.

Talk, propositions, sentences in Q-R grammar are not merely responses to putative questions, but an organized, syntactic selection of a member from each set (sometimes null), placed together to form an idea (how many, what color, what), e.g. a red book.

Interaction and Knowledge: Do we "know" the world *directly*, or do we come to know via studying how others (our parents) know the world? Isn't the infant's study primarily of the face of the infant's m/other not necessarily the birth-mother; even a father? Isn't it she who provides the *means* by which meaning "originates"?

Was it when humans began to instantiate one another primarily as faces that the origin of meaning occurred historically? Since the early statuary of Easter Island and the east coast of Mexico are not yet clearly "faced," this may well have occurred in "recent" times; perhaps when we became sufficiently upright. (J.)

Redefinition of Consciousness: Instead of consciousness and awareness being the primary, the beginning of all of knowledge, it seems clear (if not obvious) that consciousness is a much more problematical notion in the context of the idea that continuity "derives" from the external than from the internal. In other words, we need to rethink, to redefine consciousness. (What we think/realize to be consciousness must be a sort of story we tell ourselves about what we imagine consciousness to be. Consciousness, as notion or as truth, remains obscure.)

Interactionally, consciousness has to do with the ability to speak sensibly and understandably to others; i.e., to be able to enter their world of sense in a situationally congruent and meaningful way (Heraclitus' notion of "in common sense"). It is at least as much an entering their consciousness as it is a reflection of ours. Intelligibility, mutual understanding, demand this.

The problem of the "content" of individual/personal consciousness remains moot; not denied, but something we must infer, rather than something which is privately obvious or even evident (self-evident).

Consciousness is whatever is "in common sense." One's internal or "private" knowing remains peculiarly unavailable to direct analysis (Joubert's 1838) notion of the mind's dialogue being in parallel or there being a number of dialogues going on—all "at the same time").

Motoric-Cognitive: Attempts (e.g. by McNeil, 2000)) to say what is cognition, derived from the dualistic scheme which assumes that motoric-body is the more animalistic, the more primitive-natural, and that conceptual thought is somehow a translation, transduction, transfer from body-mind; or in speaking, from mind to body: how a conceptual/imaginary scheme becomes actualized.

The mistake is to believe that this is entirely "self-confined": that the schemata are all internal. Certainly this is true, in a sense, but in which senses? And how powerful, how exhaustive is this as an accounting? It depends, ultimately, on what we think schemata are, and are like: and this is where we differ, strongly, the psycho-linguist and the interactionist.

Language Development: Ontogenetically we seem to phrase the problem as the infant coming to do (be) something s/he couldn't do (be) earlier; or, the development from (pure) body toward the development of mind; somehow, we have decided—too strongly, I think—what language consists in. We seem to miss, or to dismiss, the feats of bodily development which precede and accompany the "beginnings" of language, as if they are not aspects of language; but, especially, as if they are inconsequential to this development; as if, even in the infant, language is an essentially independent process/entity.

Well, we don't really know what is consequential or causal to language. We tend to forget or dismiss as "biological" (as opposed to mental) that language is bodily-muscular – and interactional with m/other. Study those who don't get to talk ("retarded," "autistic") and you will see that their bodies are quite different from those of us who are "normal," and that they learn better in other gravities (e.g., water), to begin to realize that language development is an aspect of body, at least not separable from *it*.

Language development should not be merely the study of first words, or early sentence-like phrases, but of a more general notion of language-as-communication, of parents getting the infant to share their world-view, and to come to articulate that vision, understandably.

I sense that language development, conceived as the progressive movement from pure body to (pure) reason, must invoke a number of mystical causes to explain how mind, reason and language can emerge from such brute stuff as muscles and cartilage, or else attribute it to some inexplicable, inherent features of human nature.

What Should Linguists Do?: Within this arena of the origin of meaning and of language, there are a number of "confusions" concerning the nature and "location" of the subject matter, and what the students (linguists, semanticists, semioticians, etc.) think they are doing, ought to study, etc.

If it were truly clear what language consists of, then, e.g., developmental psychologists could study (as they claim) the development of language and meaning. But it is not clear, that newborn infants are "devoid" of meaning, and that learning, say, words/sentences is clearly or primarily what learning language consists of. (Bowlby, 2013)

We linguists take for granted that we know, in some senses deeply, what is language. But it is the parents who essentially determine it for each child; it is their view, their correctives, their observations and determinations which move development of language in some directions rather than others. Shouldn't we be studying (shouldn't it be our study) how parents (the parental "class" or generation) realize and actualize the origin of meaning, rather than the study of infants through the "stages" of learning what we linguists accept to be mature language?

The implications of these two modes of conceptualizing the task have great differences, not only in what we do, but in how to think about education, the nature of these subject areas (what predominates, e.g., language or meaning), what an individual is, what we mean by history (phylogenetic/ontogentic), the nature of experience, etc.

Why Some "Retarded" and "Deaf" Persons Sound Like "Animals": Those who don't/cannot talk do not articulate (well) with their tongue tips; but all of them (who I've met and tried to engage in imitation, and they all do), articulate with the velar tongue, using the back of the mouth (laryngeal) muscles. So they sound "guttural"—like "growling" –and we infer they are "animal-like."

(What would "retarded" or "deaf" animals sound like?)

The "reason" why (I think) the "retarded" do not use tongue tips as articulators has also to do with the fact that they have little control over external facial muscles, and somehow do not "know" where their lips and faces are in relation to the tongue. (Derived from observing 21-trisomy Down's syndrome children with tongues hanging out.)

Emotions and Meaning: In the evolutionary myths of the origin of (human) language, it is presumed that our bodies and our passions/emotions are somehow similar to and derived from other species. The phonetic articulation of the emotions was transformed somehow into "actual" language: the "aha!," or groan or pain theories. Somehow (we assume) these internal events were externalized as speech and developed into language.

Within these theories there is already assumed a meaning-relation between the emotions and the expression in speech. A groan designates or reflects or tells about pain. I know of no deep explanation of why, in other species (or in pre-human) there should be some reason to articulate the "emotions"—other than interpersonal, communicative ones. Breathing, muscular tension release, etc., are bound up with speech, and perhaps it is somehow obvious why, in these theories, they are "spoken." But I don't think it is obvious. In any case, within such theories, the origin of meaning is connected with the emotions, and the study of the origin of meaning should be directed here, probably as well as into the questions of why we think our bodies/emotions are akin to or derived from other species.

In infant humans we associate "crying" with the confirmation of life. And in the ontogenesis of meaning it is important to note that we adults already come to the observation of newborn infants with pervasive interpretative (semiotic) frameworks: *see somebody there*! (Elaine Morgan, 1995)

Whether the expulsion of air, the general excitation of an infant, has much if any meaning to the infant, we adults believe and act as if it has; not only for ourselves, but impute this also to the infant. (Likewise we "read" and interpret "character" into newborn infants' faces). That is, we believe that these creatures are inherently meaningful; that their speech-making, articulation of "cries" is reflective of something about their internal states. There are (or soon develop) cries of pain, hunger, and so on. We assume in ordinary human social contexts that these infants are meaningful by virtue of their being (physical beings).

A serious student might, at this point, ask two sorts of questions: 1) does the infant possess an intrinsic/inherent theory of meaning, or does s/he merely expel air, exercise muscles which "feel good" (i.e., the infant possesses some theory of "pleasure"); 2) if the infant (if we assume) has a theory of meaning, is it "like" ours, the adult observers?

Without going deeply into mechanisms of development, it is worth suggesting that—whatever the infants' actual nature, and this is still not well-understood—the infant is dealt with as if she *has* (a) theory of meaning, and *the problem of ontogenesis is to come to possess the same essential theory as the adult population.*

If it is the case that the infant possesses no such theory, the question of the origin of meaning becomes one of much greater interest and wonder. Puzzles in this area have led us to study retarded and autistic children at some great length, to attempt to see how they are peculiar; whether this has to do with "incapacity" for meaning, or whatever.).

I am confident, in the case of visually obvious "Down" infants, for example, that the parents see little of "meaning" in their children's faces, do not know how and are tempted to abandon interpreting meaning in faces which are, for them, not very informative. We seem to infer from peculiar facial expressions to peculiar mental capabilities? Why? Is this correct? (See Rynders and Horrobin)

If we are, as observers, creatures who impute meaning to our own infants, what sorts of observers-interpreters are we, already, of other species? Is what we see in them aspects of ourselves, of the behavior of other species? If we already see them as much simpler than humans do we not impute meaning to them (or "give" them very simple theories of meaning "fixes" to a stimulus-bound mentality)?

Is this about them, or about us?

A metaphor: Could a non-Human observing us (say, an intelligent Martian) determine that we have theories of meaning? Why?—Why not? (Especially before we became civilized, yet had already well-developed languages, as far as we now know! See: Sarles, 1985: Chap.2)

Paralanguage: Somehow we believe we know in some objective way just what language is. It is clear to those who observe the speech of humans that the stuff which emerges from our mouths includes many noises which are clearly not language (by almost any definition) and many which seem to be "commentary" upon language. These noises or aspects of sound affect messages, quite probably, but do not seem to change— like phonemes—the meaning of words. Tone-of-voice, paralanguage, voice quality is not minimally contrastive, yet it has to do with meaning in some still unelaborated senses.

To whatever extent we believe that paralanguage has to do with emotions we may consider that this is the arena of speech in which the origin of meaning (has) occurs. And, in any case, to whatever extent meaning is bound with tone-of-voice, the origin of meaning must consider paralanguage seriously.

The "status" of paralanguage (David Crystal, 1975) has not yet been developed or even thought through with any comprehensive intellectual and empirical discipline, having been relegated to its epiphenomenal position with respect to whatever is (currently) considered to be "language." It is, however, necessary to point out that language does not occur in any sense unembedded in what are usually considered to be paralinguistic variables. Language does not occur in any "neutral" (not too loud, too soft) sense, except with respect to potential contrasts; language does not occur outside of actual *contexts*, even though we try to examine language "in isolation" as if this is both possible and revealing.

Is paralanguage 5%, 35%, 95% of the stream of speech? I tend to opt for the 95% idea because it aids me in considering how to think about what is heard in speech. The "loudest" aspects of the speech signal in ordinary communicative language seem to have to do with the "distance" (literal, physical) between speaker-interactors. What does an infant hear in listening to parental talk?—something about how far away her parents are from her, or from each other? How does the infant come to know what is what; language, paralanguage? What do we hear when we record the speech (paralanguage? language?) of other species?—mostly distance, social variables, "the message"?

Is there (still) a "universal" paralanguage; an *Ursprache*? Can we tell who is talking to one another, what is the nature of their relationships, something about context, merely from the paralanguage? Is meaning "located" here, first, then to be more specified in sophisticated language development ontogenetically?

Is there any way to decipher the paralanguage of other species (discounting their bodily/resonant chamber shapes) to compare "how" they talk, with how we talk? Does thinking about this help to illuminate the origin of meaning?

Kinesics, Sign Language: Much of the problem of the origin of meaning comes back to the human body. However, to use the notion of "body" within the usual frameworks of discussion of meaning and of language already constricts and directs our thinking about the body either to something construed to be in opposition to the meaning and the mind, or to something which is biological and "pre-human". To consider the body as a meaningful, conceptual "instrument"—as the person "I am"—is a task which requires both re-thinking and an experiential re-doing, especially within the framework of Western thought.

Some metaphors: 1) "deaf" persons (formerly "deaf and dumb") seem to do very well in generating interpersonal meaning, in communicating and mutual understanding without verbal language as a medium. Sign language is seen clearly as a vehicle for interpreting one mind/person to another. Thought/mentation processes are translatable into sign language which is then interpretable-as-intended by other persons. Here it becomes clear that "language" in the ordinary phonetically articulated senses is not a necessary aspect of understanding and meaning. (This is not to downplay the fact that the human world is linguistic; but to wonder about what it is that language is and does, without a mere acceptance of traditional views. (Stokoe, 1960: 2) Some "retarded" persons who have not spoken in their lives have been taught sign-language in recent time. Some of them have learned hundreds of signs in very little time and are able to communicate effectively (if somehow in limited fashions for a variety of reasons). Minds which were thought to be "poor," even "empty," are much richer and normal then we had thought. The lessons to be studied in this example have to do with how we ordinarily judge such "retarded" persons: how we think about what they are, and can be. The fact is that we have inferred much from peculiar ("stupid looking/acting") bodies to *inferior* minds.

Somehow, in our thinking, we already connect bodies to mental processes, in complicated fashions. In my experience, we have inferred from animal bodies to their lack of or poverty of meaning in similar ways: from "bestial" bodies to "inferior" minds. Thus the origin of meaning problem, it seems to me, must be rethought in terms of how we Western thinkers already have determined it to be, because we assume/infer that animals possess no meaning. Perhaps, like the "deaf," like some persons thought to be "retarded," they merely cannot talk. That doesn't necessarily mean/imply/entail that they cannot think.

It is my view that bodies are "thoughtful"; it is our previous conceptualization of bodies which has prevented our seeing and understanding this. Toward a retrieval of Platonism at the moment when Plato banished the body from knowledge: *Phaedo*.

Especially, we have been limited, I believe in observation because we believe the universe of meaning begins from each individual, rather than the individual being cast within complicated social dialogues— which, even anatomically, are interactional.

(After being a "critic" at a Gallaudet College for the Deaf— Conference on Sociology of the Deaf):

There is a certain "stuckness" among the promoters of Sign Language use in deaf communication. They have been very successful in using earlier ideas from anthropological linguistics; teach in "native language" how to "read" then switch to second language, if the second language is the pervasive, national, commercial language.

And deaf children are now being taught via sign language, moving them along conceptually toward fully thinking and communicating adults. This seems to "work best" from the deaf persons' perspective.

But the promoters of sign language, instead of trying to bridge problems of sign-to-oral, problems of interpreters and interpretation, are trying still to placate the proprietors of language as an "oral" phenomenon, by trying still to demonstrate that sign language either is language or is the equivalent of language.

I think this effort is misplaced or misdirected since it does not further the examination of human communication in any sense bridging the gap between the deaf and hearing experience—vehicles for helping the deaf live fully within society. Rather, it is fighting a kind of battle for equality using a metaphor. It should take on the battle straight-forwardly, showing that "language" is already an aspect of the body. It is the body which is uniquely human, and it is communication toward understanding and mutual understanding which is important in life.

Linguists and the defenders of language as what is humanly unique, are trying still to stave off what they perceive as threats to rationality, to logic, to morality.

Trying to demonstrate that sign is like "real language" is silly because the owners of the concept of "language" are not willing to examine the grounds of their claims to defining language, and have no "rational" way of responding to what they perceive as a threat, except or only within their terms of what is language.

Within the problems of the origin of meaning and the origin of language, the question of deafness becomes particularly poignant and instructive.

To deny conceptual abilities to the deaf is to deny that sign language is like "real" oral language. More importantly, it is to not take the time or care to communicate with some deaf persons on their terms: or mutually, through an interpreter.

The Body: To most of those concerned with "language" the human body seems like an anchor of biological foundations. The "body" seems fixed, predetermined, a thing in and of itself whose material construction is obvious and well-known. Ha!

Within the discovery that the anatomy, the actual bony structure of the body, its form and substance, are more like a viscous fluid in equilibrium than like the hard, bony remains of the skeleton of history, this foundation is no more secure than the fluidity of a language spoken in particular place and time (i.e., muscle tension "molds" bone!) (Ekman, 2007)

It is, perhaps, comforting, and a way to shift some responsibility for knowledge, to think that the study of "the body" is given over to some groups of "biologists" who "know" what it is and how it works.

It is, in fact, likely that this new "functional, dynamic anatomy" will have a powerful effect on how we think about the human (and other species) condition.

Understanding, studying, language and the body, need thought and discussion within some context of thinking about common issues. It is not (yet) obvious where putative boundaries between "body and mind," or body and language might reside; or whether this dualistic outlook makes sense in the further understanding of meaning in the living world.

Anthropomorphism: has, I believe, to be rethought. The realization that how we think about other species has a powerful influence about how we think about humans, ought to give us some pause.

It is useful to review why this is important—this juxtaposition with other species—in our theories of meaning, language, human nature. How did (why did) we begin to think of the differences between humans and other species as having to do with "mental" aspects of being, rather than with their bodies (which is directly how we know and recognize other species)? At various places within this notion of the comparative enterprise, I find contradictions and paradoxes.

To think, for example, that so-called "retarded" humans are more like other species "intermediate" forms is to already have a theory of human progress and "intelligence," which seems, to me, to prejudge what there is to find. As Donald Griffin (1976) queries repeatedly, if other species were intelligent, had awareness, would we be able to see it in them? I think we would not, and suggest that a great deal of our own thinking about language and meaning is bound-up in this inability or unwillingness (or fear?) to observe what might be there; to devise critical methods to see anew, rather than elaborate differences and denials to justify what we have decided already (on what grounds?).

In order to rethink what is anthropomorphic, we must consider what worries us: can we no longer treat other species as expendable; edible; to be locked up in zoos? Is there a secret, sacred arena here? No doubt we have some sorts of hierarchies, of Great Chains of Being, in our ordinary judgments of life's creatures. No doubt this arena is linked with social philosophy and politics in the very broadest senses: religion, morals, government...

Why is it so difficult to admit to ourselves what we really do not know or understand in the comparison between humans and other species? What precisely is at stake?

The Neurological *Solution*: Humans are more intelligent, have meaning, etc., because we possess a "cerebral cortex." There is a tri-partite brain with the mid and hind brain dealing with more "vital," "biological," "animalistic" functions (Maclean, 2012).

This might be true in some senses, but the argument is quite circular, so it's very difficult to separate argument from content. We believe (assume) we possess language, meaning, and so on (left parietal area), and we also believe other species do not. The mode of (pseudo) comparison is to account for the assumed differences in ability and function by stating what is different between the human brain and others: a circular argument, mostly used to justify what we believe or assume on other grounds.

The human brain is "enclosed" in a human cranium and may well "take its shape" *from* the cranium. There is a general myth that the central nervous system is what humans "really" are (i.e. the CNS is "independent" of the human body, its form, etc.) The body, within this thinking, is the mere locus for the nerve end organs. Again, this is peculiar reasoning, and is based on the assumption that neurology is the bed-rock of being. Our human shapes are much more interesting (to us, at any rate), than "the neurological solution" implies. "The neurological solution" begins from assumed differences, and looks for mechanisms and/or anatomical correlates to account for what it assumes already to be true. (I prefer to think of the CNS as like a telephone interchange system rather than the seat of a homunculus! The problem of how "flesh and blood" can "think," can possess imagination beyond bounds, is not addressed seriously within "the neurological solution").

It is much more productive to ask why we look like we do, what are our shapes, how do (we) grow up and out? The muscles for talking and for facial appearance are the same and/or overlapping: this is why speech/language and facial appearances are similar; i.e., why non-speaking "retarded" persons appear "retarded." How other species appear (to us; to them) is deeply problematic, and we have to begin to query our habits of observation to begin to be able to see what and how other species see (cf., Mark Johnson: *The Body in the Mind*, 1987).

If we are to do productive comparison, we must begin from similarities, not from differences; or we will be doomed to circularity of reasoning, and possibly "new" packaging and merchandising of the same old ideas in today's styles. The origin of meaning is mostly a problem in methods of comparison.

This is neither to claim that the CNS of different species is the same or different, but to state that we shouldn't assume what we do not yet know) (Searle, 1982).

Primitive → Civilized: All the "primitive" people in the (increasingly urban/bureaucratic) world speak language much as we. The work of Boas et al in the 1920's was calculated to show that the "savages" and "primitives" were (are), in fact, thinkers and talkers much as we are. What has changed since primitive times, the archaic past when we had no tools, few tools, etc.? What sorts of conceptual changes might have recurred in the human (or the pre-human to human) condition?

First, the instantiation of humans as faces, coming with erect posture; also some shaping of sound (we, no doubt, "hear" differently than other creatures, due in part to our bodily and facial structure; bodily in lower tones).

The domestication (living in fixed-built settlements) may well (Wilson, 1989) have led to our thinking becoming "geometrized." This powerfully delimits and places boundaries on our being, creating maps based on our being creatures of particular places; and having others who are not; setting up social hierarchies; spaces for gardens, home, heaven and hell; and populate the world as the partials whom we now know as belonging to someplace other, being other, and finally wondering who we might then be.

The depiction of life—learning how to abstract life into two dimensions (for the power of visualization and depiction of modern idea. Each depiction perhaps an entire way of rethinking existence.

Writing created the idea of a temporality/history very different from that otherwise imaginable. It has led, for example, to being able to conceptualize notions like origins of meaning or of language; probably (via Parmenides) of notions like "forever" and "instantaneity"; causality and a creator-deity.

Possibly most important, the size of one's interactive cohort: the crucial point being, perhaps, when there were too many individuals to know each person in the "depth of actuality" and we began to call and sort others (and ourselves). Isn't this the major difference between primitive and civilized?

Feral Children: That (human) children raised by other species will teach us something about the origin of meaning seems wonderful but very unlikely. If, as is claimed, such children can survive, they become humans raised by some other species, and what is there to be learned?

Fascination with this possibility seems to presume some abyss between us and other species, which feral children would have bridged, somehow. If they survive, they will have learned to communicate with another species, it is thought. But we already, in limited senses, communicate with some other species, and this should be studied in detail to see what common grounds there are between us and domestic and other trained animals. We should study development of other species with respect to their species development, as well as the sign-language and other experiments which enable communication.

The feral children story seems to have held out such prizes that we have limited our imagination about how to study cross- and other-species communication. Besides, the issue of survival entails humans raising infants to be human in their own terms; entailing speaking to, caring for, touching. All infants cannot survive without adult humans; how they become human is an important problematic.

Archetypes: The story, propagated in modern terms by Jung ("Collected Works") presumes some essential ancient originary human beingness, whose features can/will be revealed if we learn to see us properly or appropriately. An origin of meaning story (or several) can be developed or detected here, because it follows easily from archetypical thinking, that there is some (Adamic) *Ursprache* which is human and pure (or one could, with sufficient imagination, posit a language/meaning system which is, say, pan hominid, or pan-mammalian, or pan-life!). If we "refine" our analysis, we will gain insight into what we are like (and what "I" am) in some more "real," Platonic sense.

I am not opposed to such analysis, but feel that there are an infinite number of schemes we might follow—derived from language or sounds or behavior—that will lead us back to different notions of archetype. Most of these seem to be dualisms in which one side is the "primitive" (body, usually) and then there is a long-term scholastic debate over what is mental, what is pure, and so on. Often these are moral-religious. My general critique is that they lead away from experience in the present, and do not seem to receive any factual basis for their persuasion. Then they mostly seem circular, and it is difficult to say whether any particular scheme is any better, truer than any other (or any worse; less true).

Having spent a good deal of thought on this issue, its theories and implications, I have been pushed to consider notions of "what history means," and suggest reading the pre-Socratics to see how the current ideas of history were "invented" or otherwise came to be. Clearly the notion of "the origin of meaning" takes on different perspectives if we conclude that the notion of creation (and a creator) was a human discovery or invention (probably Parmenides *Fragment VIII*). My personal experience with a variety of historical thinkers (including evolutionary biologists and historians per se) is that they have "weak" theories of the present, and are likely to opt or push for causal explanations of a very different sort, than for the existential and "process" persons among us (e.g., how did we get here?; not, what are we doing here?).

These questions can be raised and studied in the socialization process, where we see parents observing and interacting with their children, applying observation, theories of history, of the moment, etc., with respect to their children's behavior. I believe that there is a viable comparative study of development, as well, which will help inform us concerning what the notion of meaning might mean, on a broader basis than it is presently constructed. Parents (of whatever species) raise their offspring to become essentially as they are and see themselves being!

Meta-physics: a good deal of thought about the nature of meaning rests on the presumption that the "real" is *primarily* the physical objects in the universe, and that human "being" is derived from or made up of this material. The human condition is "meta-" or "after" physics. In some senses this notion of what is human is a "residual" idea; not merely meta- or after-, but there is also a sense of "leftover," sometimes a "more than"; a material universe compacted into a body, accompanied or enlivened by an "elan vital," a force which gives life to this "inert" body.

This thinking which pervades not only Western thought, but can be found throughout Asia in various forms (the "humors") has some peculiar consequences for the question of the origin of meaning. One is that the particular form of the human body is not very consequential to human being, and it calls attention away from the body; e.g., in development. Thus we get studies of cognitive development (McNeill, 2000)) which do not relate the beginning of talking to the beginning of walking. Maybe they are unrelated, but it seems to me likely that the interrelation of bodily and cognitive development are powerful, and are even more likely oneness rather than a duality. But this illustrates that physics (body) and metaphysics (mind) distinction is still very alive in our thinking.

Why I am critical of this and why I think it interesting, and possibly important, is that we tend to think about "objectivity" in ways which already mirror the physics-metaphysics organization (we presume) of the universe. In fact what we have is a human physics, a human biology, a humanly derived reading of everything. While we tend to believe that what works, what generalizes is a derivative of or attribute of the material world (which it is in some senses, I'm sure), it is not a human truth, but a formal truth which would apply everywhere. The search for extraterrestrial intelligence (SETI) reflects this orientation. (Other species, with other sorts of bodies, might possibly have other or alternative physics to ours. I am not a solipsist, and am not trying to deny physical reality; but am saying that all we possess—so far—is a physics which is undeniably human—not necessarily "untruthful" but certainly not "all the truth.")

Another example of the thinking of which this formulation of metaphysics seems to persuade us is about so-called "retarded" persons. Why we infer from a "strange" body to a defective mind always puzzles me. Interestingly the nature of the retardates' bodies is very poorly described. In my work with them (with J. Timian), I have discovered that they are very different sorts of beings than we have perceived them to be. And the errors we have made about what is wrong with them is very illustrative of the way we think about normality. In fact, the "retarded" and "autistic-like" are quite informative arenas in which to ponder questions about the origin of meaning. What we see as "retarded" and what "the retarded" are actually like are very different (e.g., their bodies are quite different from what we see as "normal," especially how they deal with their gravity by wanting to "preserve" it—not to move—much more than others.

Lastly, the orientation of physics-then-metaphysics has persuaded us of the centrality of the individual in the human condition. A good bit of the reason for why metaphysics seems always to be a replay of Plato is, I believe, located in this formulation of reality and objectivity. Without denying the "real," we should remind ourselves that we are social creatures to our very marrow, and "the origin of meaning" is not to be conceptualized outside of a serious consideration of sociality.

Juxtaposition Theory: In Western thought, we have seen humans and animals as different in important and interesting ways, but within a framework in which they have important commonalities. They are, in other words, in some logic(s) of juxtaposition with one another: alike in some ways but different in others (alike in body, humans have unique minds: but this is so bizarre!).

In general, and throughout most of our history, the differences have been kept pretty constant. It has been assumed that humans and animals are alike in body (="biology") but distinct with respect to mental processes of the sort that we think of as having meaning, intelligence, logic, rationality, morality, the ability to think new, creative thoughts, and so on. (see Adler, 1983). This theory, as it has developed at least from Plato (*Protagoras*) onward, also considers the social nature of humans as distinct and related to our human ability to be "objective"—to know the world, to know others, to know ourselves as others know us.

In such a juxtaposition theory—as long as the framework holds—any change on one side can have an effect on the other. If we think, say, of animals differently than we used to, then we are likely to alter our views about humans, in some (related) way.

This has happened. We now see "wild" animals not as beastly individuals stalking the primeval forests and jungles, but as feral and social. This "fact" is apparently forcing a change in thinking about humans, especially as our theories about language, logics, etc., have derived from a presumption that the unique differences between humans and others, were located in this intellectual arena. Some of the ideas being proposed about animals which have an effect, are that sociality implies communicative abilities and/or competence. Thus, other species "must" have some kind of knowing, understanding, mentation of different sorts than we had imagined and possibly much greater, possibly more like ours.

This notion implies, among other things, that the "origins" of language and meaning are not—as it was formerly considered—at the moment of historical development or emergence or creation of humans, but is somehow already present in (some?) non-human species.

In the present context what this is doing is causing us to rethink what we think is unique to humans, and why we have thought as we have, as well as what is language, what is thought, knowledge; and it has important resonance in the related fields of morality, religion and politics—as evidenced by a strong concern, particularly by Scientific Creationists and other fundamentalists in the U.S., and by the "animal rights" movement.

This shift in knowledge and/or outlook about other species may have a fundamental and powerful affect about how we think about human nature. It is my view that the shifts in the ways we teach and consider a variety of handicapped persons in the U.S., has been pushed by changes in thinking about other species. I even go so far as to suggest that "juxtaposition theory," along with current insights into the sociology of knowledge and the history of ideas, will push us to consider seriously what we mean by history, causality, etc., and is at least partly responsible for raising concerns about language and meaning and human nature in the present era.

Bio-linguistics: It really isn't obvious what "biology" is or means, what its limits are (if any), or that any aspects of language or meaning can assuredly be said to be biological or not. In a dualistic construction of being, it is generally assumable what is one or the other of, say, mind and body, but the present era should cause us to ask whether this dualistic thinking has anything further to illuminate with respect to language or meaning. (One current argument is—within a dualism of nature and culture—that we have moved so far away from Nature that our biology is not very meaningful at all; this is countered by the bio-political argument that culture and language have obscured our true nature from ourselves.)

It has permitted us to obscure the complexities of the human condition by suggesting that language is a set of isolable phenomena which can be analyzed in each/any individual, essentially independently of other persons; but especially it has obscured the fact that meaning and communication occur within social matrices, which are themselves causal and caused, and not considered seriously by thinkers about semantics.

The biology of behavior (ethology) and the biology of society forces us to reject them with some thoughtful seriousness rather than merely out of hand, as pertaining to some domains in which the study of meaning has no possible interest. Mere rejection is to presume various sorts of knowledge, where, in fact, little or none exists. Or it is to cede the power of intellectuality to a form of biological "determinism" which is at least as political as intellectual, and which will be more than a little pleased to tell the rest of us what meaning means, cast—I suspect—within a notion of being in which reason, will, personal freedom, are highly circumscribed. *Biology is too important to be left to "biologists."*

Texts: a good deal of semantic analysis is the analysis of texts. While I read and study (most primary) texts a great deal, I am wary of entering into the origin and study of meaning via textual analysis. It seems both useful and a kind of important reduction to central problems to pursue the study of being human as it is lived and experienced, rather/before than how it is discussed, written about, described, etc. (Reading as phenomenon or phenomenal)

If we study texts, we ought to ask "Why does this text work?" What lessons are to be drawn? What is the relation between context and text?—in that order. Texts seem, to this compulsive scholar, to be too easy, a kind of "good news" approach to the meaning of meaning. (If it were this obvious, the question of semantics would not arise, unresolved, at least once per generation!). Texts are, and are good or masterpieces, because they strike at something about life and living, not merely because they are in a particular tradition, or break out of another, or are transparently beautiful language. It is because they still do something to us; teach us, scintillate us, upset us, scandalize us, blind us, make us laugh, take our breath away, and overwhelm us... us!

To search for meaning in texts, before (instead of) we have searched life and living, seems a mistake. Narration over living; another form of essence over existence as Plato wanders in us saying, *Tsk*.

Pure Reason: Always we have to make the world and experience "fuzzy," translucent, if we posit some deeply essential character to human reason. Life, is then, form and structure; and true meaning remains somehow below the surface. The methodological problem, that which would reveal meaning, is in the hands of those who control the definitions of "purity" and of "reason." They tell us what "the problems" are, how to locate them, how to circumscribe them, and what "a solution" is. They also deem certain issues to be possible or capable of solution, and others not possible or not capable of solution; others, they seem to hide or to obscure, finding them useful surreptitiously and upon occasion.

Again, wary that those who gain control over the definitions (of e.g., grammar, creativity, logic...) have entered the study of meaning with surreptitious theories of meaning hidden in their hip pockets. One must join the tribe, pay dues to philosophy or to linguistics before s/he can pursue problems of reason or of meaning. Part of the dues are, in my experience, that one must accept the surreptitious meaning theories in order to demonstrate competence as a proprietor of definitions. This is to say that the origin of meaning remains obscured by battles defined within disciplinary proprietary boundaries; problems of turf and territoriality.

Again, wary that others who enter this fray are fellow teachers of those whose claim to owning definitions bolsters their own audacity and arrogance and hubris. Here, I wonder about anthropologists or psychologists who "discover" philosophy or linguistics that they are mere translators or otherwise derivative, rather than critical thinkers. Wary, I am, that we all tend to be scholastics rather than scholars and observers, arguing forever about the nature of the definitions we find appealing, rather than check what we find appealing with its occurrences in the world and in our own impulses to be pleased.

Context and the origin of meaning: There is a debate between using "context" as a residual category which "decides" certain questions of meaning, and the notion of context in the sense of studying how people locate themselves in the world.

With respect to the origin of meaning, questions concerning the very nature of context: its forms, how "it" operates, whether it changes, whether and how it applies and when (also meta-problems of context). The difficulty is that it is tempting—too early—to posit some bed-rock phenomenon or notion which will tell us how to proceed in each next place. Within an existential-anthropological biology, this appears futile.

We might begin to ask instead: why does the world seem very stable usually and very changeable occasionally? Consider a bureaucracy: what difference does "scale" make in how we "mean" when we cannot know everyone? How do we treat and conceptualize persons as types or sorts? In what senses do we define ourselves, are defined by others; how are the limits of imagination set for us, by us?

Why does context seem so complex a notion, whereas we usually locate ourselves fairly easily in our everyday worlds? Because it is so "ordinary" that it seems unproblematic?

The problem of the origin of meaning seems locked into whatever is meant by context, else we carry some hidden notion of what decides meaning or where meaning is located, while we attempt to specify some notions, features, or attributes of what meaning is.

Form and Substance: If it is true that ontogenesis in many senses involves an "increase" in meaning, some sense of progressiveness in development, then a child's perspective on form and substance is surely interesting.

It has seemed to me that form and substance (by any names) change in meaning, in use, fashions, during development. Form is a "gathering notion" at some points in development (to bring together different terms which mean the same), and then it is/becomes something "other" than what it was formerly. Once the form is possessed it is used "to refer" to the world. But before it was possessed, it was a form; a form, simply, or at least in some other sense.

Example: the plural morpheme in English is a form (actually several forms to be collapsed into one) which has, at first *no* meaning to the infant. At some point it seems to "harden," to be used everywhere. It gathers the notion of plural objects, and begins ("the origin of plurality") to represent them. What was meaningful and substantial now becomes formal. Thus, ontogenetically, the notions of form and substance change considerably, and may even reverse "roles"—from the perspective of the child: the process?—form→content→form in bootstrapping ways.

How does a 3-1/2 year old become an (appropriate) 4 year old? Is it purely a problem in developmental stages or does the 3-1/2 year old study what it means to be the "next" stage? What is the nature of this study and analysis? And then one becomes a (proper) 4 year old.

Style and Substance: I have the sense that "style" is also in some kind of interaction or reciprocity with substance; that a child sees the world in a progressive, developmental sense, as stylistics. Once what was stylistic is taken into the child's life, it has become substance. (I think this is true in the teaching art as well: that students see stylistics and respond to this by wanting "to please" the teacher, not yet being good, critical judges of what the course substance is. I think "curing" operates in a similar fashion.)

Thus to study style (or form) or substance as if they are something, or located in life's experience as one entity or another, is to misrepresent how these elements actually operate in life—and we end up battling forever over scholastic definitions, as if, for example, such notions as form, style, substance were/are what we claim they are, remote from the experiencing of them.

Grammar and Grammaticality: These are good examples of what I mean by surreptitious theories of meaning. To posit, say, that all "normal" humans know inherently what is grammatical, is simply to dismiss the question of meaning; or to place it mystically within the human condition as somehow "inherent"—to be studied by "someone else" (Who?), or to be argued about in discussions of "Human Nature"; or to be "assumed." (Chomsky, 1966)

It is also to open this arena to bio-politics and to theo-politics because "hidden" arenas can be utilized by those who want power for power's sake, to claim whatever they want. (My personal example is the study of the human face, which remains poorly understood: it is then easy to claim certain sorts of faces represent high intelligence, others stupidity or whatever. All those who want to believe or already believe in a social hierarchy will find these claims useful to bolster their beliefs, and can use "facial" descriptions as a basis for discrimination. Lack of systematic study means that any claim is as invalid as any other.

I hold that the human condition, vis-a-vis meaning and development is a quite fragile process; that whatever is normal, grammatical, etc., is in some dynamic equilibrium; in need of (constant) restating, and open to change of all sorts. As extreme examples, I suggest that "retarded" people are neither well-described nor well-understood, because our usual judgments about them presume they are inherently and permanently "defective." Careful observation shows that they are not as they "appear," and will show that our notions of "normal," of grammar, and of what is human nature are bound up in complicated assumptions and beliefs about the human condition, which must be rethought before we can shed new light on what is meaning.

On the other hand, I do not deny that grammar and grammaticality are *us*, in some deep senses. My objection is to those who by-pass fundamental questions about grammar by claiming they are somehow inherent to the human condition!

Meaning of Life: In various existential senses, life is a constant grappling with meaning whose origin seems to have sprung anew each day.

Where am I? What am I doing? Why? Towards What? How did I get here?—each day requires some answer, some sense of satisfaction, some way of pushing the quest for meaning once again below the threshold of action.

My "solution," more a leaning in a direction, is to quest for becoming; moving the questions of meaning, each day, toward a more meaningful tomorrow shared with Nietzsche and Kierkegaard. It is, perhaps, the search for where to go next, needing a meaningful now, in order to become, then. (See *Next Places*)

To and for others I propose a pedagogy, in which I, the teacher, pose the questions in which my intellectual aesthetic is translated into a sense of meaningful futurity for students. My "contract" as teacher is somehow to be an instance of themselves as an older, still thoughtful, critical, grappling persona. In this sense it is teachers who create meaning, direction, hope, a sense of future in which the students will become (including parents as teachers). (See Sarles, 2013)

Static vs. Changing World: The question of meaning arises mildly or blandly in a static world, where the institutional structures are seen as permanent, and there is presumed to be "a place" for everyone, or "a way" throughout life.

Where the world is perceived to be changing, the question of meaning is continually problematic: questions of existence, of time, of history, of origin seem sensible and occupy our attention. It is not clear to me whether they seek "solution"; whether they want discussion, temporary resolution; whether the voices which ask such questions perennially are heard in such eras. (Benjamin 2002).

"Our ordinary inaccurate observation takes a group of phenomena as one and calls them a fact. Between this fact and another we imagine a vacuum, we isolate each fact. In reality, however, the sum of our actions and cognition is no series of facts and intervening vacua, but a continuous stream. Now the belief in free will is incompatible with the idea of a continuous, uniform, undivided, indivisible flow. The belief presupposes that every single action is isolated and indivisible; it is an atomic theory as regards volition and cognition. - We misunderstand facts as we misunderstand characters, speaking of similar characters and similar facts, whereas both are non-existent. Further, we bestow praise and blame only on this false hypothesis, that there are similar facts, that facts exist, corresponding to a graduated order of values. Thus we isolate not only the simple fact, but the groups of apparently equal facts (good, evil, compassion, envious actions, and so forth). In both cases we are wrong. --- The word and the concept are the most obvious reason for our belief in this isolation of groups of actions. We do not merely thereby designate the things; the thought at the back of our minds is that by the word and the concept we can group the essence of the action. We are still constantly led astray by words and actions, and are induced to think of things as simpler than they are, as separate, indivisible, existing in the absolute. Language contains a hidden philosophical mythology, which however careful we may be, breaks out afresh at every moment. The belief in free will -- that is to say, in similar facts and isolated facts -- finds in language its continual apostle and advocate."

#11 Nietzsche's "Wanderer and His Shadow

7.

REALITY

Every time I read some of Hegel or one of his descendents who proclaim they are studying what is, or what really is, or who writes phenomenologically so I can tease myself into thinking that reading is like thinking processes or like what really is, really, I feel like I do not understand. What is the problem that this declaration of what really is, is made over and over, and over again? What is the un-real that we are now supposed to, urged to, look for the real? (I suspect, as well, that some notion of what is the present, when is the 'now' of the *'here and now,'* is much more problematic than a modest intellectual comfort would allow!)

On the other hand, I have been faced on two occasions recently with what turned out to be a positive defense of studying and teaching the world *as it is*. Perhaps I have gotten carried away with the notion of being protected as a (tenured) professor in the reclusive nooks and crannies of academe. Perhaps I have become enamored with the notion of performance; of doing what I do, essentially in the public domain, or of relating the University to society, or of looking for some audience in the *at-large*.

I have (and am) in any case an interest in the present age; in the now of here and there and everywhere; a strong sense of an ongoing present. But the problem is that the strains and straits of academe, trying to carve out a place of strength and ownership and the what-ness of an institution which is no longer in favor, wants to retreat. They are *worried*, I guess, that scholarship is being attacked—or afraid that they have no existence except within their academic genealogies, they attack me and mine for teaching the *actual*, the what is, as if this is at odds, at war with the texts which inform society, the present.

Ideas, in the books and texts of all of time - of no time within all of time - this is what they proclaim is their study. I, they say, am *pragmatic and/or a pragmatist*. I, bemused, accept that descriptive title, feeling that ideas are informed by, tested in, resonate within some *actual*, some *real*, where they can work, where they can fail. They, dealing in ideas informed by some genealogy, some history which has become its own truth in veneration, seem to find *anything actual* a little seedy, a bit tawdry, and its practitioners cloaked in veils of the same cloth: seedy, tawdry, *salesmen* turned to pseudo-thinkers, hyping some visions of what sells, driving out the good goods with an inferiority of the pragmatic, the actual, of what is.

I am sympathetic, compassionate, want to know, curious to a fault; wanting to understand where we are and how we got here; wanting to teach and study all the texts and histories, but am cast into the pragmatic, the applied: the opposite, somehow, of some poorly cast Platonism calculated to obscure as much as to light-up.

They, in the name of defending ideas, of methods, gather arrogance like the lint-balls which form on wool garments, an aura around their persons, glowing. I—always misplaced or unplaced or still searching—want to know how the world works, what is right, what is correct, what is knowing, and how do I search for truth or for wisdom, by whatever its occurring: first defend, then attacked, attack, then think and look and write and wonder even while I prefer knowing, or arguing.

Or I am posing, trying desperately to save reality by seeking synonyms and apologisms acceptable to those who think words savor power.

Framing Reality: Plato (following Pythagoras, following Parmenides...) seems to have figured out a way to frame the nature of reality in such ways as to take us away from our bodily experience, and to proclaim as (really) real, that which is unchanging, formal, idea(l)s. The real becomes the real of the imagined and of the imagination.

It is, for the moment at least, less interesting to see how this happens than to be truly astonished that it could happen at all. How is it that anyone, any particular mode of thought and being, could replace or derogate other modes? We *are* all of the above, all of our being: imagination and experience.

Moreover, this move set up the subsequent development: that we begin/began to question our very existence. If our true *reality* is that of the imagination, of the/some *essential in being* which is knowing the unchanging forms, then the actuality of being is diminished—going, going... That is, the framing of *reality as forms*, as a story about being, seems to have attacked *actual being*, bodily being which is clearly capable of snorting and farting as well as doing advanced mathematics. It is as if we find some reality by standing outside of experience and then diminish bodily experience as if giving into desires is what is wrong with life. So we have learned to define reality and then treat that definition as if it is reality itself.

This has been accomplished by splintering (bodily) experience into two opposing categories, and raising the one while diminishing the other (if done actively or passively, it will make a difference to the development of subsequent thought): mind over body, body beneath mind. By doing this—by diminishing the category—apparently we are able to make the lesser diminish to disappearance. While this solved (for Plato) the problem of death by banishing it, this framing of reality *works* by making life appear chimerical.

Obviously, we are mind and body, both, in some relationship which is from time to time, situation, and circumstance, paradoxical. Is the possibility of framing reality to include, thence to exclude, aspects of being—a result of resolving some paradox? How then do we recognize paradox? Where, in our experience, is paradox *located*?

Categories and Taxa: Categories intercept, perhaps actualize the perceptual. Categories (Aristotle: *Organum*) are about definitions located at once *in* the world, *in* language, *in* ourselves. Categories are, particularly, about how we see and actualize the world; as others do as well.

Categories are sets of words which *have/share* a commonness (into which we *read*). This commonness is at once abstract and located in the world that is actual. A category is a definition, a gathering principle, derived from or attributed to the words and their referents-meanings.

The categories are each well-delimited and bounded, but indefinite in the size of their membership: at once finite and infinite.

The delimitation of categories has to do with how others (parents, the parental generation: m/others especially) already delimit the world: thus the actual is how adults conceptualize the world. The actual and the real may thus coincide or be somewhat different. The actual consists of how we/I/you conceptualize the world in terms of categories: what is this object?

Or that one? Is it a...? What is this particular object that it is like others of its kind; i.e., its category?

Talk (i.e., sentences, phones, etc.) is intrinsically located in the actual, not in the real. Talk is to/with other persons, thus within the structure of the actual. Talk consists of words or other units (i.e., members of categories) tied together syntactically in an order which is generally not located in the actual (or irrelevant to it.) Thus a sentence is not a syntactic string of words but a string of members of syntactically ordered categories which a speaker and hearer will understand in equivalent ways. Members of categories are existentially very well constrained, and very little arbitrary. That is, in any particular setting, the words to be used are more, rather than less, definite (contra Saussure).

Goodness and Malignity:

"At first men imposed their own personalities on Nature: everywhere they themselves and their like, i.e., their own evil and capricious temperaments, hidden, as it were, behind clouds, thunder-storms, wild beasts, trees, and plants: it was then they declared Nature was evil. Afterwards there came a time, that of Rousseau, when they sought to distinguish themselves from Nature: they were so tired of each other that they wished to have separate little hiding places where man and his misery could not penetrate: then they invented 'nature is good.'"

Nietzsche: *Dawn of Day* #17

If we can control the definition of nature and the definition of human nature, can we control destiny; the idea of destiny; the idea of human nature? (Where are we, am I, within these sand castles, rising higher as the waters of narrative wash in upon my feet?)

Theories and Actuality: Three economic theories over three centuries *illuminate* (he said) many things about the city and how we live our lives. But there is somehow a gap of some size between the theories, the depictions and the actualities of living which are so much denser, more particulate than the theories (Samuel Bass Warner).

I wondered what that meant: how do people act, what do they do, and how do they conceive being and doing? What is the relation between *motivational psychologies* and social life? Have these theories (e.g., Adam Smith, Marx, Veblen) encompassed some surreptitious social descriptions in their theories of individual action? On what are these based?—new times, new societies; old theories? Where are the connections, what the fabric between self and society in terms of economic survival and/or success?

This disconnection, the attempt to claim that theories would lead to some deeper knowing, reminded me of a talk by (I. Cohen) a historian of science, talking about the history of anatomical illustration. It seems that the body, fully dissected and in front of expert eyes was still not explicable until a series of graphic depictions (not necessarily directly mapping the body) of the interconnections were gradually developed or invented. That is, we could not *see what there is* until we (gradually?) learned about seeing in some *new* ways. Is this true of the city, the actual as well?

Still we *know* what the body is: its outlines and boundaries; we understand that it exists in some senses as an entity with integrity. We can touch it, photograph it, and imagine it within the scale(s) of life as we *are* it, just the same size.

What models, what graphics, what depictions would help us to see the city? Is a city an entity in much the same senses as the body? Is either the body or the city the same as reality?—the same as the actual?

Real and Actual: I use the notion of *actual* to refer more to my experiential/existential being, and the word *real* to designate some framework of thought in which more widespread concepts of being are ensconced.

It is not at all clear that I/we experience the world directly, unenhanced or cast within expressions and theories about the world. It is not clear, even, that we live exactly within the present, bound as we are by our definitions of ourselves in terms of past notions of who we would/should be, in terms of future concepts of might or would have been. The actual is the word I use for the closest approximation to my experiencing that I can dredge out of my most careful and honest being self.

The notion of the real (and of reality) has been used, in Western thought at least, as a framework in terms of which we calculate our being. It forms a theory at once of the nature of being human as well as a measured notion of who and what we are, why we are, where we have been, and whence we go. It has seemed to me that since Parmenides we have fallen in love with the human imagination, surprised somehow that we have extension beyond our material being, and wishing to make this ability into a theory of transcendence: a deity, notions of purpose and causation, a sense of being caused more by powers and agency *outside* of the human condition, than by the actual facts of our being conceived, born, growing and changing in ways we tend to diminish even as we cast our development within metaphorical histories, rather than in noting how we live.

In the Pythagorean/Platonic tradition (*Republic X*), we already have diminished our being (e.g., we are in the habitual framework of measuring the size of our being), by contrasting life with the ideality of the *true* reality of the forms of the formal, and the ideas of the ideality.

My principal objection to the notion of the real over the actual is that in submitting to the concept of our being which is derived and diminishing, we grow ever smaller even as we increase in age and conceptual power, searching for some directed end more than engaging in living *itself*. Attempted solutions, such as Kierkegaard's suggesting that we live as if we are/were the Christ of the New Testament or as the *overman* of Nietzsche, never quite come back to our own being sufficient to the task of overcoming the real. My *meditations on...Next Places* seems to me more cast in the actual than these others. But there are a variety of visions existing upon this earth which tell and foretell how to be at one with oneself and with the earth and with others: Amerindian, Confucian which less portray the necessity of an external utopia than the Western Christian and Islamic which necessitate the directness of an eschatology to tell us who and that we are.

In the *actual* we are unquestionably existent; whereas the *real* casts doubt upon our being and forces us to think upon death (Plato *Phaedo*) as a locus for theories of being and of knowing. In the real we tend to think from our being as static, while the actual is ongoing and changing and becoming and the problematic is more in growth and directedness and living each day sufficiently.

"**But can you *prove* you exist?**" He shouted gleefully...almost. A certain deepened sense of cynicism finding no objects placed in text by-passing experience turning into a nihilism which challenged any notion of reality. The speaker, a foreign thinker from another country, another tradition, could not respond to this not exactly self-assured attack. The speaker, a Confucianist, returned to his first principles, beginning with an experientially loaded statement of his own being and presence: how else would we be here, how else could we now, think, consider? The academic-turned-scholastic wanting certainty following from texts removed from experience, finding none because there were none he could find, retreated to a plaintive self-assault secure in the knowledge of no knowledge.

What answer could *satisfy* when the actuality of the common presence of speaker and questioner did not speak for itself?

Why, I asked, did people question their own existence when existence and experience is the be-all and end-all of life and of knowledge? Is it a fear of death (or a fear of the fear of death?) which stands life on its head: easier to deny life than to deal with the fear (of fear?)? Is it a belief in texts being the beginning point of all being, writing over being, which leads us down this path toward nothingness? Is it some realization of the vastness of knowledge which no one of us can master which reduces each person to insignificance, questioning existence? Is it the sense of an uncaring Nature where chance is a cosmic jokester placing us here on earth pointlessly?

No! Existence is its own proof, needing as well the testimony of the generations, of mother and families to certify. The "*I am*" is sustained by the moral acts of others who raise us to survive when infancy is not yet its own guarantee. This is why I exist, and needs no further explanation nor apologetic. Just who is reading this or asking the question of existence, except someone who is?

Analogous Paradoxes: On hearing a talk just yesterday on *The Critique of Cynical Reason* I wondered if the Platonic paradox of examining life by grasping personal death, applied as well to the examination of cynical thought; that, to understand cynicism one must move to the outer edges of cynicism, grasping life and experience as the ultimate *cosmic joke*?

I asked the author where he found himself standing; where, that is, is his position grounded? He said he found himself *floating*, trying only to show the dialectic tension between idealism and existentialism.

I, sensing his angst—an existential Angst it appeared—suggested that was exactly the paradox: that he couldn't find grounding, having become the cynic's cynic, and was drifting toward an idealism which he claimed (& believed?) he was refuting. He, declaring (over and over and over...) the end of metaphysics, suggesting an examination of the body (*orality*), stuck in the scholarship of scholarship, withdrawing from his own experience, trying to please, berated, cajoled, condemned; but he took us nowhere we had not already been. "What if some (ghost of) philosophy entered this room in the next moment or two, in the guise of some new philosopher, would you recognize her?" I asked. He smiled wanly.

The banishment, the denial of morality, also an aspect of the position, he declared. There was (is) no morality. It (morality) always turned *strategic*. "Show me a moral person and I would believe it, accept it," he declared.

I challenged him by raising the current Christian Fundamentalist's strategy to act out of what seemed perfectly moral to them. "No," he stuttered, "they weren't really moral." I retorted that he, having banished the category of morality, would not see it even if it were to.

Is this form of scholarship of necessity a kind of intellectual voyeurism? Or what?

How Many Tracks: How many tracks—like trains—do we run in our mind's thinking, in our being's being (William James' (1892) *stream* of consciousness? It has seemed to me that most of us *run* two or more at once, simultaneously. We may run more, if idealists, if the present visible world is not the entirety; how it is, and how it might, or ought to be.

Yet we do not seem obviously splintered, clearly lacking coherence. The stream of consciousness has no clear forks, no exact places where brooklets of thought conjoin, leave, or run in parallel courses. Our minds do not split exactly, like the schizophrenic of dissociated character (Eve's three faces or Sybil's several selves).

I think about this, about those other things, the ideas running in motion, apparently much of the time, then surfacing at another place much like loons' diving. Some tracks seem most pleasant and I like to call upon them to loll in, to help to banish the unpleasantries; to put myself to sleep or fill-in idle time or the boredom of repetitive exercises. Others bring senses of sadness, or warn of panic, of mistakes, of wishes I had not had or deeds I had not done. Some tracks seem past or in some other eventness; others, fantasies which alter bodily feeling, other sheer feelings whose turn is to stimulate particular thought arenas and other tracks.

Sitting here writing down a particularity of linear coherence, my mind's tracks go on. How many? What directions do they go, on what planes, in which geometries do they gravitate? On which ones are being, imagination, loves and lusts and fears and fantasies and myths and...?

Not obviously dissociated, the foundational persona of my being asks how I hold this *thing of being* together. I suspect it is an active process—reinventing myself each little while or each next day, and that the truth of truth will not be seen until we note this modality of regeneration within our being.

How The World Works: Any one theory, any over-arching scheme for observation, description, and analysis will not tell us how the world works. Only the world can tell us, and only if we can listen and hear. At any one time, in any moment in the history and flow of history, the details are too spread out, not yet congealed or consolidated, so they are difficult to gather. In any moment there is a little here, some over there, a glimpse, a promise. Some issues are cyclical, generational, and we must study to know just where we are within them; some involved in how we know others' knowing us and our knowing. Even if we listen, even hear, to grasp the flow is to think we remain motionless in the Heraclitean river; not noticing the stationary banks, however close or distant. Not noticing ourselves not noticing ourselves.

This is not to say that the world doesn't *work*, that some sense of flow or of determinism is not everywhere actual, but that different parts, different aspects and modes partake of existence differentially: from different perspectives/histories/contexts within a variety of logics, attending now to

403

one, next to another of these shapes or frameworks; hearing corrective voices, plotting strategy, or reacting merely.

Not every person partakes in an independency of reality in any total sense. We are of a kind of oneness while yet moving in particulate manners. In figuring the working of the world, we can only remain some aspect of it, while yet finding some position without; change, yet remain grounded in the abstraction of observation from which we operate - Olympian and mundane: making the exotic, ordinary; and the mundane, exotic.

Recent attacks and implosions on the certitude of scientific knowledge seem more to stem from the insistence of questions of human (one's personal) existence, and the arrogances of *a little knowing goes a long way*, than that there is no knowledge. All this recalls to us the necessity to rethink human nature and the foundations of our knowing just at this historical moment.

Aspects of Change: Who I am in any moment has many aspects while yet being one: a *sufficient* integrity. What change is, what changes in me is no mere contradiction, no argument or antithesis, though this may also work to change me.

Here am I, yes; not, here I am, no!

What's new? What attracts, pulls, catches my attention? Fashion, style, beauty pulls. Ugliness repels, repulses; flying bats bring out the fear places within me ducking all the while. Do I yield? A question of yielding? (Is ritual, religion a non-yielding? - a resistance to a pull which tries to regenerate a stasis, a re-search for some (earlier) integrity?)

But to be pulled, even to begin to dwell outside... but, to dwell, outside? Where is that?

Here am I, yes, being struck by fancy, pulled persuaded by a form. I, substantial, contented, am altering myself? Who am I, now; then? Will I rejoin myself, pull back? Will I reincorporate, or merely grow older?

Here am I. What's new is now older. No surprise, no pull; for it is me, am I. I was not yet, now partake in... Not rejected, not exactly accepted.

What was style, was vanity, now is who I am, now changed from before; not noticed. Ready, in-ready, for new forms.

Bed-Rock: The issue of there being a purely objective world which exists outside of my/our being continues to locate what might be called *reality*. Much of the ink of philosophical history has been spilt, like the milk of human (un)kindness, over this so-called issue.

As if solving the problem of reality will tell us something more about...what much of the history problem is what it might tell us about. Maybe it is all our individual story, representation; the world is how we make it to be, and nature is a story which our minds *tell* our minds in some inner dialogue which has no participation. The Stoic, the Taoist at work trying to deal with one's feelings tamed. Sensing all there is, at war with being too sensitive for my own good. Maybe...

I reach-out and touch the world; the world pushes back. There, now, doesn't that prove *its* existence? Well enough for some. But there are others, many who have emerged particularly in the West, who are then urged to wonder about proving their own existence. "If only," muses Wittgenstein, "if only I could prove my right hand..." (My right hand, busily typing this missive, wonders if this Wittgenstein couldn't write, or eat, or wipe his...?! Possibly he was left-handed and this was a left-handed accounting for *righteous* behavior.)

In other words, much of the desired *proof* for the existence of the world of reality pushes back on offering, then finding acceptable, proof of my own (anyone's) being—and even further, of the sort of proof which would somehow guarantee the existence of some deity, who would in turn certify ours. The problem of reality is not merely proof, but authoritative certifications that I exist to know the world which exists somewhat, but not exactly completely, independently of me or you or anyone or anything. Self-authorization, sufficient authority that I trust myself to know knowing? Identity *or* reality; identity *versus* reality?

The problem of the issue is that the question of the nature of any external objective reality has resided upon the more hidden surreptitious issue of *whether anyone exists*, whether the deity exists, and so on; and also, on what might constitute proof: some complicated chain of thinking, usually, about the nature of what causality might mean, precisely. This issue has become particularly complicated, even poignant, with the rise of television, in which we have lost the sense of place, of our geometrification of world and boundaries; one's extent ironically grows globally even as our being grows more isolated.

Since Hume (1748), at least, the skepticism about knowing causality has tended to split the problem into the two camps of those who deal with science and merely assume something about reality, and those who concentrate exclusively on the place of the human: knowledge, language, narratives, and all that. A lot of issues, many of which might bear on the so-called problem, seem to fall into the interstices of skepticism, a place inhabited perhaps by the stench or perfumes of all the sensory *stuff* which both frightens and intrigues us.

The bed-rock, at bottom, is there is no bed-rock. It is either infinitely thick/thin, or retreats especially as we move toward *it*. We can model it, but cannot assure ourselves that it *is*. A right hand, give it to me and I can prove anything; everything.

The Body and the Knowing-I: Obvious! Astonishing! The Western (but others also) temptation to act as if the human—each I—is particularly the stuff by which we know knowing, and is particularly *not* the stuff which is my body-I, never fails to amaze me.

What amazes me even more is that most other *thinkers* do not think as I think, but relegate the body to some realm away from the knowing-I: material, mechanical; likened either to other living but non-human creatures, or to some machine, increasingly portrayed as a computer/robot which has been built by us to look just as we look, feel as we feel, think as we think?

The simulacrum becomes I become simulacrum. (Text-as-world.)

Perhaps the primary problem in probing the nature of reality—for us—is that we have calculated being human within a very narrow and particular calculus: an oppositional dualism in which the bag-o-bones which we are is relegated to some place in a reality which is known by some other aspect of our being: the mind—which is definitively not the body.

Perhaps it, as Plato says, *houses* the mind. And if we remain somehow within Platonic thinking about being, it is linked precisely and particularly with non-being (*Sophist*): either associated or driven by calculations about (personal?) death. Plato's philosopher is instructed to keep his eye upon life from the after-life and to work continually and rigorously at excluding the body from existence lest the desires, lusts, and loves, and sicknesses interfere with our ability to think and to know.

To know, therefore, is to know what is external to our being physical-material. The objective world, in this construction, would seem to be primarily (ontologically prior) physical and to include our being only as a kind of second-order distancing of the body. As it were, we are cautioned to watch our bodily being; a looking-out from the mind's eye or the eye's mind; location as dislocation.

If, as I think, at least some aspects of the problematic of reality are due/related to some analysis of being human. Then the notion that the body and intellection are *not* related, not the same, has to be probed at length in order to begin to determine how the issue of reality has been cast: rather, miscast!

But the body is, as Nietzsche also says, what there is and all there is, and the mind is some story about the body. The fact is that the body and intellection are one and the same. To leave the body out of our stories and theories about thinking and the mind and what is human, is to leave a great deal of surreptitious theory wandering about, infiltrating our thinking but not probed to any depth. How can we claim to be depicting reality when we do not work at accurately depicting ourselves, the interpreter of that reality?

(A century post Nietzsche, we know more, know better: the body exists within a world of other bodies; the individual physical body, the knowing individual emerges from sociality; not the Hobbesian joining-with, but our being is emergent and continuously in a complicated dialectic with others and a *moving self*.)

Nature: Similarly to the body, *nature* is depicted as being outside of our being human. Or within the Western dualism nature is the bodily expression of our being, with the emphatic claim that the truly knowing human stands outside of nature: described in the context of various terms all of which are in some opposition to nature: culture, art, artificial, linguistic (= rational, epistemological, logical, meaning, conscious, etc.).

Nature is either what precedes culture (et al), or logically what follows and is left over residually after we have done the analysis of what we are that nature is not. So even when we grant some existence to nature which is prior to being, the methodological approach is *after metaphysics*. (Or within postmodern narrative, nature becomes our projection of it; and we are either the dislocated originary subject, or our location is forever being displaced.)

Two major schemes have derived from this thinking: one historical and the other primarily technical. Both suggest that the human has moved away from nature, or is removed from nature. Thus both approaches to nature derive from an accounting of this movement away from whatever is considered to be nature (a concept in rapid flux at this historical moment).

The first removal is the historical notion that by various means we became removed/removed ourselves from nature historically: the origin of language, meaning, and consciousness (etc.), culture, art (and let's not forget that the notion of rational derives from Plato/Pythagoras in which geometry and musical ratio of the whole notes of the musical scale define what is logical thinking). In this portrayal we are moved to invent theories of how we got to think through language (restricted usually to humans...origin of language), the search for the Adamic language (because the Adam of Genesis named the animals their *true* names), and if/when we rediscover this originary language we will re-discover nature, truly (and human nature and the deity's nature.)

In this mode of thinking presumptively, the attempt is to locate nature via *unpeeling* history to find how we were originally, when we were *at one* with nature, or more simply aspects of nature. Within this theory that we became removed historically from nature, the general approach is via speculative history: the search for the *Archeus*—Jung/Buddhism, etc., and treats nature as if it is/were timeless and unchanging.

Mixed up in here are battles between the Biblical Genesis accounts of our being and the evolutionary Biological ideas which also tend to focus in this opposition on the nature of originary causality: particularly of what being human means: why modern Biology tends to focus on *ultimate* rather than *proximate* causes in interpreting evolution; some search for a *purer* human not corrupted by nature, etc. (Hobbes' *natural law*, Rousseau).

The primarily technical approach to nature has to do with some notion that we are (now) removed from nature, but less seeking some historical *return*. This has mostly to do with machines, these days particularly of robotic computers which will have *artificial* intelligence—the term is very revealing of the orientation to being human and to our nature.

The methodological mode is deeply *comparative* in which we attempt to understand our understanding as being roughly (or even actually) like a *smart* machine (i.e., it thinks like we think we think). Indeed, the operations of the machine which we know because we have designed it, give us insight into how we (must?) think, revealing our nature.

Since Descartes, the same mode of thinking is used in comparing other species to humans: there has been a conflation of machines and non-humans. We use apes (or other smart animals—morphology used to reign but presently we are more open to any large-brained or long-lived species) to tell how we are. In both cases of animals and machines, we find that *they* and their study are more revealing of how we are, than the study of humans in any sense per se.

Where do these approaches *leave* nature? In the historical mode, the presumption is that we exist somehow outside of nature; in the comparative, that we are much like nature, if not as studiable as other creatures of nature or of our imaginations. Nature *itself* isn't much probed as a concept in either approach, being *bootlegged* in our back pockets in the comparative notion, and only residual in the historical. In both cases, nature remains as some sort of unexamined bedrock, to be used, one supposes, when it seems conceptually *useful*. (Useful: capable of convincing us to act socio-politically in particular ways that we might not otherwise → Aristotle's *Politics*.)

Nature's God: In Jefferson's *Declaration of Independence* (1776), the *deistic* notion of the God of Nature is employed to keep the notion of the state independent from the concept of the nation as endowed by authority of a *theistic* God. This was done in contrast with the earlier use of the deity to justify and authorize a monarch to rule over the people. In Jefferson's notion (derived principally from Locke–"Essay Concerning Human

Understanding") Nature is a concept which is to be probed by the thinking man—this includes all *white men*, at least. In this context, nature is a concept which is (has been) useful as a humanistic strengthening over and against external authority: monarch or church. The idea of the *strengthening* is to create the possibility that we are each of us capable of entering into a social contract and thereby to rule ourselves. The method, at least as it comes to us in the present age, is that of science.

The human is an aspect of nature, and requires probing within the context of how to see our seeing as natural creatures. We are not removed by dint of language or of the deity granting us the ability to know to know God, truly. But we are natural, living like the abundance of live animals whose otherness is not incomparable with our own. Nature's God is not the transcendent notion like a Gaia who has determining power; not even the winder of the clock which gave start to the mechanical clock-workings of the 17th and 18th century and began the process which has led to the present age. How to find out who and what we are and how is the world, became the major tasks if we would approach the truth and truths of all of time. And the human is no larger, but certainly no smaller than the life which we experience.

The game of time and of history lie critically within this formulation of the world and our being within it. *If nature* - then the temptation is to take us out of any present determined and overly set by our adherence to some past which told us how we were to be even before we gave birth to ourselves. Experience is all!—Though we fight still over whether it is even possible to remain intact even while we engage the world, mostly watching ourselves watching rather than doing. Experience, then, becomes the central metaphor for figuring how we are; know; think.

The Invention of Evil: Aspects of the complexities of a world in which we each wake up one day to the realization that we exist, and realize that we have little idea of how we got here. This clashes, as it were, with the experiencing of the present moment as it appears that the story we tell ourselves about what is, is joined by another story having to do with getting here. We live either dual-ly or paradoxically or (ironically) both.

What to do with the fact of the realization? *Nothing* does not handle it, nor does its banishment. We are not only here and now, but then and there, and now and here, and it is puzzling only if things go well. If they do not go so well, there is a trouble. But there is more...

Not only here and now, but was and will be. How we got here transduces into when we will no longer be, further complicating the present experiencing. Present and past, life and death. The duality and paradoxicality multiply in complexity. And that is not so bad when things go well. We are tempted either to heighten the present experiencing or to bury and background it beneath the complexity of its ongoing realization.

When things do not go so well, when the present experiencing buzzes more than hushes, the paradox calls attention to itself, creating a valuation of good and not-so-good, of worry, of bad and wonder of judgment.

The present always asking to be judged contrastively even while it judges its own judging, often finds an upside and its opposition. The temptation to give names to the aspects of the paradox turning into poles grants them even more memory, more reality, more censorship and critique of present experiencing. Good and not-so-good transform into the desired and the feared, or the sublime and the superficial. And the notion of evil is granted agency in our lives. We yield increasingly the present to the external and judge being-not more than being-yes. We give name to ourselves as enemy, calling ourselves the evil which attacks us even as we attack ourselves in the name of...

Conceptual Change: One can come to see the world **in** radically different ways from how she did previously. In some instances of conceptual change the prior view is still partially available and visible; in some others it seems virtually impossible to know the world other than how it now appears. As teacher, I try to take/force my students into conceptual change in as many arenas as possible—with the lesson of how to do this as autodidacts when they no longer study with me. As autodidact my studies are often directed toward quite new understandings and modes of seeing. Which is/are the real?—and how do changes in knowing and understanding reflect this. When is there progress toward the real?

As a ("good amateur") violinist I frequently attempt to play pieces which are beyond my (present) abilities. And it is often not simply a case of having insufficient technique. Sometimes I cannot see nor hear nor imagine how to play a piece or section; how to *get* my fingers to do something new or different from what they already *know*.

I am playing at a particular level of competence, at the edges of my technique; but now I wish to go beyond, to be able to do something I cannot yet do. But in many cases, I now know that I am closer than I was. I have *improved* and become more capable—and believe that if I proceed in the *right* ways I can eventually come to play a passage well. The problem how to break-through, to ascend beyond the present plateau...

The moment of break-through is never obvious: one day I couldn't; the next I could, with some practice, and (usually) increased strength, and some better sense of what the nature of the next doing is. And if things are going well, the next day and the next after that, I retain the ability to play at the higher level. Now I reincorporate the remainder of my technique and knowing, knowing now that I know better and can do more.

Logic: Thinking that thinking is to think logically, to solve problems, to do as Plato's slave in the *Meno* a geometric proof; axiomatic as defining of the term itself. An historical resolution to the very idea of paradox being the path of incorrectness. Indeed, framing the very idea of what is correct and truth and knowing, logic has been characterized not only as the architectonic but as the definition of what it means particularly to be fully human. Equivalence, negation, the notion that one idea follows from others, that causality directs itself to direct ourselves, the very idea of beginning and middle, and the concept of towardness: if's, but's, and/or's, thus-es, thences, and therefores; the notion of proof which is so capable of being generalized that such proof is the same as the truth of all the ages.

There is a great deal of power here, and some large amount of truth which can be transferred to our knowing the world. But much is also left out in our hurry to know the world without attending to the fact that it is we humans who are doing the knowing (and the reporting). And there is more story to tell, more to the caveat of Protagoras that (hu)man is the measure of all things.

Ask of those aspects of Heraclitus which remain alive in our being about the quest for questions of change and permanence over which he puzzled so long ago. All is change; all is permanence—our minds so small that we cannot have it both ways at once, as if knowing's boundaries were also and always limits and limitations.

Puzzles and paradoxes; paradoxes and puzzles. So in love have we been with the possibility of knowing at all that we cannot see ourselves viewing ourselves to know when measuring is measured, and when it is not. So afraid of the fear of paradox that we had to settle upon life as an aspect of the forever, a form of life as death. So resolved (to) the paradox of change and permanence that just a bit too much change augurs chaos. If not logic!?

Consider, instead, that Heraclitus is/was correct: that all is change!

The intrigue is that the world seems, then, like Plato's cave turned inside-out. We live on the edges of our senses; just on the verge of being out of control, or, as Heraclitus put it, he *loved the senses best*? What sense here? Too much light, we try to look past the most of it to see what lies in shadows. Here I am. Take me! All of me!

If we follow Heraclitus, the more actual puzzle is not the human, nor time, nor what precisely is knowing, but that the world *ever holds still*—as it surely seems to. The "I" I call myself endures even as I change from moment to moment. The objects which tell me that even I can be objective do not evanesce like the ghosts of Geists or of Zeit. As Korzybski (1933) told us some time ago, we humans have figured out how to *bind time*. Is the "I" I call myself, some process by which we find the "I"; or merely what it is? Part of the human is the ongoing ability and propensity to actively hold things and oneself *still*.

What is logic resides at some conceptual places within the fixities of the time structures which we have cast upon ourselves framing the world. It derives from the knowing how our mothers/others know; not merely or particularly from some inbuilt propensities.

This Heraclitean move leaves the world as it (always) was, still moot, still requiring us to know ourselves and our knowing how the "I" of who I am endures even while I am in change always. Paradox? Yes. Grab it!

The response is in the neglected aspects of language wherein grammar and rhetoric battle each other for ever deeper obscurity. It sits also in the *within which* we have neglected various aspects of languaging while concocting a story of what is particularly human. This has, in its turn been a circularity which has told us "how we are that we are-not"—humans are not-animals, not-machines, not-deities, while we have neglected how we are and come to be.

Indeed, we concoct stories endlessly, while we do *not* watch ourselves watching ourselves be and become. It is as if we do not want to know knowing but are in love with narratives and poetry which have cast all of being within ancient quests and questions.

The response is located in part within the coming to name objects: we do not come to know the world in any early sense, directly. We come to name names, to name the world in the Adamic sense of being disciple to our parents who gave names to the world to give us in their turn. We know knowing, that is, as our parents frame the world; not *as it is* in any individuated sense of our being.

Knowing, that is, is primarily rhetorical—we know our parents' knowing. Then it is rhetorical: we are presented the world as a set of questions and learn the proper (rhetorical) responses. We learn that the world of being is paradoxical: it is one and many, many and one - our parents tell us so, and authorize our believing it to be, and to be as they live it and tell us it. We emerge as individual propositional logical beings within the notions of logic which have "worked" and are at work in getting us here.

The grammar of our being is no mere arrangement of categorical forms of nouns and verbs and the spelling out of their particularities. It is at once rhetorical and individuating: a system whereby the statements of our being (logical) are situated rhetorically as responses to questions put to us by those who authorize our continuing being: being like them by becoming like ourselves. And we come to be logical. A smaller aspect of our being has been taken to its greatest heights in our attempts to account for our being humanly unique-s, as if we fear rather than love knowing *knowing*.

The relation between the circularity and the triangularity does not describe reality or our *partaking* within it, but is derived from the more central aspects of our continuing being. To raise logic to its current hegemony over knowledge is to neglect asking questions such as how we come to have a consistent identity, and to wring our hands rather than dealing with Heraclitus as we intended.

Authority: In actuality we who survive beyond the birth of our birth are continually authorized creatures. The Western myth of the individual who exists as a primary ensconced in a material body is the result of the historical inability to account for human knowledge and imagination: the love of the infinite and the unchanging over the finite-in-process, and the false certitude that paradox must be resolved else the universe fail and fall.

As physical individuals we are *lethal*; we fail and fall unless there is sufficient love and food and talk and a breathing-of-life into us. Those who feed us and give us our being also empower us to empower ourselves—actuality, skill in self-creating, and the wish to go on indefinitely. Our parents authorize us, then teach us how to authorize ourselves, and others in our turn. We learn to name the objects and movements and relations of the world as our parents live that world. We grant authority to that viewing of the world, having at all times in our thinking the necessity to think as our authorities do, as well. We historically learnt how to make authors of our own concepts.

Authority is the source and foundation of our being and derives initially and frequently through life from other persons. It is, as Heraclitus, the *common-sense* in which we live the reality of wakefulness, which guarantees our continuance. In sleep, we are alone, and many theories of being (e.g., Amerindian) value this aspect of our being more highly than when we are awake. If we value Heraclitus' thinking, we can note contrastively that being in common-sense means truly that we think as others think, and think as they would think, thus authorizing the world.

The authority is also the author, the source of the thinking and writing which entices, instructs, or delights us. The author is the ultimate *rhetor*, certifying the sense of who we would be like, or as ourselves.

There is a tendency at various points in life and in history to de-authorize ourselves, then others—or others, thence ourselves. At these recurring moments of weakness and/or fear (which can be understood as the weakening of authority within or without), we may seek authority in other loci: beyond being: in the past (e.g., Plato, Confucius, the Koran or Bible)—in some temporal locus as a president or monarch or priest—or in some *place* within our own being which we (now) define as mystical or beyond being-as-our-body. Or as in Western thought we relegate bodily being to an inferior status, also de-authorizing being, and seek authority in transcendent theories and agency.

The present age is one in which we now observe the rise of nihilism—rising as Nietzsche prophesied—from the Western obsession to be truth-seeking, thence to discover that Western thought has too often been untruthful in casting our senses away from being. As well, we experience the replacement of authority with celebrity—historically, a form of corruption where every external notion of author and authority—thence ourselves—is de-authorized, also exposing us to nihilism.

My wonder and hope is whether a tradition of teachers and teaching is sufficient to overcome the fall of authority, and how to be/become the Teacher being neither self- nor other-destructive!? (Sarles, 2013)

Agency: Lying within, about, and around the notion of authority is our wishful tendency to grant agency to the variety of objects and concepts which grant meaning to meaning.

The preliminary problematic is in granting agency to ourselves and sustaining both the agency and its continuing possibility. Within this problematic we seem to be able to grant agency to all sorts of concepts which have little to do with life or living: deities, natural occurrences, mythical and mystical concepts, texts, and structural abstractions such as language, society, and community.

The inability to see how we do as we do resides, I think, in the Western (particularly) tendency to assume that each individual is the primary object in its own world (a mind within a given body). Thus the notion of having to gain or grant itself its agency seems somewhat absurd. But in the relational semiotic of the infant having to survive only in terms of the parents who feed and love it and read/project into it, its futurity, the question of individuality is at once problematic in existence and *emergent* from interaction. Whether self-agency is totally derived, some mix of intrinsic beingness, and/or in continuing interactive tension with others' viewing of oneself, agency is never continuous and guaranteed within individual being.

In developing the skills and architectonic for telling oneself that one is and who one is to be, and to continue to generate and grant this notion of agency to oneself, one simultaneously learns how to grant active being to (potentially) any concept which is like one's being: other persons (actually agency begins here as we *yield* definitional being to mothers and others), thence to anything which has attributes of personage. These include continuity of noted being, then of imagined being, the ability to isolate and to name any being or concept, the sense that others can make sense of the same concept—that one can grant it meaning. Early ones in life include the notion of today and tomorrow and yesterday, numerators, colors—most adjectives, which then take on a life of their own having noted the generality of their occurrences. (Actually this is built-into the naming of objects both in their singularity and in their universality: a *skill* well practiced by two-year olds.)

The second point is located within the learning of the language which one's parents use to describe the world, and the laying-on of that language upon our being. Here we learn - in the first instance - that names are the names of objects because...because our parents tell us that they are. Causality is itself self-directed and circular in the first instance. A book is a book, a name is the name for something, *because it is* (i.e., because we have bought into a notion of authority in already granting agency to the parent, thence to ourselves, thence to anyone/anything which makes or can make sense in that cultural setting.)

At this point we are off and running. I can do, God can do, Society and Language. The problem, existentially, is that all concepts can disappear or no longer appear, including myself—deriving, as they do, from authority and agency.

Absolute: The concept of any absolute is so bound up with humanly generated concepts of authority and agency that it is difficult to state precisely what it might mean. On the one hand there is the sense that temporality is resolved on the side of non-change and the eternal or continuing, and that space is precisely either infinite or inconsequential to existence. On the other, there is the paradox of our knowing as humans from the position of being involved in or as aspects of change, and finitely bounded. In this sense, the notion of the absolute depends on the resolution of the time and space paradoxes toward the infinite and eternal.

In quite another sense, we find little difficulty in understanding and utilizing concepts which are beyond the autonomous being of our finiteness and changingness. This can be taken to mean that we (and/or the universe) are either truly paradoxical or that within the human condition we have discovered (or are—this depends in turn on our concept of nature) ourselves and our externality.

Thus it is difficult to discern precisely whether we are talking about being human, about being human to have survived socially, about the materiality of our being which is equitable with nature and our derived knowing about ourselves, about some external agency which exists truly.

With respect to questions of change, the very concept of reality has been *captured* (and apparently remains capturable) by asserting that our senses obscure knowing and being, by claiming that the ideas of the ideal forms of rationality are the real and we are somehow subservient to them. Plato simply denies materiality, virtually banishing the body in the *Phaedo*, proclaims that death reigns over life, that we should keep our inner eye upon our concept of the absolute, and live humbly with respect to *his* depiction of the absolute. Life reality is thus chimerical. The great irony and paradox here, of course, is how we could know all of this never quite existing; always having to grapple with our being finite and having to deny actual being in order truly to exist. (It's really a continuous problematic within this construction of being and reality to grant agency to ourselves!)

Much of the history of Western (and much other) thought is then the attempt to justify some concept of the absolute as each depiction of it is variously punctured, or made to seem to skeptically doubtful that both absolute and our (now derived) being seem dubious in their turn. Since Parmenides, for example, the concept of the imagination—some extension of our being beyond our (*obvious*) mechanical-material boundedness—has caught our imagination. We play at infinite length with the unpacking of the imagination without wondering too much how it could be that we might possess that conceptual extension: analytically examining aspects of logic and other structural aspects of language without asking too deeply why these seem primary, and other aspects of our being (dualistically written out of our existence) often remain unnoted thence unexamined. (Q-R System)

This is what is particularly worrying about questions of any absolute. We have jumped from fairly narrow concepts of our being - presumably derived from some particularities of our observed and experienced existence –to some notion of the absolute. Then we grant agency and authority to these concepts and claim that they have some causal and/or determining function in our being.

While this does not seem clearly or distinctly incorrect in any overarching sense, it has certainly neglected many aspects of our being: being social and in mutual understanding, being terrestrial and in some relationships to other species, being bodily-facial, being in complicated developmental processings, being in belief systems which may determine how we see and care-for and cure ourselves, and so on. And we have used our concepts of the absolute—and our worries about how realizable and believable they are—to *justify* much of what we seem to want, much as we report on what there is. Desires/fears and the absolute seem too much in cahoots to assure us that we know knowing.

Indeed we go to amazing lengths to assure ourselves that the absolute (reality) is where we have said it is, because not being assured we often get quite discouraged and positively destructive to self and to others.

Similarly we have derived our notions of causality from (what seem like) reductions from language—logic/mathematics—somewhat less as tools to explore the universe, than as ways to justify our concepts of what truth consists in. Again, there is a battle over the very concept of truth (the absolute) in eras when our skepticism over the possibility of truth in this unchanging and non-finite sense, becomes irresolvable and paradoxical. Why not reexamine our being in these eras prior to reexamining our concepts of truth and engaging in the severe skepticisms which lead us to doubt knowing, thence our existence?

Especially this seems silly and useless when it is our existence which leads us to question our existence, rather than puzzling and celebrating it; tending to operate upon the axis of fear and wonder, tilting one way or the other.

Nature and Human Nature: Another concept caught within prior depictions of our being. There are variety of possible ideas of nature, depending primarily on whether we (see ourselves) as *looking out*, or as looking back at ourselves after we have *gone out* and now return to look at ourselves (looking out) with some newly refreshed observational and conceptual lenses; issues derived from already having grown up without specifically noting our earlier developmental being, and calling (by now) most of our being *ordinary*. Issues background themselves, our adjustments to present being captured within whatever we call comfortable, we cannot/do not *see* most of our being or beingness.

We are also caught within the conceptualization of nature as somehow different and in opposition with whatever is the human: e.g., nature is mechanical and its opposition is mind or culture or artificial and related to humans being somehow beyond nature. Nature is taken to be finite in this oppositional thinking while being outside of nature is the human condition. In this sense, nature is primary conceptually, being before whatever is human, but actually and conceptually residual in being seen as whatever is not the human; we become defined or definers less of what is, than of what is-not in particular.

Thus we search for *intelligent* life on other planets or in the universe, rejecting the concept that other terrestrial species might be intelligent, and taking the anti-natural aspects of our being (by whatever definition) and extend it to the limits of our imaginations (Sagan 1980). If, more reasonably, we see humans *within* nature, the likelihood and temptation is that we collapse metaphysics and politics, thus *reduce* the human within some prior (reductive) definition of whatever is considered to be nature. (Lorenz, 1973; Wilson, 1979)

Or we may consider the natural world primarily in speculative-historical terms—i.e., before humans technologized and colonized nature; our current living conditions being far (removed) from nature.

Similarly, the notion of evolutionary development is usually historical in the sense that the great intellectual surprise is that we ever got here. So-called *ultimate* biology (i.e., most evolutionary biologists) studies the present in terms of how the various species on earth could have (*amazingly*) survived, paying much less attention to the present or *proximate* biology; how various species actually maintain and sustain their existence beyond the very few moments of mating and extending history.

This includes the habit of taking survival to be a primary and granting it agency as the purpose for our being. As we have (since Pythagoras/Plato) raised the human over nature, the history is speculatively being rewritten to figure how we humans form some end in this notion of natural history. (How easily agency gets abducted from the human to transcendent ideas is exemplified by R. Dawkins (1976) who posits that the genes *have* the purpose of reproducing themselves, using our apparent existence as their purpose dictates.)

Within such theories of nature the difficulty of keeping cleanly separate the various thematics of nature and the depictions of theology and politics is high. Whether we want to move *closer* to nature (e.g., Rousseau, anti-chemicals), whether we see nature as *red in tooth and claw* (Tennyson and the 19th century following Darwin), whether we *bow* to our nature (usually a pessimism), or celebrate some particular line of *genetic* development (e.g., eugenics, manifest destiny, Apartheid)—overlays and interpenetrates any understandings we may have of nature.

Since our views of the human condition are stated often in terms of our "possessing" human nature, nature (itself!?) is constructed in terms which seem to predetermine how we are (to be, become). The definition of human and of nature is thus involved in a quite complicated circle of presumptions concerning how we are and how we are in relation to whatever is being called nature.

Nature: The question of where to begin: with the entire earth. The fact of the earth's gravity literally shapes all terrestrial being. We would not be the shape we are living in other gravities: we are walking, upright, two-legged creatures who are rarely in any specific locational balance (but 'always in balance'), who have/use a particular velocity. (The recent discovery of gravity in determining our human form, some three centuries after Newton's apple!)

Seeing ourselves seeing ourselves is thus doubly deceptive but equally real. We are what we are and live in the terms of that being and being seen. We see out of a shaped being toward a world which is equally what it is but could be other. *Physis* and morphology are neither direct nor simple. But what we see and/or attribute to the world overwhelms what there is and we have first to deal with that fact, story, history, politics of ideas. To know nature we need (as well) to study/know ourselves and our knowing.

Tempting as it may be to state that the "I" who I am right now who poses these questions, who would question the very concept of nature, is not the "I" who I am at all moments is at the heart of our knowing. Getting here, the effects of future knowing pressing on my present identity, the desire to be truly objective without paying all the prices this continues to demand, all contribute to the concept of nature. Can I subtract my being; how can I reduce and deduce the talk about my being, the facts of my seeing what I am wont to see, to see-through my own seeing? These are not simple puzzles, compounded further by the wondering if knowing itself is not the ultimate deception and if existence is not *really* what it seems (e.g., the current return to Cosmology—Toulmin, 1985).

The reduction of mathematics and logical languages to describe, hypothesize, and elucidate, excites and offers the guarantee of a nature which is neutral to my observing my being within my objectification of the world. But the idea that some externality exists independent of my seeing its being is no less a story than my determining solipsisms and other *-isms*.

Much is left out here. Truth is particular and circumscribed, lacking the various contexts in which meaning gains meaning. And there is the old skepticism about the truth of truth which turns upon itself when we lose faith in our own existence, and question the very possibility of knowledge. No solid foundation for knowing nature here which is not sustainable when faith in our own being falters, convincing me that the very concept of nature derives dependently upon uncovering our own place within *it*. (The sobering realization in the age of revisionism and the market economy is that destiny lies in the hands of s/he whose *definition* of human nature reigns over any enduring truth about being; why I think it crucial to study how we actually are, and to study ourselves studying ourselves).

Some notions destructive of the possibility of nature: the idea that language is *arbitrary* (Saussure, 1916), driving the issue of our knowledge of *it* back upon itself—especially within a metaphysics which assumes that the individual is the primary, the subject of the notion of nature which is fading,

fading... gone; any anti-absolutist relativism which already is cast within an opposition to that absolutism seems to devolve upon its own internal oppositional logic—not to be equated directly with cultural (or species) *relativism*s which states directly that experience is developed differently by different kinds and types. Knowing these differences does not deny the reality of nature, but is necessary to penetrate in order to know *it*.

Similarly, the notion that nature already determines who and what we are and are to be/become tends to background the nature of our experience, and to falsify the very knowing which has led to our reflections upon nature. Nature is seen as magician and mystifier given agency to create the nature of our being in order to obscure that very nature: e.g., we are our genes, who *use* us to do what they *want*. Similarly any theology whose deity has *laws* which are raised above the human condition and then used to determine it.

Also undercutting the possibility of nature are the attempts since Pythagoras/Plato to halt time or the experience/concept of process and duration, and to call attention away from our experiencing of it. This includes the essentialisms of logic, mathematics, and geometry. Not trying to claim that they don't tell us about various aspects of being, they seem to establish and defend a priori the fixity of nature which backgrounds the realities of the human's gaze and development and leads us into the vagaries of removing ourselves from our own experience, thence from the possibilities of knowing. This is to say that all presumptions (e.g., of equality, of any basics of our knowing of number, relationship, etc., are within the processes of our becoming, not directly given to our experience.).

Nature: The *filters* of our knowing nature are focused upon the apparent transparency of world-fill. Since Kant, it has been clear that nature is not precisely as it appears to the lenses of the knowing human suspending self-realization while examining the world of nature. This is not to say that there is no *objective* nature, but that we need first/also to examine our examining of *it* even while we observe, describe, hypothesize!

If we are no more than the bundles of sensations coming at us, then nature loses any substantiation; Hume's assertion prejudges the configuring of human existence. What if there is no proof of causality? Kant proffers that we have built-in to our knowing-self some sense of time and space and the intuitions which lead us to know nature at all. All a mistake, mistaken in its

423

still unexamined presumptions that the primariness of nature is its *physis*: a mind/reason placed within a body already given shape and being which we then discount even as we observe and erase and deny the nature which is outside while we deny the nature that is us.

Apparently, wanting to play in the fields of appearance, we are wont to overlook the gravity which Zarathustra (Nietzsche, 1883) figures only from afar and away and above. It is as if we each run a sale, discounting our changing physical being, even as we ponder our condition. Facts fade, the *actual* dematerializes; our being is totally/only a social construction, even and especially as we dress and groom and peer into the mirrors of our facial reflections: Narcissus rising in a cave-in; erasing the self while constructing its appearance, we gather no sense of the history of the construction of its being physical. Physical we assume, and notice no longer that we become the stature and statue we see reflected. What is the ontology, the becoming of the *physis*? To know nature, we must first know the *physis* of being human!

Two cells joined. A growth and dividing; growth and dividing enlarge and encircle; an inside, an outside now joining again. The body is surfaces; the locus of being? More growth ingesting the nutrients which it knows and uses and rejects, it intrudes, obtrudes, protrudes; formulates places and more surfaces: muscles, guts, bony prestructurings color them red and blue and yellow in the embryonic books of life. It becomes self-pumping, feeding, filtering, moving with respect to itself, its containments: a oneness, many manynesses. Which is the "I" which (I) will be?

The sex *act* acted out of theories of love, of necessity, of wanting, needing, a completion-driven sense of incompletion, a wink and stare; the true hardness of/to philosophize with a hammer, and in the twinkling of being, there is another creature. Small, helpless, it can exist, breathe for but a few hours duration. But it is imagined into being, conceived even as it is conceived; conceptualization much as conception. It is not fed, not heard, not given the breath of long life, merely as the tiny copy whose each next breath is at first so wondrous, so problematic. It is cooed to, not just the newly born, but imagined to be grown, adult, complete, a generation complete, actual, capable, real, projected by its mothers/others in the fullness of its being like them.

It is understood, treated, interpreted, not fed merely. We adults, big, treat this thing, baby, not in any terms of *what it is* as much as we study it, conceive of it now being, growing into a *real* person; real no less derived than our views of what is nature and natural.

Otherwise it dies, is lethal. The babe to whom we grant agency, personage is always in some very complicated interaction between its being physically vulnerable, and our theories of its being which are precisely the theories of being which allow it to survive, determine its survival. Face it! We humans are creatures who face it, who grant being and selfhood to the partial view of the mechanical infant which is its face. Look at *me*!

We see it, see nature, through our self-conceptions as having faced out, seeing nature not merely through our visual nerves simply bombarded in a Humean bundled sensation, but in a humanly wrapped set of interlaced surfaces which concentrate being as seeing-out, seeing others' faces, emoting emotions as expression all interpreted, just as our parents interpret(ed) us. We do not see the world cleanly as the *physis* which is our center-of-gravity of the mere surfaces which would not know face from fact. Fact is, we do know face, we face facts and nature, but all interpreted, all socialized, all semiotically configured into the social being which is the who I am who survived and learned what I was told, enticed, loved. But this does not mean there is no real.

The *physis* of the physical human is not self-generated, calculated as the *arche* and architecture; architectonic of skeletal prefiguring, except as some possibility. The excitement should be that we stray sufficiently far from being other's imagination of our selves, that we can portray nature, and now can see it, now see-through our portrayals to self-discover.

The error, I suppose, has been the excitement since Parmenides that we can go beyond the *physis* finite, and imagine a world we do not experience even while we experience the now and here and locate ourselves. We made up other creatures, our terrestrial relatives, to be what we say they are— purely *physis*—and granted with the hubris we often warn ourselves about, so little to them, that we made up what is the human without much consultation with those who truly create us: our parents, *mostly* mothers.

The excitement about being, about nature, is that we are granted agency, that we can come even problematically to grant agency to ourselves, at least for a while. Instead, we have taken that for granted while wishfully granting the exclusivities of knowing only to our human knowing. Better we should contemplate the Narcissus within than look for intelligent life in the realms of inner and outer space. It has seemed easier and more compelling to repeat Aristotle on reasoning reason, than to query how we came to be, and are; thinking upon destiny while we cannot see the present age. (Dretsky, 1993).

World-As-Text: The ostensible argument between the purveyors of nature and of being—the two cultures—is not so clear as thinking that the naturists are totally mechanical-material, and the others are totally invested in the notion of the human as a reasoning creature. No! The argument is more subtle, its blatancies more about the *politics* of nature than about reality or actuality or objectivity or knowledge.

To defuse (some of) the politics, it has been my experience that they must be dealt with early in any conversation, and continually in order to begin to pry apart what is presumption, what is known and knowing, what is wishful, and what is winning. Fact is, nature is approached by all of us as if it were a text. We do not know exactly how to *read* this text, but approach it out of a variety of experiences and history, and wishes and hope. And once we know one or two chapters, we often reread and interpret the text differently than we had in getting to the moment in which we recast what we know, as well as what is knowing, itself.

The principal difference in the claims to reality between the two cultures has to do with the notion of *textuality* of reality: the *hard* scientific rational-logical mathematical approach presumes that the mechanical-material is reality in a sui generis sense. The observer is written out as if our being human is totally independent from the nature which we observe. Any *objective* (human) creature, the thinking goes, would note the same reality. A potent example: we go further into space searching for the same sort of intelligence we attribute to ourselves (but actively deny to other terrestrial creatures).

The others, the *softies*, approach not reality, but texts which are or are-not about anything specifically, as if the texts portray or represent reality, again sui generis. The (external) object disappears or is back-grounded to the reality which is now cast as what and how we know, and this is told to us through the systematicity of a Kant or a Hegel or the doubtings of a Nietzsche or the double-doubtings of Derrida who praises writing over being and grants the history of knowing some priority over knowing... *itself.* Derrida reacts violently to the failure of Husserl to *prove* external reality. Here the text effectively has become the world, and the task of knowing has become the task of being and of any reality. Again, the human effectively and essentially disappears, does not appear... no longer appears, hidden from the view in her/his/our viewing while we read about... being? Interpretation (or exegesis) becomes all, and the issue of reality comes down to the narrative text which appeals most to us, or relieves us...

The two-culture existential problem is that the text-as-world has so preoccupied our viewing that we suspect that either there is no world, or that there is no being; or both. Instead, we might grant that we humans have a particularly human form of knowledge which is less built-in to our being than it is that our knowledge is already attached to the knowing of our predecessors. We have to probe how we come to know what they know, and how we need to know the world as they have already portrayed it; as they treat the world as obvious in their terms—which we are essentially forced to accede to as part of our socialization. Then, perhaps, we can come to know the text which is the world, and the readers of it which is who we are.

The world is *not* as they portray it and treat it; i.e., the world may be fairly like we say it is, or at least close enough that we can (and have) survive(d) today, and all of the todays in whose being we/I got here. We are not so stupid as to *believe* our fictional texts about the world, at least much/most of the time; not so misled that we treat our myths as truth, the truth mythically. We know food and feeding, and much about nurturance and sustaining, and how not to praise suicide, and what is up and where we are. (Regal, 1990)

We know actually how to learn, to be skeptical and critical, and to suspend judgment much as we tend to worship our own beliefs. We are often virtuous and brave, but often we cannot see the path from the pathetic. All of this is somehow about the world, about truth and reality. The world-as-text is not pure fiction, consistent and survivable as we are. The text-as-world (e.g., television), on the other hand, can lead us to believe our own beliefs just as we suspend the skepticism which got us to wonder *if* more than *what* and *why*.

(Admittedly, much of the criticism of religion and the postmodern to scientism, is that the implicit politics of correctness about nature easily turn toward hubris concerning who knows and can know, as well as toward the Faustian arrogance of claiming more knowledge than we actually have.)

Critical Naturalism: The important issues (thus far) in the quest for knowing the reality of reality concern the place of the human condition within/outside of nature, whether reality is the other side of the Heraclitean flux in some eternal and unchanging forms, whether physics precedes metaphysics, whether the concept of some absolute nature/reality is undermined by suggesting differences of perspective (e.g., of different cultures or species) making reality less hard, more spongy, and suggesting to the incautious and impatient that there *is* no reality in particular...anything goes.

The dilemma arises and persists within Western thought in the context of what has been meant by Plato's worries about the antinomy between truth and persuasion, and in his insistence that this be a truth-telling and truth-seeking tradition. In order to accomplish the resolution of human experience into truth vs. sophistry, he literally removed us from our sensory experience, and proclaimed life to be mere copy of the permanent forms of concepts of geometry et al.

This was, of course, made complicated last century by the realization that geometry is, itself, dependent for definition by particular presumptions of the notion of parallel lines, etc., leaving us presently without the certain Platonic foundation of geometric figures, but only with geometry as models for geometry has, so far, then turned out to be a useful guide and metaphor for truth-telling, no bed-rock of truth.

Because Plato took us outside our existence (particularly by reducing or diminishing the human as participating in some external formal reality, but not of being/creating reality in our own being) we find ourselves in some opposition to nature. Oddly we remain somewhat caught in considering our own being as different from/outside of nature even while we judge it within our own experiencing of *it*—or of *it* as we experience ourselves as knowing—several concentric/contextual circles in which now the human, now reality, is at question without considering why and how we remain caught.

The dilemma, succinctly, is that the human is generally defined residually: *after physics*, as the individual *within* the physical body, masking or hiding our sociality and usually our physical development occurring along with mental development; after death, looking back at life; different from nature, removed from nature, even while we are juxtaposed with other species considered to be natural or within nature.

So we are duple (at the least) creatures always in some vain disputes with ourselves (leading to our overtaking of ourselves in terms of good or evil or whatever is *selling* in any era). We are animals-not-animals at war with experience, seeking to transcend the worry over nature's encroaching.

The most recent dilemma stems from Descartes equating nature with machines: where earlier we had to worry only that nature (our bodies) were a threat to our *real* being, now we can wonder if our particularly human *intelligence* (and associated ideas deriving from geometry and music→ rationality) is to be overtaken by machines. Or that we are merely and *really* our brains. Experientially, Platonic essentialism comprises a variety of ways of removing ourselves from our experience(s) and judging ourselves well or badly with respect to what is nature or anti-nature.

The dilemma of reality is complicated by the necessity of our having to be removed from it, experientially at least. The concept of reality is thus often overstated or presumptively defined as being anti-experiential thus unchanging. And if it is not like this (geometry and formal), then it/reality has no meaning; doesn't exist. Nature and reality are thus defined as being whatever is not particularly human, which is not-nature, which is not-human, and on and on.

A more *critical naturalism* examines the varieties of skepticism at large in the world, wondering that the idea of human knowing has principally captivated the imagination of the concept of reality. From Parmenides to the present, we have (for example) been in love with the concept of how a finite (physical) creature can indeed imagine the not here and not just now. We transform that love of extension into our definitions of the being of reality, thence of ourselves. Yet we retain a skepticism about our ability to know, to be the infinite and at once finite. Here it is necessary to see that the skepticism is bound with our definitions, while primacy is granted to physics and to the wonder of the human imagination presumptively.

A critical naturalism would note that we are children of mothers/others, learning their knowing of the world as our own; talking first to them and through our trying to get them to understand us thence the world (not the reverse). Then we would observe human development as occurring particularly in the face-to-face (literally we are face-loving). Then we would begin to study other traditions, and begin to see our own as a tradition which has taken certain life-paradoxes and attempted to resolve them, rather than to deal with life as truly paradoxical (which would no doubt undermine our particular Western concept of reality as existing outside). We would see that children can/do learn at a quite young age, the changing and the unchanging, the one and the many, death and life, all and at once. And we would begin to relax/alter our demands upon the definition of reality without thinking that we have to either have it one way, or not at all. Life is not-not real but thinking makes it that way.

Finiteness: If we take as a given, a primary, a presumption held at the level of the totally and unquestionable obviousness, that the being of being begins with the physical body, then we take as *fact* that to be human is to *be* finite. But (we observe) we are not finite in the terms which have come to represent what is uniquely and truly human: issues which have come to define the domain of the mind—of whatever it might take to take us beyond the finiteness of bodily obviousness. While this has led us to ask about those aspects of the nature of our being which have to do with however we carve out and carve up the mental, it leads us away from much knowledge about our being, away from knowledge about how we know and what we know, about, that is, the actual or real or nature.

The concept of number, of one and two and three, and infinity, of the physical carried beyond itself mimicking our story about the humanly indefinite and extended beyond itself, confuses and excites us to see how this could be and to wonder especially about the general within the specific; the universal set within the presumed experience of what is specific.

A better *story*, a truer and more accurate depiction of how we can come to represent the infinite within the finite, is born of watching the development of the infant turned scientist and intellectual, wondering precisely the same: how to see the infinite within the finite; to understand oneself as having extension into the distance of space and time: to know tomorrow and one's future being, and relationship of mommy and daddy of oneself.

The grounds of being: one is always seen and interpreted as having extension in the world, from birth on and on and on, and in relationship; one is never merely finite. One can never interpret oneself as merely finite, either.

Sense to oneself can only make sense if one comes to believe in one's extension. To do this, one has to *abandon* one's sense of finite being, to enter into the faces of others', to recognize the constant features of facial surfaces within the changing expressions of talking heads: to see *mommy*, to see oneself reflected within her irises, and to derive one's sense of self, now having yielded it to others' definitions of one's being. Here lies individuality and personage as we have attempted to define and understand it—but always heretofore begun in/from the *wrong* place. (See Elaine Morgan, 1995) on m/other looking into the eyes of her newborn, and seeing "somebody" there!)

In language, the route is not from experience of the body looking outward at the world, but within the definition and interpretation of oneself as extended by one's parents. One does not proceed analytically from bundles of sense experience to compose the world.

One is presented the world already composed (having effectively *yielded* the definition of one's being to others): one learns objects not colors or number or other adjectives; one learns time (responses to the question 'when?') and space (responses to the question 'where?'). One learns the individuality of objects simultaneously with the universal. Gradually one derives the sense that objects are colored, have colors—the world of experience is not built up, not constructed according to some scheme within the brain, but out of the dynamic of coming to be like others, and like others state that one *is*.

The infinite of knowing is then built-in to the dynamic of learning language as the parental generation regards language: the world is not the world as the child constructs it, but in her/his coming to know her/his parents' knowing. What we then call the *individual* or the *person* is later, and emergent, and solidifies the extended and non-finite self which the parents demand of and necessitate from the infant.

The finite body is *yielded* early (if it can be called a yielding—perhaps a *joining* in imitative and face-expressive while the infant examines, strengthens, exercises, *smiles*, both within and in-relation to its mother and others, all simultaneously. The person, the infinite/finite individual which has been the puzzling aspect of our being which argues against the physical finiteness as dualism, is not oppositional; not necessarily unique in the range of life forms, but the semiotic and socialized self which is (now) transformed, transduced into the sense of being which we are calling *the* human. *It is not the finite physical with the infinite mental overlain!*

The physical which is now socialized, that one which develops the persona which is who I am, is who I am with respect to who I am interpreted to be, by my m/other: at once finite and infinite, extended in time and space—but very little from *within*. Rather I am who I am in terms of a world knowledge which is that world which others say is *the* world.

How this world of knowing and language might have had its *origins* now is also problematically transformed, and will ask us to ask questions of other species to wonder if they, also, are not any mere *physis*; as they are (all) also social, just as we: interpreted and interpreting the world as they are told it is and told who and what they are to be.

The Intuitive: The question (Leibnitz and others) of how we come to know from some sense of earlier, built-in knowing which is already an aspect of being human (brain, gut, heart...) as opposed to some Lockean (tabula rasa) sense of sense experience built-up to relate to objects, words, concepts: a construction of the world (by each individual). The skeptical problematic of Hume, worrying that we have no real-actual sense of the principle of causation, if we are experiential in our coming to know knowing. If not sense experience, then we are (led to believe) the answer is to be found in our intuitions, our feelings, our *built-in's*.

Whether these approaches to knowledge should be considered in clear opposition seems to me doubtful. The infant—born—already seems to have much of what I consider knowing: of its own body, externally and internally; a visual orientation to be interested in high dark and light contrast, etc. As the dualism of mind and body has not led us much to consider the sense of knowing which relates to one's physical body—as if the central nervous system is *set* already in some ways autonomous or automatic to the organism which is somehow different from what we think of as meaning and knowing—the way we have thought about knowing has to do with how we (the individual) begin the processes of knowing the external world with the *end/purpose* of becoming rational/human.

I don't think this way of proceeding is useful: it is circular in many ways, and does not lead us to understanding as much as it seems to direct us to one *path of solution* to a problem which itself seems to close-off quite early in the game. Whether one is skeptical about the possibility of knowledge of the external world, or of the possibility of mutual understanding, this skepticism is quite formal and structural, not out of our experience: why we have set up this problem in the first place; the finite body versus the infinite of knowledge. Bet to begin/continue by reading and studying "Woman"– Natalie Angier, 2000)

We grab experience to justify one sense of understanding the problematic and then become skeptical of how we can know, and then seem to forget or overlook how well we actually do in (to me) a world in which knowledge of almost anything seems quite marvelous—but actual. It often seems to me that we do not actually *want* a solution to the problem of knowing, perhaps because it would trivialize being beyond what the philosophers could tolerate (Heidegger, 1929).

If we need to probe knowing, it should be set in the context of the developing human—not, for example, within the metaphor of the already grown individual, akin to Condillac's *speechless statue*. It should not be set within the fantasy of the *wild boy*, but within the actuality of how a human infant (you, me) could have become/did become the knowledgeable *who* I am today.

Rather than worry about experience vs. intuitions, we should note that the infant has particular *interests*: in others' faces, in sucking (= exploring

433

and knowing its own mouth and internal faces); in seeing great contrasts and contrastive changes which it then internalizes in its own facial movements, muscles, smiles, and so on.

I theorize that the mouth and face are *where* the world is modeled and molded. The infant *gives away* much of her/his face. No doubt there is some sensory-muscular *orientation* (= intuition) to the faces she/he sees, reacting to them. Whatever the actual mechanisms, it is primarily in adapting for its reality the facial *outlook* of the mother, that its own experience and becoming is oriented: not from within, not from inbuilt intuitions by which it approaches directly the world of knowing.

The experience of the developing infant is moderated or directed by its involvement with the face of its mother (and others) with *whom* it identifies itself. Within this process of *identifying* effectively begins the process of becoming a self—the person, the being who I am and have become. The individual of birth is perhaps residual and very small. Effectively the "who I am" is overwhelmingly the "who I am" said and told and interpreted to be; the social, semiotic me, the one whom I project forward into the indefinite future, becoming.

The *universality* of language which has been rated very important in attempting to understand the process of becoming a knowing being, is located not in the intuitions or built-in's but in the (humanly universal) *processes* by which one is attached/attaches oneself to one's parents: some extended vision of the question-response system by which we are direct to know the world by responding to questions in terms of which the world as the parents understand it is presented to each infant.

Truth: The problem with truth is that by the time it occurs to us to ask specifically about truth, it has already become quite complicated. If we survive to ask about the truth, then we have already accepted and developed a number of notions, theories even, about the nature of truth. In order to penetrate the problem with truth, we have to unpack what we already believe is truth; in order to see what is problematic and what is interesting and/or revealing.

The essentialist/foundationalist complication is that truth has become associated with permanence and formal, logical notions abstracted from much of the way in which living proceeds, consistently and, well *truthfully*.

The truth of living has to do with ingesting food and air into the mouth (which is itself a large, if ordinary-appearing aspect of being), of muscular movements (including especially heart and lungs, but also balancing and the muscularity of stillness).

The truth of living has to do with constancy but also with and within change, and developing even to oneself a sense of persona obtained and emergent from interaction with others. It is about (facial) expression and sound, seeing and feeling of and with others, in order to relate to them in ways which become ways in which one is constant to oneself. Constancy seems to have little to do with that which is *internal* to the organism. The individual, that is, is derived, constructed, and develops from the constancy of how one is conceived and treated by others, and interpreted to be and to continue being. Truth is finding a persona which is the *ground* of one's being; a sense of self-reference in which the self is engaged in circumscribing itself. The truth of being, that is, is that being is in-relation with others, while the facts of being are growing and changing.

The truth of being is about conscience which is play about the emergence of one's being a self; true to oneself in constancy, while reflecting to and from others' depictions and interpretation of being. A self is a findable persona: the one which wills and talks to itself, and gathers itself into a *homunculus* which it says it is, and I am. The ways in which we find constancy and continuity, in which for example I see myself *into* my childhood photos, these ways are at the heart of being.

All of these truths precede the quest for a truth which hovers over being. Being does not merely wear the lenses of seeing and hearing any object which exists clearly outside of the self. The being which is, is *emergent* and constructed and necessitates active work in process to reconstruct it in order merely to have it appear to remain steady and findable. The difficulty in locating any difficulty with one's central being is an indication that the processes are working well and effectively. This is a powerful form of the truth of being.

It may be likened to the lack of active awareness of the inside of our mouths even while we articulate speech, eat, and swallow, and salivate, and press our tongues even while we read and think—in known places with precise pressures. Any awareness of this process is like a broken chip of a tooth, *gigantic* and focusing beyond the apparent dimension of our total being —showing how gigantic (in actuality) are the truths of being which we have backgrounded within the quest for truth even while we say we are constant and objective.

We know time and space and because and how many of who and what and what happened to the coloration of the horse which is this horse or that horse and any or all of the above, in response to the way we watch and hear the world being posed as questions our parents pose to us. When we respond contextually-correctly as they define whatever *correctly* means to them —this is, these are truths of our being. All of this is, by the time it occurs to us to ask about the nature of the truth, solidly part of the truth of our being, only to occur to us when problematic that it is aspectual to being. It is, perhaps, like violin technique, only necessary to examine when it does not work well enough in any present moment.

And the question of *how good is well enough* is also a matter of the nature of truth which we already know: well enough to sustain us, which is no small matter even though it may not usually arise when we ask about the truth.

In a peculiarity of Western thinking, much of the truth of this telling has been erased from thought about thinking as it has been placed or relegated to the material-mechanical with rules and truths which have seemed opposite to the truths of truth, or totally defining of them. But the truth of the matter is that there is no clear opposition in being body-or, body-and. We are what and who and how and because, and in-relation, and all of this is true. The dilemma is how to locate the persona which is the effective self, the "who I am" who I tell myself I am, as if some notion of a *mechanism of character* will do to tell us about the nature of truth.

Much of truth is located in deciphering the nature of being which is posing the quest and question, as if unsure or unsatisfied with the truth(s) already possessed in the nature of being; as if they are now or suddenly problematic; as if one has discovered something new or general or wrong with what was known to be true. Or it may be that one's persona, the grounding and central aspect of one's being is now seen by others with significance of definition of one's being, to cast earlier truth into present problematic. That self of self who willed the truth, who was the who I call myself, no longer serves, no longer works, no longer content but now wondering and wandering asks what is the truth? Toward an *anthropology of the ordinary...*

The mechanisms for judgment have been present in one's being since one first learned how others judged and categorized the world of objects and movement and how many of what size and how they work, and what causes what to happen; or it no longer does cause what to happen; or there arises a new issue which may have no story of cause or explanation; or the old story no longer serves as it did formerly, but they usually do when the remainder of one's world seems stable. The quest for truth arises *when* stability is itself suspicious.

And we must probe *why* the question arises, under what conditions, and for whom, and what would satisfy the quest. For the notion that the truth will *set us free* is at war with the tale that we should not know more than we should know which is what is already known - a sense of hubris which is a little Faust agitating a few of us to be all-knowing, mixed with power in decline.

The truth is not *in nature* in any simple or reduced or purely analytic process which is not so difficult to derive from the truths of being which we already possess in becoming who we are to ask the question about truth. We are not merely in-nature or outside of nature, or trying to control nature or ourselves. We are largely reflective—less in reflecting upon what we know— more in reflecting how we think others want us to be in some circularity of who and how they think we are and ought to be; less in any certitude which calms.

Eschatology and Nihilism: Of course the entire phrasing of this form of argumentation, of reportage on the problematics of truth and being and reality, is that we live within a heritage whose ideas mix most readily with the experience of what is. We openly invoke old men (mostly men) in the guise of philosophy and religion as we make most general most everything and cannot easily decipher what is mine and what is yours and its and theirs.

We are often unclear concerning who we are and who we are told to be and urged not to be. In this tradition, particularly, we become aware of our experience to some large extent through the imposition of an awareness of our impending death(s): do this, or else no heaven... God will not like it if you don't do it. (In some others we are blurrily reincarnated or actually the rebirth of someone who is already well-known and present in the thinking of one's community.)

Authority and conscience and pleasing our parents and the whys of because are all imposed upon the being-in-the-defining which is our early childhood. Love and goodness conflate with do and be it, or else. Why? *Because I say so...* to the three-year old.

Authority within oneself and the self-certification of one's own experience remain backgrounded as we are urged to yield. We gather a sense of self as much in the thinking as in the doing, and the sense of who I am, and am to be is gathered in the large from externalities, both derived and tied to others whose own reason for being seems increasingly obscure as we age.

As Nietzsche tells us over and over again, the battle of being authorized to be oneself with the limits of one's being are at odds in realms roughly called moral, which have overwhelmed those which are more self-centered, more virtuous. We praise others in their weakness, and grant ourselves power in lording it over them in our pity for them. We live in a tradition which says it praises the truth and its telling, while not creating within the would-have-been truth tellers the possibility of discernment and the staying power of overcoming one's bringing up or earlier versions of who one thinks s/he is.

In the end, we are told to say to ourselves, in the end we seek our being. Do this because; do that...for the same reason. Because I want to be virtuous in order to get to heaven—for heaven's sake.

It is so difficult to review critically, to unpin the effects on the seeking of salvation on the telling of any truth. This is precisely what this truth-telling tradition has got us to, to this moment when it has become obvious and clear that the tradition which praises itself has not told us the true truth. And now it fears that there is not truth because the possibility of truth has shown its own temptations to lie, to weaken any resolve to see ourselves seeing, and to lead us toward nihilism just as we are led to see the end more than the ongoing present. Woe is us!

Architectonic: There has been much praise, a raising to genius those to whom we look for instruction; the teachers to all of us who have caused us more to reread them than to read ourselves in our being and doing. If we know what there is, but more how it is put together in its relationships and reactions, then we (would) really know knowing. Here is often located the rock of the bedrock. Here is the locus of the placement of the concept, the notion behind the idea; the virtual Zen of the universe. Here is the plan, and here is the architect, and here is authority and agency. And where am I?

Here, again, I suspect we have victimized ourselves and our (self) understanding by granting being to aspects of our existence which we have taken to the level below and out-of-awareness, and called it *obvious* and especially *ordinary*. The architectonic and the resultant architecture of the human body, a prime example in our case of being, has been raised to a plan of what is, then extended to what must be and should be.

The critique is that the plan does not often include the flesh and blood and guts of our being, but primarily the paleontologically obvious: the skeleton. It is as if we are reverent not toward our parents and the wisdom of the aged, but more in love with the fixities of the idea of wisdom...of the ages, of what has endured, as if having endurance certifies our being. (Is anyone today smart/wise enough to be an Aristotle?)

We derive metaphorical being from the in-most, the parts which survive the vicissitudes the longest, as if they provide the map of our being. We classify the human much in relation to the bones of other species, less in terms of how they act, are, live. We call this *morphology* and render the processes of being lesser: we consider those processes as physiological if they maintain life, but have overlooked how it is to be...in gravity. Three plus centuries after Newton, we are only now beginning to discover the gravity (literally) of the human condition.

For it is by now clear—if not so well known—that the bones are not so clearly architechtonic and hard. But they are viscous and changeable, and take their shapes and maintain them only in the position of being upright, and moving in terrestrial gravity. Do not remain too long in bed, do not spend very much time in the depths of sea or the heights of space. If we are who we appear to be, then this is in great part due to what we do, and do often, and do not wear and tear down with being in gravity for more than 40 years or so. Even the concept of age and aging is heavily in relation to being in gravity, though we have related ageless to ongoing being but more to the approach of death.

More and moreover, we have granted to this architectonic the primacy of our being, while we overlook the fact that we are engaged as fundamentally in seeing others seeing us seeing others...In accounting for how we look (and much of who we are), we impute some hereditary power to facial shapes. Yet it is now known (through orthodontia, going to the non-gravity of space and cutting muscles of young mammals, and plastic-reconstructive facio-cranial surgery), that the shape of a face is in relation to muscles, which are actively *held* in various tensions and uses and disuses dependent greatly on who we are with, and how they talk and look and hold their faces and respond to our active expressive muscular movements. (Ekman, 2000)

Where precisely is the architectonic in all this? How have we managed to not see the obviousness which is how we look at looking, and overstress the notion of the looking-out; as if the facial dynamics which largely determine and sustain the who we are of our being (and whether we are, for example, *credible*) are subordinate to the architecture of the edifice. It is as if being is in our bones; even while knowing that it is not there.

Similarly we have been uncritical about how we gather information about our being, relying on the same authorities to authorize the notions of intellectuality and to repeat (e.g.) Aristotle ad infinitum as if he had and is the last word on the nature of human nature: e.g., the *organic analogy* has created more obfuscation in the framing of political organization than seems possible.

But this fact points to the implicit acceptance we have had of what is the human and what is nature, generalizing from how I am and we are, to the whole of existence. We seem to carry various speculative theories rather than actual theories of speculative history of the human with us and within us as if they are merely to be applied in the correct(ive) circumstances.

Peter Wilson attempts to turn speculative history on its head (but I suspect the body-part analogy to the notion of philosophic inversion is not unimportant). In his *Domestication of the Human Species* (1989) he lays claim to the idea that we began to geometrize being (not to think geometrically, as Plato suggested), when we began to live in fixed communities: with places, insides and outsides. Then social structure tended to harden much as the places which we told ourselves formed the architectonic of our being. Then we began to think of *gardens* of Eden, and of palaces, and of nations, of nature and culture, and of humanly formulated deities. And we raised the objects of the geometrizing of our being to transcendence and causality and began to derive ourselves diminished as they ascended to the agency and power of definition of the architectonic of being and truth and nature. (Now in this era of television have we any longer any sense of place?

What-is vs. what-cannot-be: There is a recurring temptation to depict the real and nature less by what it is or does, or in the various processes of being and doing, but more in terms of what is aw(e)ful and destructive and impossible to conceive. We are driven often when we once-believed, to deny that belief in a loaded way: a positive/negative chaos-ism replaces a once-sufficient deity; the limits of being overtake the examination of life and the world. We seem to indulge our worst fears in calculating what is. The very idea of our existence overwhelms us in a cosmology of 'if and whether'; meaning in the West, reality is at war with personal death.

Less do we concern ourselves with the public health aspects of maintaining and sustaining life itself. More we are taken with the edges of being where the polluting poisons enter being—corroding thought: a toxicological approach which focuses upon the *not-to-be*. When the tragic sense of life enters then pervades our sense of the real, then it is difficult to see and to remember seeing and doing and what might be the good. Rather being is overtaken with the chaotic cosmic excitement of how nothing could possibly *work*, and finally come to question the fact of our very existence, without which the issues of the real diminish and disappear. Here we beg to be told that we are, and that the fears we experience are the experience common to everyone.

Instead it is important frequently to ponder Kierkegaard's observation that we approach the world either through fear or through

441

wonder. It is important, in such moments, to recall the Heraclitean possibility that all is change anyway. Our infatuation with the certitude of permanence cripples us in seeing what there is, led as we are to concentrate and to celebrate the boundedness of existence. The cannot-be, the don't-be, the lack of any will to say 'Yes!' has already in its development negated any possibility of...

And there is nothing much to say except that death has its own domain; and that this is not it. (See: *Next Places*)

Leviathan: A confusion and conflation, the application of ideas which we humans invent or derive are then imputed to the concept of nature! Once granted to nature, they are then taken to apply somehow to the human condition. Since Aristotle at least, we have taken some ideas such as mind-body dualism, raised one over the other (e.g., Plato: *Republic* Book X) as if this is obvious in the natural scheme of things, and applied them to social theory (Aristotle: *Politics*). The problematic notions that there are a mind and body in each individual, that mind is placed in the body, that mind is the ruler or director of the body, is merely presumed then taken by Aristotle to apply equally well in social theory: monarch over polis as husband over wife, people over slaves.

Social theorists never get to ask, apparently, what is the status of the original opposition, or if they do are shouted down by (belief in) the philosophers. Leviathan is Hobbes' scheme for the same notion.

Such ideas presume the *cannot-be* of existence, a sense that chaos always looms just over every next horizon and must be stopped at the pass, else anarchy...will rule; there will be no rules, no order. A *natural law* theory is concocted to account for why human (males) are intrinsically competitive and destructive, rather than a theory which posits the social and mutually interactive obviousness clear in the relationship between parents and infant.

Here Leviathan is a *justification* argument, a way to claim that power invested in people cannot be sustained, cannot be trusted; that education and change are to be avoided in favor of hereditarian claims of non-change; and the worry that change goes awry and moves toward chaos. Here it is difficult to distinguish what is real and what is actual and how the world is, because we are already involved and invested in many circles of theory about being which are difficult to unpack or to deconstruct.

And the actuality of experience for those who are already disposed to see the worst (Kierkegaard's *fear*) is that they approach teaching with distrust and a sense of the destructive potential of any change. Rules become laws which become nature and the real, and we emerge as persons only to find that we live duple lives: one of experience and the other of theory about being and reality.

It is difficult to see the real or the actual. This takes much rethinking and study; but it is tempting to submerge them to theories of our being.

Pathology: There was I, one day seemingly whole, the next not so well, telling myself that all is not so good and that tomorrow all will be better. Pains, hurts, innards popping off and oozing out; the former surfaces once smooth, now growing glowing grotesqueries.

Theories of the world, of the real, bah! I want relief. This turns day-by-day into fears for my own being. Sickness alters being slashing and burning at its roots and brings the presence of death into life crying for a return to normality; to what was. The future fades as I seek ways to account for this sickness, ways to blame or to forgive and to calm the self which was just a few days earlier at some peace with its own internal dialogues. The 'ow!' of pain creates an immediacy to experience which cannot get beyond itself. How can pathology be used toward understanding and standing outside of the pain whose vast size so compresses being that all else disappears?

Additions: Upon trying to fill-in the thinking of the romantics of the 19th century (as well as my own), my puzzles remain, I think, mostly intact. We are bodies, living in the world with/of other bodies. We are what we are, and can also think, think in remove and in present here and now.

Coming upon thinkers after the skepticism of Hume (See my essay on *Cultural Relativism and Critical Naturalism*, 1991), I sense that the deeper problem is not with being human, but with the development of our theories about our (human) being.

Much is left out of our theories, constructed as they have been upon—as it were—certain *surprises* emanating primarily, it seems to me, by a surreptitious certitude about the primacy of the physical world, and the inferences and entailments which follow from that thinking.

The romantics (I'll choose Schelling for his clarity: in *System of Transcendental Idealism. I: Idea of Transcendental Philosophy*, 1800) got to worry about the precise nature of truth, particularly in our relation to knowing that truth. Although this is an old story about human nature, Adamic language and all that, it boils down for Schelling to the nature of our representations of reality, of nature: words, ideas, grammar, etc.

As this has been constructed within the context of meta-physics consisting of that which is left-over after physics, Schelling raises the issue both ways: from nature to subjective, and the reverse. So the problem is stated and lives within two domains: the problem of philosophy is now to connect them—truth (nature) to knowing, or knowing (subjective) to truth of nature.

Instead, I think much is ignored in this formulation of the problematics of nature, truth, subjectivity, and so on. It relies on some (necessary, presumptive) opposition between nature and knowing, as if the human condition resides in some loci or contexts independent (virtually) of nature. And, perhaps more important, it neglects much of the human condition, especially (but not only) the fact that we develop and change as bodies, that we live within and are virtually interpreted into being by m/others (Sarles, 2014).

8.

THE MORALITY OF BECOMING

The Dilemma:

"To give any sensible account of how it is that we can acquire standards which we turn against the society that taught them to us, we need a coherent picture of how the individual can be shaped by one's upbringing and yet become an active, intelligent moral agent -- one more reason for being cautious about exaggerating the extent to which morality is emotive and reactive." (From *Reasons of the Heart*, by Alan Ryan, a review of James Q Wilson's book, *The Moral Sense*. NYRB, 9/23/93, p. 54.)

While much of the current dilemma in understanding morality seems to revolve specifically around issues of absolutism and relativism, the locus of the problematic is specifically concerned with the nature of who and *how we are* as individual and as social creatures. An explanation of morality thus depends on a prior analysis of the human condition and/or of human nature with respect to the nature of our individuality, and how the flow and vicissitudes of life may frame our being and identity. It is worth reminding ourselves that Western thought has merely presumed that the individual, located somehow within the physical body, is the locus of morality. It is precisely this presumption which falters in explaining morality. Continuing within this presumption we are left with the either/or of fixity or change, of a morality which is built-in or which cannot really exist; we are left wandering...

A Critical Turn within a Life of Thought and Respect for Others' Thinking and Believing: Other species, we have realized only last century, are (also) social (Darling, 1934). Sociality and morality are inter-linked, perhaps *mutually defining*. This (new) understanding would seem to ask us to rethink the issues and nature of morality, a field of inquiry which has depended largely upon assumptions and beliefs about the uniqueness of humans, and upon the sense that sociality and thinking are what sets humans aside from other species. Our thinking about morality has developed

445

principally within the area in which we have particularized human uniqueness. Instead...

Being-is-social-is-moral...already! Questions of morality and freedom have been intertwined with a history of assumptions about the human condition. It has been assumed, for example, that each individual already contains the seeds of future morality, rather than morality and individuality being aspects of being which emerge from sociality. In this realm of thought, it has been the idea of the individual which confined the issues of morality. If, as appears to be case, other species are moral (act and live morally) in spite of...not *having* language, not *foreseeing* death, whence morality...?

This insight implies that almost everyone considers (even upon critical and honest reflection) that one acts and lives morally. The question of why some of us live and act immorally - as others construct that notion - rises to more puzzling dimensions than ever before: no devil, no evil...only us, only you, only me.

Taking this position, a major burden and puzzle and quandary is to examine morality without destroying its possibility by relativizing morality, and claiming that all behavior is either moral, or that there is no such thing as morality/moral behavior/being. Can we ask questions about human nature which will illuminate rather than further obfuscate the nature of morality? Can we find some contexts or boundedness within our being which we can find as particularly moral, rather than fighting within the argument over absolutes and external agency as opposed to relativism and anything goes, might makes right or its apostolic opposite...or denying meaning within life?

Survival of the Individual within Social Species: In beginning to understand that we are - by our nature - a social species, it is important to strive to understand that the so-called individual, the self-located within the physical body is *not* intrinsically survivable. Our survival is interdependent and dependent on and with m/others. Our individuality is not continuous with our physical being, but is a characteristic of our being which is *emergent*: demanded by others, acceded to by ourselves. The "I" of who and that I am, is a socially constructed self-seated in the wish, demands, and necessity of parents to have a child which/who is self-generating and not dangerous to itself or to them. The persistent problematic in understanding morality in Western thought (at least) is presuming that the primacy of our being is physical (Aristotle), then disregarding that presumption in exploring and searching for the nature of morality and moral being.

Introduction: In a world most often conceived as a place reserved, prepared, and purposed for human beings, the question of morality has seemed quite clear: locate authority—deity, parents and elders, texts, some notions of the world; then guide one's being to conform to this authority.

In effect one strives to become an agent of the authority which lays out how one *should* be, or structures much of the detail of the shouldness of being. Thou shall or thou shall not... be... do. This to be translated experientially into: I shall... yes or no. There is a sense of certainty, of surety, of there being a morality which is clear, even *absolute* in its directedness.

In a world where the purpose of our (human) being is not (any longer) clear or is considered continually problematic, where the possibilities of being moral within the context of authority seem reduced, where we might grant ourselves full authority for our (own) being, where we note globally various different approaches to morality; then we stray from any clear and clean (*absolute*) notions that authority is to be found in any certain place. Perhaps it is not to be found even in our own being—a worry for those who seek calm.

The question of morality is often then *relativized*: do what seems correct, what feels good, what doesn't hurt others, what you would have others do unto you: live a golden life, find a golden time. And we find that all of these admonitions open myriad possibilities which one or another of us finds different or difficult, without purpose and meaning, and with a sense of futurity which weakens in our very becoming. Any sense of a moral present, of being moral in our ongoing existence, is reduced. And like others swimming in the tides and murk of when is post- to the experience of the modern, we place a price on morality, sell it to the highest bidder, and look to other times, places, texts, agents for explanation and control.

This is, at least, the sort of story which we (Westerners) have told ourselves; a story which has led by now to some epic battle for a bottom line and guarantee of authority finding itself at deepening odds with the observations of *live and let live*, or let me *do my own thing* or that others understand morality from other perspectives equally valid as mine or yours or of any deity.

What sets the stage for such a battle is much of what this study consists in: an exploration of the foundations of the morality of becoming - of becoming, because it is a battle also about the question of change and eternality, of spirit and of authority, and some sense of towardness or *finality* of the human condition: becoming and moving toward one's *next place* in life; moving toward some global or universal utopia, the end and the eschatology. Often, but not always, this has involved questions of personal and of others' deaths; thence of life as questions and fears of death enter being and meaning and whatever is morality. (See: *Next Places*)

In this attempt to understand a conflict which does not seem necessarily conflictual (to me, at any rate), I have tried to gain some sense of how this problem has arisen in Western thought. What are its foci, what its directions and paths, what its arenas for agreement and disagreement, and why they seem to be operative (*to work*) in some eras and places and for some persons, but not in and for others, and particularly why (not) *now*?

The story of morality is one aspect—perhaps the major one—of a Western metaphysics which has construed the human condition and *uniquely human purpose* within the context of certain presumptions: a division of each of our individual being as being constructed (usually in opposition) of two parts: a body and a mind. The body is considered to be an aspect of nature, while the mind is seen as being outside of, removed from, advanced beyond nature.

In this depiction and setting of the human condition, the mental aspect of our being has been the locus and focus of morality: the remove from nature, the direction and purpose of life. Within Platonism (*Phaedo*) and neo-Platonism (especially Augustine) even the Christian (and Muslim) idea of the deity is constructed as a mode of creating a transcendent and unchanging deity/purpose to our being. Within the mental, the concept of language has been very powerful in the development of the metaphysical depiction of the human condition: language not only in terms of what it is and is presumed to be, but also in terms of what is has been supposed to do in the context of removing humans from nature; becoming social, civilized, and all of that (John 1:1).

The rub, especially in the context of questions of morality and human purpose, is that nature is quite different (*now appears much different*) from how we had formerly supposed it to be. Where we had earlier presumed that humans in nature were the only species to have become social - via language and its ability to remove us from nature—it now seems clear that other species are also social, communicating with one another, perhaps symbolic and removed from the present here and now which we had associated only with humans, and certainly moral; at least *within* their various species.

What then, what now, morality? What then, now, the human condition? How should we be? What should we now do? Anything?

The Present Context: With the discovery only last century that humanly related/similar species are social, there arise a series of issues about human origins and the human condition/nature including those concerned with religion and morality. In a wide sense, morality is concerned with how one lives with and treats others, and *why*; how others treat oneself—and *why*. In the context of this wide sense of morality, the fact that other species are social asks us to rethink the history and ideas of morality as a specifically or uniquely human attribute.

If, as seems correct, other species live rather peaceable social lives within species, raise their young to become social *adults*, it is reasonable to wonder whether they are not (also) moral; in some senses like humans with a morally interpretive sense of towardness in raising their young. Does thinking of other social species as moral lead us to new and/or critical perspectives from which to view the nature of (human) morality?

It is also interesting to wonder whether we *should* compare human behavior and the human condition with other species. Part of the issue to be considered here, is that this question itself has a moral aspect, reflexively raising the issue of how we have formulated our thinking about human nature. For example, the question of whether we are somehow in or outside of nature has often made sense to thinkers about human morality - as if nature and moral humanity are in some dialectical relationship. I will explore such issues in this foundational study, attempting to search for the human condition both in its living dynamics and in the stories whose heritage we share and only now find contested.

How is it, as it is often posed, that we are said to be creatures who can *transcend* ourselves? (Some pose this ability as that by which we can ask: *Why?*) Is this due to some aspect of being human which is unique to our species—as it has usually been held? Or is transcendence available—even *ordinary*—within other species? As much of our being has been *constructed* within the idea of some dichotomy between humans and others (mind and body; culture and nature, etc.), if we realize that humans are not so unique, how will this affect—help to clarify—our understanding of ourselves?

If other species are moral, do they have a god, a deity or deities—one God...or many? Our God?—each species, a God? Do they generalize, universalize; or are they *stuck* within the here and now, reactive and signaling, rather than symbolic and with some sense of happening?

If other species have no god, and if they are indeed moral, then the religious basis for human morality is not, apparently, a (*natural*) necessity.

Humans are (would be) moral with or without such a notion, being social creatures: the *death* of the concept of god, as Nietzsche put it, should have no necessary or particular effect upon our being what and who we are. That is, whatever we are, however we choose to believe we are, the entailments of ongoing sociality are already moral. We treat others reciprocally well, raise our children to possess conscience, because that is (an aspect of) our nature. In this context, there is no need to justify or to explain morality. Morality requires re-thinking, not denial or approval. Our stories about morality need to be recast.

Similarly, the question of human *freedom* is an important aspect of this discussion. How do we act as we do: tied to our *natural* or emotional make-up; or capable of deciding (rationally?) to act morally; able to grow and to decide that we can act in terms of some idea of morality, rather than being permanently tied to experience, observation, desire, or habit?

In this set of aphorisms on *The Morality of Becoming*, I examine morality as social ontology. Beginning from Nietzsche's attempts to criticize the moral form for our conduct, and to substitute some existential vision, I attempt to flesh out a human morality which is neither more nor less than the requirements of our continuing being, being together in the existent global universe, upon a now shrunken earth.

The Human Nature Issue: The issue of morality being linked to other species is not about diminishing humans by claiming that our *animal nature* is about to win some war with what is particularly human—although some *biological* thinkers have construed it that way: as a *biological morality* (Lorenz: *On Aggression*, D. Morris, *The Naked Ape*; E.O. Wilson, *On Human Nature*). Biology, in this sense, has been construed to mean—somehow—more fundamental, basic, primary; and biology is understood as opposed, somehow, to mental or cultural—entailing some notion of the ancient antinomy between change and permanence.

Rather the issue is to attempt to see the human condition as clearly as possible without being totally burdened by the weight of earlier theories and stories about the human condition which color our thinking and focus our observations and questions very narrowly. Such (Western) theories have depended in some large measure on certain ideas of what is human which have included ideas of what is not-human, tending to divide each human into two: a bodily or mechanical aspect usually thought to be like the nature of other species; and a mind or mental aspect thought to be unique to humans.

Or theories have invoked religious, political, and metaphysical ideas which have used theories of human nature to elaborate one or another view. Or these have been commentaries within some structured way of thinking about ourselves which have had more to do with solving certain intellectual problems than with issues of experience and existence.

In particular, Western thought has begun thinking about human nature by assuming that we are both related to and different from other species; what I call a *juxtaposition theory*. These ideas affect and shape very fundamental thinking about humans particularly and presumptively as individuals.

In the realm of moral questions, this leaves the larger issues of morality as located somehow—fairly mysteriously at that—in each individual. And we are left trying to explain questions of good and evil without much consideration of good and evil with respect to other persons: our significant others/mothers, families, groups, enemies, and so on. Indeed, Kant who frames the question of morality in an epitome of thinking about morality as a kind of logic or geometry, posits that we must have within each of our beings, a kind of transcendent moral law, which operates independently from experience (Kant: *Foundations of the Metaphysics of Morals*, 1959).

Morality, that is, has been cast within various forms of *idealism* as a priori structures, rather than emerging from our social and communicative experience. This does not necessarily alter our perceptions of right and wrong. But we should note that it has persuaded us to look for appropriate questions and answers in what I consider to be narrow and particular places.

As the human condition has been characterized in idealist thinking as unique due to our minds, to language and rationality, much of the issue of morality has located itself within our mental being trying to overcome experience and bodily desires. As I will attempt to show, we are what and who we are, and much of our being is in relation to and *emergent* from our interactions with others.

The Entire Earth: The comprehensive question about morality arises at this moment in part because the earth is—for the first time—conceived (and conceivable) as a singularity: "global." Morality is thus not just a question about why and how to be with respect to those who one knows or will be in some relation to, for now this includes potentially everyone (...and every thing and every species).

Or the inclusion of the entire globe in our conceptualization forces us to rethink morality because we now realize that others (entire traditions) come to (some) moral questions differently from ourselves/Western thought: different theologies, different senses of purpose and reasons for life.

And we ask ourselves: why are we like we are?—they: like they are? And is there some overarching sense of rightness and morality? Is there some sense of an absolute morality; or is all just different, relative, and perspectival? At an extreme, does it make any difference in the context of human survival if we kill one another in the name of deity, nation, right, wrong?

This epoch in global history raises, as well, questions about the appropriate contextual questions to ask: survival, a good life, life lived well, preservation of human nature, of nature, of...? Are there some persons/groups who are better/worse, more/less deserving of...? Are there too many of us? Which/who?

Who will decide such questions? On what grounds? Can we even conceptualize any sense of morality which applies to the entire earth - without appealing to privilege of...?

And there is this peculiarity of our being global which seems somehow to interfere with, to overlap, with the idea of the universal translating sometimes into holism everywhere, sometimes into variations of oppositional thinking.

Location (Locus) of Morality: One of these overarching contextual questions about morality has to do with how and where morality is *located*.

By *locus*, I mean that the ways of conceptualizing the problematics of morality have particular dimensions and directions of thought within theo-political and individual histories which often seem, by now, *obvious*.

Obvious means that certain thought modes do not get critically considered in any new situations, but are at the level of what we assume uncritically; more generally and merely applied.

For example, do politics and morality overlap or find themselves often in different loci? In the Old Testament injunction of Genesis 1:26, it says that *Man (human) is made in the image of God, and has dimension over all the other species*. This is clearly a political statement, stating that humans have control (= *dimension*) over the destiny of other species. Is this to be interpreted to mean that we also have (moral) responsibility? In this context/locus, clearly morality and politics overlap or are the same. And in Genesis 1:27, God created men and women.

And how (a *method/methodology*) do we determine how we humans are? By asking how God is? By asking how God says we humans are? Here morality is likely not located in asking ourselves, say, to observe how we are actually. More likely we are directed to texts inspired by deity (Old & New Testaments, Koran, etc.), in which (hu)man is derived from God. In these historical contexts, the locus of morality in within the reading/interpretation of the deity's saying who and how we are and are to be; often, why (e.g., to *return* to God in a day of judgment.)

In other contexts associating with and deriving morality from politics, morality derives from power and authority: a monarchy often virtually controls the definition of morality, packing and containing it within the persona of the monarch as much as possible.

If we question (as I certainly do) the idea that morality is built-in to each human individual, then we must relocate the issue of morality to sociality as a primary locus; move from the oppositional idea of mind as the locus of morality, and enter into questions of interaction, conscience-for-others, and enter new sorts of wonderments about human freedom and the emergence of the individual. This gathers, as it were, the structuring of politics and attempts (e.g., toward a democratic government) to show that freedom and individual responsibility is/are on ongoing aspect of being human, rather than some obvious given. In this context, morality is not divisible into goods and evils inherent in our individual being, but located elsewhere: e.g., in a pedagogy of dialogue; in the ongoing Nietzschean attempt to *overcome* ourselves; in a re-gathering of authority to ourselves; in a continuing development of critical self-consciousness about morality and the honesty necessary to sustain this effort. (See my "Genesis of Morality," 2011)

The Loci of Morality: As with questions and quests for being and for meaning, the issues which gather under the rubric of morality are important and not always very clear. In considering so-called *Foundational* issues, the early attempt is to locate the thinking in whose/those terms we already think we know and understand morality.

Why the morality of *becoming*? To call our attention to the fact that, in the human condition, we are in some flux; changing, perhaps growing, hopefully moving into some next places in our lives which are developing, pleasing more than before. (See: *Next Places*)

It is not enough to *wear* morality as if a permanent veil, a gossamer structure whose ability to see through it does not necessarily make it permeable. It is insufficient to be and act "good." We also project ourselves forward into our imagined tomorrow's. The ways in which we inform our becoming is at the very heart of morality.

In my thinking/being the locus of morality is primarily and necessarily within one's self and one's ongoing experience. Problematics of morality rise most usually as a set of questions about how to deal with others and with oneself; with others as with oneself. Questions of being and of relationship intersect, intermix, and complicate the domains and terrains which express themselves as moral issues. And it is difficult even to write this down, because the locus of the agent—of who I am that I say, of who I am that others say—is also intermixed, complicated... an (ongoing) study in self.

But the locus of morality is also within the human condition. We may refer to human nature—whatever it is that differentiates humans from other species, or that which has been taken to *remove* us from nature. Or we may explore the limits and possibilities of any notion of humanism and of our outermost and complete *potentials*—whatever we might be which is also somehow moral. In this context, particularly, there has been a long history and a virtual edifice of thought construction about morality as a uniquely human aspect of being, which must be examined critically and in some Nietzschean or Derridaean sense, seen-through or deconstructed.

The history of locating morality has been filled with rather particular if unexamined solutions: to place humans somewhere other than other species and to claim we are what (we claim) others are not. Morality, that is, has something in particular to do with our nature as a kind of *given*; to empty ourselves of experience; to avoid thinking that we are actors, but rather (passive) recipients of forces which have invaded our being (e.g., good and evil).

There are many ways of (apparently) avoiding complications: by acting as if agency is located primarily outside of oneself—in, for example, an unchanging deity; of acting as if morality is located in some code of laws which exist, also, outside of being. Then the *shouldnesses* of life are referable always to places or persons outside of experience; at least outside of the experience which I am; and/or which I tell myself I am.

But the complications of being oneself, especially and particularly, rarely seems simple or direct. I write this because it seems, to me, moral activity to write about morality. This is so, especially, because the prior loci of morality have seemed to me to be misplaced and constructed upon a narrow

455

understanding of the human condition—at the least, in Western thinking. Being moral may be an enduring condition, but it is also *doing*. And it seems important, and moral, to attempt to explore the truth as I understand it; even as the question of the idea of truth has itself become problematic.

For me, this means engaging in observation and thinking about other species in addition to humans, in order to (help) see our own seeing, being, and morality. This is so because, in this time, it now appears clear that other species are social; and this notion of species as social thus seems to alter radically the loci of morality, ultimately to reflect us back to think and rethink the condition of being human, and of being who I-am and you-are; who we are in various ways of being-together.

Agency: Once the question of absolutes, of the certainty of locating authority is considered critically, the question of *agency* arises to our consciousness as well. Who/where, precisely is the directedness for any action or thought?

If we consider some notion of deity as the locus of total authority, then the agency which moves us is to be found in the idea of some transcendent power: God knows and tells us what to do. We only have to query God's will, and we will know... Agency is thus granted/derived from the deity, and our own movement/thought is derived.

In the often anti-theistic humanisms which have arisen and dominated a good deal of Western thinking - at least in the arena of politics and experience for the past few centuries, agency is granted to us humans as actors. Even if there is a deity, God has granted us *free will*, and we do what we will: we are the agents, and agency is ours to use, to abuse... to refuse. If there is no deity, then agency is ours alone. We do what we want! There is no one to blame but us! There is no evil in the world, but only bad or thoughtless (or bureaucratized) thinkers and thinking; only bad or thoughtless actions.

Nonetheless, we have many habits of assigning agency in our looking and searching for causes in the world of existence and happenings. Genes do it!—we (persons) are only the outward manifestations of genic desire to reproduce. Evolution does it!—bad behavior is not my fault: a no-fault will. Culture does it!—bad parenting, peer-pressures. Literature is all of being, and all we can do is interpret how others have told us our being is. Our bodies do it!—the penis is unconnected to consciousness and is unmindful of itself (*it* has a self!?). Hormones rage! It's a wonder that there is any *me* left: the subject of my being myself can only be read *into*... me.

The question of morality and truth: if there is one truth, is there a single, obvious, graspable morality? And if there are many truths? Or there is no truth?

The problem (romantic/modern): the suspicion is that there is no locus for one's own agency in being, thinking, acting; the postmodern dilemma where lack of personal agency and nihilism race hand-in-hand to deny meaning to being and to morality.

The issue: where is the ground upon which meaning and morality play hand-in-hand?

Choice: One (I/you) can *choose* to be moral; to live morally. Or I/you can choose to be immoral; evil.

Or can I?—you?

The issues, indeed the entire domain of the morality of becoming turns to a large degree on how one deals with the issue of what is choice, and the grounds and arenas in which it is constituted.

The presumption that choice is active, available, includes the idea that the I of who I am is active, self-directed, willful; that I have knowledge, that I am thoughtful and understand the consequences, potential costs and benefits of my actions. I am a being with conscience, caring about others as well as or more than I care about myself; or I am ideological, thinking and caring about the nature of some idea(l) in which I am a player; one among others. And the others care about the idea(l) much as I, and would/should act much as I.

But others do not at all presume that the "I" of who I am is so willful; rather I construct the "who" of who I am within some construct of, say, good and evil. I am some combination of a good deity and an evil Satanic force, an anti-Christ who is at war in my being with the good which I can assert but only partially. In this construction of being and morality, I am already conceived in some sense of sin whereby my very being has been constituted at least in part by some others (parents) whose desires (for sex, to begin) overcame their own consciences: and I am some soul now embodied and living in a deepened sense of condemnation.

Most of what is possible for me to do is to redeem myself-my-soul. What choice do I have? Any choice I may seem to have is bound within a concatenation of questions about my very being - being born in sin. Woe is me! All of my so called choices are cast within a cosmic battle for my being, and the illusion, the chimera of being me also includes the chimera of choice. The only choice I may have is to give in to the evil within—rather than engaging it in battle. Some choice!

The existential, experiential problematic is, however, much more the questioning of being as being moral: a set of problematics, of situations, of anti-responses to others who seem to act morally or immorally, of whether to tell a lie and is that some shift on the entire truth, and whether this compromises my integrity so that I can no longer be certain of what I said, or meant, or who exactly it is that I am. Honesty! Honesty?

If I please others or do not; am I being moral to them?—to me?—the boundaries of treason, treachery and the questions of choosing to belong or to leave, of how long and the conditions of the contracts I make in the world with myself and with others: with children it is for life; with others? For better, for worse!?

And the sense that choice is bound up with individuality is always complicated by social arrangement and the ongoing pulls and tugs of others upon me upon you; the sense of contract and obligation and responsibility toward culture, family, society, business, the who of who provides my goods and my food and insures my well-being. And if I consider that choice is truly mine to make, then I need to have some sense of motion and towardness and an ongoing sense for the morality of becoming who I would and can be... to be updated frequently!

Laws of Nature: Rather than looking to see humans as we are—the habits and the obvious-nesses of our being which hardly permit us to see who and how we are by looking away at other species, gaining new ideas and wearing new observational lenses... Instead, we have constructed and concocted stories of how we are: removed from, beholden to, controlled by, in control of Nature.

There is some urge to see us as if we know that we exist with respect to Nature. If only we would know Nature, who and what we are would then be obvious. But there is in this quest, no less a set of jumps, a wish to locate the true agency of our being in nature much as we have done with a deity. While there are no doubt limits to our being, the idea of limits has been carried as if it were definitional of the human condition: the agency of nature. This is a form of *bio-politics*, a story about being and morality constructed, as it were, to *save us* from ourselves, rather than explore who and what we are.

The fact is, that in Western thought, we are *juxtaposition* thinkers already. In thinking about who we humans are, we implicitly are comparative thinkers: we include in our ordinary perorations of the human condition, an active set of stories about other species with which we compare our being—irrespective of the accuracy of these stories. This seems easier, morally, than scrutinizing our existence and disinterring (deconstructing?) the edifice of stories in terms of which we live our living...

Altruism: The general *biological* puzzle of why certain animals *sacrifice themselves for others* remains overwhelming for many thinkers.

The thinking which underlies most of the current sociobiological phase which ponders this question—and answers it to its apparent self-satisfaction by claiming that organisms use altruism to their advantage by passing on their genes, thus continuing the species—depends on some assumptions about the nature of our being individuals. This presumption, especially in the light of our rather recently achieved understanding that other species are (intrinsically) social, seems, to me, to miscast the notions of being, and of sacrifice.

For social beings are not independent in the sense that they look to their own self-interest (as the economists would hold). What is a *sacrifice*, then, has much to do with how any organism/person sees one's own being and identity as independent/interdependent with others'. This is not to say, that even within sociality, there are not cases of sacrifice, conscience, responsibility; but these cross various species boundaries, and are not restricted to (any uniqueness-stories of) the human condition.

Western thought merely presumes that the individual is the locus of the agency by which it does what it does, and that any interdependence derives from the (agency of the) individual.

It would be more useful to increase our understanding of why various organisms-individuals-species do what they do, to ponder questions of how they gain meaning, identity, and so on, in their own terms (See: Vicki Hearne, 1987, for the nobility of various species' being: *Adam's Task: Calling the Animals by Name*. 253.

Imagination: Given the Western propensity (obvious, necessity) for presuming that the individual is the locus of all of being, the question of how we live outside of the present here and now, remains troubling and problematic in our thinking about morality. Or, because morality requires that we have imagination and do think beyond the here and now of the being of oneself, the very question of morality remains problematic. How, it has been asked, can we imagine that which is not, has never been?

Whatever is, precisely, the individual, our morality (and our being) seem to have much to do with our relations with m/others. Upon being born as the infant which has been forming and fulminating within the being and thinking of the mother-to-be for so long, the newborn infant is not simply observed and conceptualized within any present here and now. She/he is *projected forward* (imagined and interpreted by its parents as growing up) within the variety of imagined possibilities that exist within the knowing of m/others—a grand largesse quite beyond the life experience of any one person: all the stories of others, of ancestors, of the virtues and foibles of everyone's being strong and noble, weak and lesser.

One does not, that is, ever exist only within the present here and now in the terms in which one is treated. Good/bad behavior, thoughts, occur within the imagined future that one's m/others cast/project into one's life's possibilities: gender, roles, relationships, loyalties, loves, fragilities, carings, one's self, treacheries... the possibilities of all of being cast within what is known. Even in the most limited of societal experiences, this remains large and includes the life-ways of many persons; the possibilities placed upon the infant suckling remains and continues much as work of the imagination. Within social species, that is, the present here and now includes the imagination of future becoming, and consistently interprets her child's behavior as both present and when-will-s/he become a/one's self?

It thus seems to me that understanding the beyond, the becoming, the towardness is interpreted into each moment of our being. In any understanding of the ordinary of life's ways, including morality, it is more difficult to see how we know and can remain sufficiently in the present to deal with the dangers and vicissitudes of any moment, than it is to understand the work of the imagination.

The error—metaphysical, ontological, cosmological—remains in our conceptual work, not in the life experience of any of us. The infant is not survivable without the continuous thoughtful involvement of its m/others.

Sociality—Being with Others: Sociality means, I think, much more than merely being in each other's presence, trying to communicate what each individual knows, thinks, or wants. It means (G.H. Mead 1934) that we each *have in our minds' eyes* some sense of the being of others; it means that we construct ourselves much in relation to who they are, as well as who they say we are, and are to be.

Sociality means that the next generation is not simply fed and nurtured to survive, but that infants' behavior is seen and interpreted within the contexts of *proper*, moral behavior and being. Children are continually being shaped, being corrected with a sense of interpretive towardness— toward becoming/being adults within the sense of a good person. They are not merely treated as a physical being, but projected forward into an indefinite future as real persons; i.e., much like we are already. The child is seen consistently within framing ideas of the adult it will be, eventually. It is never interpreted merely within the presence of its present here and now.

And, I think, this is also true of other species. Social behavior (all behavior) is *corrected* within frameworks of becoming whatever it means to be a proper wolf, or dolphin, or crow, or aunt to momma and papa wolf. (Domesticated species…?)

The historical-philosophical error of understanding morality as located within the physical individual has created a study of morality which sees the human condition as particularly unique, particularly in our mental capacities; and has derived its forms from whatever we have considered to be the differences between humans and others.

Humans are clearly different from other species; but we share some ways of being, treating, and understanding others. The study of morality should begin from the study of social similarities, not from the (presumed) differences between us and others. (→*Next Places*)

Sociality implies that we already know a great deal about others, (including their constructions of the world), and makes problematic the nature of individuality—not the other way round. Contra to Rousseau, we are not born free, but live in complicated relationships with ourselves, with others, with our senses of being proper and defining (frequently) who we are.

And it means that we have others with us who are self-critical and critics of our own grapplings with morality, with honesty, integrity; and with our doings in which questions of morality are often in some places and moments of irresolve.

And sociality means that individual being is in some measures of intersection between who I am that I say and think I am—and who others see and say...think I am. As I understand human processes, the quest for individuality/self is as important to others as it is to ourselves: we are, in various ways and senses individuals. But we are never only or solely individuals.

The Psychology of Morality: It seems difficult to distinguish some sense of the *psychology* of morality—the why and how of morality serving human ends and needs—from the sense of morality as independent of our (individual) being.

Thou shalt not kill, should honor thy father and mother, not covet thy neighbor's wife... are laws, admonitions, but they also can be thought to serve our existential being. That is, breaking these *commandments* also places our experiential being in some places which move us to the *edges* of our being. Killing someone (usually?) reduces our hold on life by cheapening the worth of existence; if we do not honor our parents we tend to dishonor ourselves; by imagining love we grant less seriousness to the complications of loving those with whom we enter into life-long contracts of marriage.

It seems clear that, to some great extent, the psychology of morality has much to do with the importance, necessities, utility of the psychology of morality. If we *do (not) unto others* as we would to ourselves, then we are thinking about the care of others, but particularly of ourselves, and the importance of life, presumably as some sort of gift or of its own necessity: a kind of Jewish view on the nature of existence, but also an existentially informing view.

It refers reflexively as well to the necessity of caring for ourselves in order that we may be *sufficient*—strong, self-assured (assured of self)—to care for others. As a teacher, for example, my first duty to my students is to maintain myself; no small task.

How universal, how time-unbound, how out-of-situation, how culture-specific this sense of the psychology of morality, is not always clear. As Ecclesiastes reminds us, much of life is seasonal and cyclical. To anchor morality to some unchanging sense of the human psyche may often be to deny that we exist in history. And while we take care of the individual psyche, we open vacuums and spaces for the politically totalitarian to so bind existence that all quests and questions of morality are not allowed to be asked.

And so...

Absence (of Presence): Being moral always includes, I think, being *present*: having presence to oneself as well as to others. As Kant would have it, we must be self-conscious of our own consciousness. But this is not enough because our physical presence is/seems so *obvious* that we seem able to absent ourselves even from our own presence, apparently noting that others see us and then we retreat *into* ourselves, into interior spaces where we are but at the same time are not!

This aspect of being and not-being present also has a quite long and powerful history of the architectonic of our being moral, because being and not-being have—since Parmenides—been included in the dialectic of life and death; less presence in our own presence. The issue arises in Plato's *Sophist*, a line which Heidegger rephrases in his *Being and Time*, a line which seems to underlie the thinking against being which inspires the questions of suicide from Hamlet to Schopenhauer and rephrase themselves in the 19th century wonderment of why we continue on: willings, wills to... live... power.

And as we can absent ourselves from our presence, we seem to be well-equipped, we Westerners at least, to not note the presence of others whenever it suits our purposes; whenever...

Given this propensity to oppose (thence to equate) being and not-being, it seems that we develop much of moral thought in the spaces between moments of our present presence. We wander, that is, from awareness of our presence as we act as if we are other places, and derive moral and ethical rules from spaces where we situate being, which are not right here and right now. Actually Plato (and Pythagoras) set us up for this by developing the forms and ideas in whose terms we are (morally) *supposed* to live, even as they deride actually being present: living as aspects of the ideals, of partaking in the ideas at a level much lower than the reality of the universal ideas of being (*Republic X*). Morality stands, as well as our presence, at a higher level of being than our actual self-conscious presence.

Toward any morality of becoming, it seems necessary to understand that being present and non-present in the same moments of being, constitute (a) paradox; and note that life is paradoxical across a number of apparent oppositions. If morality until now has derived essentially (sic!) from our absence from our presence, then there is also a sense of morality of becoming which constitutes our presence in our presence. The inability to see this within oppositional dualism derives from our habits of understanding presence from the essentialisms of idealism (absence), not from experience itself; e.g., Heidegger's *Dasein*).

Research: It was not so many centuries ago when we (still) knew very little about the mechanical aspects of the human body. Wherever the body was punctured, blood would spew forth as if blood and being were in some total suffusion. Only with the intellectual discovery and insight that the heart is a sort of mechanical pump, do we begin to understand the whats and whys of blood circulation; of oxygenation, of the concept of nutrition, of waste; of why, wherever there is a puncture of the body, there is blood.

In order to understand the staggering jump provided conceptually by the idea of the heart-as-pump, and the making sense of the circulatory system, one must attempt to do some sort of thought experiment, suspending belief (and disbelief) to try and see the human clearly and *anew*, to develop theories of our nature, like the theorists of old; without, that is, benefit of such a mechanical understanding.

Performing such a thought experiment is important not only to understand—and to develop a critical stance of earlier theories of our being—but also to develop a critical stance of our own present thinking. Present thinking still, for the most part, presumes an unexamined sense of human uniqueness due to language and mind - including a uniquely human sense of morality - and leaves us observing and thinking about humans much as if our observational lenses were conceptually colored by what we *think*, more than what we *see* even when we bother to look carefully.

Or we look especially at certain behaviors or aspects of the human condition, it not often occurring to us to look at others. A large amount of human behavior particularly concerning the human body and the human face, is generally by-passed and unnoted in our thinking and seeing: even as we look, we often do not see!

This is so, at least in part, because we *use* the face as an arena for making social judgments (beauty, age, gender...) and do not *see* it. One arena of developing interest in is so-called *sports medicine*, in which it becomes quite obvious that much of our understanding of the human body previously, has depended on conceptualizing the body lying down, at rest, cadaverous. We have, for the greatest part, not taken human movement in an upright position into our thinking about how we are.

The research problematic is to develop a good critical sense for how we see as we do—guided by certain habits or theories—to *see through* our own seeing; to examine how we are in the world unguided by stories and theories about human uniqueness which have allowed, even encouraged us to think that humans are unique due to our mentality—overlooking the most obvious of the obvious aspects of being human, that our bodies and especially our faces are very particularly human... and that we are the species who particularly loves and studies faces as we develop and mature (Sarles, 1985: Chapter 14).

Ethico-Cognitive Parallelism: Hans Reichenbach teaches us (*The Rise of Scientific Philosophy*, 1963) that much of modern morality derived from Spinoza who tried to develop an *Ethics* modeled on geometry and logic. Moral-ethical first principles would be stated much like geometric statements and theorems, and morality judgments would follow. Similarly with Kant (*Foundations of the Metaphysics of Morals*, 1859), this modeling seemed to follow the idea of logic within the mental, unchanging, true in a mathematical sense; knowing, thence and thus morality.

The major problem since the 1930's is that geometry and logic are now understood to be assumptive and models—one among several or many geometries—logic, a system among systems—leaving ethics...where?

It is clearly appealing to think we have a philosophical morality by which (some) philosophers can tell us how we should be. But can they? Do they have some better knowledge or better preachment than the deity or an Ayn Rand (1964) who preached respectively: *love thy neighbor* or *love thyself* as the directness of human nature and its condition?

Are there some places or ways between the either/or of Kierkegaardian morality: ethics vs. esthetics; live like a Christ lived...or...else? (How can each of us *live like ourselves*, morally?)

Self-Interest and its Moral Transcendence: "How does it happen," asks Adam Smith, "that man, who is a creature of self-interest, can form moral judgments in which self-interest seems to be held in abeyance or transmuted to a higher plane?" Heilbroner (*1953*:34) quotes Smith's *Theory of Moral Sentiments* as holding "that the answer lay in our ability to put ourselves in the position of a third person, an impartial observer, and in this way to form a sympathetic notion of the objective (as opposed to the selfish) merits of a case."

The problem with Adam Smith—and with the history of Western thought from Plato-on—is that this argument is assumptive and circular. It is based on the assumption that human beingness is metaphysics—*after physics*—that (physical) individuality is primary and prior: thus the notion that man *is* a creature of self-interest (from *Natural Law*, like all other creatures—Hobbes, 1651).

But we are not necessarily creatures of self-interest any more than we are creatures interested primarily in one another. We would, for example, not continue to exist, to survive as infants if mothers and others were (already) not very interested in our continuing being, and willing to act (*morally*) more on the behalf of their infants, than upon their own (present) wishes or interests.

The idea that we are the creatures who are objective, can be objective, derives from the history of the so-called *origin* of language argument which sees the uniqueness of humans as due to language; language leading, in turn, to knowing words for objects, leading to objectivity, to seeing ourselves both as subjects and as objects—allowing humans (alone) to be moral.

But we really don't know that other creatures don't possess language and objectivity—this all having been assumed before we knew that other species are already social, communicative—and probably in some senses objective and surely moral, even in our terms of whatever is moral (Sarles, 1985).

So if it is that we are transcendent, it is much more an *ordinary* aspect of our being human, than something which is particularly or solely human. This line of human uniqueness argument does not lead us to consider any true *foundations* of the question of morality.

Nature: Many of the questions of morality have been dealt with in the context of the human condition being understood within various dualisms rooted in the issue of our relation to *nature*.

It is illuminating to juxtapose the *Politics [1254a5 - 1254b]* of Aristotle with Jefferson's *Declaration of Independence*.

Aristotle: *But is there any one thus intended by nature to be a slave, and for whom such a condition is expedient and right, or rather is not all slavery a violation of nature?*
There is no difficulty in answering this question, on grounds both of reason and of fact. For that some should rule and others be ruled is a thing not only necessary, but expedient; from the hour of their birth, some are marked out for subjection, others for rule... the living creature, which, in the first place, consists of soul and body: and of these two, the

one is by nature the ruler, and the other the subject. But then we must look for the intentions of nature in things which retain their nature, and not in things which are corrupted. And therefore we must study the man who is in the most perfect state both of body and soul, for in him we shall see the true relation of the two; although in bad or corrupted natures the body will often appear to rule over the soul, because they are in an evil and unnatural condition.

Jefferson states simply: *[It is]...self-evident that all men are created equal.*

Are we aspects of nature; removed from nature; unrelated altogether to questions of nature? Are we, as in Western thinking, both of nature and removed; e.g., in the dualisms by which we have imagined that our bodies are like the bodies of (other) animals while our minds or souls or spirits are somehow removed from nature? Are we aspects of nature at the moment of birth, but become gradually removed from nature as we go from *biology* to *rationality*? Is the female aspect of our being more centered/located within nature, and the male more removed; as it were, civilized and rational?

Such questions have, I think, dominated discussions of (human) morality because in Western tradition we have been ambivalent about the relation of being human to being aspects of nature. Morality has been seen as an aspect of being which is particularly and uniquely human. It has merely been assumed that other—even similar and/or *related*—species are not at all moral; do not partake in morality, but are completely tied-to or dominated by (their) nature.

Human have been construed, that is, to be the only species which has been (able to) overcome its nature—either because religiously we alone were *created* in the image of a deity, or we evolved somehow (usually, via languaging and all its entailments) into the only species which have managed to overcome or to dominate or to otherwise remove ourselves effectively from nature.

Now, as was pointed out in the *Introduction*, such stories apparently have been constructed in the human imagination without much careful observation of other species in the contexts of their feral/wild/actual situational nature. Our observations of other species, apparently, has been based on zoo, specially trained work animals (elephants, camels, etc.), or domesticated species as if they represent fairly accurately the actual lives of other species.

Our observations of humans have been done largely within the context of our stories about ourselves, more often than from careful observation and analysis. Plato observed that older men—women were generally excluded from/hidden with respect to issues of morality as they entered into thinking about the human condition: or as aspects of purer nature—unfathomable, obscure, dangerous, unimportant (Paglia: *Sexual Personae,* 1990)—were somehow beyond the pulls and pushes of their own desires (*Republic, Laws*). Age had to do with being, removed from nature. Not only were the raging, desiring hormones tamed or understandable and dealable-with, but the older and experienced persons had plenty of experience with flattery and corruption (and all the other deadly sins), and had presumably survived them or transcended them, and were able to see beyond the moment and the individual → wisdom.

Social class—royalty, aristocracy, and education, etc., were often constructed within the idea that the proper or appropriate ruling types were somehow more beyond nature than the poor and (ethnically) different. That is, within our construction of the human condition, we have applied a sense of nature, and our social-political theories to different persons/groups along some hierarchical notion which parallels our sense of their removal and distance from nature: *jungle bunnies* (used to characterize some African-Americans in late 20th century America) and the rest of the racialist epithets and thinking.

Most important, in Western thinking, is the concept from Hobbes (based on Aristotle's *Rhetoric* and his *Politics*), of so-called *natural law,* which has been taken to be applicable to legal and political theories. The story is a metaphor which we are urged to ask in understanding and analyzing how the world works: how would people be in a *state of nature*—compared to how they are right now—in order to analyze why they act as they do?

The difficulty—the mistake and error, I think—is that the depiction of any state of nature has had wild swings. Until the present, our representations of nature have had little to do with humans or other species in any actual nature. Indeed, our notions of nature have principally derived from our theories, rather than having contributed to them.

The nature story (the women are *absent*, presumably keeping the kids behaving): all the solitary males are highly competitive, seeking food and sex and all their hearts' desires. They gradually acquire language (requiring *origin of language* theories, also derived) which got them to be objective (to know objects) then to know themselves by being objective, thence also to know present, past, and future. Seeing futurity (now, for the first time), they got to foresee their own deaths, got very frightened, and began to limit competition by forming societies (also, presumably, for the very first time in nature).

Thus society is (claimed to be) an outgrowth of the ("uniquely") human development of language and rationality; a society which is formulated by independent individuals coming together for mutual protection et al. And this is why the discovery was made only in the twentieth century (*Introduction*) that other species are also social is (i.e., should be!) a powerful shock to our thinking. It causes us to rethink language, society, individuality—and in the present context, the nature of morality.

The concept of nature has also been largely derived from our theories of human-uniqueness-due-to-language. So we have particular representations of nature—ranging from beneficent (Rousseau and society has bound us in chains) to terrifying (Tennyson: "nature red in tooth and claw") and many positions between, on this axis of a nature-agent which either determines us to a great extent, or from which we must work to remove ourselves further and further, until—via culture, art, the imagination. Instead, *nature* is much more interesting, probably changing as much as anything else (another issue in this discussion), and suggests to me, at least, that the human condition has been underestimated and misunderstood: morality, not the least of all.

Nature as Propaganda: Phil Regal asks how an apostolic notion of Christianity which was against politics, against the pursuit of money, against the idea of massive propagation for over a millennium until the early 1300's, could have changed/yielded/ sold out to a world view and practice which seems utterly to have reversed its stand on all these issues. Orwell's Orwell!

The answer is the invocation of Aristotle's notions of nature which presumed that the human condition is essentially political, and underwrites the pursuit of wealth. The context was the Crusades against Islam, set off after the 1st Millennium when many readers of the Book of Revelation found themselves in Palestine waiting for the arrival of the messiah, and found themselves still waiting after the moment of prophesied arrival did not occur.

The holy wars moved the Popes in the direction of needing a politically bounded sense of being—a state, and an army, which needed money, and people to engage in the wars and wars, and wars to come: thence usury, thence the rise of nature over the eye on the ideal God of the apostolic Christians; thence the arguments that a particular version of life on earth (inequality) should determine how we are and are to be.

Justification for War: One of the most compelling examples of how the *argument from nature* has been used (*is* used, still) in the context of morality is this 15th century argument used by Sepulveda as an apologetic for why Spain *can justifiably* conduct war against the native peoples of the New World. (Sepulveda was anti-native Americans as less-than-human).

"Democrates: In the first place, one must keep in mind a principle which is the basis of this and many other questions: everything which is done in the name of natural rights or laws can also be done by virtue of divine rights or evangelical laws. When Christ tells us in the Gospels not to resist the evil-doer and, if someone strikes us upon one cheek to turn the other...we should not believe that he was attempting to do away with the laws of nature which permit one to resist force with force within the limits of a just defense...Those words from the Bible are not laws in the obligatory sense of the word, but rather advice and exhortation which do not belong so much to everyday life as to apostolic perfection...

I wish to make it clear that one should search not only in Christians and in the writings of the New Testament, but also in those philosophers whom we judge to have dealt most wisely with nature and the customs and governments of all societies, especially in the writings of Aristotle, whose precepts, except for a few opinions referring to matter beyond the capacity of human understanding, and which man can understand only through divine revelation, have been received by posterity with such unanimous approval that they no longer seem to be the words of a single philosopher, but the decisions and opinions held in common by all wise men.

Leopold: Let us return, then, to the business at hand. Now show me the reasons, if there are any, by which you believe that war can be undertaken and waged in a just and pious manner.

D. A just war requires not only just causes for its undertaking, but also legitimate authority and upright spirit in whoever declares it and a proper manner in its conduct...

L. ...*But what happens if a ruler, moved not by avarice or thirst for power, but by the narrowness of the borders of his state or by its poverty, should wage war upon his neighbors in order to seize their fields as an almost necessary prize?*

D. *That would not be war but theft. For a war to be just, the causes must be just...Among the causes of a just war the most important, as well as the most natural, is that of repelling force with force when it is not possible to proceed in any other fashion...The second cause of a just war is the recovery of things seized unjustly...It is licit to recover not only one's own things, but also those of friends, and to defend them and keep them free from harm as much as if they were one's own. The third cause of a just war is to punish evil-doers who have not been punished in their own cities, or have been punished with negligence, so that they will take heed and not commit their crimes a second time, and others will be frightened by their example. It would be easy to enumerate here the many wars waged by the Greeks and Romans for this reason, with such approval from the people, whose consensus must be considered to be a law of nature...*

L. *And who is born under such an unlucky star that nature condemned him to servitude? What difference do you find between having nature force one under the rule of another and being a slave by nature? Do you think that judges, who also pay much attention to natural law in many cases, are joking when they point out that all men since the beginning were born free, and that slavery was introduced contrary to nature and as a law of mere humans?*

D. *I believe that the jurist speaks with seriousness and great prudence, but this word slavery means quite a different thing for the jurist than for the philosopher. For the former slavery is an accidental thing, born of superior strength and from the laws of peoples, sometimes from civil laws, while philosophers see slavery as inferior intelligence along with inhuman and barbarous customs...*

Those who surpass the rest in prudence and talent, although not in physical strength, are by nature the masters. Those, on the other hand, who are retarded or slow to understand, although they may have the physical strength necessary for the fulfillment of all their necessary obligations, are by nature slaves, and it is proper and useful that they be so, for we even see it sanctioned in divine law itself, because it is written in the Book of Proverbs that he who is a fool shall serve the wise...If they reject such rule, than it can be imposed upon them by means of arms, and such a war will be just according to the laws of nature. Aristotle said, `It seems that war arises in a certain sense from nature, since a part of it is the art of the hunt, which is properly used not only against animals, but also against *those men who, having been born to obey, reject servitude: such a war is just according to nature...'"*

It is only necessary to claim that some other persons—those against whom we would justify war—are in some measure less civilized or more barbarian-like-animal-dumb than we are. Any claim to morality or ethics is easily defeated as idealistic by the claim to nature, which is more *real*, more inevitable. And thereby we can justify whatever we want to do!

And if this lacks some power of convincing by justification, then we can do as Hitler—simply define a new notion of a *eugenic ideal*, a direction for the human race, and proclaim that some (e.g., Jews, gypsies, homosexuals...) cannot fit this definition. So even our idea of nature can be altered to suit ourselves or our purposes, as against whomever we would engage in battle. In effect, the idea of any morality is itself captured as hostage in a war with nature. It only remains to define a new ideal, a new utopia which excludes some categories of person... by whoever controls the claim to nature.

Freedom:

Free to be... me... you...

The locus of the nature of how anyone is to be free, how much freedom, where it directs itself, can be directed...?

How are freedom and morality connected? Are they?

Much thinking about morality has located the nature of anyone's being moral as interlocked with one's sense of freedom. One wouldn't be moral, if he/she were not free to choose!? Here the question of morality has been deeply intertwined with the notion of the will: of free will, of freedom of will; freedom to inquire, of free inquiry.

If we must obey... you listen to me... trust me... listen to God, obey the law. Love your mother; call your mother (right now!). Do what she says! If not...

Rights, responsibilities... by now my head is aching with the complications of being so complex that I can no longer think. Oh, just to be... me... you...!

Law(s) and the Scale of Society: Because morality has been ensconced in some theory of humans being different from (all) other species, and the construction of a history of development away from animals, and toward some notion of being moral and like a deity, the question of law has also entailed a developmental structure: toward civilization, toward a *higher* human way of being.

This thinking has often begun with some construction of what humans are like, *really*: really, being understood variously. The *natural law* ideas stemming from Hobbes, for example, concoct a depiction of the human condition *previous* to our becoming creatures who could exactly think, has language, could imagine the future, and so on—a competitive world of all against all. Women are not present in this depiction; men who learn through language to foresee the future, become frightened of death, and seek protection in social agreement: laws. Here, Leviathan (monarchy) is proposed to control the natural propensities of men to destroy one another.

Other pictures (Plato) begin by being concerned more with psychological factors: virtue, the control of desires (sex, power, fame, money...). He proposed an older philosopher king—those who had grappled successfully with virtue and desire, and had gotten past some of life's driving forces, to rule the kingdom.

Recent feminist arguments propose giving voice to women and others who had been made to disappear from theories of law, of virtue, of desire or to be passive within their understanding. Women would balance the boys' penchant for war, and focus questions of being and morality, law and control, on dynamics and understanding of more actual and experiential/existential forces of being.

Much has probably been left out of our thinking about laws. One important factor obscured by the stories which have had some notion of human development toward civilization (democracy?) is that codes of law develop whenever the scale of any group expands beyond the number who can be, live, and study one another in a fair fullness of their being. In small groups, everyone is in face-to-face relationships, knows everyone else in great detail, and usually have ways of punishing those who offend, whose behavior is egregious or annoying beyond toleration.

Once there are too many (usually with/after agriculture developed) - then other modes of regulation develop → laws. We deal with one another only partially, or as partials: roles, classes, clans. Like classical orchestras, when they move beyond the number which can see each other face-to-face, they *need* a conductor—someone to mark time, whom they all can see. Then laws occur; laws are necessary.

The dynamics of being change with scale, as well. When we live in the one-to-one, then we deal with one another in some fullness of our mutual existences. When we deal with partials, when there are too many, when we no longer know anyone in great fullness, then our thinking about others and ourselves change and alter—sometimes radically. The power of family to define us is likened to the small community. Much of our thinking about them and ourselves in within each other's terms: positive or not so positive, I am still the son of my parents - now dead for 40 and 50 years, still wandering and developing within my thinking. But with many, there develop distinctions and differences which affect ourselves and moral being: who am I to be? - has little modeling in the world of my experiencing advancing age; who all the others are divides into gender and color and nationality and not so classy and those who have some power of definition... about my being... older...

Laws remove us from ourselves when there are too many, when the scale of life's experiences enable us to see many, more than to see one. Then we construct them, and reflectively construct ourselves, and it is difficult to know what this might mean from time to time.

The Problem of Evil: Construed within the notion of being-as-social, the question of evil recedes, collapses, or is overtaken by issues of being, of identity, of politics, of fear, and the myriad motivations which work themselves through the human imagination-turned-into-activity.

This is *not* to say that there is *no evil*, but that our concepts of evil residing in Western oppositional dualism can only label, but never help to explain whatever the nature is of what we may mean.

Life is largely a process of self-development, emerging (as it were) from a social being which/who is largely defined in terms others provide (language as well as any sense of an independent self). In its becoming, the self develops within the context of others' treatment, definitions, outlooks both of immediate and of long-term existence. One's m/other-parents, looking at the newborn, do not merely see in the moment, but within the lifetime of possibilities, already shaping who they see in terms of who they expect, want, will love... and may hate.

In this context, notions of evil are aspects of development, as well as other aspects of the self who is becoming. As one learns the language which is the descriptor of the world as one's m/others experience it, one learns the possibilities and parameters of one's own beingness. As de Sade instructs us, with personal freedom comes the possible and potential inclusion of deeds which are destructive of self and of others, and of the moral schemes which have previously defined even reasons-for-being.

Not only morality, but the why's of being moral are up for discussion here...and will lead us eventually into issues of existence as wide as the universe of understanding.

This is to say that evil is a construal of our being, not an aspect of it. Much/most of what we call evil has to do with some developments, directions, habits of thinking (bureaucratic, etc.)—in terms of which we cast morality within terms having to do with construing of the self as an aspect of something beyond ourselves: deity, bureaucracy, authority to which we then grant *agency,* a new within which we now see ourselves and others differently from before: culture, corporation, apparatus.

This is not to say that there is no *evil* in the world, but that its understanding is not illuminated by constructing evil as any direct opposite of good. No doubt people act evilly, but there is great doubt that they (most of them—there are, no doubt, some anti-persons who have thoughtfully rejected any earlier notion of the source of their own morality, and have chosen its apparent opposite) recognize their acts as evil.

Morality and Politics: Where does one begin and the other end? In the context of sociality, being moral is an important aspect of dealing with others as they would have one do. Rather than conscience being an aspect of morality built-in to one's character, morality is seen as overlapping with politics. "Do what I say," says mom, "because (I say) it is good for you."

The politics and authority of parents wanting a child not to burn herself or fall down the stairs or be hit by a car must somehow be *internalized* by their child: to act as her parents would have her act. Maybe she recognizes causality in the world, and will eventually - for most activity. But acting with conscience is, in early life, acting as authority urges and demands. In this sense, it is not very clear that morality and politics are very different.

Later in development, things become more complicated: as one begins to develop more involved pictures of who she or he is, the urge to act morally becomes increasingly distinct from its politics. The authority previously granted to parents is now taken in and on to oneself: authority is transformed into responsibility.

Questions of what is good or bad, transform themselves from what others would have me do, to what I *want* to do. A realm of morality invests selfhood: do what others would have me do, what they say is right or wrong becomes me. Sometimes I am not very clear that when I oppose them, that I am acting badly or immorally. In some Christian (Protestant-Lutheran) families I have known well, behavior of children is often (usually) judged in terms of whether one will get to heaven - or not. God is invoked as the authority for conscience and it seems never to be clear whether good and evil are moral or political; never to be clear whether one takes on any personal responsibility for his or her behavior and being, except that some sense of authority hovers about one's head, buzzing one's decisions. In such persons, it is often difficult to separate contrary urges from immoral thoughts.

And in one's internal perorations, emerging from sociality in becoming oneself, the realms of morality and politics are never completely separable: opposition, hatred, immorality, evil—compose a slippery slope.

As Freire would account for it, the question of morality is inseparable from politics as long as those who are weak are oppressed and, having learned too well, become oppressive in their turn (*Pedagogy of the Oppressed*, 2007). The development of a true, social morality, begins when one is sufficiently *strong* to not need to oppress others merely because they are weak;

not to feel frightened and have to direct one's fears and feelings toward others. In this sense, morality includes politics, but is *beyond* politics.

Spirit: is a term whose meanings go in many different directions from some sense of personal strength, to a sharing of a sense of a deity, toward sharing - a sense of being at one with others—family, group, nationality, religion, the world, life...

In other contexts, it can be used to represent the sense that each person is truly oneself; not exactly like anyone else; a kind of independence of spirit—although in, e.g., the Cameroons, one is born and exists as if she/he actually were some specifiable ancestor—one *is* one's grandmother. Her *spirit* is alive in me; as me. Among Amerindians, one's spirit (*Nagual* is as common a word as I know) is shared among several: human and animal—and is *released* from the human during sleep/dreams.

The term, spirit, overlaps sometimes with the mind or soul: some sense of being which has permanence. In the Augustinian-Christian story, one's *soul* falls to earth, and is placed in a body. It should have been in Heaven with God, but due to the evil of sex and Adam and Eve and all that, it finds itself on earth, and needs to be born alive, baptized, and thus return to Heaven. There is a kind of evolutionary travel story among the Buddhists, where the soul's journey begins low (in some animal) and gradually rises to the state of Nirvana, when finally with death, comes the truer death of the soul.

In the context of morality, I think we refer principally to why this aspect of our being acts like it does. I, the individual, am conceived of as a complex of features, but am locatable as a central persona who acts, thinks; who may be complex but is and does and has some centrality and consistency. While everyone lives (as) a congeries of roles, spirit is at the least a centralizing tendency which can find itself when it *wants* to, or *needs* to.

Since this area of being is so complicated—yet has been made to appear so obvious and central to the idea of the individual in Western thinking—one finds it difficult to describe the nature of spirit without falling into simplistic or quickly transcendent terms. The complications arise because it seems that we are paradoxically both one and many, with variation in situational, relational, and contextual variables.

In the sort of societal theory which I propose/observe in this exploration of morality of becoming, any especial individuality which is possibly inherent within the physical organism in early infancy, is seen by mothers/others in their—adult, cultural—terms, and treated as if their constructed depictions of the child are the ones which the child *is*. To a very large extent, each of us then becomes the one which the parental generation sees, expects, corrects, and treats as if it is that person, that spirit.

Perhaps the Cameroonian notion of becoming one's ancestor can illustrate this well: my (friend/student's) grandmother died shortly before she was born. She was named *for and as* the grandmother. And for all intents and purposes she was seen and treated as the grandmother in her cyclical becoming again (and into futurity). All of her behavior was treated, interpreted, concretized into her being and becoming this other person who was known in terms of what I am calling her spirit: the senses of being and doing which is bounded and called by her name.

As it happened, all this did not *fit* particularly well this particular student, who left home (complicated politics et al), searching for herself in the midst of all her being interpreted as the grandmother whom she was supposed to be. We might say that the spirit of her grandmother—an identifiable set of habits, frames of mind, of being - did not enter her wholly.

Or we can recall Borges' story of the person who could have become exactly the person whom he would have hated, and had to kill, the person/spirit he actually became.

Importantly here, it is in this sense of the personal spirit which is the source of morality and the ability to act as if one is someone; someone who can trust oneself, and be trusted by others to act with a sense of integrity—as an integral person—standing outside of the immediate, beyond the desires of each moment, and still be human.

For many, the world of the dead is full and they surround our being; for others the spirits of the formerly living show up only at certain times or places; other spirits may be found only in cemeteries or in the workings of our own changing being.

Existentially, it has seemed to me that the important idea of spirit is to grant the fullness of existence to everyone, thence to oneself; to oneself, thence to every one; and to continue to explore this aspect of being whatever one's paths (Sarles, 1985).

The Individual: In the social world, the *individual* is not the given which is directly continuous with the physical individual which emerges from the womb, but is process and product emergent within the sociality of being.

It is never clear in this life exactly/precisely where one begins and ends. Nor is it clear, internally or within the theories of our being constructed by those who seek certitude and direction and purpose, precisely who one is; or even what these questions mean.

We live within a historically constructed edifice which has much to tell us who we are: a kind of programmed matrix of being to which we must eventually conform/join. Whatever we become, wherever we seek, the trajectories of individuality have seemed to be set out. Some peoples have models for their being—saints, heroes, martyrs, teachers... Direct being toward these anointed to become anointed oneself. Made in the image of God, we only must enter the *strait gate order* to... But in the global village, we find that there are various gates, and various paths, and what is virtuous for some often is at war—sometimes literally—with the *howness* of others.

In most of these edifices, the architecture of the individual is set within the physical constraints of being, and individuality is never the puzzle which experience teaches us it is. In the real-social world, the individual is an emergent notion: never complete, never completely *alone* even when one is alone (Mead, 1934).

The individual—the idea of the individual in sociality—is certainly one which parents demand: and most of us take on within various contexts of our being. They demand that each of us be sufficiently responsible for ourselves, for our independent being, that we can be trusted: proposing, propositional creatures which have taken on the mantle of independence and freedom which says that they do not have, at every moment, to tell us how to be. How independent, in what times and places, how much we return to interdependence varies in different traditions.

It is for these reasons that morality is confusing: that one is not immoral because the devil dwells within us; that one is not immoral because she or he gives-in to evil. Much of what *seems* immoral has to do with the confusions and complications and internal wars of being independent and inter-dependent; mistakes are made, judgments are made, one's being is structured or is not.

Whenever (it has seemed to me) individuality is constructed so that direction and completion are not only possible, but likely or necessary, then the issues of morality overwhelm politics; we begin to praise/condemn acts more than persons; and everyone's being is diminished to the boundaries of toleration and beyond.

Paradox: Part of the contextual problem of considering issues of morality within Western thought is that we are accustomed to thinking that morality is a horn within some dualistic architectonic. This sense of thinking as dialectic sets up a universe of the two-sided either/or of life within the penumbras and lights of *good* and *evil*.

The world is arranged into two kingdoms (Augustine A.D 386) is filled with the Deity and the anti-Christ and Satan; our very being is construed to be dual: mind and body—with the mind as the locus of the good, and the body as bad, evil, and sinful even as we are supposed to be born in sin and fallen to earth. The mind, mental, mind, spirit, soul is an arena which is unchanging, the place in our being in which we could know an unchanging and eternal God. The body is *yucky*, and the locus of change and can only distantly partake in the reality which is the universal and unchanging. Each of us is some combination of good and evil, always at war with the devil within - to determine how to be and to survive to escape from this earthly world: life itself is not life itself. By the time the bodily actuality is dealt with, it too becomes an aspect of the place of the mental, a social construction rather than anything mortal or experiential.

One exercise which may illuminate the limitations of thinking dually—leading, hopefully, to a sense that the temptations of duality have more to do with the fact that various life paradoxes are aspects of the human condition—is to begin to consider the nature of being from a curer's perspective. The perspective of curer, an attempt to relieve, to change, to restore, prevent, make whole often turns upon a triality: a sense of beginning, middle, and end.

Every illness or disorder has an onset, a set of pathologies, and experienced discomfort, an actual break of bodily bone or organ, a spilling of blood, an orifice where none was intended. Then one attempts to change: conditions, contexts, experience: curer and patient. There is a *yielding*, a surrender to condition, to curer. Finally there is a restoration, or a new newness, a cure, a disappearance of pain or discomfort, a staunching of the flows of liquids green and red; a sense of boundedness that one calls oneself. And this process seems to want to organize itself in a sense of three; and this sense of three may place in some perspective the wanting to split into two, eventually to desire backgrounding to disappearance the one over the other of the opposition of body and mind, of life and of death, of nature and art and culture and the experiencing of life which seems so often to subordinate itself to the essence of our being.

The paradoxes of being, many of which we experience only occasionally as truly paradoxical, but nonetheless are apparent in all moments of our being what and who we are: girl, boy; one, many; now, then; on and off; awake, asleep. These, different traditions have dealt with often by banishing the one, or attempting to background the one and to foreground the other so successfully that our bodily experience remains almost hidden to our being; or so subordinated that we have developed complex theories to tell us who we are, rather than observing what and how we do. Wakefulness over sleeping (the opposite for many Amerindians) we take the simplicities of logic, the regularities of geometry and try to apply them to life and experience. Reality, likewise, is formal; the ideas stand in the light in whose shadows experience and the senses, pale and seem to tell us that what and who we are is not what and who we are.

We take, then, these resolved paradoxes and construct them into theories of sociality, of politics, only rarely coming back into the mode of discovering that we are; and that we are, for example, moral creatures who tend to act in terms of our stories about our being, more than we explore our being to understand the nature of our morality.

Immorality and the *Or of Being*. Questions abound! The wonderment of how to be; and how to be moral, and why others, some others, act against;

against the law, against their mother's wishes, against the laws of God and nation, against one's own self-interests—all these seem to set the issue of morality as residing within some oppositional dualisms: good and evil, God and Satan, construed within some Manichean clarity of this or that, of Plato's question of identity constructed always as an either/or. The *Or of Being* seems primarily to be constructed outside of one's being and experience.

Inside one's own being, morality and immorality do not seem so clear: break laws, disappoint others, tell lies, screw others lest they screw you—or before they do—Hobbes' war of all against all in this too short life; all of these raise the questions of the *why's* of existence. I would like to be good, if only I could discern always what that means. Are we reduced to questions of meaning? Whose?

Are we engaged in some ancient wars between thou shalt not, and thou shall...?

Or in some quandaries of being and identity which cannot yet tell us the limits of our being who we are?

Or are we engaged in a methodological problem: knowing and not-knowing how to proceed in asking/answering such problems?

Or are we engaged—as of old—in always trying to balance questions of desires and rationality whose war seems to entice us unaware... until it is too late? Do we settle into the living room of life seeking some harmony between the places which threaten to spin us out of control: the abysses of total Sadist freedom vs. the boredom of all of being, being foretold: safely seeking safety? Or do we move to explore the possibilities of life's fulnesses, treading on the edges as we try to move them to accommodate being, even while being tries to punch holes in existence?

Nietzsche wondered out loud if those who broke the laws of life's commandments weren't explorers in the first instance—looking for excitement—instead of the simply or merely immoral.

The Immorality of one's Child's Sickness/Death: Much about the nature of human life remains at the level of mystery. Some think it should remain this way, claiming that mystery is the voice of the deity whom we should believe and not seek further to pursue any Faustian ambition.

There is, for example, not much of which is obvious or clear about the nature of time. Korzybski (1933) claimed that the human is the time-binding animal, following Aristotle while claiming to overcome his thinking. What is clearer, closer to our actual experience, is the nature of generations: we have parents/grandparents, we have children/grandchildren, and we locate ourselves in life often, perhaps principally by our sense of relation to *our* other generations.

It seems, to us, appropriate in thinking about a life, to think that it should consist of infancy, youth, maturity, and old age, and death will follow a long life, well-lived. If any of these is not met, if a sense of a life is interrupted and cut short, then we think that this is some sort of tragedy, and have invented various ways of making tragedy handleable: heavenly returns, an end to suffering, etc. But these are stories which seem to emanate principally from within the sense of being as of one's own generation. One expects grandparents, then parents, to cease life before oneself.

What presents itself in moral terms has to do with the descendent generations; who should live beyond oneself. In this context, one senses that generational time has itself a moral component. Perhaps it frames morality in some senses: one's children and grandchildren should not sicken and die; it is immoral. It is often cast in terms of the constructs of nature of life - as unnatural, as against nature, opposed to our sense of what is a life.

The death of one's child can be survived. It can never be right. Do the seeds of morality reside here, in the generation construction of what is a life?

Why Ask Why? Morality is often construed as the uniquely human ability/burden/opportunity to ask about the *why-ness* of being: why do this; why not that; why, why...why?

Somehow in our construction of the presumptive human whom we try to solve and set straight, we have equated the rational with consciousness of a world which wants or needs explanation. No mere facts, please, but a universe where we want to know how come this or that, or the shoulds and can'ts of the restrictions to our being completely free. "Don't do that; stay out of the street; don't hurt him; be gentle with her!"

In the comparative sense of what human means, it remains the case that we don't know whether (other) animals are moral. As they are social, one suspects that they raise their young with some notions in "mind" of how they "should" (not) be at any point in development. The cubs and ponies of the world apparently get reprimanded when they do dangerous things or otherwise "step out of bounds." I mean that there are boundaries on their existence, perhaps similar to how we both grant increasing space but within certain restrictions of danger and what moms can tolerate. If, as I suggest, other species raise their young to be much like themselves—and the range of possibilities within development "exceeds" the actualities—then it seems likely that other species are moral; not necessarily in ways so different from how we are. (Sarles, 1985, Chap. 1)

But to return to the case among humans, the notion of *why* arises to our thinking that it has a life of its own, not within a self-invented grammar of a language within each human individual, but within a concatenation of questions and responses. Children do not invent language or the world it represents, but adopt the words for the objects as their mothers/others say they are. Language—including the whys and why-nots—is adopted by authority. Why say this or that: because that's what it is called/I call it!

Much/most of early developmental use of the why's of life is to explore the boundedness of categories as well as the boundaries of what is allowable, acceptable, and contextually meaningful as belonging to the individual (child), to the politics of social situation, and an increasing sense of the context of context in which meaning grants itself. Much of it has to do with the development of social conscience without which hardly any infant can survive: "Do what I say," says mom, "and start believing that you mean as I mean, and will to do what I think is necessary for you to be a safe, moral child/person!"

At some point of self-consciousness, the why of "who I am to be" begins to take on a new life. And I truly begin to wonder who and why I am, or why anything is as it is said to be, and why-not that.

Will develops from a sense of conscience in which a social imperative of internalizing the mother's sense of propriety and of avoiding danger becomes one's own. And at later points, this increasing size and power of the individual persona comes to grapple with one's own conscience; no longer *smothered* and trying to come to terms with the who I am and why not that's, which actually set the scene for the usual discussion of human morality.

Being within Comparative Thought: Within the usual strains of Western thinking, it is difficult for us to realize that we ordinarily think of the human condition *within* the context of comparative thought. Thinking of humans as particularly unique—due to language which allows us to think or possess consciousness, to our large brain which makes us smarter than other creatures, opposable thumb which allows us to work, of any of the other features by which we have tended to separate the human from other species—this form of thinking about humans is already and presumptively comparative in its very formulation.

Whether we accept the comparisons as particularly valid or yielding of insight, or as negative and invidious, the fact is that we are comparative thinkers. We have-in-mind other species when we think of humans; and we think humanly when we think of others; usually to *raise* (some-all?) humans in some direct or not so direct line of hierarchy or complexity. But - to reiterate and to underscore—when we think about humans we have other creatures already contained in our thinking, how we go about asking questions, judging the reasonableness of responses, and so on. We are not so good at seeing the human condition as it is, because we approach questioning and observation already with a fairly well developed metaphysics.

We have tended, for example, to concentrate not on the human body in its variety of complexities, but to grant grand possibilities to the human mind/brain, already construed within the dualism of body and mind, which is used to separate us from other species—within the claim that humans alone possess minds; while, in the same breath, we somehow claim that the human body is just like (e.g., in nature) the bodies of other species.

That is, we take to the study of humans, assumptions which foreclose our seeing much more than we have already assumed about the human conditions—not the least that humans are the *only* social species, for which we have over the last two and a half millennia concocted elaborate stories ("natural law" and all that) which have attempted to explain how we are, based largely upon the dualistic assumptions of our presumed differences, rather than from experience and observation of how we are, get to be...and so on.

Many of our stories of the human condition even banish the possibility of our experience informing our knowledge of ourselves. Thus it is no exaggeration to claim that we see ourselves particularly, narrowly, wearing strong/colored lenses informed by how we have thought we are, rather than seeing how we are.

The fact is (actually!)—and here we have to fight the Platonic inscription of the control of the very idea of reality and the making of reality into an idea—that we are creatures who *love faces*, as much or more than we are the smartest critters to have walked the face of the earth. Get real! Faces will *explain* smartness much or more than the mind.

Kant Couldn't: The problems with morality expressed within the context of the uniqueness of humans due particularly to our mind and rationality, is that morality has become a kind of subtopic cast within the nature of whatever is (*considered in any place or time*) the *rational*.

Kant—as (all) others in the Platonic-Western idealist tradition, begin to look axiomatically at our being creatures which/who partake of the logical, rational, geometric notion that humans alone have a sense for the forms and ideas which we understand through our reason: realms which Kant wanted to purify, thence to grant agency. There is a realm of physics, of logic, or morality/ethics, each of which has its own purity of being: and its own agency (Spinoza *Ethics*).

As rationality is taken to be an attribute of each individual mind, the question of morality tends to begin with an exposition (Kant: *Foundations of the Metaphysics of Morals*) concerning the nature of what rational has to do with morality. If—as I observe, as the ethologists of the world have decided—other species are already social; if, as I suggest, humans are *also* social, rather than being social due particularly, solely, or principally to our (unique?) rationality, the problem of morality is not due to rationality in any a priori or particular sense, but is an outgrowth or an emergence of our sociality.

Thence much of the question of the nature of morality devolves upon our understanding of the nature of our sociality; how we as individuals *emerge* from this sociality; why we act as we do with respect to issues of conscience, of right-ness, of justice, and so on. It is not that we are not rational, it is more that rationality, like morality, is a *consequence* of our being social, not the reverse.

The Western story: as we develop, we become more rational, thence more moral. Rationality and morality become attributes solely or particularly of each individual—essentially independently of our relations or interdependence with others: being children of actual m/others who are themselves children of m/others; having our being and behavior observed and interpreted within complicated (moral) frameworks within but also beyond the present moment; having objects presented to us both/and as particular and universal. Whatever might be *built-in* to the individual in some sense of continuity through a very large and rapid period of change, seems to be subordinate to the sociality in terms of which each so-called individual comes to interpret and develop one's personal sense of self.

"Morality" (now italicized) has much to do with what parents *need/demand* each child to believe/do: carefulness (jumping, burns, electricity, drugs, cars), being hurt/hurting others, self. *Conscience* must become an attribute of the child; conscience, thus morality, a similarity of understanding shared by child and parents, and a sharing of activity and of responsibility; thence of respect for others, and of oneself. The self, the person *emerges* as parents *demand* that each child act as if a responsible person, especially for oneself: toilet training, proposing ideas in the forms of word combinations, sentences.

Morality is intrinsically social, and becomes an attribute of each individual self as the society would have it become. Morality, thence, immorality, has to be understood first within its social context, and only then seen for *what it is*.

Comparative thought—the noting that other species are also busy raising their young in their own terms to become responsible *persons* within the ongoing notion of any particular species—is what all species who have the concept of raising their young to become competent adults, have in common. That these ideas of morality seem to differ considerably, should help lead us to see our own seeing of morality; then to see how we raise our own young to become like we are and would be.

Moral: Social or Individual: The question of morality seems to arise differently depending on whether we assume/believe that humans are intrinsically individuals or intrinsically social (or some "mix" and what is meant by social and social-individual): this seems, almost, to be an involution. All questions of motivation, what is intrinsic to human nature, etc., become historical-social, if we are somehow intrinsically social because our existence is not separable from others in any clear sense. The tensions which exist are derived *from* sociality—the very idea of self-as-independent-individual is a social idea whose "motives" are not independent, either. That is, the concept of what individuality is, can be, is a socially-derived notion. What is good, bad, conscious are negotiable, changeable.

The problem of morality (social-interactional) is to work, always, at the *concept* of individual/self which is sufficiently "strong" or transcendent to see beyond any and all extrinsic definitions of itself; yet not to "fall in love" with oneself at any point in one's development (as did Nietzsche).

The Freedom to... Existentially, perhaps the most interesting thing about humans is that we are capable of continuing to move on, to grow, to *overcome* ourselves as it were. If we can or must, as Kant holds, put our spirits into the development of some moral ideas which transcend the ordinarinesses of our being flesh and being social in and to our cores, then we are more interesting than our being human merely or obviously allows us to be transcendent. We often can and do overcome our desires, experience, observations of the ordinary and the worst, to think and act in behalf of, to act nobly, to act (as some thinkers about animals claim—Vicky Hearne, 1987) out the destiny of being human at its highest.

Examples: To take on the tasks and responsibilities of being and doing the sacred work within the secular—curers, preachers, teachers who are given and yielded the spirits and bodies of others within the context of helping more than hurting—is to act morally, if one truly does these tasks. To be a(n) m/other to someone else: to act on the others' behalf at least as much as upon one's own is truly moral. It is not overly strong to suggest that our very (human-social) existence and survival is dependent upon the morality of others: human infants are *not survivable* by *themselves*. (The question of the self is obviously at question within the idea of the social being definitive of being human! Physical being, individuality, and the self/person are not coterminous within the human condition, even though the approach of metaphysics has held these to be the same or to follow one from the other, as it were, naturally.)

If we are not, as Rousseau held, *born free*, then isn't the idea of freedom some chimera of anti-scientism, of religious thought, of a politics of thinking wishfully or toward some aspect of self-interest? Indeed, the notion of social means that we are not exactly born free. It is not society which has us in chains, but sociality is the human condition. How can it be that we are both social, and with the possibility of being free, acting freely? Is it truly the case—as some materialists who see the human condition as if we are basically and only the physical condition—that we are determined or limited in our being much as by a toxin or oxygen?

One answer is to look around, and to note that we have come an amazing distance in our knowledge, and do not live much like the so-called primitives from whom we undoubtedly sprang. If this is about freedom, then we have had much of it (Phil Regal, 1990: *The Anatomy of Judgment)*!

The more likely correct response is that our individuality—thence our possibility of freedom and of morality—is *emergent*. As we exist *within* sociality, the definition of our being is not totally intrinsic to our physical being (which is itself socially contingent even for survival). The issue of freedom and of morality even as possibility is bound with the notion that we become individual within sociality: both the self and the wishes, motives, and activities of m/others is that we become individual even as we grow and grow up. Indeed, growing up is to take on those aspects of being which we have equated with physically-given individuality. Our parents/society want us to become creative, self-generating individuals, selves who are free, competent, propositional creatures, much like themselves.

Socially, we are useless, dangerous, destructive, unless we are free and individual: ourselves and not anyone else. What is only at issue from society and theo-political *arrangement* to another has to do with how freedom is placed contextually, or how much freedom is given or possible; how long the umbilicus of self-determination can be extended or stretched without other forces coming into play which attempt to reel-in the boundaries of self-determination, or to limit their elasticity. And it seems (to me) not particularly different with other species.

So, to claim as Kant does, that to derive morality from experience is necessarily incorrect, does not jibe with our being able to transcend our experience. That is who we are, and we can get beyond ourselves. Transcendence is this life. It is within the ordinariness of living experience that we become moral and can find the places in our being in whose terms we can (and frequently do) universalize morality. Experience—which is social—is not (in spite of Rousseau) necessarily limiting of freedom. On the contrary, our notions of freedom are developed, refined, practiced within the ordinariness of being.

Transcendence: this is it! Freedom: is a search within being and experience. (→ *Next Places*)

Why are Humans Moral? Are we? (Nietzsche, 1889, *Twilight of the Idols*) Do we need to ask this question: Why does morality arise? From fear of death? One another? Oneself? Fear of time, of change, of loss?

Nietzsche's antidotes about personal strength, increasing knowledge, all of that about which devolves the concept of power, the why-ness of our existence, under attack in a human universe devoted to supporting personal weakness/meekness rather than strength which grows in such ways that we can stand to accept our own past in which we were less: the pity of pity.

The "Overman," dedicated to the idea that tomorrow will be more difficult than today, and yet we will live it... live through it!

We are dedicated not merely to accept, to survive, but to search for understanding, control—of oneself, of one's evolving dedication. Like preparation for the Olympic Games in which they will always occur in the next time period; in which one must stay in shape, prepared, as it were, to compete for the gold medal, the universal-world cup; not merely to be and experience, but to be and experience to the very edges of being and experiencing—and beyond—without falling into the abysses; but to say where they are and what they are like.

But even at the edges of the abyss, to plunge ahead, as if one can roll up those edges like a carpet, and push it over to one side of the universe, to view it anew, each day thenceforward, in a more benign form till it becomes another piece in the furniture of life, to be unpacked, moved, or rearranged on necessary occasions.

Isn't Being already moral? Isn't morality *natural*? Don't other species have a moral sense for themselves and for others in which they are "careful" about what they do? Why do we think we need some greater, some divine to tell us how to be? Do we not require that, or do other species also have a divine—*the same* divine?

Doesn't the question of divine, especially *for* humans, arise when we seek to reject the natural—about other species, and about what we think are the natural aspects of ourselves? It is a rejection of life, and a deeply puzzling paradox: to have to reject life in order to live correctly—to survive in the after?!

But the psychology on which this rests, which it presumes, is and is always tending toward negativism and pessimism. It seems always self-fulfilling: expect the worst...

And it supports a view of nature/natural which remains separable and independent from us; from humans and human nature.

A second paradox: the view of nature which we conceive of as separate from humans, persuades us that "it" (Nature) exists, and possesses its own power, correctness, and morality. "It" selects who will survive, who exists and, because it arises as a counter-divine; it becomes its own higher law which "dictates" not only what *is*, but what *ought* to be. What odd twists in our thinking! The creation of a sphere of our being which is distinct from some other sphere: then we grant *agency* to that other: now we are two, effectively independent, even *pure*.

Doesn't the question of morality, the notion that there is an issue, a separate or independent aspect of being which can be identified or labeled as *moral*, arise only when there is *trouble*?

Doesn't the persistence of the notion derive from a time of trouble—as an aspect of a solution to that trouble which has then come to take on a life of its own?—whether or not it ought to continue to apply?

Doesn't the issue of morality, as such, arise only when there are sufficient numbers of individuals that the concepts of "danger" and "stranger" take on real meaning? Isn't it the lack of present knowledge of one another, in very full aspects of being, that even creates the possibility of harming someone else; that one needs to have a "code" of conduct, which is relegated to self and is out of the present time of every one-to-one interaction?

Doesn't the question of "seeking oneself" make sense only when there is a dawning that one is one-self, in some sense independent—individualizable self with a life-line, in which the line seems its own; and from which it seems to be longer and longer, to reach out beyond itself? (Nietzsche *Genealogy of Morals* #13)

The Will to Power: The actualization of oneself, the sense of movement being directional, moving on, growing; transcending the sense of self we had just a moment ago, leads in various directions.

It may lead as well to a totalitarian take-over of all the world's peoples and powers—Hitler, Faust... It may lead to such a take-over in the name of power and the purity of the human species (eugenics), of the deity and of a church structure. It may lead each of us to attempt to fill and to live our lives with some senses of fullness. Or it may lead us to quit growing at various points in our being: out of frustration, a weakness to discern where we may go and grow or some sense of inability to do what we think necessary.

And this sense of the will to power is often not any place in our being per se, but is contrasted dialectically with who and what we are-not or cannot be. It may attempt to destroy rather than to overcome what we experience as weakness or hesitation; often acting as a way to excuse ourselves from self-growing. Or it may be used to justify the varieties of ways of self- or other-destruction which a growing sense of power and its attendant strength would presumably overcome.

Where, precisely, the will to power turns toward acts of destruction and evil toward oneself or others seems to have to do with the enabling and increasing *strength of character*, in whose terms we can overcome ourselves without having to overcome others. Here, Epictetus is probably the greatest teacher; the traps of personal history and the stucknesses of vengeance toward others and toward this history being the greatest disablers. And the nurture and feeding of one's fear-places can grow to the dimensions of the entire universe. (→ *Next Places*)

Even Evil: Whether we consider *good and evil* the opposites of some force of being which is/are essentially of the same cloth, whether we see them as so different in their opposition that they represent the religious notions of a living deity and a condemned devil. Even so, these issues construe themselves differently when the nature of the human is understood as intrinsically social.

It is the ordinariness of goodness and the banality of evil which begin us in our understanding. Not that there are not good persons and those who act out of destructive and vengeful tendencies, but that these aspects of our being develop *from* our sociality rather than contribute *to* them.

It is that our relationship to others defines, shapes, and constrains our relationships to ourselves: not the reverse. As we learn the language presented to us by our mothers (and others), so we learn the nature of conscience in relation to them, in and through them to us.

It is not that our character is (so) inbuilt, but that it *emerges* from the relationships. Knowing, being, the shaping of who we are is in-relation. The one, the "I" who emerges self-consciously, is not the one who is born and would die without the others who feed and sustain and grant the "it" of one's cells' continuity in life.

Much of the developmental period known these days as the *terrible twos* is a clash of wills-in-the-balance of being oneself or being as one's parents' demand, can tolerate, support, despise. Be nice; gentle—is at odds with the wonderfulness of the toddler becoming able to do and to say and to be someone; some one—one's *self*—somewhat independently within a continuing dependency. The *space* of future Being is developing. "Do what I say," the parent laments, "or you will get hurt, hurt yourself!" "Be strong, but not too independent, lest you become a moral monster, and no one will be able to stand you!" "Grow and become yourself, but do not sacrifice all of my being" is at some obliqueness with, "I love you," and "Love me"!?

All of this is to say that *conscience*, the foundation of morality, is an aspect of being social, remaining social, becoming what one's parents want and demand, while becoming sufficiently in-dependent to become oneself and to do that which (one's parents and culture say) is sufficient and necessary to be safe, to be whole, to be oneself. It is from this experiential (and learned) developmental sense that the person emerges, the one which is moral, which is the seat of morality in becoming. If we do not develop independence sufficiently, if we do not develop conscience, but that is moot because (almost) all of us do.

What we mostly mean by morality, then, derives and rests on this originating but emergent conscience which is already an aspect of human sociality. We are moral creatures by our social nature!

The complications and arguments about morality, the questions of evil, then, derive from this sense of conscience in some ongoing intersecting, adjusting, and battles with the emerging self-findings, and the pull of remaining social while growing up. The process is more a matter of centrifugal—becoming *oneself* and centripetal—becoming and remaining social within those becomings; than any either-or (→ *Next Places*).

Morality and Will: How strong, how independent, how separate is each individual from every other? How is one interdependent, how is being dependent; where and when is freedom located? Much of this has to do with concepts of the *will*.

Rises the voices of the stoics within us telling our being that we will to survive, no matter what. No matter what? Is will necessarily linked to what we need to do in order to survive? What do we do in order to flourish; in order not to hurt others; in order that others flourish as well or more than we?

Where are the intersections between meaning and being where "I will" joins with "I should"? And just who is telling who: some inner dialogue between my will which asserts itself to rise to the kingship of all of my selves over—some inner dialogue which has figured ways to be integral and to have integrity? Is my will strong enough to be able to yield? To surrender? When, and to whom?

Isn't it the arena of the sacred within the secular which is the ground for this sort of peroration? To curers we yield our bodies in order that we may be cured, become well, end the sensing which is our hurt—will or will not. Teachers we yield something about our spirits: hoping that in some sense of surrender, we can become stronger, learn, grow, a sense of progression and a moving beyond—a carving out of an arena in which our wills might flourish. To preachers we may yield our souls, and grant a sense of agency to something and someone who is outside of being—a surrender to our own ideas, a diminishing of will, a containment of ideas and feelings (of feelings, thence ideas?); I believe, but not in my own sense of will.

The world is full of human (and other) bodies, to which we grant personage. Do we grant them all the same? And if they are not all the same—as they never are? Then in the granting of sameness, we actively replace differences in being with... with what? We do this, I think, *willingly*.

Will, in its moral sense, seems always active, requiring a doing; a kind of circularity and cycling which grows more than diminishes; or which may compensate for diminishing in other arenas of one's life where there may be no possibility of control (Epictetus 108 A.D.). But one may also be actively passive, willfully calming. In these senses, the seat of will is an inner dialectic more than any inner dialogue.

In the contexts of morality, the question of will often goes beyond dialectic; towards polemic, between self-care and self-caring.

What are the Difficulties in Treating Others Decently or Well? Is it something about ourselves or about them? Does their existence, does their possible presence cause us, somehow, to think and treat them ill? Is it in the moment; is it in some idea of the future, of the past?

How does the idea of "what is" translate itself into "what might" or "should" be? Is it a game of time—constructing what is the present—in terms of an idea of that present from some earlier moment? If so, then which is *the* reality; the existence which is each instant, each "now"?

If one's anger or anguish is aroused, what is the nature of the battle by which one "controls" him/herself, and doesn't re-batter his child, friends, self? A battle with herself—but how? Two exact present selves—one good, one evil? Two (more?) selves, constructed somehow differently? But how? Stories to oneself about experiencing some present? Some idea of the present? The present-not-the-present? (Borges, 1935)

Morality is Actively Concerned with the Negative: What we don't want to be, to do, but think we *ought* to do, to be. Perhaps this is a pre-occupation, a diversion from some positive sense of being and doing; e.g., if we can "have" a moral sense, we may never have to grapple with the fact that our actual Being is emptier, less complete than we admit.

But how do we have or experience our actual being? With reference to others? How do we measure: what is enough, too much? What is the nature of a scale? Isn't the debate about absolutism-purity an argument about where such a scale can be found?—and who might *own* it?

Perhaps we are really different, say, in different eras. In some we are truly fearful; truly patient; deeply greedy. That is, these *are* our conditions: they inhere in our beings, in our nature. In other eras, we are, say, truly dialectical; hopelessly greedy. Educational traditions would act as if some prior notion of human nature were still existent; and attempt to "train-in" and "train-out" what they considered correct, right, or virtuous. The "felt-tensions," the dualisms of experience, the conflagrations of life and death would then have different manifestations.

In what senses do we know that this is *not* true?

When is it claimed that some part of us is moral, what does that mean? What is *not* moral? Writing is moral! I sit here inventing tales to persuade, to instruct, to change, to make people 'better," to have them not destroy others or themselves; to be inventive, to create "better" institutions, to teach, to appreciate and love their life-ways; to hate and explore the deepest abysses of melancholy, to investigate their own histories and to "grow"—but for what? To entertain myself on an almost spring morning? For myself and my children, and J. and my dog... What a curiosity!

Looking for Causes: If it is true that the concept of cause (causality) is, for example, *a linguistic trick*, what then? Would the world be any more of an illusion? Other people? But here we are, ready or not, illusion or "yes." Life is nonetheless difficult even in an affirmation of it. Besides, some of us drift into the notion that the pain is explicable, and merely drift into a new form of causality. Life, moral life, the search for the individual which is oneself?

Perhaps life as that search, but having to treat others well in order to *find* oneself!?

And if the world truly is an illusion? Still, we live. (Ask your m/other!) And much of thinking about morality turns upon the dialectic between life as some form of sin and life as some form of gift. Whether we live to overcome something not much of our own doing; whether we live to fulfill the sense of possibility and of promise; increasingly of our own making.

Life-Morality: A series of workings-out of varying forms of fears of life and death. Essentially negative in the sense that fears are "negative"?

But what's positive?—a struggle? Winning? Losing with grace and style? Surviving—but what cost to determine what costs? Health, hurt, good feelings—all modifiable in real/conceptual terms which depend on others to tell us somehow that we are, and set the grounds for being and judging. That is, the primary moral problem is not moral, but esthetic—concerning how we organize, form our judgments; decide, for example, what we distinguish between ethics and esthetics.

The Path from Morality to Nihilism: If one seeks perfection (is it possible not to, in some sense or other?), and one becomes tired, gets discouraged or weakened, it is persuasive to tell oneself that there is no perfection.

For the utopist of means and strength, this self-telling is rejected, and one casts about for new ways (or old ways which will work in the new present) to seek that perfection.

For the weakened, for the person who has few means of sustaining ideality through some present experiencing (which she or he may call "reality"), it is increasingly plausible to enter a phase of denial; at first denial of perfection. But, depending on one's ability to live well-enough in some experiencing, the temptation (toward temptation, etc.—it is a slippery path!), is to move towards denying meaning: toward denying the possibility of meaning, towards denying any possibility.

Morality—a Weakening? Nietzsche believes (*Genealogy of Morals*) that the discovery—invention—of morals was a weakening, and a mistake. To see the world in terms of good and evil, to contemplate a wrongness to our being and to call it sin, is in many senses destructive, and for Nietzsche, particularly *self*-destructive.

To judge (it is necessary to judge, is it not?—aren't we arguing the grounds and how often?) is itself a complicated notion. It is to have (in mind) some framework of not-being; some way of not-liking or enjoying a moment. It is, minimally, to seek a change-of-state; simply from, say, hunger to satiety. The question of judgment comes in when one knows outcomes; when one has "experienced" a state-of-being which (from memory) one calls the "source" and seeks a change, a "solution." In this sense, the discovery of morals and judgment are not very different from what we usually mean by causality.

But the road from judgment to sin is not very straight, and depends on certain self-judgments in which a change-of-status is "preferred" (self-observation)—or would be preferred, except... And the question of the ambivalence contains the seeds of conscience, of *self-hatred* in the sense that a change which was preferred is now argued against.

In the context of the individual and society debate (in which thinkers from Rousseau argue the individual *versus* society), a second judgment of self is seen as coming in from the outside, from society (at least from one's significant others) equals Freud's super-ego.

But from a social determinist position, the earlier notion of ego preference also has a social base and causality, so this represents (this conscience) no necessary "loss," but a further development of socialization in which it is necessary to judge one's "feelings" (and to judge what is a feeling) in a "new" sense of preferred states.

It is a part of understanding others in their terms. It is, it is true, a kind of weakening of the self—in a universe of individuals—but can be seen as yet one more place in a world of becoming. If it is seen as enabling as much as weakening, we have overcome Nietzsche's problems, and can still admit to being social as more than self-*destructive*. Nonetheless, it is an important exercise to think through Nietzsche's objections to morality, to go back to origins, personally and historically, in order to investigate one's self critically, to understand the ambivalence; neither to accept nor reject, but to *use* that understanding.

Invoking Morality to Justify (*Politics* of Morality): A "good times" strategy to account for how things are or how they work when it is otherwise inexplicable; also, an "excuse" for not digging deeper to see how/why motivation works. But *the fundamentalists and biologists* use this perceived emptiness to enter the field of government and politics. (If they are wrong?—it works in pessimistic eras as it sets a moral groundwork which, it claims, is "natural" to humans, and especially, will *work*!) Also, a move by authority, and obliged to give thrust and/or justification to why they do what they do. (Why do we seek such accountings?)

Moral Claims: Hearing a "moral philosopher" talking about morality, it became crystal clear that he was using the term "morality" as an invocation; to sanctify some claims about human being and behavior.

Somehow it is not sufficient to merely be, to enjoy life as wonderment. One must find "meaning," a sense that life is... for something other than what it is or seems to be. Is this the case from fear (of life, of death, the fear of fear, of yesterday, of tomorrow, today?), from difficulties in extricating who "I am" from whom I was told to be, or said to be, or that I told myself I was; that which created the existential tension between what others think I am, what I am, and what I imagine others think? (What I have learned/been taught about imagining!)

If one were truly *free*, would one need to make moral claims?

Morality-as-Corrective: Many believe that things go wrong because of immorality; that, if we were all moral, that we would do right; or, that in some battle between right and wrong, we would somehow know which was which.

But this boils down to a question of knowing, and entails a push to an absolute—to Platonism or some other form of surety. (As, for example, "Creationism" is a purism, so it perceives science as an "impure" purism.) This entails, in turn, a stopping of time unless one uses, as model, an ongoingness which is somehow stopped: e.g., Kierkegaard's form of Christology—to live as Christ would live, one can do, just do, as/what he would in each new moment. (And I wonder what Augustine would do in a secular era.)

In any case, all notions of correctness are tied to humans saying, giving testimony, saying which texts to invoke, and/or interpreting those. The question comes down, then, to which humans, living, what/whom to believe, and on what grounds.

Is my own moral stance, in any sense amoral, or a political stance about the morality of others' claims? It would be easier in living day-to-day, to grab onto a sure thing—and, this is part of my morality, that what is easy can never be moral—per Kierkegaard. Is it part of J.'s morality too?

But what is difficult is not then definitional of being moral. To be moral, for me, is to think about morality with as much toughness as I can muster, and, to do this, requires knowing all that I possibly can about myself-as-observer with respect to arenas in which I live and interact and react. It is an attempt to gain freedom in a constantly renewing way, and to do that with respect to the others who substantiate my being: in order for me to go on, to grow in any positive sense, it is virtually necessary for them to go on, as well. (Sarles, 2013)

"Biological Morality": (D. Morris, *Naked Ape*, 1967, p. 99; K. Lorenz, *On Aggression*, 1966) A notion that in a two-part, double-aspect creature there is a "more natural, biological morality" that determines how we really (at bottom) are, or ought to be.

What we turn out to be and seem to be is, to a large extent, *appearance*. It is the other side, the non-biological tune, to which we *dance*: "social," "cultural," "learned"—whatever term is selling in the arena of anti-biology, of non-biology gone self-destructive, is that which is what we see and seem to experience. But this is claimed to be false!

The bed-rock, the real, *is* (claimed to be) the biological: that which we are, truly. It is ancient, it is claimed, thus more natural (or natural, thus ancient—circles abound).

In such theories, the "present" is weak, obscured, an aspect of something "other"—since these biologists are basically and primarily convinced of the notion of life-as-survival: how we got here, not what are we doing here (ultimately, historically). Since the rational, the strong-willed thinking self is "in," or requires a strong theory of the present, our conceptual abilities are down-played.

Nature/natural, being an equivalent "self," has its own morality which is both proper and correct, a guide to living and to continuing in some sense of "species' destiny," which appears to drive their theories, and to continue, as it were, its own "biological morality." (This appears to be a form of *bio-politics*!)

The one certain thing about humans is that we are extraordinarily susceptible to believing our stories about ourselves and acting in their terms! Why, how, do we give up one set of stories about ourselves and accept another as if they were hair or clothing styles?

Do we forget, or do we recast our theories in new circumstances so they appear to not be very new or different? Do they appear "progressive" such that we reject those which are "proven" false?

Are we discussing truth or meaning or...?

Morality—a Life-Strategy toward a Definition of Futurity: The notion that life is (at least) double-headed—an *is* and an *ought*—provides a dialectic which is both sustaining and the foundation for a theory of history, and entertaining, too? (Kant, 1959)

Loss of Morality: an explanation for modern times!? But which morality; whose morality? Confused with a felt demise of civilization?—use of drugs, breakdown of family, loss of belief in higher powers? A crisis in morality?—or in the meaning of meaning? (Sarles, 2001)

Perhaps a loss of *fear* is a/the most powerful motivator?

Relativism: Pragmatics, situation ethics, ethical culture, the idea that morality is not absolute in any sense whatever—seems to frighten whoever searches the world for its clarities and absolutes.

The fears: a cosmological fear that I am unsure that I exist, and the idea of a clearly moral-morality underscores my existence; the conservative (nostalgic?) fear that there is no truth unless there is some sort of guarantee—from science, logic, determinism, that there is a world which "works"—then all will become politics, and if all become politics, then any measure of truth will become claims and charisma; fear that there is no authority (left) in the world. Everything is as good (bad) as anything else: no morality, no paths, a cynicism leading to nihilism; no meaning, no point of anything, no reason to live—or to allow anyone else to...

The strengths: to counter previous claims of anyone (religious, political, moral, strength of arms, my mother...) to know precisely what is correct for everyone, for all time; a critical view that we do live in history, and that our experience is valid in some sense or other at least for ourselves; not to be bent in the terms of some (usually prior) metaphysics or claims of ownership and architectonic of the *real* standing outside of ourselves (some battle between "logic" and being); to admit that different persons, cultures (species, genders, ages...) have somewhat differing rights, responsibilities, levels of authority and/or vulnerability, and that morality sometimes differs with respect to such differences (e.g., a right of the terminally aged-ill to die; of a woman to decide if a/her fetus survives).

Morality-become-Economics: a measure of life and living in terms not of what is worthwhile, but what is worth money: when is morality a *commodity*?

Is it analogous to the bureaucratization of all institutions? They come to serve their self-definitions in terms of survival within those definitions and forget to wonder what they are for. Is it, then, a loss of any sense of purpose which results in an apparent loss of morality?

Bureaucratization of Morality: A kind of *technologizing* of being seems to occur whenever an/any organization rises above individual being and experience. Part of this is an aspect of *scale*: when there are too many persons to know and experience everyone in any community in the fullness of their being (~1500 individuals?), then we begin to deal with *persons as partials*; to fill-in their characters from more general schemata derived, it appears, from our own *location* within the bureaucratic structures.

Once we become *members* of any bureaucratic structure, we seem to begin to think about many things differently from how we would have previously; e.g., our minds become *bureaucratized* and we begin to think about ourselves and the world as the organization within which we exist, thinks about it. Questions of why we do what we do become submerged to the organization's outlook, goals...attempts to survive as an organization. Whatever independence (freedom) of thought has been gained throughout our lives until this time is subverted and otherwise changed as we see ourselves as a member rather than as our (previous) selves.

This is all complicated because being social and being independent are (always) in some tension/harmony. If, for example, we diminish ourselves within (a) marriage to the other or to the relationship, then we become less than equivalent partners within some notion of contract; or as a priest/nun, dean or president, or senator, or a cog within the wheels of any other organization, then we change and often decrease our sense of independence/freedom.

The fact of harmony can be thoughtful and done *well* if we do, indeed, retain some sense of self and a grounded position outside of our being within the bureaucratic organization. If we lose this sense of self and exterior being, then we become less mindful, less able to *see* what we have become.

It is as this point that our minds become bureaucratized, that our moral sense is also shaped less by our independent self and more by the bureaucracy. But this is not obvious to the person who is within the organization because (as Kierkegaard points out in *The Present Age*) one has already begun to see futurity as being (at some level) successful within the definition of the organization.

The mind change is less in any particular terms of the organization, and more in terms of what is means to be continually successful and surviving within the organization. One suspends various forms of judgment, subservient to whatever is policy; and subserving one's judgment to any next policy—no longer noting or even noticing that one changes even radically, even suspending what would otherwise have been clearly in the moral sphere in an earlier time in her life. Even, in the Nazi case, finding it necessary to kill, having now redefined formerly human beings to the realm of the less-than-human. No evil left here; only bureaucratic banality which has swallowed up any possibility of morality within a particular definition of goals and objectives.

And here, any organization can also lose any reason for why it existed in the first or second or last place, taking on a life of its own which has replaced any moral/meaningful being.

In the modernity of experience which is constantly attempting to rewrite itself in some sense of post: post-modernity, beyond being—the "*I*" *of I would know and be* tends to get lost and disappear, leaving hardly a trace. The "I" of my being gets desperate in this game of hide-and-seek, tempted to destroy being in the name of morality, not being able to see itself having yielded to self-criticism...

Bureaucratization of the Spirit: As anyone *joins* a bureaucracy, s/he undergoes a shift in thinking about being: a sense of yielding to the definition of one's being in terms of the structure of the bureaucracy. One does what needs to be done in the terms of the apparatus of the bureau.

Perhaps the greatest shift in thinking about oneself is that one tends to do what one does increasingly and primarily with respect to one's own duration and *success* within the organization: within the organizational definition of one's being.

Here there is a moral shift; a tendency to suspend moral judgments of oneself with respect to one's significant others or to one's self judgments. Increasingly one judges oneself with respect to how one succeeds within the definition of the bureau (school, government, church, military...). If the bureau itself has some duty or mission or vision which informs its being in some senses morally, then each person within it may be acting morally.

If it has, as many organizations do in certain historical/political moments, lost this sense of moral vision, then the operative, the bureaucrat, has yielded one's moral sense in the act of yielding the definition of self to the policy of the organization: a structural answer to being.

While this loss of vision can be widespread and long-lasting in certain situations, its actual situation is generally obscure to those who have joined it and yielded to its definitions of themselves. Here, activity can be justified in the name of the government or church—or of simple and obvious *necessity*—to continue to succeed in its terms.

Here the notion of evil is degraded to banality (Hannah Arendt, 1963), and the worst and greatest immoralities—the killing of millions in various holocausts—is experienced not as immoral, but as sorts of organizational necessity.

Loss of Morality: Equals an attempt to gain personal strength? (= Immorality?)

If, in a world of unfairness (everyone's world to some degree), one decides to gain and show strength, to shift the unfairness a little more towards his/her side and purpose, how else then to oppose what there is perceived to be?

If that which is, is opposed; and that which is, is believed to be moral, how could anyone oppose the present, that which is, except by being immoral?

But this is not the case at present. The current loss occurred, it seems, when we (our nation) opposed a "communistic" force perceived to be evil. Since they were evil, immoral by definition, the nature of morality was constantly being defined and redefined in terms of how we depicted them—metaphors of holocausts, the A-bomb, world imperialism. This loss must have occurred as our morality became reactive and oppositional to that depiction of immorality. Perhaps it occurred because the definition of morality became obviously political, and ours, becoming politicized, lost its groundwork and its fervor.

Perhaps, it was that the imminent threat of world destruction altered our individual outlooks. But, how?

Morality and Strength in Teaching as Dialogue: Am I sufficiently strong in and of myself-as-teacher to overcome my wishes and needs to control, to be authority to my students, to subvert my own teaching self; to not oppress my students but to set situations in whose terms my students can empower themselves; thus ending the cycle of oppressor-oppressed which Freire (2007) says is the story of the world so far?

Conscience: Is a notion by which others teach us (force us?) to judge ourselves as they would have us judged.

It is at once the wellspring of what we call consciousness (as well as conscience) because it is a set of stories in terms of which we tell ourselves how others think and act. It is experienced as articulable awareness: what we tell ourselves what we are thinking (as well as *how* we tell ourselves what we are thinking.)

To whatever extent conscience is the outside-in-us, it is available to be infused with a sense of other persons (parents, teachers, God, etc.). It is an aspect of self which is not-self, and which - at some point in our lives— we can tell ourselves, has such-or-such characteristics.

Conscience is a repository of comfort; the seat of loneliness. It is a powerful aspect of our "will," the depicter of the future and the confirmation of the present. Its power fades with age, and we increasingly invent the outside, or rely on memories of how it *worked* in times past.

Is Morality an Error? Are all moral systems mere interpretations of some putative *outside*, some G(g)od, some great person, some extrinsic agency in whose terms we are to judge and be judged? (Nietzsche, 1886).

Do we create these judges? Are they real, or metaphors and stories about how we can or should conduct our lives? Are they mere canons of and for judgment?

Is this judge an aspect of our own selves, of our characters? In what sense do we have aspects? Are we not *one*?

Even rejecting all God-nesses, all canons for greatness, for *should-ness*, it seems to me that we are in various senses moral, already in terms of our surviving as social creatures. If sociality is a given, an inherent aspect of human (and most terrestrial existence), then our being in any continuous sense, is intertwined with others' critical judgment and support of that being. To sustain/to be sustained is to appear "correct" to them; to our parents, families, others with whom we interact. The roots of morality reside within their construction of correctness and the reciprocity of our ability and willingness to accede to that construction.

What is the difference between this and an intrinsically individual/anarchic notion of self?

Our stories *about* morality are thus derivative from this sustaining experience; stories to ourselves about how we struggle to be correct enough. This is the *first root of morality*—from the necessity for human approbation.

The *second moral root* derives, and in a certain sense, uses the "moral" approbation to place us on our own, to individuate us within a social (now-equals-moral) sphere. Whether it is language, or something about language, it seems that continuing sociality demands an "as if" participation of "individuals."

The paradigm of social correctness demands that we demonstrate "will"; that we talk as if we are individuals, and—in that process—come to be. Again, whether it is talk-to-ourselves about what we are, or some deep actuality of person-age, whether metaphor or reality, this is the second root of morality. Within the tensions of social correctness and willful individuation, there arises the moral dialectic: the *shouldness* has discovered the "shall-not." (Morgan, 1995)

All else seems to follow, being *details* in the ongoing resolution of the social → personal dialectic.

Today I will be Perfectly Moral! Already partially drugged on the caffeine in my coffee, on the brightness of the day, on hoping I will do something interesting, profound, important, and not anything too stupid, harmful or hurtful. I grapple with being moral.

But, will I know; how will I know? Will I tell myself; will someone else tell me? Can I query a higher power? Or is this "it"? Better to forget today, and try for tomorrow when my judgment will be more removed and objective? And the happenings have already happened, and I am not crippled by the necessity of ongoing judgments. No wonder it is easier to look for signs and portents to tell us what the being-of-morality is.

Relativism: A bad word? A notion of destruction? Morality must be absolute? A single concept? A single plan of action? A single *truth*?

Will not everything fall that is good or correct, if we suggest that there are two—or more—moralities? One for each people or "culture"—will this not reduce to one per person; perhaps a new one each day, or each situation? Will we not be lost? Why did we ever think we were *not* lost?—a notion from pathology, from the curers? They have no notion of wellness, of being found. If things are not too bad today: well, wait!

Is the problem that two moralities will conflict, rub heads, clash horns, intrude on each other's territories? Then what will we do? If both parties fight in the name of absolute morality then neither will yield, and morality is indistinguishable from power and politics. And the winning morality will claim its victory is morally correct. Untold numbers of human beings can be maimed and killed in situations where morality and power become fused (or confused).

Is the problem that truth and rationality and clarity (and logic) fail when there is admitted a possible plural view: no science; worse, it is feared, no possible science. A world dominated by whatever is anti-reason: feelings, whimsy, faith. Based, it is feared, on whoever whimsies are selling in the fickle marketplaces of flesh and all that is worrisome and corrupts (*Phaedo*). Feelings lie; flesh tells its own truths; sickness and sex obscure clear vision: the worry of the logician.

Is the problem one of control of self? Will I lose control over reality? Isn't absolutism a response to a prior, an earlier motivation?—that one is always on, or approaching, an edge; that if control is lost, one is lost? But what is it "to be found," to know *where* one is? How is this to be grasped?

Moral Cycles: Almost every generation, and once per generation, there is a moral outcry, a Jeremiah which proclaims the ruination of whatever is social, and whatever the moralist finds informed by her/his texts and inclinations.

Let us break into such a cycle, say, just after a great tragedy where millions were killed. And many of us experienced this tragedy on a fairly first-hand basis (e.g., just after WWII).

We are horrified as the extent and basis become known (legal, moral, political, etc.). We mourn deeply, celebrate survivors, and take safeguards to ensure that such tragedies will never recur. We locate, explore, castigate the enemies, the perpetrators, the causers. Their survivors castigate themselves, accuse the accursed, *recivilize* themselves... and wish it had never happened. (And we try to *forget* who bombed Hiroshima!)

The mature, the powerful—the accusers and those accused—age, grow old, begin to die off, to lose their power of influence, of the ability to tell how the tragedy had come about; how they had fallen into the habit of separating persons into an "us" and a "them," and how they had *regathered* all people into an "us," and why and how to expiate their guilt and their memories of guilt; and how they turned that guilt into the energy of renewal; and how that had worked. And they became old, and weak, and their stories lost the force of personal experience and the depth of personal witness and testimony.

Their children's generation matured and became powerful, and became the testifiers and the story-tellers; and their testimony derived from the experience of *their* parents. Their own experience was positive. They didn't like guilt because they had no personal fault: they hadn't caused any tragedy; they didn't have to go through any depth of processing their own need to understand and to forgive themselves. Being the children of guilt-ridden parents was often unpleasant and complicated by affairs beyond their ability to control; to understand. And they were different kinds of persons, a different people from their parents.

There were others around. These people used to be different, to be weak. And they got more populous, stronger; and because they were different, some of the differences became an issue; and because they were stronger, their ideas clashed, or they seemed to clash in the lives of a generation now come to power lacking the experiences of falling into tragedy, of the expiation of their own culpability and guilt.

And it was clear (to them) after a while that their own beginning to lose power with their own age was due—not to aging—but to some sense of external competition, of someone other.

They had become so accustomed to fending off the first sign of self-guilt that they turned these signs into the derogation of others, not of themselves. And they learned that if they told themselves stories in particular ways, of how their own weaknesses were due to some enemy, some inferior being, it made them feel strong again. And they began to construct their own stories about themselves in even more self-justifying terms, which gradually took on the signs of truth, of clear truth, of obvious truth, of a truth given to the true and righteous—of the truly moral.

As their own fear born of forgetfulness and of weakening, of aging, of mortality fed upon itself, the moral stories of self-justification became clear, obvious, and totally convincing. And any perceived opposition to them and their stories became opposed to them and to their morality: thus, immoral.

And since they had forgotten that the last tragedy was supported by their own parents on moral grounds, they proceeded to judge their own morality and others' immorality, and that seemed proper, correct, and inevitable.

After there was a great tragedy, and those who survived expiated their guilt by punishing the guilty, and they understood for a little while, and in the next generation they forgot...

This is the effective cycle! J. objects by asking what happens/happened to reflective thought at each and every point in the cycle. No denial. But, effectively, i.e., the actuality in terms of which the tragedies actually occur, people get hurt and killed, is translated into action by an instrumentality, a "military," which operates reflexively and reactively. The power of action somehow leaves reflection aside and beside.

Death—a Relief: Time stops. It just stops. No more; no more. Dying by degrees, by minute moment-to-moment changes, some lead ahead, some toward...

Time stops. No more time; no more dying by degrees; no more being sick about sickness; no more sickening, no more dying.

Death—a relief!

Death—a Directive and a Direction: At some moment around the age of 7, most of us come seriously into the idea that knowledge is also foreknowledge of our own demise. What was (just) previously a question of being, and only of being, now becomes a question of being with respect to non-being. This realization that one is (I am) going to die is often awesome (more in some traditions than in others!); and it tends to inform present being, and future towardnesses, with framings, dilemmas, and a space of viewing present being.

We can live for *life's sake*. We can truly explore any sense of soul or self which might be worth saving. We can explore being to find the mortal-fear places, the feelings of strength which can endure endurance that might have been ill defined and only roughly delimited in an earlier invention of our being. At about age 7 we turn both inward and outward in new ways, now realizing the end of being; that being ends.

And the sense of morality, framed against being, gains new stresses as being defines itself anew. What to do, how to be, draws lines about itself like stick-figures expanded. The question of why I do what I do rises from the chest of breathing to the glottis of self-expression, and often sticks there.

When gods are Invented; When God is Invoked: Being is sufficient when the effort rewards itself and renews to a sufficiency for which we have stories and ways of adjustment. And for which we have a time-sense which can contain our being.

When either of these (stories, adjusting) alters in such ways that are perceived to be insufficient—either the stories no longer work or they "forget themselves," or time is too narrowed and there is no space in which to be and to move, then we invent modes of being which are "other." There is "me, the insufficient," and now there is another me which is at least sufficient, and which I can call myself-not-myself: God.

It is best to have myself-not-myself, but never to call upon it unless one does *not* need to. But the mere accession of another self-aspect has taken its toll, has had various costs. One is already tempted; that temptation itself being the actualization of self-as-other. One is also weakened. Having yielded to the first temptation is also a path of transfer of self in which a possible perception of an internal battle—of self against oneself—takes over from self and the external world of other beings, and of being other.

In this internal battle, God is invoked whenever one feels a loss of self. The battle is lost whenever one feels further weakened rather than strengthened by an invocation.

Morality and History: Do these co-exist? Can they? Most moral systems derive from some notion of history, of what is past. Behavior and ideation in the present are directed, as it were, from stories out of the past.

The hope of a *messiah* is not different from a theory of the present which no longer works; whose stories no longer inform, no longer have sufficient strength to overcome fears and trepidations; no longer show us any way which is stronger than the reflex of activity which is moment-to-moment and day-to-day. The problem is that historical moralities do not guarantee the future. The present—in times of trouble—simply expands beyond the filling of consciousness: we become weak and susceptible. Having lost our futures, our selves, we call upon God, but can no longer hear, even if…

But, teacher traditions do possess a futurity. Painted as the quality of living, of how to. The sage is near the end of the best life. All of each present is directed toward our personal becoming; toward, rather than from. A sense of history invented; informed, as it were, from the future.

The trouble, here, is that there is only one future if there is only one model of teacher-sage (Confucius, e.g.), only one sense of curriculum. In fact, however, moral systems compete with medical and various intellectual-social theories of being. A present difficulty is that many aspects of the curriculum are no longer merely competing but are being attacked from within. As the world shrinks, the theology, the medicine, the arts and sciences are all seen to have alternatives. And these alternatives usually "divide" differently in other traditions: e.g., medicine is not different, necessarily, from morality. (Sarles, 2013)

"There is something in the consciousness of literati that cannot stand the notion of someone's moral authority. They resign themselves to the existence of a First Party Secretary, or of a Fuehrer, as to a necessary evil, but they would eagerly question a prophet. This is so, presumably, because being told that you are a slave is less disheartening news than being told that morally you are a zero."

Joseph Brodsky—NYRB, 3/5/81

Brilliantly, sadly, true!

Moral Systems in the Global Village: The world has become small enough that we can see how large it actually is. There are different idea markets, different moral "systems" which work to sustain large numbers of persons through productive and "full" lives. There are many ways to teach right and wrong and to live them out; many ways to treat others and ourselves. It is difficult if not impossible to say that one way is the truth, or more of a truth than any/every other. If my way is moral, and another says her/his way is moral - but we are different and opposing—what then?

Were these systems workable and working only in smaller world-times? Do they depend on national or religio-cultural boundaries whose erosion and disappearance places such moral systems in apparent competition? Did the major systems emerge and become major because their moral authority became politically persuasive? Do they not become political whenever threatened; or when the opportunity is perceived?

One political question, perhaps a political dimension, concerns the dependence of morality and persuasion for its claim to truth. How important is a claim to truth, especially to absolute truth, necessary for its being and for its continuity? Will we see an epic battle over the control of (the nature of) truth? Will it not reduce eventually to control over the definition of nature; especially, over the definition of what is human nature?

Morality and the Size of One's Life: *Humility*—have it! *Be* humble! Does an ego possess some inner desire, some burning need to grow? How big is big? When should one be reminded to be humble?—when the world sees too much growth, too quickly, that it threatens some necessary equilibrium?

The world, society needs arrogance—if only to go on. People need new energies tomorrow to do what, today, has already been done. Who can do that in a universe of increasing humility? How much humility is there? How much should there be? When is there too much?

Is there a general demographic approach to humility? In the Tower of Babel story, humankind was increasing in arrogance at a rate which so alarmed the Almighty, that He destroyed the ability for group cohesion; destroyed the arrogance meter and forced humility upon those who would have been so arrogant as to take on the marks of deity. If y'all don't humble yourselves, it will be done to you, and your pretentious edifices will collapse of their own weight: lessons upon gravity?

So humble! That's how humble. Somewhere between self-destruct, non-procreate and proclaiming self-as-God, that's how humble. How are we to discover just the right amount?—to not go under? Why do Nietzsche's screams of false morality rend the intellectual fabric of our times?

If we possess too little or too much humility, does it affect the size of God? Vengeful God, loving God—but, now, also a humble God. Who can afford to have a deity who isn't all-knowing?—who isn't sure? If God doesn't, who does? Same problem: no measure of humility. If God decreases, don't we have to increase in arrogance to protect our (and God's) kingdom? Wouldn't God want us to?

Don't go too Faust!

What is the largest size ego one can have, and still get to heaven?—the smallest size, and still go to hell?

The "modern" fundamentalist problem with the "heliocentric theory" is that the earth has diminished radically in conceptual size. Humankind has, instead of inheriting the center of the Universe, gotten saddled with a planet. If the earth is not the center, then we are too small, perhaps too humble to deserve the deity who created us. Worse: the earth is full of others, not-so-humans, whose effective power relative to us humans has increased, further pushing us down to their levels. Not humans, not special, not a free ride to Providence, but apes: born only to ape, to copy, not to reason and to imagine. If God did not create us in His image, then—my

God—is there no God? Bad enough to lose faith, but to have erected an entire edifice borne by reason to justify it: the worship of Nature becomes blasphemy. And we won't get to Heaven! A case of too much humility! Not sufficient ego to believe the strong thoughts to ensure eternity? Will the destruction of Science do the job?

Moral Psychologies: (1) The Psychology of Sin: in a world view in which one *sins*—in which one has "original sin" merely for existing—the problem is redemption: how to achieve grace, or whatever there may be (which will get us out of this *mess that is life*)?

It helps to confess, to seek absolution. That is the best one can do! One is able to conduct one's life or not, stay in good health, sleeps, and sins more-or-less as an activity of life. One expects to fall—and one does, and can find some relief, or one cannot. One seeks a way which "works": which is not disruptive in life-threatening modes in which sin and redemption seek whatever due they need. In a deep sense, life *is* sin, and one does what can be done.

Within such a world view, it is difficult to reject the system without rejecting oneself. And to reject oneself is psychically destructive. To not destroy oneself, one has to attempt to destroy the system. If one destroys the system in such a way that she/he also destroys *meaning*, then one destroys oneself in the aftermath of a critical nihilism.

Psychological rejection of the web of meanings—into which one is cast—seems to drive one to seek vocation, to create meaning or to discover how others continue to exist in a world apparently bereft of meaning. Why do they not despair? This question becomes: How do they not despair?—and does their way have any sorts of "authenticity" and "genuineness"? Moreover, the problem is to translate their "How?" into a persona whose development has been "other"; to find "how" for oneself, without accepting or rejecting the moral authority of someone who has come to it directly and, in the first instance, without thoughtfulness.

(2) The Best-Motivated Self: In the ontological world-view in which being is not yet complete, in which one is also and always becoming; in changing times the problems of redemption and of perfection are muted.

One could be responsible to oneself, if only that self could be located and *held still*.

One attempt to solve this ontological riddle is, in effect, to deny it; to find a self which one calls, *Oneself*—the real me. It is a vision of self which declares "the kind of person I am and am-not," the living equivalent of *eternity*.

In a changing world, in a universe of being and of becoming, one never *is*, finally. "Oneself" is tentative, at odds with its external treatment as well as with its conception of itself. It is moving—in flux—*becoming*. Moving towards what? Towards the "best-motivated self," which is the aspect of self which one likes now and will enjoy being in the futurity of looking-back to each now, from whence it came and which "caused" it to become.

The best-motivated self is a view of self moving into an uncertain futurity in which she and he, I and you—will also know and love and like that emerging person. It is neither the "I" of today, nor yet of tomorrow. It is as much a critic's view of oneself—an outside, a "towards which," which one's most trusted others will find even more and ever more interesting, absorbing, vital.

It is my best motivation for you, for me, as well as yours. It is at once a clash of what should be and who should be, *from* whom and *for* whom. That each tomorrow should not be less, not be worse than today, towards the self that we can like and is worth liking: the best-motivated self.

Where life and death both motivate, and where one seeks to transcend each previous day, in terms that are possible and actual!

(3) Who I Am-Not: Who am I? I have searched and searched and searched unto the ends of the universe of being, of thinking, and of imagination. I have queried the real world and every unreal world. Some have said who they think I am; others have responded by saying whom they thought I ought to be; a very few have said who they would like me to be; a couple have said who they thought I would like to be (coupled, in each instance, with whom they thought I should be). And so it has gone... Fleeting! It is fleeting!

But am I not moral? How should I know? Does it help to know who I am-not?—to know why I am-not them?—to know whom I have not been, and will not be?—to fight constantly to not-be, to not-be in an active, willful, oppositional way.

Perhaps, in a changing world, there is no precise way, and one can measure only whom one is-not. Is this not a morality?

The False Morality: will the false morality please stand up and reveal itself?

The fate of humankind resting upon a paradox: a logical trick!?

And what if it is solved?

Judgment and Motivation: Telling a story to oneself about others and about oneself; telling others, etc. What stories shall be told? Will they be true? How will we know?

The dilemma: that there are several dilemmas. How good and solid is my own motivation? Do I do "good"? Or do I do that which I (or others) call "good"? Are these the same? Are they consistent or steady?

Or do that which pleases me and persuades me (or a significant other), is good? Or if I am of a negative cast of character, do I call good that which displeases me and causes me pain? (Is pain a clear designator of penance?)

Are others good? Do I call them good if they please me? And so on.

Who am I to judge? Who, then, can judge? God only knows; God only knows? Who am I, then, to judge who God only knows? What if I have chosen wrongly the false god, the evil one, the Satan? Isn't this a judgment too? Whose?—mine!—mine? But who am I?

The View from Death (Plato: *Phaedo*): The acceptance of personal death, looking back to life. Accepting what is, still—mind, soul, the knowing existence, the continuing… the true. Realize what is not—body, sensation, perception; that which is not-yet knowledge: opinion, uncertain, fallible and falsifiable.

True?—from death: that which gets us to this acceptance of personal death; to be able to view life from that acceptance, and to discard the trappings, the momentary and evanescent. This thing—this death—it's not *bad*. It is clear, so brilliantly clear without time, without disease, without passion. It is, so to speak, heavenly.

Not only is it what is, but it is what is meant to be. Why would we die if it were not meant to be?

What of life—from death? Murky, confused, confusing... Why? Time, disease, passion... If death is clarity, life is obfuscation and illusion. The antidote and remedy: rid ourselves of those aspects and yearnings which are life... from the view of death.

The *actual illusion*: this view of life-from-death is a view of death-from-life. There are no theories from death. Death merely is; it has no theories! If life is an illusion, our theories of life-from-death cannot inform, and only accelerate.

The actual paradox: theories of life-from-death persuade us of their truth for living; e.g., morality is living correctly to die right. How to know the being of morality?

Manufacturing War: 1) Creation and selection of an enemy; 2) Legitimating of moral suspension in the case of an enemy; i.e., that it is right to end lives if "they" are enemies; 3) Justification of death, usually by dehumanizing enemies; or by claiming "they" will attack us; 4) In the name of...

Managing Information: easy in a bureaucratic society, even when putatively "free," because everyone is more dehumanized than otherwise, and prepared to act "properly" with respect to information.

Hell is here; on earth. (If it were not, we would *reinvent* it!)

Politics of Religion and Religious Politics: Machiavelli (1531 *Discourses*, Bk 1) says religion is, in essence, a device with which and by which one manages and preserves the state. Conversely (perhaps) the state is a device by which an essential religiosity conveys and preserves its messages.

The view of the state is that religion keeps the immoral, moral; in line and less dangerous to the state. The religious view is that it enables the state: that the state, itself, must be morally *underlain*, or it will fall of its own weight.

Somehow, these two find a wavering balance in which a potential war lies over a next horizon, perceived morally or politically depending on where one sits. Apparently, a great deal of what we call *freedom* can only be preserved within a religious-political tension. Is this because either side considers freedom carefully and seriously as it considers "the other side" to be competitive with it?

The Great Should: Why is not enough merely to live one's life?

We/our wills are always at battle with... what?—with what we *should* do! Where resides the Great Should? Is it an aspect of oneself (how many are we/I?)? Is it what others tell us we are; what they want us to be; what we should want to be...?

If our parents and teachers "guaranteed" some sense of the future, in whose present are we living? Must one reinvent them to find the Great Should? Has one merely embodied it, to be an aspect of oneself with which to conduct the battles of life, to remind oneself that he/she is? (→ *Next Places*)

On Doing Battle: Being engaged with what is wrong, what is bad, one must spend great efforts on studying the enemy; that which is (considered) evil.

If the study as well as the battle is engaged, one must beware lest one begin to fight in terms by which that enemy constitutes itself. At the point, perhaps just before or slightly beyond, one has in effect taken on the mind of the enemy and has become that enemy. The battle has been lost, yet it appears *reasonably* to be won.

Here, texts will no longer help, since they are now read from the "*other*" point of view. In the name of remaining moral, one has become the self which was formerly hated. (Why Satan often wins, virtually in spite of himself!)

Responsibility: Who am I that I should be responsible for you? Is the idea of taking care of someone else, someone other, merely another means of seeking identity and confirmation of one's existence? In order for me to truly be me, you must *be*...?

Do I have a right, a reason, a motive to feel that I have to do for you? —or do I feel that I will get something in return, a *quid pro quo*; responsibility a reciprocity? (Cicero 51B.C.)

Do I respond to you and for you, for myself?—to quiet my yearnings and anxieties, to focus them within manageable constraints, to place them in the pigeonholes of my life where I can file them under "Responsibility," and become a "who" which can do what that "who" does and is supposed to do?

Neither statement (I am that I am; I am who I am) "works" without some notion of responsibility, because my being requires that others be, as well, and certify me. And that is my responsibility toward them.

Love: Oneself, others, one other, community, the deity. What is the problem? Why is it difficult to turn the other cheek, to accept humility, to give away... what?

The problem has to do with integrity and the sustaining of one's own self while caring for others; and is not difficult under good circumstances. What drives the withdrawing from love is the fear of bad times and bad circumstances. Narcissism is the steeling of one's character against any threat, but so is humility—and they are twins: out-of-love.

To love, one must balance being whole, a certain arrogance, with yielding aspects of wholeness to others, to one another. The balance is precarious as the boundaries of one's wholeness are subject to the vagaries of everyone-in-relation. One becomes reactive to situations, and while one's view of integrity may continue, the actuality may be changing, and one becomes remote from his/her vision of self. Then, love cannot come from anyone, directly; because one is not located anywhere, exactly.

Love requires the study and knowledge of oneself continuously, throughout life. Love does not and cannot stabilize or settle down.

Teaching and Love: How great is love when are there conditions? As a teacher, I try to carve out intellectual spaces which also demand futurity and hope. As I love myself, I can be mentor and guarantor of your idea of your futurity. If I do not love myself sufficiently, then I am of little use to you. The conditions of being student to this teacher are many and involved. The possibility of self-love enables me to me moral, as the Teacher. (And J.)

But this is because teaching (as curing) resides in the realm of the *sacred*! I promise to imbue in you a sense of being able to grapple with futurity—a sense of hope—if you *yield* a sense of your self/spirit to me, the teacher; your teacher. Yielding is a sense of love; a suspension; a form of self-surrender.

To be moral as a teacher, then, requires me to do well—for you and for your futurity; to be sufficiently strong within myself that I can eventually subvert my teaching so you can re-find yourself within it and become an autodidact, a who you would be.

But to be moral-as-a-teacher is quite different from being moral outside of the realms of being which are not sacred; which are secular—where the politics of our being remain open and negotiable.

Arrogance and Humility: I cannot do what I do—except that I believe that I can do it; I could not get to do this, except to have believed that I could; I cannot move on except to try and to believe that I can, and to make it a study, puzzles to be discovered and their solutions sought—arrogance of a sort, trying to be as good as I am and to try to improve. To teach, one must deserve to teach, and (on certain days), I believe no one can deserve to teach, least of all, me—humility? (It is crucial to have a good friend – to support this notion every day of teaching: thank you J.)

Need I create another me so I can believe that I solve this problem in balance once and for all? Is that solution what many people call "God"?

Hatred:

"One does not hate as long as one disesteems, but only when one esteems equal or superior." (Nietzsche, 1886, *Beyond good and Evil* #193)

A recipe for healing: By hating, one raises the object(s) of hatred beyond their worth, especially with respect to oneself. In order to judge well and clearly one must see others as they are, and this necessitates a lessening; an abandonment of hatred. (Or hatred as a hatred of self, using others as surrogates for a derogation of self!)

Pity: From a handicapped person—I don't feel pity for anyone, per se. "They" are what and who they are, and have to do what they can with what there is. I can as much give pity as I can receive it—but it doesn't help.

I feel the most "pity" for victims of systems, institutions, governments…who have extruded some in order to maintain the others with respect to those systems; true innocents. (But those, I try to teach.)

The greatest pity I feel, occasionally, is for myself, and (occasionally) that becomes so awful that I am forced to reject it and to move on and out. In truth, I often fall in love with my self-pity, and know well how to nurture it, caress it, and make it me. (And, ask J!)

Anger at Others: There is none. One is angry only at one's images of others, in terms of how they impinge on other aspects of oneself (Epictetus 108 A.D.).

This doesn't make others unreal, but claims that anger is a self-perception whose "cure" necessarily involves a change in self; both inside and with respect to others. The "confessional" is a statement to some other of how one is coming to be, or says one will. The difficulty in changing, reducing anger or other strong feelings, is that they are ours, they are us, and we come to cherish them.

The dilemma is how to love ourselves less and to imagine we love others more. The sustaining solution is to seek how others are – how they may "find" the best Next Places in themselves - to discover how oneself is—often—and not merely to promise them, but to promise them as oneself…

Atonement: Is this a necessary aspect of living?—If only to account for how one "got here," to accept an always less mature past as the real, and to be able to move on. It involves compassion not only for others, but particularly for oneself; it requires a kind of forgiveness of oneself which is not an excuse, but an attempt at understanding. It is a remembering, a recounting, which enables one to forget sufficiently to be able to live tomorrow.

Atonement must balance with self-hate, the me which I would no longer be, no longer wish to claim, but... to deny self-hate is a dangerous error, to disclaim it is to fall in love with those aspects of self that we learned to hate when we were small. Thus, to deny self-hate is to deny one's history or to have altered it in a way which no longer informs one's present. It is to live in the narrowest senses of time, and in the deepest whimsy; the core of one's living being on the surfaces of one's eyes.

Meaning: Requires a searching, a study of where one is, how one got here, what/who shaped one's being and perceptions—*before* one can quest for meaning in any sense independently. To opt for nihilism is to have said that there is no meaning: therefore I don't exist.

But this is *silly* and simply distracts us from understanding. To deny meaning is the obvious solution of the would-be brave who can recover courage only by negating their culpability, and worshiping their own imaginations (or who seek war in order to let someone else teach them courage).

Meaning is in becoming what one would.

Meaning is in the study of that becoming; doing; being.

The Will to Power: There have been a variety of solutions to the problem of being oneself: primarily for and toward oneself; primarily for and toward others; a dialectic of internal being and dialogue; an often constant set of nagging voices occupying the domains of morality when they seemingly have more to do with questions of strength and resolve and patience.

The will to live, not to commit suicide; to go on... and on: The puzzle of Europe's romanticism, wondering why we are so afraid to die that we would do virtually anything, everything, to avoid it. Kill others, inform, torture; the fear of the very fear of dying...Why do we go on knowing that in the end there is the end of knowing?—of being?

What is this will to live (Schopenhauer), to power (Nietzsche): is it a positive sense for being, a wanting to go on—more than it is a fear of dying? Is it a weakening of character; a lessening love of being, once we discover that we are mortal—or an increasing sense of weakness, a yielding to the places of fear within our being? How do we, can we overcome and transcend being sufficiently? ...To do what?

Or do we come to love life less and to love fear more?

In those of totalitarian bent, does the will to power overtake the fears of willing to live, or do they become informed negatively: as an overcoming, a shaping, a response to fears which sublimate themselves within power over others? And oneself?

Insurance: Another of the complicating dialectics of the moral life has to do with insurance; with predetermining the future and the nature of our being and eventfulness within it.

In the most basic, perhaps the clearest senses, we live each moment as the bodily, sensuous beings we are. The stories about morality which are our heritage, have, instead, downplayed the life of each moment in some sense of temporal being and flow, and have stressed the senses of our being outside of time; the permanence of our identity, the universality of being human as opposed to being precisely who I am. Within this concentration of our being removed from each present, existential moment, there is the temptation not only to live in some removal from present being, but to insure that very little bad will happen to us in any characterization of futurity.

The Western dialectic/paradox of life and death is overwhelmed by an eschatology; a concern with death over life and living only as a preparation for our souls to return to heaven. In the context of insurance, the removal from our very existence has tended to essentialize life as a set of structured categories—a "who" I am as determined fully (gender, ethnicity, race, age...). Insuring the future has had the powerful effect of removing ourselves from ourselves.

Here one wonders if insuring cars and houses and lives and health and old age also contributes to downgrade and to background the present of our existences, and to praise categories of being over experience.

And if insurance removes me from me, does it remove me as well from others? Linked somehow to insurance is the question of *charity*, of taking care of others if they cannot take care of themselves; of whether they would take care of me and of us. The question is one of communality and of community, and rephrases the questions of the locus of morality.

Am I/we more moral if we/I save for old age; or if we contribute to communality in each year's possibilities?

Is the world sufficiently stable to insure that insurance does what it claims; that others will feel and act upon the obligations I feel...and does insuring the future contribute to stability or to instability?

Blasphemy: To take the name of the deity in vain is blasphemy! To take the holy—the concept of the transcendent being that is above nature—and to reduce it to the mundane and ordinary is to blaspheme that deity.

How complicated is this idea of blasphemy which some religious thinkers is the major, and even for some, the only *crime* worth raising to the basis of morality. From the agnostic idea of the deity having agency over us, as something *created* by humans in our image, to take that image of deity over us and to claim that to invoke her/his name is blasphemy. How complicated!

The case of Salman Rushdie who has/had been condemned to death for blasphemy...and understandably for his depiction of the scribe in *Satanic Verses*, 1988). The character of the scribe is of he who wrote the words that Mohammed is said to have said, and to have unwritten those specific words, perhaps to have altered them, to have erased some, to have altered the meaning or the context; to have undermined the deity by transforming the idea of the deity; by transforming the truth of the deity, of the truth of the idea of the deity. No longer can we trust that we can get directly (or indirectly) to the words of the deity.

If the crime of blasphemy has conditions or levels of awfulness and of treachery, perhaps this would rank the highest! For to take the name of the deity in mundane circumstances may be terrible, but to undermine the idea that there is a deity, or that we may not have her/his true words, is to penetrate the concept of blasphemy more deeply by several steps of priority.

It would be more beneficent to claim that there is no deity—or that any particular deity is false—but to erase the words of the deity even in her/his writing extends blasphemy into treachery.

In the Christian world, there is a direction for solution, a place where the mundane and the holy may meet to divide up the profits of our being: a domain where Caesar rules reasonably; another, where the deity rules... by some jump and conviction of faith. In the city of man, reason is said to rule, and the deity may be invoked or not; preferably not (Matthew 21:22). Blasphemy is herein preserved for the city of God, and one needs know upon whose maps and terrains one travels.

But, suffice to say that all of the concept of morality may be *condensed* in those who believe in belief, that the only morality is gathered into the concept of blasphemy.

Beyond this *moral filter*—a screening of the externalities of being taken into oneself; and a hard/harsh decision made whether any event is to be counted as good, or as evil: Beyond this moral filter, all else is *detail*. All else is background and backdrop to the panorama which is moral being, and being moral.

Politics as Religion vs. the Political use of Religion: Was Ronald Reagan a politician using religion or a devotee using politics to further his religious convictions?

The Genesis of Morality: I propose that the idea of a moral foundation of the self has, until now, remained fairly vague; lacking much of anything like a "mechanism" which would account for our being moral by-our-nature, or via our interactive experience. The mechanisms of emergence of the infant from an attachment with its m/other; this Mead informed idea (1934) leads to the development of the social self, a self which is (also) moral.

My thinking and observations suggest that it is now important to re-study the human in our actuality, and attempt to free ourselves from the dualist traditions which have framed the study of the social-moral self. How to go about this study? Dewey (1923), in his less philosophical practice, points to some procedures by which we might continue to engage our study of ourselves.

All of this is important to an understanding of the moral self. (I might even make the case that much of the development of religious thought works within what I think is a gap in theories of the self.)

In developing a self, Mead (1934) suggested that a child is somehow different from, not directly continuous with its earlier physical being. The physical infant/child undergoes a very significant change, an *emergent transformation*, on the way to becoming a social self. The self that is, which one is, is thus (already) social. "The self has a character which is different from the physiological organism proper. The self is something which has a development: it is not initially there at birth, but arises in the process of social experience and activity, that is, develops in the given individual as a result of his relations to that process as a whole and to other individuals within that process."

How can I attempt to extend this idea?—that the social self is (also) a moral self, and that one's moral being is (also) emergent? How this occurs involves the emergence of the social self, which I will dub the social-moral self.

Mead (1934) suggests that it is somehow through the use of gestures that we develop language and reason, and become a social self. But the mechanism, how this might actually occur during development, has remained unclear. And the parallel question of morality seems more an afterthought, not usually posed as a problem in becoming or of development within the contexts of interaction.

Why this has not been clear or obvious occupies much of the foundational story of the Western tradition, and it continues in a debate which is currently heating up. The physical child is presumed to be primary, what is beyond or me ta physics to be debated: mentalist, spiritual, ideas. The individual has been held to be primary (that is, until Mead), and continues to dominate the debate about the human to this day, with occasional nods to the idea of having others who confirm us, at least our knowledge.

Continuing as well is the attempt to embed the idea of the human within presumptions of superiority: humans are considered to be unique: the only species that has achieved language, rationality, knowledge, understanding, consciousness... and, moreover, is the (only) moral animal. This thinking includes an implicit depiction of other species as lesser, usually as non-moral. How humans are, has been and continues to be prescribed by our differences, more than how we actually are, and has neglected a great deal of our being in our understanding of ourselves.

How do we proceed to (re)study the human? Dewey (1923) frames the issue of knowing as our experience:

"No one would deny that we ourselves enter as an agency into whatever is attempted and done by us. That is a truism. But the hardest thing to attend to is that which is closest to ourselves, that which is most constant and familiar. And this closest 'something' is, precisely, ourselves, our own habits and ways of doing things as agencies in conditioning what is tried or done by us... the one factor which is the primary tool in the use of all these other tools, namely ourselves, in other words, our own psycho-physical disposition, as the basic condition of our employment of all agencies and energies, has not even been studied as the central instrumentality."

This is to say that our study will include ourselves in the study of interaction. Perhaps this is so obvious within our being and experience, that its neglect should not surprise us. But we need to remind ourselves of the contexts in which we consider ourselves, and the pragmatist attempts to move outside prevailing modes of thought.

Most of the thinking which has gotten us here embeds the dualistic concepts of mind and body which pragmatism contests. Dualistic thinking has presumed the notion of the individual child facing the world alone; the major question of how we are has had to do with how we know the world. As Dewey says, how we are, what our human agency is remains virtually unstudied. As long as we are pulled into the sort of debate of mind vs. body, our selves will remain outside our discourse and thinking about being.

Within the traditions of thinking about the human, the mechanisms of how we are have remained elusive: theme and variation on pure reason and ideas within the idealist-mentalist tradition. More currently, postmodernism demands that narrative and representation is all. Currently, as well, the locus of our essential being is the brain on the oppositional physical-body side. I suggest that Mead's ideas can lead us, with some history and observation, to a clearer and more accurate understanding of the human condition; in the context of this essay, toward a sense of our moral being.

Where to begin? In a growing body of literature on child development, there is recognition of Mead's thinking that relationships are part and parcel of our being who and what we are. The infant is said to become attached to its m/other. The development of the self is now seen as an interactive process, from which the self emerges; a process of co-regulation.

The early life-relationship is between/shared by the infant and that person who takes deep and continuing responsibility for (usually) her infant: the m/other. It is in the involving relationship between infant and m/other that the child enters the relationship - enters deeply or becomes the m/other in many senses, attaches in current rhetoric, and emerges as a social self, but also as a moral self. I will add that the infant becomes student of its m/other's being and relating to the infant and the world.

As the seat of the social self, the infant gradually emerges as a social-moral self. How does this occur? What are some of the dynamics, the sine qua non of our continuing existence?

"The heart-stopping thing about the new-born is that, from minute one, there is somebody there. Anyone who bends over the cot and gazes at it is being gazed back at." (Morgan, 1995)

The moment when parents first meet their newborn is quite amazing. They look at it, check its gender, note its parts, then dwell upon the face. What they actually see is facial and optical tissue reflecting muscles, reflecting light.

What they bring to their observations, however, is centrally important to our story. They do not merely see that there is somebody there; they read, interpret into, ascribe being to their infant. Whether there is anyone there, gazing back—or how this comes to be—is part of our search for a moral mechanism and the social self. But, for the m/other, the operating presumption, informing and absorbing idea that there is somebody gazing back, is crucial for our understanding of the social-moral self.

Mead's idea of emergence is that a social self emerges from the relationship with its m/other: there will be someone there, as the infant becomes it's self. It will be able to refer to itself as "I," it will know itself, begin to know the world, etc. It will also be a child with some sense of responsibility for itself, in terms similar to how its m/other would have taken care of her/him: the basis of morality, I suggest. How does this occur?

To elaborate Mead's insight into the idea of an emergent social self, I first want to suggest that the physical child is not survivable without the relationship with its m/other. Data on this goes back to the 1930s, particularly in the work of Rene Spitz (1957), who examined children in foundling homes, and found that up to half of them did not survive to two years of age. TLC, and the notion of the m/other, somebody, actively reading, working with her child, updating, responding— mothering—is an ongoing part of the narrative of emergence. Much is changed, much changes, much is added to the child. The infant-m/other relationship is a *sine qua non* for our continuing being.

The individual, that is, essentially does not exist, is not coterminous with the physical self. Mead was correct in specifying that we are social selves. In searching for mechanisms of that emergence—moving back to Dewey's concerns—I think it is important that we ponder something like "an archeology" of the body. We have to resituate ourselves in our present, examine where and how we are, and how we got here, much beyond reflecting on how we are now, as adults.

To enter somewhat more deeply into the question of our emergence it is useful to ponder Dewey's sense of human agency. How, for example, do we speak or move, remain in balance? The muscles which we rely on in our ordinariness are quite amazing. The great violin teacher, Suzuki (1968) thinks that ordinary speech is as complicated as performing on the fiddle. Those of us who are of some age, recognize the changes which being-in-gravity wreaks upon our facial and other tissues. All this to say that our habits of our human agency are much more complex than we presume, and these require our rethinking and analysis.

It is also useful to follow the arguments of Dewey's close colleague, F. Boas, especially his student Ashley Montagu (1971), whose book called *Touching* takes us ever more deeply into an appreciation of what an infant is and does; and more of what we take as obvious and habitual: Taste, smell, sound, an enormous fixation on the face of its m/other, glancing there during most moments of agitation, for re-attachment to its m/other... to itself.

Since this early period of attachment leading to the emergent social self, seems to occur very rapidly, in practically no time; since, the habits which Dewey postulates and ponders enter us and/or we become them, I would like to add to our thought several ideas, perhaps they are more observations, about the new-worldly experience of the infant. Mere observation may be insufficient, especially from our current framings of space and time.

How are we? How did we get here? Look in the mirrors of life, but also rethink our own early experience. Some questions:

Why does the world of experience speed up with age? A year in our older lives passes increasingly quickly, while a year in the life of a small child is very enduring. I suggest, therefore, that with little experience, the sense of time, eventness, duration is very long, at least relatively, for the developing infant. There are few contrastive events in an infant's life. What we consider to happen quickly, the infant experiences as drawn out very considerably. Bring this idea back to Dewey's notion of our habits and agency.

With respect to space, I suggest that the infant experience is much more Brobdingnagian than ours. I infer, for example, from what happens to our tongues whenever there is slight irregularity in our teeth: a chip, a seed, a dentist probing. Our tongues seem to refocus much or most of our being, demanding, as it were, that the errant event cease and desist. I infer from this that we continue to experience as Deweyan habits, the sense that our faces are really, really large; that infants experience their m/others' facial surfaces, eye movements including focus on the faces and eyes, in minute detail. A smile is as large as the experience of fireworks up close (plus the explosive noise of speech).

As space and time effectively diminish/speed up as we mature, at the level of Deweyan habits, I suggest that thinking about the emergent social-moral self, the architectonic of human agency is not directly inferable from our usual observational stances. The infant during the experience of attachment with its m/other is very fully engaged.

Further, I suggest that the infant is less directly a student of the world, as most of our theories of development have assumed. Rather, the attachment relationship involves the child first as student of and to its m/other, thence of and to the world: as she depicts it to her child.

During all these processes of early development, the m/other is doing, handling, feeding, observing her infant and interpreting its behavior, wants, and needs. The infant is changing, growing, and m/other is also changing in her observation, and estimation of her child. She is realistic in her readings, but also and at the same time, has a number of ideals, future-directed senses of what the child will be and become. Importantly, for our quest, is that m/other and child are a kind of singularity.

M/other's glances, for example, effectively direct her child to look where she wants, then back at her. Much of this process is about sound, but also involves faces and eye directives and games. It entails a continuous confirming of the child (seeing somebody gazing back). The (vast) facial movement of a child's smile, for example, is welcomed by m/other's own smiles.

On our way to the emergence of the social-moral self, I suggest that the m/other utilizes the attachment process to direct her child to the world. But the major point here is that the child attends to the world through its study of its m/other's facial movements and voice. The infant does not directly study the world, but develops through the sense that the m/other is providing questions and context to the world, and her child is responding by organizing and beginning to understand the world...as its m/others sees and directs her experience of the world to her infant.

I call it the *Question-Response System*, and think its study will tell us a great deal about our language development: beyond the (fairly simple idea from Dewey's perspective) that the essence of language is sentences, creativity, and all that. Its pursuit will also, I think, free us from the ancient/current habit of implicit comparison with other species whom we presume to be mentally inferior to ourselves. This only excuses us to not observe our selves, and to presume that we as observers are somehow removed.

Meanwhile, the child is growing, changing, beginning to develop the muscular abilities to move: sitting, crawling, beginning to walk, then move, then move quickly. The ease of caring for an infant, until the moment when he or she can move independently, seems amazingly simple in the hindsight of guarding against the infant hurting itself. Until this point, m/other could literally leave the child on its own. It was safe to do this. Later, however, after several months, after the first steps of about a year old, the infant is increasingly dangerous to itself. Fingers in electrical sockets, touching a hot stove, running, trying to go downstairs... What's a m/other to do?

It is at this point of development, that the self begins to emerge much more clearly: a sense that the (now) toddler, has a sense of itself, knows much of what there is in its world, is involved and entranced by its existence, has begun to speak, and is on the way to figuring how to call itself by the impossible-to-teach word of self-description: "I."

The child begins to have an internal dialogue, begins to be able to gather memories which for us, to this day, wander in our heads as our first memory; the first event that I have in my memory...who I am. It begins to have, to be, a self; a self which exists within the (always) social context of its m/other, and gradually including others.

At this moment of development, every m/other has a deep dilemma. The child can be safeguarded from itself only to a certain point. She can put him (usually, him) on a leash, keep it from wandering into dangerous territory; try hortating or even screaming. But there are limits on what anyone can do. The (moral) problem is in somehow getting the child to take care of itself.

But what does the child know of itself, of taking care? The very idea of the self indicates that the child has a sense of itself which is independent of the world, especially its m/other, and in interesting ways, independent from itself.

The problem for the m/other is to get her child to take care of itself much as she would do. Here, I suggest, is much of the idea of the emerging social-moral self. The child now sees itself, but always within the context of m/other. It is becoming more separate, has an increasing sense of its own boundedness and continuities. But its viewing of self is within the moral necessity of taking care of its own being.

This is to say that the very basis for our moral being is located in the necessity of the m/other to have her developing child take on the moral equivalent of her responsibility for her infant. The child must begin to see itself as its m/other *would*: a sense of conscience, a sense of/for itself which sees itself.

The seat of morality is located in identifying oneself as oneself—a deepening sense of self—always within the context of how others see us, and would have us be. In the early years, the power of the m/other to confirm and direct her child is pervasive.

This experience of the child continues, and expands to other persons—family, community, etc., as the child develops and grows— with others seeing and judging the child in many ways, but most always including various judgments about the self-as-moral. Who am I, and who I am, includes questions and judgments about m/others and others. Who am I thus includes questions of what am I to do.

It begins from the sense that one has/is a self, that one has to take care of and for, but within the context that taking care of oneself is much as one's m/other would have one do. It derives from, is located within the directly moral commitment of the m/other to her developing child. It is not merely m/othering, but brings to the interaction and care of her child, innumerable pictures of her child—in each immediacy, in the very idea of each next moment; in a while, tomorrow, and toward the idea which she brings to her observations of and responses to her child, of it developing and becoming a person... much as she is and would be; much as the child will. She includes a deep sense for the idea of futurity, of hope, of the possibilities, but also of its evanescence.

The foundation, the genesis of the self, the genesis of morality, is thus located in the emergent transformation of the developing child with its m/other. It study and implementation is increasingly focused beyond the mere study of the child, into the study of its early relationship with its m/other.

My observation or wonder is that without taking seriously the Meadian idea of emergence of the social-moral self, we have been left without any way of accounting for our morality; or being-moral. The sense that the individual develops as it were, independently, has left us wondering how it can be, even might be, that humans are moral. This is much of why, I think, we are continually tempted to look outside our being, outside of life itself, to account for our moral being. Attempting to locate mechanisms for our moral being is thus crucial in establishing us as naturalistic subjects.

It is the morality, the actual morality, of continuously being parent to a child that is the locus of morality. It is an aspect of our being social, that we are also moral, as it were, by-our-nature. It resides within the complex of experiences of the moral ongoing involvement of infant with its m/other.

9.

LIFE PARADOXES: EITHER-OR, REALITY

Heraclitus, famous for holding that "all things pass and nothing abides; you cannot step twice into the same stream," also insisted: "It is wise to hearken to the Logos and to confess that all things are one!" For Heraclitus, change, "the clash of opposites," is essential to the unity and stability–the continuity– of reality. But the tension between continuity and change is not simply an ancient philosophical conundrum. It is also at the root of the most pressing questions of our time.

We wrestle with the tensions of tradition vs. innovation in the law, in religious thought, and political life. The pace of change in scientific discovery, religious thought and practice, technological advancement, environmental transformation, and globalized culture is accelerating at such a dizzying rate that our abilities to cope are tested to the limits. But the key to our thriving and flourishing as human beings–perhaps, to our very survival– depends on how we find continuity in the midst of such rapid change. The constructive engagement of the seemingly "clashing opposites" of science and religion may hold the secret to our well-being and our future.

H: Life is a Paradox!
J: Life is full of Paradoxes?

Who we are vs. how we look like we do (who we are to others).

Introduction: Much discussion lately, and over the eons of thinking about the human, consider the notion that much of life seems to be about opposites in our lives: e.g., good and evil, night and day, sleep and wakefulness, change and permanence, life and death, female and male, pathology and health, right and wrong, hot and cold.

(Note that the very idea of opposition—paradoxically—places sometimes very different ideas into kinds of juxtaposition—in a relationship—where they seem, at least, to be *obviously* "opposed.")

They seem to have reached a time of greater attention as most of the world's traditions are increasingly wandering in(to) all of our being and thinking.

Interesting, in some cases, this has raised the importance of one side of some opposition or paradox to positions of importance or power in our lives and thinking—while the other "side" has been made unimportant, attacked, reduced, derogated... wrong.

"Attacks" on the morality of women over issues of contraception and abortion are a case in point—making it seem obviously or purely political—but this, I think, oversimplifies what is occurring. The notion of paradox often seems to heighten the importance of the relationship, and focuses on the differences as gaining more or less power.

I propose that this is occurring within a great or more encompassing notion about reality: e.g., permanence is "real," while change is an "illusion"—some form of whatever is seen as opposed to reality (ideas deriving mainly from Plato and Pythagoras, but alive and thriving in Christianity/Islam).

How is this occurring? The rise of "strong" religion—especially in the Western tradition—has raised the idea of permanence to a literal defining of the nature of reality—while change is either reduced to very little importance, equated with "chaos," or used to bolster the notion that death "defines" the actual human condition while life is some sort of chimera. (Augustine – "City of God" an important developer of these ideas: "fall to earth.")

But some of these pairs of opposites are not merely opposites—and we have to already see or know that such opposites have a bond or enduring similarity—in order to note the paradox.

If, as many have attempted, we combine these in some sense of structures which have meaning somehow, we think we have gotten closer to the actuality of the human and of the human condition.

And to the extent that they are "life paradoxes," we have to deal with them. For example, the question of male and female is not merely an idea, but an actuality, a fullness, which sets our lives in order, gives it direction (or not, but usually actively).

The paradox of change vs. permanence can operate in our very being to cause us to wonder and wander in each moment of our being: the present, past, and the often agitating directives of the future, and each of our futures.

This is to state that life paradoxes are fairly ubiquitous in our being, and enter into our thinking about being in powerful, but usually obscure, hidden, or merely habitual ways. They come into our thinking or thoughts in odd and often interesting ways, but usually float along, as if they are mere parts of being, not all that different, say, from our ability to move or use our limbs to accomplish what we might need to do.

This is *not* to state that they are unimportant in our being, but that they rise to "power" in different ways in different times in one's life, or variously in the "histories" of different traditions of thought mostly about the human; but they usually include some sense of the human with respect to other parts of forms of life-nature.

Occasionally, in history, these oppositional pairings have not merely been lived or noted. They have risen to "importance" (kinds of transcendental centrality), in thinking about the human, existence, and the world. In some contexts or "traditions," one side or aspect of a paradox has been taken as *the* truth—the way things are... actually. Instead of a paradox, the notion that life *is* a paradox, they have effectively been raised in import as a kind of explanation of how things are, or the how the world is.

In such cases, the attempt has been made to *resolve* them: to claim that one or the other of some pair is more... real, actual, the ways things are. Instead of placing or of seeing all oppositions as within the broadly human condition, one or the other has been chosen as preferred, destined, as least bad...

Western thought, an important example in framing our understanding of the world and of ourselves, has focused, particularly, on *resolving* the change-permanence paradox on the side of permanence. What is changing is somehow less real, less true; and the overarching reality is that which does not change: the idea of the deity is, probably, the most pervasive and powerful notion which has arisen from this re-solution to what I will be labeling *life paradoxes*.

In the traditions which seem to want/need to resolve life paradoxes on one side or the other (e.g., dreams are *real* in Amerindian traditions, waking is real in Western thinking, while dreams are some sorts of commentary on real—awake—life), the very definition or idea of what is (really) real, arises to define itself.

Permanence is the really real; or change is what there is. As we shall see, both are *the case* in the human condition (at the least), and the attempt to resolve them—in this case, particularly, on the side of permanence, has created some powerful ideas and thinking which resonate widely and often powerfully. (Christianity and Islam take the notion of permanence as the really real; which *often* interprets life and experience as questionable, as chimera or dream.)

In the East, where the ideas of Confucius and his heirs continue to dominate in many senses, the question of change and permanence or continuity, has been considered to be *complementary* rather than oppositional. No need to firmly or finally resolve the question of time and change once and for all: there are moments of and for change, and others in which permanence reigns. Consult the "I Ching" whenever the paradoxes of life seem problematic or an issue in anyone's life experience. (This is further *framed* by the notion that everyone wills to live the longest life—wisdom will *increase*—and needs to work at that.)

I call them *life paradoxes*, because they seem to derive or arise from our being or experience, more than they are givens in our existence. Life and death seem to arise from our early *realizations* that we/I will eventually die. If we *choose* to *focus* (primarily) on life, or upon death, our thinking and ideas expand and often pervade much of the rest of our being.

It is similar—though less obvious in our usual experiences—that we regard the time of our waking lives as the actuality of our being, and dreams are considered to be some commentary upon our waking, presumably *conscious* being.

I learned only gradually while doing anthropological-linguistic work in Southern Mexico with some highland Mayan (Tzotzil) Indians many years ago, that the life of dreams is considered or understood by some to be *more real* than what *we* (Western thinkers) consider to be *the real*. In continuing conversations with Amerindian thinkers, this idea seems to be quite widespread: dreams are or occur when our (*true*) "spirits" leave our bodies and re-enter the worlds where we share spirits with (other) animals. (This, in turn, raises deep questions about our being, and relationship to (the rest of) nature.)

(An *incidental* note: most Amerindians I have known and inquired of, seem to have quite a few other *persons* in their ongoing being: i.e., they are actively in their thinking. I have J. always present, for certain, but others move in and out—or I can invoke their presence in my active thinking, e.g., now dead parents on their birthdays (else-wise too, but not obvious) in my ongoing thoughts/thinking.)

This is to say that the framing of this discussion takes us upon a journey which is about the real or actual of our being; what is truth, or not (or whether there is clarity or obscurity, or both). This discussion, particularly as it takes place in the current time of the rise of religious thought and activity, may enable us to understand the human more as we are, than how we may have said we are.

Male and Female: Female and male. An oddity, opposition? A life-paradox. This is how I am, what *they gave me*; a peculiarity of being, being one or the other in some anatomical senses. Not a "surprise." (Or an enormous surprise? To be accepted/rejected?)

Oddly, interestingly, most of the notions we have of the nature of the human—and all that follows from this, which is most everything—is a male('s) story. The metaphor for how we are and know, is usually a little boy looking out at the world: how does he get knowledge of the world? Whether or how that is in any ways different from how little girls know—has not much been raised in the human nature discussions. (*Knowing* you can or will have a "your own" baby—a girl's "notion" from about age 2 on—doesn't often arise in what knowledge is! Questions of how we conceive of our futures— maturity, mating, birth, death...—don't seem to have much gotten into our theories of knowledge!)

We look back to Plato, Pythagoras, and Parmenides (usually anti-Heraclitus) to find out how we and the world are: the paradox which reigns over reality, dwells here on change *vs.* permanence. We don't much consult the women philosophers (note that philo-sophia *is* a woman!), or return to the Delphic Oracle who was depicted standing naked above a hole in the earth's surface, receiving all of knowledge, of what there is, through her orifices: "know thyself," she advised/admonished.

Instead, we in the West have decided that our knowledge is through our minds: reduce or get rid of the body, banish bodily being to discern how we are, really. Banish women from the frameworks of being human; their bodies are "changing" all the time, anyway (as if men's aren't!) And to find out how we are, look rather at animals, and "see" how we are "different" from them, "unique" in existence. Rather, look mostly at domestic animals, who are obviously dumb, and think that what is human is somehow smart: language, rationality... all of that.

Men carry the sperm which they "need" to spread, to push into the woman, in order to carry their genes forward into the world, and keep the world... afloat. Women are receptive, passive. Fuck them! Men do what we *have* to do. Not much thinking in this depiction, after all. (What to do with/about one's sexual impulses: a major life-setting issue! "Go to the world with the mind alone"—advised Plato. Make those lusts/loves go to hell. (Maybe easier to "blame" women for men's lusts?)

The fact that women bear men's babies, doesn't much penetrate their actualities, particularly after birth. The after-birth experience of women is seen as solely passive. Knowledge, being: the individual child develops, gets language, gets to know... essentially on its own.

But the (early) relationship between m/other and child is thoughtful, continuous, and intense; the momentary and daily interaction of the women and her child are virtually total.

The notion (of biologist Elaine Morgan)—that from the moment the baby is born... there is *somebody* there—involves the seeing/projection into her child, in that moment, and it only gets more "complicated!

Man and woman, we are all involved in the realities of the interactions which got us from birth, to knowledge, to this moment. Yet, all this is virtually absent, missing from the story of our being; we have resolved this paradox on the side of the man, at least in Western thought.

In these days of the "rise" of religious thought and activity, I wonder that women aren't being pushed down, in a deep sense, because they represent the future: life, inspiration, her child who will go forth into the world, and become the future. In the religious contexts which the West has promulgated, this moment is largely a return to the past: to authority, prophets/prophecies, texts, all of which are taken as ways and means to tell us how the world, how we, "really are," and how reality really is.

Life and Death: Writing on this day, June 6, 2006, I am reminded of the text in the Book of Revelation, to protect us against the rise of the Evil of all of being and time: 666.

This paradox of life and death seems to reside in the minds and being of all humans (others species?–likely) from the age of 5 or so, on. "I"—the sense of self, myself, my self, will no longer exist at some moment, in the murky future. This thing, me/I, is now alive—breathing, moving, thinking, relating to others. Not now, but someday will die: later... or sooner.

(This clearly raises all the questions about being—ourselves. What is this self, the person I call me, myself, I? How do I "know" the present and past, foresee the future in which I have to take care that I continue to be? ...but, no matter what, I/me/myself eventually will not continue to be in all these senses of self, actuality? How do/did I get to be me, how locate, remember, imagine, project...? How does this relate to human agency, which, as John Dewey reminds, us is mostly thoughtless habits, which remain backgrounded in the "obviousness" of being.)

For many Christians and Muslims—particularly—involved, obsessed, convinced that life is more an aspect of death, rather than or less than part of the ongoingness which is life/living: especially "my" life. (Not to underestimate the power and importance of the life of some others: family, friends, deep enemies, the dangerous, etc.)

Christianity and Islam are, deeply as far as I (can) understand, concerned with death: the resurrection of Christ, the God of the Koran is *the God of the Day of Judgment*. Perhaps, obsessed, directed by the most primary of all questions: what is (really) real—death or life? Death is a heavy favorite in Western thought: ways to get over the fear of death (ways to create that self-same fear so conquering it rises to the center of our beings—and advises us that non-being is more real than being).

Intellectually, it got its major shape from the writing of Plato—who provided Socrates with the role of celebrating the overcoming of the fear of death in the dialogue *Phaedo*; more in the *Apology*. He had been condemned to death for *screwing up* the minds of his students—the elite youth of Athens. His solutions ("Republic X": go to life with "the mind alone" – grant the mind perpetual life, and death will (fear of death) will be reduced to practically nothing. Ideas are real, higher than our being, which is only a copy. The senses, our senses, our very being is a shadow; the light of our knowledge remains murky, at best.

For the rest: solutions and/or directions—live a good life, take good care of self (and others), do good works, love... life, others, everyone, nature... oneself... sufficiently and life will become good, sufficient, a celebration.

(And then, there're those women who can bring new life into being through giving birth—the ongoingness of life—a sense that death doesn't exactly "exist." Life just takes different forms.)

Or those whose sense of life is "shared" with nature: sharing of spirits with other species, a commitment to our mothers—the earth is our mother. We are responsible to life, to the earth, to our mother, for at least seven generations. A widespread Amerindian philosophy.

And there are those followers, descendants of Confucius and his descendants, who puff-up life to its ultimate: wisdom, growth, go on for-ever in life. There is always direction, ways to go within life. Death...? Live long enough, well enough—by any/many definition and the idea/fear of death will diminish! Move, do *tai chi*, *qigong*, get into the ideas of the martial arts. Or, for the Jews: *l'chaim* (to life)!

Change and Permanence: Whether because of its usual relatedness to life and death, or because this paradox intrigues and itches us (particularly in certain moments of history, and each of our lives).

In Western thought, the paradox of change and permanence is (very) central to all of our thoughts both about our being and about the world. In some deep senses, it is invoked or used or to define what is (really) *real*.

In the history of ideas, it was (and remains) a battle between the ancient puzzler, Heraclitus—who thought that all was change ("you can't walk in the same river twice"), and the tradition of Parmenides/Pythagoras/Plato who developed the "idea" that what is real is permanence.

(Being brought up in a secular Jewish family, this didn't arise much in my youth. At that time in American history, death was fairly "hidden," not much discussed—only slightly less obscure than homosexuality during this period, 1930s, 40s.)

The paradox reigns in our lives: how can it be, how is it, that we are both the same person as we have been all our lives; how do we find or locate ourselves each day upon awakening—yet we are changing in each and every moment (or the world is changing)?—Especially in these times of rapidly increasing globalism.

Most of our theories about the human (being, condition, nature) have hovered about-upon this paradox. The locus of the New Testament and the Koran are concerned with death: but not merely in the paradoxical sense of death vs. life.

As these "ideas" have "worked out" in Western thought, the so-called dualism of mind and body has been invoked or thought to account for the human (often, the world). How can the (physical) body be able to think or understand the world outside of its purview, the senses? Aristotle's response: only humans have symbols which allow us to go beyond the here and now; whereas animals have signs (also children) tied to the sensible here and now. (A central issue for any attempt to solve or "get around" Western dualism; I think Q-R system will do this!)

Some years ago J. *got into* the "I Ching" and we realized that Confucian/Eastern thought didn't dwell on the either/or of change and permanence: instead, change occurs or can be chosen from "time-to-time," and permanence at other points. And, I got the sense that certain traditions of (Western) thought seem to keep their paradoxes unresolvable: while the East seems to "resolve" the paradox—both… and, in some ways and moments.

Once Heaven (the afterlife) became the answer or metaphor for our "real" being—mostly via Augustine—and we "fell" to earth via our parents' sins—the paradox got resolved: Heaven, God, death *is* permanence. Life (change) is "but a dream." Baptism, abortion… whew!

Or, as Pythagoras developed the idea, permanence is "higher" (more correct, real) than change: more like the rational (mathematics). As more rational minds are more like permanent (=the persistence of math/geometry), then males are smarter than females—because women are continually changing (whereas men don't have the monthly cycle)—so a lovely paradox, has been turned into a political-religious-philosophy.

One more thing: why permanence becomes more "real" in this moment—very rapid change (as right now) seems to turn to "chaos" for many people, as they grab/grasp for permanence—usually they "return" to the usual prophets, texts, authorities to tell them what is what.

(Heraclitus is helpful to help us try to discern if and why anti-female tendencies are rising in our times!)

Certainty and Uncertainty: a "sub-topic" of change and permanence. The notion of permanence contains within it (as it were) the idea that the universe is open, immense—but it is also bounded or complete: Heaven is a term or metaphor for the notion of permanence. The idea of God (or Gaia)—some "force" which "exists" irrespective of humans/us or anything else. Pray to the deity: He (most often "He") created us, will sustain us. Our "souls" are aspects or, or related to the deity. Everything that is/was/will be is already determined: it is permanent and also certain.

In this apparent (or derived) opposition (an "apparent" paradox?)—the parallel with change is equivalent to "uncertainty." Change implies some moment which is the "present"—a sense of memory which was/is the "past"—and the impending ideas of a future: which is (certainly) uncertain.

This becomes complicated because it overlaps with the paradox of male-female. Females are "always" changing (monthly cycles, blood, etc.) represent (actually) the future with babies, etc. Males are seen (see ourselves?) as more stable, consistent.

But an important aspect of outcome of this thinking, is that the reality of the world can be (and often has been) interpreted or understood, as the power of the past (time stopped!) to determine our world: prophets, texts (e.g., Biblical), truth is more believable (at certain moments of history) as it represents what has already occurred, or determined (e.g., God "created" man)—this is all (seemingly) certain.

One and the Many (Parts and Wholes): (atomism vs. holism) see Plato's "Parmenides."

Good and Evil: (Not givens in the world: derived from the acceptance of paradox(es) being resolved and/or resolvable!) Related often to *Light and Darkness.*

This oppositional pair seems, to me, less like a Life-Paradox, than some sort of derivation from (the lack of) an explanation of how/why humans are moral creatures.

The ideas underpinning the opposition between Good and Evil are that we are not moral creatures (by our nature)—thus we have to define, take-on, become Good persons, else we will decline into Evil.

And this basically already possesses a Western religious orientation that God represents or instantiates Good and Satan (or the anti-God, anti-Christ) represents or instantiates Evil.

It presumes the idea of God, taking-off generally from the Adam-Eve story. There are various traditions here, each following a different prophet—such as Mani—who developed such ideas and carried them to very high importance—*epitomes.*

Wakefulness and Sleep (Night and Day): Sleep (and "Dreams") the real, more real than wakefulness? Or is being awake what there is, all there is, knowledge, truth, etc.?

These questions arose in my life while working with Mayan Indians (Tzotzil) in Chiapas, Mexico. In sleep, the spirit leaves the body to join with the spirits of all the other animals/beings. These questions came up when a Mayan friend/informant I was working with had a problem with "returning" of spirit upon awakening.

In Western thought, wakefulness is the truth, what there is, etc. Dreams are, if anything meaningful, commentary upon (real) life—as in Freud.

Appearance and Reality: Parmenides?

Mind and Body::Body and Mind: Maybe—like Good and Evil—derived from other issues or paradoxes. Mind separated from body in the Western traditions. But this duality is strongly implicated in a series of "unanswered" or "unresolved" questions about human being, which make humans "different" from all (other) animals due to the "mental superiority" of humans. How to resolve these paradoxes, or help make them "go away"?—a central task of my (forthcoming) *Body Journals*!

Perhaps it's what I've been reading, as I'm dedicated to (trying to) edit *The Body Journals* for publication. I thought/think that maybe it's best to state "very simply" that we are bodies in the world along with other bodies. But this observation/idea is a very hard "sell" in the world which takes the idea that we (humans, at any rate) are basically-fundamentally minds which find themselves "embodied" (Merleau-Ponty, 1963).

A "Western" idea flowing particularly from Plato (*Phaedo*) and reverberating in *the Republic*, where the idea of permanence over change is used to justify/solidify the idea that the mind reigns.

When the mind reigns, the problem becomes one of placing the body with respect to explanations of the human basically/intrinsically as a mind.

10.

IDENTITY AND BEING

A direction/solution to the problematics of Identity and Being.

"The heart-stopping thing about the newborn is that, from minute one, there is somebody there. Anyone who bends over the cot and gazes at it is being gazed back at."

British biologist, Elaine Morgan (1995)

The Issue of Being and Identity...in this Time: A mere perusal of the global or local scene forces one to wonder who and where we are. Like Dicken's *Tale of Two Cities*, the times are the best and the worst. Many of us live very well, at least ostensibly. Many of us live quite poorly in terms both of money/style of our lives, but particularly in the fact that being who we are seems more and more to involve struggles which have appeared but recently in our experience. *Who I am* and *who we are*—rise persistently as questions which demand asking; demand responses.

Many of us participate now in a global culture, within a kind of cosmopolitan outlook which centers somehow upon America, perhaps as some kind of icon of being. Others of us look backwards to Biblical and other holy or theo-political texts; to philosophy; to geography; to ethnicity; to language and some force which will gather our being within it.

I/We look forward with hope but also with a trepidation that all is not exactly well. Death and taxes: well, death is being pushed far, farther into the future even as many of us survive what would have been old age, now turned into an age of middles, with many years of life yet to come: productive vs. mere survival; healthy vs. being supported increasingly by technologies which may support our vegetative being, but do nothing for our being, our identity. Insured; Medicaid; social security; Medicare... *life insurance*.

It was in my imagination of my futurity, it seems almost clear in retrospective and hindsight, that at this point in my life I would be able to look back and judge that all was well; or not so well. But it rarely occurred to me that this time stretching out to years would need work, filling, more than a rest for the not-so-wicked, not all that good. The ordinariness of life's vicissitudes has become problematic; summation no longer helps. Who am I? What do I do here?

A cursory glance around the world looking back wonders why all these modern peoples like to look back to find themselves. Why do our mirrors no longer tell us that we are what we see and what we do? Rather we take the pictures which we generate inside our own heads and believe the stories which we place about them: the 'what was' or 'must have been' ('would have,' 'should have'...).

Who I am fades into the history of some collective sense of myself even as I gather its strengths, its insides and outsides. Experience and existence falter, blur. Weakness and courage find no home within our flesh. There is no longer any home, no one at home, no place to pitch our tents. Me? I? We? You? Who?

I and We: The paradox of the one and the many, of individual and society, particularly me and universally human naturally me, is one of the dozen and a half or so which affect - perhaps they help define - our very existence. Whether this entails issues of the universe, of being human, of the very nature of life processes! The paradox of life ←→ life as a paradox?

I am that I am. But I am also an aspect—a persona, a role, another— who is significant in the being of some other(s). Who is the real me where my energies and definitions of being find themselves located, is clearly bound up with the way in which such paradoxes arrange our notions of identity? (Or we arrange such paradoxes by solving, resolving, compartmentalizing life experiences in which various issues seem opposed, different, but within the same domains.)

The temptation has arisen in different (theo-political) traditions either to *resolve* such paradoxes: to say/believe that I really truly am the I which *has* a soul, the I which *occupies* the body which is born and eventually dies; or to say that I truly am she which/who is the child of my family, the believer in my religion, heir to a certain geography or ethnic history, a language, a gender. But some (e.g., Confucian) traditions attempt to *complementarize* rather than to resolve paradoxes: yin and yang, change and continuity in some complex of existential resonances.

These *tastes* in the handling of experienced paradoxes often seem to me related to how different traditions handle progress and utopic issues: whether life is seen as sufficiently/infinitely long (Confucian, Jewish), or utopia/heaven is available only after dying (Christian, Islamic, Hindu). Resolution of paradoxes is possible and often compelling within the strictures and structures of life defining death defining life; but may be complementarized within the idea of the longest life as sufficient to itself.

My observation and experience are that being and identity are (really, truly) paradoxical: yes! and yes! But, at many places and times in our lives, one or the other seems important or dominant, while the other side of the paradox backgrounds itself, disappearing. And, as the reader can discern already, talk about paradox already seems to contain its own paradoxes. Western thought—to which I seem heir though thoroughly critical—bathes the paradox by resolving being in the complications of being. I am that I am! The individual has a soul placed in the body; the soul transcends physical being; the physical me is not me?

And we seem to be left with our being problematic: confused and caught in a vast set of dualisms beginning with mind and body, and going directly or indirectly to issues of essentialism and existentialism—experience. So I talk with you through an essential medium which certainly seems, at the least, to transcend physical being. But your trust in my existing much as you underwrites the possibility of mutual understanding—and illustrates the complications of the paradox of the one and the many.

Meaning and Identity: The quest for identity seems equally to be questioning/questing after meaning in a moment in history whose gatherings bring us all together in the arena of global being.

The facts and perceptions of others' identities reflecting and impinging upon our own seems virtually to cause us to react and question and feel even that life is too full, saturated. Perhaps it is, as Gergen (1991) has said, that technology and the pace of life itself so fill us with the sense of speed that we can no longer absorb even our own being. Perhaps it is that the age-old questions about death and life which had formerly been ensconced in socially scripted roles, no longer come wrapped: everything is up for grabs. Perhaps, as Nietzsche warned us, the Western quest for truth has seemed to prove to us that the truth we sought turned into truths each of which revealed some senses of emptiness or incompleteness. We now see-through history, see through our own presentness/presence, and revel in the futility of seeking meaning. Now this flashes signs back at us that whatever meaning was or seemed, it is now tied inextricably with our senses of being and of identity.

I am me, a son to now dead parents alive in my memory, a husband of many years counting but always a new day, a father to two children and their friends, a teacher, neighbor, a (relatively new) grandfather tempted to think that this is really who I am and was meant to be, a colleague, a worker, an ethnic of sorts of sorts alive and resonating with what it means to be a man, a secular Jew, an American, a world cosmopolitan citizen, an intellectual of sorts seeking and questing for all of knowledge ready and/in waiting for Faust's temptations...

Being No One...In Particular: There are modes of anonymity; there are processes by which one becomes no one rather than everyone. There is the question concerning these times in which the kinds of thought and organizational construction which seem to be operating in these moments, tend toward reducing being: going, going... gone.

And if institutions and governments replace me with a number, with a location, with a fairness which distributes being as if it were a not very precious commodity, where then am I? Does anyone care?

Is it that the entire world has become a caricature of Chaplin's movie *Modern Times*? Have we modeled being upon the efficient machine, attempting somehow to capture the dualisms of Plato and transform the mind into a computer which directs the body which is us, and which is stupid? Located, doing... but no longer needed to think out its being? If we organize to beat off the organization or the capitalism which promotes—it seems—these movements away from being, do we recapture our identity? Lost? Me?

Why? What motivates me so that a few dollars, a little party of celebration would give me the sense of who I am that I am anybody at all?

Incentives? Incentives! Meaning quests replaced by the carrot dangling marketers who psychologize us in our minimal moments and captivate our being. No wonder Nietzsche and Emerson wanted us to need to transcend and overcome our own being which seems to be in a mode of reducing being. No wonder.

Is it change itself which turns us away from being students of our own being? Is it the experience of changing *too* quickly which urges us to look for fixes and guarantees which experience itself cannot contain? Is it the sense of loss of control, having imagined that we had found it once, twice, which moves us to seek for surety: looking backwards, looking for deities, looking anywhere but into our own being, trying to unpack the histories which have propelled our being into this moment? Globality? Bureaucracy? Wanting anchors in a too-fast world?

Where am I? Who am I? If I am certain today, will I be tomorrow?

Doing or Being: Am I a person defined largely by what I do—an instrumental definition of oneself in which one can determine who s/he is by noting what one does? Or am I a person who wanders about my being, trying—Oh so hard!—to be someone in particular, trying to engage myself and my life in its living being and processes?

The modernist Enlightenment model of externalizing the principal actuality and reality of being and attributing being to that externality, leaves us in various senses objective and free, even from our own being. As long as we do well and do good then we are in effect free; even from ourselves, even from engaging in the arduous task of self-examination to make sure that we are good persons. We tend to attribute our own being to the realities of our being: genetically endowed in such and such ways and destined to become just who we find ourselves being; being attached to nature, being creatures of a nature which we find in various places outside our own being, we do what nature *tells us* is our own nature—a play upon play upon words! Multiply, seek to save our genes, we are responsible to the necessity of preserving and serving our species. Do whatever we need to do to be ourselves.

But, but where am I within this instrumental definition of myself, at this point in existence, in *my* existence? Whence have I come, where am I now, will I be going with some sense of towardness which seems to me thoughtful; some sense of an on purpose rather than being thrown about cast as it were upon the waves of the oceans of life's vicissitudes? What now? What next? Why? Why not?

On Purpose: To put this instrumental notion of being and identity in another seeming context, I ask what purpose to my being one way or another, or yet a third. Why do this or that; think that I think this? It is often tempting to think that the thoughts I think are cast upon me by the necessities of existence. No whys—just that's. Not wise, I surmise.

Some confusion between the sense of teleology of an external agency, a deity, a nature which is like deity immutable and unchanging, and my sense of my own changing to be banished like Heraclitus, drowned in the river of paradox. It is as if my being is floating in a canoe drifting dreamily: "row, row, row my boat, gently... life is but a dream." A nightmare. Better to admit that my suffering is part of my being that I need to update, to see whom I have become, to examine habits of being contra being and to find my location where myself might be... might be being. Better a sense of purpose I impose upon my-self's *self-ing*. Jump in, the water's fine!

The Selfish Gene: The being who I am is hidden to myself, driven by some specie's *necessity* to stay alive: I am no more than a set of genes bent on conserving, preserving, spreading myself as widely as I can, and will. No Camusian problematic here; no worry about the Shopenhauerian problematic of suicide. I have automatic and autonomic systems driving my genes in the passing lane down the Autobahn. Whatever it takes to do this, this will be proper, appropriate, moral. The questions some active I of my brain's mind asks may swerve the real me of my genes from the task of human nature.

But this is a diversion. Really my genes ought to take care of themselves, and I my body like the body of Plato am not much more than the place in which my genes and Plato's spirit happen to find themselves. Not my problem...unless it interferes with my proper tasks of preserving myself to preserve myself within the futurity of being human—a Sociobiology in which mind doesn't really matter and being is some illusion which my genes use to do their business.

I: THE ONE

On *meditations on...Next Places*: The issue of who one is and what it means to be me - or anyone - is much more complex than any mere naming or signing of one's name, affixing authorship or individuality to any piece of work; including *oneself*.

Who I am, what my possibilities and necessities, my dependence and freedoms are; all these areas are issues of being and of identity. They are issues not only of structured thought, but also of each person's ongoingness.

This does not mean that there is no continuous or central or integral me which is the "me" I usually say I am, that *one* which is the authoritative author of my writing(s). It is just that I am in many more relationships than that one with myself; as it were, *alone*.

I not only have a theory about my being—now and then, tomorrow and beyond—but carry it with me, as me, sighting the visage which is myself as well as those whom I know, and who have tried to tell me who and that I am: parents, spouse, children... significant others. I am one and many; many thence one. The paradox is who I am.

Identity/being is paradoxical.

Who, then, is anyone else? Do we remain stuck in some Cartesian meanderings about the so-called *problem of other minds*? Do we approach being as some skeptics who, like Plato, really are dubious that my knowing something, some object, does not translate to knowing that/what someone else knows? This epistemological skepticism—doubt about the very possibility of knowledge—has been translated into doubting that others know, implying: 1) that the seat of being is the individual (the *thing* I call myself), and; 2) that others are, like objects, mere externalities to my being. Instead, it now appears clear that we humans are social in our deepest senses, and that me—the individual I call myself—is not only invested *in* others, but is invested *by* others; in life in my living.

But this is all too quick! I exist within the time of my and others' being: some senses of being as passing through; some notion that who I am (and others are) has much to do with the conjurings which we call memory; a will to live...

Part of being who one is in *projecting forward* some sense of future being, of oneself as seen into the world which is not yet. My *meditations on...Next Places* attempt to entice us to meditate on who we are as who we might be, or might want to be, intend to be, or not to be...next and next.

Looking backward at the photographs of one's personal biography, one is able to say that this picture is of *me*, of someone in my immediate family, or of someone *else*. I do not think that this ability to *see* continuity into one's photographic being is a very obvious fact of being. Merely it is a quite common, almost universal ability, which is usually not thought about because it seems so simple to us. But it is not so simple.

Rather, we have learnt to see who I am as some complicated notion of who others say I am, who I have been told to be, who I say I am—to significant others, and to not very significant others.

It is like looking in the mirror, and saying to oneself that one's reflection which is twice the distance as it would be looking at anyone else, is precisely who I am. Here, it is clearer, I think, that one sees a mix of who I am, who I would like to be in some narcissistic senses, how I think others see me. Clearly, one sees some mix of what is, how one imagines that others judge one's appearance, and so on. One can read beauty into one's visage; as well, one can see and foreground that which is unpleasing and carry that vision back into one's image of s/himself.

And here I am writing about being me, as if there is a separable self which can contemplate the being which is myself. Is this yet another paradox of being? Or are there multiple selves?—and able still to find...*the self?*

This issue is, perhaps, made quite complicated for the Western mind because the question of identity is subsumed within the Platonic dualism of mind and body. In this tradition, the body has been effectively *banished* from the issues and quests for who one is, and granted to the realm of the mind-soul-spirit which has had effective hegemony over the body. Identity and being have been located within issues of mental uniqueness of humans: language, rationality, knowledge—as if these are all essentially mental processes. This is to say that much of what I will call *actual* being has been omitted from the Platonic quest for the nature of identity. Similarly and related, is the Platonic dualism of matching being (of the individual) with the non-being of death (*Phaedo, Sophist*), rather than examining being within life in all of its complications, including especially being in the world with others' being in the world.

As a partial critique and corrective, my *meditations on...Next Places* explores being and identity as if life itself reflects and is reflected in the mirrors of others' faces and of their saying and affirmations of who I am, and of who I am that I might be—and will to be.

How to update judgment of oneself is not removed from the updating of who I am per se. The problem of how to move on to one's *...Next Places* at any moment in one's life trajectory is a meditative one: how to enter into one's being, such that one can do this better than that, that one can do this?

THE ESSENTIAL CHARACTER

Looking at the photographs which were taken
of that person who I am
who I call...Myself
I see an identifiable person: Me.

I was and I am
each yesterday; every now.

How have I changed: which visages gone,
which remain?

Do I see
the same person I am, now?

Who was; who now?
Where will the next place be?
How will I get there?
How will I know

I have arrived?

What lost
given up, gained
...what cost?

The Beginning and End of Being: At the risk of being part of the problem, of being ironical rather than critically foundational, it seems important (for me) to state that the Western predilection for presuming a picture of being which entails a vast framework of assumptions, lies at the heart of the problem of being as we have inherited it. It is as if we have either lost something in our existence and (changing) being—or it is that we have some necessariness of towardness in order to fulfill something about being human. If not...

...then we are not whole, not complete; we have no direction, no deity, no morality, no center to our being, no way of dealing with others or even with ourselves; there is not meaning in life, no meaning in the meaning of meaning. Life is a fall from a heaven in which we must either return to (that conception of) heaven or face the damnedness of an existence which has no meaning. It is as if we cannot be participants in our own existence because we do not and cannot *own* our own being. The freedom for which we are urged to search in our own being becomes chimera and condemnation.

Return to nature! Return to heaven! Are we so captivated with the idea of our own capture that we will not see what we have willed not to see? That we are children of m/others, that the language in which we come to think is the self-same as theirs, and that it is generative beyond any finiteness, even in its finite structures—this remains invisible in our presuming what we need no longer presume.

For the truth of being is an *emergent* truth. We are not (very) continuous with the fetus which is the individual self, become person within the context of others' imaginings of our being. The mechanical, material, physical individual is not the mark of our being in time, in every here and now. The (surviving person) body is itself conceptual as well as physical. Life and being are intrinsically social: a body being in the universe of others' bodies being. But all the m/others also will us to live as individual beings, interdependent, but also independent, and free to ask all these questions, to carry on the searches of identity.

The Enigma of Being/The Being of Being: Heidegger's *Being and Time* (1927) takes up the question of being, attempting in some fundamental sense to situate the questioner asking the question of oneself. "What is the being of being?" he asks. What is the place or point of reference from which all else flows? When is the 'here and now,' which resides somehow in one's being? Where is 'one's being' which knows all of this?

The enigma, deriving from some passages in Plato's *Sophist* and reflected upon in Aristotle's *Metaphysics*, reflected most recently in Wittgenstein's thoughts *On Certainty*, is that the very existence of the existent being seems to have to be *assumed*.

The existent being flows from a Western skepticism about the very nature of knowledge; even of the possibility of knowledge, principally of the world of nature, external to being. The "*I am*," and "*you are*," and "*it is*"—the ontology of ontology—must *already* be presumed to exist even and especially for us to begin talking about any *it*. Are we any better off understanding the nature of being—of objects and persons—than in invoking a transcendent deity or Gaia or history or what have you...which is another reflection of the dilemma?

The enigma of the being of being is not so un-understandable as all that. After all, we seem to be able to do what Heidegger says is (intellectually, philosophically) problematic. But to see my position takes a bit of review, and a concentration more on the nature of our own (human) being than on any necessity, first and *a priori*—to say that the world of objects *is*.

In a sense, this is a move back to the idea of Protagoras that (hu)man is the measure of all things. But it is also a critique which attempts to place in proper perspective and importance some issues about human nature and our own being which have been uncritically presumed to this time—without, I think—lapsing into any easy (formalist-idealist) solipsisms. The first order of discussion is about the locus of the problematic of being.

A more thorough understanding of the being of being human is first in order. This is so because the being of being is the locus of our own knowing; and knowing about being, the without-which talk could not occur (at least in the terms in which we have made language central to knowing, thence to being!), seems like the central issue in the being of being: what is the *it* about which, from which talk begins? (In Platonist problematics: what is the difference between being and non-being?—a more technical issue which I will take-up again later.)

The shift in understanding comes partly through the late works of Wittgenstein (1953) based in no small part on the work on comparative thought of Malinowski, (in Ogden and Richards, "Meaning of Meaning, Appendix 1, 1923) thence upon the knowledge gained about other species being (also) social. The first issue is about the nature of humans being social; radically altering our views about the nature of language: not primarily to know objects; but to talk (first) with one another, thence about the world.

The comparative (thought) view alters—also radically—our perspectives about our own viewing of ourselves. By going away and immersing ourselves in the viewing of others (cultures, species), we can *return home* to viewing ourselves often with new lenses, and in so doing can *problematize the ordinary*.

In turn, this enables us to see ourselves somewhat anew, seeing as interesting and/or complex...various aspects of ourselves which had been so *ordinary* as to have remained *below* or *out-of-awareness*. Examples: the ways in which we understand (phonemically, cognitively) our native languages; ways in which we *use* faces to judge character and being; the thoroughness of our knowing our own mouths and articulatory apparatus. Third: the importance we have granted to certain aspects of the human condition being particularly unique and radically different from other species, the raising of (certain views about) language to primacy, have to be rethought.

Briefly, the problem of the being of being is located in each of us—as young children—coming to know who and that *I am*. In the development of each of us, there is nothing obvious in parents'/others referring to a child, that s/he should understand that s/he is an "I." "I" is not a reciprocal term; in any interaction, each person is a "you," or a "she," or a "he." In effect, each child has to *invent* s/his own being as an "I." This, quite specifically, is the locus of the being of being. Once a child knows s/he is an "I" then reference is clear, if not obvious. (But it does not necessarily or always reside in articulated language; e.g., it occurs among the deaf in sign language).

Thus any deepened understanding of the enigma of being requires study and understanding of how any child gets to know about oneself.

This includes a rethinking of the nature of grammar; of the locus of meaning, and so on. Grammar (Sarles, 1985, Chap. 9) is not—as Western thought beginning from the physical individual—developed within each individual, as it were, independently. Grammar is about m/others presenting the world as a set of questions to which the infant learns the proper (to the parents) *sets* of responses. Meaning is located in, derived/inferred from such response sets. Parents merely assume/know the reality of the world of external objects and teach this to their children with the authority of their authority: why?—because I say so!

Purpose: Why am I? What telos, what meaning, what direction, towardness, do I have? What telos, meaning, direction does fate and destiny have for me?

What difference does it make if I have no purpose outside of my own being who I am? Does/doesn't the question of purpose already take me outside of my being in order to figure out why I am who I am?

In tune with the order of the world? Is there one order; many? Out of tune is *being* the attempt to improve one's intonation?

The Aristotelian attempt to judge present being in terms of some oughtness of existence, seems, like mysticism, to take us outside of ourselves. We arrange, we concoct some sense of the real purpose of life then live our lives as if this were an overarching truth. Then live our lives...?

But if there is no purpose, is there no point of my life; beyond this moment? What is a life lived well? Where can the purpose live; where is purpose proposed and enacted: acted upon?

The Origin of Consciousness: The temptation has been to equate being human with having consciousness. How exactly it happens that there is a thinking "I"—or my brain or my genes create the chimera that I think that I am and can think—remains an arena heavy with theory and with less observation and thinking about how I get/got to be conscious.

There has been a metaphor since the mid-17th century which has been much used (if not critically), enabling us to probe *immediate consciousness* (Hegel's term—Bergson's methodology). Condillac's (1932) protean notion is that the way to understand understanding is to wonder how an exact replica of my being—the *speechless statue* only cast in alabaster (the stone color seems not to be fortuitous)—could become a human (me, you). That is, the question of the origin of consciousness is still largely dominated by the idea and metaphor that consciousness is to be understood particularly by imagining that I can examine my thinking right now: even as I suspend or bracket (Husserl, 1913) my thinking about that thinking.

Instead, it occurs to me that the way toward understanding consciousness is to see how we humans go about it: from infancy (as the fetus) to developing bodily-intellectually. Much of the bodily development has been by-passed or neglected by those who seek the origins of consciousness, as if the body has little to offer being: a form of the *speechless statue thinking*.

Instead it seems important to examine the nature of the newborn, to watch the infant being watched, responded to, interpreted by others, and responding in turn. The eyes: the infant sees in her/his mother's eyes the self reflected. (Try feeding an infant while engaging s/his eyes!)

And watch a new m/other meet her child, and "see into" her/him that "*somebody*" is there (Elaine Morgan, 1985). If not... survival ...not!

The other powerful metaphor/methodology which informs thinking about consciousness is that of Plato whose notion of being is intertwined with epistemology: we are what we know. And the known is external to us: generalized, universalized. Knowing the world of objects (the objective world), we reflexively come to know our own knowing. But we have never found ourselves—the "I" who is conscious of my consciousness—within this casting.

My first subject matter is (simultaneously) other persons and myself: How different (if at all) these are/is debatable? I come to be distinct, especially when my m/others demand it, treat *me* as if I am, and urge-force me to be some-one. In the *beginning*, I may be no more than the constancy with which my m/other sees (in) me. I respond, she interprets, and gradually I become *me*.

Rather than considering the one which I am, the two of Plato, the three of Freud, it seems to be that I am intrinsically many: the question of self-conscious consciousness then comes down to how I find/generate a self which is constant and aware (conscious) and can find the self which others interpret and want me to be: this moment, tomorrow.

The fact is, it seems to me, that the demand of parents (m/others) for me to be independent-creative-consistent, is more powerful and extrinsic to my being (a body-mind) than that which is internal to my being a (potential) being.

I am that I am: When, it says in Genesis, Moses asked God for his name, he is said to have said, *I am that I am.*

In a discussion by the psychoanalyst, Erik Erikson, the question of *The Galilean Sayings and the Sense of "I"* contrasts this statement with the reports of Jesus having introduced rather than ended a number of his sayings with *Amen, but I say unto you.* The primary issue of the essay is how we know what we are: the "I," the "me," the "is" who I am...Being and Identity.

Being and Non-Being: (Nihilism from first to last and back again to first— the argument against the sophists/orators.)

Much of the confusion and argument about the being of being has centered about where knowledge is located, what it consists in, who can know it... and how.

Part of the argument seems to reside in the sort of battle which Plato wages against the sophists (*Sophist*) which concerns the nature of *true truth*. (In the post-modern climate of nihilism, the notion of truth is itself at serious risk, and demands that some new idea of its grounding be established if we are to proceed intellectually or actually.)

Plato analogizes the formal truth of logic and geometry as being located in the unchangingness of figures and of ideas as represented by the universal idea of any object. This becomes the *real*. Just as Plato suspected, in controlling or framing the idea of the real—at least within the formality of dualist thought which he posits—a potential battleground over the nature *reality* is set up. These days it is often called the battle between existence and essence: note that existence is about knowledge being in or flowing from the human, while essence flows from the idea of objects; and humans also become objects, as it were, by an osmosis of ideality.

Plato is worried most specifically—as is Heidegger—that the sophists cannot distinguish between being and non-being (an issue raised originally by Parmenides). It is not, as I used to think, about death directly, but flows as all else—from objects—to our own being. It is about the being of being, the referential knowledge by which any of us (and all of us) can talk about what is and what isn't... and, especially recently, how we know all this. Or that we cannot—the failure of Husserl.

The problem (of course) is that knowledge of objects is not at all obvious: either we have built-in, preformed abilities to know (pure reason, or...—not a solution!) or we derive knowledge from experience somehow, or (is it possible) that we really do not and/or cannot know (or be)?

In the beginning of the modernist philosophical era, Descartes solves or obscures this problem for a while, by assigning it to the examination of our thinking—something about language. Gradually, however, the question of our own being as subjectively knowing anything has penetrated the question of knowledge in ways which, at the moment, seem to have no apparent direction for solution.

As I have suggested, the understanding of the being of being is located in the human coming to know oneself as an *individual*. The grammatical shift is that grammar is not merely the set of all sentences, or the collectivity of words about objects, but is a process by which children come to know the world of objects and sentences in the complex of the Question-Response System.

Children do not know the world (in any sense, merely), but know the system in whose terms parents describe (and operate in) the world. In the context of human sociality, language is—early in development at least—toward mutuality of understanding, with the being of being located (in each individual's experience) in the knowing of her/his m/others, which s/he *has* to understand in approximately/essentially the same way as they.

Independence of the individual person thence *emerges* from this relationship, rather than preceding it as the Western tradition has had it. The problem of the being of being is located in understanding how humans operate in the world, rather than being knowledge theoretically conceived by philosophers in their especial wisdom. The problem of being is in knowing how to see human development as it is!—including a problematizing of the ordinary from comparative thought.

Two arenas of example may aid in seeing the problematic anew: the ancient debate between the philosophical and the oratorical tradition, and the ongoing debate within the context of Artificial Intelligence as the logical analysis of language vs. the engineering approach of expert systems.

The question of identity in the present age shifts the question of being and non-being quite radically toward the existential in a world in which existence has no apparent viable philosophy which includes doing and living. (Gergen's *Saturated Self*).

Authenticity and Integrity: Am I the genuine article? Have I forgotten to say '*No!*' whenever the odors of life's free lunches waft before my nostrils' tendrils? Has my *stuckness* in the past been thoughtful, forced? Have I preserved some sense of being in the present which is strong enough, self-pleasing enough that I can say that I am who I am, knowing mostly what this means; and meaning it?

Am I on the take: morally, intellectually derived from others who define who and that I am? And if I have based my life's living on others' stories—heroic, martyred, brilliant, prophetic—is it enough to be me precisely, to live as they said or as they (would) have lived?

For whom/what do I do what I do? Do I please my own sense of self-being by pleasing and doing for others; or by isolating myself like a hermit in order that some inner sense of self-being finds itself and emerges and emerges? Is there no place to stop and to call myself completely who I am? Is there some place to stop and to call myself who I am? Stop the world! Get off! Get a life!

Get a life worth living seems to ring hollow, reverberating in my thinking that who I am, what I do falls short... of what!? Wisdom is a term which rings hollow: Bing-Bong, bing-bong, bing... bong!

Do questions, agitations, and issues of authenticity and integrity arise much because of the various asymmetries of life's relationships? As teacher to others, I am perceived as steady-state, as being precisely who I appear to be; a tower of knowledge and strength, a purveyor of others' hopes and imaginations and inspirations toward their own futurities. And I am—to myself—in varying degrees, at various angles to my students' perceptions of the "me" they see. If I am authentic, honest to them, can I remain authentic to myself, except as my students' teacher? And to the "me" who I am...to myself? (Sarles, 2013)

Is there some way, some way of being, of study, of finding a notion of the mentor-within, which could direct me directly to my boundaries of my integrity so that I can know at all points just precisely who and where I am; and am-not?

Authority: The question of and quest for being and identity entails authority—the sense that one is sufficient to oneself; that one effectively holds the ground upon which one finds oneself occupying. In a deep sense, authority in pomp, authority in its yielding, sits in relation to this sense of ground. And it is an arena where the one and the many portray together the power of being who one is and we are.

Authority resides in the sense not only of who and what one is, but also in what can happen with respect to one's ground: if, for example, I move to occupy a place where others might want to be (or not want me to be), what then? Can they move me out? How easily will I move? What context surrounds the places of my being? In these aspects of authority, the existential-processual elements of what is and might be, the "if," and would, powerfully circumscribe who one is; who one might be: the child growing, the teacher's student who will (someday) overtake the teacher; the king and the peon, the question of relation between policing and the polis.

Authority possesses a sense of social legitimation as well as of context. The scepter of Agamemnon in the Iliad represents the authority of kingship—which has its underpinnings and justification in the acts and assumptions of others, as well as a philosophical apologetic as, for example, in Aristotle's *Politics* where he uses the mind/body dichotomy-hierarchy to analogize the authority of king over polis as mind over body (the *natural* order of director over directed). Who is perceived and treated as if proprietor of the place and of the podium? Who yields and how?

And in other traditions such as the Amerindian where space and place have no proprietary claim upon us or us upon them? Or in the martial art of yielding of *Tai Chi*, where power and authority are located not in the occupation of the place, but in the ongoing ability to yield, to absorb, and deflect, the authority is located in the wise: s/he who knows, but also can *do*. In the Apostolic forms of Christianity and Buddhism, identity rests in the concept of selflessness, of giving up all earthly authority: authority is precisely ironic as the more thoroughly one asceticizes her/his existence and reduces one's dependence on the power of others to authorize one's own authority, the more complete one is; and likened to the deity.

Who writes is the source. Who becomes and develops and grows into the author is on the way to the power which defines and declares self-being and identity. Not only source, I-the-author am responsible for the words and the ideas and the thinking, the declaration and defense of this set of ideas, of analysis, of the mode of thought and the ways of thinking-through.

And within the concept of the bodily transcendent, the idea of taking one's power and creating authority within the idea of deity has been awesome in its power of taking our own authority, authorizing some idea of a deity, who in turn grants us (lesser) authority. This, like in monarchical schemes of authority, asks us to yield authority in the name of being frightened (mortal, sick), so that we will be taught to live well and properly in the name of the deity. The solution to being, says Kierkegaard, is not to disciple ourselves to God, but to live like God would live.

Authority is certainly the growing and coming to the power of one's being, a wrap-around identity.

Being and Time: The Western-idealist assumption that humans are distinct from other species due to our minds, has carried with it some powerful notions about our being in time. It has been thought that our physical being—like the physicality of other species in/of nature—exists particularly or only in the present here and now: some sense of the *immediate*. Immediate consciousness, an ongoing sense of phenomenology has been cast as opposed to the sense of past and of future; of memory and of the imagination.

Similarly, this thinking has developed the idea that humans are the generalizing and universalizing species: opposing the particularity and singularity and individuality of objects. We know human, while others existing in the present of immediacy only know this man or that woman.

Given this duple form of (our) being in immediate time, and of the notion that immediacy also entails individuality and particularity, a favorite method of exploring our subjective understanding has been - from Hegel's *Phenomenology of the Spirit* to Bergson's thought, to examine the contents of immediate consciousness, as if this would reveal much about our being and thinking.

Future and past, universalizing from the one to the many (and back, reflexively), has then been cast as a human ability which is beyond being: transcendent, concatenating, above the existential.

As Martin Krieger asked me some years ago upon first reading Hegel, what/where is the transcendent, and I responded that *this is it*, I have been probing to find out what I meant by that ever since: Toward an *anthropology of the ordinary*.

This seems to have left the problem of human understanding in its subjectivity as having to do with the nature of our understanding the objective/universalized world. And how we have come to be able to be both objective (to know objects) and to universalize them. The nature of our mind, then, is presumably reflective of how we do this.

Since my own understanding of how we come to know the world, is through the *Question-Response Grammar* (Sarles, 1985)—that is, we come to know the world as our parents-m/others regard it as being, learning simultaneously the particular and the universal in our coming to name objects in infancy (as our parents regard them)—this quest for our consciousness seems misplaced and simply incorrect in the human condition.

This notion of coming to know the world as our parents have constructed it (back eons, perhaps shared somehow with other species), means that it is probably more interesting and problematic to understand how we operate at all in the present, rather than to understand how we universalize, or live within the contexts of past and future. (I have supposed that we need to have ways—and ways to have ways—of knowing that we live in each present, perhaps a kind of memory itself; remembering to remember that we have to be present in our presence.)

But I also think that we live in the present in various/many ways, and to single out some sense of the immediate-immediate and give it priority, is to oversimplify the human condition.

This is all to say that the problem of being and/in time belongs in the first instance within the problem of *Context*, not of Being and Identity.

Am-Is-Be-Being: Multiple existential confusions between who I am which I carry with and as me even as I experience the present—ongoing, yet evented. The me I say I am to the various others who have or want to know, or to whom I confess and present myself—as in teaching, parenting, friending, even as I sit here watching the black symbols appear upon a mostly gray background; the me I tell myself I am contrasted with the sounds and feelings of right now playing against a future which aging seems to be shrinking even as I work at stretching it out; the senses which locate myself into the various parts and parties which I also am, and certainly am; the doing which confirms that I am, is, and be.

All of this is matched, contrasted with some ongoing sense of being in the world, of the world, against the world, changing it and me, and wondering about history and futurity and the human condition and the election next week and whether meaning and being will endure.

And If I Am-Not? There are some who live in mortal fear of mortality...or of immortality. It is difficult sometimes to distinguish whether or not one exists; whether or not one is or is-not.

The understanding, the realization that one will die (I will die, it is only a matter of time and of circumstance!), can easily dis-inform existence and identity. I am, am I-not?! Or am I?

Is this thing I call myself merely a shell, a temporary housing for a soul which (I hope, oh God knows I hope) shall carry my soul back to heaven? Oh dear Augustine who said that we had *fallen* to earth; that life itself is a cosmic error perpetrated presumably by the female who was tempted by evil to sup at the tree of knowledge; and here I am supping alone and feeling doomed rather than being at peace with the God of all souls in heaven.

If indeed, if in fact, I am—that this bodily existence which is full of feelings and desires which threaten to overwhelm me, all of this being is suspect, a momentary fragment in the firmament of all of time's being whose enduring must last until my return. Return? Return? To what? What is this here and now? What, this earth? Who cares, should I?

And if I do not really exist? And if I do? What then?

Wither existence? Withered existence, a return to Cosmology.

A Lament: of the narrative textualist whose reality derives from outside and remains outside of her/himself.

Freedom: The notion of human freedom has been cast within the romantic-idealist tradition as the human ability to transcend the immediate of time and particularity. This has left the concept of freedom located intrinsically within each individual, and played into the *Natural Law* notion of Hobbes (from Aristotle), that we are by nature bound to immediacy, and open to pursuing freedom more out of fear than of love or desire or our intrinsic nature. In *nature*: we are held to be rather fixed, unfree; in society, especially civilized society (implying an evolutionary history of the development of freedom of the individual, and the sense that this will be inevitably progressive in the unfoldings of history), we must seek our freedom by overcoming our nature, and the social ties which seek to *imprison* us, as it were.

Instead, it appears that we (like other similar/related species) are social by our nature. Freedom and individuality are emergent, even as we remain somewhat interdependent throughout our lives. Again, like being and time, this seems to be less an issue of *Being and Identity* in the first instance, but more a problem of *Context*.

Context: As being, identity, and meaning seem inextricably linked, the question of how meaning gains meaning rises to our thinking. Outside of the usual or normal senses in which objects or thought have meaning and names—names, thence meaning—there seems to be some loci or spheres of our existence which inform or frame meaning more specifically. Call this *situation*; call it the *loci of context*, it is usually a *residual* area saved (as it were) for the infrequent moments of our experience when we seem to have to appeal to some elements outside of the ordinary to tell us what means the meaning of some issue.

The *same* word or notion may take on different meaning, depending on context. The idea of any temporality—piece of a sports game, a division of a musical piece, a discipline—seem to determine when what is ordinarily sameness, turns upon difference. When is something serious, commentary, a joke, is not obvious from *outside*; outside, that is, of whatever is or determines context.

Much of the meaning of being and identity resides here, in the context of context.

Justice: Whoever said that life would be fair?—a palliative said by others, said to cheerlead oneself on those down days when one's sights are cast down and away; sad days, sick days...

Justice: issues of power and control—In the world of inequality of our being, then s/he who is most important deserves the most. Here, the issue of justice reduces, reverts to the question of importance. Structure (the breadwinner, the mother, the hope for the future—the progenitor, the womb, child, royalty-aristocracy, the source, e.g., of religion and purpose, the teacher); Process (curers and healers, priests and pastors, and rabbis as carriers and interpreters of the *law*). Who one is, who one knows; who one is *not*, does not know!

Justice: within some sense of equality and the so-called rule of law applying equally to every-one, no one is *above* the law. Importance of personal strength, endurance, integrity, and hope (sustaining).

Justice: questions of evenness—eye for an eye. Mutilation and wholeness. Punishment and asceticism.

Existence, Essence—Who's on First? *I am, therefore I think* might seem somehow to replace Descartes' dictum with its proper or appropriate antinomy, but in the issue of anyone's being, thinking is not a precedent issue. There is no easy Either/Or of being which will solve the issue of being and identity; no internal deity which will tell us finally that we are and who we are. For we are creatures whose generation is a powerful aspect of our continuing existence, and whose maintenance of sociality virtually circumscribes being.

What this does *not* mean is not that there is no point of departure for who I am; not that there is no subjectivity or a me which is precise enough to say that and who I am. My being does not require or necessitate a deity to say who and that I am; parents and community are usually sufficient.

To date (in Western thought, at least), the issue of being particularly or uniquely human has been used as a framing architectonic for examining the concept of being: I say *the concept of being*, because much of the actuality of our being has been neglected in favor of the notion that our being would be revealed particularly in our being particularly human. The method of thought and investigation has thus been always in the Platonic/Pythagorean line: speculating (from some narrowness of observation of other species) on how we are especially as we are different from other aspects of nature: species, machines.

The issue of identity arises now to some large extent because it appears with more extensive observation of other species, and with the developing fields of *brain* and of machine *intelligences*, that our arena of uniqueness has been narrowing. This developing problematic of identity shows how fragile and speculative has been our concept of the human, faltering and hesitant at any moment of attack upon our sacred constructions rather than any celebrations of our continuing development and extent.

There is reasonableness and objectivity within one's being which is often and usually sufficient to the tasks of ongoingness. One is someone. But that one is also many: I alone; but also I and mothers, brothers, spouses, children; children and teachers. As being is enigma (Heidegger 1927), so it is clarity and certitude.

The narrowness and particularity of the debate on who and how we are essentially/existentially has revolved as well on how we have constructed the notion of the ideal. Not finding continuing purpose in the purposiveness we have hitherto constructed to account for life's directions, we seem weakened rather than hopeful. In the case of the either/or of existence or essence, we are tempted to seek purpose outside of being in any present age; the ongoing present. Rather than enlarge the nature of life's experiencing, we seem wont to focus on ends and eschatologies as they seem to frame being within the dimensions which our ancient frameworks have found more amenable to their theorizing.

The fact is that we are bodies living within the world of others' (bodies); living as well within the mutuality of understandings which have hitherto been constructed as the dualisms of mind/soul and body.

The Grammar of our Being: One of the confusions of Western metaphysics, located within the presumption of mind and of body, is that each individual is the primary locus of knowledge. We must, say the Kantians, be like nature to know the nature of the things of nature. Since, they think, objective knowledge is of nature, since we exist bodily in the temporality of the here and now, how can we know infinity and be outside of our own physical being; symbolic, imaginative; able to see ourselves being ourselves even as we are?

Part of the response and answer is to note that the physical individual exists within the social construct of m/other(s) responding to *her* infant within a depiction which is at once immediate and simultaneously projected forward into myriad expectations of what it means (to her/them) to be a person.

Being is not merely vegetative survival, but requires the imaginative seeing of being an infant within the contexts of gender, adulthood, the morality of becoming as m/others construct those notions, and the idea that the infant will be much like its parents through life; not just in this moment. Humans (other social creatures) simply do not exist in the moment. The human body is itself symbolic, with a beyondness which is limited but not bound: Promethean in its possibilities and towardnesses.

The question of who I am is frequently conflated with who I would be?—who can I be?—and who is it that I am?

In the "major" traditions, it seems, the question is implicitly answered as a kind of "built-in" to the self which is given physically as a presence in the world. In other traditions, who I am is sometimes a cyclical being (e.g., I am my grandmother), in other places it's an aspect of the spirits of other species whose quest I must journey upon. In all these cases, however, one "finds" her/his identity as if it is a set of old or new clothes which one can try on, and if it fits, must wear it... forever.

I wonder, instead, if being and identity isn't an active process, a mode of generation, of "having" to be someone. I wonder, that is, if the idea of having an identity isn't foisted upon oneself by one's parents/family at a point of several years of age: requesting, then requiring one to act as if s/he is someone. I think this mode of considering identity bears certain similarities to Aristotle's "self-caused-first-cause" and may find it reduced to the "homunculus" explanation for how thinking occurs. But it takes primary "causality" away from the (physical) individual, and sees sociality as the locus of the force-which-begins and requires the physical individual to generate her/his "own" sense of being, else this entity is not truly a person in that setting.

Who I am is then forever at some odds/harmony with whom I am said and told to be, who I think I am and tell myself I am, who I want to be—to fulfill what I am told is my destiny. Identity, that is, may have certain kernels of itself, but it is in part at least always on the move. (A way of understanding Heraclitus: but, if self is the locus of change, then what is nature?)

Who am I? Who are we? Who am I that I am-not you? Who are we that we are not-they?

Alternatively, the problematic of being raised by Plato in *The Sophist* and echoed over and over again within Western thought, and given its most recent shape by Heidegger in *Being and Time* is the opposition or antinomy of being vs. not-being: that is being has been contrasted in Western thought with death; and existence has been sometimes in harmony with, but often opposed to experience in life.

This philosophical heritage has provided us with a conceptual baggage heavy with history, even foundational in its power truly to frame the problematics not only of being, but even of the very notion of reality which has been shaped in our thinking to include within existence both life and is opposition in some grand dialectic. Not for nothing has Western thought been described as an eschatology, a seeking for finality in cause, in truth, and —in the Nietzschean ironic—the truth that our attempts to describe being have been mostly an interesting fiction.

If we are, as Heidegger claims, an *enigma* to which only poets (such as Holderlein) can possibly be witness, then there is little testimony to our very existence. Overburdened in the West by an urge to explore the eschatological much as the ordinarinesses of our being, we want to live either in the middle range of the Aristotelian harmony or upon the edges and extremes of existence which will illuminate, excite, confirm that we really are! (Nietzsche, 1883)

And the others who we are-not. Only, we are sure but much less sure in these days, we are not-animals. Can we explore being without having to ensure ourselves at each moment that we are rather than our being-not?

To-be or not to-be? Is that the question?

The will to live—an active process from Schopenhauer to Camus; a passive structure granted to our sociobiology (Wilson, 1979); to give-in to death (give up the ghost); to suicide.

Being within Experience: A major issue of being concerns the formation, sustaining, and/or alteration of one's/our identity. Much of Western thought is summed up by Rousseau in *The Social Contract*: "Man is born free, but is everywhere in chains." In this particularly Western summation of being and identity, the notion of the individual is granted priority: even the absolute definition of identity. What is the social, any relationships or commonalities with others, is taken to remove something from the individual—to lessen him or her. Questions of role, of social identity, nationality, culture have tended to be backgrounded, called into suspicion or altogether neglected in this tradition.

In an elaborate history of law and so-called "natural law," it is presumed that the individual (a priori given), at some point in linear history, discovered (via language) that s/he had to come into relationship in a social "contract" with others, or risk annihilation at the hands of others who found themselves competing with him for food, sex, and the other necessities of existence. Within this Western story, that is, sociality "reduces" being and identity. In this setting, the "problem of identity" is often cast as the necessity to heighten individuality and its attendant aspects: usually "political" issues such as competition, power, and so on.

But this is, like many other stories, just another story of being; but one to which many are partial, and one which others find onerous and destructive to being.

In other contexts, the notion of identity is equally or primarily a social-political idea. The question of "who I am" is deeply embedded within my relationships to others, theirs to me, and the issue of what identity we share or significantly do not. Some aspects of being which we may share may not always be related to identity in an important way; but others may be overwhelmingly important in particular times and circumstances: language, gender, religion, color, health/sickness, age, geography or nation, history. In some times and places an effective bond of identity may be woven through opposition to some others' identities which we may oppose, or which may define and oppose us.

In some times and places, that is, the notion of identity has seemingly more to do with sociality and communality than with individuality. Whether and when the concept of identity fits both individual and group will be explored in various ways. In combating the primacy of the idea of the individual as the locus of identity, various theorists have attacked the individual, and claimed that there is no real individual (Marx 1845), or that the individual is an aspect of a deity, or that we are primarily within some covenant or other relationship.

Within (Western) philosophy (Garcia: "Individuality"), the question of identity is cast within the issue of the one and the many, and which is *primary*. The thinking usually proceeds from the one to the many in a kind of pyramidal organizing scheme much like the notion of military or the efficiency models applied to organization and business schemata during the past century.

This seems to follow from the sorts of metaphors by which we derive the notion of the deity and grant agency to that idea, granting and organizing me/us within it. Similarly, within what is being called "modernism," there has been a tendency to praise and to raise the idea of the individual ("genius") who is creative, or the orchestral conductor over the players. That is, within the comparative contexts of the one and the many, the idea of the primacy of the individual is not only structural, but the dynamics of description tend toward identity of the individual as representing any group or organization.

The recent tendency within the context of business organizations to talk about the "culture" of any organization has been effective in considering the dynamic elements of organization as a function of group-thinking as opposed to other models of the organization (but even this concept reflects the expansion of the individual head or boss effectively controlling the business within the context of her/his particularity of outlook).

The general Western mode of thought follows or parallels the kind of hierarchic thinking which was developed by the Pythagorean-Platonic attempt (successful to this day!) to "solve" the "problem of death" and of knowledge by banishing the body from personal existence. That is, within the focus on the identity of each individual, certain aspects of our being have been backgrounded to the point of virtual disappearance, while those which focus on the (individual) mind as the locus of being and of knowledge have been raised to primacy. So even in pursuing the notions involved in our very knowing, the focus has been placed on particular aspects of our being, and located within each individual—not noting, backgrounding, or not admitting that we are human bodies located together in the world of other similar human bodies.

Usually the experiential ("actual") issue of identity shows up however within the context of an either/or of the paradox of identity. We/I are both an "I" and a "we" in a variety of ways, in and through time. I am not any less a "me" and myself than I am her son and his father and a citizen of a variety of jurisdictions. In addition I/we are heir to "name" and to a variety of ideas and literatures some of which extend being, but many of which substitute certain ideas about being for "being itself."

The quest in Western thought (and in perhaps most world theo-political "traditions") has been to attempt to "resolve" the paradoxes of identity on one side or the other of them. Western thought, for example, resolves the paradox of reality being while we are awake or asleep on the side of wakeful existence, and the question of change and non-change on the side of permanence. Identity—for example, the Christian notion of individual "soul"—is restricted to individuality, while one's relationships are backgrounded to enabling or to be "blamed" for existence (the "sin" of one's parents causing my pure soul to "fall" to earth).

Here, perhaps especially, the questions of being as one's actual existence and experience come into some odds with theories about being. And as literature and philosophy have come into our lives and into the practice of politics and law and it is often very difficult to distinguish who I am, from who I am told that I am, from whom I am treated as.

And the possibilities of governing others is variously restricted or strengthened depending on how the idea of the individual is lived-out or acted-upon by various constituencies/citizens.

The Actual Individual: Apparently (this notion of) identity is not merely built-in to (individual) being, but requires affirmation, new, or changing ways of telling oneself who one is; that one is. Perhaps it is the case that we can effectively "lose" either our identity (Oliver Sacks: *The Man who Mistook his Wife for a Hat*) or the means for "re-generating" our identity. Death (and suicide) is—in many traditions—the ultimate definer/destroyer of identity. But in other traditions, the identity of the individual is seemingly eternal and/or can be recreated within the lives of one's descendants (e.g., Cameroonian animism).

My sense and observation is that this is no mere aspect of the (physical/physically bounded) organism; nothing which is (essentially) born-in or inborn. As Ashley Montagu (1985) reported, most infants will perish if they are fed food alone. More seems "necessary" in the human condition: to be touched, talked to, "loved"—and to love, talk, touch in return. Whether "tender loving care" is what is necessary, is what we shall explore. Whether others can give, grant, or confirm our identity is at issue. Whether others can confirm us at all points in life is another issue and whether they will or won't, can or cannot.

An early introduction to this idea was from reading an ethnography of the Murngin people of northern Australia (W. Lloyd Warner 1937), who on the occasion of condemning an "errant" person to death, could expect his actual death within three days or so. In this case, a death sentence was sufficient for the person to "give up the ghost."

Whoever one is, the definition and continuing support of one's being by the others who are significant in one's life, is apparently necessary in one's continuing existence; at least or especially in cultures in which the interaction is "high density". True for infants in most/all cultures, the remainder of us have defined—have had defined by others—the idea that we are truly and sufficiently "individual" that we can survive, want to survive, have "a will to live."

In America, the definition for many men, at least, of who they are, has been within the notion and confines of a work situation. Many who retire, die within a short period (six months or so) after retiring. Who they are is apparently heavily related to what they do, or how others in that work arena confirm their being.

And in many long-term marriages, the death of one spouse is not survived long by the other. Thus the boundaries of one's being and identity are not always and not necessarily within the boundedness of one's physical being.

Being: Western thought has held that the identity of the individual is overwhelming and obvious, (*ought* to be obvious, almost as a moral necessity) an aspect of the physical body. The mechanical-material aspect of being—was considered to be primary; life and thought was held to be "after" (me ta) physics.

The metaphor of being and identity (and there have been a number of "metaphors" through and by which we explain ourselves to ourselves), is the comparison of our being with the same physical self (as if) without being: without that "life force" (a *vita activa* or whatever). We are without life, akin to a stone. Condillac's 18th century invocation of the speechless statue, which presumed that we come to being already fully adult in form, and then posits what we "need" to become fully human is informative. Like Pinocchio, who merely needed a human body to become a real boy, the thinking about being and identity does not give very much attention to the developing child who grows and changes radically. Rather we seem to seek out primarily those aspects of our being which have as much permanence as that we grant to our very appearance.

The generalizing and universalizing tendency to find out "who and what" we are, has since pre-Platonic times been comparative in bent. Being, in Western thought (contrasted, say, with Confucian thought), has invoked visioning us relative to non-being, and in implicit relation to our being fully adult (complete) when compared to the material being without the life principle.

We have tended, that is, to seek the nature of our being and identity, with respect to non-being or death (*Phaedo, Sophist*) and to the animating force which "grants" us life (Aristotle: *de Anima*). Western thought was and remains enamored of eschatology and the directness of life toward death, and has been likely to attempt to define identity with respect to however the path toward and the "realm" of death has been depicted in any era.

Similarly the physical basis presumed for our being has convinced us that the persistent aspects of our being are variously "masked" by the changes which blind us to our actual being. This has led to the rise of geometry and the varieties of formalism and idealism which lead us to value being-as-object over being-as-living: statistics, I.Q. scores, and the rest; essentialism over existentialism and experience. Thus the pursuit of who we are as being and identity has been cast within various metaphorical frameworks whose seeing-through or deconstruction is necessary to see who and what we are. (The problem as it arose for Plato had to do with the apparent observation that each person likely will invent a different form of reality given even half the chance—thus the problem of any facticity and truth of being and the world is relative to whomever…

Doing the Buffalo Dance This parable from the Mesquakie of the Great Lakes region offers an ironic view of Native Americans caught between two cultures. It is from "Native American Testimony: A Chronicle of Indian-White Relations from Prophecy to the Present, 1492-1992," ed. Peter Nabokov.

Once there was an Indian who became a Christian. He became a very good Christian; he went to church, and he didn't smoke or drink, and he was good to everyone. He was a very good man. Then he died. First he went to the Indian hereafter, but they wouldn't take him because he was a Christian. Then he went to Heaven, but they wouldn't let him in because he was an Indian. Then he went to hell, but they wouldn't admit him there either, because he was so good. So he came alive again, and he went to the Buffalo Dance and the other dances and taught his children to do the same thing.
N Y Times Book Review 5/10/92

At certain moments in life—one supposes—the problem is more particularly how to "come alive again," and to *do it*!

The Body Politic::The Organic Analogy: From the first pages of Aristotle's *Politics*, the relational equivalence is drawn between the individual and the social-political.

The reasoning is *directional*: from the individual to the social, establishing or highlighting the primacy of the individual. Methodologically, the inference can be drawn that how we think about the individual; how we decide what individual contains, means, or entails, is applicable as well to the political.

As the individual → is the social-political.
Individual → thus/thence → the social.

As the outlining, the specification and location of the individual is the physical body (materiality, *physis*), the body is thus primary in establishing the very nature of being. While the physical nature of the individual body is (within the human condition) essential and obvious, it is used, methodologically, for little more than to establish and to locate the subject: the political body. Then, the facticity and implications of bodily being are simply dropped, not attended to, dismissed, suppressed, downgraded

581

As did Plato, Aristotle uses the body to establish the essential locus of our being, then proceeds (again, methodologically) to *empty* the nature of the individual by effectively *banishing* the body. In the dialogue *Phaedo*, Plato wants to pursue the nature of being (as knowledge) and to "purify" being he literally banishes the body to "go with the mind alone" toward knowing and thinking; ridding us of the necessity of messing-up thinking with desires, sadness, or sickness.

To add injury to insult, the mind is then granted directive power over body within the hierarchy of being which Plato develops to idealize the unchanging forms of being, thus including the human soul as if it were like the idea of the circle or triangle, of the universalized word representing the idea of any object: the idea of the table, of the man, of identity, of being, of existence. With the body effectively banished, existence even is turned back upon itself: an idea more than being-as-doing.

This leaves us investigating and/or understanding the human condition particularly as the mind—having used the body to locate the essential being (me), the body is then made to disappear whenever we discuss what and who I/we are. I am essentially my soul/mind—and the facts of bodily being, that others see me particularly as me as I appear bodily, and whatever else being a body entails (a great deal!), simply fall away from our thinking about identity. This leaves us living—actually—as bodies, even while we tell ourselves that we are our souls, essentially.

The very notion of the essential "me" is dependent on ridding the context of discussion of identity of the body in order to rid identity of the changing aspects of being. This does not rid the problematic of identity of the fact of our continuing being, being paradoxical as the Heraclitean river (being continuously me, even as changing each moment, each day, month). It just resolves the apparently loathsome fact of paradox of identity, and makes human existence a subject in the province of philosophy and narration, but not of existence.

In translating or extending the notion of the mind (less body) to the body politic, the analogy is taken from the concept that the mind effectively "directs" the body. What Aristotle analogizes the to the mind utilizes the notion of directing within a hierarchy and elevates all of this within some concept of nature—"nature" taken to justify or to underline or (as in some laws) to "enforce" the actuality of the concept (as in: natural must be real; we can't fight or change nature or human nature; we are natural, in nature).

Analogs of the mind are those parts of society which "direct" the polis, the body of the politic: the monarch/king directs the people; just as the husband directs the wife; parents, children; and people, slaves. The body of the politic is the fact/means by which we locate ourselves. Once there!

Then the body is banished as having desires, causing sickness, death, and all of our attention is placed upon the mind/king which directs and controls the body politic—which, like the body, always threatens to do something which will muck up the clarity of the mind-alone. The *polis* becomes focused upon the king as representing all else, the citizens' thoughts, wants, needs, are backgrounded just as they are downgraded in importance.

The king—Leviathan in Hobbes' articulation—is effectively granted and given power to draw attention to itself as the director, the effectuator of the notion of unchangingness. Having used *physis* and the material body to locate us, the body politic to locate the idea of the state, to justify it/them by the use of the notion of natural, then this is abandoned.

The lesson drawn within the Aristotelian tradition of how/what human nature means, is to locate the human by its body (=not other species); thence to draw out not what is human which includes its body (literally, how we distinguish and locate humans), but to say what is particularly human by how we differ (putatively) from other species strictly within the domain of mind: humans are the reasoning creatures, that one which possesses language, intelligence, can think, can foresee futurity—the only one which is social.

All apparently wrong; but oh so seductive! That is, to deconstruct the issue of identity, we have to see how we have and continue to be Platonic-Aristotelian within our thinking; to note difference within hierarchies of dualism analogized to the putative mind-body split, thence to *make disappear* those who are not higher within and directive dualism; even to abandon our own bodies to decrepitude rather than to examine and to work (with) them as we age.

Interestingly, the facts of our social existence are particularly downplayed within this "use" of the body politic to analogize sociality to the individual. This is so because the facts of our being children to our parents, the fact that we are not survivable without love and affection and talk beyond the mere food we may be given, is virtually written-out within this tradition. So the facts of our social existence, the relation of our human being with the other species with whom we have most (morphologically, behaviorally) in common, the facts of their prior social existence still have not come into the common mentality of most of those who think about the human condition.

And even for most of those who think well across species, who are comparativists, even for those, they tend to focus on the individual or the species as delineated by their bodily (analogized or directly physical), rather than at the nature of their experience. The facts of any actual paradox of identity—being one and many—rarely enters into the discussion of what is human, why we live or should live as we do, and what is our destiny.

The Endangered Authentic Self: An unfortunate side effect of the almost constant presence of the media in our lives, the psychologist Kenneth J. Gergen suggests, is a loss of the small, subtle, authentic responses to life that compose a personality.

"The media expose society to a massive array of self-representations. Our manners of friendship, family relationships, romance, and animosity are documented, scrutinized, rhapsodized, and satirized. We see how the lips are pursed in moments of quiet anger, the fingers move to the mouth as expressions of serious thought, and the tongue flicks backward in moments of cautious reflection. As these images are exposed increasingly to the culture, they become the standards for expression; a subtle Miss Manners for the world of informal relations. They inform the culture, for example, as to how sadness is done -- its duration, its modes of expression, and its proper intensity on various occasions. Indeed, in failing to meet these commonly recognized standards, one cannot properly define oneself as "being sad"—either to others or oneself... Our actions are suffused with the sense of metaphor, and we ourselves lose the ability to differentiate between their authenticity and their artifice."
N.Y Times Book Review: Oct. 20, 1991

Like cartoons, the depiction of our being and identity in the popular media has tended to take on various lives of their own: the issue of movement in cartooning being several lines surrounding a figure or parts of a figure; talk being in balloons overhead or in captions. Are movies and video very different: the relation between what we see on a screen or CRT and what we see in everyday interpersonal-interbody interaction is not precisely one-to-one...or is it?

Human Potential: There has been a virtual movement in the past generation toward *being all one can be*. I sense that this movement which found its principal home and support among those who thought of themselves as Humanists—trusting in the human, but within some dialectic about being agnostic or atheistic—has been to a large extent a way of substituting a personal progressive scheme for one which was politically or socially progressive. It has been, that is, a way of directing life with a sense of purpose without falling into the politics of utopia or teleology.

It developed to some large extent within the beginnings of looking for a mode of health which seems, certainly in retrospect, to derive from South and East Asia: a sense of holism within the context of wellness. It opposed the Western allopathic medicinal approach of moving to relieve symptoms, to derive thinking about health *from pathology* without any necessary notion of health or sustenance or what each person might do to remain well or in shape. It derived as well from a hope and wish to shed the puritanical hang-ups that many of us had had about any possibility of enjoying life, especially the possibility of enjoying rather than enduring sex. It was a movement which brought medicine and talking therapies to the fore on the tails of a retreating religious outlook whose preachments went beyond souls to the restricting of anything which even felt of hedonism. And it was Kierkegaardian in the sense of a growing distrust of organized religions which took us out of our experience. It was apolitical if not anti-political, asocial if not antisocial, in which we entered into our own individuality as completely as could be imagined.

This human potential movement, created a cadre of professionals: a group of persons who we took to be somewhat greater than, somewhat beyond being in the sense of ourselves being...They were somehow clinical and removed from the ordinarinesses of everyday life, a bit beyond ourselves. They were a group apart; apart from us. Like teachers they gained our respect, and we yielded to them some aspects of our being; surrendered our bodies, our spirits in some increasing asymmetry, based on the promise that they would help us to gain our potential and be all we could be.

But, like other utopic schemes, the directedness and line of the potential did not always find placeness where any of us could see direction. We thought that someone else knew something we did not, and that any sense of transcendence—Emersonian/Thoreauvian, Nietzschean, Zen or martial arts master—would somehow reveal itself in some obvious ways. And they did not... for most people.

So most of us are seeking other directions, other mappings for our own and others' futurity, seeking our *Next Places*: some of us in old, older, oldest places and texts; others of us in self-overcoming; others of us still seeking the directions which being seeks itself.

Me, Myself, and I: The search for who I am—especially and specifically—goes on. I am who I am for days on end, and then it occurs, suddenly it seems, that I forgot something, or there was an accident, or I did not attend to being as somewhat dubitable, or something seemingly important slipped from my tongue. I acted inconsistently with whom I had told myself I am. Do I have to "re-construct" my being, that it was apparently a construction whose identity was riddled with lies or vagaries or pressures to be somehow other?

How pleasantly easy it must be to be someone other than I: consistent—s/he knows who s/he is!—ease with self, others. More to the point, being seems enigmatic (Heidegger): Me, myself, and I seem more multiple than triple. Life is more a trial, than the certainty with which I can say exactly who I am.

On other days I seem to be the Rock of Gibraltar; absolutely certain of being who I am, was and will be... and it/I seem O.K.

Self: I am...much of who I am... has its amoeboid loci concentrated in who others say I am, and am to be.

It was the pragmatists—from Peirce to Dewey and G.H. Mead—who said that we are, we carry, some deeply productive senses of self, of the I of who I am, as other's images and depictions of self (oneself, myself). There seems to be, still many years after they both have died, of not being my parents' son. I operate, in various ways, themes and variations of what they saw in me, what they wanted to see, what they liked and didn't; and also a good bit of who they saw in themselves and would have, and did or did not.

They lived, much, in terms of an ethnic enclave in America's melting pot, responding to questions of their being as being ethnic, Jewish, or anti-that model of their being, but located well within its grasps and hooks. It was not religious it didn't even seem particularly anti-religious, perhaps strangely now in the retrospection of trying to rethink myself. But frequently, my off-balance grappling with self-esteem to harmonize with their modes of operating, and logics of observation and criticism.

The point is that the self I call me carries yet, is propelled as if upon unending waves of the logic of self-determination, some picture of who I am which sits within a household dynamic of many years and many places ago.

By now, worked over, working over the significance of who I am with respect to those whom I consider significant: family, the few friends who have stayed with me, and who I have stayed with; the university in which I perorate and peruse and visit, and might have wished to belong; at home not at home, like Buber's lament that certain times possess no stakes for the tents which we would have pitched, for which we would...

Self, me, a Marxian congeries of roles which others have assigned to me: a 'would-have-been worker' afloat somewhere within a bourgeois mentality. A truth in here! But how broad, how deep, how changeable, how connected to history, to my history, to the experiences I have and watch the self I call myself, having?

Risk: Most days I feel it is important, often necessary, to place my being at some risk. Perhaps it is that life is never so certain—or that I feel that life is somewhat uncertain—that I must test, must risk, must challenge being as invested in issues of mortality. Perhaps this sense of the necessity of risking is intertwined with questions of social morality: that a driver of an automobile "should" or "should not" do something; that I "will-not" be intimidated by something or someone. It is as if I were still a teen-ager: not imagining or not being sure that I care about futurity.

Maybe it is that I'm particularly "nervy" or narcissistic, this stuff of personal risk. I'm not at all certain that it is "merely" physical risk - but this is an important component of whatever it means to "take a chance." This business of risk reminds me somewhat of one of Chamfort's (1860) aphoristic tales about a Napoleonic general who used the moment of entering into battle literally to challenge his body to quit shivering from fright. It was as if his sense of being who he "would" be overwhelmed his sense of who he was— actually?—so that he could overcome by some sense of "nobility," his actual-physical reaction of fear.

The miles each day I walk or ride my bike, down-and-up many floors of steps, I am very careful not to take unnecessary risks. It is only that some risks seem quite necessary to take, and to make myself... whole? A self... challenge? An integrity-check? Mere or not-so-mere stupidity?

Shells and Shills: He was bright and charming and had developed a slick presentation having to do, of all things, with therapizing the human condition by offering it new ways of being and thinking. And, no doubt, he was effective for many who suffered. He made gobs of money, in demand for large and small groups all over the country. He was developing an enormous reputation.

Only it was all hollow within. The man's external presence and presentation was just that, and hardly more. Mostly less.

He had become, at an early age, the sort of virtuoso that Kierkegaard had warned us against being. He was slick, meaning that others found in him something that they wanted to see. But he found, increasingly, that he was their person, their invention, and there was very little inside him, and what there was, was rapidly emptying out... gone.

II: SOCIAL-UNIVERSAL:

Being Alone: I am always alone::I am never alone!

What are the boundaries/connectedness between aloneness and loneliness?

No *one* else can occupy the ground of my being here and now. Do I? Can I? That my body is here and now only asks me to ask if I am my body; or do I have a body; or does my body have me?

How can I be both me and we if I "am my body"? Doesn't the materiality of my bodily being contain and restrict being to the here and now, and limit knowing to the stimulus and the potentiality of response? What is the body? What did Nietzsche mean when he claimed that "I am body alone, and the mind is some story about the body?"

Is my body (also) aspects of others' seeing me, and reading into me the character and person whom they see, and I respond - me and my muscles shaping the bones which harbor and are the face you see and is me—and you? My face: mine or the "you" who read-into-me the person I want to be?

I wander alone in the primal forests of all of time and of being, and I am never alone. You are in my thinking. The very language which I apply to thought; the very language which speaks the ideas I generate in my head, generates the ideas which speak the language which I formulate in the terms you might understand that I understand. It is all so complicated. No either/or!

But I often feel lonely. I—difficult to separate from the we (J.) who have been "married" so long that the complications of knowing me from her are vast, so vast. But often lonely; sometimes isolated. Much more than the sense of being alone.

No joy, in many senses, of seeing the sights of the world, or experiencing what there is, unless there is someone else with whom to experience. Not the existential loneliness of a Sartre who never, like Heidegger, was very certain of being. Not like conceiving life as an infinitesimally brief moment in the sands of all of time which I am as likely to spend in a hell as in the heavens of any imaginings. More the sense that if I am to remain growing, learning, moving on in my being, that identity must in some senses be kept fragile, boundaries somewhat blurred, a kind of naive who can (still) see something freshly even as my lenses harden.

We: In many senses, life is so situated that I (beginning from the sense of the primacy of the individual) am mostly some aspect of one or more "we's."

Although I am physically "alone" at this moment, my spouse will return in just about an hour. And when I am "alone" and no other person/body is present within the confines of what I call my home, that other is present within various aspects of my thinking and being: present within me.

The antinomy, the notion that the very physical body which is me cannot be shoved aside within the presence of my presence, merely presumes that the physical and the mental exist in quite separate domains; that the body, for example, does not possess intellection in any deep senses that the body cannot think.

Nietzsche was the first to refute this idea seriously in *Also Sprach Zarathustra*, by claiming that the body is all there is, and the mind is something, some story about the body. But this issue had risen earlier within the writings of Montaigne and others who wondered about the issue within the context of whether humans alone possess language (Montaigne: "Apology for "R. Sebond".

Historical Positioning: Powerful perhaps in even beginning to consider the nature of identity is the position within history within which we consider the human condition. Do we think of history as beginning with the birth of the newborn, trying to fill-in and develop all of knowledge, essentially de novo - the general epistemological-psychological view? Or do we take the general anthropological-cultural view of the transmission of culture from one generation to the other, as the beginning question of our inquiry?

The question of identity thus flows to some extent from the positioning of the observer/theorist, leading us to concentrate on epistemology and development of the individual as the principal or sole locus of being or upon the relations and transmission of knowledge via culture, via teaching, and teachers. In both cases, the tendency also flows from this historical positioning to define the problematics of identity.

Theologically this has led to the Christian focus on the birth (Jesus, each and every child) containing already its most essential aspects (soul), and the Jewish notion of the Covenant in which each person is especially identified within the context of relationship with others.

Intellectually, it has caused us to focus on certain questions or issues rather than upon others: epistemology or culture—but not both. And it has shoved questions of ontology—of being in the some ongoing present with towardness—*aside*. Or it has caused the tendency toward a totalizing solipsism as in Bergson, to self-examine one's adult being as if it represents all of being in some essential ways—to the exclusion of others.

In, for example, Locke's *Two Civil Treatises on Government*, the notion of the empty slate is useful in order to beat off the idea of hereditary monarchy, because it proclaims a new person and a new day as the foundation for government. And it tends to create the sense that individuality and discontinuity is always revolutionary, perhaps also that it is always necessary in the human condition. There is, no doubt, something very important in this thinking because the tendency of the social/cultural overtaking individuality tends to freeze any present age and time into a version of the past.

Part of the solution—if there is any—of the idea of the *present age*, is to take seriously the fact that we are paradoxical creatures, and always noting that the transmission of culture is not necessarily opposed to creating a new present in each life in each generation: a both/and.

Within the very act(ivity) of historical positioning, the sense of distrust of the other node of any paradox can often be overwhelming: as if—as some colleagues have noted—one's children's maturing is causal to one's own demise.

The question, perhaps in the "unraveling" of philosophy, is what else is entailed within the positioning of oneself in delineating the human condition at one node or another of human existence!

The Existential Angst: I think, therefore I am! I am, therefore I...? I am that I am. I am who I am. I am. Am I not?

The skepticisms about being have driven the Western consciousness since Parmenides first contemplated the contrast/comparison between being and not-being. This drove Pythagoras to substitute the formalisms of logic and geometry for being, and led him to concentrate on the nature of our existence which is non-temporal: the quest for being which climaxes this past century with Heidegger who attempts to locate being and time in some complex interweaving. Plato then seems to externalize existence in his solution to the problem of death; now taken back into the life of experience which then denigrates and distrusts itself. Time (and change) became the enemy of existence and being, and the aspects of being which are/were permanent and not susceptible to change overtook any notion of actuality. (Where is Heraclitus in a global world which is so-changing?)

The senses—so obviously open to occasional mistake—but otherwise so central to much of who we are—are downgraded to aspects of superstition and the surreal. Our bodies are banished from existence, to the extraordinary, and the actuality of our being—and the ways in which we both are and know we are, no longer count much in the exploration of being. The lament that within the antinomy of change and non-change we are ever tempted toward one and away from the other: either the senses or they are non-sense.

The arising of the severe skepticism which directs us toward the sense in which we think about being, and away from being in any sense per se. 'Do I exist?' begins a period of separation of our being from ourselves; our 'self' from our being, and calls any sense of attention away from the others in our lives who are now merely residual in being. How do I know that I exist? → How can it be that I exist?—denigrates the presence of being and reduces us to some mere copy of self. The image in the mirror, the more real that the narcissistic visage which finds confirmation in its glassy copy.

"Give me an arm," wails Wittgenstein and I can "prove" existence, proving only that the need to prove our very being rises above being itself. Why is life not sufficient unto itself that we think we have to spend eons in providing its "proof" in order to reassure us that we are? How have we exteriorized existence such that it could occur to us that we might not be? (Just who/what is the 'I' that is posing this kind of question?)

The turn to the deity to provide solace in lieu of the impossibility of providing proof not to being, but to our skepticism which does seem to want to trust being, then distrusts any proofs which offer to tell us that we are.

An undermining of the challenges of life? A yielding to the wish to deny life by acceding to some eschatological demands to keep us focused on endings? Being-as-not-being!?

Authenticity (Individual): The problem of identity, at least in Western thought, relates to our inability so far to *find* some core of genuine being - a homunculus, a decision-maker, a driver of the rest of our being which is coherent, clear—at the least to itself, to oneself. Where is *it and I* located? If I cannot find myself, how do I know who I am; that I am consistent and possess identity to myself? Is it perhaps possible that I am shell and not substance? Who do I tell myself that I am? How do I locate the wants and wills and will-not and who I am-not that tells myself that I am me...that I might mean what I say? Where is the *'me'* who told the story, yesterday, that I am responsible for today?

It is certainly obvious that any notion of the self is pushed and pulled, shaped and framed by the relationships in which one is placed or finds oneself. I am child to my parents, still many years after their death; student, but lessening gradually to my teachers, husband to/with my spouse, father to my children, teacher to my students, colleague to my colleagues, friend to friend, and there are plenty of those with whom I disagree, or am anathema. Just exactly and precisely *who is the 'I' who I am* rings somewhat hollow in this realization.

Perhaps I am not anyone precisely, but a result, a development which is yielded from the myriad *roles* into which I have found myself cast. I am...no more than... the self who others have told me that I am: some amalgam, perhaps a residuum, a particular who that I am told I am—and I accede to—or I do not. Attempting to be (and to remain, sustain) husband to my spouse, teacher to my students, father to my children, in which some of these relationships are more, some less dynamic and/or consistent, I might find myself essentially residual to my own being.

I think here of one of my teachers (G.L. Trager) who proclaimed at some point during the period when I studied with him, that he felt he had to represent the *school* of scholars who looked to him as their mentor. But his representation seemed stagnant, somewhat older in thinking than my teacher's teachings to me, who had come later to him than many others. And this seemed to pull him back into his history—a *yielding* of self as I experienced it, and some sense of demand on my loyalty to him, to join him in this felt regression. Not exactly inauthentic; but neither true to the person who had till that time been growing intellectually, and changing conceptually. This seemed, to me, a decision to not grow any longer.

More a psychoanalytic movement toward the genuine person, the subject to whom and about whom one can be objective, includes a sense of dynamic and development which has various stages of being, each of which are variously granted temporal hegemony, then proceed to shape the future experiencing of one's being: oral, anal, genital solidify being.

The body as the residual, Jungian locus: What is, as what was. If I am not precisely located anywhere in my sense of being myself, then I *must be* located in the body of my being at some moment earlier than my knowledge about my being. The metaphor that knowing emerges from physical and material being—takes us back to the beginning not of ourselves, necessarily, but of Western thought. Rather than study the body in its intriguing developments and possibilities and talents, we attribute to it all those aspects of our knowing being, which we cannot somehow account for within being itself. It (goes our thinking about being) must be more archaic, older, built-in already to our being a body. As the metaphysical story goes, we transcend bodily being as we increase in knowing—but we seem not to acknowledge that we are body throughout this process, and are body this moment, and will be.

Rather than grant primacy to our social being, we seem forever trapped in thinking that being-as-knowing is preceded by being a body. It is somehow easier to deny the very possibility of reality than to admit that our bodily being is social to its core. We do not, after all, merely exist in continuous fashion unless... unless our parents feed, love, speak to us, sustain us.

If not... then we die early and do not persist. That being which is 'me'/'us' which persists is that one which is the one which is loved and sustained. We exist within the contexts of the social: the person who I am is (includes) that one who others say I am; includes their attempt to get me to grab my own being as an independent being. But this is not in any deep sense derived from or continuous with my *archaeus*, with the body, with my biology which the true I of my being will transcend. The locus of my being is emergent: the "who" of who I am exists within a variety of existential/experiential processes—partly from the outside (including the sociality of granting the "me" who is the core of being the sense of continuity and persistence). To say that this has some necessary *authenticity* which precedes the processes of being who I am is necessarily to buy into the notion that meta-physics is truly *after physics.*

The "who" I am which is the core of my being is constructed and maintained in various ways. Like the Heraclitean river which is at once the same and changing, being goes on and is yet the same. What has been absent in this quest for identity is the sense that paradox is to be resolved rather than lived. (But, then, living occupies only the other side of the paradox!)

The Stoic Self: The lessons of Epictetus the slave, the crippled and lame, stuck in the prisons of life in virtual and total isolation, decided that he alone determined his understanding of the world and his experience. He decided that all the power in the world was available to him because he, alone, had the power to decide how to understand his condition, his being. And, lo and behold (as they say!), he became very powerful, wrote, taught, ruled. He was no longer ruled, no longer enslaved, but survived and prospered. And it is his words and ideas which also survived to teach us some of the lessons of the alone, the private, the solitary, and the deprived.

It is, I think, a philosophy for the extremes of isolation: being condemned to life in a real prison, to total isolation from the noises and the others of our being. And, in order not to give up, to die, to give in to the definition of others over our being, to agreeing that the dreams and hallucinations which become as much of experience as the intercourses of daily life in the by-ways of commercial life. In order not to give up, it is useful and perhaps necessary for each of us to summon the lessons of Epictetus within. Only I can determine who I am and would be and only I know how and why I got here and only I can move into my next places with some critical thought and, and... hope.

I deeply appreciate the fact that some of us are thrust into situations where we find ourselves in total isolation. Some of those who do have so aggravated *the-powers-that-be* that this is done with purpose and malice, vengeance and a sense of true grievance. But many of those who find themselves in such scenes also were *strong enough* to bring it upon themselves with some reason, some anger. They know, somewhat, already, what opposition means, even though knowing this does not relieve the sense of total isolation.

Others of us find ourselves being the marginalized more or less by accidents of gender, age, color, language, or the givens of our being someone who was never wanted, never loved. For these, the isolation is often fatal. There is no reason, there was no opposition. Simply the facts of one's being have been somehow... wrong.

And there are others—teachers, as a peculiar example—who find themselves alone in crowded worlds. It is those who operate within the idea of the *sacred* within a world of secularity and human bodies wandering about each other's spaces. If one asks (or is asked) for others to yield or surrender some spiritual/bodily aspect of themselves to another presumably for their greater good (teachers, curers), then the person who asks becomes more and more a continuous and authoritative persona.

More and more, s/he becomes the invention of the other. And there is less and less that returns to one's own definition of self which is ordinary within, and changing much as everyone else. The isolation of authority, desired as a socially useful and important role and way of being, carries within it a possibility, even a likelihood that one becomes quite isolated and separated from the persona whom others may respect, even love.

Call Epictetus immediately: Epic 911!

Authenticity (Social): Who are we: you, and them, and I and all of us?

We are the nation of..., we are the speakers of..., the children of..., the members of...

We are in relation with..., in covenant with..., servants and/or masters of...

We are a genealogy. We look alike, act like, believe in the same...

We are-not...!

The issue of identity at the level of the group is understandable and experienced in several ways. In the sense of a psychology of being-individual which is (often) considered to be primary, then a group is understood to be made up of a number of individuals who are then "members" of the group. Issues of consent, how freely given, how much is yielded or given up or sacrificed are often raised here.

I "work for" my university, but resist being a member of the faculty in a number of senses. My identity is (to me) an academic-anti-academic; my bags remain half-packed. In many senses, this notion of identity presumes a fairly strong assumption of strong individual "free-will" entering (as it were) into contract—with some idea of retention of the individuality if and when things work out well, or do not.

Such groups (extended to entire ethnic, religious, cultural, or national groups, identity by profession or work) or referred to as "low density" by Edward T. Hall (1983) in the dynamic/processual sense of "reserving" aspects of being which are preserved for "oneself."

Other groups or culture are, in the processual and membership or sense of roles, considered to be "high density," where the interactions between group members is primary to one's being and identity. I am, primarily and principally, a member of my family with no deeper longing than to be a good son/daughter, spouse, father, cousin. Or I am, primarily, wed to a church, or committed to a particular tradition of politics (a "born again" Christian, a born Stalinist, a member of the clan of...) which shapes and frames my being as totally as possible to be what I am told and aim to be fully.

If and when and I continue to live the life which is committed to my being a..., then life is *genuine and authentic.* The knowledge of what this consists in is derived from parents and others who also "belong to" and live their lives within this commitment to being a "good..." Or it may be learned from the study of informing texts (Koran, Torah, the Gospels) or from engaging in study with the teachers who represent this knowing and tradition.

Its reality is, in effect, "guaranteed" by the others who praise its virtue as well as "reward" one for living her/his life in this way. In the Confucian tradition, it means committing oneself fully to, and remaining "on the Way" to knowledge—a kind of utopia within life where growth is promised no matter how long the life - leaning toward continuing experience. In other traditions, the utopia is promised, but is not available within life ("The God of the Koran is the God of the Day of Judgment.")

In no case does the notion of the authentic life, of any true authenticity seem to be an essential or built-in aspect of being, although Plato and others in his long tradition, claim that aspects of character are innate/genetic or givens within the life of any individual—thus the idea of "education" to bring out that which is already within the individual in some sense of precognition. And we still are engaged in debating the "nature-nurture" battle on various grounds in which the limits and boundaries of the life condition are granted agency, thence "needs," thence a sense of the fixity of any social condition.

It appears, to me, that the concept of "authenticity" as a social idea is always available within various gathering ideas, and requires the affirmation of those in any context who are considered "significant" and informing persons—who treat, that is, the structural notion of the authentic as if it is truly authentic.

Members of my study group on *The Body*—who are curers—claim that the beginning and end of curing is to meet the authentic, the spiritual person, the inner-, the... Then the person can begin to cure her/himself, using the curer to enable.

Frozen Identity: For, as Mr. Hoffman (*Gray Dawn: The Jews of Eastern Europe in the Post-Communist Era* by Charles Hoffman—reviewed by J. E. Young in the NYTimes Book Review: 9/6/2009) makes clear, Hitler and Stalin both won their wars against the Jews. (They did not extirpate every last Jew, but in a way accomplished something almost as historic: they displaced a millennium of vibrant European Jewish civilization with a grotesquely malformed version of it. Where Hitler had reduced a thriving culture to pictures of skeletons and piles of corpses, Stalin allowed most Jews to live, but only after he had beat their Jewish brains out by purging Jewish intellectuals. With their writers and cultural figures murdered, their literature and art outlawed and all Jewish religious learning banned, two generations of Jews grew up defining their Jewishness in Stalin's terms alone. If this is all there was to being Jewish, the third generation is now asking itself, why bother?

In his interviews and biographical profiles, Mr. Hoffman shows that for young Jews in Hungary, Czechoslovakia, eastern Germany and Poland, the only Jewish ritual left is asking what it means to be a Jew, and answering with national variations on this theme. In the case of Czechoslovak Jewry, for example, he finds that a return to Judaism means not an embrace of the religion but a return to a traditional, if studied, ambivalence toward Jewish identity. Even the impulse to reclaim an otherwise unknown legacy seems to be due less to a flickering Jewish flame than to the Jew's need to reassert some ethnic identity in the face of other ethnicities so menacingly resurgent around them.

Indeed, one would have thought that if 45 years was long enough to forget how to be a Jew, it might also be long enough to forget how to hate Jews. But as Mr. Hoffman soon discovered, anti-Semitism and all the other old national hatreds were never really extinguished by Communism, merely *frozen in time*. When the thaw came, the traditional conflicts bloomed with a vengeance, picking up exactly where they left off 45 years ago.

While some of Mr. Young's comments about the re-invoking of anti-Semitism seem overdrawn (*exactly* where they left off 45 years ago), his other points seem very telling. In the present context, they raise questions of how much of identity is *generated* (as it were) from within, how much of it reflects various external or extrinsic definitions, and how this changes (and, amazingly, may not) over time.

In the context of a discussion between Lutheran-Christians and Jews held at a Lutheran Seminary in the Twin Cities several years ago, I discovered that the Christians ability to freeze in time the notion of Jewish identity had much to do with the very elaborate histories which they had of the past two millennia of Christian life even as they had only two moments of Jewish being in their thinking: within the context of New Testament stories of the era of Jesus Christ, and then jumped to the present moment. The Christians thus had rather full histories, while the Jews had virtually none, and presumably did not exactly possess being (or identity) during this immense period of time. The *Jews of the Lutheran construction* was truly frozen in time, occasionally permitted a brief thaw to be placed back into the deep freeze when(ever) the situation demanded that their own identity be rethought.

And the Jew's *own* identity? Do they (did they?) ever possess an internal/integral identity without reacting to the extrinsic and partial placing of their being within the Christian context? (Isn't much of Jewish identity within a Christian world dealing with the quest for eternity and messianism without any promise, and without any palliative for the fears of death which seem to fuel the verve of Christian life?)

Anthropological Nihilism: If there is no true authentic, no really authentic, is life and being and identity really a sham? Yes and No!

There really is no (really truly) way of stating that life is meaningful in any *a priori* sense. In some larger cosmological sense that many current fundamentalists around the world seem to take to heart, the question of whether we even "exist" is considered quite seriously. In Augustine's version of Neo-Platonism, we "exist" as souls prior to our "Earthly Being"—but it is virtually a mistake (our parent's uncontrollable, sinful desires) that we find ourselves as bodies upon this earth, and it is absolutely necessary to return to Heaven where our souls find abode, or they will effectively disappear, and we will be lost (lolling forever in limbo, thrashing ourselves in those other... places)—or God will be lost because our souls get lost... Meaningfulness is, within these traditions, not precisely available. We do what is necessary, think how we ought to be, in order to "get out of this life alive."

The anthropological nihilists, noting the wide variety of attempts to discuss the authentic, seem to be of two minds more directed, apparently, by whether they are optimists or pessimists, than whether authenticity is a form of clothing which can be found and worn, provided us in our existence. In this position, there is simply no sense of human identity, no meaning to being in any *a priori* sense.

For the pessimist, this leads to the cynical view that how we live our lives (*my* life!) makes no particular difference: there are structures, details, we fall into patterns. But—in the end—nothing makes much difference. An intellectual nihilism which may be quizzical or destructive, creative and/or productive, but it is all for naught (*me?*). One does her/his best; or not. Since meaning is not at all an obvious possibility, the pessimistic sense is that there is no meaning available in being. Vocationalism seems silly; destiny is always prefigured. A great sense of strength and endurance is available in this configuration of being in the meaningless "as if," because what one "makes" of oneself has no relevance unless one "invents" her/himself... and others.

The more optimistic—a kind of realist-idealist—looks around and expects that the world is always falling apart; but it isn't always. Things actually work, often, frequently. Expecting that they would never work, this position holds that somehow meaning and identity is somehow being created; that the world which is only a set of stories "about" being—an "as if" world—functions much better than one would predict if there were no meaning available for individuals or groups to structure or to understand being. But they do and they can, remarkably!

And this becomes the subject matter, the foundational project about the nature of identity and being.

Emergent Identity::Emergent Literatures: A current issue of identity has to do with the sorts of literatures and peoples who are recently emergent from colonialized and imperialized situations. Where the British or French or American, Portuguese, or various ethnics held sway over various internal populations of the world, those indigenous peoples were under the control of essentially foreign, alien, external powers.

The question of identity of post-colonial or emergent peoples has several phases having to do with the linear history of the indigenous people(s) in any situation, with the various adjustments to the colonial situation—especially but not only as oppressed peoples—with the development or overthrow of the colonial powers, and with the (re)establishment of identity after the colonial powers have lost their power and withdrawn from the areas in question.

It is usually the case that the colonial situation endures over several generations, so the question of identity prior to the colonial take-over is not directly available to the current people except through the memories of prior generations—and even then, after they had already become older than they were during the phase of the original colonization. So the question of "who we are" in any present which is post-colonial, is referenced to memory or to literature or other sorts of documents.

Secondly, during the colonial phase there are also a variety of adjustments and reactions to the colonizers. In retrospect—there seems to have been a rise in anti-oppression literature—a *"poetry of oppression"*—which characterizes the very important moments just preceding the release from colonial bondage. Some persons experience great oppression - and did during all phases of the colonization. Others were injured or killed during the initial phase - and may be remembered: especially some have "risen" in memory to the status of *martyrs*.

Still others simply moved on in various aspects of a diaspora which they and their descendants may remember and celebrate, or continue to mourn and be lonely for the "old country."

Still others ("Raj Indians") served the colonial powers more or less happily at various moments in the situation: as servants, slaves, as brokers, partners. Depending on various factors, various persons identify "with" or against or, at different times, were relatively neutral or unconcerned with the colonials. And, to further complicate things, bringing current peoples "back" to issues of identity remain alive at least as possibility for great periods of time—especially if other peoples in the present living situation respond to or define them as "other" (e.g., "Blacks" in America increasingly are defining themselves as African-Americans).

Thirdly, the moments after the colonial phase—probably with a period of development having much to do with an older generation or two who had more-or-less "successfully" adjusted to living with the colonizers, aging and dying off. The next generation, or the one after that, begins to redo and revision themselves—not having had to deal personally with the reduction and humiliation—both issues of (negative) identity. Or, as in immigrant America during the 1920's and 1930's, there was in many populations the wish to assimilate as quickly as possible, and not to be "Greenhorns" (ironies of what it means to be "green"). A sense of "loss" occurs in the third, especially the fourth generation, seeking to find what it means to be a...

In any case, there occurred in the colonizing situation a sense of loss of one identity, without—for many persons—any concomitant gain of new identity. Out of this—as well as actual physical or psychological beatings—

arises the sense of oppression which arises especially near the effective "end" of the colonial situation. Some people(s) seem to experience this "loss" as the end of hope—e.g., many Amerindian people with despair, suicide, and the loss of any "work" or reason for being. Others get outraged, and become the martyrs and poets of oppression who will (in memory, retrospect) become heroic figures - often defining who and what "not" to be, and in some cases, what it means to be... noble, a...

Since any actual (national, religious, ethnic) identity in the context of an emergent situation occurred in the lives of persons long gone, the question of who they were, how they lived their lives, their aspirations, experiences, strengths (and weaknesses), is not any longer directly available to the experience of the current people(s). This leads to the notion of "emergence"—the sense of something new (in the sense of "levels of organization" and of "systems")—rather than to a newly "emerging" or "post-colonial" situation, although much of the grasping for identity continues long after the colonial situation, to be *poetry of oppression*. That is, identity for the immediately post-colonial is an identity "derived" strongly from being opposed to the oppressors, rather than being found within oneself, one's generation, history, literature, or other traditions.

When this period of the experience and the testimony of those who experienced colonialism directly has disappeared or faded with the aging of those who were directly oppressed, the question of identity rises importantly and insistently in the lives of many persons. "Who am I, that I am a (religion, nation, culture)?"—"Who are we?"

There seem to be a variety of patterns in whose terms people seek and *"find"* themselves—depending on various circumstances: geography, and/or nationality; varieties of history and/or "roots"; religions; language; "color"; messianism; mysticism; philosophies (metaphysics, cosmologies—ontology seems to presume that the question of identity is either backgrounded or we shift from some structural notion of identity to a dynamic or processual sense of being).

A digression about Existence: The Koran, the Old or the New Testament re-reading of the Book of Genesis can certify that we do exist—if, as I have observed, this is some sort of "lively" cosmological question. In the Christian *panglossialia*, the question of existence seems to precede or at least accompany the issue of identity, since the "purpose" of being on earth is due to the "sin" of one's parents, and the "fall to earth" of one's (bodily) being is held in some senses to be a mere cosmological error.

For the rest of us, the question of existence is puzzling, but is rather more shaped by a variety of adjustments to the immanence of personal death. That is, in most traditions the question of one's existence seems not to be so very powerful in informing the issue of identity (but more later).

But the invocation of historical texts is a primary and usual move in forging identity in moments when meaning and identity seem to be fragile or in some crisis. And the post-colonial situation is one of these moments. The use of these texts (theological, philosophical) is at least two-fold: first, to certify being—ownership of the texts means that we have a history, thus a continuing present and presence; second, to inform us of the actuality and reality of being—how we are and are to be. If the deity is in place and is thinking of us, has a purpose and a plan then in order to have identity, we need to study the plan, then live our lives in accord with the stated purpose.

The plan can be used in many ways to state, to justify, to change our thinking and behavior, and so on. But, particularly, since the notion of the deity precedes us (usually), this acts as a guarantee that all is alright in the universe, if only we learn to act *properly*—and that there is some proper way(s) to be: "in the image of God" (Genesis 1:26). It also sets out a fairly clear methodology for identity—"in the image of God," and we need to determine what God is like (from a study of the scriptural texts), and we can derive ourselves from within this idea.

Within the philosophical textual history, the problem of identity seems a bit more complex, since one can live in "accord with Nature"—and the method from Aristotle is to determine what "Nature" is and/or what is our human nature. Or, from Plato, we can find ourselves as being of a class of slaves, or carpenters, warriors, or philosopher kings—as a kind of given—locate our identity within these ancient configurations of a sort of congenital caste system and destiny, and act accordingly. It is, perhaps, not too strong to state that much of the scholarly work in the modern Humanities essentially follows these plans, and even leads to this exercise.

Other modes of the search for identity (and it is not too strong to state these as "methodological") in the post-colonial situation include the "messianic"—where we search out or hope for some "white knight" figure to "rescue" us from our own fear and selves. This move is, perhaps, more out of desperation than some of the others—but is very appealing ("cargo cults," etc.) particularly in the time just around the time of the departure of the colonizers. In the moment of the Christian calendar "millennium," the temptation is to defer till that moment the question of identity, when the "rapture" will take us (back) to Heaven. In either sort of case, the problem of identity is able to be, as it were, "deferred" until the messianic moment which will apparently, grant us our rightful and proper identity.

National and cultural identities are variably historical, geographical, and theological. They grant forms of identity to a collective "us" as we "belong to" or derive from that history. Some senses of history seem to inform present identity generally or usually; others are more or less "useful" at particular moments or in certain contexts. The Jews in diaspora, at least in the Christian world, always remain in some senses in a colonized situation.

The claim to Israel is particularly a geographical-historical one, in which the notion of identity is informed not only by the ancient covenant with the "people" of Israel, but also with the geography. Here, the Jews are no longer living in a colonized situation, but are living out the judgment and justification of claim to *their* land; even providing a kind of centrism of definition of identity even for the other Jews remaining in the diaspora. The Jews are, probably, one of the most interesting cases in all of history, in having been able to maintain a collective identity—using some very consistent ploys, but occasionally and contextually new (e.g., mystical) ones.

Similarly, the post-colonial peoples seem to find strong claims and bonds (in the present) from the historical sense that they "belong" to the land, thus to one another. If one can trace parentage to the land on which one sits (or would like to "return"), this seems to be very powerful in granting current identity to many of the areas of the world experiencing national or "nativist returns."

The power of history ("roots") to inform present being is particularly strong in the case of American "blacks"—a term now transiting to "African-American." In a "post-slavery" situation, in an earlier context in which slavery seems capable of stripping identity from being as completely as imaginable, the issue of identity has been particularly poignant.

In many senses, the notion of being Black is an extrinsic idea, as identity often is in a colonized situation. One is "seen" as being...Black, and treated as if inferior. There (has been) no geographical or other bond (slavery has not been "useful" in granting positive identity) tying those who are seen as being Black together; no intrinsic collective sense of being. Slavery had effectively wiped out historical memory of being African, of even possessing "language"—a mark of even being "human" as those of Aristotelian/Platonic Christian heritage have calculated humanity. So the first (methodological) task of restoring identity to Blacks, was to show that the former slaves still possessed aspects of their (former) languages; that their form of English was not totally derived from whites (the creole conference in Jamaica in about 1970). And this, with Haley's 1976 work on *Roots* has been fairly effective in getting Black identity on the map. Why/how the notion of history informs present identity remains less clear, than that it works to do this (why "revisionism" works, as well), at least in particular contexts, generations, moments of cultural history.

"Color" has occasional utility in forging a "positive" (i.e., it serves to provide a unifying collective identity: the "White" race (which, in a majority situation in America only serves as an oppositional category to Black, or "persons of color"); a sense of the Platonic hierarchy of what is beautiful or desirable—the longing assimilation of various (male) Ethnic-Americans to some American "ideal" in the 1960's being portrayed as marrying the WASP "Bitch."

"Darker" has often been an observed category which has tended to discriminate against the darker—although there seems to me no reason why lightness has been more positive, except that lighter (or self-hating darker) people have gained power over the informing notions of beauty, power, etc. (e.g., Manichean ideas of white and black as good and evil, etc.)

Language, just as geography, is occasionally important in identity— e.g., the growing debate over "the" language of America being English, vs. the growing competition with Spanish; the situation in Quebec in which French has become the more official language—but it also threatens to divide as much as it unifies.

Finally—for a while—the temptation toward "mysticism" is quite powerful in forging collective post-colonial identity (or other moments of crisis in meaning). I would include under the notion of mysticism the variety of ways of "escaping" from one's being and identity in which the search for identity is located (methodologically) in realms of being and ontology which are in various ways different from what is accepted as "ordinary" experience (grant that "ordinary" experience is somewhat variable from place to place and culture to culture).

Some of these I think of as very similar to theology, but without the informing texts being dominant (e.g., numerology overtaking the Old Testament for some Jewish mystics). Most forms of astrology appeal methodologically to mappings of the heavens and their reflections in our being: calendric, auspicious events. The notion of our being in some relation to various "saints" whose great deeds or thoughts or forms of martyr continue to inspire ours (or "great" persons or great deeds or great writings - but here mysticism overlaps with textual history).

Drugs and other intoxicants are useful in cementing bonds, giving and sharing blood, "sacrifices" of various sorts, oaths, promises, collective witnessing or involvement in "horrible" acts—or more simple "rituals." Shared and unusual/privileged experience also serves to unite in various contexts; as can the prohibition of the same sorts of experience: denial, forms of asceticism; notions of strength, nobility, inspiration (having experienced the same "teacher," guru, oracle, or sage).

The counter-balance notion is put forth by Nietzsche who says we should be living at the edges of our being: comedy and tragedy, the Dionysian as critical commentary upon our being and identity. Issues of "masks," issues of the various critical positions upon the ordinary: the sublime, the anarchic, the avant-garde (post-modern)—all that is critical upon the present and every modern, seeking for sites of critical alterations upon being; the ordinary as extraordinary, and as problematic.

There is a "power" of the mystical to radically inform experience as we move from an "ordinary" predictive-causal world to a "prophetic moment" or time, when the very framing of reality and of being (thence of identity) is done (once again, as method) by appealing to the life or deeds of some *great* prophet. Present experience is virtually shaped (and shapeable) in terms set out by the claim of some prophet (prophetic figure) concerning "what would happen" in the context of the present moment (e.g., millennial). Questions of the variety of transcendental possibilities, of idealities, and of the real all arise within the notion of the mystical—the strangeness is that futurity and history can become the operative reality if and when...

This section should not end without mentioning that any moment of collective identity includes the possibility/likelihood that there is great power "available" within any collective identity because group identity includes a "yielding" of some aspects of the individual identity which are able to be "used" in the sense of the "good" of the group, but also in any other sense of the utilization of power: i.e., power—like technology—can "travel" independently of the membership of any group. Whether such yielding of power is summative or even beyond itself is an interesting question.

Post-Colonial Identity: During colonization, there is some external force which has overtaken one's people, culture, and/or oneself. One's prior identity has in many senses been suppressed, forgotten, mystified, hidden, or obscured more-or-less actively by that force. It may be the British or the Chinese, the Spanish or even us (in the case of Indians, or maybe of our children).

During slavery days, the sense of one's being is particularly defined by the incapability of one to define or to actualize what s/he may "want" to do or is wont to do—but is entirely captivated by what others want one to do. Similarly "they" cast one's being in their terms, which they then attempt to "operationalize"—then, adding the final insult to any earlier sense of identity, they try to convince me/us that we ought to be like them, to be them—at least to be like they want us to be.

In some cases, one is truly encouraged to "join" the captive force: e.g., children becoming adult within their "own" society. But in many circumstances, one remains "other" within a colonized setting. Even in these cases, a few (e.g., "Raj" Indians of South Asia) become a "serving class" loyal and fairly successful in becoming the model of the "good" colonized person or type. Even in post-colonial moments, these (and often their children) become and remain "conservative" to the former notion of an external force which is above them; to whom they remain as loyal servants.

For others, in colonial moments, their identity was bound-up in rather complicated ways with being colonial-anti-colonial: nothing much to do about their situation, but always tossed about in a sea of waves in which being was always chancy and somewhat external to themselves. In certain moments of rebellion—especially in the past few decades in many places in the world; in these moments of multiculturalism in America—there is a kind of *identity of heroism* which one can pertain to—a kind of "poet of oppression" in which one asserts her/his being as being opposed to whatever the perceived/actual colonizers. But even here, perhaps especially here, one's identity is principally worn like clothing that can be put on (but also can be removed), and is difficult to take "into" oneself.

Now, at long last, the colonizers have been overthrown, or they have left for any number of other reasons ranging from sheer inertia, to the decline of their interest or ability, such as a decreasing market for cotton, or even on some notion of morality of no longer wanting to enslave.

Now, we who formerly cast much of being, the idea of our identity, as opposed, as trained by some others who treated us as if we were poor cousins or worse, now they are no longer. I, who was opposed, weaker/poorer, remembering perhaps in the marrows and the cells of my being that I was not-not anyone else, but who my ancestors might have been; now that I am-not the oppressed, still I am me.

I am "here," but the location is not very clear. I discover that I have spent much of my quest for my being in not-being the others. Much of me is invested in the oppressors and I have become somewhat like them in the shadow of their being my invention. And I remain not so clear about who I am and am to be to and within myself. I find that I am either much older—or much younger—than the mirrors of life's reflections tell me I am. But who I am seems amazingly up for grabs. What to do? Who to be? My parents' parent's parents? My sense for belonging to the land where they reside(d)? The others whom they liked and were like? It seems like being very young once again.

Can I be like I am told my ancestors were and would have been, but who did not live through the colonial experience? Is being in the world, now of experience? Can I find once again the deities of the texts which are now paraded about publicly which were once hidden or suppressed and only whispered about? The moments of post-colonial realization are so giddy, so full of possibility. The actuality of today and tomorrow and the facts of being who I am still—how heavily do they weigh against those newnesses of being which are reborn... but out of opposition, now out of myself!?

The relation between the not-being of Plato's Sophist and Hamlet's not-to-be are both eschatological—and the not-being of the oppressed and colonized seems complex. On the one hand, the question of death (a quest *for* death in the realm of eschatology) frames being always in reference to the not-being of an existential question. On the other, the question of identity from the view of being oppressed and colonized, leaves the issue of existence and being lesser, reduced—but in the direction of death and non-being? (Let us recall that *woman-is-life and the future*.)

For some people(s), at least, the moment of the stealing of identity and overtaking, may be like or likened to a death - of who they have been, a robbery of their existential history and a moment of the necessary recasting of their futurity which is, perhaps, unimaginable in any moment, and for a while. Like the victims of any holocaust, those who have had great losses of relatives have indeed lost aspects of themselves; many of them will mourn this loss and their own ("surprising") remaining in the world as long as possible; so the question of existence in the context of being and not-being-who-I-imagined-I-would-be seem very similar in some senses: death and the murder of one's self-image into futurity are not so different.

Several generations, some centuries later: the *recovery of identity* is, perhaps, likened to the Platonic quest for identity, in the first place—and why the question of identity in Western thought is so wrought with the possibilities and likelihoods of the thought path running from skepticism about truth, to skepticism about knowledge, to a cynicism, and now to a nihilism which is close to living within a vision of death.

Global Identity: We met in Minneapolis not so long ago; all of us.

The colors and languages, cultures and talk about the literatures of the world which were in the just ongoing; now, arising and coming into our attentive and tuned mentalities, all these came together in an uncommon common space in the midst of America's northern prairie. Shades of shades from pales and pallids to the darks and darkers of the reflective skins and minds talking about the peculiarities of our being together in this space in this time: "emergent" literatures.

A sense of excitement touched this crowd, thinking that was no very ordinary situation, occurring as it did in the regulated regularities of the academic yawn. The invitation to discuss began the days: an administrative refugee from the Italian south of Europe; a South Asian, a Portuguese-American whose thoughts translate themselves even two generations removed, still in that language; a Larsen/Jenson/Johnson local person who had earlier in life been an ordinary Scandinavian-Minnesotan, an Englishman with the "wrong" accent displaced his yearning-learning to the Asiatic. This refugee from the Pale of Soviet settlement and the pogroms of the deeper Dnieper began the story:

"I want to remind us that we are all visitors here, visiting upon the Indian soil of Ojibwe (Anishanabe) and Sioux." Preparing the soil perhaps, readying the day for the principal speech later which would be the itinerary of an Ojibwe gone west, now returning home where we are visitors. We are all visitors. And we are all here. Here!

The world, the globe, some community, speaking all in this common tongue called English, we all guessed. We—all in the room together. What is this "emergent," this moment of return from the colonized lives which had not so long ago painted the global maps in shades of red: the red of the British empire, the red of the Soviet ambition, the red of the blood of the persons and peoples who would not survive being when they were forced to be other; all visitors in the land of those who have been called red of skin? What has emerged that we are here today, together, a gathering of the world? How did we come to be here?—how can we all be in one place?

"I want us to consider that we are—*we* are—the global community. This moment is interesting, exciting, heady. But others who do not seek voice only, but seek once again in the contexts of power are studying the forms and content of global community; not necessarily seeking to diminish us yet again, but seeking to elevate themselves because: destiny, god's will, avarice, greed, the loudest voice! It is important to speak, but speech floats away like the smoke of a cigarette briefly lit, very soon ashes. What do we do here? Talk? Proclaim? Teach?"

The formerly dominated and displaced peoples, colonized, robbed, plundered, gradually enforced peaceable administrations whose time had so not recently passed. The south of Asia—the teeming India—the Africa colonized of Spain and Portugal and Netherlands and Germany and France, the women who are and were and remain colonized by the men who would seek power. Something about power in this time after colonization, in this time wishfully looking forward wishing to live less in the anger which looking back always instructed; still informing worry.

Finally being able to speak, to have found a voice which no longer wailed of daily oppressions and acts of diminution. Gaining a wavering strength of articulations and syllables which spun the tales as if certainly historical. All here, gathered, gathering.

"Emergent"—a notion of newness, not of a history predetermined. Not "emerg*ing*" as a butterfly from some protective custody cocoon. Not "post-colonial" as if the "post" remained the outpost of the colonized troops set upon the peoples to remind them they were victims. Victims. Now, here, the time of no-longer victims; no longer seeking to find their reduced selves out of their anger at who they were not allowed ever to be; no longer writers and poets of oppression storming out of themselves. Now looking backward very little; now staring outward very little; now a time of discovery, of looking inward and forward out of the experience of our being. Being here together, in Minneapolis—of all places.

"I am who I am," stated, restated, reverberating to the corners of the space in the room inside all of our being together. "I am who I am," moving from one to another and back astonished to discover that we were not talking past each other but *with* one another.

Questions, talk, not still of whether and the dubiousness of some other catching us, or catching us up. Questions rather of how and how soon and just now and right how and right here; and it doesn't much matter that we are speaking English, but that we understand one another, then ourselves.

The quietening of arrogance that I have suffered more and most; of shame and guilt that I have not and do not suffer still every day, but still do; of pity of others and of self in the knowledge that pity is borne out of the poetry of oppression still oppressing; of worries that enough and sufficient sense of who I am is neither too much nor too little.

Knowing we have plenty, that many others seek retreat in this moment which we experience as global community. Reacting to power of the past and present, sure that there are numerous outsides, but none with the power to state who and how and where anyone's being is truly located: nationalism, messianism, retrieves of who I think I was that will tell who I am now to be.

Rather we in this room which expands and expands, grows to the edges of all of our collective being, tell one another that the literatures now being written by people of the 3rd and 4th and 5th worlds to the end of geography are now seeming to be of a more singular piece. I do not seek who I am without joining your search for who you are.

We do not, we who gather here, seem to be blaming. We are not looking back to find some authentic bit of self-reflecting in the pools of history. We all seem to be past those pasts. We are not any longer devoured by our reduced and oppressed selves gnawing at one another. Rather we are seeking for some newly emergent ways of seeking. And we seem to expect now that we will find one another as our paths join, as our trajectories collapse the strands of divided temporalities across the bands of bounded spaces to find ourselves in the same search.

A newly neoromantic utopic vision? Some ideal form of community wanting to reduce our longings of transcendent self to live like the proverbial sheep—in peace? There were moments that expressed that sense of being: wishful, hopeful. But very little of this emerged from a sense of incompleteness or a mystical return to a simpler time in an Eden.

We were mostly, I think, well-trained in the cynicisms of futile longing; brought up to be critics; skeptical especially of our own yearnings, and knowing the 'no' and nothingness of nihilism. The writings, the idea that the angers of past wrongs no longer gnawed at the being of the authors of all of the most obscure places on the earth; an earth whose face we begin to know in the exquisite detail of the grand variety of human life upon it. But we were surprised—now and again and over and over—that the cynicisms we all expected had fled from our being together in Minneapolis.

We came away with the sense that something surprising was happening. And the surprise was ourselves.

Narcissus:

> Vanity, vanity, all is *vanity*.
> Vanity, vanity, all *is* vanity.
> Vanity, vanity, *all* is vanity.

Within the cycles of the roundness of time looking forward looking backward I look out now upon my visage and think it is myself. It pleases me this visage does. It is made in the image of...

I am this visage which is my image which is me looking back at myself, reflecting the way in which I see others seeing me. They are pleased; I am pleased; they are pleased, I...

Am I... not?

Negative Identity: (derived, e.g. from the definition of the oppressor who tells me/us that I am "lesser than")

I am precisely who I am-not. It is not so clear whether this is an "active" who I am, or something derived and left-over from who I am not *permitted* to be. I am a residual being, left over after the others who are real, claim all the turf of being—for themselves. I am slave, at least in the necessity to grapple continuously with their definitions of me/us as having more validity than any which I might generate to myself.

I am sometimes pariah: the *other* whom one is not permitted to be: the Jew, the bastard, the fallen woman; a kind of extrusion and residuum from the categories of being allowable within the imagination and construction of existence.

In my own family I was both desired and a kind of accidental left-over from a set of parents who spent much time and energy finding out who they were: caught in their identity battles, each one, and with one another.

Terrorized, threatened, loved, what chance have I to find out who I am in any way particular to my own being?

In Borges' accounting, we all have to imagine that we could have been other than we are; that in our search for identity it is crucial to imagine that we have/are an identical twin to/of ourselves. This twin is the precisely oppositional force to the being who we happened to turn out to be, that the twin would find it compelling, even necessary to murder this person who I tell myself that I am.

In the case of "identical" twins in fact, the mirror-imaged left and right-handed pair whom others cannot distinguish, it had always seemed to me (growing up with such a pair of close friends—M. & E. Rivo), that they saw one another as the extension of their own visioning, and could not but help be the mirror of themselves. Each was, perhaps primarily, the reflection of the other. (And there are reports that when the twins grow up and move away from each other, many of them move far apart in their appearances within the first several months of separation = not seeing one another!)

In the colonial and/or racist situation (or youth or age), the category of being is so powerful, that all who fall within that category as the vision of our lenses of seeing construct their appearance, are all other: lowered or raised from where we place ourselves within our various hierarchies of being. It may happen that the particular one or ones of the others whom we happen to know personally, are all "good" persons, but this is often to judge every one of the others as an *"exception."* The lines and category boundaries remain and are unshaken within the possibilities of our personal experience. (Sartre: *Jew and Anti-Semite*, 1944.

In fact, a "neighbor" who lives just below our apartment in a high-rise building, complained not to us about some noises which he thinks come from directly above his head, but to the external "authorities," the management of the condominium. Rather than tell us what he is experiencing, so that we might (being "good" neighbors) attempt to change our habits or behavior, he accuses us of causing him grief. And we are grieved and we grieve because the concept of neighbor is reduced to one of an external legal structure in which we are presumed guilty, and we begin to think not about the problem of noise, but too much of the time to think that we are "not guilty"—being defined by another who has taken public a problem which he presumes we are causing. And we spend our energies defending ourselves, being defined already as "other" than we think we are.

In any moment of transformation—personal, legal, political—the problem of change, even when desired, is that our vision is heavily constructed with these categories as active actualities even as we look out our eyes. How are these categories (lines) constructed in our being? Mostly they agree with the category lines of others (of "our kinds"), so they are learned established as our identity with, with respect to, against.

Identity when the Oppressor has Disappeared; No Longer Appears: When the gaze of the other attempts to define us, when this other is not at all me but the reflection of the other in whose eye's mind I shine or am obscured, am beautiful or frightening; when the gaze of the other remains only in my mind's eye then, still I remain, wondering and worrying the who of who I am.

Who am I? Who did I suppose myself to be? Who will I be? Who can I will myself to be? These questions never quiet themselves, always murmur, whispering on, unawares but persistently.

Dreaming in Cuban: A book by Cristina Garcia. Reviewed in the NYT Book Review (5/17/92) by Thulani Davis.

Cristina Garcia's marvelous first novel, "Dreaming in Cuban," is, as its title suggests, about the specific mysteries of place and the hidden passions people often carry into exile.

The members of the del Piño family, scattered from the Cuban village of Santa Teresa del Mar to Havana, Brooklyn and Eastern Europe, live in exile from home, lovers, family. Only Celia, the family matriarch who stayed on in her seaside home and who welcomed change, has managed to understand who she is and in what language she dreams. When Celia's husband, Jorge, finally gives up on her beloved revolution and goes to New York, she replaces his bedside portrait with a picture of Fidel Castro, El Líder, and seems to pay it no mind. The politics of the Cuban revolution and its aftermath, divide Celia's family, as it did many families, yet at the same time some other inability to keep the family together continues its deadly work.

Only the unseen communications of Celia's and Jorge's spirits bring solace and healing to their children, who, for their part, accept these telepathies as commonplace and reliable...Celia's daughters, Felicia and Lourdes, are both given to extremes; each is driven, almost hurtling through time, by vengeance and painful memory. In Cuba, Felicia has her mother's lust for poetry and romance but suffers from months of syphilitic madness, finally committing acts of violence after days of dancing to the seductive voice of Beny More, the king of Cuban balladeers—and making oblations to the still-lively African gods in hopes of salvation. Lourdes, blindly loyal to her father, a compulsive eater and a fanatical anti-Castro convert to American patriotism, runs a bakery in Brooklyn and dreams of taking her place with the nouveau-moguls she sees getting rich in the United States. Their brother, Javier, who ran off secretly to Czechoslovakia, finds he is fragile, too, when he loses his family. Celia's grandchildren can only be described as lost and abandoned by the obsessions of the parents. Of these. Lourdes's daughter, Pilar Puento del Piño, a would-be-painter and student In New York becomes the secret sharer, a distant repository of the family's stories and some of its demons...

Ms. Garcia also tracks the subtle changes in language as the del Piños cross borders and decades. 'Pilar, her first grandchild, writes to her from Brooklyn in a Spanish that is no longer hers. She speaks the hard-edged lexicon of bygone tourists itchy to throw dice on green felt or asphalt.' Lourdes runs around the island asking people what their hourly wages are and telling them what they would make in the States.

While taking very seriously those ideas that have truly riven so many families in recent years, leaving many obsessed with the politics of Cuba, Ms. Garcia also portrays the costliness of such an obsession and the fading of the light between mothers and daughters, between loves, as communication fails. The language of such love songs as once were sung must be saved, Ms. Garcia seems to say, so that we may make songs in exile...

This question of leaving what was as an ongoing aspect of one's life is always complicated in its doing. Whether Cuba or China or America the question and quest of leaving is rent with difficult issues because one's own history is bound up with the lives—real and in one's ongoing imagination—of the others from one's childhood who run around still in one's ongoing thoughts and dreams. It is not so different - growing up and leaving one's parental home—this leaving and being in exile from one's home country either: or church. The life of the exile never precisely sunders the connections with the "old country" no matter how cleanly and surgically disconnected is the "new."

This was illustrated in a beautiful and poignant way by Florian Znaniecki and William Thomas (1918) in their study of *The Polish Peasant* in Europe and America. Most of the first section of the book, I recall, consists of letters between a young man who had emigrated to America from Poland, written to his mother who remained "at home." At first, the young man writes and sends home money—he had come to America because hard times had come upon Poland and there was no work there. His early letters were full of love and yearning for his family and the small town in rural Poland which were rooted strongly in his dreaming.

Gradually, he takes hold, gets some land of his own, marries and has children, and the letters evolve as gradually and magically as his own growing accustomed to his being in this place. Slowly, slowly, it becomes his home and he is at home in his adoptive land. Slowly, the tone of the letters to his ever aging mother, alter: his concerns for her well-being express themselves as loudly as ever, declaring his undying love and wish to see her. But, ever so slowly, ever so clearly, his need and wish to actually return home—his dreams in Polish, as it were—fade and become less and less compelling. Gradually his life as a farmer in America, a life full of a spouse, children, and the need to maintain a farm, crop, animals, trees, fills his life and thought to the brim. He, ever so slowly, has become an American rather than a Pole. His dreams, too, translate themselves into American. And his children, his children will themselves have very few dreams of Poland; and when they do they will be situated in an American visioning of Poland and being in English. And his children's children; and theirs?

Assimilation To and Fro: In a book review of *Bone* by Fae Myenne Ng, entitled *Dying to be an American*, (NYT Book Review 2/7/93, p.7), the death is that of the middle sister in a second-generation Chinese family. She is an apparent suicide, dying of a high apartment plunge while overdosing on Quaaludes. But the book is principally about the Chinese family.

We were a family of three girls. By Chinese standards, that wasn't lucky. In Chinatown, everyone knew our story. Outsiders jerked their chins, looked at us, shook their heads. We heard things...
...A failed family. That Dulcie Fu. And you know which one: bald Leon. Nothing but daughters....
...This theme is the difficulty of cultural assimilation. And Leila (the oldest sister narrator) implies in several misty passages that jumping was Ona's only escape from being "stuck" in Chinatown. The youngest sister, Nina, had already escaped to New York City...In America, a magical injustice reigns. 'In this country, paper is more precious than blood,' Leila's stepfather, Leon, tells his friend You Thin Toy.

In order to get to California, Leon had to invent 'paper' ancestors; his wife married him only for his green card; when he tries to visit a grave, he discovers that it can only be done with the proper documents. Families are destroyed in the scramble to cross the impossible ocean, and then they are reassembled out of several pieces in America's Chinatowns, mysterious sovereign colonies where the census taker doesn't go and a social security number is merely a strange token of a civic religion.

How to be someone else, an *'other,'* like all those others who are American? The three daughters, trying so hard to be; equally hard to not-be; not knowing so well what it means either to be or not to be American. Cursed/blessed by being girls—only girls—within the Chinese context; not so sure what it means to be girls within the American context. Much of life remains unclear to obscure within the experience of that second generation; hyphenated, yet leaning; ready to fall in one direction or the other; not so sure what it means to be.

But assimilation also obscures the facts of (the politics of) birth order. Being the son of the middle daughter of her three-girl family, and the husband of the baby of yet another three-girl family, I am pretty certain—if I know that someone is a child of such a family—which child I may be dealing with: 1, 2, or 3.

Pride and Meaning: The rise in Islamic Fundamentalism (NYT Magazine: 5/31/92) has been blamed on the wish, the need to restore some sense of "pride" in being Muslim, to the millions of those who have felt aggrieved by the West defining them as being "lesser" and "backward" in contrast with the West. After the Gulf War (1991) and the ignominies visited upon them/theirs by the Israelis, they feel some need for "finding" themselves. In the absence of any direction or vision for the future which arises from their ongoing lives—a sense that vision is particularly owned or controlled by the West (Europe and America, particularly), the direction for any viable solution is seen to be in a "return" to a fundamentalist Islam.

Similarly, America which has at present little sense of its historical existence, or that this history can inform the present, is often looking for what will give them/us prideful meaning.

The question of what grants anyone/people pride—or how anyone grants pride to self—then becomes the important study.

Yield and Surrender: Diminish or Grow? The perspective of the parents, the teacher, the spouse, healer—do as I say, or I deem best, for you! Then you will grow, flourish, prosper.

Believe in country, deity, the prophet—submit to the truth of it and you will be righteous, go to heaven, be saved: grow, flourish, prosper.

If you go through this surgery, then you will soon be whole again!, says the surgeon, we will cut out this minor irritation for the integrity of the entire body. Submit to my will, to my scalpel.

So complicated, so confusing. To yield to my (teacher's) superior - knowledge, experience, connectedness with the rulers of the universe—to surrender my will to the deity who—God knows—knows God.

Dogma derived from some other place, some other time trying still to claim that today is the day of all other days, a blip upon some eternity. Believe me; trust in me!

What is the distance between believing others—in others—and believing oneself, and in oneself; and in locating precisely where and who that is? When is it important/useful to suspend belief and disbelief, to yield and surrender one's critical spirit in order that one may develop, grow, heal?

Integrity, authenticity, authority... (Sarles, 2013)

Generational Identity: The issue of general identity seems to arise most clearly when a particular "generation" undergoes a (radical) transformation, and the following, descendent generations see themselves to some large extent with reference to these "patriarchs" (in some cases, "pariah-archs") or matriarchs.

This clearly arises in situations where a generation migrates to a "new" place, when one generation gains money or great power. It arises as well, when a generation loses money or power, is subjugated (colonized), excluded, exiled, "falls." And there are situational variations depending on how "direct" one's relation to the "originary" line is perceived to be—by self and by others.

The lives of the "originary" generation are markedly different, the "personality" characteristics much different between the "first" generation and those subsequent. The first or establishment can be said to be more "ambitious," more "adventuresome," "stronger," if this is the generation which establishes itself "positively." Or it may be the pariah generation if it "loses" everything—or was considered weak or sinful or unlawful. Those who had great political ambition, who had great yearnings for money or power, and managed to obtain what they yearned for, become in effect a defining generation. (Machiavelli, 1531)

The next generation is usually brought up by those who had the great yearnings, not themselves to have great ambitions, but to be like their parents were—*after* they had obtained power or monies, or migrated. The "first" generation of migrants, for example, had in their own upbringing a range of experiences which are essentially unavailable to their children - living now in another place/culture, or within a totally different "life style" from their parents when they were children. So the upbringing of the second generation is cast within the parental experience of "after" their rise or fall: perhaps, within their memories rather than their actualities. Often this generation is brought up to "preserve" what had been gained, rather than to be ambitious on their own account.

By the next generation—the third—members of this generation are, in effect, natives to the new land, or to their being as landed gentry (or relatively less affected by the downfall of their grandparents—sins last in collective memories until the fourth generation, it says in the Bible).

By this time, the reason for being one of descendants of the transformed generation is not any longer clear. They are not children of the newly rich or famous or of those who migrated newly into new lands. They are citizens; they are in a particular social class or setting whose reasons are simply what they are - no one got there; they are there! (Testimony of being seems to become less valid and powerful as the age of the generations extends beyond the parental and personal experience gains more its own validation.) By this time—as in the case of the Rockefeller fortune—there are numerous grandchildren who are heir to money, power, or tradition, and instead of there being a patri/matriarch, there is a convention deciding how to preserve or split up the heritage, and wondering how to revision it within

621

the disparate experiences of the various sub-lines. In the cases of "royal families," the Shakespearean plays demonstrate still very clearly the problems and possibilities of preserving a single line of hereditary monarchy in a clean or pure sense.

The fourth and subsequent generations have a tendency to seek out their genealogies and roots, having lost the reasons for any identity. Many of these simply "disappear" as members of any line or group, understanding their line of descent as an artifact of their existence. Others wonder "who they are" and begin to seek out literal family lines, or genealogical chartings, or "returns" to the home land and the ancestral home or ideology or religious tradition. In other words, history is now becoming tradition, and has to be restated and revised in a sort of messianic way to make it again "alive" for those in the subsequent generations. It is possible for this virtually to disappear, or to regain great power of "authenticity" in the hands and minds of those who want badly to recreate their being within the history of some genealogy.

As we now witness in the varieties of returns to national and ethnic history in Europe, the former Soviet and elsewhere, the idea of history can remain very lively in the thinking of the current generations, e.g., the national museum of Anthropology in Mexico; the sense of greatness of 12th century Lithuania, the sense that Confucius or Christ or Mohammed will be waking and walking among us any day now. When and if any current generation moves from what I might call a "predictive" notion of the future to a "prophetic" moment in which they carry in their thinking the notion that their heritage or religion is fully informed, full-time by the idea that they are members-of or believers-in, then they are effectively "back" in an (updated) "authentic" version of their system of genealogical being. (This is not very different from being a "vocational" thinker of any sort when, e.g., a musician carries in her/his thinking full-time some line or lines of music which can no longer be "turned-off.")

Life Paradoxes: Attempting to look most broadly and comprehensively at the world's traditions, I have been struck by the observation/fact that most of these traditions have tended to "resolve" certain of what I will call "life paradoxes." Except for the Confucian tradition which seems to "complementarize" the (experiential) paradox, for example, of change vs. permanence, other traditions have effectively "decided" to choose one or the other of a number of life paradoxes (20 or so!) and take seriously only one "side" of the apparent oppositional positions. That is, most of these traditions have apparently resisted or even abhorred paradox, even or especially at the level of personal/individual experience.

"Life-paradoxes" are about the experiences we (all) have that seem in their phenomenology to consist of two more-or-less clearly oppositional phases or aspects. While we are awake, we "know" about sleep; while alive, about death; when picking up a particular object know that it is also generic and a name of a class and category, and that I myself am at once and also a man, human, and a one-of-many; but man also an aspect of knowing woman; and on and on. The most human of the all-too-human, the face it itself an example of the Heraclitean paradox of change and not-change: I am who I am and look like I do to others so that they treat me and identify me as a constant me; but my face is changing in each moment's expressions, blinks, and articulated movements.

Sometimes, in life experience, these paradoxes seem oppositionally "heightened," and we are more or less aware that we are duple in our thinking and being, or especially confronted with some desire or need, say, to change even as we hang on to older versions of one's being. At other times, the other "side" of the paradox fades into some experiential background or back burner simmering perhaps, but not totally disappearing.

That is, by calling certain experiential realms or events paradoxical, I do not mean that such are necessarily in full time opposition. The paradox of life and death are not necessarily opposed in all of life's moments. "Waking up" at age 7 or so to the "fact" of one's mortality is the first moment of paradox. And for many persons, the question of death is neither constant nor nagging; while for others - often within certain theological outlooks—death can overwhelm living.

As sex is duple in the world, our lives are in effect sexually "resolved" paradoxes, even as anatomy. As we are both awake and asleep, it remains unclear which is the actual or real, which is more commentary: both are necessary for survival - but, perhaps, waking takes care of the conditions for sleep, while the reverse is less obvious. As I am one (individual) and many (son, husband, father, teacher, neighbor, citizen) the quest for identity wavers between who precise "I" am, and who I am within various "communities" and in various relations which are not much less constant than who I am, precisely as I am (as it were) alone.

As change is, as they say, a "constant," the notion even of granting myself identity and continuity in life is palpably paradoxical. However, large traditions have "decided" that paradox is not somehow acceptable, and have opted to resolve some/many/all paradoxes on one side or the other. Some, particularly the Confucian, have instead "decided" to "complementarize" certain paradoxes (the yin/yang of the I Ching involving moments and dynamics of change).

Western thought, for example, has "chosen" to call the very idea of the "real" that which is universal, non-changing, and awake. It seems to call upon the eternal - a very defining concept for its depiction of the deity—as the real, while the life of change (which is our life), is downgraded to the mundane, or to those aspects of being which do no more than imitate or "partake" in the real (Plato *Republic X*).

Amerindian traditions tend to make real those aspects of our being which are loosed during sleep: our spirits which we are said to "share" with the spirits of particular other species. In many of these Amerindian traditions, in order to find out who we truly are, we must go on "vision quests" which enable us truly to see and know what is our nature, being, and identity. Vocational "urges" are similar: decisions at some early moment in life which are made "for" life.

This granting of active "agency" to entire traditions is a kind of observational gathering notion—as on the face of it there is no particular reason to think that Western thought would, in any sense whatever, be anything in particular: but it is! This means, of course, that each person, family, grouping constructs the world as if it has this agency—a structured/structural idea in which everyone's acting as if (a story, a shared myth), makes it so.

In the context of opposing theo-political traditions, a powerful way to see (to heal, to bridge) differences is within the context of the variety of life paradoxes, in which the concept of paradox is "to be grasped" and understood within the existential, rather than to resolve experience into a set of either/ors, thence to hide or to banish much of our experience from our very existence.

Existence: Probably the most powerful life paradox is concerned with the issue of existence: of life and death, life vs. death, death over life, and so on. Questions of identity intersect directly with existence, because when existence seems, in one's experience, to be problematic, then the question of identity arises also in ways often entirely new to one's prior experience.

The originary experiential issue of being and identity arises around the time (age 7 or so) when one becomes rather fully aware that death not only occurs, but that it is also my personal (physical) destiny. "I am but I will not-be," is my hind-sight statement about how this arose specifically in my knowing-knowing. The events in my life, specifically involve a classmate in 2nd grade who died. More powerfully, in its effect on my being at age 8, was the sudden death of the father of a neighbor-friend who spent the afternoon and evening of his father's accidental death with my family—we knowing the nature of the event, he remaining uninformed until an older sister arrived at our house in great grief at about 8:00 P.M. to take him home. This latter event greatly shaped, surrounded, informed my thinking, dreaming, and some activities for years afterward... perhaps still.

Some of us, until age 7 or so when the issue of death may enter our knowing but does not smash into us within the context of a virtual paradox, may have "known" of death. But the idea of going away, to not/never return seems, to me, a quite ordinary experience in the early development of every child. Early on, disappearance and appearance are as if magic *anyway*. Parents show up, then do not. Siblings are more constant perhaps, but the concept of constancy and change is not at all clear without some inner notion of identity, which is the towardness of social interaction—not, I think, any given within one's early (bodily) experience. The very idea of a "mother" is one of a recurrence toward a constancy. Many of those children whose mother "disappears" actually, become autistic, not any more relating to others. That is, the question of the constancy of identity—in the social sphere which is the human—does not seem to me to be a given of our existence. Instead, the notion of identity which is the "who I am" is an *emergent* fact in our existence.

For the rest, many stories about existence have been constructed to deal with, solve, resolve the problematic(s) of being. One popular mode has been to "banish" the body, thus to banish any actual experience. Being is divided into two (mind and body—often with an intermediate area or "interface"—usually, the "emotions), and only one part is thought to be particularly human, e.g., Plato/Aristotle calling "the human" what is particularly different from other animals or is considered "unique" to human: mind, language, etc.

Or, in Plato's terms, (changing) human being and experience is to "downgrade" itself with respect to the unchanging nature of the pure or true reality, which is of ideas and/or forms. Thus experience only or merely "partakes" of the real in some form of mimicry or imitation.

In the Christianizing formalization of Plato's ideas, Augustine creates the notion of our being as "fall to earth" through the sins of our parents who could not control their desirous nature, following the Adam and Eve who were tempted and fell to the Satanic seduction.

In effect, then, existence has been *made* a form of cosmological "error" or "mistake" and the solution and resolution to the paradox of being alive/dead has been to resolve on the side of "death"—but with the idea that our "real" being is the mind/spirit/soul which is "alive" by itself without our bodily existence; thus problematizing the issue of the body by denying it as completely as possible.

Amazingly, Plato's "solution" to the paradox of life, is to deny life, the senses, and all of knowing which is not derived from the truth of ideas and forms which have an eternal existence quite apart from our being. Plato's "vehicle" for carrying this story into the future world has been Christ, and later, Mohammed—both fully "alive" in present thinking. Any paradox between life and death, in this tradition, has been to resolve on the side of death, and life is the "placement" of the soul in a body to be "returned" to eternal heaven as surely and quickly as possible.

Other traditions—parts of Africa (e.g., Cameroons) is to take the concept of the person and "transfer" it from one generation to a next: from a grandmother who has (say) just died, and grant her being and identity to her granddaughter who is then raised as much as possible within the social construct of the character of her grandmother. In effect, one's being is already pre-constructed, and one becomes what others see one as: in these traditions, as if she is already who she will become. Here, there either is no death, or it is of no particular consequence.

In Buddhist traditions, one (one's soul, again in a dualistic paradox which is effectively "resolved") is "reborn" any number of times, with the idea of towardness of perfection or utopia—a Nirvana—giving direction to our being. Eventual (but projected into some usually far-off, just beyond the possibility of our imagination, future when we will be relieved of life. In these traditions, life is taken in its essence to be very difficult, and needing to be dealt with effectively.

The major difference between the West and the South of Asia is that the body is to be banished in the West, and to be entered into as fully as possible through some meditative and physicalist "Zen." That is, Buddha makes/enables us *disappear* from our own existence by an extended paradox of existence in which complete "entering" into it bodily makes it "disappear."

The two major traditions (which I have some sense for) which move toward some utopic moment within life, are the Jewish and Confucian. Both seem to deal with death by pushing it toward as distant a futurity as is imaginable, thereby hoping it will fade from present thinking. Perhaps it is that old age will "live itself out" and seek death more than life at some point. Perhaps it is that the sense of life as bond and as "covenant" between persons so certifies life and life's meanings, that death of the individual diminishes to the fading point.

But, in these two traditions—alone among the great theo-political traditions—life v. death is not resolved, but "handled"—treated as a given, but reduced in any moment's active awareness as it is pushed within the idea of life as infinitely long. In the Confucian traditions, as long as one remains on the "way" to true life and knowledge, there is not only remaining and continuing life, but there is also continuing growth. That is, the sense of life as good and sufficient "in and of itself" in some paradox in (active) foreknowledge with death, seems to be filled with some sense of progress and towardness which is positive and *interesting*, with a sense of developing skills; toward whatever enters into the concept of "wisdom" in any era.

This is all to remind ourselves that death—rather the foreknowledge of one's death which enters one's awareness around the age of seven - has to a great extent driven theories of being and of reality, how to live a life, and where the notion of life itself has gained in meaning. The wish to resolve this paradox, either a wish to banish thoughts of death, of somehow to "handle" whatever we all might experience as the fear of impending death, has driven and directed various of the other theories of being, especially from around the time of Heraclitus in Western thinking.

The traditions which have done this "successfully" and reduced the sense of fear or directed it toward some interactional-political theories, have grown very large and powerful: the major traditions who apparently needed some gathering idea of "agency" which has grown out of the experiences of paradox in each of our lives.

Politics of Paradoxical Theories of Being: When a *felt* or otherwise experienced paradox is "resolved," a side of portion of the paradox is foregrounded and/or granted primacy, while the "other" side is backgrounded and/or diminished, possibly to point of its "effective disappearance." Our lives, predilections, concentrations become particular, even as we continue to live (as) the vanished opposition: what I tend to call our "actual" lives.

I'm am not at all sure that what one/we experience as paradoxical extends to all the human condition—rather, some paradoxes seem more particular to certain traditions, and may be absent in others. In those traditions which have tended to complementarize what others experience as oppositional (e.g., Confucianism with respect to time and change), the experience of life remains within life, but in the West, the paradox of mind and body has literally been interpreted Within the neo-Platonic Christianity and Muslimism as real being existing only within or on the "day" of one's death.

The fact is that we all are awake and we sleep; often on most days. When we are awake we think and dream; and when we sleep, we seem to think and dream. But in most traditions we have "granted power" to one way of being/thinking/dreaming more than the other. In the one case of sleeping, we are presumably all "alone" (Heraclitus) and not moving, not in gravity or at least supported not from bottom to top but more equitably across our bodies. And when we are "awake," we are "in-common" sense with others (Heraclitus), but also supported either by our feet or our rumps, and having to maintain that weighty protuberance—the head or cranium. In sleep, we care less about balance and our loci. When awake we must know where and whence - i.e., about location and orientation and navigation (Don Griffin, 1976). Any "maps" of being are quite different from sleep to wakefulness, awake needing to be "reading" continually, and sleep being based on memory, or memory alone?

By granting hegemony or even reality to the one or the other of wakefulness and sleeping, the politics of our being are then "extendable" to other arenas of experience. If we grant power to dreams, for example, we likely grant power to those who "have" the best/worst dreams (those which are somehow visionary). Particularly, the power of definition of whatever is reality is often granted to those who claim to interpret them well or properly. These interpretations are then granted political or other reality; others act in terms of that reality; and on and on. (Does that understanding of the real then feed-back into dream life, toward new interpretations?)

Similarly, within traditions which have resolved the issue of sleep and dreams on the side of wakefulness, the politics (e.g., in Plato) convince us that certain types of persons or of experience, predilections or abilities are more worthy of the human condition than others: varieties of hierarchies—toward action, or contemplation, or taking care, of compassion or pity, or transcendence.

Once some aspects of our being are downgraded into the less real, that is, then it seems that the hierarchy is established in our thinking, and the assignation of the importance of anyone's being is available to shape experience, as well as our thinking and evaluation of that experience.

Paradoxical Tics: A friend, now deceased (Dr. Bill Pew) taught me how to control whatever are facial "tics," those involuntary movements of some facial muscles which seem occasionally to "shoot off" as if they have been given life beyond the vessel which displays them. They are, apparently, muscle movements which give to one's expressive observers the sense that something has happened to the face which is out-of-control, pathological, something gone awry.

Bill's idea, which I (and Buddhist thought) has extended to whatever is the experience of "pain," is that the muscular "tic" has in effect taken on its own being within us. This, I think, is not such an unusual event. But it "usually"—up to the moment of its reoccurrence against our "wills"—it usually goes away, like pain. Give it time! Relax! Have a good night's sleep. The paradox of the experience is that we are at odds, even a minor war, with ourselves: I am two, not one; or I have lost "control" of my (former) being.

The solution, paradoxically, is not to fight the tic (or pain) which has by the moment of which we speak, become consistent and insistent, but to attempt to come to some terms with it. One doesn't fight the pain, but accepts it, and does not want it to become "an enemy" within us. Nor would one fight the tic. It is there. It is, paradoxically, me... as well as who I tell myself I am.

One should try to find the muscles which are themselves the source, the cause, the tic itself. In discovering these muscles, one begins to attempt to "cause" the tic." Rather than fighting it, one not only accepts it, but tries to "own" it. Gradually, Bill said, the tic would disappear as it no longer owned a space in our (collective) life.

Emotions: I am how I feel, what I want, all that I need...raised to the level of necessity. Some Rousseauian battle about whether we are truly rational or truly emotional creatures. Is this then extended to the question of truth being from knowledge or from esthetics, but not both?

But there is some slippage in constructing the notion of identity (rather than identity-itself) based on some either/or, likely a paradox in which being is either rational, or it is emotional/esthetic but not both, and more. It is as if we must choose from the categories rather than query our experience to see whence these categories derive, and how they grant us being.

Within the Western construction, we seem to be caught within the dualism of mind and body, where the emotions act as an "interface" category, in the occasional attempt to reconcile how a mind and a body which have virtually nothing to do with one another, can co-exist.

I suggest, in this context, that the apparent opposition between mind and emotions granting us identity, tends to rise as reasonable or interesting particularly in those eras when a mechanical model of the universe (as in the 18th century), seems to have resolved the nature of our being by externalizing the bodily aspects of being; as it were removing being from our being by claiming that the body (alone) is understandable, and the methods by which it is are quite independent from our experiencing.

For those interested in identity and being (all of us—but some have decided that the "problem" is promised to be solved outside of any experience, or that we have reduced being as a problematic virtually to zero), this seems, within a framework of dualist and oppositional thinking, to leave the question of being as a war between the mind and the emotions: one or the other is either more "basic" or "fundamental," or we are born essentially as bundles of emotions, and what development is, is the gradual overcoming of emotions, and the learning of rationality (Piaget 1952). Some in this tradition (Freud 1918) think that we never truly overcome the emotions, but they have been "stuffed" deeply within our being, always at the ready to emerge. And I don't think any of this is precisely incorrect.

But it is not revealing of our being, as it tends to take "small" truths and extends them to all of being: either-ors all the way to destiny. The body, as an experiential aspect (dynamic, developmental, changing), simply "disappears" or does not appear as a subject of study; e.g., the fact of our faces interacting and reacting with/to others' faces: a centrality of being human.

The strength, the shaping, the "use" or situational and contextual aspects of the emotions and feelings and what they contribute to our being, also have tended to be explicated within models of pathology, rather than strength, or merely the "what is." "Feeling" is as much about knowing where I am located and what is my balance, and about how I know how others in some shared space "feel" their bodies, as it is about some war between esthetics and knowing. It is an aspect of knowing, just as rationality is an aspect of whatever is feelings and esthetics.

Hidden, as usual, in this oppositional formulation, is a surreptitious story in Western lore, about the nature of our bodies being ancient and primitive and harboring still some aspects of animality and nature, which we are "supposed" to have overcome in becoming modern and civilized.

Much of the "postmodern" critique of modernity is that we haven't much "overcome" anything, falling into war and hate and revenge and all those usually negative emotions which continue to plague us just when we thought we were on the verge of a rationalist-utopic moment in world history. But, again, this model has been constructed as if we existed within some larger gathering schemata of history and progress, and have not in each generation asked us to query those schemata of our being which we live in actuality, and to wonder about how and why that is.

The pessimisms of Adorno (1970) and Horkheimer (1947) over our propensity for war and destruction instruct us particularly that a mechanical-rational model of humankind is not sufficient or correct in any essentialist, outside of experiencing, senses. They do not tell us how we are particularly well in reacting within whatever seems to be oppositional to the ideas which had been selling in the prior period, when all went wrong.

In his utopic works, Plato (even) warned us that those who live on the edges of their emotion-driven desires, are apt to get society into great trouble: power as the most addictive of the ambitions, and all. Ridding ourselves of the body, of the desires and emotions, by stating that they have no power and meaning in our lives seems as incorrect as stating that the most human of all our attributes is the (uniqueness) of human reason.

The answer to emotions, body, rationality is Yes, Yes, Yes—and there is more. But aspects of changing, growing, learning, maturing, include channeling and shaping emotions, figuring what is possible and permissible and "what works" within what contexts—personal, interactive, and so on. To say what is inborn, or primary, or why the philosopher king of age 50+ no longer experiences or gives into her/his desires, does not illuminate questions of identity—or remind us that life is in the living.

Birth Order: The fact is that we are, among other senses of being, *political* creatures. Our politics carry over to, affect, and are affected by our personal psychologies. If we are born into or are taken into an existing family entity, as most of us are and have been in some form or other, the situation—politically, psychologically (and so on)—differs as each child enters the scene.

Likewise, the scene changes and is changed as a "new" face/person enters into any relationship, extending it, compressing aspects of it. (This extends to family pets, as well.) And, in certain times and places the fact of being an only child are also important in understanding the psychology of being.

In a nuclear family of male and female (if any/many now exist), the first child enters a formerly adult relationship. The child has the potential of full attention—at the least s/he doesn't much share it with other children—of the parents. As any relationship is complicated, adding a third person doesn't directly simplify it. This first child deals directly with the parents, unmediated as it were. As children are children of their families' (thinking, logic, outlook) the power of parents to define much of the child's outlook and being is great in many areas of present and future being (e.g., religion, culture, etc.)

A next child deals also with the parents, but also with and "through" the older sibling: whether a second child deals with the parents directly or alone, the image and knowledge of the being of the first child has some undoubted "presence" in the interactions. There is not only one dyad between second child and parents (and each parent and each parent dealing with the marital and parental relationship), but the children are in some complex of dynamic and historical relationships with one another.

By the time a third enters, this situation gets multiplied, rapidly on its way to becoming a full-time corporation/bureaucracy. At this point, not only do further children experience the world through and in the terms of their older siblings, but in many families the energy necessary to oversee younger children is no longer available, and some of the older children (especially girls and often the oldest) become a kind of surrogate mother—as if this family has become a kind of corporation with differently managed smaller companies within its structure. Here, birth order per se is less important in terms of family politics than the surrogate mother and her relationship to younger siblings, and her own relationship to parents. What are otherwise a manifold set of relationships in larger families become largely reduced.

The question of how familial politics affect or determine the psychologies of various children in terms of birth order—or of only children—is interesting, deep, perhaps profound. The modern University is, for example, full of oldest or only children; most faculty are oldest or only.

They are, perhaps, the most "ambitious" or yearning or responsible or need to belong to a "mother" institution. Other professions are more care-taking: youngest children (social workers), and so on. In other words, birth order certainly seems to affect or direct ambitions or outlooks on what to do in one's life.

One infers that the oldest/only children are more directed toward the ambitions of their parents, tending to see a world in which parents' interpretations are more actual than later children whose interactions with the parent's understandings are interpreted as well through older siblings. The world of the oldest and only is, perhaps, the adult world in their terms. And other children find themselves constructing that world with different contextual twists and turns.

But the most told story is about the politics of the siblings. Both my mother and my spouse grew up in three-female families: mother, the second and middle; spouse, the last and baby. The story of same-sex threesomes is about the disappearance in many ways of the middle child and a sense of deep resentment for all of that. The "smartest" and most ambitious in worldly terms is the oldest, and the youngest is the most intuitive and caring for all the others, always remaining as well, the baby of the family.

Existence: Writing mornings, my usual take on existence is how my body feels upon waking: a renewal of self-acquaintance, a looking forward or not to the day to come, an impending sense of euphoria or a sense of the dismal...as this is the day I have to have a root canal. Usually my bodily feeling confirms itself, and I am: simple as that.

At other moments, the notion of existence does not seem much to appear: neither dread nor diligence directs itself to think about the 'me, myself, and I' which in one large sense is who I am: all of existence; my being. The world is my creation, much as I seem to create myself each day (—is each day new?).

Meeting some of those who believed, who healed their ills and woes by praying to some idea outside of their being, my later youth wondered about what they were up to. Healing? Praying? Why not go to the doctor for some pills and palliatives? They said to one another: "Jesus is in the tent tonight," and they greeted one another to the left and to the right and sometimes shook and held each other's hands. And some went forward to be touched by the preacher, while others did not. I watched wondering.

Years later when I was an anthropologist, we received a note from an evangelistic preacher stating that "creation science" should be taught alongside of "evolutionary science." It was then that I began more seriously to consider that many folks are more wondrous and questioning about existence—their own existence—than I had ever thought. They, trying to convert me, said that I had never thought.

Death, the fear of death and love of the concept of death informing life and the 'who and what' of the 'I am': a cosmology; an about my being from the depths of the infinite of the universe. A magnificent sense of the largeness of my being tempered and captivated ten seconds after by the vast diminution of my being; ever being. I was so happy to know that different traditions thought about life and death differently and seemed to blunder through life pretty well. But, wondering about existence even as I awoke, vulnerable to the problematizing of my sense of myself just as the cobwebs of thought were being brushed from my insight! Imagine!

Existence, the love of the imagination as it represents life within our being...

The Social Me: I am → I belong. I am my mother's child. I have a covenant with the people of...This is our land; our nation; our god; our house; our child; our (mother) tongue...

I believe. I believe in.
I accept.
I love.

Others see me as. Others see me as *a*. Others do not see me, notice me, note me.

When I look in the mirror; when I look in the mirror I see looking back at me the features which my brother and sister see looking back at them, looking at me. I see in me, I see as me, I am the one which is the many.

And I? And I!

(A major difference between men and women in relationships?)—at least in late 20th century America.

There is (for G.H. Mead, and all of us?) no sense in which we are not social in our identity. But we are not only social, and not always social, in the same ways.

Freedom: The paradox between individual and social identity begins to show up in this question of being "free." Whether we are engaged, in this context, in thinking that freedom and being are especially or only to be located within individual being and possessing the "freedom of will" to do exactly as we "want"—can be balanced against the sorts of freedom which are available by yielding some aspects of identity to membership in some group. In this sense, who we are is in some ways clearly restricted, but having yielded some limited aspects of self, we are "free" to do—especially to think—exactly as we want to.

If I "give myself" to some particular image of the deity—in becoming a nun or priest for example, or in joining a political party—this may be restricted to certain limited aspects of myself. This may leave "me" with great freedom of intellectual or geographic freedom, or it may open up great arenas of possibility. Similarly, the discipline of any deep study or skill, opens up vast possibilities once the art or craft is developed sufficiently that one doesn't have to spend all energies developing the skills necessary to do or to make something: musical or other performance, and so on.

How much of "oneself" is yielded in developing the discipline or skills necessary to gain the ultimate freedom to develop oneself is a complicated issue: delayed gratifications, studies toward real knowledge sufficient to be a "real" professional leave some so involved in preparation that they never "get" to where they might be going. Others (say, Olympic gymnasts), the preparation is often so all-enveloping during the years of growing-up, that the few years of performance are over before age 20, and skills for living life "itself" were never granted much attention.

There are certain models for being which particularly seek-out the freedom of self, of movement within any restricted or restricting definition of self, which raise the question of freedom of the "will." The Stoics, particularly Epictetus—a cripple and former slave—urge themselves to find ways to take the most constricted external definition of self, and to explore the possibilities of freedom within which will "release" the individual from the bondage of definition and treatment by others as being one thing or one way.

In the context of the realm of the social-political, the question of freedom complicates itself with respect to the sort of features which characterize location within that group: are they "voluntary"—harkening back to issues of free-will? Are they "given" - aspects of the bodily anatomy: sex, size, color, irregular or anomalous features of one's surface vs. being within some preferred esthetic of appearance or being, age? Are these features related to a desired or earned state of being: (grand)parenthood; marriage (divorce); being a public (or hermetic) person, fame, power; a failure, an addict, a criminal or cop?

Being of Several Minds: Some (post) modernists claim (Gergen 1991) that it has been technology which has so complicated and filled our minds with so many ideas competing as it were for limited mental capability, that we are over-full beyond the brim with thoughts and meaning hurtling hither and yon. We are "saturated" with images which find no solidity, no framework, no compositional mode which is frameable as any singularity; no me, no more.

The (formerly: romantic, scientific/mechanical) modes of our being truly an integrated individual are no longer experientially available to us. We are so overfull and overloaded with images blowing our minds asunder, that we cannot find ourselves; not our *true or authentic* selves. We try to reach back in time to the most primal of our human (or other) instincts, reach out to the agency of the deity within, ask a head or other "shrink" to limit and delimit our being so much that we can find who we are truly. And I know what he's saying; feeling a bit like I am operating on 6 cylinders in a twelve cylinder world, with carbon incrustations corroding the formerly faithful six. Where a good night's sleep or an orgasmic experience would have cleared the self of the webs of yuck accumulating in my psyche, now they merely gather, grow, grub, and fester.

But I wonder how much of this is new in the world; how much is temporary, or born of a time of simpler expectations. I wonder about some simple concepts which have multiplied within us only gradually, now come to our attention because the ground of their competition might demand that we take sides or make hard choices.

A term of great sway and practical power comes "to mind": the term "rational." Most of us moderns → post-moderns have in our little heads at least four "meanings" or contextual soundings: one in philosophy ("logical"); one in psychiatry ("crazy"); one in economics ("greedy"); and the "rational person" in law (who is "reasonable" as a good and responsible citizen).

In most of our collective minds' meanderings, these 4 notions or meanings assigned to the same term seem to reside unmolested by their competition for attention with the others. All are true, all are persuasive, used for the proper occasions within the sensible contexts in which they "make sense."

Is this era the one where we note that they all cry out for attention at the self-same moment; the time when we want to resolve the kinds and sorts of contradictory confabulations which had earlier been able to demand their own conceptual space. Perhaps we are trying to stuff additional meanings into a shrinking space. Perhaps something is changing about the context. Perhaps…

I have wondered since meeting the mind of my spouse whose mind is so very full, if much of the idea of the saturated self—for at least many of us—isn't partly a problem of "scale."

She, having grown up in a village of some 600 persons, knew everyone there, and in some depth of their being: their family histories, all the players in their lives, the frivolities and foibles and phantasmagoria of all of their imaginations and habits.

Being the daughter of the town inn-keeper(s) she got to watch many of them, and hear each day's gossips brought up to the news of each newsy moment. And she knew just what to serve when, in the full barroom after work, someone for reasons she would know but I never could fathom, someone yelled "a round of drinks for everyone," she would serve them all what they wanted, and in her head tally up the costs, and never (as far as I could tell) make an error in person or in money: a whiskey and a tap beer here, a Miller or a Schlitz or a Bud or a Genesee or a Red Cap pale ale, or a shot of Old Overholt (I made that up: *my* grandpa drank that!), or of Scotch or Jack Daniels, or...

And she knew which women waited in the car, or if not the spouse—just who it was, and where everyone else in town was likely to be; who was good or bad at what, and only learned much later what the nature and quality of judgment of 600 persons ensconced in the mental boundaries of a small town, meant in some larger world: not a great deal! But this knowledge filled up her head, saturated her knowledge peopled with the people who knew her back, kept track; delimited her being, and likely outlined-limited her possibilities.

I, who grew up in a larger city—in an ethnic community of some 20,00 or so persons within a city of close to a million persons, knew very few people in such breadth and depth. And we moved from one neighborhood to another several times while I was growing up so that the persons I knew—sort of—changed; or the locale changed, or I changed, or they did. But most I never knew, nor could know.

Even though there were many, many more, I actually knew many fewer than she, and in much less detail. My mental clutter, at least with respect to people-knowledge was sparse, spare. And I had learned, apparently, to let this knowledge go and fade into narrowing memory with little residue.

So I wonder if the self of those who have matured in a small community is indeed already "saturated" by having in mind all those persons in myriad detail in manifold relationships, while the self of those who grew up in large, large, largest communities isn't greatly reduced and focused. What we witness, now, is the increased pressure on the self of the "selfish" to expand what and who they know, working on a self which is not accustomed to such great pressure to contain so much.

I wonder, as well with respect to the engorgement of technology in impacting our being, if we hadn't Descartes some places in our thinking that the human condition isn't particularly located in that conceptual, metaphorical space that machines were-not.

639

Whatever our existence is, is underwritten by Descartes as the ability to think. And now machines occupy that formerly clear space, with a sense that they will fill it increasingly until there is no space left: they—computers, robots, artificial intelligences—will do the thinking. And there will be nothing left of us, or for us. Some have even suggested, seriously I guess, that the time of the human body and its evolution is effectively over, and that the mental processes will go on among the artificial minds: minds over matter, and this earthly portion of our existence is over, and, well and good?

How much of our being, that is, has been imaginarily constituted by some (implicit) contrast within the Cartesian framework of our existence being our thinking? It seems now that artificial intelligence expands so rapidly, that we diminish variously with respect to its growth. We might, one supposes, find new ground and hope for being, rather than revel on the sandy soils of our having defined ourselves largely as the one thinking being in the universe.

Identity and Context: As the concepts of identity and meaning are virtually dependent on the definition of the accompanying term, and both actualize themselves within a variety of notions of context, the issue of context is directly relevant to thinking about who I am and who we are.

Like, perhaps, the search for the ground and grounds of our being, the issue of context is both an umbrella-like presence, and an idea behind all ideas which is hidden even in its revealing. I find it useful to think of some aspects of context more as a "residual" notion, a what-is-left-over when all else is understood. In other senses (although the question of what means "otherness" is particularly at issue within the framing of what and where is context), the sense of context comes with a kind of powerful-not-so-powerful "everybody knows this" sort of agency, in which the meaning of a particular word in any setting "depends" on the "context" or the "situation."

Politicization: Some of us wander blithely through life thinking that most tomorrows will be...better; at least not any worse. We live within some implicit scripts of life's ways being forward or upward; at least mostly straight ahead.

Some moments, sometimes, however in life's cycles or progresses gain our attention so clearly, so powerfully that they reflect upon our lives, revealing reflexively that we had been living within some schemes of being which now seem silly, useless, false. And we are left... wondering.

It may have been an unexpected illness, an accident which had nothing to do with our being cause or even very involved. It may have happened to someone upon whom we depended or were involved so that our very being became at some risk. Such events seem to raise powerful questionings in our being, bring us to some crisis in life. Even for some, these days, becoming age 40 crystallizes the facts of life by raising the hints of death's approaching, teaching us or at least demonstrating that we had fairly successfully hidden to ourselves the reality or unreality of life and of death.

But some such critical events seem more social, more political, more due to eventfulness way beyond our ken and experience: a revolution, a police vendetta visited upon someone close, neighbor or friend, an acquaintance of an acquaintance. And, often just of a sudden, one begins to think that something happening is way beyond oneself: beyond control, having little to do with personal being or identity. One begins to think that forces exist outside oneself which are catching one within their webbings; one is seemingly told who to be, who one can be, cannot-be. And the stories one told to s/himself still at work within seem increasingly without meaning, false, downright misleading, lies that you and I believed about our being.

And we are becoming politicized: belonging to some party, an outlook, a history, a citizen of a place, a believer/reader in an ancient text which apparently explains how we are and should be, and that we are like others who are just like us. We begin to act, to think, to be as we are defined, as we are told to be who we think we are told to be who we are.

Justification: The issue of being and authenticity is bound peculiarly in Western thought, at least, with the notion that there is a judging public to whom and for whom any movement needs to be explained and somehow justified. Justification is beyond explanation of what, and bends over toward the why of any activity or action. Going to war demands justification; i.e., we are civilized, they are barbarians (from Sepulveda to this day invoking Aristotle over Christ). If there is no justification, no sense that an action entails or contains some sense of justice, then there is the reactive feeling that the judging public will not approve, will not support, and eventually one is left hanging in the wind, alone. No mere declaration or assertion will do even, apparently, in telling a story to oneself.

An Indian (South Asian) friend/neighbor called Deleep R. claims that this is particularly true of Minnesotans, perhaps all Americans; but not true of others. Minnesotans cannot/do not merely declare who they are and that they are, but walk around any statement of who we are, perhaps try-out the effect of out statements of identity on others. He thinks this feeds-back on ourselves. Others, he says (referring particularly to others of his countrymen) simply state who they are, and go on about their business. Period! Does this extrapolate to Western thinking?

Justification is the idea that what I say is, truly is; what I say there is to do, should be done; that what the justification claims is fact, is truly fact; that there is authority, and that this authority serves our purpose. It is as if the *further* we can push from ourselves to some exterior authority a rationale for some otherwise dubitable claim or activity, the more it is possible to accept its premises, and to act upon it. It is as if we push responsibility far enough away from us, then we bear less and less of the responsibility for ourselves, our thoughts, and actions. Now we can hurt or kill and even convince ourselves that we are moral, still.

Being and Truth: From Bergson (1911), the issue of knowing that I am, who I am, and so on, is the most obvious and direct aspect of being one can know. He attempts to draw out the quest and question of existence by appealing to the notion that our most direct awareness is the passing of one moment to another (like a movie frame perhaps). This raises, in turn, the question of what holds steady. Of a sudden, at the beginning of the 20th century, we find ourselves doing a restatement of Heraclitus' paradox of "not being able to step into the same river twice."

Somehow, establishing that and how we are, seems to captivate the question of being. Once, we establish that we are, and probe how we are and how we know, then we will apparently be set to understand how we go about knowing truth. (This also works inversely: if we question the possibility of truth—modern forms of nihilism or meaning crises—then we are also or in turn driven to question our existence.)

This seems to mirror the sorts of skepticism which has beset Western thought from the "beginning"—from Parmenides to Pythagoras to Plato. It has been a skepticism about knowledge resting particularly upon a skepticism about the possibility of knowledge—of objects—and, again, particularly about the possibility of others knowing precisely that and what we/I know related to a skepticism about being.

The skepticism is deeper that any mere doubt about knowing any one thing more-or-less precisely, but a doubt about knowing anything with any sense of surety. Within this framework of skepticism about knowledge, there seems always to be a suspicion that we may not exist, not possess being - and the philosophers from then onward (the essence of being philosopher, philosophical) have considered truth an aspect of, or dependent on some reasonable solution to the problem of being—as if it needs to be a problem rather than some mere notice, observation; a declaration.

But none of this makes the "problem of truth" any more (or less) clear.

Being as Knowing: Preliminary Digressions: The quest for and question about knowing is cast differently within different metaphysics, assumptions, notions of nature and of the human nature which we might hold in common. In a mechanical world—like Descartes' world—where we are some pointed mind casting about in and at some impersonal universe, the notion of knowing is all about knowing the universe which is "out there." Nothing is of great or particular interest within one's being or within oneself, or even about the *self which I might be*.

Knowing resides evidently within some notion of language; and language is all about the external, mechanical world. And that world—about cause and effect—has endless truths and knowing which is monumental and as permanent as the everness of action and reaction and the geometries and logics which try time.

In the more feminine and feminized viewing of the Oracle at Delphi who counseled us to "know ourselves," the question of knowing is directed less at any world external, and more to the vessel which is ourselves knowing what it means to be ourselves; oneself.

In this context, knowing oneself can never be cast at me, the individual, existing solely, because this is not the human condition. The human condition is changing and includes others, mothers, the knowing of the world but always with others' knowing *knowing*. It is always organic, organismic, including the history of how I got here and where I am, and where is there to go next. The locus of knowing begins with the sense of the quest of knowing oneself.

In the eschatological world in which the knowing of life is always interwoven with the fears and fascinations of death, knowing is directed toward some end; toward escape, toward doom, toward escaping from doom, toward escaping from the concept of doom—transcendence layered like a global onion; knowing flits from core to periphery. Nietzsche's proclamation of the "death of God" attempts to deconstruct the notion of eschatology—the necessity to seek the end of—to live at the edges of all of being, and to state what is the beyond which is not the end. Bataille (1943) lives this out only too well, succeeding by becoming the unexpected (but welcomed?) Faust who solved all the problematics of knowing, and finally became bored in the beyondness which was precisely a mirror of the end which he had told himself he had abandoned. Knowing collapsed upon itself.

Critical naturalism considers knowing within the nature of our nature, attempting not to see how we humans are unique within life, but as we are. We have oversimplified ourselves and our being, and need now to see us as we are, have been, as well as the complications of our unfolding. It lives within the viewing of us both inside and outside, the viewing of the viewings, and the problematization of what we experience as mundane and ordinary.

The Others' Me: They—my mother, spouse, kids, friends—see me as a *'who I am'* which is consistent. It is, for them, very much the same; not anyone else. And whoever I am, from the perspectives of my being who others see me as and say I am, it is always *right now*.

No matter how I think I am, or which of the many 'me's I feel like I am or would rather be, these others treat me *as if* I have real identity. Am I actually the *as if me* that others see in me; see *into me*? If their envisioning of me are static, at least not very dynamic, what does that do to my imaginings of *'the me'* who I (think I) am?

As a teacher, I am constant and authoritative, a consistent being to my students' construction of me-the-teacher. Inside, I am *ordinary to myself* even as I try to remain the authority of constancy and stability that the students grant to my being as their teacher. They try to please me, the teacher, even as they might actually please their own constructions of me. (2013)

Watching an infant come to grasp the constancy of its mother—thence, perhaps, itself—it dawns that the process is akin to taking-in the features of the mother into oneself (one's face), then responding to the constancy of the other to confirm oneself. The process of being constant thus seems to involve and entail the yielding of some senses of self (superficial—as definition), the taking-in of some senses of the other (constructed into some forms of my holism), then responding to the other of my construction as if it is essentially the other. Not very different from the circularity in terms we invent any aspect of transcendence.

The others' me seems thus to be the locus—at least a locus from which we can find constancy—in terms of which we are who we are with enduringness. Rather than this part of being me located within, it is peculiarly located outside of my physical being within the knowing that the others' me is palpable. They know who I am. The problem remains, then, in how I may use this idea of the others' me, to generate my idea of me.

Group Identity is Enduring beyond the Individual: Within the notion of any "we," the quest and question of identity has enduringness beyond the being of any particular individual. Perhaps this notion is appealing for some of the especial or super-reality of group identity.

As differentiated from Plato's "solution" to the problem of death accomplished by ridding the individual of its body, and granting to the soul or spirit a sense of enduring eternality, the idea of the one's enduring also exists within the idea of any group's genealogy. I have a son to "carry-on" my name, a daughter to remember me and praise me to her children in her turn. In some places, a death is proclaimed not to be a death, but a rebirth in the life of a grandchild born at the time of the death, who is then given the name of the grandparent, and treated as if s/he is that person.

Aristotle (*Politics*) takes this endurance of a group beyond the being of any individual, to give primacy to the idea of the state. But, as I mentioned elsewhere in this work, this move doesn't solve or resolve the issue of being, but merely attempts to locate it in one or the other place—often obscuring the fact that the primacy of being one or the many is paradoxical in our existence.

Identity and a Group: Family, Country, Race...: I am an American. I am for, hate, will do, will never be for that sort of thing. I pledge allegiance to the flag. My hopes will never flag for the old red, white, and blue. I am a citizen. I love America; I love the idea of America. Like my friend who loved humanity, the question of loving people is always at some risk in the context of concept over persons, of structure over personal and individual being.

I am a Catholic, Jew, Protestant, free thinker. I approve of, or cannot abide, just because I am a "who," precisely, am "I." I am white, black, just the right proportion of each of those. There is no concept of race; no purity. Who am I? Who am I without these gathering concepts? How can I be me, when I am so many? And all the things and -isms who I am-not and can never be so startles me that I cannot hope to find myself. Who will tell me who I am to be? (Don't forget that I wear/have an artificial eye!)

Imagined Communities (Benedict Anderson, 1983) the question of the concept of the engulfing nation and why we accept/reject it.

The "I" who responds to the Others' Me: If we are talking interesting puzzles, here resides one which goes on and on and on. When I look in the mirror, even, just whose version of myself do I think I see? When first I saw my facial image reflected in my mother's eyes - literally - what precisely did I see? When I saw myself reflected in her face and critique and whatever love she could afford to give me, was this a "me" which I liked? Despised? Got sustenance from? Defended from? Did this response/reaction change from time to time?

Is maturity a growing need or necessity not to see myself as my m/other would see me? To forget or forgive this version of myself? To alter my mother in my own view such that her envisioning of me was moving... and growing, or not?

Family, spouse, children, friends, enemies—imagined or real: where do my reactions to them reside? Is this residential neighborhood of my being, my real or actual home? Does the "I" which I call myself consist in major part of some blend of my reactions to the "me" which others say I am? What can love or hate or toleration or my disappearance from anyone else's eyes mean in my own story to myself about who precisely I am? Is there a core of being located here? Is "it" merely located here, generated anew every so often; is it changed and updated; or a vision of the past notion of who I was or said to be, which now reigns over my being?

Identity Projected Forward: I wandered about in the world a victim, a slave to the various of my addictions, wondering why and how I had become so in love with certain substances, particularities of thought: caffeine, tobacco, alcohol, to name those substances which are adjudged "legal"; and various obsessions including the various dependencies which sought me out successfully (or which I sought out!).

There has/had been an argument about the nature of addiction, cast as within Western thinking between the notion of physical or physiological addiction—a passive attachment and "need" of one's next "fix" or "trip"— as opposed to a psychological addiction in which one presumably gets in the habit of thinking that one needs to have a cigarette in hand with one's coffee which one needs to have to wake up in the morning or a drink which acts as a soporific to sleep through the night.

Instead, I have wondered if the question of addiction is more one of how one thinks about one's being and identity "cast forward" into one's image of self in futurity: the "moment of addiction" being that time when one (can) no longer see oneself or imagine oneself into future being without the substance or object of obsession which is "causing" or promulgating the addiction. That is, one's future image of self seems to be (at least passively) involved in determining one's identity as it plays out in each present moment.

Body, Body Politic, Body of Knowledge: It is not easy to say where we begin to state and to think about the relation between being and identity, because the framing of both seems to be intertwined; intertwined, that is, within several virtual loci in which one locus is presumed, then the other(s) derived from that presumption.

We can charge Aristotle, conveniently, for developing this model of conflation. The (physical) individual body is first presumed to be nature of our entity-ness: an establishing principle. Having presumed that each individual person has existence, we then divide being into two parts: body and soul, granting (both dualism and hierarchy are derived from Plato/Pythagoras) that the soul has power over the body. Identity is thus shifted toward whatever the soul is or does.

The concept of "nature" which is used to bolster this thinking, is not only invoked but is also given a sense of direction and towardness: human nature is what each individual tends toward—here, the male adult.

At about the same conceptual moment, the concept of the nation-state is given primacy over the individual, because it exists more generally: irrespective of the existence of any particular individual(s). But its nature is taken to be analogous to the individual (body). It, too, is dualistic in its nature: the director (mind) having hegemony over the citizens' (bodies). Thus the "nature" of the state is of the "body politic" in which the physical (body, citizens) is presumed or taken as given; then, the/its proper form is declared to be some form of monarchy—a directing mind "over" the body politic.

In this web of circular and circulating presumptions, the question of what is a good or proper person/government is conflated. Aristotle (*Politics*), having presumed the primacy of the physical body—then having hidden it—takes up the "problem" of the direction, thus the nature of our *true being*.

On the way, the question of whether there are "natural" slaves—inferiors, thence superiors, arises. Although there seems to be nothing like "proof" of their inferiority offered by Aristotle, there is the conclusion that there are and must be: I infer that the idea of superiority of mind over body, of monarchy over citizens, leads fairly directly to the idea that slaves who are principally bodies in terms of their treatment in society, are now taken back to their originary being: body equals slave. As body is natural, slavery/slaves are natural.

In any case, the web of intertwining body with body politic, now moves back again to body and seems to establish, at least to offer justification, for there being slaves, and treating them as lesser; i.e., as subservient.

Since, the "fact" of one's identity at birth is nowhere clear, this "methodology" of intersecting body and body politic permits us to dis-identify any particular person by equating identity with an impersonal body-mind, to raise being to the body politic where the individual is made virtually to disappear, then back again to the person who can now be declared to be a slave or not. Here one disappears under the weight of her/his external definition.

Nature and Culture: A story in Western thought, at least, is that we are some mix of culture and nature, or some mix of good and evil, of mind and body—an oppositional sense that we are particularly some one way, with some other crying to be let out or threatening to take over some more or less *real* me.

And when there is some opposing or other side to our being, then there is likely to be an arena of interface, where the two sides may find one another, or they may even be subsumed to the area between.

Capping this tradition is the hierarchical tendency to value one—or the other—side of being; occasionally in different moments, or in some complementarity of yin/yang. (Much of this seems due to the unwillingness or incapability of theorists of being to figure out what to do with the fact that much of life is truly paradoxical, and to confuse or to conflate different modes of being with their having to be oppositional; i.e., life/death, male/female, one/many, and so on to the number of *20 or so*.)

In the Platonic-idealist tradition, I am really-truly mind, language, rationality, text, deity, purity, form, and the other—the body, nature, dirty, Satan-anti-Christ is opposite and threatening to the real me. One suspects—within this metaphysics—that one has the real exactly the opposite from what it really it (In Sarles *Next Places*: "The Terror of Beast Within"). Or, worse, that as we are composed of both parts at once: that nature is always trying to overtake the real me, and may win out, needing then to be exorcized, or I may need to be imprisoned.

In a theory which is variably social then political then...theme and variation on Hobbes vs. Locke/Rousseau, the question of who I am is taken to social and political theory. Who I am is intertwined with the issue of freedom and liberty. The real "me" is the "me" who is totally free to do with what I will, what I want. (As Hobbes derives directly from Aristotle, the Hobbesian attempt is always to take the theory of being, of one's identity, and to metaphorize it into social-political theory: the Body Politic and the Organic Analogy.)

As the mind is free and reigns over the body, thus it has been held, is the king over polis, man over woman, parents over children, and polis over slaves. Here the question of the dualism depends on which side is credited with being the *real* I - the really human in Aristotelian theories of nature is the mind.) But in Hobbes, retold via Paglia, the really us is the body, and the interface is located in sex and the erotic. The opposing theorists are variably Locke and Rousseau who presume us to be born free, and it is society which has placed us in chains.

Tender Loving Care (TLC): Human infants *do not* survive on their own!

They do not survive in "their own terms." If they possess such "terms," they do not ensure survival. Surviving infants (us, et al), survive in terms largely defined/shared, interpreted by their parents.

Whatever TLC consists in—touching, smell, talking to and with—is some set of terms which creates/breaks boundaries and categories in whose terms we survive. (Ashley Montagu, 1967)

The individual "I" thus exists in terms largely constructed by parents. This does not mean that I do not possess (prior) terms, or that my terms of identity are not "emergent." It does mean that Rousseau's notion of "born free" has little meaning, derived as it is from "natural law theory" rather from study of the developing human condition.

M/others draw the boundary conditions for the emergence of identity, but do not necessarily specify in any continuous and structured manner, the nature of one's identity. They "project being into" their infants; "demand"—as it were—the conscientious/conscience of any other within particular contextual sense of being: e.g., not being a great danger or threat to self or to significant others. Stay away from the fire! Do not bite your mother!

With the development of Attachment Theory—ideas from G.H. Mead of "Symbolic Interactionism"—it has become clear that the m/other-infant relationship: the infant "joins with/becomes" its m/other and "emerges" from this relationship to become its "self," eventually. (Mead: 1934)

Beyond these contexts, however, the nature of identity has great "spaces," its limits often needing and getting continuous or particular or sporadic redefinition—particularly in those arenas which are interpreted as TLC: touch, smell, talking...

Sex and Being: This is what I got; what they gave me. Is this who I am?

They looked at me early on with sex and gender in their eyes, dressing me as a boy/girl, addressing me as girl/boy. How earnestly did they look in the eyes of the new-born - buggy and bassinette to see what sort I was? And I? How did I respond to them looking at me with gender in their looking's lenses? Did they judge me within a gendered frame? Didn't they always refer to me as she or he?

I *learnt* girl and boy pretty early on; learnt to tell myself, that is, what I am? I learnt early on to think of son and daughter, of being father or mother, brother or sister. I was shut out of women's/men's rooms after a few years. I was restricted in who I could touch where, what I got to smell, where.

Within reach of hands and fingers probing, feeling, feeling pretty good, better than most places, would change, often swell the boyish sort further out, unlayer the girl beneath the beneath. At some moment in time, sex solidified into gender and became a "who I am," further complicating the quest for who am I.

Who I Am-Not: The "I" who-am-not seems to be primarily comparative in origin and in its driving force. Am I not-time and not-space in the same senses in which I am not my spouse or my dog or my students or parents or friends or enemies? Am I not-lightening or a distant star in ways similar to how I am-not a chimpanzee or an octopus or a poltergeist, a Martian, or a weatherperson? Am I natural; in nature... not?

Yesterday I was the "me" that I am in this moment except that I am-not. Tomorrow, similarly, I will be; then, someday I will not-be. What power, what necessity to discover who I am that I am-not?

Is the issue of phenomenon—the reality of the existence of objects which I also am-not—the sense of the *residual* in terms of which I discover I am? What!—discover? What difference between knowing and discovering the "who I am" that I am-not? Isn't this issue of the constancy of being the "who I am" that I remain even as I am as in-change as the Heraclitean river, derived from the language of the particular and the universal—at once this one and in the same moment every one?

Do these vagaries of life's experiences for the infant to whom all is contrast (it seems) freeze into phenomena and persons much as the faces which they face back, become identities: m/others and others? Then, once I am, the others are, and I am, and a *circle of being*? If identity is circular, how does being increase, change, grow, freeze, problematize, adulterate?

If an infant's mother "goes away"—even for a few hours—and "returns," does the infant "know" that this is the "same" person? Does the infant know that she is the same? Constancy, duration, how do they become me while I still live in many senses as change?

How do chemicals become me? How do I become myself? Am I in some state of tension at the ready for myself becoming not-me?

Loss: Of limbs, of life, of youth's imagination of who I would be! How afraid in the depths of my being am I of, say, becoming blind or deaf—both of which conditions reside on the margins of my present being? What if I have an accident; become senile? Is this like whatever else I call fear within my being? an exaggeration, perhaps, or something of quite another kind? Are these sorts of loss similar to the "loss" of another person who is significant to me?

In the arena of the construction of being and identity, is the posing of this sort of question likened to the asking of questions about toxics and other limits to life—in the informing of being: the conditions of not-being used to define who I am? Does this help our understanding? Is it unavoidable, either methodologically or in the living of life? Is this about the issue of what one "needs" in order to truly be? Is this different from what one is, or defining of it?

That is, if it is the case that I need so much food to survive, or cannot tolerate some other condition, does this contribute to any positive understanding of who and what I am? If I am overdosed on carbon monoxide, or given the hemlock which began this entire tradition of questioning, what does this tell me about who I am?

Now it is certainly the case that I need to avoid or to expel those things and substances which might harm me—to take care not to expose myself to the killing wind-chills of deepest Minnesota winter or to the baking heat of the hot deserts of the world. In what senses does this not-doing—a positive kind of knowledge, in general—active in the construction of identity?

In my own person case, I have not been able to see out of my left eye since I was a small child, it having been destroyed by a thrown stone. And I have worn a prosthesis since that time, making me appear to be relatively alike in appearance to most other folks of my ilk; not different enough in general to be seen as damaged or "other." But it has made me especially self-aware or aware of self perhaps in ways that have led to the asking of the fundaments of identity.

Consider: that I *know* that I look different from how others see me (in my mirror, in my memory of a face with one eye gone, a socket of light rose flesh which does not look back; in my intellectual being which wonders what eyes have to do with being human and being me, and how are others with two eyes or with none?) Consider that I know that I am different, that I have lost an eye? What means the possible bitterness, the sense of what might have been?—actually I don't think I experience this sense of thwarted being very deeply. But others—those who lost an eye at a later, more grown-up moment in their lives—apparently do *mourn* such a loss. For me, personally, it has led me to muse on the nature of appearance, and how the interpretation and *looking-into me* has led me to look for in-sight.

In terms of the loss of others, is the mourning of the loss of a limb akin to the loss of a significant other? What, in me, has changed when someone I love, dies? What, in me, changes when a significant person no longer enters my life: accidentally or on-purpose? What sense of loss turns into treason when a spousal person or a loved sibling decides that a relationship is null and void. Where does that leave the other; the bereaved; me? What does mourning tell us about our own identity? How is it that others have entered us in ways that their disappearance causes us to have powerful feelings of loss?

It must be that the centrality of our being includes—or begins from—the inclusion of others into our very (physical) being! While the sense of loss—of their death—has a reality separate from our being, the fact is that we *feel* the loss, often powerfully. A friend reported, on the occasion of a spouse leaving, that she felt that she had a large, painful "hole" in her chest. Did "time" heal that hole? Was the hole she felt different from an actual lesion? What is the relationship between the hole and being whole?

How, that is, do we have or develop an inclusive sense of the entirely or wholeness of our being? Clearly it entails "taking-into" our being (physically), the fact of whatever "significance" of others means to us. The loss of a person who is important—one whom we have included in our sense of being who we are—is an aspect of our being. S/he is in our being, in our thinking at least potentially (as is obvious at the moment of loss).

What then is a loss? Is my eye more important in the constellation of my being who I am than my beloved? Will only loss tell? Tell what? Whom?

Drugs: Drugs alter one's being and sense of identity in various ways.

If we focus on the alteration, then practically any ingested stuff, any activity which we "use" or which occurs to us, is a drug: food, sex, power, a sense or loss of will, excretion as well as constipation; washing our bodies, shaving or cutting hair, picking a pimple—all of these are alterations. But we usually mean, by drugs, something broader or more specific.

The concept of "alteration" presumes already that one somehow "has" a *continuous* identity, but I think that one's sense of permanence is also an emergent phenomenon. Going to sleep, another day, are concepts which may have little continuity for an infant. One observes that the infant's m/other's face/presence is the link of being which *provides* ongoingness into the infant's experience.

So, alteration!

We have, find, want not to have, to have some of us approach the world as wondrous, transformative others do not?! (Kierkegaard's axis between those who approach the world through fear, the others through wonder.)

The world has settled down, I want to rile it/me *up*. Do drugs alter me, my perceptions, the world? What is it, how do I keep myself continuous: a sense of my self-image, carried forward, projected into the futurity of imagining me into each tomorrow?! Is this sense of continuity which I (have learnt to) carry in myself into my futurity, where drugs gain their power, their interest? Is my continuous 'self' complete? Boring? Exciting?—can I wait till tomorrow? Do I want today to be over? Am I bored to tears?

Coffeed to the point where my metabolism speeds at just the right momentum for me to write and live my day at twice the speed of...

Liquored to the point of soporification so I can sleep the sleep of sounding quiet...

...so I can taste the elixir of coffee, and live my life at a pace which I can barely keep up with.

Cigarettes I quit so many years ago, still reverberate in my being, wondering that I cannot stand the smell of its smoke with some temptation to breathe deeply the smoke of tobacco and feel whatever my body yearns for: a yearning!? An alteration, steadying the nerves of... what nerves? What am I reading about my body's feelings, feeling incomplete?—with what solution in my *feelings' mind*?

Hooked on drugs? Hooked on the image of my own being carried and projected forward into the future sufficiently that I live my life as risk-free as possible, or on the edges of existence challenging the cars as they cross my path and the ideas of time in which I want to play in these moments. Drugs, living on edges, wanting to dare the dark urges, titillate them a little, a lot... all the way to hither and yon and beyond the being which I know, perhaps to know much more, and to know all there is. (*They say* that for older folks a bit of wine each day is a really good idea, especially red wine!)

The Historical Me (from Jung to old-age): There is always the present temptation, especially when the I of who I am right now is less satisfying than the sets of I-images in my being tell me they might be, or should be, to look to history for explanation or for clues of how to *undo* the self I think I am.

The most prevalent stories—from South Asia and from the Western quest for directedness in life's passages— make some claim that I am in some trajectory from lesser to more. Where I began mostly in nature—likened to another creature whose spirit I am or once was—now I am further along, more progressed, with a sense of towardness: on the road to utopias, Nirvanas: a return in the West, an escape in the South of Asia. Some form of an end and endedness, an eschatology, a finishing is held out for us to aim: human potential, maturity, but not always wisdom which is more processual and passing than an endness.

The search, then, is not toward one's *Next Places* in the world of being, but back in history: back to another life; back to the traumas of infant's repressions and recessions; back because the present being of my being *un-satisfies* me. And rather than explore the senses in which my pictures of present being are not satisfied, I look for older-younger images which I will work at changing or explicating. Here, one hopes/believes that history so determines present being, that a change in one's putative history will somehow affect present being. "If only" turns into a possible doing, and being.

I suppose there are ways of doing this well or usefully. My wonderings have more to do with the costs which attention to these ideas of history take from critique of the present. Does present understanding yield to past misunderstandings? Does critique turn into blame: of one's parents (I have found that it has been useful to *forgive* my memories of their being in order to move on.); of the traumas I occurred even before I had the sense of being sensible about my own being—variation and theme on lost innocence.

Similarly my wonderings and skepticisms are less, I think, about the possibilities of exploring the who of who I am, and more concerned as spouse, parent, teacher, citizen about remaining critical and thoughtful in the here and now. If I yield to dreams or history or the vast variety of numerologies and mysticisms which appeal to several of my sensibilities, can I also remain critical in the present? I think that one cannot do both with any depth, and I seem to have made my commitment, at least for the nonce.

And, since most of these schemes of skewed development have implied for scholars and politicians of the mind's perorations, a sense of history—usually from some depiction of nature as other animals toward this utopic sense of what it might mean to be fully human (away from animals and bodily being toward soul/spirit and a visage of the transcendent deities). We find ourselves in this quest for the historical to be burdened with heavy luggage: racist in theory, usually racist in hard facts paralleling the histories we have sought to draw; and racist in the practice of comparing ourselves—the Brahmins—with the others, the *'they*'s of the world, the untouchables and the would-be, should-be slaves to our fantasies of wanting to be (practically) perfect!

Geometrizing Being: In his *Domestication of the Human Species,* Peter Wilson (1989) claims that humans first became the sort we see today—hierarchized, grubbing, thinking imaginatively about the spaces and places which occupying self-consciously notes—when we first established fixed domiciles. It is not *in* the human condition, per se; but something we came upon; a process of our ontology rather than a process of our primary developmental being.

This piece of speculative history *shows* us several things: 1) the fact that we carry already in our thinking about the human condition a variety of presumptions about being human, most or all of which may be mistaken—that is, that we are speculative thinkers, but of particular sorts; 2) the apparent fact that we are the only species who thinks, which has some Kantian sense in our heads which matches the external universe of our being, is likely not the case. We have learned in's and out's by living *as if* there exist particularities of space and place; 3) that boundedness and discontinuity are as real as anything else, setting up perhaps the paradox of the one and the many and of continuity vs. change (perhaps much of language origin finds itself in this experiencing and geometrizing).

Indeed we tend to operate in the world as if these places which our geometrizing of the world keeps on constructing are powerful. But they are as much metaphor as anything else: Eden, heaven, the kingdom, America ...hell.

Much of our identity is bound up with the construction of the places which attach us to them: we have effectively *lost* something—memory?—when certain places no longer exist or are destroyed much as the death of a significant other.

Much of life is given power and definition for religious thinkers who want to *return* to heaven, to nationalists who gain their identity by being of this or that land, or wish to return, say, to Israel. It is interesting, frightening, exciting to return to one's childhood home. What aspects of oneself are attached to the spaces of one's existence that the metaphors are often as real as anything else in our being at home in this life?

How does place give us meaning and create within us some sense of belonging or not? And, at least in contrast to the Amerindian sense that the earth is our Mother and that she cannot be parceled or valuated or sold or bought, how do we construct our thinking being to be able to abstract ourselves from the land to which we ever might think that we belong, and might return to?

God *Said*: *In the beginning, in the beginning...* we are so lulled into these words and thoughts as if they represent some reality that we follow by thinking that we are the creatures who primarily think... *was the word, the word*. And the deity was said to *say* that the world should be created: talk, not doing. And still we talk about being, and steer clear of being itself, herself. A *man's* story?

In the beginning we emerge from our mother's womb; from the vagina which wrapped about the penile punch some nine months before. That was some (sense of) beginning.

In the beginning, we became (I guess) human? Created as it says in the Old Testament story of Genesis; evolved from the long line of life and living creatures: continuous, yet discontinuous; we seem to want to focus fully upon the differences, the particularities...the word we think that God spoke which moved the powers which made the world for us humans in the image of, with dominion over it. Thus spake!

> I am who I call myself; whom others call me?
> If I was in the beginning, and always will be, who am I now?
> (How do I know?)

Transforming Knowledge: ...and if a man tells a woman's story? Is this the same as if/when she tells it?

It depends, I suppose. I used to try to imagine what it is like to be/have a vagina, to be able to/to have a baby, having lived through/*gone through* much of this experience with J. Much of the experience I can think, in my most imaginative construction, that I could (as the saying goes) *walk in her shoes*. But, I could not merely remove my genitals and formulate a vagina; and even though one can do this (have it done) surgically, is it vagina or a close approximation? Was/is it sufficient to say: this is who and what I am, in order to know the experience of another, a mother?

But who can tell anyone's story? Can I (even) tell my own? Certainly not in the detail which I experience it. Much of what I tell (and I seem to talk incessantly) has to do with others' theories of being, of experiences which are generalized and universalized to the stars. Some of it seems to be an invention (mine, J's?).

I think much of it depends, as well, as how men and women *construct* one another, one and the other: how much in the context of opposition, where the male constructs the female he would want her to be, then responds to her through the vision and lenses; or precisely not want her to be, and then responds. The gaze of the male defines the female who then has to react, defensively perhaps, in and to his terms if she seeks love and approval.

Certainly the way in which women tell woman's story is quite different from the way in which men have been telling it. Perhaps this is principally about power and equity; perhaps it is more directly experiential. How could a man tell the difference? (Natalie Angier: "Woman," 2000)

And where/how does one draw her boundaries. Women are part of men; mothers at the least. How have men constructed the idea of man that we do not love and lavish the women inside our experience? Are men so *powerful* that they need not; so incomplete that they cannot; so denying that they must not?

Can a man tell woman's story? Somewhat. Not really; not exactly. Can we find a couple who can tell both stories; or have couples moved their boundaries of being sufficiently so that male and female have moved to un(re)cognizable spaces and places?

On the other hand, it seems important almost always to continue in this quest for understanding others and oneself. Who is to be able to know where one's next visions and next places reside, and what notions of being and identity we have to surmount to continue to grow in our understanding? Or being older…

…or being Gay!

In at the Womb (from egg-zistence to embryology): The vast puzzles of being, might receive heightened awareness of the developmental aspects of our being if we take embryology more to the heart of the task. Two cells—an egg and a sperm on one level—two cells joining and sharing and beginning (perhaps) the process by which I am. No free fall from the space of heaven's home for the spirit of later imaginings: just two cells—not at all dull, but not all that *interesting*, either.

Growing, ingesting, taking in nutrients, expelling and extruding the wastes of development's excrements, the cells divide and multiply, fold in such interesting ways. Who one cell is, now become where that cell finds itself, the neighborhood, what everyone else is and does: being embryology sounds more and more like the culture of interaction's theories. The outside folds in: three layers depicted in three colors remember me of the course I took in embryology so many years ago; but fresh still in many ways, and striking in my amazement. Purely mechanical → increasingly mental, rational, I have always thought we heightened this directional idea of development and underestimated, even dis-esteemed the physicality of our being by mechanizing it.

We have left the theorist of our own development in the hands of some directorial homunculus whom we now think of as genes. They—that is, the genes, seem to have a life all of their own; but they are not available for consultation about being and identity. Shy? Conceptual slippage about the question-*why* and the retort-*because*?

It, my embryo, ma and pa (blush, Augustine!)...me. If those aspects of my developmental being remain in the conceptual background, has that fairly formally blinded us from noting that the body whose hands and fingers type out this stuff? And we remain in the either or of opposition and antinomy even as my type types; not remembering to remember why there are chairs in the world's places. Fingers...type...stuff.

A Patina of Identity (derived from the deity, mom, flag, sausage): There resides within being a deep temptation to splinter off edges of my being and let them fly like satellites about the nearest celestial body.

I virtually cry every time I look at the flag and imagine the wonderfulness of the state, thence of me. I am proud to be an American! I feel deeply about citizenship, about being a "good" citizen to some concept of a nation which I experience at some level. Similarly to the concept of being citizen to the world...

I love(d) my mother, and her apple pie (especially lemon meringue), her ability to spell well even when she didn't know what words meant, her angers and fits which were many and voluble, her analytic skills which went everywhere but never too deeply, and her involvement in being a historian to all the characters who had ever shown up in her life, keeping them afloat and updated each day even many years after they had died. One thousand miles from her was the necessary minimal distance at which I could live. May she rest in sufficient turmoil to maintain her own senses of being!

I love the sense of fullness of the fullness of my stomach having ingested a fully satisfying meal: of sausage as the ex-Soviets seem to say. More, I feel a sense of nervous incompleteness when I have fewer than 2 heads of garlic in my cupboard or the other spices of my life are running low. Then when I possess the garlic, then I am. And hot sauce, I am.

Am? Am what? Am I garlic, yet unprocessed, yet unsmelling? Do I constantly diminish myself in the context of 30 spices adding up to me? Can anyone be said to be living a life, to possess a real identity and being without coriander and vinegar, cumin and caraway? Nations go to battle over spices, as well as over gems and other minerals which oil the wheels of commerce. Do I go to pieces over minced garlic mincing about in the onions of life? Capsicam, therefore I am?

The Essential Self: a Residual Notion? Dig deep! Dig underneath the patina of my being. Look, look into the mirror of my mind's eyes reflecting and see Narcissus looking back at me wondering who I am. I am me; am I not? If not me; who then?

Am I an aspect of the deity whom I invent, who invents me, whom I trust to confirm me in order to confirm the god of my invention who tells me that I am?

Am I my parents' child? My spouse's husband? My dog's "master"? My children's father? My students' teacher? My colleagues' colleague? The *actual* composer of these writings? The inventor of the concept of myself? Myself?

Then who am I? Is there anything left over of the "me" who is principally defined by others telling me who and that I am? (And if they no longer tell me and confirm me; what then?)

The Necessity of Being a 'Who I Am': This truth-telling universalized Western attempt to seek the essential and continuing of being wants to take itself oh so seriously. Pure reason! I think, therefore I am! Bah and not a little of the humbug whose humbling and huddling grows out of the ashes of being. A humble hubris.

Yet I seem to want/need to find myself and keep that self intact and locatable and reliable. I need/want to trust myself. I want/need to know what I believe so I can at the least trust myself to remember who I am and what I said. Do I "mean" what I say? What I said?

The Moral Necessity of Being a 'Who I Am': I in the world with others, some of whom seem to "depend" on my being who I say I am saying that they are, and they are who I say they are. But if I think they depend on my saying, on my being, then do I deny that they are? Do I project into them my imaginings of who they are? What then, of them?

If I do not mean what I say, if I am not at all certain that I am, saying that they are, then am I not being moral with respect to their being?

Isn't being moral more truly to establish that I have trust in their being? (J.)

Intention: There is some "methodological" urge abroad in the land to find the *"me who is"* by attempting to locate the "I" who "intends." If I say this, I intend that it influence you, change you, effect you somehow... otherwise, I wouldn't have said it?

This move to locate being by/as intending is an attempt to understand the nature of communicating as if there are (already) two of us individuals cleanly and independently saying to one another what we "mean" to say. This seems to me a form of stimulus-response argument, an elaboration of a telegraphic metaphor of mutual understanding: I send, you receive. Thus we must both be...

The "information theory" which gave rise to this thinking did not necessitate the physical presence of both of us—sender and receiver—further rarifying or further purifying the problem, depending on how we come to the issue.

What this approach does tell us is that the problematic of how information gets from one person to another remains interesting. But it presumes much about the nature of personage and being which we need to begin to understand: residually, there must be sender and receiver whose (physical) primacy is guaranteed, i.e., "unquestionable," not capable of becoming problematic in our thinking about being.

Intentionality brings "back" into our awareness, on the other hand, some notion of the "will" of the Stoics and of the theorists of the 19th century whose "will and idea" terminated into the "will" to live and to power (Schopenhauer and Nietzsche). But it resonates, so far, within a captious presumption about the locus of being, being passive. At the least, it raises into our awareness, the fact that being and "doing" are coterminous in the human condition (and in law).

But, this is all recollectible within (political) theories of being in which the intention and power of the individual is to be gathered or subsumed into the state; in which the individual being has to be diminished or subjugated or educated to the greater good of the greatest number, rather than the contractual notion of the individual whose identity is discernable and in at least some areas of our being, "separable" from others.

When I think that I intend that you understand me: do I set all the terms for your understanding of "me"? Are we both located within many larger frameworks of understanding (e.g., spatial-temporal, in some particularity of relationship, etc.) in terms of which most our words are "about" the contexts rather than directed from or toward one another? Do I "seek" love or power or the mere filling of time or variations on these whose intention weakens itself even as it proceeds to play itself out?

Integrity: I think that some of the virtues, especially "honesty," are extremely difficult to pursue.

I think that the issue of "integrity" is central to the question of identity, of knowing about one's boundaries and central foci and directness, and of maintaining them in the context of many reasons and persuasions to alter them, thence one's sense of self.

In two areas of my life, particularly, this has been very clear. In violin play—"good amateur" play—it is the case that one easily becomes *pleased* with her/his level of performance, and calls "good" that which is pleasing. One apparently adapts at some "plateau" of competence and calls that "who she/he is." What I can do well-enough, I (have) gradually have come to call "good."

The other place where I have become particularly aware of the issues of integrity associated with an "honest" reading of myself is in my teaching. At some point, I "woke up" to discover that my teaching had become largely "memorized"; that I was not consciously engaged in my teaching, but was pandering to an audience out of my desire to please them; whose pleasing would then please myself. I was becoming a good (I think) "low-paid monologist." (Now having produced a book on teaching in which I drew a quite-fine Teacher, I feel the necessity to work harder at my own teaching, Sarles, 2013)

I wonder in how many other arenas of life one settles-in to some self-conception of honesty which is more actually akin to one's prevailing practices and adjustments? How can one be "careful" and live "carefully" with respect to issues of honesty and integrity?

But integrity is also concerned with the boundaries of being whole and complete; of not being destroyed or of being a destroyer of oneself. And yet one changes, perhaps grows, moving toward some "next place" in life. How is one then, with respect to her/his integrity?

Can I be me and still move on? Can I not move on?

If, as in the asymmetry of teaching, others regard me as complete and integral and essentially non-changing, how then do I regard myself? Can I confirm/disconfirm what they think, and still remain loyal and honest and integral to myself? How can I be simultaneously of two minds, without forgetting who I am? And just who defines and sustains who I am?

Equally, if others see me as changing, or want me to change, do I find myself resisting that felt wish, and saying like a deity: "I am who I am"?

If, like Kierkegaard (1854), I see the joining of a church as being a disciple, the giving away of myself to some external, largely political structure, do I seek to live my life like Christ (is said to have) lived his?

Or like Nietzsche in his "destruct" mode against the power of Western thought upon our self-definitions, to transcend ourselves; or like the Catholic nuns and priests who deny themselves (their senses, feelings) to live more fully; or the variety of ways to enter into and enhance bodily experience (yoga, Zen, martial arts, Alexander Technique, Feldenkrais) even as we attempt to enter "fully" into each moment; or by being a musician—even, for me, occasionally, when the music plays itself over and over and over in my head's "hearing"—then who am I?

What are the boundaries and edges of my being? Who am I really? A structured me? A process me? A path and trajectory who is not anyone else? I am only a "difference?" A role? An actor upon the stage of a theatre in whose plays the scripts ran out of good lines some time ago?

Near the beginning of Jasper's *Nietzsche* (1935) in which N. is said to have said that even the most evil of us have to tell ourselves stories which allow us to sleep the good sleep each night.

Culture: Bypassing the dynamics and processual aspects of being, we are apt to search out some mechanisms which seem to grant us a particular form or nature. Culture, language, society, family are often claimed to determine who we are. We are, for example, Catholic, Protestant, Jew, or Muslim if we are brought up in a family which is.

If we revolt against that identity, it is not that we are not Catholics, but that we are ex- or once were or failed at whatever our family "raised" us to be. Overwhelmingly our identity is taken to be attached to the orientation or identity of our families.

This is often extended to local or national or historical or "racial-cultural" identities where we are who we are perceived to be and/or with whom we "identify"—we often have no "choice." At certain moments in life, at particular moments in "history," the necessity to be some "thing," some cultural or religious member or participant seems overwhelming. At other moments, the issue is moot, or there is no issue. Like gender, personage and being often is the crucial issue. But in other moments (or in particular cultures or traditions) the identity which is less individual and more external, is the one who we think we must be. Or others think this is who we are and must be: we become the *other* that they demand we are.

In such moments, in the context of the externalization of identity, the quest for who I am is often submerged, virtually to the point of disappearance. As with, say, menopause, the person who is the woman is no longer threatening-threatened and may gradually discover herself once again. Being a Jew in the midst of a holocaust translates only roughly into being a Jew in other moments, or into being a cultural Jew or an ex-Jew or into not-being a Jew in myriad ways.

The issue of who I am in contexts of culture, tends to weaken and disappear under the virtual weight of extrinsic perception and definition. It is not that I do not occupy myself with issues of who I am in particular during those moments, but that they diminish with respect to issues like "who I must be," and "who I am said to be," or "who I wish I were-not."

Love and Friendship: The conundrum of "love" so complicates the issue of identity that one can barely recover the sense of the problematic of being from its voraciousness. The notion of love is—in some respects—contrary to the very concept of personage and being: one yields aspects of self to someone (or something) other than oneself. This is said to be a "romantic" idea, the "falling" in love; the imagination that the object of our love has overtaken concern with the self.

Love implies that none of us is sufficient (ever?) to oneself. We yield ideas of integrity and wholeness to the sense that we are incomplete. Rather than the (e.g., South Asian) notion of a "contract" with some other being, we Americans seem to want to "fall in love" with a person. Here the quandary of what is identity reaches for the question of whether one's being is located within oneself, or located directly in the being of another, or in some relationship(s).

If we locate being within the physical person who is (also) myself, then the question of "being in love" is clearly a diminishing. Whether one lets loose of part of oneself, whether something which was oneself is now "yielded," one becomes less than.

This notion presumes that one was in most senses a complete—an unchanging being before she/he "fell" in love. But, in a world construed as always in some flux, the idea of being in love, might be as aspect of a growing sense of oneself. The question of identity then alters from the location of being and identity strictly within the confines of the (physical) individual, suggesting that identity is an ongoing incompleteness, or that identity actually is more complex than the usual treatment of it has implied and entailed.

In construing the problematic of love principally within the notion of being in-love or of "falling" in love, the problem is also skewed (as in most American ballads) within the romantic idea that one is never possibly "complete" except when one is involved and invested in a (usually) sexual relationship with a partner/spouse in some sense of marriage beyond the contractual nature of sharing goods, children → some notion of "family."

Once one moves beyond the idea of love as (purely) romantic, the question of the "Eros" of Plato (*Symposium*), of the love of companions and companionship, of wanting to be "with" someone often, occasionally, to enter into some communion/commonality with them, to eat/break bread together, to have a party, celebration; towards community.

Wrestling with Irony: In a recent report, it was told that a local high school girl (12-14 years old) was wrestling capably with the boys. In the midst of some hue and cry about the morality of this, it dawned with a shining sun moment on the crowd of would-have-been moralists, that boys wrestling boys must also be sexual.

Memory/Forgetting: Am I what/who I remember? If I remember everything that has ever happened to me, wouldn't the clutter so fill my being that there would be no space for the present, for the new? How is it that I remember some of the 1930's, '40's, '50's, '60's, '70's, '80's, and the 1990's and...

Some of older (condo) neighbors seem to dwell increasingly within (on) the past? A few seem to have "fallen in love" with the past, using the (putative) present only to think upon how wonderful was the past: parents, small children... eventful. Then, they are diagnosed as senile or with Alzheimer's, and their sense of the present does seem slimmer than many of ours. But their inner sense of being and identity seem possibly clearer than ever: just not very *interested* in the present?

As noted by C. Darwin in his notebooks on "Mind, Memory...", older folks often are able to (and interested in) recall events which seemed otherwise to disappear through their earlier lives: as if the clutter of some present experience covered over certain aspects or detail of memory.

Living in southern Mexico for two years, where many persons were not literate, one was impressed (*amazed*, more like) by the vast detail of the memory of the non-literates. Without books, without the possibility of any records which are not within one thoughtful grasp, one has to know/remember *everything*—or it effectively did not ever exist. With writing, with literacy, one "trusts" to records, to encyclopedias, to the references of one's life (including other persons), the details and facts of one's life experiences. Does this require effective modes of forgetting?

When I play/perform music, I need to have at my disposal several "modes" of thinking about my playing. Especially, I need to immediately "drop" or forget what I have played, and both to remain in the present of the performance and to be looking a little ahead (but not too far!). Just who is the "I" who is performing? Who conducts, directs, forgets, remembers to remember where I am at this moment, dropping it, not getting panicked in each present by an error in the just past, or worrying about an especially difficult passage to come? I do, in this form, however, perform a text, which has a beginning, middle, an end. I have "studied" it at length, and "know" it well. "Know?" I can locate myself at any moment within the text, etc. And performing with others? Who am I, exactly, that I blend with another, with several, trying to play well for myself, for them, for a good performance?

My teaching as dialogue (2013) is an improvisatory art. Some ideas are outlined, students are apprised of the general topic, of an issue in some potential dispute. Then I ask a question, challenge some idea, and play off the responses—others' retorts to those. Watching how other students react or do not, I may ask another question or argue a point. The form is "made-up" largely as it goes, rather than being very specifically pre-planned. How do I remember what I am up to; find gathering notions, sum up... all in the "heat" of a discussion which has no very discernable structure?

Is it, indeed, "structure" which provides a sense of memory like the narrative of the novel which dramatizes the world and gives it some particular sense of direction, of eventfulness, of happenings which I then give meaning as it reposes in my memory?

Has, for example, the art of reading and writing led us to this form, which now in the land of television-media and the virtual presence of the bodily image is rendered less important? Doesn't the presence of the bodily image itself carry memory? How? Has the overwhelming use of the lecture form in teaching derived from the print medium, but is no longer necessary and is the less convincing? What is the relationship between memory and what is convincing?

A picture worth a thousand words? An unforgettable character?

How Many am I? Father, son, husband, teacher, student, neighbor, citizen... all of these and more am I. How can I be all of these and remain particularly and especially myself?

Most of the works on being and identity seem to strongly presume that the "I" of my being who I am is at once a centrality to my existence and quite particularly alone in the world. (Shades of Aristotle defining the psyche as being that portion of being which the breath of life is!) I am isolated; I am at war with myself—all of this presuming that the otherness of being who I am with respect to is less essential to my being than my work particularly at exploring who I am alone.

But I am not *really* alone. Rather I am in a variety of discourses—some with myself, admittedly; others with a spouse of many years whose boundaries in our being are at many points in some dispute and obscurity which seem dynamic and less fixed than the sense of being secure in my actual being who I am. Here, the integrity of being is apparently secured within the relationship: sometimes stationary, more times moving—consistent in relationship to children.

Denial: Denial already presumes that there is more than one of me; that my identity is manifold such that there is a sense of my identity which can deny aspects of itself while still functioning and able to say *I am who I am.*

Certain aspects of being become backgrounded, placed into arenas of being which are no longer "in awareness"; once central, now more firmly who one is. Example: The mouth which was once quite central in our being infants - as large as large can be, I suppose (but cannot "remember" except I note how its awareness grows when I chip a tooth or have a seed stuck between two teeth)—now that the most complicated art and muscular practices of speaking are "second nature," they are not much in my awareness. Like any other function which we do at the level of balletic complicatedness, they now appear unproblematic, then apparently "simple." But they are not simple... We are adept!

Within the complicatedness of being we have rehearsed, performed, and memorized (as it were) many dramas of life; many of which are remembered in some detail, but many of which are placed in that area of being which is not any longer on any surface we find regularly; or are in places which we can no longer seem to locate. The "who I am" now has no particular interest/access to such places, and, it seems, that many of them are unavailable and inconsistent with who I say I am, now. I can literally deny that is how I am, even though some "trace" of my being may still linger like faint perfume in my being; to arise, perhaps, when "I" least expect or least desire, or at least say that I do... or I don't.

All the trails and trajectories of thoughts and desires which have pulsed the fasciae of my body—awake, asleep—all them are "there" somewhere. In my necessity and zeal to tell myself who I am, some of these I do not permit, do not allow, do not admit to the my selves of present being.

No! Old thoughts, habits, would-have-beens; the vengeances of little-boy hurts and the wounds of bigger-boy slurs, the frailties of my being which I cannot and would not admit... these lurk no doubt in being even as I tell myself they do not, and would not.

Hope, Transcendence, and Progress: Who will I be? How will I be? How do I will myself to be?

The idea of a God was constructed to place one into orbit beyond the ordinary of each today: one "solution" to questions of hope and transcendence is to critique the *idea of the ordinary*. Life is itself transcendent: we must come to be able to note this—to see our seeing—even in our oft seeming quest to *stop* the world.

The idea of futurity: some "guarantee" of the future, is planted into us by our parents who "see" us *forward into the future*, becoming much like them, heirs to their knowing and being. This works in our lives for a while, at least until we are able to survive (as it were) on our own. At such a point, we need to recast the idea of futurity, for others, but especially for oneself.

Teachers can also "guarantee" futurity. Like earlier parenting, this requires authority granted to the teacher: varieties of the yielding of the self to another, who will point toward the substance of the teachings; knowing then defines the direction of the future.

Transcendence entails thinking about one's *next places* in the world with some meditation, some sense of purposefulness and the possibility of growth rather than any mere management or hanging on. The "loss" of hope, like entering into Dante's *Inferno*, involves the yielding to issues of death; issues, that is, constructed from some particularities and traditions and stories and questions of "why" am I here, subtlety replacing the drama and inner dialectic of why I *am* here.

Progress is the most subtle of all the tempters, deriving from the experience of youth growing-up to the images and suitings of being the adult which the former adults had "read into" one, then having to construct oneself within an effective stasis of being. The existential problematic has much to do with how to balance and use the change which is (always) occurring, and grant it some sense of towardness; some continuing vision which is from life. Like pain (after a certain age), the issue of death can become an enemy, rather than a partner within one's being. How to use this idea to further inform living, is life's problematic; and progress is a word which elaborates it.

The Actor: "Striving for the widest variety of identities, he [Laurence Olivier] had run the risk of being no one and consequently often felt he had failed to locate the contours of his own adult character...I don't like myself." (D. Spoto, 2001)

Actors often wonder, as they assume one personality after another, just which might be their own; library shelves groan under the weight of theatrical autobiographies redolent of self-doubt, of performers confused about their identities. Having devoted a life-time to the convincing assumption of different manly personae, Olivier had become a man ever more remote even from himself. His emotional history reveals a pattern of timidity, insecurity and withdrawal that he constantly sought to overcome onstage; it is sentimental to expect him, because he is an outstanding actor, to be a man of great feeling and emotional depth. Not many actors are. An actor's life involves maintaining continuous emotional openness in the face of rejection, a warp to the strongest temperament.

Remembrances of the prohibitions of "graven or false images" in the Ten Commandments, one wonders if the question wasn't particularly about being oneself; that if one attempts to "act" out the being of any other, of taking on the notion that one stands outside of oneself, that if theatre overtakes life itself, then being is weakened, cheapened, and one no longer can know (or like) her/himself. One either has no identity in particular, or one cannot remember with any surety, who s/he is. Or one does not continually seek her/his own being, a task which is life-long, and ongoing.

But the temptation to "live outside" ourselves is always present, available, even urgent for reasons which are at once personal, political, and whatever is called theological. Internal to our own being, we are filled with "desires" and "impulses" which from time-to-time are raised to political and economic theories to justify our acting upon them. Theoreticians of utopias from Plato to Skinner have sought ways to temper or control them, or to wait for public service until we are "past them" after some age: whatever is 50 and "golden."

In fact, we live with others' (bodies), and are creatures who respond to their faces (particularly), and are at least in part derived or emergent from others' expressions responding to ours. Who I am is not exclusively derived from some self-dialogue or depiction floating in my originary being from prior lives or ancient archeons located in the belly-buttons of being. One is in continuous interaction with others, with one's "traces" of parents and friends and the teachers of our youth with whom we spent much time, and with I thought I was, and would be, and who others thought I should or should not be. And I am in some continuous inner dialogue with who I will be next: derived from some earlier vision of self which I still practice, or look for some continuous or transformative experiences. (→ *Next Places*)

The sense of growth and movement which characterized our early lives—before we thought about thinking about—does not necessarily "want" to halt its being in our own. Maturity is not a state of stasis. Development is not just for children. But in times and societies where adulthood is constructed as a status, where the responsibility for one's being is burdensome and without any possibility for growth or change, one seems to "buy" a sense of the bureaucratized self as if it were life's cloak; as if the "grim reaper" of actual death visits us early disguised as a clothing salesperson, and we are tempted to become the clothing which seems to fit us.

As parent, as friend, as teacher, and all the other characters I am, I also "play" just as if I were an actor in my own life. It is not that I live as a permanent, continuous, and identifiable self: an identity, a sense of being which was granted me, and I need only "find" it, discover it, as a destiny which will stand up to be worn, once and for all. Even in those societies in which the roles for everyone seem like "givens" for all persons in all of time, they need to be studied, forced and reinforced, and each person needs to be treated as if they are who they will become; as they are willed to become.

Unlike Laurence Olivier, unlike those who are paid to enter the cast of characters who appear on those platforms which we all agree are the illusions of life - the stages of being—the rest of us enter into outlines and drawings of characters who we will truly call "ourselves." The actor in us brings home, rejects, tries on, and enhances the roles one plays in one's own life. As being, as identity is in part an act derived from various places in the being of beings, then one's own being involves an ongoing search for the wonder of oneself.

Will: The will to live, the will to power, the will to will... Camus (1942) said that the only real problem in life is whether to suicide (*Myth of Sisyphus*).

Can a one-year old "commit" suicide?

Caught in some epic 18th century battle between rationality and the emotions (say, between Locke vs. Rousseau, Leibniz, and Kant's cant), the question of will seems now like an archaism best left to the Stoics whose Libertarian offshoots have cheapened being by confining life to each of us: as if we are solitary individuals wandering in that primeval forest of the one-on-one; where competition is all of being. Can one truly be "self-reliant?" (Can one not-be?)

Perhaps we are caught in the English language in some deep confusion between the "will" of self-will, the "will" of futurity, and a variety of plays upon whether I do what I have said I would; some border between the contingency of "would" and the morality of "should." There is also some lingering sense of the possibility that we would be monarchs of the world, that I "will" this, I "will" that to happen... and it does or it does not.

And there is some magic, some mystical ideas deriving from the pouting of childhood where "no" often meant that parents did not want you to, now at war with the arenas of freedom: the necessity and responsibility of saying "no" to oneself... if and when it is "appropriate."

I am caught a bit as well in the zone between what I can assert and actually make happen much involves me, me: typing this word, eating, drinking, sleeping; and the loci in which I have no power, or almost none, and can find some if I can and will!

I will the world to be better place!

I will help make the world be a better place!

...but God's "will be done"—an abdication, or another way to will, or a passive release and acceptance; is there a diminution of self in the light of this?

In the context of *Teaching as Dialogue* (Sarles, 2013), the issue of will arises in such interesting ways. In teaching, there is already an "asymmetry" between Teacher and students; an asymmetry of power in which the Teacher can will the students to empower themselves; and can with some skill work at this. And the students can, and some of them will overtake their Teacher. This I will!

The borders between "will" and "cannot" are tender, often excruciating. Perhaps the ultimate issue of being resides here: active/passive, redoing the world/myself.

Like Epictetus—there is a method: redo my own conception of the world to fit the picture of myself which can survive whatever happens (I can only "allow" or "permit" myself to be defined!). Then one has the power of self-identity to do whatever s/he can to redefine the world; literally to "will" it to be what I will.

The problem—as with Ayn Rand's "Libertarians" (Tea Party)—is that there are other persons in the world; and we are (already) interconnected with them in various manners; and our interconnections may/should increase. I cannot do all I can merely if I do not hurt or interfere with others. My mere being "interferes" with the being of others. Why should parents raise their young?—ask the socio-biologists—unless they "gain" something in return? The only "gain" is in enhancing their own human experience, not—as the socio-biologists claim—in passing their genes on to next generations, following Aristotle, who thought that generation and the preservation of the human "race" is what we exist for.

Will creates its own senses of the purposes of being; and these often need updating in the course of any/everyone's life experiences.

Embryology: The egg and sperm—each half-alive and half-a-life in the potential *wouldness* of Aristotelian purpose—meet in the warmth and darkness of life's wombs. They grow and divide, divide and grow, and multiply into the shapes of future being. Persons? Shapes, undoubtedly.

Enlarging, multiplying, the shape becomes a spheroid-blastula, which then invaginates, turning into itself on one side. The in-turned will become the guts of life's processings. The outside remains the structure of our being what we are—skin, skeleton; the stuff which frames the other stuff of our being: the architecture of being human.

Now we are an inside, a place which will "pass-through" the externalities of air and water and subsistence, the foods of our continuing being. In the places between form the "middle-stuff," the mesoderm of muscles and blood; the heart of the matter.

The heart of the matter is that this growing, living thing is not only enclosed in its "m/other," but it is in various forms of interaction with the living (already) being which houses it. The question of the activity, the passivity of the mother is at issue here. Is this a passive nesting place, a locus for the exchange of tissues and food merely? Or is it a more active locus where the being and identity of the mother is blended somehow with the embryo—an embryonic being? Already a social being?!

What are the paths between the joining of genic "material" and the development of being? Is the splinter between the material biology of a new being and the still imagined being of an actual person so complete that we do not ask how they are one as each of us? Is the biology of being, pure structure; even as the persona of being is a fictive generation of that structure?

Is the biology only a limit on our being, even as who we are determines our life experience? The gap between these two ways of thinking about being remains a yawning abyss, even as the competitors of theology and philosophy battle over the turf of definitions: biology comes first, thus has primacy; or, being is all in the rational which we become; or neurology will fully explain our being; or, we are fully self-determining; or, after age of 50 or so, who cares?

I remember my first course in embryology, all described in three (primary) colors: blue (ectoderm), yellow (endoderm), and red (mesoderm), and have wondered at the intellectual gap between those in the curing arts who think of almost everything (diseases, etc.) as composed and analyzable in terms of three—as passing-by the oppositional philosophers who everywhere see in two's. This is, perhaps, why I try to think in terms, of two and three, but also in five's, and about 20, and lots, and too many to count.

When, how does any "cell" have heart, act like a liver, course in the veins of life's dynamics? Is being any different: made-from, but not made-of?

When does potential become…?

Parenting: Who am I that I am someone's father or mother? The fact of an infant's being who s/he is 24 hours every day; that, as infant, s/he is quite completely dependent on me/us, is breath-taking in its actuality.

I say us, because though I may be mother or father, others are involved and invested in this infant's being, and continuing to be. Sometimes they, too, are present. But at other times I am alone the parent of this creature who also possesses being in essentially the same ways in which I think that I do.

Who am I: Exactly/Particularly/Precisely? Is this question sensible: sometimes, always, to everyone?

Is my identity a given, a quest, a both am and a-changing?

Do I have purpose; destiny; past, present, and futurity? Can I not?

(Do I have a history before I have memory of my history?)

Where/what exactly is my extent? My being interpenetrates the being of various others (whose being interpenetrates that which I call my own): do I gain extent as others; lose as they forget me, as they die?

Wisdom: Beyond the skills of living, having gained the knowledges which are available in knowing, I think it more a pursuit than any state of being.

Unless wisdom is pursued actively as a search, a quest, then its possibility fades and blurs into the not's of existence, of which there are many; even now they increase::Wisdom cannot be pursued actively, it is an outgrowth of being and living just beyond sufficiency. (A parable or a paradox?)

Marriage and a Marriage: On the sufficiency of sufficiency: if one is somehow "complete" unto s/himself, then there is no possibility of marriage. If one is not sufficiently *some-one*, then one cannot enter fully into a marriage.

Marriage is in a way the living-out of the problem (paradox) of change and permanence. It is a contract which is made for the life of the participants; it is an ongoing relationship in which the participants—and the relationship—are in continuous flux. As it involves children, the relationships are continuous (mother/father); as it involves children, the relationships are in flux.

How many is/are a marriage: you, I, and the relationship; the history of you and I before marriage; the history of you and I becoming married; the history of the marriage; the present of you and of me; the notion of the futurity; the relationship of the relationship with respect to each child; to the children, each one; to the children's relationships with the marriage; with you, and with me. (Pity poor Kierkegaard who could not deal with the possibility of his incompleteness! Pity the idea of a deity who could not!)

Updating and living (mostly) in the ongoing present. Does the power of the history permit us to look at ourselves and bring us into each day, together? Or do we move along propelled by the stories in whose terms we calculate the relationship... only to awaken one day to find that this history has little remaining meaning?

Marriage is a most subtle form of relating; details of one another's facial expression are memorized in such exquisite detail that the vast changes of aging visages are rarely noticed, but incorporated within the memorized ongoingness. Similarly outlook, vision, habits, annoyances are incorporated into well-honed adjustments as the time of relating paradoxically packs nuances of expression into the history which is increasingly well-rehearsed and the performance of each day applauded.

A conversation: when all else (sex, food, sleep) is *handled*, the essence of any marriage is a conversation; a long conversation, a theater of performance in which each of the partners is both player and audience. Like the identity of any person, a marriage can relish the boundaries and edges of being comic and tragic, or pack all of being into the middle ground of not much new—at least to any observer.

A long-term marriage becomes very fast, very subtle. Its dynamics and details are not available to anyone outside the relationship: even its children (at certain levels, perhaps especially to its children); and grandchildren. So much history; too many habits.

It is perhaps most obvious in a marriage, that the partners have imbibed each other's being to a powerful degree. It is not very clear—perhaps most/least of all to the participants/partners, how much each lives within the construction of the other; within their construction *by the other*.

Can't live with 'em; can't live without 'em...the history of the marriage has overwhelmed present being, for at least one of the partners.

In love: a romantic fable; an ongoing necessity? In love with one's vision of the other; of their vision of themselves? In love with the romance of the original romance (revisionings even at home)? Looking for: good feelings, a sense of deep understanding? A wish for more, always more? A looking-out for the spirit of the other looking out for yours: no one on earth like her/him?

An appreciation: for the sharing of home, children, for a place of safe-haven and the safe-guarding of the soft-spots and sillynesses of one another; for the incessancy of demands that we both remain in the present.

Bad habits...

Lying: One of those attributes claimed for humans alone *because* only humans have propositional language, and lying presumes positive propositions. This is probably a lie! Does lying presume a prior truth; the possibility that there is some (obvious) order of truth? What does lying have to do with being and identity?

If I can lie to others, this implies that there exists some concept of truth, particularly of my knowing that there is truth, and that any statement is not true. What then does identity have to do with knowing and telling the truth?

A great deal!

Much has to do with one's sense of steadiness and consistency in the world: not only who I am, but who I am with respect to other persons, places, the artifacts of which one knows and applies, the uses to which things are put, the places which one knows, and the spaces between oneself and others. As one can play with gravity, with one's bodily parts, altering the aspects of relationships, testing the boundaries which others hold to one, truth gathers itself. And lying constructs its possibilities.

To be someone other, to grow up, to live within some older and ancient vision of being, to not be "loyal to oneself"; all of these are able to be lies about the focused locus of one's being. The problem in stating who I am—especially in lying about it—is that others and myself must have already a consistent if not clear vision of what and who I am. Thus lying about identity contains within it, at least at times, the impossibility of moving on in the world.

If I "pass" as someone I am not, then who am I really? And to whom do I lie? To them? But what of me?

Lying seems to presume, then, that I am very sure of my identity; or that I am fishing about in the world trying on the clothing of becoming who I would be, if I would be.

The Uniqueness of Being… Human: So steeped in Western thinking that Plato created, that we seem only to elaborate certain possibilities of our being within his framework of not-being other. I am not exactly who I am, but who and what other (species) are-not.

Much of the definition, the space of being is thus framed by whatever we claim are the features and aspects of (other) animals by which we contrast our own being. And the very study of being and identity is also thus restricted and captivated; in this contextual history, by the claim that others do not possess the mentality to think, to act rationally, to be capable of seeing the formal and ideational structures which define the truth of truth. They are—we have claimed—without sociality, without morality, without the sense to come in out of the rain.

Thus the question of identity has been bounded and framed by the architectonic of being-not or not-being like others. Less is it framed by the noticing of what and who we are actually: bodies in the universe of other's bodies; always changing without falling over the edges of any universes; fragile but not always frail. See *Body Journals*)

Homo Faber: (Arendt 1968) The idea is that we are what we do. Only (the human uniqueness story goes) humans have opposable thumbs, only humans know and create objects (are *objective*), thus we are what we do and make. Arendt distinguishes between work and labor, labor being more animal-like because instantaneous and ongoing (without duration like other species, historically), and work being making those objects which endure for long periods of time—particularly beyond the life of any individual, granting reality to history, etc.: architecture, furniture, moving toward the technologies of today.

We evolved into humans via labor, asserted Engels (Harman 1964): so labor is not only an identity marker, but it is also a motive for history; even a driving force; progressive, one presumes, and with a towardness which is invested in the definition of the human condition.

Before the notion of the market and the industrial revolution, the idea that each of us would live and do as our forebears: a kind of heredity of being-as-vocation, destroyed in the 18th century. Now, what? A conflation of who I am and what I do.

What am I to do? Do, be? Be, do? (Doobeedoobeedoo!)

Essentialism and Existentialism: The question of identity impaled on the horns of an ancient Western dilemma with being, particularly with being and knowing. How, asked Plato, could I know, and know what you know, that you know, and all that? How could I be anything of interest, of endurance: identity thrust within some Heraclitean puzzle of that old man river? Will I durst place my little toe in the river which both is and isn't, to see if... If what?

My dear; my soul; myself!

If I am not already, the essentialists argue; placing us in juxtaposition with the forms and ideas of all that is out of time: the circle of the circle, the triangle of the triangle, even the essence of the bed upon which I was (actually) made, which obviously precedes one's existence (*Republic*: Book X). Existence, a mere copy of the essence even of myself. My soul!

The problem of identity and being, reduced to the problem of change and non-change, some philosophical issue hung up on the problem of knowing how we know?

Yang and Yin: An Asian notion that we are paradoxical and complementary and living aspects of more than one: two, too...? Full of yang, we begin life, gradually taking on more yin, becoming less yang, or developing some harmony; *in* some harmony.

This idea at some odds, a war when cast within a Western dualistic mentality where two seems to have to mean that one must oppose the other.

The difficulty is that the battle has some tendency to destroy the entire category: no more yang, nor ying... nor being, much less identity.

In Hegelian terms, the opposition occurs as dialectic, having to *go* somewhere; even, one supposes, when there is nowhere to go.

In Norwegian droll: ying-gle, ying-gle! Yang-gle?

Loyalty: The existential problem of loyalty has to do with remaining alive in one's version of the *present age*. Whether loyalty is to someone, a group, even some previous picture of oneself, the issue of abandoning one's thinking being in each moment, centralizes and focuses the issue of being and being loyal.

Does loyalty mean remaining consistent to some idea or person which/who is outside of one's being; of being consistent to some sense of purpose or ways of organizing being or thoughts of being and/or the world?

And if not? If one is not loyal, does this mean that any center of being is floating like waves in front of a fickle tropical storm?

The Schlemiel, Schlamozzel; the Tzaddik...: With apologies to all and to none, the mixing of the jerks and scions and best persons of all of being, this Jewish sorting of characters in the world indicates that many people/groups do *characterize* the world. Probably most of us do!

How I would love to be the thoughtful, the wise and blessed tzaddik, but worry that I am even now acting the part of the schlemiel, writing this heavy heady stuff which may end up sounding like so much...trash. Oy veh!

So...what identity? Some accident of my anatomy, overfeeding from a mother who wanted me to have at least 40 pounds avoirdupois in excess of... god forbid I should get sick, and could lose the 40 before anything serious would... a schlub, I think I was and see myself still as with fat so overhanging feet that I cannot see them. But then, the feet cannot see me either, so...

Some accident, I became one day the class clown, the over-serious never-serious, the one who, the one which... some accident of fate that on the very day... I became the character whom they all remembered... and from which there seemed to be very little escape. No me left! Instead, I found myself (I think a she-friend once said in annoyance) *up my ass*; up my own ass; and I couldn't even see myself seeing myself. Not their idea of who I am; fighting their idea; locked forever at about age 12…

What's a guy/gal to do? Seen within a limited universe of characters, I had to become one of them. How should I become someone I wanted to become, and not the one that became the me frozen into a time beyond which it never seemed to fit me; to fit any picture of me I could find within… and so I seemed to be at some war between who they said I must be, and a who I couldn't yet delineate; and for whom I search, still. Am I locked within that ancient-seeming universe of schlemiel and schlemozzle, a being within only from without?

Identity Crises: I cannot fathom whether this issue of identity arises within other cultural constructs, but in the American doing of the Western tradition, the question of who I am seems often to occasion a crisis. Perhaps because I was told that I was to be someone, that the one which I thought I was no longer seemed to fit me; even to belong to me, or I to it.

Other cultures have, perhaps, handled the moments of changing identity by ritualizing them, or by not concentrating on one or another aspect of my disposition.

Intuition: *Better some things you shouldn't know*, my mother used to say as I occasionally seemed, to her at least, to ask questions verging on some forbidden areas surrounding which she had erected barriers.

Intuition often seems to reside within these arenas considered by some to be sacred or sacrosanct, forbidden or frightening, and beyond any creed *to live and let live*.

Whether I was seen by her as a super-sensitive because of the loss of an eye or some other sense of my being damaged which impinged on her own life's boundednesses, or I was just wreaking some small measure of petulance of the do-gooder's teenage angers at the status quo, or I really was treading on dangerous grounds, I am not at all sure. But I think I really trusted my intuition, at least until I came to be educated to what intuition might mean.

Maybe it is my dealing with fate and personal destiny within a life which seems fully bounded by what it is, and the problem of figuring out how to live it well—and living it (am I caught in the inability to grapple with some distinction between being abstract and being an abstraction?). But it is true that I was asking all the kinds of contextual questions which I can stuff into the arena called intuition. And when I was more ignorant, all of this seemed like a good idea.

Trust me!—Do I really trust myself? Swaying somewhat uncertainly on such an axis where inebriation meets intellection, I find solace in walking the tightrope of knowledge and intuition. Trust me!

Or perhaps I follow or walk parallel with Kierkegaard's own declared axis of the paradoxical amble between fear and wonder. I fear I would be the last to know precisely where I am, and how frequently I fall off this balance beam of life's concentrations like the aging gymnast whose weighty shoulders bear one's weight but overbear one's grace.

Intuition! I thought I trusted myself until I knew that others think that knowing and intuition are at some odds, fight wars of never-ending claims to where there is knowledge, of what it might consist, or even in these days of trust-diminished perhaps by the blazing images of television's pictures worth thousands of words, each harboring the possibility of thought, until there is no thought of thought left. Intuition!

One of my teachers tried to make the distinction fit between what he called *line vs. point integrators* styles of putting atoms of knowledge together into useful knowing. Line integrators were the proverbial cooks who read the recipes of life line-by-line, adding each ingredient in the quantity and order specified, and coming up with a luscious if not inspired moment-by-moment creative dish. The point integrators would intuitively *wander* from place to place gathering ingredients, throwing in a dash of this and a sprinkle of that, looking, smelling, dreaming perhaps of what such a dish could be—and (voila!) it is either a magnificent creation, or... it didn't work this time... or ever.

It was safer and surer to be a line integrator because the recipe is tried and true. Do what it says, and it will do what you already expect. Even a jerk can cook this way.

But the intuition of the point integrator requires... *genius*, creativity, a sixth sense of knowing which no recipe can intuit. Somehow intuition resides in some space where there is genius, creativity, originality. But there is also space in this construction for the fool and those who are too stubborn to follow the rules and recipes for a life lived sufficiently if not well. (Do I sound like Dionysus beating up on Apollo, still seeking the thrills of driving drunk?)

Alas, the Enlightenment! Alas, Aristotle's trying to take over the definition (mostly successfully) of humans wanting most of all to know, by our nature. And knowing, in his oppositional thinking became pitted against whatever else. And intuition became the fall guy for whatever there is about us humans which isn't knowledge: thence against and contrary to knowledge. And what was there to trust about my intuitions which would be at war against knowing?

I, who have been accused of being the ultimate rationalist!?

On Re-seeing and Seeing: How we see others (ourselves?) is very complex. We have forgotten to see our seeing in Western thinking: the idea that we are the creatures who love faces, and love to love our ideas of faces—others and our own. Narcissus turns in all directions... in love.

I, who clearly do not look like I appear, am engaged in a life-long fest of love with the complexities of appearance: of how I appear to others, knowing that it is much an artifice, and that I distinctly do not look to myself how I look to others. The artifice is a molded and painted disk of plastic crafted to look like my left eye. And look like my left eye it does...for others, and usually to myself looking hard in the mirror to find myself... there.

It is so clear that we *see-into* faces much of what we find there: age, character, beauty, gender, ugliness, power, and pity. We find there, one's mother and brother, even after they have been dead many years conjured up in this dream, in that reverie; not only looking back but usually in some relationship, loving, judging, wanting to be pleased offered as a smile.

In a course I teach about thinking about categories of people and the pluralisms abounding in the world, I try to engage my students in various exercises to get them to see their own seeing. The one which is about re-seeing, is to be teaching the class for several sessions; then to proclaim to them that I am not precisely who I appear; that I am handicapped, and that this handicap is visible to them.

"What," I ask, "is wrong with me?"

I try to lay out some groundwork for seeing their own seeing, try to suggest that watching their own views change about a political candidate, or their perceptions of others' age, or whatever is loveliness to them which has altered over their own experience, is available for critical review, perhaps, if they can watch their watching, re-see their seeing.

Only a few, in most classes, have noted their own noticing that my eyes do not always move in tandem: a lazy eye, think some; cross-eyed, but not very. One might well say that I have a *glass* eye, and I tell them that that is correct. Usually I am not challenged in this telling, but am ready to permit them to touch this eye-thing which is hard and not sensitive like a real eye. (Oh! - the vicissitudes of the authority of fact and truth!)

I suppose I should try to take a video recording of the students looking at me and their re-seeing, as they alternatively stare, and rethink, and re-see me as a one-eyed person, contrasting with their longer term vision of me as regular and ordinary and whole. It is *in* their eyes, and it is notable, and very powerful in my visioning of their re-seeing. And nothing has happened, and they now see differently. And they possess the experience of re-seeing their teacher.

If only, as a teacher, I can help them to see that much/most/all of their seeing is open to re-seeing; and to ask how they come to see; and how others did... and do.

Biology of Being: By this time, the question of how and who we are, embedded so firmly in the dualism of mind and body, has made this title seem to have some meaning: something deep, obvious, unquestionably not very open to any *reasonable* question.

But to say "biology" is already (within the thinking of the oppositional mind) to think that there is something else, some otherness of our being which is importantly not-biology. And once into this *game* of dialectic and dialogue, one finds oneself suspended upon an axis which is itself not so obviously located anywhere; and if it were to fall to ground, one is suspicious that the fall would be long, longer...

I understand somewhat the idea of living and of life—just recently a newborn grandson born of the daughter who was born to my spouse, and all that. I understand the concept of poison, of damage and limits to our being: hot, hot, I tell my granddaughter who knows the term to be whispered so loudly with that special intonation, but doesn't yet really know HOT! I have some knowledge and experience with death: of other humans, as well as that of the animals and plants, I call food. I know something of the mechanics of the body, but not much of how to interpret or reinterpret them to be able to move, to be strong. I have increasing experience with/of an aging body, and so on. But, the biology of being!?

Biology: deep, sexual, intuitive, dangerous, a kind of sense of out-of-control, hidden even to my own ability to know knowing... women, wine...wow!

Nature, other species, smell to me, and smell a lot to one another, one notes and supposes, trying to experience what four legs does to the power and processes and predilections of smell. Ah-h-h!

On first coming across the dish, I was (I think) told that sweetbreads were breasts instead of thymus. What a good dish, what a good idea! Now knowing differently, I only think cholesterol, and no longer sup the sweetness of that bread.

Biology of being is to say that there is nothing that I can do about it: no-one could change it. No plastic surgery on being; no culture; no society, no change, no sir! It is the race of racism and the color of coloration, and the excuse me, because I couldn't help myself! Help yourself, one might have said, but no longer to any avail. No excuses accepted here.

No interpretation if it really *is* biology. Biology is what it is. The biology of being is really what it is. Really!

Models/Teachers for Being: The conceptual difficulty with not having a philosophy of dualism - of the nature of the freedom of becoming whatever

I might—is that the direction for living well and upright, seems nowhere available.

As life is the continuing authorization of being, the strength and wisdom needed *not* to succumb to one's youthful models and visions, is not always available to perception or to the practicalities of being. This is why living in *an unscripted time* (the present age) requires the judgment and conceptual authority of those whom we grant the title of *Teacher*. (Sarles, 2013)

These Teachers, living in the sacred spaces of those who are permitted to touch our spirits, can act to inspire others; they live in the present within the context of their students living in their own futurities; thus *inspiring the future*—as it were. It needs to be within their construction of wisdom to construct themselves that they may authorize the being of others.

The world, which I hold to be intrinsically secular, involving persons as bodies living in the world with other persons, invents certain positions of authority, which exist in the realm of the *sacred*. The *sacred realm* includes those persons (who effectively occupy positions) which can touch the body or spirit of others: family, but also curers, preachers, and teachers.

In encountering the sacred personae one *yields* some aspects of his/her being (or suspends some aspects of judgment), hoping that greater benefits will result: much as the surgeon causes a lesser hurt or disease in order to prevent or cure a larger one.

(*A scripted time* exists when most/all people regard the existence of some transcendental text or other authority - deity or monarch - as determining of the notion of present and future; in which it seems apparent, even obvious, of what a good or proper or successful life might mean.)

In *an unscripted time*, the problem of models is duple, at the least: how to be an effective model for others; how to direct and conduct one's own life so one remains useful for others, and does not thereby destroy oneself → a search for wisdom!?

Interdependence of Opposites—the Romantic Solution to Being: "Be careful who you choose to conduct war against," says the old Russian proverb, "because you'll become just like him."

The questions surrounding the categories of opposites and oppositions often make me wonder what press of likeness surrounds those adjectives which seem—like the general against whom we war—to gather; much as to divide.

Good and *evil* find each other more often than either of them finds anything (anyone) else. No wonder Orwell warns us against the possibility that one concept elides into the other: mirrors, reflexives, or the very seat of morality and all of being.

In the romance of romance, it is told and seems not unlikely that one will find true love and being with that person who is precisely one's opposite in character and disposition. Here we sense the concept of harmony and the blending of those traits which would in most other contexts leave us each alone blathering about the impossibility of the other: fact, a palliative, an adjustment which would ask us to abandon good judgment in order to...get along?

The fact is, I think, that none of us is consistently that clearly one or another of any single trait if we remain within our own existences. If, on the other hand we grant agency to ourselves in the name of some transcendent, mystical, or divine persona, then we can package ourselves to ourselves in the context of clear and clean opposites: a trick? Perhaps.

The existential problem of oppositional thinking is that we often seem to be driven into some axis of opposing, pushed down to the ends of our being in order not-to-be something or someone: *enemies*.

We become Platonic essentialists, as it were, trying to fix who we think we are in order to clarify continuously who we are-not. What a fix! But how simplifying when the complexities of life's living, of dealing with the present within the larger interpretations of yesterday and today, myself and others, play upon self-understanding. So much easier to float, to decide to be one thing or another specifically; easier when who I would-not-be stares back at me threatening body or spirit.

Then there is the story of Jorge Luis Borges who asks us to consider our life-ways such that who we have actually become could have had another history and destiny so entirely opposed to that which we have become actually, that that persona would have to kill off the actual us. A tale of caution about loving so much the axes of our being that we forget often - to be.

What I actually witness a great deal is that romantic thinkers, used to oppositional and polemical being, mostly create a polemic; then create their enemies essentially in their own terms: straw men and women. They then do battle with whomever they have created, often killing the others without ever much understanding.

Giving Voice to Others (the Anthropologist-Linguist): There are various senses in which I have lived my life (live my life) as someone who exists principally to give voice to others who are different, lesser in some sense or other, or who have less access than I to the sources of life's tales.

They do not write, or cannot be heard, or cannot sometimes even find the muscles which would express their minds' perorations: children, various of the handicapped, physically or mentally, others of other cultures or places or genders or those who have experimented so much with their being that they cannot find where the place and locus of others' being usually resides. This I do gladly, hopefully well.

This choice of giving voice to others seems heroic, noble, and sometimes arrogant and stupid. If being moral is to live life so others can live their lives also, then giving voice to others seems good.

But there are some difficulties in maintaining the sense of my own being which is less clear to the *"them"* whom I try to represent, than it is to myself. They do not know, do not appreciate, the "them" whom I told the world about have now aged, now disappeared, now gotten their own voices. My path which seemed clear, pristine at the first, now is well trodden, even worn down, and the meaning of giving voice has captured my own being which can now only peek out, trying to find the path which it once chose and now unchosen. Who cares? Only me?

This self-appointed martyr, would-be prophet, would—it seems—wants to be told how wondrously special s/he is; still needing a soulful massage. The troubles I went to... for you and you and you—are you grateful? Am I?

I was/am a sophisticated naive: able to study, to try to understand the voices which I had chosen myself to represent to the world to which I thought I had access. I would never hortate: praise the poor and pity the incapable; not I. I tried to find their souls, the beauty in their being beyond their appearances which everyone else had already judged as inadequate, wrong, foolish or worse.

I trod some path of relativistic absolutism in which everyone who was born of humans (and most of the rest of life) had/has a right to exist in her/his own terms: some wedding of universality of rights and the right to universality: a holism; a confusion?

I study them, studied their studies, studied my own study of their being... leaving me where?

Like the teacher who would engage in dialogue with the world of all the others, I found that the asymmetries of my being did not reside so simply and restfully in obtaining the position of *grande naive*. No, not at all.

All that happened was that I aged, and began to reside in that part of my being which seemed to be the place which would give voice to others, while I was less and less able to give voice to my own... voice.

Seeking still for the strength which others think I must have in order to represent them, to teach them to have that strength of head and resolve which grants themselves their own voices without destroying me - or me trying to raise myself over them - so I can always be the voice which might give them voice.

Bittersweet! What lessons for continuance and being?

Author: There is some battle occurring which has to do with *being and authorship and authority*. In the attempt to sunder our relationship to the edifices of thought which inherit themselves within our being, a recent move has been to deny that the idea of the author has any meaning, any authority.

In the work of Foucault, Barthes, Lacan, there is the sense that the author (he, she—is the author gendered; cannot s/he be?) is, like the Marxist idea of identity of all of being determined by forces external to personal being: in place, time, intellectual direction, the child of particular parents—and that there is no way any (human) author can get past or transcend this.

Similarly in the behaviorist work of B. F. Skinner, and the banishing of the notion of the mind, there is virtually no one *at home*—leaving the peculiar problem of deciphering the "who" of Skinner's writings. It is a recent form of the ancient battle between the mechanists and the mentalists for control over the definition of our being. Only now, the material-mechanical is extended to movement and to behavior: the battle rages within - over the definition of what is behavior; the temptation is to extend it to culture and to our political being.

And this is the complication of the move to remove authorship and authority from being and from texts: that to attempt to destruct or to deconstruct the edifices of old which greatly determine who we are and how we think, the move to remove the author from thinking or intending her/his works, effectively (for many) destroys the power of the work over our thinking.

There is much to be said for locating any author within the themes and variations of her/his social forces: I keep telling myself in an apologetic for my lack of bravery, that I might have been a terrific *poet of oppression*; but I will not let myself feel that oppressed, and I am not so oppressed, actually.

And I deeply appreciate it that others are (on recently hearing a reading by the South African writer (Breyten Breytenbach). I am, no doubt, a guy; but my closest friend (J.) is a woman; and the boundaries of our being and thinking are complicated and intertwined. As a guy, probably, I am the one who does the writing... And I am handicapped, not being who I appear. Not being who I appear to be, am I not *freer* to be my own invention?

Am I (not) fortunate not to have been much educated to literature and philosophy, to have had anti-religious parents whose anger extended freely to their children's bodily being?

How much am I, is anyone, my own invention? How much has this changed over the years? If I had been more successful, early on?—two of my friends who were briefly successful as writers never seem fully to have recovered from this fling with fame! How brave, weak, ambitious, tired!

How lucky to have been trained in science and technology, to think that the new is truly new, and that originality and creativity are where it's at, before stumbling on the edifices of thought? To have had a mother who thought the religiously orthodox to be old-fashioned and more dangerous than quaint? To be a teacher? To have been trained early on to be a musician, and to think as if I were playing, performing, hearing scanning, musically?

Amanuensis? Lacan posits, apparently, a language within our being which mirrors and doubles language; the place from which and in which our thinking writes itself. An unconscious which seems to serve as an explanatory device for some, of how we can think. But I, I pick up my fiddle, and fiddle; sometimes in reading and playing a text of some history, I do it, play it, read it. And I know very well that most people cannot even begin to imagine doing this; that getting to the place in playing that I am and can, takes much study and practice and thought; that it moves on and is on occasion something like transcendent, and I can see and do and hear universes better than I could. (As does J.)

And this is interesting; and has something to do with the being of an author...or composer, because I the reader am here clearly also a doer, a performer; and the puzzles of reading take on in this context some realizable occurrences. Not only do I understand the text, but I *do* it. And we have not much theory for *doing* literary or philosophical texts. If we did, wouldn't this problem of the author become somewhat transformed?

And I the linguist, returning to how we know language, and how I know to get inside the cognitive structures of speakers of some/any other language, to see how they construct and hear and understand sound, then speak it.

Yes! And much of what Barthes, Foucault, and Lacan agitate themselves about is the kind of knowledge we gained and learnt (and taught ourselves) when we were very small, and placed in those *out-of-awareness* places in our being; those places where we have much of our knowledge but use it simply to do, and not to raise to consciousness except upon occasion when a linguist can bid us to tell ourselves about what and how we know. It is much like all the technique which I (hands, eyes, arms) possess that I can play the violin, but which I can just *call upon when I want to*. If the out-of-awareness is not much less mysterious than the idea of the unconscious, it is less metaphor and more body-referable.

The *trouble* began, I suppose, most directly with Saussure, who kept telling us that language is *arbitrary*. What he meant is that any word is as good as any other for expressing or symbolizing or saying what anything or idea is: mesa, table, tabula... whatever.

What this notion has been taken to mean is that all of being is relativized and there is no ground for anything, including being. Actually, in the dynamics of being, there is very little arbitrary in the selection of any particular word in any given context; and the issue of absolute or relative seems, to me, to be located in the general issue of context.

But this eventually leads (as most of our edifice is crafted upon) back to Plato's stealing being from experience and the body. In violin parlance, once we tune to A, and tune the other strings in fifths to that A, then we are pretty relativistic. But the A is something like an absolute, and the limits of arbitrariness are quite close: something of a statement about the human body... And so the attack on authority and the author seems, to me, weak, even if well-motivated in the attempt to deconstruct the edifice of Western thought and to see the human condition more cleanly and clearly.

Now, then, it is important to ask ourselves about the author, and to educate ourselves to reading much as if we were doing anthropological-linguistic fieldwork: attempting to enter into another world-view; coming home to see ourselves while wearing new lenses; going away... returning home...

No Nerve: A warrior. The metaphor of my child's version of the American Indian, of Castaneda's depiction of myself as my shamanic Don Juan; Maxine

Hong's idea of the Chinese(-American) woman as the person who could always seek inside herself and find the strength to do what needs to be done, the spoof of Garrison Keillor's child characters in Lake Wobegon being just slightly above average—all these visions spin in my being: wanting to be a warrior.

The routines of living can wear one down. Mere living, the question of loving each day sufficiently that I can love myself sufficiently for... *Today is a day made by God* doesn't much work for me. Bleak Minnesota winter days, the only luck is that it is not SO deeply blustery cold. Bleak sense, that life becomes harder, I become older, and soon can see that there is much work left undone. Were I the warrior that I tell myself I would be?—what then?

Perhaps I am in some dialectic with the warrior whom I would be, at odds with the martyr into whose sacrificial places my moods would settle more graciously. A cause to which to dedicate my life, myself, a sense of injustice ruling the world, to which I would give myself. But I sense that this would require exactly the kind of yielding and surrender of the sense of myself as warrior that the warrior in me would find so self-destructive. Later, perhaps, but not now.

I want to be garnering strength, to sleep the deep sleep which refreshes but does not diminish. Yes, the sense of self as warrior requires refreshing, a kind of arrogance which remains bounded and within control; a sense of increase, a hardness sufficient to protect the necessary places of love and naiveté and softness which can understand others; some sense of synergy and growing.

I wonder how much those who wander into the political places of power and control of others more than of themselves, have actually lost much of their nerve, practicing control but over others when they have lost some of the same sort of control over their own being.

I wonder how those *great minds* which discipled themselves to others' meanderings, took on the great problems, but settled for distancing themselves from their own paths and solutions. I wonder, that is, how Heidegger and his followers came to unravel being, precisely in the name of being and its study!?

III: REFLECTIONS IN IDENTITY

Appearance and Being: Aspects of the problem of being who one thinks and says one is, is that being human is being social. And being social means that one's identity is in many senses and contexts also *social*: that although one is (it surely seems) one's own physical skin-surrounded self, one is always in the world seen, reacted to, interpreted by others. Indeed, G.H. Mead was certain that we (the "I" I say I am to myself) carry the *other(s)* with us no matter where we go or how isolated we might become in the living of our lives.

An important fact of our being is that others see and hear us. And they not only see us in any momentary frame of being, but carry within their own beings some sense of who and how we each appear to be.

I look interesting, odd, ordinary, anomalous, pretty, old, gendered, kempt, like my others' grandpa, not very well, one or another *race*, bursting with energy...

The fact is that I appear to others in some terms and categories which they (and somewhat reciprocally I) carry in my being's judgments. I not only *appear* to them, but simultaneously judge who and what and how I am in at least some senses which may well become aspects of how they respond and thence appear (back) to me.

Such terms and categories are, for many of us in many of life's contexts, very powerful; so powerful, in fact, that once we literally see someone as (gender, race, age), it is practically impossible for us to *see-through* our categories of their appearance, that we can *see* any particular person: a very complicated problem in life, excruciating in attempting to teach by dialogue; and a doggedly constant problem in distinguishing identity and appearance—for others, for oneself.

One of the complications of being social, of engaging in face-work is that the categories of others seeing us has some effect on our being; in terms of how we are seen, responded to—and perhaps most importantly—how we then think of ourselves. Appearance and identity is very complex in terms of how we understand our own identity—and then others... and then ourselves... others... ourselves.

Much of what we do in the human condition is *face-work*. (This is true at least in societies in which the scale of our being many is beyond the 1500 or so persons who would, in a small mostly hermetic town, know one another in a fairly complete and ongoing detail—but then detail is one of the issues here.) Infants mainly are students of faces; we identify one another principally as and by faces—prisoners cover their faces—memory of others is much in terms of faces and expressions... *face-work*.

Ironic it is, is it not, that the study of faces has not ever gone very deeply into its dynamics. Somehow, the complexities of the facial aspects of our being are so *obvious* to us in terms of out-of-awareness processes of our thinking, which they are very difficult to see; to see ourselves seeing ourselves and others: *categories*.

Cosmetics: It is not easy to be precise in expressing the notion of what is *cosmetic* and what is not. Perhaps the definition is in the eye of, the gaze of, those who behold us. And if we apply or use any cosmetic, it is most always with the concept in our minds that the gaze of the other is the context in which we do our cosmetic work.

We try to look attractive, extraordinary... if we would otherwise look unordinary—younger/older. To talk clearly about cosmetics, we need to develop, to study the concept and actuality of the nature of gaze: of what we see in one another, and thence (I think) in ourselves. That is, cosmetics is a *derived* art.

Are we discussing the nature of appearance with some reference: say, *nature*? As our usual natural reference is other species, do they use cosmetics? They do groom themselves, and, for some, one another; for appearance, for health, to relieve themselves, to feel better. Smell, looks... is it cosmetic to go around peeing on every (significant) object?

Does it make a difference in other species, how they cosmetize: if they are attracted to faces or to asses, or to the perfumes and noises of our constructed selves? And are these selves *constructed* in other species? This is often what we mean when we invoke the notion of nature: that we are what we come with; that we are totally passive in our being what and who we are.

Surely, cosmetics has to do with social analyses, with volition, with knowing about appearance.

We humans, the naked ones living in the oddest climates on earth to which we are often ill-fitted, we humans adorn and cosmetize ourselves. It is one thing to stay warm, one might say, but another to stay warm artfully: to throw upon our bodies a skin or fur with the idea (in mind) that others will see us. Judge us? Judge us in ways that we now judge ourselves, applying cosmetics, plying appearance in order to place order upon how we appear.

Passing: I suppose all or most of us *pass*, at least occasionally. We portray ourselves as someone or something we are not exactly. But as we pass, we also pass *to someone*; we require that others *read* us as someone whom we are-not, as someone we might be, might like to be; as someone they might like us to be; we might like to fit into someone else's picture of who or what we are. Occasionally we might like to be so far in another's background of attention that we can virtually *dis*-appear.

I have, since age seven, worn a prosthesis. For many people, a prosthesis literally aids them to do something that they might not otherwise be able to do: an artificial hand which can grasp, or a leg to stand on. No, in my case the prosthesis seems primarily to be—as they say—*cosmetic*. It makes me appear to others as if I am regular, ordinary, not a freak, not a handicapped person.

But my actual, real appearance sans prosthesis is hardly like most others. I have no left eye—a flap of white-pinkish skin covers a gold ball inserted there by an ophthalmologist more than 70 years ago. And this image of myself I carry in my mind's eye (i.e., where appearance locates itself).

But I also wear the prosthesis most of the time, so when I look in most of my life's mirrors, I see the "me" which is prosthetized; two-eyed as if I were passing as ordinary. Ordinary to others, sometimes ordinary-passing to myself in the terms which others bring to my judging; carrying, as well, that factoid of appearances not so clear reality that I look quite, well, *odd*.

Passing, looking at the world looking back at me, as if I were just like all the others and their apparent appearance categories...

Passing (Adrian Piper): She occupies the borders between whatever are the races: black and white. She seems black (African-American) to some others; often to herself. She seems white to some others; less often to herself. Caught, freed, not finding a locus of her being except in the reflections of others seeing her...face. And writes a poignant piece about living this experiencing and how it reflects back upon her own reflections of self.

Inside...who knows? Her writing *pensamientos* concern history and those others, those genealogies which have passed as white, and how she might or might not want to know them, having chosen mostly to pass as white; i.e., as *majority*. Much of her so-called family has broken off, does want to know they are black, does not want to know her, a woman who lives on the edges of the margins, ready to fall off, and dangerous to all the others who might try to maintain her precipitous identity.

Facing, as an academic in a philosophy department, the stares of others who judge her first, it seems, according to whether they know or recognize (*re-cognize*) her as one race or the other. Some judge her as lesser.

Some others, one supposes find her especially *interesting*, perhaps brave to fall over the line and see herself as black even when she is not exactly black. Exactly! But she mentions no one, no colleagues who find this issue of passing intriguing, challenging. In her terms, at least, they mostly judge, and judge her less than she appears.

Identity is always problematic, but it gets stranger in its liminalities. Neither fish nor fowl?

How is it that others see us? *Directly*? Not possible!

Masks: I grew up listening to the William Tell overture celebrating the triumph of good over the various evils which abounded in the world of radio's machinations, as the masked Lone Ranger jumped upon his horse, shouted Hi-Ho Silver, laid his silver bullet on the table, and gathered to him his faithful sidekick, the Amerindian Tonto. "Da-da-da da-da-da da-da-da-tada..." rings still in my mind's ears. The mask itself seemed to be an ambivalent/ambiguous symbol, designating the intrinsic goodness of the persona while asking us to ask why anyone would need to cover his real visage. A real visage!?

Days of work, days of rest, holy-days and holidays, the sense of what is real and what is not reacts and contrasts and intersects with who and what anybody is. If, as in the Mardi Gras and the theaters of life, one puts on a mask, then one is not who s/he is ordinarily; one has license to be, to do.

Sex, dance, debauchery, the *Bacchae* runs to the intoxicants of life which: alter life, make it possible or worthwhile, cast any of us in the multiple possibilities which might be, just might be life's story of being and identity. Who would know just which of us is the real me; the one which is my destiny; the one which Borges seems to think would so hate the one I have become that he would destroy the me which I am... think I am.

Masks may, like cosmetics, enhance more than change, invite or excite much as they alter the being of our being. In the world before the incandescent bulb, the faces of our being are at least double: in the reflection of the Sun's light, and in the light cast by the fires of evening's fires or moon's monthly flights. Most of us, especially those of darker cast, have actual reflective masks which differ considerably from light's light to dark's night lights. And in the darkness of intimacy and of sleep, who knows exactly which visage illuminates itself in our touch whose knowledge is not lesser.

Made in the *image of God*... Thou shalt not worship graven images: dolls, animals, what are the pictures, depictions, of others whose flesh is removed from the images which can be carried about in wallets, shown on television and movie screens, and posted on posters.

If we would like to come to understand masks, we might like to study why we like to study our own visage reflected in life's mirrors. Beyond Narcissus, we carry in our being the experience as memory of years past and how we looked and must have looked, and wonder how we recreate still the visages of parents long dead looking still at us through the masks of death to discern who is truly me.

And the ambivalence of wanting to see-through the masks others wear while wanting the masks we see to be truly you...

Pictures in Our Heads: I enjoy playing with students responding to appearance in some of my classes. I tell them sometime after they have made some judgments about me and my teaching and my subjects, that I am not exactly who I appear to be.

Who I appear to be? How do others see us? Do they see us *filter-free*? Do we see others without lenses crafted by experience and the sense that we must see how, what others see? What, for instance, is female or male-appearing about a face; do genitals translate into facial features? Beauty, age, trust, race... do we see or we see-into?

How well-constructed these gazes of others into *the "I" that I call myself*? How well-motivated? How accurate? More about them than about me? Does the "me" I think I am get reconstructed in reflecting and responding to the gaze of others? Deconstructed? Do I need reflect that which I see in the others' imaging of my visage? Where does this process begin and end?

Do they see me more than their construction of me? Me?

Do I have a self, a "me," which is stronger, more perduring than the "me" they see in... me? Me and my facial image; now there is a real relationship in some dance with the "me" they see in me, and the "me" I am!

But...my class. At some point in the course, usually in ones on the *Body* and the one called *Issues in Cultural Pluralism*, I say that there is something *wrong* with me: I am a handicapped person. "What is wrong with me," I ask.

The *look* of *embarrassment* is multiplied by most of the students in the room; such looks shared by 20 or 30 or 40 persons are impressive, educational about what facial expression is. To see a similar set of facial movements spread over the visages of all those persons is to begin to see faces. The look of embarrassment is, I think, much ado about requiring, demanding that they change something about how they see me; about how they have constructed with some sense of comfort and a completion of business, me; a "who I am" to them.

And I am telling them that *I am different*; that I am handicapped; that they are wrong; that their images of me are not the "me" who I more truly am. And they are embarrassed. They stare at me, at my body, dissecting me, stripping me several ways, wondering what they have missed or what they have added to their internal depictions and gazes.

Or is it that I have told them that I am less than normal that they seem to be embarrassed. They stare at me, stare at their own stares, trying to redo them even as I watch them, collectively.

I wonder now, but now in the excitement of seeing so many faces reconstructing their visages of my visage... if this is like the time several years ago when we told our neighbors of over 20 years that we were selling our house, leaving their neighborhood, moving out.

Instead of interest, instead of their somehow helping us to redo our images which had been gathered, padded, fleshed out in the children and the loves and the sicknesses of all those years watching and participating in the neighborhood, instead of all that, they became quite upset and angry. Angry, I think now, because we were asking them to redo their images of their neighborhood where we, and the safety of their knowing us and our house, were about to force them to change their images of their neighborhood. I wonder if this is similar to asking students to re-see me.

A few students respond by looking askance: not about to risk telling me that I lack any body parts, am crippled, am less than how they see me, seeing an older man. One asks about my eyes. Don't I appear to be a little bit cross-eyed; one eye seems, to her/him, to wander a bit independently of the other. I say s/he is on the right track. Faces going blank, going into that *calculated neutral* in which they try to construct their faces so as to become totally impenetrable.

Another asks if I am blind in one eye. "Yes," I say. "Which one?" Pauses. "The left one," a student offers. I now relieve them now, taking the edges off their being asked to say what is wrong with me, by saying that my left eyes in actually plastic: a glass eye.

And now I see the entire group redoing their images of my face; of a half-blind person whose left eye is some sort of hand-made disk seeming to look at them; but it is empty... blind. This is an amazing moment, seeing 40 students staring so hard now to see me anew: the man with one glass eye, seeming to see them, but seeing blankly.

It is like being undressed, I guess, in the gaze of a curer, of someone who wants to see-through my exterior. And it is powerful, especially in my seeing these stares which last and last, and for which I have given them *license* to stare in ways which are not so usual, but for which they are all quite prepared.

So they now see me differently; see a different me. And I am left wondering how we *construct* images of others, being more and more certain that we actively construct rather than merely mimic or reflect others' visages. If we see - through stereotypes, comparing who we see with some kind of image we construct: directly or by some sorts of comparison with what we expect, remember, desire or cannot bear.

I wonder where such images *reside*: how to guide them toward more empathy or sympathy or understanding or teaching students how to see-through their own habits of seeing.

So powerful these ways of seeing others; so permanent, so seeming-sure, yet so easily and obviously altered, changeable in the proper circumstances, given the appropriate contexts...

If we see the beauty in others, can they remain beautiful to themselves?

Illusion, Magic, and Simulacrum: For many persons and peoples, the striving question is that of death, whose awareness in one's being meanders amoeba-like in the depths and processes of being and identity. Who am I?

Am I? ...the question rings and rings, round and round, often producing panic in the young whose feeling states to themselves that they are, but maybe they are not. If this is real, what is that? If that is what is this? Chimera, illusion, trust the senses to distrust the touch of hardness which is the world! Woe is me! Whoa to this line of thinking.

Theater, illusion, seeing the antics of persons who, I really do know, I do really believe, are just the same as you, the same as I, cavorting upon those places we see as life's stages. Yet we see them *as other*, as different from the "me" and from the "you" who the ordinary knows to be ordinary. Call it a stage, call it theater, and we are taken by the idea and the unreality that those others truly are other, captivated and commanded by acting out the play, whose author and authority wanders in spaces others than our own.

The ongoing temptation is to think that the reality of theater casts precisely a commentary upon the reality which is ours: the real reality. And if we study staging just right, approach it with a sense of correctness which illuminates the edges and liminal moments of existence's dubiousness, then it will like Plato's back-lit, top-lit cave bring the light upon our knowledge of our own being.

Life is all a stage, Shakespeare's believers quote and try to believe, leaving it up to my older intellectual brother (Erving Goffman, 1950), to describe to our own knowing: perhaps he described a method, perhaps he found new ground from which to observe our own being... perhaps. (Goffman and I were both students of Ray Birdwhistell who was the most outstanding-involved student of Kinesics: the study of human interaction).

But others—living more upon the *edges of their being*—having early, it seems, given up the idea of the deity as an explanatory device for various reasons, seem to want to believe in more certitude. Artaud's (1938) theater of cruelty, Bataille's (1943) attempts to implode his inner experience, want to take us to the extremes of being to find the regularities.

One wonders (I wonder, not having had so strongly to reject the idea of God which my father had never taken into his heart), if this trying to reflect back upon reality the erstwhile mirrors of being as if death were somehow reflective upon life, rather than (simply) owning its own turf within our existence; isn't fundamentally *ascetic*. Somehow, if we cut into being just enough, if we slash our senses just short of insensitivity, our bodies will have to tell us who we are, that we are, playing upon the boundaries between existence and un-existence, we tell ourselves, will mimic precisely the borders of reality and non-being. Then, with the hope of the futility of the fantastic, we will truly know something... truly know.

But, but, I who can love the mystical-seeming feelings of the presence of greater being, the poet and musician of composition's musings, think we are missing much of our own experience, yearning for illumination in mirrors and in smoke. We, as the Delphic Oracle tells us, need to look into our (bodily) being, to know ourselves... knowing illusion, magic, and simulacrum. We need to see ourselves seeing, to know that we have developed (develop still) in the idea of life which, as Kierkegaard suggested, wanders along the axes of fear and wonder. We wonder less, fear more, and think that exploring the edges of fear will instruct us, or gird us. It is as if the solution to life's questions and still-unfathomable aspects were to be found in *de-sensitization* rather than in study and understanding of what we are, already.

We have, many of us, given up upon the reality of external reality, and seek within ourselves (the self, the subject) as the sole creator; taking on the Faustian task without wanting to take on the costs of these exercises; a modernist form of the Tower of Babel, a hubris which finds it more tempting to quote others, than to work to find ourselves, our being, quotable.

Gregory Bateson (1972) who called himself also an Anthropologist, wrote in his metalogue *The Message: This is Play*, that children know (already) much about the rough-necking which is understood as play—not serious—and the seriousness of other similar behavior, which is *not play*. I wonder, as well, if there aren't levels of knowledge (already) in our meta-language and in the contexts of domains where ordinary being is given direction and interpretation.

What seems to be happening in this moment of severe critique of the modern is that we are engaging in changing the very locus of the meta-language and contexts, the very nature of the metaphors which help us to understand the questions and issues of our being. The search upon the edges of being—magic, illusion, and simulacrum—while always interesting and often enjoyable, should not be sacrificed to the principal task of illuminating our being. Rather, they exist also in their own rights. We do as well.

On Being Beautiful (Ugly): There are certain persons-others upon whose faces we *dwell*. Those whom we might call beautiful seem to pull our eyes *in* to their features: not merely to glance for a brief moment before pulling our eyes' attentive selves away perhaps to return shortly, but literally to remain fixed: to dwell. Those whom we are also drawn to, but in senses almost (directly) opposed to those whom we might dub beautiful, we might call *ugly*. Some of these have literally different features - anomalies, let's say: a cleft palate, a missing tooth in these days of dentally reconstructed features, a missing nose or huge blotch or colored spot, or whatsoever draws our attention in to its peculiarities so that we would dwell there, but find in it more a sense of repulsion which seems to cause us to look quickly away, then return, and virtually have to fight our own eyes' tendencies to dwell. Others are not so beautiful or their faces seem nondescript or they fit into some stereotype or caricature which seems to be carrying our heads about: ordinary; e.g., we feel no need to dwell there. Our eyes are *free*.

We seem to have little insight, no sense of these forms of freedom when it comes to those we tell ourselves we are *in love with*: spouses, children, parents, especially for me these days: grandchildren. It is as if the idea of significant others places our responses to their visages outside of the usual habits in whose terms we see and judge; judge, then see.

How do such judgments affect our being and identity: surface and/or depth? And what part do they play in determining the identity of those who are often judged to be especially beautiful or powerful or particularly odd or ugly? (And, one might ponder, what does any of this have to do the integrity or authenticity or centrality of the *'who'* of who I am. It is as if the external faces are, at least for those whose visage pulls us in to dwell, a mask, a uniform, a story about being.)

If, as I have seen until recently, those who have been judged "retarded" have had few people dwell for even a brief second upon their facial surfaces. Most people look away from them, past them, through them; anywhere but not upon their surfaces. What is it like to live one's life without anyone else seeing one; seeing one's surfaces, looking one in the eye: is it some denial of other's being? And if I am not seen by anyone, do I miss that seeing? How do I (anyone) construct myself with or without the glances? How do those who appear to others beautiful, then respond? Do they think of themselves as beautiful; special? Do they, like the Marilyn Monroes of the world, resent the fact that beauty is only skin deep, and that their depth of character never has the possibility of showing through to others? (See: John Rynders and Margaret Horrobin on *Down Syndrome!*, 1974)

Becoming/Being the Gaze: Upon discovering this past century that the history of ideas and of politics and the discourses only of some of those who have preceded us, still operate within our thinking, shaping being, we ponder and wonder who and how we are.

We sense only too much that the ways in which others see us has much to do with how we are. Which others? What conjoinings of conceptual powers enable others to see me as of a certain sort or type or not much to see me at all? (Recall that almost no one notices my artificial eye!)

And we have realized as well that most of our antecedents do not much appear in our being. Only certain ones show up still, and they are primarily of *certain sorts*; and certainly not of others. Not many women, not many persons from the continents of the Americas or of Africa have weathered the ravages of whatever significant history means and has meant (changing in these days?!) Events, power, gathering ideas which excited many persons; some thinkers whose ideas have been invoked time and time again as if no time—still produces the ideas which whatever classicisms developed: and develop again and again. It is, in Western thought as Whitehead tells us, as if all of thought has been merely footnotes to Plato.

Those of us who do not appear, who are we? How is it that we do not much appear; or that particular sorts of others do? Is this mostly situational, like showing up as who we are in the moments of our birth; mothers are present, but fathers often get much of the credit; and who am I? Is it much to do with how others see us; or do not? Do we become, are we becoming; am I the product as it were, of others seeing me, or not seeing me. Are we visitors to our own lives, products of the gaze of others; struggling either to please their gazes or to find some sense of ourselves which we might please... if...

The fact is that we are students of faces and gazes and interact and judge others as their faces, much/most of the time. Some of the time we are, so to speak, *accurate*. We read faces, read into faces, and sort persons as some age, gender; much of the time we also see-into faces categories as types of persons, and do not much see any sense of person or persona, *blinded or bound* as we are by our typing of them! And they often share these same types, it being difficult to know exactly whose types we see, thence become. If it fits and we wear it, does it only seem to fit; does it become us, the gaze, or is this some complex of circularities in search of meaning and identity? (→ *Next Places*)

Charisma and Presence (Walter Mondale, Nelson Mandela): There are some persons who seem to walk into a room and virtually command by their mere presence that we dwell upon them, pay them attention even as we suspend much attention to ourselves. It is almost as if these *charismatic* persons appear to us upon the stage where we are audience, becoming passive even as we stretch our being to join in theirs. They are more than present; they have *presence*.

It is as if they have, I think, ways of bearing themselves which indeed seem like their being on-stage. It has to do with the ways in which they carry themselves—varieties of tensioned muscles and bearing—which is *regal*. A sense that they are, indeed, special, and that the others will become audience as they move through the world appearing. It is in their faces—varieties of tensioned expressions—carrying, like beauty, some sense that we must and will look at them in order to glare but with some greater sense that the persona will give us something back; like beauty but with an offering, a recompense.

Whatever it is, this charisma, it does not necessarily translate from actual presence to television. I have been in rooms with Walter Mondale whose actual presence is close (for me) to exciting—and truly interesting in the sense that the promise of his charisma is delivered in his actions and his talk. But on television he appears flat and too slow.

Are we talking about actors upon stages? Is it some mere projection? Or is charisma indeed some sense that the person who projects it really does have/contain a sense of energy, a sense of knowledge, a set of promises which might, just might, be?

The Reflected/Reflective Self: *"How we are represented by others - shapes how we represent ourselves, what is real to us and the worlds we imagine; images and representations are a formidable cultural force."*

...so a review of *Black Looks: Race and Representation* begins. (NYT Book Review, 2-28-93). This is, says B.S Madison, "particularly important-powerful-poignant among black *victims* of *white supremacist culture* precisely because *representation is so important a force in self-identification, particularly for people of color.*"

But why? How does a majoritarian (*supremacist*) culture effectively control the representations, thence the very definitions of being people of color? Is this sort of statement a fact, a lament, an analysis? How is one/does one become the *other*?

As social creatures, all of us are *susceptible* to extrinsic, representational definitions of our identity. An angry glance—when we are young—from parents, is powerful in our being: taken in, responded to. Similarly with loving, approving glances. At once so obvious, to simultaneously inexplicable, the power of others to affect and to define us is not at all clear.

We humans are, I have thought, *students of faces*: dwelling upon them, using them to read/project character into others... loving/hating them, we sprinkle vocabulary upon facial movement like seeds of grain strewn and sewn upon the great plains' unending horizons.

We seem virtually to absorb into our being the emotions we read into others' faces: the seat of conscience, a necessity even for our survival!? If we see anger or fear, we are supposed to stop what we do: don't walk into the street; that's hot; don't move; be careful! If not we may not survive: fear, awe, caution, taking into our being what we see in others' visages.

But, then, at various points in being, we are supposed as well, to become some*one*: at various points and turns, to be more-or-less independent creatures—the problem of the one and the many playing itself out in each of our experiences.

Why entire populations: how does the gaze of the male determine the inner sense of being female? (Is this all changing – in these times? Is there some drive, some intrinsic sense built on the reading of emotions in others' faces, which we not only absorb but then use virtually to define ourselves?

What about the majorities: males, whites, the necessity to become supreme is problematic for all and each of us. How does character spread from individuals to populations? How does reflection generalize into representation? And in these globalizing times, might we become more a "single" appearance?

How do any of us grow into a self-sense of power even as we are all susceptible to extrinsic definition: the glance, the slur, the stare, the calculated inattention?

Is the locus of these questions the quest for meaning and for who and how the significance of the significant others gains power over our self-definitions? Context, will... hope?

At some point in our being, the glances of m/others translate themselves much into words into stories about m/others' glances, and seem able to replace visage with virtuality; "is" becomes "about," reflection becomes representation.

Is it that we are totally derived from the beginning, as it were: that what we see in others' faces reflecting our own being *is* our own being? (Fanon: *Black Skin, White Masks*, 1952)

Representations: At Home/Not at Home:

As a writer one doesn't belong anywhere. Fiction writers, I think, are even more outside the pale, necessarily on the edge of society. Because society and people are our meat, one doesn't really belong in the midst of society. The great challenge in writing is always to find the universal in the local, the parochial. And to do that, one needs distance. William Trevor. (NYT Bk Review: 2-28-93)

Who belongs anywhere? Is this a time, asks Martin Buber (1952) when virtually no one is at home; when we do not find any place to even pitch the stakes of our tents. There have been other such times, he claimed: times of change, of upheaval, of conceptual wrenching, whose vast landscapes have, this particular time, extended virtually everywhere upon this earth.

I, the anthropologist, feel less at home, more a *visitor*. Even in the midst of the city, I am usually away from the action. Even in the hum, even in the roar of people's doings and comings and goings, I am often alone. For the past several years, living in an aerie, seeing many people moving below, quite abstracted: they, me, us. For me, at home *is* away.

And for those who have moved, emigrated, immigrated? For them, what? Some people—whole large peoples—seem to be so tied to the sense of their geography that they are only at home when they occupy some place: actual, virtual!? What is a place; who am I? Who are we? Ethnicity, religion, language, I have no being particular to myself which is not always generalized to others' particularities?

Adoption: We fell powerfully in love with the creature who showed up at the airport in the Twin Cities of Minneapolis and St. Paul. She had been born some eight months earlier, and there was the possibility of acceptance or rejection. There were some questions of health and background, and we advised our grown-up daughter and son-in-law to *go for her*. And they did. And this one night in July we found ourselves—some 20 persons at the airport awaiting her arrival. (Today–some 22+ years later!!)

The Chemicals which ARE Me: I am utterly sure and certain... I am utterly confused and distraught by the apparent fact... that I—the "I" that I am—am a chemical factory: the Dow Chemical of downtown, the Sandoz of the upper Midwest. I now seem to eat a banana, not at all to find enjoyment or some hidden (to myself—a suspicious notion in the chemical-context) Freudian joy in its phallic swallowing, but for its potassium. On calcium!—that I do not ingest gradually the bones which support the cranium which might contain the symbol-making places, which direct the fingers whose ideas... well, this is as silly as Alice wondering.

Tits and asses reduced to fats and glycerol's and all the other "-ols" and "-teins," whose productive packages tell me to think they deserve a second glance; what truth is this chemical mass whose mess will one day be reduced to the dust from which it arose by any name.

I waver between the hardness of hard truth and the obliquity of "so-what!" even as the rDNA chemists are making a moneyed revolution against the biology which I could more easily recognize as something like myself. Looking in the mirror, I more and more see my facial twitchings as the creakings of kekule rings and dead denucleated cells I used to call dandruff, and find myself now longing for a view of the mystical aura. The only sadness remaining the "inorganic" vision of the organism I call myself, is that my genome is itching unbearably and my fingernails cannot find the precise places whose scratching might relieve it. (Would you try, please, just a little to the left...)

The power in reductive thinking is not merely in its correctness, I think, but also in the fact that we in this era are so uncertain of the reality of our being, that reduction seems to promise a ground upon which to deposit the chemicals of the contract of our being. Woe would be me!

Insuring the Future: It seems easy to hold as mystical, the divination of the future. It seems difficult to understand in any way with clarity the notion of what will be, shall be, except as extrapolated from the present which was future, and the past which one would be; by now, has been. Even the semantics seem complex.

If only the savior on the great white horse will appear once more on earth. If only I am lucky. If only I meet the love of my life. If only I get well. If only I can accept my fate. If only I can understand my fate to have been other. If only I am open to my life as destiny. If only I hadn't, they hadn't, it didn't, or it did. If only...

What's new? Nothing under the sun! What's new is perception bound in the wonderful words of the Book of Ecclesiastes, within the unending, unbeginning ebbs and flows of the seasons to sew, to reap, to plow. What's new is everything. But generation is seasonal; as the seasons ripen, I grow old. What's new? Less and less of "I."

Heraclitus said that everything is always in flux, and that the world as moving stream appeared paradoxical. But we thought—Pythagoras, Plato, and each I of the stream of the West—that paradox was to be resolved in life as in logic; in life as if it were as aspect of logic. But Heraclitus is correct. Everything is always in flux, and much of it appears to be stable. And this truth is not to be resolved, but lived.

As scholars perhaps we should be more aware of the discovery of insurance, but we are not. Insurance, security, the futurity of our being is all taken care of; less and less is left to chance! We need no longer to trust to the divinations of star gazers; indeed, in fact, we have bought the future, and it is becoming us... who we are.

And it is difficult to see-through the notion that we somehow possess the future, because most of us have a proprietary stake in it. Like trying to understand the Amerindian lament that the ownership of land is against any and all principles of life: the earth is not for sale! We have taken the future and are trying to possess it. Little do we note that the concept of ownership freezes the future and so shapes present being that it is difficult to discover and sustain who we are, or might be… If only…

Guaranteeing the Future: In an *unscripted* time—such as this time—it does seem that certain significant others in our lives may so exemplify and futurity as to *inspire* it. It is neither small nor trivial that our m/others breathe life into us; humans are not survivable on our own until we are about 8 years old. Not merely food, but sustenance of the spirit is necessary for the continuance of individuals of social species; including humans. It is not very simple to distinguish the "I" which is my own invention from the "I" whom others have said I am, and am to be.

Those who have a good chance to inspire, to virtually to *guarantee* the future seem to be those to whom we are willing to *yield* or to surrender aspects of our spirits in order that we may grow and go on. These are *sacred* aspects of our existence in a world of chancy secularity. It is hope, the sense of towardness which the teacher underwrites as s/he may enter into dialogue with her/his students. Its guarantees are to be studied and explored and lived within the peculiarities of the asymmetries of students' granting continuity to their teachers, while considering themselves ongoing and ordinary.

In an unscripted time (such as the present age), it seems helpful, perhaps extremely important to create Teachers—to set the possibilities of life's chances, so that Teachers can create themselves. Otherwise, it is difficult to see our being forward, and we find ourselves on the various precipices of Dante's Inferno: losing meaning; lost future. (Sarles, 2013*)*

Not Here, You Won't Be: Some years ago I played violin in a neighborhood chamber orchestra which performed occasionally in an *Old Folk's Home*. I said to my seat partner once—a woman slightly older than I—that I would hate to live in this place. She replied, casting her looks about at the 'oh so few' old men living, surviving, that I would not have to worry…

Immediate **Consciousness:** In order to unpack the mind, some thinkers from Hegel to Bergson have thought that we could somehow *examine* our *immediate consciousness.*

It is as if what is happening in/to our minds in the fairly well-bounded here and now is available, perhaps obvious to us thinkers who are *having* the experience, thinking our thoughts. Our phenomenology would then be ascertainable—presumably some summative function over a period of time or a duration. Then we would know something about our thinking, about the reality it refers to.

The problem is, I think, that it is not at all this simple: that to think that immediate consciousness is particularly revealing of itself; its thinking, thoughts is only a small part of the story of thinking.

With respect to questions of being and identity, some ways of being who we are/I am are always somehow present or being generated (if we consider immediate consciousness more an active, less a passive mode). The fact of my being, the facts of being who I am, the contexts in which this all might make some sense, seem to me to be ever-present, even though *backgrounded*. Similarly, I almost always need and seem to know how and where I am going.

Even if I appear passively listening to someone else speaking (perhaps particularly then), I am busily generating, coding, decoding ways of understanding, moving my vocal muscles in some ways analogous to modes of speaking and unpacking.

We know from phonemic theory that the so-called rules of cognitive mapping are operant, and that they are so beneath the sense of consciousness which the notion of immediacy implies, that they are not only not available for examination, but we don't even *know* these rules in any direct senses. Here, I'm thinking of such obvious rules as the ways in which we form plural morphemes in English: /z/ after voiced ending consonants, /iz/ after affricates and vowels, and /s/ everywhere else. We do this virtually without error, know it as well as we know our very existence. Yet how can we say it/they are not part of immediate consciousness. Such rules may not *report* themselves to us actively, but...

And we know a great deal about what is not being said or thought: contrastively (when we think female, male is not far behind; but the contrast is present in its virtual *availability*). When I think myself, the other is virtually present (Mead 1934). How can we say even that our (own) immediate consciousness is more directly ours in any proprietorial sense, than thinking others through ourselves: the question of the identity of self is dependent upon knowing others? Perhaps we're looking for immediate consciousness precisely in the wrong places. More probably it is too simplistic to proceed this way; maybe this is why it seems necessary to follow this exercise of *thinking-out* being and identity.

Possibly an analysis of such a study as this—to the extent that it begins to be a sufficient analysis—is more useful to note what is *in* our minds.

Besides, the existential problematic has more to do with using or playing our minds than with their examination in some temporally delimited senses.

Spirituality: Besides some construction of myself as scientoid and/or humanoid, the "me" I tell me that I am seems to be a very spiritual person.

I don't mean spiritual in the sense of looking for my soul to be carried to the heavens of my dreams of return to any heaven: I remain a skeptic about life being more that what it is.

Nor do I mean spiritual in any mystical sense of trying continually to find more (than what there is) in the numbers or symbols of horoscopes or the progression of saints or cycles; I think that entering into mystical realms might be interesting, but it would not allow me to be or do what I am.

It seems, my sense of my own spirituality, more to be a sense of connectedness, interest, and some strange responsibility for everyone, extending sometimes to life itself; all of life especially in these times of radically transforming of the earth, and the ways in which we think about the human condition, and the transference of genetic material willy-nilly from species at one end of the earth into others and others... and others.

Sometimes this sense of spirituality seems to fall squarely into the various excesses of desire and hubris so well told in the story of the Tower of Babel in olden days, and more recently in the variety of Faustian urges which the quest for knowledge seems to feed.

Here I often feel guilty as charged: I do want to know everything in some way or other; but less, I think, as ambition or competition, and more because this is an aspect of the ways in which I have chosen to pursue what I do and who I am—toward wisdom, a veritable needing to grow and to understand more deeply the human condition and these times; a nagging set of worries that I have been susceptible to my own defining in order to please others; less to develop an esthetic whose self-pleasing would be self-satisfying.

And I am not always clear whose boundaries I find and those which find me in the ongoing dialogue which I have with J., she with me. It is she who has the critical mind, a (woman's) sensibility and obligation. Perhaps she has captivated me. Perhaps we once discovered exactly this sense of spirituality in one another and are living out its paths and trajectories.

Maybe this sense of spirituality is from young youth, a sense of the search for some purpose in life's living; a direction, a sighting of the martyrdoms which might fulfill a life well-lived, a useful life, a good life. Perhaps this amounts to an inversion of the fear of death. Perhaps...

The spiritual sense of being a teacher, now Teacher, is that I have a fair degree of power and control over those who might study with me. The question remains of what to do with these understandings: about hope and futurity, and being able to stand upon one's thinking feet in any and every present. And so I write.

I think spirituality—mine, at any rate—is also about wanting, needing, being fascinated with all those I meet and see: mostly the humans, but also many of other species, and even the machines which we have created to extend us, enlarge us... replace us?

I go places to see the places, to see what is there, and inevitably I am entranced with the people, engaging my imagination of the human condition to enlarge itself to include each new person; each new people I find in my wanderings, or who arrive in my town. More, these days, people who arrive in my town.

Also, I imagine spirituality—mine—to be truly transcendent; again, not to any sense of deity, but with an amazement and enduring wonder that this is all happening. Sure, I am, that it does, even when I know that many others are not so sure, and continue to worry less about living it than its dying. Life is a transcendent form, and how that is remains a fundament for my puzzlings.

Authority and Celebrity: We note in this moment of history's *storying*, the diminution of authority and the rise of celebrity. The quest for importance has become much less what one does than who one is. Much of the world has thus become de-authorized, and the locus of meaning and of power do not find any *location*.

Some portion of this de-authorization seems very important in that it enables us to exist within our own present experiences. It has the power and possibility of lessening the importance of prior, even ancient texts (and personages) in our ongoing lives. But it may also diminish our own possibility of authority by empowering us in the small, and leaving large vacuums into which any number of totalitarian forces may enter.

Kierkegaard's attempt to move us into our own existence and experience (*Attack Upon Christiandom 1854*) shows us that we are tempted to grasp authority by discipling ourselves to some institution which claims the authority. Thus, he says, by joining the (Lutheran) Church, we veritably worship the Church more than we worship the deity. We should, he corrects, live like a Christ lived his life, rather than worshiping the history of his existence. In this way we fill our own lives and infuse them with deity rather than living in the shadows of some external authority which has little or no actual effects upon our being.

On the other hand, the diminution of the authority of others, does open up the possibilities for us to grow beyond their authority. But mostly this does not and will not happen because we seem to grasp and grapple for a lessened and diminished picture of the possibility of authority in our own lives, and quit our *life's work* early. We have lost the concept of vocation, trading upon virtuosic talents which sell easily in the marketplaces of being and of knowledge, rather than considering how to live and work as if we will live the longest lives.

Whereas the loss and diminution of authority is a mixed bag, the question of celebrity is most often negative and more problematic. It revolves upon the question of respect (others and self)—if one has no celebrity-hood, why would others study, follow, listen to that person? Is this not a definition?

But the question more clearly follows the path of self-respect and self-esteem: when one is a person in her/his own right, then one can understand and appreciate others in their right. Questions of power and yielding follow from this, rather than existing in their own right; i.e., in teaching or studying with someone.

The problem in growing older is to be able to maintain and to sustain one's own sense of power sufficiently to be authority to oneself; not a simple task in a world which worships celebrity almost as deity.

Testimony: Although we often think of the notion of testimony as occurring particularly in courts of law, it seems clear that much of life involves testimony; testifying, as it were.

One gives witness (the religious context is perhaps, more explicit about this aspect of testimony) to some acts, some ideas, some beliefs that one has seen, done, heard (of). As the testimony is *believable*, much else is believed. That is, the notion of testimony is linked (inevitably) with believability.

Some of the power of testimony can be inferred by my witnessing of the power of the holocaust (WWII) on young people's thinking and being. Right after such a terrible activity (killing of millions of innocent people), almost everyone is horrified and believes clearly and definitely that the events occurred as reported and witnessed. We all knew someone in WWII who was killed; walked down any street in America as children (in my case) and saw the gold or silver stars displayed in the windows indicating that a young person of that household had been either killed or wounded in the war. The war and its consequences were burnt into my being; and my identity.

But the power of testimony has waned. Those who experienced the events directly are now old and feeble, and nowhere near as believable as they were to those of us who walked down the streets seeing gold and silver stars and knowing of the haunts of war and death. Two generations have passed—been born, grown—not knowing the events directly or by the testimony of those who had *been there*, and the situation was/is no longer as believable. Testimony thus entails being believable; believability entails having some experience(s) which would lead one to be receptive to testimony and to witness.

Testimony, in any senses per se, thus boils over to the *character* of those who have witnessed and give testimony. And much of life—personal, social, etc.—turns on the issue of who and what is *character*.

Character: There is some sort of battle brewing between the sense of oneself which seeks out a persona, a being and a way of being which is large enough (Kierkegaard) for *the longest life*: a character whom I can live and live with; a sense of my being which I can say that at age 50, 60, 70...100, I can look back at my life and self and say that it was good and well enough done—as if I were a person of great strength and good taste.

This sense of character, of character tasks, Kierkegaard opposes to tasks of virtuosity which can be done with technique and pizzazz at the earliest moment of one's life—when it becomes obvious that one can do something which is desired, and do it well enough... one can show off, scintillate, and seek out the 15 minutes of fame which Andy Warhol says each of us is due.

Character is inner, virtuosity is about becoming celebrated in a world whose attention shrinks even before the minute fifteen draws us over the edges of fame. Virtuosity seeks fame; character seeks... itself?

This dialectic seems so correct to me, particularly as I age; particularly as I do not seem immune to the stylistics of being whose clock runs yet, runs still; wanting flattery, wanting fame, wanting love; yet knowing more and more that if is not inside of me, inside of my character, then life empties.

The trouble with character has to do with the tendency of many to see it as a structural aspect of being: one has it, or one does not. Some wish it to run in families, genetics, and all that. Others see it as kind of discipline that one can impose upon oneself; with the hint that certain sorts of people do this better than others—a field in which racist thought unfurls itself in myriad unfurlings.

The advantage of the concept of character is that it places some sorts of demands on the processes of being which tell us that there are and will be and ought to be moments of accounting for who we are and what we do. These help us to remember the moment, to pay attention to what we do, engaging in, expanding toward others and toward the sense of moving on as growth toward character.

Stubbornness: Questions of integrity, battles of the will, shrieks of *Yes, I will!*—and *No, you'd better not if you know what's good for you.*

Questions race around my thinking and being having to do with whether it is better if I yield, give in or give up, or simply to act *reasonable*. Or should I gather my strength to fight this battle, and maintain my sense of self, of being, of dignity?

But how do I separate out what is mere politics (I win or you win, I lose or you lose!) from some other, perhaps larger, longer-term sense of self and of other? If I lose today, will I win tomorrow?—or do you see me as permanently weaker? If I yield on this issue, will we find compromise on others?

Is stubbornness more about issues, more about identity and politics? *This is correct! Why should I change?*—or—*Will you care less for me if I...? Will you respect me more if I am stubborn, or if I come to agree with do, do what you think is... right?*

Is stubbornness a defense against the loss of meaning, of the sense that I am somebody, of whatever is integrity? Can I remain stubborn without reducing myself, or being reduced by others: disciplining myself as opposed to agreeing with some others (Kierkegaard)?

If I am not stubborn in some arenas of life's being, do I remember that I exist at all? Which? When?

Projecting Being Forward: Living in the moment, living toward the future, dwelling in the past, *when are we?*

The time of the senses, it has been said, is in the present here and now: what we see, hear, feel, smell. For other species, it has been claimed even, that all they do is to live in the present here and now, respond to immediate stimuli, and have no sense of past, or future, thence no *conscious* knowledge that there is an ongoingness other than to experience it.

The entire Western theory of our being and knowing resides in this belief, assumption that human being means knowing about the time of our lives. Indeed, the study of being human consists primarily in examining these senses of our being as knowing creatures.

But this is all too easy, too simple. Much of our being has to do with *projecting* our being *forward* in time to some other moments, to some next places, to tomorrow, next week, forever. Maybe this all begins for us with our parents imaging and imagining the sorts of creatures we *will* be when our m/others realize the pregnancy. When we are small, the idea of being male or female is carried forward in their seeing us, into seeing into our futurity: older a day → 50 years. Much of their understanding of us, of their interpretation of what proper behavior might mean at any particular age/stage in our being, *depends* on their readings of who and what we are—but usually, I think in the context of their forward projections of what we move towards.

Much of this think about our being comes from watching children, and watching our own watching of our children. But much also comes from grappling with the notion of an *addiction*. What does it mean to be addicted to any substance—as opposed, perhaps, to using some substance (or behavior) but possessing the volition (still) to not *have to use* it: drugs, power, gambling.

I observe, I propose that much of what we call addiction is the taking-in to our forward projections of our own being, the substance or behavior which is coming to be addictive: having to smoke the next cigarette (the most powerful addictive drug?)—i.e., not being able to imagine ourselves without that drug; seeing virtual pictures of ourselves with a cigarette dangling or held just so in our hands. Is addiction (merely) a physical reality, or doesn't it have to do as well with the difficulty of seeing ourselves in this or that context. Does the drug or behavior literally define us to ourselves?

Consider that many people die in the first several months after retiring from a job of many years; that many long term spouses die shortly after their significant others; that I am still occasionally in some existential search for a cigarette some 30 years after quitting smoking, *actually*.

Just who is the "I" who became addicted? My being, my tissues—lips, tongue, lungs which crave? Who is the I that is looking for the fix which I tell myself is the necessary pleasure of my continued existence; the without-which-I am not?

As for other species, their sociality seems to tell us that they too project forward the meaning and being of their young: that futurity is a social issue, much as an individual and existential one. The point of growing up is growing up to be a proper (*noble*—V. Hearne 1987) individual—but individual in the understanding and imagination and forward projections of the others who interpret our being into the futurity which is, for them, right and proper. Otherwise they could not discipline us, and we could not exist.

Why do Boys Grow up to be Criminals? As it states so clearly and poignantly on the window of the Nancy Drew store in Chicago's Loop, it is difficult for boys to grow up at all because they all have mothers. Because they all have mothers who want them not to grow up?—mothers who do not (yet) want them to be men?

Nietzsche wondered if many criminals weren't looking for some excitement, and tended to be just those persons who have some verve and nerve and courage finding themselves entering a world which equates maturity with boredom: many of the most talented, most adventuresome. Not finding legitimate directions for their interests, going contrary to law fills many of their wishes, their needs.

Boys will be boys!

Is it some sense of fantasy, of the ideal and transcendent which pushes boys into the beyond—beyond each next beyond? Do they entertain in each moment the possibilities more than the actualities of their being: now forever moving to what's next? Is growing up precisely yielding *the 'what would be'* to 'what is right now'?

Perhaps it is the hormones pumping, egos and testicles, and muscles challenging limits, which drives boys to crime. Perhaps the pumped up feelings need release—and the object is always just around the corner. Perhaps!

But it is not always so clear what is crime and what is criminal, although many of those suspecting the worst of boys will be boys nabbing tits and grasping asses think it is all so clear. It is not always clear what is the right and what is the law. And there are questions of justice, of what is fair, and what is fair game. Do unto me and I will do unto you; but if not, then...

Many of us blame it on culture, on society, on class. Poor kids produced by poor parents seeing the BMW sitting on the street in its elegance waiting for each me to ride in it, to own it, to be owned by it. Why someone else; why not me? Why not, why indeed? Why should I lose the sense of any future at age 14 when the guys I used to go to school with see a bright future, a long adolescence? Why do I feel, why should I feel robbed of my life, just because my parents are poor, the wrong kind? Whose fault? Whose laws? Is this too sophisticated for the boys who rob to analyze the workings of the world, having had to grow up too soon?

Bad habits? Back to sons of mothers who indulged their sons so proudly, not setting clear limits, not forcing, not disciplining their sons, themselves. Listen to Nancy Drew!

Laws are made (mostly, still) by men. What is crime anyway? Do not kill, do not dishonor thy parents even if everyone else does!?

Many of us are really afraid of boys turning into men, growing muscles and speed and strength and cunning. Afraid early on that they will hurt themselves turns into cold fear that they will hurt others; hurt me and you. Afraid early on that they would be unhealthy turns into fears that they abuse drugs finding life on high, looking for a higher life. Better they should seek the deity? Follow? Lead!

Drugs.
And they grow up, still on the edges of gaining and losing control, aware of the authority of others who might do them harm and take their money and years of their lives locked up in the jails of life's vicissitudes.

The girls? Lacking nerve? Tied to their roots, being; being natural wanting to reproduce; looking for esteem, value, meaning? Or are they beyond the need for meaning? Or are they *not* boys?

Or do many of us value precisely the kinds of verve and nerve in boys which only very few will find outlets for? And the rest commit crimes?

Maybe, just maybe, we do not like kids very much. Discerning this, boys commit crimes... or do crimes commit boys?

Discipline, Disciple, Disciplined: 'Readin', ritin', 'rithmetic,' rules, regs... the list of r-ginary words goes on and on. Do it *right*! Be right! Go about it right!

From the disciples of the deity, the believers in whatever is the righteous and the right, to those who wind themselves up to be and to do right, to those who are forced and made to see what right means - then to do it, to those whose study is proper because it reflects the world properly and gives them sustaining powers to follow what is proper, the domain of *discipulo* leads on and on.

Follow the appropriate path, the trajectory from here to where, the subjects and objects of our being are the disciplines and studies of what there is: the trivium, the quadrivium from music to math to history and language; where is there, and here I am is ensconced in particular courses of study → disciplines.

Now confused, now bureaucratized, now departments and political turf in universities in journals in books which sell because discipline means audience and big bucks, the question of the disciplines of being and identity remain problematic.

Is teaching, for example, a course of study, a way of being, a doing? Is it important, trivial necessary for what? Is a biology which used to study organisms and populations a subject matter that it is now rapidly being reduced and replaced by the chemistry of genes?

In the study of our being and identity, do we do psychology of ones and many? Do we do an anthropology, a sociology? Do these major problematics of our existence fall into the intellectual-existential cracks of anti-awareness because they have no clear disciplinary locus?

Do I need to know, in order to know a discipline? Do I need to be a geographer or a physicist in order to become disciplined? Launched upon a life of study properly grooved in the particularities and proprietaries of knowledge and custom? ... For what?

Do I disciple myself to a subject matter much as I would disciple myself to some particularity of a deity? Would I learn more or less about being?

And in those various times and moments when the idea of being grooved into disciplinary narrowness seems old and confining, do I then become inter-disciplinary? Should I study others, with others who possess knowledge garnered in the disciplines of our times' times, attempt to understand what and how they think (and do not think, specifically and residually)?

Or should we attempt to move beyond history, trying oh so hard to live in the ongoingness of the present age?

First Full-Consciousness (age: 7 or 8) and the awareness of personal death—could this be the first moment when we could survive alone?: Oh, it seems so complicated to even talk about one's thinking about one's thinking. *Do it*, I say, and leave it at that. I reach down into the parts of my body feeling and reporting to me that they are the "I" which feels them feeling, and peculiarly this does not always seem to be the case. Am I hungry —or do I feel a part of me, my stomach's reporting that it wants food, wants relief, satiety? For most things, most of the time, this does not seem to be too much of a problem, even though it/I remain unclear even to myself (especially to myself—to myself?).

Where are the grounds upon which the "I" which watches myself watching, has full awareness of the rest of my being; the "I" which is the energy of movement, the "I" which goes to sleep, and gets up, and thinks, worries, ponders, loves others and myself? Is it all arranged, so to speak, in those first moments when we realize that the "I" which I am and call myself has some very finite limits in the world: that it will die, and go away, and return to the dust from whence it is said to have come? Here? Away? Do I arrange it all in that moment of first complete awareness of the finitude of my existence? Others may have told me, but I did not fully understand (I do not fully understand) until...

Bill Charlesworth, a colleague, friend, and kind of person who mirrors, complements, and challenges my thinking, also thinks about humans along with other species, regardless of whether they are like us or not. Bill, having traveled much of the world in some Catholic sense of charity and love to the hovels and favelas of the 3rd and 4th and 5th worlds says that children might first survive about the time they are 8 years old. Younger children (4 or more) may occasionally latch on to an older one and be taken care of, but they do not truly survive on their own until they are age 8. And, Bill reports, the oldest child that he was fairly certain told him a direct truth was probably age 7. Survival, truth, knowing, awareness of the presence and certitude of death, all come together with the first consciousness of being alone as myself facing personal death.

Hyperreality (Baudrillard, Eco): The observation that the so-called artificial can define us in such ways that the identity of, for example, journalism, photos, novels, television, i-phones can become more actual than our experienced actuality and identity.

One can write/read books in which the action takes place in fictional or in real space; then there is a reversal. Fact is less real than fiction? Who would know? What difference does it make? Where does imagination reside? ...beyond the here and now?

With modern computing/media techniques, even photographs which used to be thought to express some sense of the actual, can be altered in various ways to tell stories different from the original.

But, one wonders, what did a portrait on a photograph taken after the shutter opened for 1/100th of a second actually portray? How do we see what we do? Does a 1/100th of a second represent something that we know, living (as we do!) in the streams of our ongoingness? How fast are we? In reference to what? Where are the *bottom lines* of the actuality of actuality, upon which we know fakery, or when we are being tricked?

What are the dimensions of magic, theater, illusion, surreal, that we know that we are being (have been) *fooled*? Fool, fool, foolish: verbs, noun, adjective: pun...intended.

Art, more real than life!?

The text-as-world (TAW): the Bible, Koran; Plato, Aristotle, the Buddha, even Confucious. The work and words of texts as *laws* which tell us what to do, how to be.

The world-as-text (WAT): CNN. Stories of the world at war justify the war.

Is this all about justification?—testimony of the reality of our being? Affirmation, reaffirmation? Authority, agency? A sense that if reality is external to us, then we are... Aren't we?

Wasn't the world always hyperreal? (Yet I struck these plastic keys on this keyboard with lines on them depicting letters which I then made into words, which I arranged meaningfully when I typed this question.)

Since Plato (Parmenides, Pythagoras) discovered how to foreground logos and language by denying the validity and actuality of body and change, the paradox of permanence in change has tilted to the envisioning of non-change and the idea as the only (or overarching) reality. Western thought is (always) susceptible to hyperreality becoming (new) reality defining/redefining itself as it goes.

Heidegger: only the poet Hölderlin could witness our being.

The question seems to be, within the notion of Western dualism, whether some approach to the nature of our being is somehow more serious, deep, all-seeing into the nature of our being. Obviously this pertains, reflexively, to this writing about *fundamentals*, as much as to any other claim.

Within dualism, within an interesting and peculiar sense of historicism which has proclaimed the bodily aspects of our being to be located outside of history, while the anti-bodily or mental resides progressively as history, some approaches to the human condition are said to be *privileged*.

Sickness as defining of Identity—Review of Georgio Pressberger's The Law of White Spaces (NYT Book Review, Feb. 28, 1993, p.13): A healer's writing on the meaning of being with the sick:

"Every tale turns on a moral dilemma, and the physicians-scientists who must make agonizing choices are often baffled and outraged by the way choice seems to make up the entire texture of moral life...The extremities they confront in their practice create in them an extremity of need. The physicians are finally the unacknowledged subjects of these case histories, which themselves become episodes in the history of the soul."

Who *gets to* write out the nature of identity, of history? Who gets to construct the theories by which we seem to construct ourselves? The young, the old; the brave, the scared and frightened; the well who see futurity beyond a particular moment of diseased being, or the sick who wish the sickness away and lament (their version and present experiencing of) the human condition, or those who find themselves as the curers and healers and see the rest of us almost solely at the most difficult and agonizing moments of our being? Pessimists-optimists?

Do we need to spend all of the energies of our thinking-being contemplating death, robbing life's experiencing as we guard against the extremes; not seeing each new day as having its full measure of whatever life is in its fullness and it possibilities. Is life's story in its theories of identity constructed to center its fail-safeness, neglecting the very interest and excitement of the mundane and the ordinary; tempted to celebrate the *outsides* of the boundaries of our being?

If life's stories are written by teachers, how different it is and would be; like perpetual new parents imagining the vast future of their child's wonderments, the ideas of the ongoing stretched into perpetuity; driven by the celebration of change rather than by its dreading (Sarles, 2013).

The Ages of Identity (within a lifetime, over history): I used to know that cultures provide certain moments of effective change: of ritual and practice and declaration that one is someone and something new; that the past is over effectively, that one is mature or old, that one has reached some moment of power or impotence or importance: circumcisions, puberty rites of Bar/Bat Mitzvah, cleansings and cuttings and scarrings, wearing and cosmetizings, growing hair and letting blood, the right to stick and to be stuck, to have children and to raise them then to let them go to have children and to raise them; to regather them (Bateson, 1936).

And each of these moments and momentous changes I used to call an *age-grade*, and think that these were very powerful in establishing new identity and in bracketing the old in various kinds and modes of containment. Now I am not so sure, not willing nor wanting to enter the modes of old age and dispensal and disposal of my character's and characters' beings.

I see that it is all *culture*, that it is all definition/experience, that the world of oneself is a kind of market of ideas about who and am and can and will be, and if I do not will to be that which I can be understood to be, then I barely have existence.

The New Age & other forms of Millennialism: What a relief to proclaim that this age is truly new: a new age, a not-what-was, the end of some era declared—the fin de siecle, a postmodernism, a millennium, the now is the best which was always yet to be. What a comfort!

I will be what my heart has always desired; the deity will arrive again on earth, the white knight, a new job, a new life. All will be alright as if I were born again and now have the real opportunity to do myself and my life better; the right way. Help! I am drowning in my being, in my history, in what I might have been, in what I am now but cannot nearly abide. Get me outta here!

Help us! The jerks who got us here didn't know what they were doing. How did I get wrapped up in their schemes? Not my fault. Not my fault? Time...time to start all over. Another life... looking for Nirvana through the lenses of all my experience/our lives. What's *new*?

Dependence of Being and Identity on Memory (loss of...): If identity is a complicated collectivity of more-or-less related notions, then memory is... It's what?

We wander, I think, in the knowledge that older (usually) persons having suffered strokes sometimes seem to have *lost* their memories. Or perhaps they have lost their *presents*. Like the persons who wander in the world seemingly aimlessly, not seeming to recognize anyone or anything; who seem helpless almost like newborn babes (Oliver Sacks 1985). We think our infants do not think, and have theories that their development goes from the totally unknowing, purely reflex-biological to the knowing rational, dependent on memory, which depends it seems on identity; on remembering who one is and that one is.

Korzybski (1933) claimed that man is the time-binding animal. Is time then memory; does memory bind time? Or does the knowledge that one is who one is binds memory?

Names: Names, nicknames, *malnombres*, the name I am which I was given. Some places grant us new names whenever we want or need them, or when some significant event has placed us into a new or next place.

Approaching the age of 60, I think I am (finally) getting used to the idea of Harvey being me, being my name. What is the difference between it (Harvey) being me, and being my name? Isn't it time for a confluence? Or should we get sundered; a sundering, splitting celebration between me and my name. (Age 81 at this time of editing!)

I tried during my teen-age years to switch to my middle name, Burton. A few of my friends, I recall now so long, tried calling me Burt. But that didn't seem to fit so well, either. Fit what? I continue to ask.

Harvey, Harv, Harvella (my sister-in-law Shirley Andrews continued to think and say). Uncle Harvey sounds O.K. for my nephews and nieces—kind of affectionate—but we live fairly far away so its sound doesn't actually resonate out-loud very often. Loudly in my head, I can hear it clearly in the sound forms peculiar to each and every one of them, now including their spouses: Mary, Jack, and Peggy; Betsy and Jeffrey, voices of generations. Memories of my parents and others saying my name, sometimes fitting, sometimes not; sometimes with affection, much in neutral, and some fair bit in anger.

Why, I used to ask, was my name so *un*-common, wavering between wanting to be special or not so very unique, and wishing to be a Bob or a Jack or some name which didn't have a large man-sized rabbit for its most common social referent. Harvey?

Not too many years ago, I realized that this name wasn't really mine precisely, but my parents; mostly my mother's I think. Harvey, Burton, the most anglicized names my mother the Anglophile could imagine; so *waspy* as to remove any question of origins from her so, so-assimilative imagination wanting not to appear different, ethnic, Jewish; or that her ambivalence would be reconciled not perhaps in her generation, but in the next…next.

I realized not so long ago that names are *generation-backward*, given by parents whose life experience with the very same name (I guess) is so different from my own. What seems exotic or regular, in a name-fluid world of America to one generation, may turn out to be ordinary or so, so peculiar and unusual within the experience of the *namee*.

J., who was brought up being Jan or Jan-Marie, or Janis-Marie has not so many years ago changed her name to Janis. Only the old of acquaintances call her Jan and I am always tempted to correct them, to bring them into the present: "Her name is Janis." Get with it!

But in some families, in some entire societies, naming is much more historical, continuous, related in an obvious, clear way: John, Jr., John *so-tospeak* III, IV, like they were kings, queens, popes of other droppings from heaven. In Africa some places, children and grandchildren turn out precisely to be their antecedents, and there is no pretense that one is discontinuous in any way from the ancestor: an interesting way to banish death, it seems to me to be.

In Mexico where we lived for two years—three decades ago—the Mayan people there seemed to have various names: at birth they were given secret names known only to their fathers until they survived for 40 days (lest they would not, and someone would steal their souls, which were bound so intimately with names). Then they were given other names, new names which might serve for…years. The name and the self and the soul: which is which is which?

And Harvey Burton has as well a Hebrew name, given to cover all cases, one supposes: Chayim Berel; something about life which at some level of my existence has seemed important in developing an existential notion of our being and identity. To Life! *Salud!*

Do not take the name of God in vain continues to wonder me as if my spirit would disintegrate like brain tissue turning to a murky viscous fluid running down the leg of being.

I resent it when the modernist world of medical/dental practice calls me Harvey, as if they would treat me like their less-than-peer, a sense of their noblesse oblige which I would hate in myself.

I tell all my students (who can deal with it) and colleagues that I am Harvey. I do this less out of intimacy than out of a sense of self- and other respect: something about formality doesn't guarantee quality; that our institutional life has to do with titles and offices taking away being and granting official identity being step after step on the road to becoming an *apparachik*; better call me Harvey!

Evil: I have never thought this was a very *useful* concept. I presume that the idea of evil arises from our thinking dualistically, from trying to resolve the paradoxes of life without noting that we are *truly* paradoxical.

Do the good and the pure exist as overarching truths which generate their opposites, necessarily when we fall short of our own definings of the good, the pure? Or is evil, most usually, some form of banality, which Hannah Arendt noticed (1963) as some outcome of being bureaucratized in our thinking: being some instrumental or structural notion of our own being in whose terms we act virtually without morality, except in terms of the structural definition of our being? Where does this leave me/us?

Like human nature, I assume that the control of the definition of good and evil and purity is the *power* to define our being. And our living, our being existentially and ontologically fades into our thinking about ourselves, rather than thinking out our lives and living them.

As Jaspers says in his book about Nietzsche (did Nietzsche actually say this, or did Jaspers?), that it is pretty easy to turn one's acts into some form which allows one to sleep at night. In a directly Orwellian sense, evil can turn into good quite easily this way, and we would never really notice; never really note this.

Logic of One's Family: My father is, I think, doing better in my construction of his being and his influence and relationship with me. Some 20 years, now, since he died. And in my thinking he is *improving* in many senses: better motivated, more benign, more thoughtful and comprehensive in his vision, his relationships with others and the world (including, especially, me) more clearly and well-motivated. My mother (dead some 10 years) not as active in my memory at this point, I think, but always it seems lurking just beyond every horizon of being.

 I think I am in various active discourses with them; with their memory working in my thinking about them about me. The point is, I guess, that I think not only of them, but to some extent (large, small, increasing?) in their terms. Love 'em, hate 'em, I seem in various ways to be like 'em: a son of their family, of their thinking about me thinking about them thinking about...

 It is, I think that I think within the logic of their logic, granting importance to the things they thought were important, downgrading most of those thinks and things they found immaterial.

 I find myself disagreeing with them (my reconstruction of my memories of them) on many issues. But I also still construct them—especially facial expressions—in great detail, at various points in their lives' movements. I am not precisely governed by them, their memories within my thinking being; but I am not precisely free or outside of their thinking either.

 Perhaps it is that I don't exactly want to please them, please my memories of them; but I don't exactly want to displease their places within myself, either; perhaps especially. It seems to me not to be a question of operating with the logic of the family in which I was raised to be me, but of conditions, of processes, of growth, change.

 Is it a sign that I am more mature if I grant my memory of my father greater pleasantness in my present being?

Twins: The magic and metaphor of the study of twins keeps telling us that there is more underneath the two-ness of their being than all the one-nesses in the world. Some story about nature and nurture, about eggs splitting and splintering, about the destiny of our being—being predetermined by our genes, by our inheritance. Maybe!?

But where, then, is the twin I would have had, might have been? Where does the identicality of identity reside in the person each twin is and would be? It is said (anecdotally, the social scientist of my former being would admit) that when identical twins grow up and move away from each other, that one can see in their photos their appearance changing away from one another within six months of their splitting. *My twins*, my teenage neighbors and friends (Mort and Elliot Rivo) always seemed very different to me. But, to others...and to themselves?

They were the *classic* mirror twins: the right-handed seeing the left-handed seeing one another. And I wondered if the one twin did not see himself more in the other, each thinking that he was the other, that the other was he! Didn't they each believe that the other was himself, he the other?

One is mindful of Borge's story of identity in which our present being is mostly particular, incidental, perhaps accidental to our identity. We could have gone other directions, heard different stories of how and who we are; told ourselves that we are/were someone quite other, even, Borges suggests, *opposed* to our present being. At the storyline of oppositional extremes, Borges says we might have turned out to be precisely that person, that being who we would most hate; that one who would find it necessary, absolutely, to murder literally the one we have turned out to be. I infer on cooking this idea, that that oppositional other - to whatever extent s/he is the one especially whom I would hate, would hate me - that that other resides somewhere within the "me" which works so hard at banishing my twin would-be in every way every day!

Body as Locus of Individuality: Western thought has had this very peculiar propensity to focus on the *individual* as the repository of all of our essential being. But where and what is the locus for this notion of the individual: in the physical body, a reality or a concept which is then finally abandoned as the locus for much else of knowing or being. Plato worried about our own knowledge and absolutely *freaked* about the possibility of anyone else's knowing: our knowing, their knowing, and on and on.

Somehow (*Phaedo*) the effective banishment of the body from knowledge and intellection was posed by (or posed) this surreptitious locating of the mind within the physical body, only as locus with no particular contribution of body to the remainder of our being except as some impingement on the mind: desires, sickness, death.

Banish the body, banish fears of death, and so on: the primary text for (modern) Christianity. We remain, apparently forever caught in this skepticism about the very possibility of knowledge, about issues of whether the real is really real. I think most of this is resolved once we admit the facticity of the body in our very intellection, and in the intellection of others, interaction with others, their development, and so on.

Our identity (and our knowledge) is also located within the body living within the universe of other(s') bodies. The facts of our being are there as well as the certification that we got here in the past, and exist in the present... and will in the future.

This is to say that much of our being and identity is bound up with bodily being; not just with a locus of body to *identify* being, a fact then used to obscure much of our actuality and set up a war between the putative body (as desires, sickness, death) and the mind which we think somehow is the depository and repository for the mind which then constructs its own sense of the body. (→ *The Body Journals*)

Much of our identity is *invested* in our bodily being, a most complicated aspect of our being, and to use it merely as locus for circumscribing the real self is to see ourselves seeing ourselves but never to close in upon the actuality of being.

Creation of Image of Political Self (Teddy Roosevelt, 1st president to have done this successfully) NYT (2-38-93): In some senses, I suppose, people have always known that *image* is much of identity. It is not exactly the "I" of my imaginings or being which one's parents see, respond to, and interpret. It is not this sense of who I am that they attempt to mold and form and help enable me to become some sense of reasonable and responsible and moral person in their terms. It is more about the issue of whose terms in which I find the "I" to call *myself*.

It is even much more complicated, perhaps by the conceptual language of time in which I can possibly talk about the nature of my being: in and over time. The "I" which I say "I am" endures; at least seems to do so to me.

How did I get here?—is much of knowing that and where I am, right now. How did I get here seems to demand and receive a sense of self-history which is continually being regenerated, checked, and kept in the places below awareness which seem, nonetheless, to *ground* the being which/who I am right now.

I can (need) to rely upon a complicated historical construction: others who shared my experiences form important places in this sense of my history—for some a problem after they have died or moved away; a need for some of us to check with them that my formative experiences really were. And some sense of carrying the "I" which I am into the indefinite futures which inspire, at least do not kill off the present here and now.

Image: Me to me, me to others. I appear, they respond. Do I look like me, like how I should in their terms? What terms are my own? Do I see into the reflections of my visage looking back with accuracy? Do I even know what *accurate* would mean, more fascinated by the experience of the mirror looking back looking in, than with any sense of accuracy with what I see.

Older, most always older, most of us see today's image. But some of us want to see something which we call younger or longer ago, or more mature...or something we are not nor ever were. "I look *interesting*," my neighbor told me once. Students and faculty at other colleges and universities where I visit, say *hello* to me as if I am someone they know or ought to know, falling into some imagistic stereotype of a professor. All image? Or an image which my other behavior does not embarrass or chagrin?

So others see me. They see masks and images which they construct much as I upon the visage I call my face, which they seem to call *me*. And with photography upon the art of portraiture, someone figured out how to arrange this image, this face upon my being, so that others saw what they wanted; then they saw what I wanted them to see. It was like, this Teddy

Roosevelt attempt to control and define the image of his presidency, like a universalizing cosmetics.

I try to find whatever you want to *see in me*, whatever will attract you, not repel you, fit into whatever will make you think I am your president, whatever will help you yield your power and your vote to me - and to be that person sufficiently. I am me, the image you hold of me.

And where am I within the knowledge that you will see in me what I want you to see, and very little more or other? Who knows? Hidden, really to you, I may be clear or not at all clear to myself. Meek, diabolical, a terrorist within lamb's likings.

But people have known masks, and mirrors, and magic for a long, long time. They knew perhaps with the purposive of manipulation. Or they thought that different visages really were different: image and reality—where do we play within the actual, the surreal, the sublime, the image? What confusions between who I am, who I appear to be to others and to myself in some complex of orderings? Who is to say precisely which is image and which is not? The question, once opened, reduces to questions of agency, and who is the actor in the construction of the life of the person I call myself; or the image I call myself.

Here we play within the notions of the real and realize that it can be constructed thoughtfully; and this at once disturbs us as if we have found ourselves out to be of dubious being and identity, and reaffirms the necessity of wandering through this sort of thinking-out of ourselves; and the wonderings of how others do…and what, just what now will keep the world afloat!?

IV SEEKING FOR IDENTITY

On the Horizons of Being: Life often seems to be a visitation to one's being. I—the real I of my would-be—find myself glancing almost off-handedly at the self whose living I seem to be doing: an occupant, as it were, of some address, any address in the city or metropolitan area—take your choice.

I, looking backward from the various vantages I used to tell myself were the places of judgment of the life-lived, to see if it were done well enough. From age 40, much of it appeared to be mistaken, but not all so bad; careers appeared open, the possibility of success hanging out like a lawyer's shingle: here I am, open for business, buy my wares (I come along for free!).

From age 50, it focused already within the fantasy of life's vicissitudes, finding sufficient integrity and honesty, but not seeing much future; already having found Nietzsche's fantasy of being a posthumous author pleasing, pleased that there was more work to do, not to be sent to a house of nuts whose squirrely work would be to irrationalize my being. At the very moment of reaching 55, the rest of my life appeared reflecting backwards to this moment of rushing, hurrying me on... towards?

Approaching 60, there is no apparent reason anymore to sum up a life; rather more to live it, and to let the horizons I view become moments in which I can see growth once again. Less debt, more concern with sustaining the work which has been launched long ago yet concentrates still in these moments: sum-uppance!

Life is finally becoming less a visitation, the horizons less distant from being, itself. Lights at ends of tunnels beginning to ignite and spread and devour the tunnel through which I once would look blurrily, bleakly; now, no more and less and less... on most days. (Editing at 81...working so...hard! Fun, I tell myself. Finally.

Ways of Creating Identity: History; ethnicity/religion/nationalism; language—mysticism, millennialism, texts; counter-identity...:

When the many (*a people*) are seeking for some sense of who they are, for the yielding or dropping of some sense of who they have been, toward a new or newly sustaining identity, there are a number of favorite/usual ways to proceed. One can look to commonalities with/against others in the contexts of family, of religion, of nation, language, history...

Each of these moves require each person to *yield* something of his/her own being. But this yielding is often or usually desirable because prior senses of identity have been somehow less than *satisfactory or useful* or *sustaining*. While all of us live in multiple identities—self, family, son/daughter, (gand)parent, cousin, student, etc.—there are times when one or more of these identities become more or less interesting or more or less problematic. For example, the loss of a significant other, the gaining of a new friend or a marriage, will raise questions and make problematic various senses of who one is.

Some of these may be desired or desirable, while others may be imposed: a marriage or birth; a death or the presence of some external force seeing oneself (me) in terms which *solidify* some aspect of one's identity, positively or negatively (e.g., race, religion, nationality in the context of fearful or hateful *gazes*).

Gathering ideas seem to be few—and repeat themselves over and over again in history, appealing at various moments to populations who feel some sense of ennui, of ordinariness in the face of change, or of death, or some other ominous force appearing on the effective horizons of their being.

These appeals are often textual: reference to an ancient text such as the Bible or the classicisms of sometime which is granted hegemony or golden-age status compared to a present which is considered dull or derived, depraved or suffering beyond their collective endurance.

Examples of the Greek-Platonic and Aristotelian traditions have arisen over and over again in the Western tradition. Indeed, appealing to Plato is perennially useful when we feel that we have lost our way. Aristotle is invoked over and over again whenever we may wish to assert our hegemony over others by proclaiming our essential humanity while some others are said to be, by nature, slaves.

That is, even the appeal to nature is usually a *textually concocted* notion of nature, rather than one which demands that we return to experience and observation.

Recently, an Allan Bloom (1987) lamented *The Closing of the American Mind* even as he wished us to *return* to the Platonic texts for present day guidance. Read the Bible or the Koran, and find the truth of our being and identity therein; rather than engaging in the ongoing reading of the *Book of Life*. In 11th century France, Cuger was able to take Plato's *Timaeus* as his text and to create in actuality the idea of the cathedral which would cement aspects of Catholicism for centuries.

Other returns bespeak of an originary or creation moment, before some experience of the present which is not working or serving some group of people very well. The loss of meaning among some Amerindian tribal peoples, leading to excessive use of alcohol, a high rate of suicide among teenagers - is spawning a looking backward toward some *originary* moment before the presence of Europeans: a moment of some power, of truth, of the actuality of being *ab-original*: the real people.

Then, once established, this idea will be taken into the present where the people will live their lives in harmony and conjunction with the figure of the aboriginal.

Returns to notions of natural law, of man (sic!) in nature, are quite similar. We have been soiled and soiled by, e.g., our sociality (Rousseau), and we need to return to (some depiction of) nature in which we were more *true* to our *given* nature. In this context, especially, it is clear that returns have an intrinsic political power to raise those whose claim to history are significant, thence to lower claims of others who have helped to perpetrate and solidify their own power.

Claims of genealogy or family lines direct to someone who was famous or powerful operate similarly. For whatever reasons, the power of the concept of history to influence present identity is often if not always persuasive to many people, especially those who (says Kierkegaard) do not always reside happily in the ongoing present age.

Other rallying cries which work from time to time, and in particular settings include religion as a kind of cultural glue, the nationalisms and ethnicisms of place and relationship. The conditions under which these operate seem to be fairly limited, often depending on the perception of an oppressive outside which is said to be oppressive to the rallying force which would bind people together.

The power of Israel literally to define the nature of the Jewish bond is arguably the most effective and inspiring in history—for others (again

Amerindians, the use of historical place to inspire is just emerging, especially around the massacres at Wounded Knee in South Dakota.)

The story of the Balkans which is occurring at the time of this writing is the story of groups of Serbs who have been so frightened by the threat of slaughter, that former neighbors and friends have found it within their ordinary being to rape and ravage and damage solely on the (newly established) grounds of group and ethnic identity.

The (psychological) dynamics of when someone becomes something, some group, are often astonishing, and should lead us back to questions of mob activity and *hysterias*. When they occur, they occur quite rapidly and almost without warning, especially when while we remain unaware of their potential power, and the cyclical facts of each new generation having to be, as it were, retaught the various facticity of their history, and the ways history can be used to inform present being and identity.

Language, class and caste, and culture can be used similarly, given appropriate conditions for their emergence.

When such conditions either do not apply or are not useful to rally individuals or smaller groups into larger identities, *retreats* into various forms of *mysticism* are often powerful. I do not think that mysticism is necessarily very different from other gathering ideas of group identity such as texts or religion or nationality. Benedict Anderson (1983) instructs us that all of these notions are in many senses conceptual more than actual. That peoples will define and defend the nation as if it were actual and even sacred should return us to the issues of this entire exploration into identity. It is certainly clear that imagined or as-if identity is at least as strong for most of us as our experiencing being.

By mysticism, I mean that we can construct various ways of being which are not so much based on texts or living, wakeful experiences as upon acts of the imagination, of drug-states, ecstasy, dreams, and so on.

The idea of a fall to earth from heaven and the soul's return to God has had extraordinary power over self-definition and the judgment of one's *actual* experience. Indeed, this reflection upon what I am calling mysticism should cause us to reflect upon what we mean by the actual: and for mystics at least, and relativists at most, should ask us to explore (more) precisely what we mean by being and identity.

Is it all derived from varieties of intellectual nihilism which I think we have to grapple with (and to reject!) from time to time? And this leads me, at least, back to Kierkegaard's axis of being: fear vs. wonder—where the wondrous examine mysticism, while the fearful become and attempt to placate or otherwise deal with it.

Again, this points us toward grappling with the facts of being paradoxical creatures in a world whose major traditions have become major precisely because they resolved certain paradoxes in ways which have led to their power and hegemony, not the least over the posing of questions of identity.

History in the Context of the Balkans: In a review cast as a "Readers Guide to the Balkans," (NYT Book Review 4/18/93: 1) Robert D. Kaplan says:

*"History, like hate, is the product of memory, and memory is composed of unforgettable detail -- sights, smells, sounds, exalted emotions, grim statistics and cruel memories. A memory is not subject to condensation. It loses all meaning. It becomes just another lifeless fact that can never convey **how** people have come to think and behave as they do.*

The Balkans are a region of pure memory: a Bosch-like tapestry of interlocking ethnic rivalries where medieval and modern history thread into each other. More complicated and less visually exotic than the Middle East, the Balkans are unsuited to the reductions of the television camera...Whereas the Middle East is a game of checkers -- Arabs versus Israelis, with a modern history that began only in 1918 -- the Balkans are three-dimensional chess.

So in a sense the ascendancy of the Balkans as a news story in the 1990's means a victory for print over television. Yet it is not only the television correspondents who can't do much with the Balkans. Neither can the newspaper pundits, since the region is not an extension of America's own ethnic and racial obsessions, the way the Middle East and South Africa are. The Balkans are truly foreign. They require pure intellectual curiosity, nuance, not op-ed polemics. There is no getting around it. To understand the Balkans, you have to read books.

The key word for understanding the Balkans is **process**: *the process of history and the process of memory, processes that Communism kept on hold for 45 years, thereby creating a kind of multiplier effect for violence. Balkan violence is not a phenomenon of "modern hate," like that in Algeria and the West Bank, fed by rising economic expectations and demographic stress. Southeastern Europe is a caldron of history -- of unresolved border disputes and nationality questions created by the collapse of the multinational Hapsburg and Ottoman empires.*

By "process," I mean the fact that in the Balkans each individual sensation and memory affects the grand movement of clashing peoples. For today's events are nothing but the sum total of everything that has gone before. Process is something that is more emotional, physical even, than rational. It often has no direction: the asides and footnotes can be more meaningful than the main story line. You have to **feel***. You have to be able to imagine all the details of the past. That is why the best books about the Balkans are old and frequently eccentric -- granting access to a psychological universe that no television camera will ever penetrate."*

Transforming Knowledge: The case of women is quite different from the question of and quest for group identity.

It is women who hold the key to the future. Why, then, this strange historic battle in which men (qua men) have taken power away from women, arrogating to themselves control over the public world?

Men's toys: phallic symbols, power over things, weapons of being and the possibility to destroy more than to construct: out of some cosmic vision; out of weaknesses, whose nurturing are never admissible?

Men—always treading bluntly on the edges of control, ready to lose and to let loose of themselves, muscles grown big out of weakening. What sense of justice here?

Grown strong, the men, seeking vengeance for their lack of power over the determination of the future, carried always backwards into each day's experiencing? Lost, each day? Lost in some visions and structuring of life's would-be's never to reside in today's living?

Utopias, the onwards of what would-be, capturing and captivating the imagination? Living: in one's imagination? Out of fear? How can this wish, this need for control be out of strength; for strength, true strength is set within the ability to step-back from one's visions of the 'what would-be' to see how one is that he is also other; that m/others have created him and his looking-out? Control out of the in-ability to admit that he is on the verges of control, that there isn't any necessity to his existence, so he remains busily trying to not-worry, not to worry means constructing the possibility of meaning outside of himself, for there is nowhere within?

Life, men's life, a robbery of existence?

(And, if men could/would become women, and women would/could become men: what then?) Or/And: single-sex relationships...

Fear: There is something, something often powerful, to the stuff of fear. Perhaps, as Franklin Roosevelt said, "the only thing we have to fear is the fear of fear." Perhaps!

Much as I hate to admit thinking reductively, analytically to the smallest 'nth of my being, there is also something to the behaviorist notion of pleasure and pain: that we tend to do what produces the sensation of pleasure in us, and avoid pain. There is something, as well, to the notion of training - as opposed to education: hard work at working hard at some skills at which we become better; in some senses in spite of ourselves.

But what is the stuff and the experience of fear so great that we will do most anything to avoid its happening and reporting within our being? Pain seems quite direct, immediate; its occurrence demanding within us for instant ridding, powerful, nagging if it persists even as we demand its banishment.

Fear seems to be some variety of bodily experiences which some call feelings, to which we react much as if they were actually painful: pulling and punching at our nerve endings, catching our full attention and overwhelming all other aspects of experiencing. Pain acts powerfully in the present here and now, often acting as definitional of the possibility of placing boundaries upon itself.

Causes of fear? A good question; a good way of questioning? Death, economy, authority—these seem to have been and to remain best sellers in the game of causation. If we seek labels, then these will serve us.

Why fear death?—some have said. It (death) is a new aspect of experiencing, of being, of Plato, astoundingly, found something like a practical solution to the problem of death: banish the body, have the soul attach itself to ideas and forms outside of actual experience, return the soul whence it came. Life experience is merely an illusion, a chimera, and fear is transformable.

And remarkably it has served many, and continues to. It seems to depend to some extent on working on the young to get their fear factors operating in certain contexts: do as I say, say parents, or you'll go to Hell! And this fear seems to train, to operate upon bodily fears so they are readily, steadily available just in case one is feeling too little humility, or not sufficient pity for others. But it works in others to get themselves to play with means and ends in very peculiar ways, virtually the opposite from humility and from pity: whatever *works* to allay the fear?—one wonders.

Insanity: A sickness, an adjustment which hasn't worked out so well, a sane response to an insane world? It is not so clear what insanity *is*. It is not so clear that insanity is a state, or a set of processes, or a set of feelings which so overwhelm us that they call attention to their own feeling's thinking and enter us into realms of thinking thoughts odd from the perspectives of others' thinking. How odd!

So confused by now that the physicians have taken over the diagnosis and care of those who are seen as insane. How sad the future of those diagnosed as schizophrenic, as if the diagnosis truly lays out future possibilities as time is confined, and each new day is not much new.

How complex that the idea of insanity is so peculiarly linked to the irrational which is the other side of the rational, whose definition has become so dispersed: rational = logical; rational = the legal responsible citizen; rational = the economic person who maximizes profits and takes care of number one. And the oppositional notion is the irrational, crazy, and insane who don't much partake in the oppositional categories at all: just clinically strange and estranged. An esthetic? A sickness? How is it that any of us is truly sane?

Public Life or Retreat from Public Life? The headline in the alternative weekly newspaper seemed to me to scream out: *MAKE THE WORLD GO AWAY (WHY HOME SECURITY IS BOOMING).*

The American population, first the rich who lived out in the exurbs of our lives, but now all of those middle class especially suburbanites who live with their houses facing back into their individual yards, are able and eager to buy electronic equipment to make their homes *secure.*

A box insert quotes itself, saying: *The building of electronic barricades marks a natural step in our retreat from public life—perhaps the most significant one since the advent of television, suburbs, and the backyard patio.*

In the Twin Cities, we are just about to build our first walled-in, gated community, like a country club. Only now we build walls and gates. Like Mexico City suburbs where the favelas are the slums, where the poor-poor live across the street, and armed guards are placed at the gates of the development, we are becoming classed and anti-classed, afraid and insecure. Public life is to be gone into with great caution. We move away from others, to the few others like us whom we might trust, and even those we face away from. Do we not diminish in this construction of the anti-public, while preserving some sense of who we might be (if anyone) by who we are not?

Poets of Oppression (Saids' *Culture and Imperialism*): In my own search for identity, I thought I might have made a pretty good *poet of oppression.* I just could not see my plight or my work as occupying the position of arguing against any dominant force from which I found myself directly excluded. While I have never precisely been in vogue or in power, neither have I been fired upon for being either who I am, or who I am not in a general sense of identity; more I have tried to be me as a kind of occupation, or one might say, a preoccupation—life as its own study.

But this is not to be critical of such poets of oppression. I am a supporter of those who argue against oppression: easier to support a Gandhi (a Christ) or a Martin Luther King who wanted to overthrow oppression by non-violent means; but I can relate to and join with those who would oppose oppressive power by whatever means it might take. Perhaps I have taken the easy way out by exploring power itself, and claiming the role of teacher within this context rather than putting my life on some line, dug-in some firmament more firm than conceptual. Perhaps I am a coward.

Perhaps. I weep for those who have been destroyed in the name of...I search instead for how it is that any/all of us become the who of who we are and each of us is. How is it that anyone can kill in the name of some social identity without even taking on some sense of the personal, of some sense of the responsibility which seems, at least, to be in the domain of the personal; the wish to go on, to not die? How can one not die while killing anyone else? I would rail against the killers in the name of...

I think that oppression is born of *weakness*, of some lack of strength and surety that one is... that one is oneself in a sense which is sustaining. Plato moaned that it was personal desires which undercut anyone's ability to know, to tell the truth, not to be deceived or to have deceived oneself. But I think it is more difficult, more complicated than this.

Strength sustaining and sufficient: how to be sufficiently strong that one does not need to hurt others in order to protect those hurt places in oneself? Sufficient to find places of self-sufficiency that one can pursue and tell of the integrity of self which rebounds upon it-self? How not to sell-out to...? But this is so complicated by questions of loyalty, of family, of senses of deity and transcendental agency, and my response seems so...American; stoic, willful, and all. But if not...then oppression?

It has something to do, this poetry of oppression, directly of oppression: of one's parents even when/if they acted of the necessity that I be protected or protect myself. How to not be oppressor—Freire's wailing lament—in my turn, when I have learned principally and primarily the lessons of oppression? How to see-through my own tendencies even as I have the size and strength to strike out and strike through: self-control, control of self when others would oppress me also in the name of nation, of deity, of culture, of race and gender and all the collective concepts which rally identity for...but also against.

The 19th century problem of Nietzsche was to overcome the tendency toward peace by focusing on the weaknesses of others rather than upon their strengths - or, in my interpretation - upon teaching them in some dialogue so that they can become strong enough even to subvert their own teachings so others can become strong enough. No great sense of pity; rather than of understanding and invitation toward becoming autodidact: strong enough to, strong enough not to, strong enough not *to have to*...

In this historical moment when an entire generation has grown up in countries in which oppressors and colonizers had left some 40 odd years ago, a new time: beyond the time when one had to be and write the poetry which would lament and heal and wonder us about the odd paradox of power of oppression: strength and killing and wounding out of weakness; kindness and understanding arising from the once-oppressed (Sarles, 2013).

Hierarchies of Identity: Prestige, importance, authority, others dwell upon your being. I was born to be... me, one of *them*, the prince or princess, the ugly duckling who would. Here I am; there go the *swells*, the good-looking, those who know, those who are rich, those who control, those who would and those who resent and plot.

White, red, yellow, black, brown; black, brown, red, yellow, those without much color—the mad rushes rushing to establish that I am one of the '*we who are the right kind*'. If only I can convince you that I am: the Kohens, the Levites, the Israelites, who gets to sit nearest the Torah; who gets to stick it to some them who are supposed to lie passively and be stuck, and act as if they like it. If only they can be convinced to convince themselves that they... *like it*.

Realizing some two centuries ago that this notion called culture could be taken with language to establish a sense of history which could be used to foretell the past into the present, reigning in life, and reigning over others who thought they were peasants. The idea of a Church which could also be used to establish the notion of a fact that I am to subjugate myself to the deity...thence to those who are said to (say that they do) represent the deity, be angels or some other form of demi-semi-god.

Realizing that some language—German, for example—could be said to have had a long history, a noble history, a destiny, a higher calling, calling it higher over and over again... *inspiring*. The French bought the story then, resenting it now and then, and warring seemed necessary. Who would wage war and in whose name?

The Chosen: *Chosen* to give all of us the word and word of the one god bringing down the resentment of those who are not and were not and think they never would be, inventing their own story of god and their own texts and tests, born to be born again. The battle of life vs. death fought over texts and claims, and life cheapened and empties out. The arrogance informed by belief in one's own greatness informing others who then believe it. Pace Paulo Freire.

The Foundations Project:
As I have become a director of the John Dewey Center for Democracy and Education (www.johndeweycenter.org), I have become actively thinking and working toward the idea of a global Democracy—deeply concerned that changing times are complex, and not obviously pre-directed, granted our complex histories. The Foundations Project is an extensive exploration of these changing times; and our being within them. As we are busily exploring the idea that the entire world is becoming an encompassing concept—the means to understand what is happening, how to enter, to help create a global world has become a possible, even urgent, undertaking.

In addition to the so extensive development of new technologies and so many media, we are parts of the world driven—perhaps principally—by the vast changes in issues of gender: the pill. The other most major gathering force has been since the 1969 "man on the moon" insight that all people(s) are parts of the same world. Today, we have the Internet…

The Foundations Project is a series of ways for exploring how we are, how we think, how we are changing very much, as we are coming together globally. The ten chapters of the Foundations Project should help us to re-enter our own thinking, hoping to deepen, expand, and grow ourselves as significant players/members of these coming times.

BIBLIOGRAPHY

Adler, Mortimer J. (1993) *The Difference of Man and the Difference it Makes* (Fordham U. Press)

Adorno, Theodor. (1970) *Aesthetic Theory* (U. Minnesota Press)

Alexander, Frederick. Matthias. (1923) *Constructive Conscious Control of the Individual* (E.P Dutton Company)

Anderson, Benedict. (1983) *Imagined Communities: Reflections on the Origin and Spread of Nationalism* (London-Verso)

Angier, Natalie. (2000) *Woman: An Intimate Geography* (Anchor Books)

Anselm (1033-1109) *Proslogium* (Arthur J. Banning Press, 2000)

Aquinas, Thomas (1274) *Summa Theologica* (5 vol., Christian Classics, 1981)

Arendt, Hannah (1963) *Eichmann in Jerusalem: A Report on the Banality of Evil* (Penguin Books)

Arendt, Hannah (1968) *The Human Condition* (U. Chicago Press)

Artaud, Antonin. (1938) *The Theater and its Double* (Richards, trans., Grove Press, 1994)

Aristotle (384-322BCE) *Politics* (Reeve, trans., Hackett, 1998)

Asch, Solomon E. (1990) *The Legacy of Solomon Asch: Essays in Cognition and Social Psychology* (Psychology Press)

Augustine, Saint. (A.D. 386) *Early Theory of Man* (Oxford U. Press, 1968)

Augustine, Saint. (A.D. 398) *Confessions* (Oxford U. Press, 2009)

Augustine, Saint. (A.D. 426) *On Christian Doctrine* (Oxford U. Press, 2008)

Augustine, Saint. (5th Century A.D.) *City of God* (Penguin Books, 2003)

Bakhtin, Michael. (1982) *The Dialogic Imagination* (U. Texas Press)

Banez, Domingo (1966) *The Primacy of Existence in Thomas Aquinas* (Chicago: Henry Regnery)

Bataille, Georges. (1943) *Inner Experience* (SUNY Press)

Bateson, Gregory. (1936) *Naven* (Stanford U. Press)

Bateson, Gregory (1969) *Steps to an Ecology of the Mind* (U. Chicago Press)

Becker, Carl L. (1932) *The Heavenly City of the 18th Century Philosophers* (Yale U. Press)

Benjamin, Walter. (2002) *The Arcades Project* (Rolf Tiedemann, ed., Belknap Press, 2002)

Bergson, Henri (1911) *Creative Evolution* (Dover, 1998)

Berlin, Brent and Kay, Paul (1969) *Basic Color Terms: their Universality and Evolution* (Center for the Study of Language and Information, 1998)

Berlin, Isaiah (1990) *The Crooked Timber of Humanity: Chapters in the History of Ideas* (Princeton U Press, 2013)

Bloom, Allen (1987) *The Closing of the American Mind* (revised edition, Simon & Schuster, 2012)

Boas, Franz (1940) *Race, Language, and Culture* (Forgotten Books, 2012)

Borges, Jorge Luis (1935) *A Universal History of Infamy* (Plume, 1979)

Borges, Jorge Luis (1985) *Ficciones* (Grove Press, 1994)

Bowlby, John (1969) *Attachment* (Basic Books, 1983)

Brown, Roger (1970) *Words and Things* (Free Press, 1968)

Buber, Martin. (1937) *I and Thou* (Touchstone, 1971)

Buber, Martin (1947) *Tales of the Hasidim: The Early Masters* (Schocken, 1991)

Buber, Martin. (2002) *Between Man and Man* (Routledge)

Camus, Albert (1942) *The Myth of Sisyphus* (Vintage, 1991)

Cassirer, Ernst (1955) *The Philosophy of Symbolic Forms: Volume 1: Language* (Yale University Press)

Castaneda, Carlos (1968) *The Teachings of Don Juan: a Yaqui Way of Knowledge* (Washington Square Press, 1985)

Castaneda, Carlos (1991) *The Second Ring of Power* (Washington Square Press)

Chamfort, Sebastien-Roch-Nicolas (1860) *Complete Maxims and Thoughts* (Oxford, 2008)

Chomsky, Noam (1966) *Cartesian Linguistics* (Harper & Row)

Chomsky, Noam (1967) "A Review of B.F. Skinner's *Verbal Behavior*" in Leon A. Jakobovits and Murray S. Miron, eds., *Readings in the Psychology of Language* (Prentice-Hall, 1967) pp. 142-143

Chomsky, Noam and Halle, Morris (1968) The Sound Pattern of English (MIT Press, 1991)

Cicero, Marcus Tullius. (51 B.C) *On the Republic* (Oxford, 2009)

Collingwood, R.G. (1938) *Principles of Art* (Oxford, 1958)

Condillac, Etienne Bonnot de. (1930) *Treatise on the Sensations* (University of Southern California)

Conway, Flo and Siegelman, Jim (1978) *Snapping: America's Epidemic of Sudden Personality Change* (Stillpoint, 1995)

Crystal, David (1975) *The English Tone of Voice: Essays in intonation, prosody and paralanguage* (Hodder and Stoughton Educational)

Damasio, Antonio (2010) *Self Comes to Mind: Constructing the Conscious Brain* (Vintage, 2012)

Darling, F. Fraser (1937) *A Herd of Red Deer* (Oxford)

Dante (1317) *The Inferno* (Signet, 2009)

Darwin, Charles (1872) *Expression of the Emotions in Man and Animals* (Penguin, 2009)

Dawkins, Richard. (1976) *The Selfish Gene* (Oxford U. Press)

Derrida, Jacques (1967) *Of Grammatology* (John Hopkins U. Press)

Descartes, Rene (1644) *Principles of Philosophy* (Reidel, 1983)

Dewey, John (1923) "Introduction" in Alexander, Frederick Matthias, *Constructing Conscious Control of the Individual* (New York)

Dewey, John (1916) *Democracy and Education* (Free Press, 1997)

Dretske, Fred (1993) *Explaining Behavior: Reasons in a World of Causes* (Bradford, 1991)

Dretske, Fred (1999) "The Mind's Awareness of Itself" in *Perception, Knowledge, and Belief* (Cambridge U. Press, 2000) pp. 158-77

Durkheim, Emile (1893) *The Division of Labor in Society* (Free Press, 2014)

Eibl-Eibesfeldt, Irenaus (1989) *Human Ethology* (Aldine Transaction)

Ekman, Paul. (2007) *Emotions Revealed: Recognizing Faces and Feelings to Improve Communication and Emotional Life* (Times Books)

Epictetus (108 A.D) *Discourses* (Penguin, 2008)

Ernst, E. & Canter, P.H. (2005) "The Feldenkrais Method: A Systematic Review of Randomized Clinical Trials" *Phys Med Rehab Kuror* 2005; 15: 151-6

Fanon, Frantz (1952) *Black Skin, White Masks* (Grove Press, 2008)

Feuerbach, Ludwig (1841) *The Essence of Christianity* (Prometheus, 1989)

Freire, Paulo (2007) *Pedagogy of the Oppressed* (Bloomsbury)

Freud, Sigmund (1918) *Totem and Taboo* (BiblioLife, 2009)

Gallop, David (1991) *Parmenides of Elea: Fragments* (U. of Toronto Press)

Garcia, Cristina (1992) *Dreaming in Cuban* (Ballantine)

Garcia, Jorge (1988) *Individuality: an Essay on the Foundations of Metaphysics* (SUNY)

Gergen, Kenneth (1991) *The Saturated Self* (Basic Books)

Gibson, J.J. (1963) *The Senses Considered as Perceptual Systems.* (Boston: Houghton Mifflin.)

Goffman, Erving (1950) *The Presentation of Self in Everyday Life* (Anchor)

Griffin, Donald (1976) *The Question of Animal Awareness* (Rockefeller)

Grimm, Jacob. (1822) "Deutsche Grammatik"

Habermas, Jurgen (1976) *On the Pragmatics of Social Interaction* (MIT Press)

Haley, Alex (1976) *Roots: The Saga of an American Family* (Vanguard, 2007)

Hall, Edward T. (1983) *The Dance of Life: The Other Dimension of Time* (Anchor)

Haraway, Donna (2008) *When Species Meet* (U. of Minnesota Press)

Harman, Chris (1994) "Engels and the Origins of Human Society" *International Socialism* 2: 65

Hearne, Vicki. (1987) *Adam's Task: Calling the Animals by Name* (Knopf)

Hegel, George W. F. (1807) *Phenomenology of Spirit* (Oxford U. Press, 1976)

Heidegger, Martin. (1927) *Being and Time* (Harper, 2008)

Heidegger, Martin. (1929) *Kant and the Problem of Metaphysics* (Indiana U Press, 1997)

Heilbroner, Robert L. (1953) *The Worldly Philosophers: The Lives, Times and Ideas of the Great Economic Thinkers* (Touchstone, 1999)

Herder, Johann Gottfried von (1791). "Treatise on the Origins of Language" in Rousseau, J-J. and Herder, J.G. *On the Origins of Language* (U. Chicago Press, 1986)

Hesse, Hermann (1943) *The Glass-Bead Game* (Macmillan, 1983)

Hobbes, Thomas (1651) *Leviathan* (Hackett Publishing, 1994)

Horkheimer, Max. (1947) *The Eclipse of Reason* (Martino, 2013)

Humboldt, Wilhelm von (1836) *The Diversity of Human Language-Structure and its Influence on the intellectual and spiritual Development of Mankind.* (Cambridge U Press, 1989)

Hume, David (1738) *A Treatise of Human Nature* (Oxford U Press, 2000)

Hume, David (1748) *Enquiry Concerning Human Understanding* (Hackett Publishing, 2003)

Husserl, Edmund (1913) *Ideas* (Routledge, 2012)

Inge, W.R. (1918) *The Philosophy of Plotinus* (Forgotten Books, 2012)

Jacobson, Roman (1930) *Child Language, Aphasia, and Phonological Universe* (Oxford U. Press)

James, William (1892) *On the Stream of Consciousness* (iUniverse, 2009)

James, William (1902) *The Varieties of Religious Experience: A Study in Human Nature* (Trinity Press, 2013)

Jaspers, Karl (1935) *Nietzsche: An Introduction to the Understanding of His Philosophical Activity* (John Hopkins U Press, 1997)

Jaworsky, David (17 July 1980) Review of "Robert Oppenheimer: Lectures & Recollections" NYRB.

Johnson, Mark (1987) *The Body in the Mind: the Bodily Basis for Bodily Meaning, Imagination, and Reason* (U Chicago Press)

Joubert, Joseph (1838) *The Notebooks of Joseph Joubert* (NYRB, 2005)

Jung, Carl J. (1947/1954) *Collected Works* (Princeton U Press, 2000)

Kafka, Franz (1961) *Parables and Paradoxes* (Schocken Books)

Kahn, Charles H. (1981) *The Art and Thought of Heraclitus* (Cambridge U Press)

Kant, Immanuel (1959) *Foundations of the Metaphysics of Morals* (The Library of Liberal Arts)

Kierkegaard, Soren (1845) *Journals* (Princeton U Press, 2014)

Kierkegaard, Soren (1846) *The Present Age* (Harper, 2010)

Kierkegaard, Soren (1854) *Attack upon Christendom* (Princeton U Press, 1968)

Keleman, Stanley (1987) *Embodying Experience* (Center Press)

Kirk, G.S, Raven, J.E. (1983) *Philosophy of Mind* (Queens U Press)

Kohlberg, Lawrence (1981) *Psychology of Moral Development* (Harper & Row)

Korzybski, Alfred (1933) *Science and Sanity* (Inst. Of Gen. Semantics, 1995)

Leibniz, Gottfried (1686) *Discourse on Metaphysics* (Hackett Publishing, 1991)

Leibniz, Gottfried (1703-05) *Preface to the New Essays Concerning Human Understanding* (University Notre Dame Press, 1991)

Linden, Eugene (1974) *Apes, Men, and Language* (Saturday Review Press)

Locke, John (1690) *Two Treatises of Government* (Cambridge U Press, 1991)

Locke, John (1690) *Essay Concerning Human Understanding* (Hackett, 1966)

Lorenz, Konrad (1966) *On Aggression* (Mariner Books)

Lorenz, Konrad (1973) *Behind the Mirror: a Search for the Natural History of Human Knowledge* (Mariner Books, 1978)

Machiavelli, Niccolo (1531) *Discourses on Livy* (U Chicago Press, 1998)

Maclean, Paul (2012) *The Triune Brain* (Springer, 1990)

Marx, Karl (1845) *Theses on Feuerbach* (International Publishers, 1995)

McLuhan, Marshall (1967) *The Medium is the Massage* (Ginko, 1991)

McNeill, David, ed., (2000) *Language and Gesture* (Cambridge U Press)

Mead, George Herbert (1934) *Mind, Self, and Society* (U. Chicago Press)

Merleau-Ponty, Maurice (1963) *The Structure of Behavior* (Duquesne)

Montagu, Ashley (1957) *Anthropology and Human Nature* (Boston)

Montagu, Ashley (and Floyd W. Matson, ed.) (1967) *Human Dialogue: Perspectives on Communication* (Free Press)

Montagu, Ashley (1971) *Touching: The Human Significance of the Skin* (Harper Collins, 1979)

Montagu, Ashley (1985) *Living and Loving* (Tokyo: Kinseido, 1986)

Montaigne, Michel de (1580) *Apology for Raimond Sebond* (Penguin, 1988)

Morgan, Elaine (1995) *The Descent of the Child* (Oxford U Press)

Morris, Desmond. (1967) *The Naked Ape* (Dell Publishing, 1969)

Nabokov, Peter (1992) *Native American Testimony: A Chronicle of Indian-White Relations from Prophecy to the Present* (Penguin)

Newman, John Cardinal (1902) *University Sketches* (U California Library)

Niebuhr, Reinhold (1941) *Nature and the Destiny of Man* (Scribner)

Nietzsche, Friedrich (1880) *Wanderer and His Shadow* in *Human All-Too Human* (Cambridge U Press, 1996)

Nietzsche, Friedrich (1881) *Daybreak* (Cambridge U Press, 1997)

Nietzsche, Friedrich (1882) *The Gay Science* (Vintage, 1974)

Nietzsche, Friedrich (1883) *Thus Spoke Zarathustra* (Cambridge U Press, 2006)

Nietzsche, Friedrich (1886) *Beyond Good and Evil: Prelude to a Philosophy of the Future* (Penguin, 2003)

Nietzsche, Friedrich (1887) *On the Genealogy of Morality* (Cambridge U Press, 2006)

Nietzsche, Friedrich (1889) *Twilight of the Idols* (Oxford, 2009)

Nietzsche, Friedrich (1968) *The Will to Power* (Vintage)

O'Connell, Robert J. (1968) *St. Augustine's Early Theory of Man: A.D. 386-391* (Belknap)

Ogden, C.K. and Richards, I.A. (1923) *The Meaning of Meaning* (U. Cambridge Press)

Paglia, Camille (1990) *Sexual Personae: Art and Decadence from Nefertiti to Emily Dickenson* (Vintage, 1991)

Parmenides (480 B.C.) *Fragments: On Nature* (U. Toronto Press, 1991)

Pascal, Blaise (1669) *Pensees* (Penguin, 1995)

Peirce, Charles S. (1878) *How to Make Our Ideas Clear* (Academedia, 2005)

Piaget, Jean (1952) *The Origins of Intelligence in Children* (International U Press, 1974)

Rand, Ayn (1964) *The Virtue of Selfishness* (Signet)

Regal, Philip J. (1990) *The Anatomy of Judgment* (U Minnesota Press)

Reichenbach, Hans (1963) *The Rise of Scientific Philosophy* (U California Press)

Rorty, Richard (1967) "Philosophy as a Kind of Writing: An Essay on Derrida" *New Literary History*, Vol. 10, No. 1, Literary Hermeneutics. (Autumn, 1978), pp. 141-160

Rousseau, Jean-Jacques (1762) *The Social Contract* (Penguin, 1968)

Rushdie, Salman (1988) *The Satanic Verses* (Penguin Viking)

Ryan, Alan (1993). "Reasons of the Heart" a review of James Q. Wilson's "The Moral Sense" NYRB 9/23/93

Rynders, John and Horrobin, Margaret (1974) *To Give an Edge: a Guide for New Parents of Children with Down's Syndrome* (North Central)

Sacks, Oliver (1985) *The Man Who Mistook His Wife For A Hat* (Touchstone, 1988)

Sagan, Carl (1980) *Cosmos* (Random House)

Said, Edward (1993) *Culture and Imperialism* (Vintage, 1994)

Sarles, Harvey (1985) *Language and Human Nature* (U. Minnesota Press)

Sarles, Harvey (1991) "Cultural Relativism and Critical Naturalism" (in *Cultural Relativism and Philosophy*, Marcelo Dascal, ed. p.195-214.)

Sarles, Harvey (2001) *Nietzsche's Prophecy: the Crisis in Meaning* (Humanity Books)

Sarles, Harvey (2006) *Next Places* (Syren Press)

Sarles, Harvey (2010) *On Heraclitus* see: johndeweycenter.org.

Sarles, Harvey (2012) *Genesis of Morality* (not in-print)

Sarles, Harvey (2013) *Teaching as Dialogue* (Trébol Press)

Sarles, Harvey *The Body Journals* (ms. in preparation)

Sartre, John-Paul (1944) *Anti-Semite and Jew* (Grove Press, 1962)

Saussure, Ferdinand de (1916) *Course in General Linguistics* (Open Court, 1998)

Searle, John (1982) *The Mind's I* (NYRB)

Schelling, Friedrich Wilhelm Joseph (1800) *System of Transcendental Idealism* (U Virginia Press, 1993)

Simpson, George Gaylord (1961) "One Hundred Years without Darwin are Enough" *Teachers College Record*, vol. 62, p. 617-26

Skinner, B.F. (1938) *The Behavior of Organisms: An Experimental Analysis* (New York: Appleton-Century)

Skinner, B.F. (1948) *Walden Two* (Macmillan, 1968)

Smith, Adam (1759) *Theory of Moral Sentiments* (Liberty Fund, 2009)

Solomon, Robert (1979) *History and Human Nature* (Harcourt Brace)

Stokoe, William (1960) *Sign Language Structure* (Lindstock, 1978)

Spinoza, Benedict de (1677) *Ethics* (Penguin, 2005)

Spitz, Rene (1957) *No and Yes: on the genesis of human communication* (International Universities Press)

Spoto, Donald. (2001) *Lawrence Olivier: a Biography* (Cooper Square Press)

Suzuki, Shinichi. (1968) *Nurtured by Love: a New Approach to Talent Education* (Alfred Music, 2013)

Swadesh, Morris (1971) *The Origin and Diversification of Language* (Aldine Transaction, 2006)

Tennyson, Alfred Lord (1844) *In Memoriam A.H.H.*

Terkel, Studs (1974) *Working: People Talk About What They Do All Day and How They Feel About What They Do* (New Press, 1997)

Thompson, D'Arcy (1917) *On Growth and Form* (Dover, 1992)

Toffler, Alvin (1980) *The Third Wave* (Bantam)

Toulmin, Stephen (1985) *The Return to Cosmology: Postmodern Science and the Theology of Nature* (U California Press)

Trachtenberg, Alexander (1942) *The History of Legislation for the Protection of Coal Miners in Pennsylvania, 1824–1915.* (N.Y International Publishers)

Tu Wei-Ming (1985) *Confucian Thought: Selfhood as Creative Transformation.* (SUNY Series in Philosophy)

Warner, W. Lloyd (1937) *A Black Civilization: A Social Study of an Australian Tribe* (Harper & Row)

Whitehead, Alfred North (1925) *Science and the Modern World* (Macmillan)

Wilson, E.O. (1975) *Sociobiology: The New Synthesis* (Cambridge, Ma. Harvard)

Wilson. E.O. (1979) *On Human Nature* (Harvard U. Press)

Wilson, E.O. (1998) *Consilience: The Unity of Knowledge* (Alfred A. Knopf)

Wilson, James. Q. (1975) *Thinking about Crime* (Basic Books)

Wilson. Peter J. (1989) *The Domestication of the Human Species* (Yale U. Press)

Wittgenstein, Ludwig. c1940 "On Certainty" (Notes)

Wittgenstein, Ludwig (1953) *Philosophical Investigations* (Oxford)

Znaniecki, Florian and Thomas, William (1918) *The Polish Peasant in Europe and America: 1918-1920* (Boston: Gorham Press)

www.ingramcontent.com/pod-product-compliance
Lightning Source LLC
Chambersburg PA
CBHW050156240426
43671CB00013B/2154